ILLINOIS TRIVIA ILLUSTRATED
BY
BILL NUNES

ISBN 0-9646934-9-6

© 2005

Special thanks to Bill Jacobus and Marillyn Watts of Belleville, Harold Zeigler of Granite City, Jackie Rader and Dan Oberle of Edwardsville, Arleigh Jones of Tuscola, and my wife, Lorna Nunes

Front and rear cover courtesy Illinois Secretary of State; inside front cover courtesy David Viere
Made in USA by Corley Printing of St. Louis (314) 739-377 – Distributed by Partners (800) 336-3137

Other books still available by Bill Nunes include:

Sixty-Two Nationally Prominent East St. Louisans – 2001; 72 softbound pages, 45 pics; also contains the stories of how E. St. Louis was founded and the 1896 cyclone. Originally $9.95, sale price $5.00 plus $2.00 shipping

Southern Illinois: An Illustrated History – 2002; 288 softbound 8.5 x 11 pages, 600 pictures; satisfaction guaranteed. Covers everything from Alton to Cairo. $20.00 plus $2.00 shipping (available October 1, 1995)

Illinois Crime – 2003; 288 softbound 8.5 x 11 pages about true crime (Capone, Dillinger, Sheltons, Birger, James Earl Ray, etc.); 600 pictures; includes full-length novel *Illinoistown*, set in 1950 East St. Louis/Southern Illinois; romance/gangsters/Cold War intrigue/murder mystery – originally $20.95, sale price $12.00 plus $2.00 shipping

Incredible Illinois – 2004; A remarkably interesting & detailed illustrated year-by-year history of the entire state; 296 softbound 8.5 x 11 pages with 700 pictures. Covers history, geography, railroads, mines, legends, lore, landmarks, counties, towns, gangsters, KKK, labor violence, inventions, famous firsts, sports, media stars, writers, artists, notable women, and more. Satisfaction guaranteed! Originally $20.95, sale price $12.00 plus $2.00 shipping

Bill Nunes, 3029 Mark Trail, Glen Carbon, IL 62034 (618) 288-5185   bnunesbook@aol.com

TABLE OF CONTENTS

PREFACE

After writing nine books about the great State of Illinois, it suddenly dawned on me that I had a head full of oddball facts that might prove to be interesting reading to people who find themselves snowbound, laid up for a few weeks due to an operation, or who want to bone up and try to win a million dollars on "Jeopardy."

I have long been interested in trivia, dating back to when I first started teaching history at **Collinsville** High in 1964. The snooty math instructors at the lunch table chided me, saying that all history teachers did was drone on about a bunch of useless facts. I countered with a pithy line about history's human drama and fascination of things past, but it was like water off a duck's back. I closed with a limp "the pursuit of trivia is no mere trivial pursuit" – a clever play on words that went over their heads.

Since then there has been a veritable explosion of interest in trivia with an endless number of editions of Trivial Pursuit board games. The bookstores now have many volumes at any given time on the subject. *Who Wants to be a Millionaire?* and *Weakest Link* were popular quiz shows that demanded knowledge of factual minutiae. Newspapers regularly run columns about local trivia. Schools and churches have discovered that the easiest and most profitable fundraiser is a team trivia contest.

For this book I mined nuggets of information and gleaned (stole) tidbits from an endless array of books, newspapers, WEB sites, encyclopedias, the Jeopardy show, almanacs, sports digests, pamphlets, etc. I have also picked the brains of some of my best friends - none of them math teachers. A list of sources can be found in last year's *Incredible Illinois*. Citations are omitted for these facts are widely known by many.

It is impossible to know everything, so it's likely this tome has some errata. Please do not bet on the veracity of these Q and A's, for there is only about a 99 percent probability they are correct. This information is for educational and entertainment purposes only. Hopefully the book will sell well enough that I can print a second edition and correct my mistakes. Please E-mail me if you find any errors at bnunesbook@aol.com. If you are really angry about an unforgivable goof, give me a call at (618) 288-5185 (No collect calls, please.) Do not ring me up during Jeopardy hours M-F, 3:30-4:00 p.m. central time or during the Super Bowl.

Note: In this book I highlighted the names of towns other than Chicago because they usually get slighted in books about Illinois.

My apologies to those long-suffering grammar teachers who are fighting a valiant battle to maintain standards with students who end e-mails with little or no punctuation and write sentences like "How R U?" and "C U 2morrow." I am not one of those people who sleeps with the Chicago Manual of Style under my pillow. Due to the nature of the beast, this volume is written in a colloquial style with partial sentences, dashes and semicolons. My only excuse is that I surely must have been absent with mononucleosis the month that sentence structure, syntax, and punctuation were taught when I was in the 9th grade.

I pondered long and hard about whether to list the answers after each question (spoiling the fun for true trivia buffs) or at the end of a section (thus the tedium of constantly flipping pages for answers). I decided there were probably more people who would buy the book for interesting information than would use it in a trivia contest. Mine is also the method used by Robert Cromie in his 1992 Illinois trivia book. Feel free to use any of these questions in a local trivia contest.

Please pardon my unbridled penchant for boosterism and my unabashed Illini-centric view of America. To paraphrase a line from an old Ronald Reagan movie, I'm half American and half Illinoisan.

Thoughtful reflection tells us that we owe much to those early pioneers who "fought the elements, bridged the streams, subdued the soil and founded a state." Theirs was a difficult task. In the words of historian Bruce Catton, "the cowards never started, and the weak died along the way." May we always honor our rich heritage and preserve their memories.

It is my fervent hope that this tome, in some small way, will engender readers' curiosity – enough to the tipping point where they want to learn more about the rich and unparalleled history of our state. We all need to understand that the past is our present and future as well.

This book is dedicated to my friend Paul Simon who passed away last year following heart surgery. We first met when he came to speak to one of my classes in 1969 while he was Lieutenant Governor and I was teaching history at **Collinsville** High. He loved Illinois, and he loved Illinois history. He was a great public

Author Bill Nunes and Senator Paul Simon at Fairview Hgts. Waldenbooks

servant and Illinois is a better place because of him. Paul was one of my early supporters, was a contributor to last year's *Incredible Illinois*, and he bought copies of most of the books that I have written.

Illinois Trivia is more than just hard cold facts. It is different from other trivia books in that it sometimes includes lengthy explanations and the author's feelings and opinions. Hopefully, this will generate discussions and heated arguments about the topic.

While in a broad sense this book is helping to preserve Illinois history, there is a greater need to help preserve historic places and buildings. To get involved, contact the Illinois Historic Preservation Agency at 1 Old State Capitol Plaza, Springfield, IL 62701 217 – 785-4512. A one-year subscription to six issues of their magazine of "Historic Illinois" plus a copy of the full-color Historic Illinois Calendar costs $10.

WHAT IS IT LIKE TO TAKE THE JEOPARDY TEST?

I have flown out to Sony Studios in L.A. on several occasions to take the "Jeopardy" qualifying test. After failing the first time, I passed the next two times. I have never been called to appear on the show. One contestant said that he passed the test on six different occasions before he was finally called. Once you pass the test, your eligibility is only good for one year.

The test is given at the same place where the show is taped. Usually about fifty people take the test, and of that number only about five or six pass. The test takers sit where the audience sits during the actual show. They are given a sheet of paper with 50 numbered spaces. Alex Trebek, on video, reads the questions while contestants print the answers. There is no penalty for misspellings. Contestants have eight seconds to write their answer before the next question is read. There are 50 different categories, and the questions are quite difficult. There is one question each on history, literature, art, architecture, potent potables, Shakespeare, geography, famous women, etc. It is far different from the actual TV show where many of the questions are easy.

After the last question papers are graded. No time is allowed to go back over questions one might have left blank. While the papers are being graded, contestants fill out questionnaires and they are asked to write down five interesting things about themselves. These become the basis for questions Alex asks of each contestant after the first commercial break on the actual show.

The papers are hand graded and it only takes about fifteen minutes before officials come back. Contestants are allowed to miss only fifteen questions out of the fifty. When question number sixteen is missed, that paper is discarded. Contestants are not told how many questions they missed. All the officials do is read the names of the five or six people who passed.

It is a great feeling to hear your name read because the others in the audience, realizing how difficult the test was, give those who passed a rousing round of applause.

Applicants who failed are asked to leave while those who passed are given interviews and play a "mock game" with about twenty questions.

The whole thing only takes about an hour. In all three times that I took the test, there were more men than women who showed up.

Potential contestants are told that if they are called, they should bring several different outfits because three shows in a row are taped. Surprisingly, contestants must pay their own travel expenses and hotel bills.

GEOGRAPHY IS DESTINY

Q   How many glaciers shaped the terrain of Illinois?
A   Four - with the last one, known as the Wisconsin, sculpting much of the topography as we know it today. They began 100,000 years B.C. and ended 15,000 years ago. Glaciers typically move about a foot a day.

Q   Illinois has numerous moraines. What are they?
A   Ridges of ground up rock and dirt left behind by glaciers; the **Bloomington** moraine is one of the state's largest.

Q   Where was Illinois' first city?
A   Ancient Cahokia had a culture that flourished from 700 to 1400 A.D. Archaeologists believe the site surrounding Monk's Mound may have contained as many as 15,000 people.

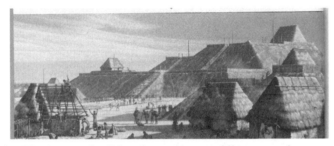

Artist's conception of old Cahokia (courtesy Interpretive Center)

Q   The Pecatonica River has canyons of limestone that are 250 feet steep. How were they formed?
A   By the process of erosion that took thousands of years

Q   Which is older, the Rocky Mountains or the Illinois Ozarks?
A   Illinois Ozarks

Q   How many feet above sea level is the lowest part of the state?
A   Parts of Alexander County along the Mississippi River are only 279 feet above sea level. Most of Chicago is slightly over 600 feet above sea level.

Q   The Missouri River empties into the Mississippi south of what Illinois town?
A   **Alton** – Mark Twain once said that the Missouri River was "too thick to drink and too thin to plow."

Q   According to native **East St. Louisans**, what is a Mississippi highball?
A   A glass of water

Q   What Native-American artifact resembles the shape of Illinois?
A   An arrowhead

Q   Where is the state's only quaking bog with aquatic and terrestrial flora?
A   **Volo** Bog State Natural Area

Q   Where is the interesting rock formation known as the Three Pagodas? (see picture below)
A   Along the Mississippi River bluffs near **Alton**

Q   What artificial lake was formed by damming the Big Muddy River?
A   Rend Lake near **Benton**

Q   What is the north-westernmost town in Illinois?
A   **East Dubuque**

Q   Where is the unusual rock formation known as the Horseshoe Upheaval?
A   – Near Eagle Cliff in Saline County. It was once 3,500 feet under ground and was brought to the surface by a geological upheaval/anticline. This area is part of the Illinois Ozarks, a range older than the Rocky Mountains. The resulting rift valley became a part of the Ohio River valley. This fault system was responsible for the salt springs in the area near **Equality**. These springs attracted deer and bison in early pioneer days. Before that, it was a gathering area for Ice Age mammals such as the Mastodon, Saber toothed tiger, Pleistocene Horse, Giant Bison, and Giant Sloth.

Q   How many square miles of water are in Illinois?
A   652

Q   What is the most northeastern town in Illinois?
A   **Winthrop Harbor**

Q   What town in 1990 replaced Chicago as the nation's second largest city in terms of population? (A) Los Angeles (B) Houston (C) Philadelphia (D) Miami
A   Los Angeles

Three Pagodas rock formation near Alton (courtesy Teich postcards)

Q   What is the state record for the highest temperature?
A   117 degrees Fahrenheit in **East St. Louis**, July 17, 1954

Q   What is the most southeastern town in Illinois?
A   **New Liberty**

Q   What southeastern Illinois town rests on the site of an **old volcano, the only one in Illinois**?
A   **Herod**

Q   What is the state's only naturally formed Lake?

A   The **Chain O'Lakes** on the Fox River, formed by melting glacial chunks.

Q   What town at the juncture of two forks of the Vermilion River was the site of an important salt lick in pioneer times?
A   **Danville**

Q   What town in Bureau County is situated on a glacial moraine that forced the Illinois River to make a 90-degree turn at that spot?
A   **DePue**

Q   What town is situated at the confluence of the Fox and Illinois rivers?
A   **Ottawa**

Q   When were a large number of trees in Illinois killed by Dutch elm disease?
A   1953-54

Q   What town was originally called Six Mile Prairie because it was six miles from St. Louis?
A   **Granite City**

Old bridge over the Embarras River at Newton

Q   What Illinois town is farther south than Richmond Virginia?
A   **Cairo**

Q   Although Chicago is called The Windy City, where does it rank among other cities in the USA?
A   Sixteenth – Great Falls, Montana, is the windiest

Q   What is the state's largest man-made lake?
A   **Carlyle Lake**

Q   What is the origin of the name **Park Ridge**?
A   This Chicago suburb has a slight ridge that separates the St. Lawrence River and Gulf of Mexico watersheds.

Q   What southern Illinois wetlands area was designated as one of 15 important wetland sites by UNESCO in 1996?
A   The Cache River Basin

Q   What site in Tazewell County (near **East Peoria**) has been declared a National Historic Landmark?

A   The Farm Creek Section which is an exposed bluff that reveals stratified sediments dating from 75,000 years ago. Evidence of two glacial episodes have been found there.

Q   Where are the rock cliff Mississippi palisades?
A   Along the Great River Road near **Savanna**

Q   What are the three most important man-made lakes in Illinois?
A   **Carlyle, Shelbyville** and **Rend** were all created by the Army Corps of Engineers for recreation and flood control.

Q   Where is the "driftless" part of Illinois?
A   It is in the extreme northwest corner of the state. It was an area that escaped glaciation and the terrain is rugged.

Q   Why does northern Illinois receive only about 34 inches of rain a year while southern Illinois gets closer to 43 inches?
A   Because much of Illinois rain comes up from the Gulf of Mexico, and the northern part of the state is farther from the source.

Q   How many square miles does Illinois contain?
A   56,400

Q   Lake **Shelbyville** was formed by building a dam to hold back what two rivers?
A   Kaskaskia and Okaw

Q   What Southeastern Illinois town picked up and moved inland after another severe Ohio River flood in 1937?
A   **Shawneetown** – there is now an old Shawneetown and a new Shawneetown

Q   What small town in Pope County is at the juncture of the Ohio and Cumberland rivers?
A   **Hamletsburg**

Q   Near what southern Illinois town is Swallow Rock on the Big Muddy River?
A   **Murphysboro**

CAVE-IN-ROCK

Q   Near what southern Illinois town is Saltpeter Cave, also known as the "Mammoth Cave of Illinois?"
A   **Pomona** - saltpeter (potassium nitrate) was used by pioneers in making gunpowder.

4

Q   Where in southern Illinois is the "Big Sink" – a large depression covering 100 acres?
A   Near **Cave-In-Rock** in Hardin County

Q   Did Garden of the Gods, south of **Harrisburg**, make *U.S.A. Today's* "Top Ten" list for scenic picture taking?
A   Yes - The Garden of the Gods has been rated number six on the list. The massive sandstone cliffs and rock formations were formed about 300 million years ago by the ancient Michigan River.

Q   What type of rock are the formations at the Garden of the Gods composed?
A   Sandstone

Q   Where is the rock formation known as Indian Head?
A   Mississippi Palisades State Park near **Savanna**

Q   Where is the rock formation known as Giant's Table?
A   **Mount Carroll** in the driftless region

Q   Where is the rock formation known as the Devil's Nose?
A   Starved Rock State Park near **Utica** between **LaSalle** and **Ottawa**

Q   Where is the dual rock formation known as the Twin Sisters?
A   Mississippi Palisades State Park near **Savanna**

Q   What is the correct pronunciation for the town of *Cairo*?
A   Kerro – according to historian Baker Brownell

Q   Between what two parallels of latitude does southern Illinois exist?
A   Between the 37th and 39th

Q   Name the Quad Cities.
A   Davenport (Iowa), **Moline, East Moline**, and **Rock Island**

Q   How many states border Illinois?
A   Five – Wisconsin, Iowa, Missouri, Kentucky, and Indiana.

Q   What town was named for an oxbow bend in the Rock River?
A   **Grand Detour**

Q   What town in Pulaski County was named for rocks that were a navigational hazard on the Ohio River?
A   **Grand Chain**

Q   The configuration of the Chicago River divided Chicago into how many parts?
A   Three - the north and south branches merge together and the Chicago River flows lazily into Lake Michigan. This T configuration creates a north, south, and west Chicago.

Q   What three rivers come together to form the Illinois River?

A   DesPlaines, Kankakee and DuPage

Q   What is the approximate length of Illinois?
A   390 miles

Q   Why were there no trees on the Illinois prairie?
A   It all goes back to the story of **Paul Bunyan** and his blue ox, Babe. Babe was a real brute and measured seven ax handles and three plugs of chewing tobacco between the eyes. Paul was a lumberjack and he cut down all the trees on the prairies of Illinois, Iowa and Kansas and then dug a dozen rivers on which to float the logs to the mills.

Q   What is the southernmost town in Illinois?
A   **Cairo**

Q   Where is the geographic center of Illinois?
A   The town of **Chestnut** in Logan County, northeast of Springfield

Illinois River and Swallow Cave near Ottawa (courtesy Teich postcards)

Q   What river enters the Illinois River at **LaSalle**?
A   Vermilion

Q   The state's second capital at **Vandalia** is located on what river?
A   Kaskaskia

Q   Does Bald Knob in **Union County** qualify as a mountain?
A   Yes – it's 1,030 feet high.

Q   What is the second highest point in Illinois?
A   Williams Hill (1,054 ft.) near the town of **Herod**

Q   What river joins the Illinois River at **Havana**?
A   Spoon River

Q   What river joins the Illinois River just north of **Beardstown**?
A   Sangamon

Q   Where does Illinois rank in terms of population compared to other states?
A   Sixth – about 11.7 million people

Q   The Illinois River joins the Mississippi at what town?

A **Grafton**

Q   What Jackson County town has a geological feature consisting of a narrow ridge of inclined strata called the Devil's Backbone?
A **Grand Tower**

Q   How many counties are in Illinois?
A   102

Q   What is the most famous lighthouse in Illinois?
A   Grosse Point lighthouse overlooking Lake Michigan at **Evanston**

Q   What town near **Naples,** on the route of the old Northern Cross Railroad, is located on the Mauvaise Terre River?
A   **Jacksonville**

Q   Into what river does the Big Muddy River empty?
A   The Mississippi, south of **Grand Tower**

Q   How long is the Illinois River?
A   About 275 miles

Q   What term is used to describe rock that is closest to the surface in Illinois?
A   Bedrock

Q   What happened to the name given by the French to Lac des Illinois?
A   Some nitwit changed it to Lake Michigan.

Q   On what river is our state capital **Springfield** located?
A   Sangamon

Q   What percent of Illinois land was forested in 1818?
A   Forty percent; today it's less than ten percent

Q   Why was the Chicago River a subject for Ripley's *Believe It Or Not*?
A   It became known as the River That Flows Backward after engineers in 1900 reversed its course so it would not pollute Lake Michigan. (Apparently it is OK to pollute the Illinois and Mississippi rivers.)

Q   What are four nicknames for the state of Illinois?
A   Sucker State, Prairie State, Land of Lincoln and Inland Empire. We are also justly the Crossroads of the Nation, but Indiana erroneously claims that moniker.

Q   How did the name "Egypt" come to be applied to southern Illinois?
A   Most gazetteers say it's because southern Illinois is triangular shaped – like the Nile delta in Egypt; the name became fixed when towns sprang up and were labeled **Thebes, Karnak and Cairo.**
   This author's first encounter with the term came during the third and final day of my Labor Day weekend honeymoon at the DuQuoin State Fair in 1960. At a local store I purchased a new Ray Conniff album, "Say It With Music." I didn't think much about it at the time, but the label on the LP cover read Egyptian Music Company. Having lived in *East St. Louis* all 21 years of my life, I had no idea what the Egyptian mantra was all about.
   A more unpleasant explanation is that the people who lived there were thought by outsiders to have the curse of "Egyptian darkness," low mental ability because they had settled there from the hills of Kentucky and Tennessee.
   The most reasonable explanation is traced to the year 1824 when the crops failed in central Illinois and many families were forced to journey southward to secure food and seed. When asked where they were going, they replied, "We're a-goin' to Egypt for grain – like the Israelites in the days of Joseph in the Old Testament."
   To this day people from Chicagoland tend to look down on southern Illinoisans as rednecks, hicks and hayseeds. Being an East St. Louisan, this author had to deal with epithets about East St. Louis being the "industrial rear end of St. Louis."

Confluence of the Mississippi & Ohio rivers (courtesy Teich postcard)

Q   What is the only mountain chain in Illinois?
A   Illinois Ozarks - in the southern part of the state

Q   What is the origin of the word *prairie*?
A   It comes from the French word for *meadow*.

Q   What was the cause of the 1881 flood that changed the course of the Kaskaskia and Mississippi rivers?
A   Most probably it was melting snow and torrential rains up north. Another story has it that an Indian brave fell in love with a French girl while working for her father at **Kaskaskia**. They eloped but her father caught them. He tied the Indian on a log, face up, and sent him downstream. As the Indian was floating away he yelled his curse: "You will die by another man's hand, and your town will be swallowed by the

Battery Rock in Hardin County

mighty river." The father was later killed in a duel.

Q   Where is the state's second largest Native-American mound?
A   **Lebanon**, Illinois - Emerald Mound

Spoon River – photo by William Ulmer

Q   What river town is the westernmost city in the state?
A   **Quincy**

Q   What is unusual about Carroll Rich Cave in Union County?
A   It bears the inscription "D. Boone 1776" on its walls.

Kaskaskia in 1830 before disastrous 1881 flood

Q   What county in Illinois was named for an English earl who refused to draw his sword against his fellow citizens during the Revolution?
A   Effingham County

Q   Where is the state's second largest human-made lake?
A   Rend Lake in southern Illinois

Q   What dam holds back the waters of the upper Kaskaskia River?
A   **Shelbyville**

Q   What three main rivers form the boundaries of our state?
A   Mississippi, Wabash, and the Ohio

Q   What is the Native-American translation of the word Wabash?
A   White water

Q   What part of Illinois is actually west of the Mississippi River and connected to Missouri?
A   **Kaskaskia** Island - as a result of a flood in 1881 that changed the course of the Mississippi River. Naturally those dastardly Missourians tried to claim it for themselves but lost the court battle. Kaskaskia was located on a narrow peninsula that separated the Mississippi and Kaskaskia rivers. The raging waters cut across the neck of the peninsula and cut a new path for the river leaving most of Kaskaskia on the Missouri side.

Q   What town once owned a place in the Mississippi River named Bloody Island because of the many duels fought there?
A   **East St. Louis**

Q   Where is the third largest college library in the United States?
A   At the University of Illinois - only Harvard and Yale have more volumes.

Q   Why does **Glen Carbon** have a Meridian Road?
A   Because it sits astride the 90th meridian, one fourth of the way around the globe.

Q   Where in Illinois is there a rock formation called the Devil's Table?
A   At Giant City State Park near **Makanda** – it's a flat topped rock formation.

Q   Where in Illinois is a rock formation known as the Devil's Stairway?
A   At Ferne Clyffe Park in **Johnson County**

Q   Where can one find the largest Army Corps of Engineers project **in all of North America**?
A   **Alton** – at the Melvin Price Lock and Dam # 26

Q   Where was the birthplace of HAL, the evil computer of *2001 A Space Odyssey* fame?
A   The University of Illinois at **Champaign-Urbana**

Q   Where is the lowest geographic point in Illinois?
A   Bird's Point - at **Cairo** where the Mississloppi (my childhood pronunciation) and Ohio Rivers meet

Q   Does northern Illinois ever have earthquakes?
A   On June 28, 2004, a mild quake shook the area near **Ottawa**. It was the first such quake in 30 years.

Q   What town is built on the Valpariso Plain, one of the largest terminal moraines in the world?
A   **Chicago Heights**

Q   Where in Illinois can one find a prehistoric mound that is the most significant Native-American archaeological site in America?

A   Cahokia Mound/ Monk's Mound is on Route 40 between **Collinsville** and **Fairmont City**.

Q   There is a 100-foot high bluff on the Illinois River near **Ottawa** with the name Starved Rock. How did it come by that name? (picture on right)
A   The Chieftan Pontiac made war on the British and Americans during the French and Indian War in an effort to stop their encroachments on his land. In June of 1769 he tried to seize the fort at Detroit but was unsuccessful. Realizing he had failed, he made peace with his enemies. In 1769 he went to the Spanish fort in St. Louis, commanded by Sieur de Bellerive, the Frenchman now in the employ of the Spanish. Pontiac heard about a party being given at **Cahokia** by the British. Bellerive warned him not to go because he was not liked by the British. Pontiac went to the party dressed in a French Army uniform given to him by the Marquis de Montcalm. Some Englishmen hired an Illini to kill Pontiac in exchange for a barrel of whiskey.

During Pontiac's walk back to St. Louis he was killed, his skull crushed by a tomahawk. His body was taken to St. Louis and buried there, although there is no marker to indicate his final resting place. Pontiac's tribesmen, seeking revenge, made war on the Illini. The Illinois

A   It is a flat floodplain of the Mississippi River about seven miles wide stretching from **Alton** to **Chester**, bounded on the east mostly by limestone bluffs.

Indian encampment at Starved Rock

Q   What mistaken belief did residents of **Murphysboro** have about the nearby Ozark Mountains?
A   That the rugged hills would protect them from tornadoes. Over 400 were killed by the disastrous 1925 tornado.

Q   Where is the part of Illinois known as Little Egypt?
A   It consists of the 11 southernmost counties in the state where cotton and tobacco were once grown. Some claim the boundaries go as far north as the B&O Railroad tracks in **Caseyville** and **East St. Louis**.

Q   The limestone bluffs at **Edwardsville, Glen Carbon, Collinsville, Swansea** and **Caseyville** are submerged and replaced with earthen bluffs composed of windblown dirt from the west. What name is given to this type of soil?
A   Loess

Q   How many drainage basins are in Illinois?
A   Seven – with each being drained by Lake Michigan, the Mississippi, Ohio, Embarras, Kaskaskia, Big Muddy, Rock, and Illinois rivers

Illinois and Michigan Canal from Chicago to the Illinois River

Indians tried to escape their enemies by seeking refuge on the flat-topped surface of a place the Indians called The Rock, on the Illinois River at old Fort St. Louis, built by LaSalle in 1682. It was a good fortress about 250 feet long and accessible only by a narrow winding path. According to legend, the Illini were encircled, starved into submission and killed, giving the place a new name, Starved Rock.

Q   Where is the highest geographical point in Illinois?
A   Charles Mound in Jo Daviess County – 1,235 feet

Q   What and where is the American Bottom?

Q   How did the Embarras River get its name?
A   According to folklore, the river was so tricky to navigate it would *embarrass* even the most experienced boatman.

Q   Where in Illinois can one find Louisiana bayou country?
A   In the extreme southern part of the state at Horseshoe Lake, Mermet Lake and the backwaters of the Cache River

Q   Where in Illinois can one find karst land formations?

A   Monroe County - around **Columbia** and **Waterloo**; Calhoun County in central Illinois and Jo Daivess County also have this pockmarked terrain; the depressions are the result of small collapsed limestone caves.

Q   What is the state record for rainfall in a 24-hour period?
A   Sixteen and ½ inches fell on **East St. Louis** on June 14th in 1957

Q   What is the annual amount of rainfall in northern Illinois compared to the southern part of the state?
A   The southern tip gets about 44 inches annually while up north it is only about 35 inches a year.

Q   What is the state mineral of Illinois?
A   Surprise, it's fluorspar – not coal. Fluorspar was mined largely in Hardin and Pope counties.

Q   What signs are seen as precursors to earthquakes in southern Illinois near the New Madrid fault?
A   The smell of sulfur and the appearance of sand boils

Q   If there are large coal deposits still left under about ¾ of the state, why has mining activity dropped off so much?
A   Environmental concerns due to the high sulfur content of Illinois coal shut down many mines after 1950.

Q   What were the names of the old trails that went from **Shawneetown** to **Kaskaskia** and from Shawneetown to **Edwardsville**?
A   The Kaskaskia Trail and Goshen Road

Q   What U.S. highway, built in Illinois in 1926, became the most famous in the world?
A   Route 66, going from Chicago to St. Louis, Missouri, then on to California

Q   What problem or weakness was there in the 1818 Constitution of Illinois?
A   It did not clearly prohibit slavery, as required by the Northwest Ordinance of 1787.

Q   What was the Grand Illinois Venture?
A   It was a 1767 scheme by easterners to float consumer goods such as cloth, ribbon, thread, shoes, pepper, mustard, and fishooks on barges down the Ohio River and sell them to settlers and Indians. George Morgan of Philadelphia was a leader in this enterprise that only had moderate success, in part, due to Pontiac's Rebellion.

Q   Land in Illinois was surveyed and platted in square townships according to the Ordinance of 1785. How is this possible if the earth is round?
A   Correction lines were inserted to account for the curvature.

Q   Why did Lewis and Clark make winter preparations for their Journey of Discovery at the mouth of **Wood River** instead of La Charette in Missouri as originally planned?
A   The Spanish governor had not yet received official notice of the transfer of the Louisiana territory and refused to give permission.

Q   What was an important daily ration to the men of the Lewis and Clark expedition?
A   One gill, about four ounces of whiskey per day

Q   Why can't tourists visit the actual campsite of Lewis and Clark?
A   The Mississippi River has since shifted east, and it is under water.

Q   What was one of the westernmost battles of the War of 1812?
A   The Battle of Campbell's Island in 1814 was a fight between Chief Black Hawk and his British allies and American Rangers near Black Hawk's village at **Rock Island**.

Q   How did Illinois acquire about 63 miles of Lake Michigan shoreline?
A   When Illinois achieved statehood in 1818, Daniel Pope Cook fought to ensure that the boundary was pushed northward which gave us 14 more counties. Wisconsinites, of course, claim we stole it from them – which we did!

Q   What two southern Illinois counties are known for their

Potato Hill Bluff at Valmeyer

deposits of tripoli, a chalky substance used in making plastics and for polishing glass and metal?
A   Union and Alexander

Q   What was used to construct lock #1 on the Illinois-

Illinois mastodon about 16,000 years ago (Illinois State Museum)

Michigan Canal at **Lockport**?
A Locally quarried limestone

Q Where was the center of U.S. population in 1960?
A A marker was placed in a field near **Shattue** in Clinton County, not far from **Centralia.**

Ancient bit of geology at the Farm Creek area near East Peoria

Q Where was the center of U.S. population in 1970?
A On the Lawrence Friederich farm near **Mascoutah**

Q Where is the "continental" divide in Illinois?
A At **Summit** on the outskirts of Chicago. When rain falls, water in the eastern part of town drains into Lake Michigan. Water on the western side eventually drains into the Mississippi River.

Q What is the general slope of the state?
A Northeast to southwest - in a gentle topographical slope

Garden of the Gods near Harrisburg by Bruce and Lori Eisenhauer

Q How many miles of Lake Michigan shoreline borders on Illinois?
A 63

Q What is the land between the Chicago River and Illinois River called?
A The Chicago portage – Marquette and Joliet carried their canoes across it on one of their voyages.

Q What Will County town is situated at the confluence of the DesPlaines and DuPage rivers?
A **Channahon**

Q Illinois is part of what larger geographical area?

A Central Lowlands.

Q What is the second largest city in Illinois?
A **Rockford,** but **Aurora** is closing fast

Q What is the extreme breadth of Illinois?
A 218 miles

Q Near what Illinois town on the Illinois River is Starved Rock located?
A **Utica** – the site of Robert LaSalle's Fort Saint Louis; some people get Starved Rock confused with Buffalo Rock which is farther east.

TRIVIA SUBMISSIONS FROM CHARLES E. BURGESS OF BETHALTO

(Burgess occasionally does book reviews for the Journal of Illinois History)

Q What was the first county established in Illinois after the area passed from British to American control?
A St. Clair County in 1790, when the Illinois area was part of Northwest Territory, named for the Governor Arthur St. Clair

Q Identify a St. Louis-born journalist and author best known for his "Poems of Childhood" and for his "Sharps and Flats" column in Chicago newspapers before the turn of the century.
A Eugene Field (1850-1895) – who wrote "Little Boy Blue" (come blow your horn)

Q Identify a judge, editor and early Illinois state treasurer who founded in **Vandalia** the first literary magazine published in Illinois.
A James Hall (1793-1868)

Q Identify the sailor, merchant and banker who settled in **Alton**, befriended Elijah Lovejoy, pioneered Illinois railroad construction, had a town named for him, and founded a school for young women.
A Benjamin **Godfrey** (1794-1862). The school was Monticello Female Seminary, now the location of Lewis and Clark Community College

Q Identify a father and son (not the Daleys) who both served as mayor of Chicago.
A Carter Henry Harrison, Chicago mayor 1879-87, re-elected 1893, assassinated during the Columbian Exposition. His son, Carter Henry Harrison II, was Chicago mayor 1897-1905 and 1911-1915.

Q Identify two close associates of Abraham Lincoln who collaborated in a 10-volume biography of the martyred President published in 1890.
A John G. Nicolay, a Pike County newspaper publisher who served as private secretary to Lincoln in the White House and John M. Hay, a lawyer and aide to Lincoln in the

Civil War years, also a respected poet, ambassador and U.S. Secretary of State during the Spanish-American War.

Q Identify the abolitionist Presbyterian minister and editor who was fatally shot while defending his press at an **Alton** warehouse.
A Elijah P. Lovejoy, born 1802. He was slain November 7, 1837. The incident has become a major symbol of the struggle for freedom of the press.

Q Vachel Lindsay's poem "The Eagle That Is Forgotten" was an elegy for what Illinois governor?
A John Peter Altgeld (1847-1902), governor 1892-1896, whose most controversial act was pardoning anarchists convicted of a bombing at Haymarket Square, Chicago.

Q What three locations have served as capitals of Illinois?
A **Kaskaskia** 1818-1820, **Vandalia** 1820-1839, **Springfield** 1839-date.

Fannie Butcher, Harriet Monroe, Carl Sandburg

Q What is the name generally given to the literary movement of the early 20th century that saw the emergence of such noted writers as Sherwood Anderson, Vachel Lindsay, Edgar Lee Masters, Carl Sandburg and Theodore Dreiser?
A The Chicago Renaissance. The poems and prose from these and a number of other writers are usually described as "realistic," "naturalistic," or "a revolt from the village."

Q French-speaking, Canadian-born merchant and fur trader Pierre Menard (1766-1844) was the first Illinoisan to hold what state office after the first election when Illinois achieved statehood in 1818?
A Lieutenant Governor - 1818-1822

Chicago Mayor Carter Harrison Sr.

Q What University of Chicago professor has written several books and won the Nobel Prize for economics in 1976?
A Milton Friedman

Q The characters "Lucinda Matlock" and "Davis Matlock" in Edgar Lee Masters' *Spoon River Anthology* (1914) are based on what members of the poet's own family?
A His paternal grandparents, Squire Davis Masters (1812-1904) and wife Lucinda Young

Masters (1814-1910), who farmed in Sand Ridge Precinct, Menard County

Q Identify the pioneer Methodist circuit rider of Kentucky and Illinois, who was defeated by Abraham Lincoln in the 1846 election for the U.S. House of Representatives.
A Peter Cartwright (1775-1872), a presiding elder of the church in Illinois for 45 years

Q Poet and Lincoln biographer Carl Sandburg (1878-1967) was born in what Illinois city?
A **Galesburg**, where he attended Lombard College and published his first collection of poems on a private press.

Q Who was a noted 19th century athlete born in **Byron**, Illinois, attended **Rockford** schools, and had a long and successful career as a pitcher and manager in early major league baseball?
A Albert G. Spaulding (1850-1915), who also became a manufacturer of sports equipment and publisher of sports guides

Q What was the name of the "little magazine" edited by Harriet Monroe that provided a vehicle for dozens of "modern" poets?
A Poetry: A Magazine of Verse, established in 1912, continuously published since then.

Q Identify the Baptist minister who founded the first higher education institution in Illinois and published the first comprehensive guides to the state.
A John Mason Peck (1789-1858). Rock Spring Seminary opened in 1827 near **Shiloh** in St. Clair County and became Shurtleff College in **Alton** in the 1830's. Peck published A Guide for Immigrants in 1831 and editions of A Gazetteer of Illinois in 1833 and 1837.

Q The Chicago Cubs last won World Series championships and National League pennants in what years?
A The Cubs last world championship was in 1908 when, managed by Frank Chance, they defeated the Detroit Tigers. The Cubs' last were pennant winners in 1945, but lost the World Series to the Tigers.

Q O'Hare Field is Chicago's major airport. For whom was it named?
A Lt. Comdr. Edward H. "Butch" O'Hare, Navy pilot killed in World War II

Q Name two early Illinois governors who wrote histories of the state.
A Thomas Ford, governor 1842-46, A History of Illinois From its Commencement as a State in 1818 to 1847 (1854); John Reynolds, governor 1830-1834, Pioneer History of Illinois (1852, 1887) and My Own Times (1855, 1879).

Q In the westernmost campaign of the American Revolution, Kentucky militia officer George Rogers Clark captured "without a shot" **Kaskaskia** and nearby French villages in what year?
A 1778

11

Q Chief Black Hawk, who led Sac and Fox tribes in seeking to regain northern Illinois lands which he felt had been taken by unjust treaties, was defeated by Illinois militiamen in what battle?
A Bad Axe, Wisconsin, in 1832

Edgar Lee Masters home in Lewistown: photo by William Ulmer

Q Before it became a state, Illinois was administered as a territory 1809-1818. Name the territorial governor.
A Ninian Edwards (1755-1833) was governor for the entire period, later serving as one of the state's first U.S. senators (1818-1824) and as minister to Mexico

A young William Jennings Bryan

Q Name the Chicago salesman and merchant generally credited with being the "father of the mail order business."
A Aaron Montgomery Ward (1843-1913)

Q Name the lawyer and editor, born in **Salem**, Illinois, who became U.S. Senator from Nebraska, three-time unsuccessful Democratic presidential candidate and U.S. Secretary of State.
A William Jennings Bryan (1860-1924)

Q Name the U.S. District Judge for the Northern District of Illinois who became the first Commissioner of Major League baseball in 1922, serving until his death.
A Kenesaw Mountain Landis (1866-1944).

Q Identify the farmer and blacksmith resident of **Grand Detour**, Illinois, who invented a scouring steel plow and developed one of the world's most successful manufacturing companies.
A John Deere (1804-1886)

Q Name the French trader and the Jesuit missionary who first explored the river routes along and through Illinois in 1673.
A Louis Joliet (1645-1700) and Father Jacques Marquette (1637-1675)

Q Name this novelist, born in **Oak Park**, Illinois, who won Pulitzer and Nobel Prizes before his suicide at age 62.
A Ernest Hemingway (1898-1960)

George Halas (courtesy Chicago Bears)

Q Name this pioneer of professional football in Illinois who holds the record for most seasons as head coach in the National Football League.
A George Halas, coach and owner of the **Decatur** Staleys (1921) and Chicago Bears (1921-1967)

LEGENDS. LORE, GHOSTS & WITCHES

Q Why is **Alton** said to be one of the most haunted towns in all of Illinois?
A According to author Troy Taylor, there is a three-story brick structure on State Street in Alton called the Mansion House that had been used since 1834 as a hotel. It was converted into a hospital by an Ursuline order of nuns from St. Louis. Because numerous Confederate prisoners died there, the place is said to be haunted by ghosts who still walk the halls. The building currently houses a number of private apartments. Alton erected a "smallpox needle" obelisk to commemorate the Confederate war dead.

Q Why else is **Alton** so haunted?
A The ghost of Elijah Lovejoy, the murdered newspaper editor, still walks the streets. It is also thought that the body of pirate Jean LaFitte is buried along the banks of the Mississippi near Alton. LaFitte is the man who helped Andrew Jackson defeat the British at the Battle of New Orleans. One must also account for the dead Indians that were devoured by the Piasa monster.

Q What mystical beliefs did Native-Americans and early settlers have concerning tobacco?
A The Illinois Indians raised tobacco, but used it only for religious and ceremonial use. They never smoked for

pleasure until the white man came. Tobacco in early times was thought to have special value for curing rheumatism and removing warts. Tobacco was part of Indian mythology for they believed that when one of their members died, his spirit was helped on its journey to the "Happy Hunting Grounds" by a sufficient amount of smoking. It turned out that the variety of tobacco native to Illinois was not the type that the settlers generally enjoyed. They preferred leaves from Kentucky and Virginia plants.

Q   What caused the town of **Kaskaskia** to be destroyed by a flood in 1881?
A   According to an old legend, a curse was placed on the town by a local Indian who was not allowed to marry a French maiden.

Q   What eerie event in old Prairie du Rocher is replayed over and over?
A   A woman, whose last name was Chris, claims to have seen a ghostly funeral procession going silently from the old Fort Chartres to a cemetery in **Prairie du Rocher**. Those who believe in the supernatural say that the woman saw a replay of a funeral that dates back to when the French occupied the fort. According to the tale, a local man got into a violent argument with one of the officers of the garrison and was killed. The commander at Kaskaskia advised that the whole sordid affair be kept as quiet as possible and suggested that the local man be buried in the

Tower Rock in the Mississippi River near Giant City

middle of the night at the Prairie du Rocher cemetery.

Q   What is the best-known Indian legend of **Tower Rock**?
A   There is a small island in the Mississippi River near **Grand Tower** in Jackson County called Tower Rock. According to an Indian legend, there was a Wyandotte brave who was loved by a Fox Indian maiden. But she told him that she had already been promised by her father to a warrior of the Fox. She climbed Tower Rock and leaped to her death, 100 feet below. Saddened and despondent, her true love followed her in death, giving this place the name **Lovers Leap**.

Q   What spooktacular events in Chicago have led to a supernatural tour business?
A   Richard Crowe began a Supernatural Tour business in Chicago. The two-hour adventure covers haunted sites and things like the curse of "Cap" Streeter, ghost ships on Lake

Michigan, the ghost of the water tower, "cement shoes" during Prohibition, and the mysterious **Lake Michigan Triangle.**

Q   Does Alton have a similar "unexplained mysteries" tour business?

Starved Rock State Park on the Illinois River

A   **Sonny Irvin**, owner of A-1 Limos and conductor of ghost tours of the city of **Alton**, was chosen by Fate Magazine to be the grand prize in their yearly "Haunted Weekend" contest. In doing research for his tours, Sonny worked with **Belleville** psychic Shirley Blaine who assured him that the Blaske Building was another haunted site. The building was constructed in 1916 by Sparks Milling and was used to house their offices. Several people reported paranormal experiences in the basement of the building including moans, groans and unexplained squeaking doors. The building is currently owned by Con Agra.

Q   What is generally considered to be the best ghost story in all of Illinois?
A   **Resurrection Mary** – the town of **Justice** in Cook County; its Resurrection Cemetery the home of "Resurrection Mary," an active poltergeist first spotted by residents with overactive imaginations in 1939; the ghost belongs to either Mary Bregovy or Mary Duranski, both of whom were killed in separate car crashes coming home from a dance.

Q   According to **East Alton** lore, who is the "woman in black?"
A   She is the ethereal woman blamed for explosions at the Equitable Powder Manufacturing Co. She was seen near the mill preceding explosions there in 1895 and in 1923. Witnesses claim she was shrouded in black and wore a waist length veil over her face. One local resident swore he would shoot her on sight but when he encountered her ghostly apparition he couldn't move. He reported her passing like a "cold wind swishing past."

Q   What was the main use of Equitable blasting powder?
A   In local coal mines – it was highly volatile and accidental explosions were frequent.

Q   What is the Legend of Tonti's Gold?
A   An old French legend relates that Henri Tonti (sometimes spelled Tonty) possessed a large hoard of gold.

13

Fearing that it would fall into the hands of the Canadian governor who dismissed him, the angry man buried a cache of gold on or near **Starved Rock** on the Illinois River near **Ottawa**. Tonti revealed the location of the gold to a priest who administered the last rites before he died in 1702 from yellow fever. The priest told associates about the gold but did not reveal its whereabouts. He drowned a short time later when a canoe he was paddling on the Illinois River overturned.

The land on and around Starved Rock is honeycombed with holes that have been dug over the years by those who sought this fabulous wealth. With the thousands of visitors each year to the area, now a park, it is possible that the site is trodden upon by dozens of unsuspecting feet annually. The gold may still be there today – who knows?

Q What kind of home remedies did the early French at Cahokia, Kaskaskia and Prairie du Rocher use?
A The early French were a superstitious lot and often relied on someone in town who was said to have a "gift" for healing. They usually tried to heal with herbs, spices and incantations. For sprained ankles or wrists, a string with eleven knots was tied around it and healing took place in three days. Babies with teething problems had a rattlesnake vertebra tied around its neck. To raise a fallen palate the hair on the top of the head was pulled tight and drawn into a knot. For sunstroke the patient was bathed in a lotion of river water and salt. God was often brought into the cure with either the healer making the sign of the cross or by a recitation of Hail Mary.

Q Are there such things as haunted churches in Illinois?
A Apparently – the town of **Lemont**, a Chicago suburb, is home to St. James of the Sag, Cook County's oldest church; erected on site of old Indian burial ground and said to be Illinois' most haunted church; ghost monks have been sighted at the cemetery near the church, performing Gregorian chants in Latin.

Q What ghost plagues the town of **Midlothian**?
A In Cook County, its Bachelor's Grove Cemetery is said to be the most haunted spot in area; some say ghost stories are concocted to scare off youths who vandalized the place; Madonna of Bachelor's Grove is a female ghost who walks the grounds at night holding a dead baby in her arms.

Q Who is the ghost of the **Woodstock** Opera House?
A The town's theater has seat DD 113 that is always reserved for Elvira, a female ghost who haunts the scene; she hanged herself in a bell tower after being jilted back in 1903.

Q What is the story of Lakey's ghost, told by southern Illinois historian John Allen?
A The story of Lakey's ghost is based on the murder of an early settler near **McLeansboro**. The quite personable man was cutting logs one day for the purpose of building a cabin. His neighbor came to see him and discovered that someone had dispatched the man with his own ax and severed his head from his shoulders. Lakey had no known enemies, and the murder was never solved.

Shortly after Lakey was buried, two men were traveling along a road that bordered Lakey's Creek, and they suddenly were joined by a headless horseman on a black steed. The gruesome companion silently rode with them until they crossed the stream. Near the center of the stream, the ghostly apparition turned away and disappeared into the mist. It was then that the men remembered that *ghosts are unable to cross moving water*. This incident was repeated often with other travelers, and it was said that the headless horseman was looking for his killer.

Q Why is **Collinsville** haunted?
A The ghost of **Robert Prager**, who was lynched for repeatedly making unpatriotic remarks during World War I, walks the streets of that town.

Charles Hertel

Q Why is **Belleville** haunted?
A Belleville is beset with a similar problem due to **angry citizens lynching David Wyatt**, a black man who had shot and severely wounded the County Superintendent of Schools (Charles Hertel) for refusing to renew his teaching certificate.

Q Why is **East St. Louis** haunted?
A It is said that late-night screaming can occasionally be heard just west of the Casino Queen and near the downtown section of East St. Louis. It was here that a bloody riot took place in 1917, killing nine whites and 39 Negroes.

The hanging of the African named Moreau

Q Why is **Cahokia** haunted?
A Cahokia residents have reported the ghostly apparition of a slave named Moreau who was executed in colonial times for casting spells on white French settlers.

Q What is the mysterious Blue Pool area of the Mississippi River near **Alton**?
A The Blue Pool is an area similar to the **Bermuda Triangle**, but it is on the Mississippi just north of Alton. It is legendary for its depth and in earlier, more superstitious times was said to be bottomless. There have been so many fatal swimming and

boating accidents at the Pool that locals claim it to be haunted.

Q   What is the story of **Edwardsville's** Hexabuchel area?
A   In Edwardsville there is the area known as Hexabuchel. Hexabuchel translates to "**witches back**," and it is at the north end of town by Old Alton Road and 2nd Street. It is believed the name came from a woman who once lived there who was thought to have the power to cast spells on people.

Q   Who was the most famous "witch" of southern Illinois?
A   John Allen says the most notable witch of southern Illinois was **Eva Locker** who lived on David Prairie in **Williamson County**. Witches are said to be human beings who have made a pact with the devil in return for super-natural powers. A woman was said to become a witch by drawing her own blood and then making a pact with the devil by dedicating it to him. Eva cast spells on those she disliked, causing them to suffer a variety of maladies that ranged from warts, boils, uncontrollable twitching, and fits. She could milk the cows of her neighbors by merely hanging a towel on a rack in her kitchen. Five minutes later she would twist it and wring the milk into a bucket.
    Charlie Lee of **Hamilton County** became a noted "witch-master," called upon to nullify witches' spells.

Q   Why is the Big Muddy River so crooked?
A   Henry Dillinger and George McKinney of **Murphysboro** were great pioneer storytellers. In one of their tall tales they claimed to have scooped out the channel of the Big Muddy River with their own hands. When they were asked why it was so crooked, they replied that they worked on it day and night. The straight part was dug during the day, and the crooked parts happened at night, they explained.

Chicago's Fort Dearborn where Indian massacre took place

Q   What name was given to the hairy monster spotted roaming around near **Murphysboro** in 1973?
A   The Big Muddy Monster

Q   What southern Illinois town experienced the strange phenomenon of crop circles in 1992?
A   They started in Europe and spread to America – those crop circle hoaxes appeared in the town of **Troy** and reappeared a year later.

Q   What southern Illinois town was featured in a 1978 story by Luke Grisholm about a UFO attack?
A   **Chester** – the article was in UFO Magazine and titled, "The Night An American Town Died of Fright."

Q   What was the Chicago connection to Orson Welles' "War of the Worlds" radio broadcast in 1938 that scared people to death?
A   The radio program said that Mt. Jennings Observatory in Chicago had spotted a UFO landing on the east coast. Chicago is flat as a pancake – there is no Mt. Jennings in the Windy City.

Q   What is the **Washington Park** (a suburb of East St. Louis) ghost story about Henry Lee?
A   Halloween was always a fun, but scary, proposition back in the 1940's. My head is still filled with spooktacular memories of ghouls and ghosts, witches and goblins. Carving the Jack-O'-Lantern was unfailingly a highlight of the season. I would help my mother select a medium sized pumpkin. Mother wanted one that was symmetrical and

Bob Then's Shell service station in Washington Park

blemish free, but I usually talked her into buying one that was misshapen – one with character. Once we got home, mother cut the obligatory round hole in the top and scooped out the innards for making scrumptious homemade pies. Then she gave me a butcher knife to carve the face on front.
    "Don't cut your finger off and get blood all over my clean floor," she lovingly warned. I had the choice of making it a "happy face" or a "spooky face." I usually opted for the sinister design with a menacing look.
    It wasn't easy for kids in my neighborhood to go trick or treating. My older cousins, Donnie Madelyn and David Lee Nichols, warned me that witches were on the prowl and they liked to swoop down on their broomsticks and snatch kids off the streets. They would then whisk them off to some horrible cave, plop them in a cauldron of boiling water (bubbling with lizard tails, newt eyes, and salamander toes), and make stew of their flesh.
    "If you ever encounter an evil witch that begins chasing you, be sure to take off your left shoe and *spit in it*. That breaks the evil one's magic powers and she'll be forced to search for a different victim," they explained.
    Being caught in the clutches of evil monsters wasn't the worst thing that could happen to a kid back then. We also had to contend with **the ghost of Henry Lee**. According to the legend, Henry was a religious man who attended the Assembly of God Church on Forest Blvd. He worked the

15

night shift in Washington Park at the East St. Louis Bridge Company, next to the B&O tracks.

It was Halloween Eve in 1930. Henry Lee lived in a desolate area called Jackass Flats. He loved going to the shallow Spring Lake next to the L&N tracks to go frog gigging. A long pole with a two-pronged mechanism on the end proved useful for plucking the slimy green amphibians from their murky habitats.

One fog-laden night, Lee was walking home from work, carrying a kerosene lantern to light his way through a heavy mist that was thick as pea soup. He accidentally stumbled upon a group of moonshiners who thought he was a "revenuer." One of them quickly picked up a shotgun and fired. The powerful blast knocked Henry clean out of his shoes. The unlucky fellow never made it home.

After the incident, on every subsequent Halloween, people reported seeing a ghostly apparition wandering around the area, carrying a lamp. The headless spirit of Henry Lee was just trying to find his way home.

Kids in my neighborhood were afraid to trick or treat in Washington Park. We usually made our rounds a few blocks away in the Lansdowne area where we were less likely to run into Henry Lee. But one year, when I was eleven years old, I foolishly mustered up the courage to go looking for Henry Lee. I took along a Brownie box camera so that I would have proof of the encounter. It was a spooky Halloween night barely lit by a crescent gothic moon. The cold night mist settled on my hands and face and sent a chill down my quivering spine. Undaunted, I made my way along Old Caseyville Road, hoping for success – yet praying that the grisly story had been a mere figment of someone's imagination. Suddenly, out of the ink-black darkness of Hades, there it was. My hands trembling, I hurriedly snapped a picture and ran as fast as I could back to the safety of my home. When the roll was developed, I quickly shuffled through the snap shots looking for my prize. I gasped in shocked disbelief when I came upon the picture. All that could be seen in the photograph was a lantern about three feet off the ground, slightly to the left of *an empty pair of brogans*.

Q   What is the legend about southern Illinois dogwood and redbud trees?
A   Historian Grover Brinkman once told a story about the beautiful dogwood and redbud trees that flower so prominently each spring in southern Illinois. The back-country legend holds that Christ was crucified on a cross made from the dogwood. He took pity on the tree and said that never again would it grow large or straight enough to be used as a cross. From that point in time, the blossoms of the dogwood took the shape of a cross with two long petals and two short ones. The markings at the end of each petal are said to represent Christ's nail prints.

Q   How did **Thebes** lose out to the town of **Cairo** as the county seat?
A   According to a story told by Abe Lincoln, it happened thusly. Thebes was already the county seat, but a rapidly growing Cairo challenged this. The two towns became bitter rivals with Thebans suggesting that upstart Cairo was no more than a mere daub of mud on the tail of the state. Before the deciding election was held, a Cairo man devised

a clever scheme. He wrapped a boulder in a green hide and in the middle of the night had a mule drag it along the ground. The next day he showed the marks to some citizens of Thebes and suggested that **the marks had been made by a large serpent**. Some of his confederates began to spread rumors about missing dogs and calves. The people of Thebes were all up in arms and organized a great hunt to find the monster. They were so caught up in the moment that they were out in the wild on election day and most never made it back to their precincts in time to vote, throwing the election to Cairoine interests.

Q   What is the story of "acid bridge" and the "Seven Gates of Hell" in St. Clair County?
A   The Southwestern Illinois Tourism Bureau claims that the Louisville & Nashville Railroad tracks east of **Belleville** off Rentchler Station Road are haunted. A long time ago a group of children in a buggy were run over and killed by a train at the crossing. Now, the story goes, if you drive over the crossing at the spot and put your car into neutral, your car will be

Section of Elija Lovejoy's printing press on display at the *Alton Telegraph*

pulled back up an incline and onto the tracks in harm's way.

The Seven Gates of Hell are seven railroad bridges on or near Lebanon Road east of **Collinsville**. Legend is that if you drive fast enough over all seven of them you can enter hell.

Then there is "acid bridge" where supposedly a carload of teenagers, high on LSD, drove off one of the bridges while trying to enter hell. They unexpectedly found it after a terrible crash.

If you are one of those who likes to read this colorful nonsense, log on to the Haunted Illinois Web site at: www.dawghouse.topcities.com/illinois.html

Q   Has there ever been an exorcism in **East St. Louis**?
A   Yes, but it was not successful. J. Dwyer came to East St. Louis from Ireland with his parents in 1913. He was delivering ice on a horse-drawn wagon at the time the 1917 race riot broke out. It scared him to death, and he was a white man. His brother was on the police force at the time and was a pallbearer for Frank Wadley, one of the police detectives killed by blacks at 10th and Bond. Dwyer's brother quit the force a few weeks after the riot, ashamed of his complicity in the violence.

Dwyer lived with his aunt on 11th street near the Louisville Railroad tracks. Her rented house, built in the late 1870s, was **haunted by a poltergeist**. They experienced loud knocking inside the walls at all hours of the day and night. Auntie got a priest from St. Henry's, the church for German Catholics, to come and do an exorcism. During the exorcism, the knocking rose to a crescendo, and the priest fled in terror, leaving behind his rosary. J. Dwyer says he can prove the story is true because he still has that rosary. After that, the knocking increased triumphantly, and continued thusly, non-stop.

A few days later, the family moved to a cousin's house in Washington Park and Dwyer took a job at American Zinc in **Fairmont City**. Out of fear he never passed the old house again.

Three months later, it was the scene of a brutal murder-suicide by the new Irish tenants. Not long after that the house mysteriously burned in the middle of the night, causing the deaths of several Irish tenants.

Q   According to the Native-Americans, where did the Great Spirit Manitou dwell?
A   In northwestern Illinois – they called it Manitoumie

Q   According to noted author Troy Taylor of **Alton**, what are the ten most haunted places in Illinois?
A   1. **Bachelor's Grove Cemetery in Midlothian**: This small south side Chicago cemetery has been the source of more than 100 documented reports of supernatural activity over the years.

2. **The Old Slave House at Equality**: Hickory Hill, where slavery once existed in Illinois, has been regarded as haunted by former slaves who were chained to the floor in an upstairs room nearly a century ago.

3. **Abraham Lincoln's monument and tomb in Springfield**: The site of the first ghost stories ever told about Lincoln. The President's restless spirit is believed to haunt here.

4. **Pemberton Hall in Charleston**: The first woman's college dorm in Illinois is thought to be haunted by the spirit of a former staff member named Mary Hawkins.

5. **The McPike Mansion in Alton**: The decaying home of one of Alton's mayors is said to be haunted by a number of ghosts.

6. **The Avon Theater in Decatur**: This 1916 movie theater is still inhabited by the ghost of a former owner and a score of other spirits.

McPike Mansion (photo by Robert Graul)

7. **The Peoria State Hospital at Bartonville**: This former mental institution is haunted by a myriad of ghosts from the past, from former patients to staff members and is home to one of northern Illinois' greatest ghost stories – the Bookbinder's Elm.

8. **Voorhies Castle near Monticello**: This once "haunted house on the prairie" was a stately mansion that was mysteriously abandoned by the owners for decades. It gained a reputation for its many ghostly encounters.

9. **Greenwood Cemetery in Decatur**: This seemingly tranquil graveyard is home to numerous legends and haunts, from a spectral bride to the spirits of Confederate soldiers.

10. **Archer Avenue on the South Side of Chicago**: This stretch of roadway is home to one of America's most famous ghosts and most elusive vanishing hitchhikers – Resurrection Mary.

For more spooktacular information dial 618/465-1086 (1-888-GHOSTLY) or log on to:
www.prairieghosts.com/ghostbooks.html

ILLINOIS PREP SPORTS

Q   Why did Antwaan Randle El - **Thornton of Harvey's** outstanding point guard and quarterback - end up at Indiana U. instead of the University of Illinois?
A   Because U of I and other colleges who recruited him wanted him to play at another position beside quarterback and didn't want him to continue playing basketball. Ironically, he gave up basketball on his own. He currently plays for the Steelers (but is not a quarterback).

Q   What is the nickname for the prep sports teams of **Danville** High?
A   "Vikings"

Q   When legendary coach Duster Thomas of **Pinckneyville** led the Panthers to a state basketball title in 1948, what was his reward?
A   A new Packard automobile

Q   What northern town's high school prep teams are called Porters?
A   **Lockport** – interestingly, no one has come up with an acceptable logo to go with the name.

Q   What is the winningest prep basketball team in America?
A   **Centralia** - back in the mid 1990's Collinsville and Centralia played each other and each team had exactly 1700 victories. **Collinsville** won the game and took the title, but by the end of the season Centralia had more wins and took the record back. There is a team from the East that is closing fast on Centralia.

Q   What is the prep sports nickname for **Newark**?
A   "Norsemen" – because they have a significant Norwegian population. Children's author Nelson Waterman was from Newark.

Q   What team won the IHSA soccer title in 2001 by defeating **Edwardsville** 1-0, not giving up a single goal in tournament play?
A   Sandburg High of **Orland Park**

Q   What town was the first to win three prep basketball titles?
A   **Rockford**, when it defeated **Paris** 53-44 in 1939

Q   What town's Nevco Company is noted for making scoreboards for college and high school sporting events?
A   **Greenville**

Q   What is the nickname of St. Charles sports teams?
A   Saints

Q   What connection does NBA star Kevin Garnett have to prep Illinois basketball?
A   He was a South Carolinian but came to Chicago so he could play for **Farragut High**. He figured it would be easier to go straight to the NBA from high school playing for a big Chicago school rather than from some small jerkwater town in the South.

Q   Did Garnett's team win state his senior year?
A   No – the powerful Peoria Manual team won it.

Q   What is the nickname of the prep sports teams from **Coal City**?
A   "Coalers" – Coal City is near Joliet.

Q   How did **Centralia** get the prep nickname, Orphans?
A   Back in the 1930's their basketball team was playing in a holiday tournament at **Pontiac** and they were stranded in a blizzard. A sportswriter for the *Bloomington Pantograph* called them "Orphans of the Storm."

Q   How did Dundee prep sports teams get the nickname "Cardunals?"
A   Because players came from the towns of **CAR**penterville, **DUN**dee, and **AL**gonquin.

Q   Who coined the term "March Madness" for the IHSA basketball tournament?
A   H.V. Porter back in 1939 – this may have been its first ever use nation wide.

Q   What team has made the most appearances in the state final basketball tournament?
A   **Quincy** – 29 times

Q   What team has appeared the most in the title game?
A   Thornton of **Harvey**

Q   What team has the most regional basketball titles?
A   **Quincy** with 55

Q   What team has won the most IHSA titles?
A   **Peoria** Manual with five

Q   What team has lost the most state tournament games?
A   **Quincy** with 30

Q   What team scored the most points during a quarter in a state tournament game?
A   Collinsville with 37 points against Carbondale in a 1994 super sectional; Carbondale scored 30

Q   Who has the AA tournament record for most points scored in a four game tournament?
A   Marcus Liberty of Chicago King with 143 points; Pierre Pierce of Westmont has the A record with 159 points

Q   Who has the record for scoring the most points in a quarter?
A   Brandon Watkins scored 20 for **Westchester** / St. Joseph against **East St. Louis** in the 4th quarter of a 1999 quarterfinal.

Q   What is the AA tournament record for most overtimes?
A   Six – **Alton** prevailed over **Edwardsville** in a 1997 sectional game. **Carrollton** defeated **Bluffs** in a seven overtime game in a Class A 1997 sectional

Q   What was heartbreaking about Collinsville's 1957 title loss to **Herrin**?
A   **Collinsville**, led by All-American Terry Bethel, was undefeated 34-0 going into the game and had previously defeated Herrin; the Tigers, however, paced by John Tidwell, were also a very good team with a 30-2 record.

Q   Who was the star on the 1950 **Mt. Vernon** team?
A   Max Hooper

Q   Who was the star of the **Lawrenceville** teams of the early 1980's?
A   Marty Simmons

Q   Who was the star of **Springfield's** team in 1967?
A   Dave Robish

Q   Who was the star of **Collinsville's** 1978 team?
A   Kevin Stallings

Q   Who was the star on the Lincoln of **East St. Louis** teams of 1986-88?
A   LaPhonso Ellis

Joliet Central High School

Q   Whose tip in just before the final gun gave **Rockford West** a thrilling victory in 1955 over **Elgin**?
A   Nolden Gentry

Q   Who were the three big stars of the **Peoria** Manual team of 1997?
A   Frankie Williams, Marcus Griffin and Sergio McClain

18

Q Who was the shot-blocking star of the 1973 **St. Anne** team?
A Jack Sikma – also a big scorer

Q What town in Vermilion County hosted the first prep night football game in the state?
A **Westville - 1928**

Q Who was the shot-blocking star of the 1980 **Effingham** team?
A Uwe Blab

Q Who was the star of the magical 1944 **Taylorville** team that went undefeated and won the state title?
A Johnny Orr

Q What coaches have the most state basketball tournament titles?
A Bennie Lewis of Lincoln **East St. Louis** has four in the "AA" bracket and Ron Felling of **Lawrenceville** has four in the "A" bracket

Q What prep sports teams are called the Maple Leafs?
A **Geneseo** – "rake the Leafs" became the common rallying cry of opponents.

Q Who scored the most points in a single high school tournament game?
A Delbert Doehring of **Strasburg** scored 72 points against **Dieterich** in 1946

Q What do many enthusiasts think is wrong with the prep football playoffs from 6A down to 3A?
A The finals are all dominated by parochial schools that have no attendance boundaries, making the playoffs less competitive.

Q Darius Miles of **East St. Louis** went straight from high school to the NBA. How far did he take his Flyers in the 2000 state tournament?
A They captured third place

Dike Edleman at the University of Illinois: was a prep star at Centralia High School

Q Who was the star on the **East St. Louis** 2003-04 prep team?
A Tommie Liddell who averaged 16.5 points and over eight rebounds a game.

Q Who was the only team to defeat **Belleville West** in the regular 2003-04 season?
A The Terriers of **Carbondale**

Q What is the nickname for **Jacksonville** High's gym?

A The Bowl

West Side Senior High – Rockford (courtesy Teich Postcards)

Q How did **Carbondale** fare in the 2004 state tournament?
A They took fourth place

P.S. Some other interesting prep sports nicknames are: DeKalb Barbs, Roxana Shells, Rochelle Hubs, Pekin Dragons (previously Chinks), Rock Island Rocks, East Rockford E-Rabs and the Wethersfield Flying Geese.

RONALD WILSON REAGAN

Q In what Illinois town was Ronald Reagan born?
A He was born at Tampico in 1911.

Q What is Ronald Reagan's connection to **Galesburg**?
A His family moved there when he was four years old; incredibly, **Nancy Davis (Reagan)** also lived for a while in Galesburg, being adopted by Loyal Davis, a Chicago neurosurgeon and Galesburg native.

Q To what Illinois town did Ronald Reagan's parents move when he was nine years old?
A **Dixon**

Q What amazing feat did Reagan accomplish as a life guard at **Dixon**?
A He was credited with saving 77 lives.

Q For what Chicago sports team did Reagan do radio broadcasts?
A The Chicago Cubs

Q Reagan was able to broadcast Cub games on the road without being there. How was that possible?
A He secured information about the progress of the game by ticker tape and described the play-by-play just as though he were actually at the game. Most fans didn't know the difference.

Q How did Reagan get into the movies?

A   While doing spring training games for the Cubs in California, he decided to take a screen test, thinking he could make more money as an actor.

Q   In what movie did Ronald Reagan meet his future wife?
A   *Hellcats of the Navy*, co-starring Nancy Davis – 1957

Q   How many children did Reagan have?
A   Four – two with each wife; Michael was adopted

Q   Are all the children still living?
A   No – Maureen died from cancer a few years ago

Q   In what 1940 movie did Reagan portray George Armstrong Custer?
A   *Santa Fe Trail* – with Errol Flynn

Q   Name the Reagan movie where he portrays a scientist (John Galen) who suffers from epilepsy and is afraid to commit to the woman he loves?
A   *Night Unto Night*-1949; most viewers found this one too metaphysical; Broderick Crawford co-starred

President Reagan at work

Q   Name the Reagan movie where Ginger Rogers and Ronald Reagan team up to put Southern KKK members in jail?
A   *Storm Warning* – 1951; Rogers visits her sister (Doris Day) and is horrified to learn that Day's husband is secretly involved with Klansmen; Reagan plays the heroic District Attorney.

Q   What was the name of the 1942 movie where a sadistic doctor cuts off Reagan's legs?
A   *King's Row* – at first the Reagan character wants to die, but at the end of the film Ann Sheridan and Robert Cummings convince him to lead a productive life; some think it was Reagan's best role.

Q   What are Reagan's two most memorable film lines?
A   "Where's the rest of me?" from *Kings Row* and "Win one for the Gipper" from *Knute Rockne*

Q   What was Reagan's last movie?
A   *The Killers* - 1964

Q   What title did Reagan give to himself as a movie star?

A   "The Errol Flynn of B Movies"

Q   How long was Reagan's film career, and how many movies did he make?
A   50 movies – from 1937-1964

Q   What role brought him into the spotlight?
A   Football player George Gipp in *Knute Rockne – All American*

Q   Why was Reagan told he should only make two movies a year?
A   Friends said it would push him into the 90 percent tax bracket and he would be working for almost nothing.

Q   Did he violate that rule?
A   Yes – in 1939 he made seven films and in 1940 he made six films.

Q   Why didn't Reagan serve in combat in World War II?
A   His eyesight was too poor, so he made army training films.

Q   What two big name television shows did Reagan host?
A   "Death Valley Days" and "General Electric Theater"

Q   Why did Reagan switch to the Republican Party in 1962 after being a lifelong Democrat?
A   As part of being the spokesperson for General Electric, he went around to all the plants and talked with the workers and management. He saw firsthand how high government taxation and excessive regulation hurt business. After giving a speech, someone remarked that he sounded more like a Republican than a Democrat.

Q   What was Reagan's first "political" job?
A   President of the Screen Actor's Guild

Q   How many terms did Reagan serve as governor of California?
A   Two

Hellcats Of The Navy

Q   What **Rockford** native ran (and lost) against Reagan as an Independent in 1980?
A   John Anderson

Q   What incumbent Democrat did Reagan defeat in 1980?
A   Jimmy Carter

Q   What did the Iranian government do shortly after Reagan took office in January of 1981?
A   They released hostages taken in the attack on the U.S. embassy and held prisoner for 444 days.

Q   What did Reagan think about using the government to solve America's problems?
A   He said that the "era of big government is over."

Q What title did he have as President?
A "The Great Communicator"

Q What two records did Reagan set when he was elected in 1980?
A He was the oldest man ever elected President at age 69; he was also the first divorced man (from actress Jane Wyman) to win the office.

Ron and Nancy Reagan

Q Who tried to assassinate Reagan after only two months in office?
A John Hinckley, who was later declared insane

Q What was Reagan's famous quip to doctors just before he went under the knife?
A "I hope you're all Republicans."

Q How was Reagan struck by a Hinckley bullet?
A It ricocheted off the limo

Q What **Centralia** man received a severe head wound in the attack?
A James Brady – Reagan's press secretary

Q How close did Reagan come to dying?
A Doctors said had he arrived at the hospital five minutes later, he probably would have bled to death internally.

Q What was Alexander Haig's humorous and odd comment to reporters after the shooting?
A "I'm in charge of things now here at the White House."

Q What "first" did Reagan achieve regarding the U.S. Supreme Court?
A He nominated Sandra Day O'Connor, the first woman to sit on the high court.

Q What new national holiday did Reagan sign into law in 1986?
A Martin Luther King's birthday

Q What was Reagan's re-election campaign slogan in 1984?
A "Are you better off now than you were four years ago?"

Q What two other world leaders teamed with Reagan to spread freedom and democracy?
A Margaret Thatcher of Great Britain and Pope John Paul II of Poland

Q What were Reagan's two most successful military ventures?
A The bombing of Libya (we never heard a peep from Kadafi after that) and the invasion of Grenada to rescue of the medical students stranded after a Marxist coup

Q What was Reagan's greatest foreign policy failure?
A Sending the troops to Lebanon where over two hundred of them were killed by a suicide bomber

Q What was Reagan's most memorable line regarding foreign policy?
A "Mr. Gorbachev, tear down this wall." (Berlin wall)

Q What was Reagan's famous quote about trying to negotiate arms limitation treaties with the Soviets?
A After two Soviet heads of state died in office, Reagan said: "I'm trying to negotiate with these fellows, but they keep dying on me."

Q What was significant about the S.A.L.T. Treaty that Reagan negotiated with the Soviets?
A It provided for a reduction of nuclear missiles on both sides – a first

Q What was Reagan's famous quote about trusting the Soviets after signing an arms reduction treaty?

Reagan just moments after being hit by assassin's bullet

A "Trust, but verify!"
Q What huge change did Reagan make in our policy toward the Soviet Union?
A He scrapped détente, which had been followed by Nixon, Ford and Carter, and replaced it with a policy of

21

rolling back communism. Reagan labeled the Soviet Union the "Evil Empire."

Q   What was Reagan's code name with the Secret Service?
A   "Rawhide"

Q   Did the Soviet Union collapse on its own, or did Reagan give it a big push?
A   When Reagan was first elected someone asked him what his policy was going to be regarding the Soviets. His response: "How about we *win* the Cold War, and they *lose*."

Q   What caused the big deficits during the Reagan administration?
A   Huge amounts were spent to bolster the military since the Carter administration had made cuts in that area. Democrats, who controlled congress, only went along in return for huge increases in social programs.

Q   Is the charge by Democrats that Reagan did little about the AIDS epidemic fair?
A   Probably not since his administration earmarked more money for AIDS research than any other disease.

Q   Did Reagan ever do anything about high taxes?
A   Yes – he reduced the rates from 78 percent to 28 percent. Their current levels are about 35 percent.

Q   Why was Reagan not too worried about the large deficits when he left office?
A   He knew the economy was doing extremely well, and that an expanding economy would erase the red ink, which is exactly what happened during the Clinton years.

Nancy and Ron Reagan

Q   What was Reagan's favorite activity at Camp David?
A   Watching movies with Nancy and eating popcorn

Q   How did Reagan endear himself to American women in recent years?
A   After he announced that he was in the early stages of Alzheimer's, a book was published containing his love letters to Nancy. They were sweet, witty and romantic.

Q   What term is being used by historians to describe the Reagan presidency?
A   Morning in America – his optimism reflecting the bright dawn of promise for our future

Q   What was Reagan's vision for America?
A   To him we were an example for the rest of the world - a Shining City on a Hill

Q   What was the biggest scandal during the Reagan years?
A   Ollie North and the Iran-Contra Affair

Q   What name came to be applied to Reagan's "trickle down" economic policies?
A   Reaganomics – some called it Voodoo economics

Q   What great success is generally given to Reagan's policies concerning the Soviet Union?
A   The collapse of the Soviet Union and victory in the Cold War

Q   What Reagan policy was the most controversial?
A   Strategic Defensive Initiative (SDI) – the proposal for a defensive shield around the U.S. to protect from nuclear missiles; critics called it Star Wars

Q   What surprising action did Reagan take when the air traffic controllers went on an illegal strike?
A   He gave them 48 hours to come back to work and fired them when they stood pat.

Q   What kind of a victory margin did Reagan achieve in his 1984 re-election bid?
A   He won 49 of 50 states against Walter Mondale, the greatest margin in history.

Q   How did Reagan turn the issue about his age around in the 1984 election?
A   During one of the debates Reagan made the comment that he didn't think age should be an issue in the election. Accordingly, he wasn't going to hammer Fritz Mondale on his youth and inexperience.

Q   What was Reagan's famous line about abortion?
A   It was a Dennis Milleresque, "I notice everyone who's for it has already been born."

Q   What naval vessel has been named for Ronald Reagan?
A   A new aircraft carrier about the length of three football fields

Q   Does Reagan have an airport named for him?
A   Yes – the old National Airport in Washington, D.C.

Q   What monetary tribute do many think should be made?
A   Place Ronald Reagan on the ten-dollar bill instead of Alexander Hamilton

Q   What candy did Reagan make famous?
A   Jelly Bellies

Q   What was Reagan's approval rating when he left office?
A   The highest of any president since scientific polling was instituted.

Q   Was Reagan the only president born in Illinois?

A   Yes – Lincoln was born in Kentucky and Grant was born in Ohio. There is a good chance that Chicagoan Hillary Clinton will be our first woman president.

Q   Does Reagan hold the record for gaining the most in popularity points after leaving office?
A   Yes – he gained an astounding 20 percent

"NOT WITHOUT THY WONDROUS STORY" - ILLINOIS HISTORY

Q   What is the official language of Illinois?
A   Surprise – it's "American," not English.

Q   How did early Illinois acquire the nickname, "The Graveyard of the West?"
A   Because of its reputation for fatal diseases such as cholera and danger from Indian attacks. People tended to settle along river valleys and these were breeding grounds for mosquitoes. Since there were no screens, flies were also a constant problem.

Q   What percentage of pioneer children died before reaching their fifth birthday?
A   Half

Seal of the French Jesuits

Q   What Europeans "discovered" the Illinois River?
A   Marquette and Joliet – yes, the Native Americans already knew it existed - (PC)

Q   Illinois Indians were decimated by warfare with what tribes to their east and west?
A   The Iroquois in the east and the Sioux in the west.

Q   Where was the first "civilized settlement" on the Illinois River?
A   Fort Crève Coeur (broken heart) built by LaSalle and Tonty

Q   How did the fort get its name?
A   The difficulty in getting it built and the numerous desertions nearly broke the hearts of the men involved.

British Union Jack

Q   How many flags have flown over the land of Illinois?
A   Three – French, British, and USA; some might want to include Virginia which claimed Illinois at the end of the Revolution; Desoto made vague claims when he discovered the Mississippi, but the Spanish never colonized Illinois

Q   What shocked Anglo-Americans about the way the French in Illinois treated their slaves?
A   The French worked alongside them in the fields.

Q   In general, how did Anglo-Americans view French inhabitants in pioneer Illinois?
A   They saw them as a collection of uncouth, lazy, partiers who mixed readily with "inferior" races.

Q   What was one of the few Illinois tribes to side with the Americans in the Revolutionary War?
A   The Kaskaskia

Q   What term of reproach was used to describe easterners

Chief DuQuoin's house - a reward for signing the 1803 treaty

that migrated to frontier Illinois?
A   Yankees – those who came from the South or West were called "white people"

Q   What friendly chief was a big help to the American cause in the Revolutionary War?
A   Chief Ducoigne (DuQuoin)

Q   How many electoral votes does Illinois have in presidential elections?
A   21; California has something like 55 votes

Q   How is the number 21 determined?
A   Based on population, it is equal to our combined number of U.S. representatives and senators.

Q   How many African-Americans fled to **Cairo** and stayed at the close of the Civil War?
A   Many of the "contraband" returned to the South after the war, but about 3,000 stayed on.

Q   What major company opened a large factory in **Cairo** in 1881?
A   Singer Sewing Machine - cabinets

Q   What incident in November 1909 put a damper on the effort of the "colored" community in **Cairo** to seek equality and desegregated schools?
A   The lynching and burning of William James

Q   What was Lincoln's greatest achievement in the realm of foreign affairs?
A   He largely persuaded European countries not to give diplomatic recognition to the Confederacy.

Q   How did Union soldiers tend to vote in the 1864 election?
A   Eighty percent of them voted for Lincoln

Q   What are the only two historical figures that have had more books written about them than Abe Lincoln?
A   Jesus and Napoleon

Q   When the Civil War ended and a military band offered to play Lincoln a tune, what song did he request?
A   "Dixie"

Q   What woman operated a notable writers colony in **Marshall**, Illinois, (Clark County) from 1949-64?
A   Lowney Handy Turner – the men and women that she tutored had little income and lived in barracks and tents

Q   Who was her most noted student?
A   James Jones who wrote *From Here to Eternity* and *Some Came Running*

Q   How long did it take Jones to write *From Here to Eternity*?
A   Five years

Q   How many Pulitzer Prizes did Carl Sandburg Win?
A   Two – one for his biography of Lincoln and another for his poems

Q   What would be the best way to describe Sandburg's political ideology in his early career from 1900-1925?
A   He was a socialist and a radical who espoused direct action revolutionary tactics.

Spring Valley Mine #5 near Seatonville – 1901-1924

Q   What famous Indian once worked the lead mines at **Galena** (originally called January's Point)?
A   Blackhawk

Q   How many **Springfield** families were in the Donner Party of 1846 that became stranded in the Sierra Nevada mountains on their way to California?
A   Three – Unfortunately, they tried to take a short cut, became lost, and resorted to cannibalism in order to survive the snow and cold.

Q   What boon was Donner Pass to railroad builders?

A   It was the only pass through the mountains that engineers could find that was suitable when the transcontinental railroad was built from Omaha to Sacramento in 1869.

Q   What were the three dominant groups in early **Galesburg**?
A   Yankees, Irish, and Swedes

Q   The state seal has a group of laurel leaves in the lower left hand corner. What do they represent?
A   The great achievements of Illinois citizens; a crown of laurel leaves was the prize for winners in the Olympic Games in ancient Greece.

Q   What three prominent Illinoisans are mentioned in the fourth verse of the state song, "Illinois?"

James Robert Mann

A   Lincoln, Grant, and Logan – "On the record of thy years/ Abra'am Lincoln's name appears/ Grant and Logan, and our tears, Illinois, Illinois/ Grant and Logan and our tears, Illinois, Illinois."

Q   For what two pieces of national legislation is James R. Mann of Chicago remembered?
A   The 1910 Mann White Slave Traffic Act (transporting women across state lines for immoral purposes) and the Mann-Elkins Act that expanded the power of the Interstate Commerce Commission regarding the power to regulate railroad rates

Q   In 1850's Illinois, how often did most towns elect a mayor?
A   Annually

Q   During the national Railroad Shopmen's Strike of 1922 when 400,000 workers struck for better wages and working conditions, what two Illinois towns had the state militia sent to them to suppress violence?
A   **Bloomington** and **Clinton**

Q   What Mississippi River town was given permission to have the state's first gambling boat in 1991? (A) Quincy (B) Alton (C) East St. Louis (D) Rock Island
A   **Alton** – the *Alton Belle*

Q   What two towns were forced to remove the Christian cross from their city seals in 1992?
A   **Zion** and **Rolling Meadow** – the Supreme Court found the symbols offensive to minorities.

Q   What 1833 incident harmed **Jacksonville's** aspirations to become the new state capital?
A   A cholera epidemic that somehow missed **Springfield**; Jacksonville thereafter was seen as an unhealthy place.

Q   For what is Dr. John Bennett best remembered in Illinois history?
A   He was a Mormon turncoat who wormed his way into the confidence of leaders at **Nauvoo** and then spent the rest of his life exposing Mormonism.

Q   What is the most remembered thing about the personal life of Edgar Lee Masters?
A   His unfaithfulness to his wife and his many affairs

Q   What was the best-selling book of 1923 in homes where coal miners lived?
A   *The Autobiography of Mother Jones*

Q   What was the principal means of power for boats on the Illinois & Michigan Canal?
A   Teams of four to six mules

Q   What Illinoisan was considered *the* master of patronage politics?
A   Mayor Richard J. Daley of Chicago – according to Richard Ciccone, no big-city leader in modern American history has ever been so nationally famous and so perceivably prominent as Daley.

Q   What is probably the most offbeat thing film critic **Roger Ebert** has done?
A   He wrote the screenplay for *Beyond The Valley of the Dolls* – a sexy/tasteless Russ Meyer production.

Q   How did Karen Hughes come up with the title, *Ten Minutes From Normal,* for her 2004 book about Republican politics?
A   The book is about the hectic 2000 presidential campaign.   The day before the election, at the end of the campaign - totally exhausted - she was finally on her way back home.   Someone in her travel group made the comment that they were ten minutes away from **Normal**, Illinois.   She vowed that if she ever wrote a book, that would be her title.

"Mining in Illinois" by William Schwartz of Eldorado

Q   What is the touch of irony in the death of Eugene Williams, the young African-American whose death led to the Chicago race riot of 1919 that left 38 dead?

A   His death was more or less accidental. When his "raft" drifted into the "whites only" section of a segregated beach, onlookers threw things to drive him back. One missile struck him, causing him to lose his grip, and he drowned.

Q   What Illinois prison has been referred to by some historians as the "Andersonville of the North?"
A   **Rock Island**

Q   What famous fictional character visited **Rock Island** Prison?
A   Ashley Wilkes in *Gone With The Wind*

Q   What did some Confederate prisoners do to secure release from **Rock Island** Prison?
A   They swore oaths of loyalty to the union and were sent out west to fight in the Indian wars. They were called "Galvanized Yankees."

Q   What town saw the 1881 lynching of a prisoner in the **McLean County** Jail?

Illinois Sanitary and Ship Canal under construction circa 1894

A   Charles Pierce had been arrested in **Bloomington** for stealing a horse and rig. During an attempted escape, he killed the jailer. An angry mob, frustrated by the failures of the justice system, dragged him from his cell and hanged him from the limb of a nearby elm tree. As Pierce slowly choked to death, one man slid down the rope and sat on his shoulders to insure strangulation.

Q   What was General John Logan's nickname?
A   Black Jack, due to his swarthy complexion and long black hair

Q   What college did writers Philip Roth and Susan Sontag attend?
A   The University of Chicago

Q   For what Chicago newspaper did Langston Hughes write dozens and dozens of articles?
A   The *Chicago Defender* the most influential African-American newspaper of its time

Q   How did Illinoisans vote on an 1855 proposal to decide whether the sale and consumption of alcohol would be outlawed?

A   Overwhelmingly *against* by a majority of 14,447

Q   What were the two main reasons for the founding of **Belleville** in 1814 on land donated by George Blair?
A   To move the county seat closer to the middle of the region and to undermine the economic and cultural dominance of the old county seat, French Cahokia

Q   Beside coal, what else did **Bellevillians** export to St. Louis in 1850?
A   Beer – Stag beer would later become prominent

Q   James G. Randall wrote an excellent two-volume biography of Lincoln back in 1946. What was his controversial "revisionist" thesis?
A   The Civil War was avoidable, and it was brought on by a generation of "blundering politicians."

Q   What school music teacher from **Meredosia** was responsible for leading a famous cavalry raid in the western theater of the Civil War?
A   Ben Grierson – ironically, he hated horses; General Sherman described his exploit as **one of the most brilliant of the entire war**.

Q   What did Grierson do after the war?
A   He commanded a Negro military unit in the southwest (10th Cavalry) that the Indians called the **Buffalo Soldiers**. Grierson lived out the last 20 years of his life in **Jacksonville**.

Colonel Benjamin H. Grierson

Q   What Democrat gave a magnificent 1861 speech in Chicago that probably prevented civil war in southern Illinois, an area sympathetic to the Confederate cause?
A   Stephen Douglas – "Every man must be for the United States or against it. There can be no neutrals in war – only patriots and traitors."

Q   How did the military site in Chicago come to be known as Camp Douglas?
A   After Stephen Douglas died, 60 acres of land that was once part of his estate was converted to military use

Civil War Governor Richard Yates

Q   Where did many observers think the first great battle of the Civil War would occur?
A   At **Cairo** – Illinois troops quickly arrived on the scene via the Illinois Central and took possession of Bird's Point and built Fort Defiance. U.S. Grant then occupied Paducah, Kentucky, at the mouth of the Tennessee River. Grant arrived a scant two hours ahead of Confederate forces.

Q   During the Civil War Confederates were called Johnny Reb. What were Union soldiers called?
A   Among other things, Billy Yank

Q   Name two important Illinois sites where there were Civil War battles.
A   There were none, although frustrated Rebs occasionally tried to shoot at northerners across the Ohio River from Kentucky.

Q   What **East St. Louis** businessman and alleged gangster lived in a **home surrounded by a moat** on the outskirts of **Collinsville** in the 1950's and '60's?
A   Frank "Buster" Wortman

Q   What was the Broyles Oath?
A   This legislation, passed in 1952, required state employees to sign a paper stating that they were not members of the Communist Party. It was named for the **Mount Vernon** legislator who sponsored the bill.

Q   What Chicago company published Great Books of the Western World in 1952?
A   Encyclopedia Brittanica

Q   Why was Reagan called the "Teflon President?"
A   None of the bad things that happened during his tenure stuck to him – he remained as popular as ever

Q   What name did Hugh Heffner originally choose for his magazine?
A   *Stag Party* – he changed it to *Playboy* just before publication in late 1953

Q   What college or university did Hugh Heffner attend?
A   University of Illinois – he wrote for a campus humor magazine and was a cartoonist

Q   What other function did barbers perform besides cutting hair in frontier Illinois?
A   They were bloodletters – illness back then was thought to be caused by bad blood so people were bled. Sometimes leeches were used for that purpose.

Q   How long did frontier women stay in bed after giving birth?
A   Ten days – anything less was thought to be dangerous

Q   When *Tribune* journalist Henry Demarest Lloyd wrote *Wealth Against Commonwealth*, what Robber Barron did he lambaste?
A   John D. Rockefeller – Lloyd's sons donated the money to build the **Winnetka** Public Library in 1910

Q   Ernest Hemingway grew up in the **Oak Park** suburb of Chicago. Which of his novels or stories uses Oak Park as a setting?
A   None – he never wrote a story set in Oak Park

Q   What was the historic significance of the Escobedo v. Illinois U.S. Supreme Court case in 1964?
A   The court ruled that Escobedo should be set free because he was denied his right to legal counsel before he made a confession to police.

Q   In what year was it necessary to send in the national guard to quell a Chicago riot because police used billy clubs on African-American youth who opened fire hydrants so they could splash in the water?
A   1966

Q   What apology did the Beatles make to the world at Chicago's Astor Towers Hotel in 1966?
A   They apologized for creating a firestorm by claiming they were more popular than Jesus.

Q   What act by the U.S. government in 1827 by the U.S. government was responsible for the creation of **Ottawa**?
A   A grant of a ten mile stretch of land for the purpose of uniting the waters of Lake Michigan with the Illinois River; Ottawa became known as "Chicago's twin"

Q   When the U.S. government began offering land for sale in various parts of Illinois, who bought most of it?
A   Eastern speculators who then resold it in smaller parcels to homesteaders at a profit

Q   Who were the "Corkonians" in **Ottawa**?
A   Irish settlers who came to build the Illinois and Michigan Canal and eventually settled there; Cork is a county in Ireland.

Q   When did the U.S. government first begin surveying the Military Tract in western Illinois?
A   1816 – but it was not available for settlement until after the Black Hawk War

Q   What did Presbyterians and Congregationalists call Baptists and Methodists during the era of frontier Illinois?
A   "Primitive" religions

Russian Orthodox Church at Benld by Dan Oberle

Q   How much did George Washington Gale pay for his 8,978 acres for the settlement of **Galesburg**?
A $1.25 an acre

Q   What famous remark was made by a Chicago policeman after Pablo Picasso's sculpture was unveiled in 1967?
A   To paraphrase, he said, "I like it, whatever it is."

Q   How did William Jennings Bryan of **Salem** get the nickname, "the Great Commoner?"
A   After he gave his "Cross of Gold" speech at the 1896 Democratic convention in Chicago, a railroad company offered to let him use a private car for travel. Newsmen took notice when he turned the favor down.

Q   What do many political observers think might be the next amendment to the Illinois Constitution?
A   Tort reform – two previous efforts at lawsuit reform have been declared unconstitutional. Several Illinois groups claim that excessive jury awards and frivolous lawsuits cost each taxpayer $3,000 annually.

Q   What two counties in particular have been hit hard by doctors leaving because of high insurance from excessive jury awards in malpractice suits?
A   St. Clair and Madison counties

Mother Jones Monument at Mt. Olive

Q   What percent of all class action lawsuits in the USA are filed at **Edwardsville** in Madison County?
A   Nine percent – a truly astounding number

Q   Why does this make tort reform in Illinois more difficult?
A   Nobody wants to kill a cash cow.

Q   During Prohibition, what five Illinois cities were targeted for cleanup by the federal government?
A   Chicago, **Peoria, Rockford, Toluca, E. St. Louis.**

Q   What was the first large-scale commercial mining district in Illinois?
A   The Longwall Mining District

Mining Towns and Principal Rail Routes of the Longwall Mining District, Illinois (ca. 1910)

Q   What were some of the towns in this district?
A   **Cherry, Streator, Seneca, Braidwood, Gardner, Cardiff, Roanoke, Peru**

Q   Why was it called the Longwall District?
A   It was named for the type of mining carried out there.

Q   At its peak around 1900, how many mines were operating in the Longwall District?
A   44

Q   What Illinois town has twin peaks of mine slag called "Jumbos" preserved as landmarks?
A   **Toluca**

Q   Mining towns are usually rough and tumble. How many taverns did **Toluca** have in its heyday?
A   Thirty-three

Q   When Adlai Stevenson ran against Ike in 1952 and 1956, what was his biggest problem with communications?
A   Although he gave marvelous and insightful speeches, they often bored or confused average voters.

Q   What did Stevenson think of television ads for campaign purposes?
A   He hated them. He did not want to be packaged and sold like a breakfast cereal.

Q   On what bill did U.S. Congressman William Bissell and Dorothea Dix collaborate?
A   The Ten Million Acres bill of the 1850's, whereby the federal government would make land grants to states if money from sales was used to build better prisons and facilities for the insane. After about four years the bill finally passed but was vetoed by Franklin Pierce.

Q   What is Republican Senator Everett Dirksen's most famous quote?

A   "A billion here, a billion there, and sooner or later we're talking about real money" – Dirksen was a noted fiscal conservative.

Q   What was Dirksen's greatest speech?
A   The one he gave in support of the Marshall Plan

Q   What was the highest position attained by Everett Dirksen?
A   Senate Minority Leader

Q   Did Dirksen ever make the cover of Time Magazine?
A   Yes, in September of 1962

Q   In general, on what things did Dirksen support JFK and where did he criticize?
A   He was supportive of his foreign policy and critical of the New Frontier domestic policies.

Q   What important pieces of legislation during the Johnson administration did Dirksen shepherd through the U.S. Senate?
A   The Civil Rights Act of 1964 and the Voting Rights Act of 1965

Q   What style of architecture was used in the construction of Eastern Illinois University at **Charleston** in 1896?
A   Tudor-Gothic

Q   What is the identity of the man in John Hallwas' book, *The Bootlegger*?
A   Henry (Kelly) Wagle – a well-known bootlegger and the most celebrated citizen of **Colchester**, Illinois

Q   Did reformer Dorothea Dix ever visit Illinois?
A   Yes – she visited the prison at **Alton**, a poorhouse in **Galena**, and successfully lobbied the Illinois legislature in **Springfield** to provide funding for the Illinois State Hospital For The Insane at **Jacksonville**.

Dorothea Dix

Q   What battle on the Mississippi River led to the promotion of Illinoisan John Pope to command Union armies at the Second Battle of Bull Run?
A   The strategic capture of Island Number Ten near New Madrid

Q   Why did an angry **Charleston** mob lynch Adolphus Monroe in February of 1856?
A   They were angry because he had murdered his father-in-law, Nathan Ellington, who was a popular public official.

Q   In what Illinois town is Frank Lloyd Wright's famous Tomek House?

A **Riverside**

Q   What mining town in Bureau County had a race riot in 1895?
A   **Spring Valley**

"Jumbos" gob piles near Toluca

Q   What was the cause of the riot?
A   African-Americans were brought in by Spring Valley Mining Co. to replace striking miners. Italian miners attacked and drove the dark skinned workers out of town. Most took refuge with other black families at nearby **Seatonville**.

Q   How can it be argued that the *Titanic* was responsible for the Eastland tragedy in the Chicago River?
A   Author George Hilton blames the 1915 tragedy on a fatal imbalance due to the installation of safety equipment installed *after* the sinking of the *Titanic*.

Q   What is the usual explanation for the disaster where the ship turned over "like an egg in the water?"
A   A large rush of passengers on the deck to one side of the boat

Q   How many Confederate prisoners died at Camp Douglas in Chicago?
A   4,000

Q   During the Civil War there was an outbreak of violence in Illinois between Democrats and Unionists that ranks second only to the draft riots in New York City. In what town were nine men killed?
A   **Charleston** – 1864; six Union soldiers were killed, two Democrats and a Republican civilian. It was all about differing loyalties, a polarizing political climate, and soldiers trying to force Democrats into taking loyalty oaths.

MURDER!

The 54th Regiment Illinois Volunteers offer **ONE THOUSAND DOLLARS REWARD** for the apprehension of John H. O'Hair, Sheriff of Coles County, J. Elsbury Hanks, John Frazier, James W. Frazier, Henderson O'Hair, James O'Hair, Jesse O'Hair, B.F. Toland, and B.F. Dukes, all of whom were engaged in the brutal murder of Major York and four soldiers of the 54th Regiment and the wounding of several others, in Charleston, on Monday, March 28, 1864.

Joshua Fry Speed

Q   When Lincoln first came to **Springfield** as a lawyer in 1837 he had no money and no place to stay. Who be-friended him?
A   Joshua Speed, a store manager, offered to share his room above a store with Lincoln. The two were close friends for four years.

Q   What other Illinois towns have had race riots?

Corngrowers Liberty League Poster

A   **Springfield, Chicago, East St. Louis, Decatur, Virden, Pana**

Corn Growers
Attention
●
ARE YOU SATISFIED WITH YOUR CORN ALLOTMENTS?

Can You Operate Your Farm at a Profit Under the Allotments Fixed for McDonough County?

Do You Believe in Independence for the American Farmer?

Attend the meeting of corn growers of Western Illinois at the Court Room next Monday night, April 18, at 7:30 p. m. A full attendance is desired from every township in McDonough and adjoining counties. Come prepared to express your views.

This matter is of utmost importance to every corn farmer in the corn belt. Tell your neighbors and come and take part.
●
CORN BELT LIBERTY LEAGUE

AAA

Q   Where was the center of this protest?
A   McDonough County, with headquarters at **Macomb**; farmers tend to be very individualistic and often resent government interference in their lives.

Q   At the beginning of the Civil War, what kind of paper money was being printed by the U.S. Treasury?
A   None – all paper money back then was printed by banks

Q   What New Deal agency was the Illinois Corn Belt Liberty League opposed to?
A   The Agricultural Adjustment Act –

Q   When did southern Illinoisans begin to discard grain farming in favor of orchard production?
A   During the early 1920's due to falling grain prices from overproduction

Q   French Icarians bought abandoned land at **Nauvoo** after the Mormon exodus. Where did their ideas come from?

A Etienne Cabet, who wrote a novel, *Voyage en Icarie*.

Q What were their utopian beliefs?
A Communal living, egalitarianism, and the elimination of money, private property, immorality, and crime

Q What Illinois university town saw the worst rioting by college students after the shootings by national guardsmen at Kent State in 1969?
A **Carbondale** – rioting students burned down Old Main

Q What was the name of the patriotic LP recording put out by Senator Everett Dirksen, shortly before he died in 1968?
A "Gallant Men"

Senator Everett Dirksen

U.S. GRANT – OUR 18ᵀᴴ PRESIDENT

Q What was Grant's first name?
A Hiram – the papers for Grant's appointment to the U.S. Military Academy were improperly filled out as U.S. Grant and that name stuck.

Q Were Abe Lincoln and U.S. Grant good dancers?
A No

Q What was the reason for most of Grant's demerits at West Point?
A Sloppiness of dress – none for disobedience

Q How did Grant meet his future wife, Julia Dent?
A She was Grant's roommate's sister when he was stationed at Jefferson Barracks south of St. Louis. The family lived in nearby St. Louis and it was love at first sight.

Q When did they get married?
A August of 1848 in St. Louis

Q What was the low point in Grant's career?

A In 1855 Grant was cashiered from the military for drunkenness and went back to his fiancée in St. Louis jobless, penniless and in disgrace.

Q What did Grant name the home he built in St. Louis on his farm?
A Hardscrabble – the land on which it was built was a wedding gift from Julia's father.

Q What was Grant's main source of income on his farm?
A He cut timber and sold it for firewood.

Q Did Grant own any slaves?
A Yes, three of them given to his wife by her father

Q Did he have any children at this point in his life?
A Yes – two sons, Ulysses Jr. and Freddie; a daughter named Nellie was born later at Hardscrabble.

Q Since Grant could not make a go of it on his farm in St. Louis, when did he move to **Galena** to work in his father's tanning business?
A 1860

Q When did Grant go back into the military?
A After the fall of Fort Sumter he attended a meeting in **Galena** and was impressed with a pro Union speech given by attorney John A. Rawlins.

Q What was Grant's first job in the Civil War?
A He formed a company in **Galena** and went with them to **Springfield** where he trained and drilled them at Camp Yates; they became the 21ˢᵗ Illinois Volunteers

U.S Grant, Julia Dent, and four children

Q After arriving at **Cairo**, what nearby town did Grant take without firing a shot?

A   Strategic Paducah on the Tennessee and Cumberland, rivers, barely arriving there before Confederates took the city

Q   In what **Cairo** building did Grant have his headquarters?
A   The famous Halliday Hotel – now a landmark

Hardscrabble – Grant's home in St. Louis

Q   How did Grant earn the nickname "Unconditional Surrender" Grant?
A   When he captured Fort Donnelson, the Confederate commander asked him what were the terms? Grant replied, "No terms except immediate and unconditional surrender can be accepted."

Q   What was ironic about this incident in Grant's life?
A   The commander at Fort Donnelson was Simon Bolivar Buckner, a West Point classmate and one of Grant's best friends during the Mexican War.

Q   What commander was with Grant at Fort Donnelson?
A   General Lew Wallace, who later wrote the novel *Ben Hur*

Q   What Confederate cavalry leader escaped Grant's clutches before the surrender at Fort Donnelson?
A   Nathan Bedford Forrest – the man who (after the Civil War) **helped form the KKK**; Forrest was a demon and the one Confederate commander Grant truly dreaded.

Q   What was Forrest's famous dictum?
A   "Victory goes to him that gets there the firstest with the mostest."

Q   Grant had always smoked a clay pipe. How did he become a cigar smoker?
A   The newspapers reported him having an unlit cigar in his mouth during the campaign against Fort Donnelson. After that, admirers kept sending him boxes of cigars as gifts.

Q   What did Lincoln say when critics wanted him to fire U.S. Grant because of his drinking?
A   "I can't spare this man, he fights."

Q   When Lincoln began receiving false reports that Grant was drinking again, what was his famous reply?
A   To paraphrase: "Find out what brand he is drinking and send a case of it to each of my generals."

Q   What close friend and commander was referred to as "Grant's right arm?"
A   William T. Sherman

Q   General Lee's favorite horse was "Traveler." What was Grant's favorite horse?
A   "Cincinnati"

Q   What was Grant's most brilliant campaign of the entire war?
A   Vicksburg – in campaigns against Donnelson and Shiloh, he had made mistakes, but Vicksburg was flawless.

Q   Why was Vicksburg such a strategic stronghold?
A   The city commanded a high bluff overlooking a hairpin curve in the Mississippi River, controlling all river traffic that went past it.

Impressive Illinois monument at Vicksburg

Q   What message did Grant send to Lincoln after the fall of Vicksburg, July 4, 1863?
A   To paraphrase: "Once again the Father of Waters goes unvexed to the sea."

Q   Was Grant at the battle of Gettysburg?
A   No – Gettysburg was being fought at the same time as the Vicksburg campaign.

Q   When was Grant promoted to General-in-Chief?
A   After the capture of Chattanooga – 1864

Q   What Southern general, who was with Grant at West Point, the Mexican War, and was present at his wedding, warned Robert E. Lee to be wary of Grant?
A   General James Longstreet – the man who failed Lee at Gettysburg

Q   In MacKinley Kantor's novel, *If The South Had Won The War*, what happens to Grant?
A   In this "what if?" book, the author has Grant falling from his horse and being killed when his head strikes a rock. Stonewall Jackson survives his accidental shooting and

lives to "save the day" at Gettysburg. The Grant incident is based on an actual event where his horse threw him at Chattanooga, badly bruising his leg.

Q When U.S. Grant took command of the Army of the Potomac in the East, how badly did his troops outnumber Lee's?

U.S. Grant in 1865

A Lee's strength was about 50,000 while Grant had 100,000. In fairness to Grant, it should be remembered that other Union commanders had greatly outnumbered Lee and didn't get the job done.

Q What campaigns was Grant involved in against Robert E. Lee?
A Wilderness, Petersburg, Cold Harbor, Spotsylvania Court House, Richmond

Q What impressed Robert E. Lee when he surrendered to Grant at Appomattox?
A Grant's kindness and generosity and the fact that Grant would not let his men celebrate the triumph over their southern brethren. Grant also ordered that Lee's men be given food.

Q What unusual subject did Grant bring up at the Appomattox surrender?
A Trying to be polite, he reminisced with Lee about their time together in the Mexican War.

Q What gift was Grant presented with when he came back to **Galena**?
A A brick two-story house worth $16,000

Q What friend of Grant, from **Murphysboro**, is considered America's greatest "political general" in the Civil War?
A John Logan – a brilliant orator, capable politician, efficient and brave officer

Q What exactly was a "political general?"
A When the Civil War broke out there was a shortage of soldiers and officers. Politicians who gave speeches and formed a company of volunteers were given leadership positions, despite not having any military training from West Point.

Q When did Grant first draw attention as a possible Republican candidate in the 1868 election?
A When he broke ranks with President Andrew Johnson, disagreeing with his harsh reconstruction policies

Q What were Grant's main weaknesses as President?

A He lacked knowledge about governmental affairs, was politically naïve, and made the mistake of appointing his military friends to cabinet positions.

Q What fortuitous circumstances saved Grant's son from being killed at the Custer massacre in 1876?
A He was attached to Custer's 7th Cavalry but was granted leave to go to Washington, D.C. for the birth of his daughter.

Q When delegations of Native-Americans came to visit Grant at the White House, what name did they have for him?
A The Great White Father

Q Did Grant give consideration to running for a third term?
A He thought about it but then said *no* and went on a tour of Europe instead.

Q How close did Grant come to getting the nomination in 1880?
A He led on the first 35 ballots but could not gain a majority and lost out to Garfield as a compromise candidate.

U.S. Grant statue in Chicago

Q Why did Grant move to New York City, the site of his famous tomb?
A To be near his son Ulysses Jr. who lived there

Q What caused Grant's death?
A Throat cancer, undoubtedly from smoking all those cigars

Q Who paid Grant money to publish his memoirs?
A His friend Mark Twain – sales earned the family $450,000 in advance royalties and sales the first two years.

Q Did Grant complete his memoirs before he died?
A Yes – he died a week after they were finished.

Q Where is the best Illinois statue of Grant?
A In Lincoln Park, Chicago, an equestrian pose unveiled in 1891

Q What direction does Grant's tomb overlooking the Hudson River face?
A South – toward Appomattox

Q What is the latest book out about Grant?
A *Grant Comes East* by Newt Gingrich – a novel

STEPHEN DOUGLAS – THE LITTLE GIANT

Q   When did Douglas, a Vermonteer, first come to Illinois?
A   1833. He had read about Illinois in a book of western travels.

Q   Douglas started in Illinois as a schoolteacher in what town?
A   **Winchester**

Stephen A. Douglas (Illinois State Hist. Lib.)

Q   Did Douglas become a big booster of Illinois?
A   Yes. He wrote letters to family and friends, urging them to move here. He said the state outstripped others in artificial and natural advantages and was the "paradise of the world."

Q   How did Douglas become a lawyer?
A   Like Lincoln, he was self-taught, and back then the only qualification was good moral character and an oral examination before two judges.

Q   Did Douglas own land in Illinois?
A   As an investment, he purchased town lots in **Beardstown, Meredosia, Bloomington** and **Virginia.**

Q   How contentious were stump debates back then?
A   During one heated 1838 debate with Whig nominee John Stuart, Douglas was grabbed and tucked under Stuart's arm with his head sticking out; Douglas retaliated by biting a chunk out of Stuart's thumb.

Q   With what women did Douglas socialize in his early political career?
A   The future wives of Abe Lincoln, John McClernand, and Lyman Trumbull

Q   When Douglas went to **Carlinville** to attend a public hanging in 1840, how did he make the most of the occasion?
A   Ever the opportunist, Douglas gave a speech to the crowd before they left. Some say he delivered the speech from the gallows.

Q   Did Douglas ever serve in the military?
A   No. The Blackhawk War had ended before he arrived in Illinois and President Polk thought him too valuable an ally to let him resign as a congressman and fight in the Mexican War.

Q   Were Lincoln and Douglas ever on the same side as lawyers?
A   Once – they were co-counsels in an 1840 murder trial in **Dewitt County** and got their client acquitted.

Q   How did Gustave Koerner once describe Douglas?
A   Small size, broad-shouldered, short legs, and muscular – with a large head full of thick black hair.

Q   What two "islands of abolitionism" were towns on Douglas' circuit when he became a judge in the early 1840s?
A   **Galesburg** and **Quincy**

Q   Were Sidney Breese and James Shields friends or foes of Douglas?
A   Shields was a friend, Breese a foe

Q   Was Douglas an expansionist and believer in Manifest Destiny?
A   Yes – he wanted a republic that was ocean bound.

Q   In the Oregon Country dispute with Britain, did he favor compromise at the 49th parallel or did he advocate "fifty-four, forty or fight?"
A   He favored war.

Q   Did Lincoln and Douglas agree on the southern boundary of Texas?
A   No - Douglas thought it was the Rio Grand while Lincoln claimed it should be the Nueces River.

Martha Martin – Douglas' first wife

Q   How many terms did Douglas serve as an Illinois congressman?
A   Three

Q   What were Douglas' vices?
A   He was careless of dress, smoked cigars, drank whiskey, and chewed tobacco. He could also cuss when necessary.

Q   Who were his close friends?
A   Like Lincoln, he was a solitary man and had few close friends.

Q   What city did Douglas move to in 1847?
A   Chicago

Q   Who did Douglas marry in 1847?
A   Martha Martin, a cousin to the man he sat next to in Congress. She was from North Carolina and at age 22, twelve years younger than her husband.

Q Did Douglas ever own slaves?
A When his father-in-law died, Douglas' wife inherited a Mississippi cotton plantation with 100 slaves.

Stephen Douglas circa 1860

Q When was Douglas first elected to the U.S. Senate?
A 1847

Q What did Douglas believe about the question of slavery in territories that belonged to the United States?
A He believed in popular sovereignty – that the people of the territories should decide for themselves.

Q Did Douglas have any children?
A His wife bore him a son in 1849 – Robert Martin Douglas.

Q When Douglas introduced his bill organizing the western areas into territories, what change did he make in the Mormon Territory?
A He changed the name from Deseret to Utah (named for the Ute Indians), primarily to forestall anti-Mormon opposition.

Q Freesoilers branded Douglas a "doughface" for his compromise stance of the question of California, New Mexico and Utah. What was a doughface?
A A northerner with southern sympathies

Q Douglas was a strong supporter of the Compromise of 1850. Why was its passage vital?
A It postponed the Civil War 10 years and gave the North another decade to outstrip the South in population, industry, banking, and railroads.

Q Why is Douglas called the "Father of the Illinois Central Railroad?"
A He envisioned a railroad that would run the length of the state and down to the Gulf of Mexico, uniting the region economically and helping to lessen sectional differences.

Q Senator Sidney Breese had a scheme to establish the city of **Cairo** at the confluence of the Mississippi and Ohio rivers and connect it with a north-south railroad that went to **Galena**. What addition did Douglas make to this plan?
A That a branch line run from Cairo to Chicago

Q What charge did critics of Douglas' make of this plan?
A Douglas only suggested it to enrich his land holdings in Chicago.

Q What change was made before the Central Railroad bill passed Congress?
A The northern terminus in the west was moved to Dubuque since **Galena** was declining rapidly. The southern terminus was extended to Mobile, Alabama.

Q Why was there strong support from New York and Massachusetts in the Douglas railroad bill?
A Easterners had invested heavily in Illinois internal improvement canal bonds, and the railroad would be an economic boost to the state.

Q When did the state legislature grant incorporation to the Illinois Central Railroad?
A 1851

Q Did Douglas make a profit from his railroad bill?
A Yes, he sold his Chicago lakefront property to the railroad at considerable profit.

Q In what ways was Douglas ahead of his time in 1850?
A He was fascinated with the telegraph and wanted lines extended across the entire country. He also wanted to explore the possibility of "aerial navigation" with hot air balloons. He had close ties with the Smithsonian and thought mechanical science should be taught in schools.

Q Why did Douglas advocate the building of a railroad across the Isthmus of Panama?
A He was an Anglophobe and believed that such a venture would help us in our struggle against British supremacy in the Pacific.

Q Did Douglas support Louis Kossuth in his attempt to free Hungary from Austrian domination?
A Yes. He knew that America was the model and example for liberal movements in Europe trying to establish republics.

Q Did Douglas have any more sons or daughters?
A A second son, Stephen Arnold, was born in 1850.

Q Did Douglas build a home in Chicago?
A When he sold land to the railroad, he kept a tract of higher ground with oak trees and a commanding view of the lake. He built a small cottage on it until a larger house could be built.

Q When Douglas campaigned hard for the 1852 Democratic presidential nomination, who were his main rivals?

34

A   Lewis Cass of Michigan and James Buchanan of Pennsylvania. When none of the three candidates could secure the nomination after 46 ballots, the convention turned to compromise candidate Franklin Pierce of New Hampshire.

Q   Did Douglas and his wife ever have a baby daughter?
A   Yes, in early 1853, about the same time Douglas learned he had won a second term to the U.S. Senate. Sadly, his wife died shortly after giving birth.

Q   What did Douglas do to get his mind off the tragedy of his wife's death?
A   He took a prolonged trip to Europe and the near East

Q   Why did Douglas fail to meet the Queen of England?
A   He would not give in to her demand that he appear before her in "court dress" instead of civilian clothes.

Q   Why was there such a storm of controversy over Douglas' Kansas-Nebraska Act?
A   It repealed the Missouri Compromise line, forbidding slavery north of the thirty-six, thirty line, and said the people of those territories could decide for themselves the issue of slavery.

Q   What phrase was used to describe this principle?
A   Popular Sovereignty

Q   What Illinois man, who had just about lost interest in politics, had his career revived as a result of the Kansas-Nebraska Act?
A   Abe Lincoln – who adamantly opposed the extension of slavery into the territories

Q   What is meant by the term "Bleeding Kansas?"
A   Southerners and northerners, in an attempt to make Kansas a state to their liking, turned Kansas into a battleground. A good example of this was the murder of proslavery men by abolitionist John Brown and his sons.

Q   What did Douglas do in 1856 that surprised many?
A   He married a second time to a Washington belle, 21-year-old Adele Cutts. Douglas was 22 years her senior.

Q   What immediate effect did the marriage have on Douglas?
A   He seemed a new man. He took renewed interest in his grooming habits and stopped frequenting saloons. His new wife took an active interest in his politics and was on hand for many of his speeches.

Q   Did Douglas, like Lincoln, have a good sense of humor?

A   Yes, but he was inept at utilizing it in his speeches and debates.

Q   What Massachusetts Senator blasted Douglas in his "Crime Against Kansas" speech?
A   Charles Sumner – in the speech he said some pretty vile things about Douglas, about the South in general, and about South Carolina Senator Andrew Butler.

Q   What happened to Sumner?
A   The next day, Preston Brooks, a congressman and a relative of Butler's, attacked Sumner with his cane, nearly killing him.

Q   Was Douglas a presidential candidate in 1856?
A   Yes, but he lost out to James Buchanan.

Q   How many times was Douglas elected to the U.S. Senate?
A   Three

Douglas' Speaking Dates in 1858 Senatorial Campaign
Douglas spoke in the towns marked •
The seven debates are marked ⊛

Q   Did Lincoln and Douglas consider the African inferior to whites?

A Yes

Q Who proposed a series of debates between the two men contesting the 1858 Illinois U.S. Senate seat, Lincoln or Douglas?
A Lincoln

Q Who selected the Illinois towns?
A Douglas – he sent Lincoln a list of prominent towns in each Congressional district. **Springfield** and Chicago were left off the list because Douglas had already given speeches in those towns.

Q What towns were on the list?
A **Freeport, Ottawa, Galesburg, Quincy, Alton, Jonesboro, Charleston**

Q What town on the Illinois River was the scene of the first of seven Lincoln-Douglas debates in 1858?
A **Ottawa**. The last debate was at **Alton**.

Abe Lincoln at the time of the debates

Q What was the most common topic discussed in the debates?
A Popular Sovereignty

Q What was Douglas' famous "Freeport Doctrine?"
A At **Freeport**, Lincoln asked Douglas: "Can the people of a United States territory, in any lawful way, exclude slavery from its limits prior to the formation of a state constitu-

tion?"
Douglas' reply: "The people have the lawful means to introduce it (slavery) or exclude it as they please, for the reason that slavery cannot exist a day or an hour anywhere, unless it is supported by local police regulations."

Q What were the repercussions of the Freeport Doctrine?
A It cost Douglas support of the southern Democrats in the 1860 presidential election.

Q What was Douglas' most effective charge against Lincoln?
A That he was an abolitionist in disguise

Q What do most people forget about the 1858 Lincoln-Douglas debates?
A The constitution at the time provided for the *indirect* election of U.S. senators. The people elected members to the legislature and then the legislature selected the U.S. senators. When the people went to the polls on November 2, the Democrats won a majority of the legislative contests. Thus Douglas won out over Lincoln.

Q How did Douglas alienate his southern base of support?
A He criticized them for their extremism and said, "It is folly for you to entertain visionary dreams that you can fix slavery where the people do not want it." Southerners didn't need Douglas and his popular sovereignty because they had the Dred Scott decision that said slaves were property and they had the right to take them wherever they pleased.

Q What did Douglas have to say about John Brown's raid on the arsenal at Harper's Ferry in an effort to start a slave insurrection?
A He warned that extremist actions like this, if supported by abolitionist Republicans, would lead to a bloody sectional conflict.

Q When Douglas secured the 1860 Democratic presidential nomination at Baltimore, what did the southern delegates do?
A They held their own convention at Maryland and nominated John C. Breckinridge of Kentucky.

Q What now became Douglas' main goal?
A To preserve the glorious Union. He was equally disgusted with northern abolitionists and southern secessionists.

Q What religious charge hurt Douglas in the 1860 campaign?
A Some insinuated that he was a Catholic since his wife was a "Romanist" and his sons were being raised Catholic.

Q What was unusual about the election of Lincoln?
A He received a large majority in the electoral college but, like George W. Bush, received a minority of the popular votes.

Q What was the only state carried by Douglas in 1860?
A Missouri

Q   What effect did Douglas' whirlwind campaign, that saw him visit 23 states, have on his health?
A   The exhaustion, strain, and stress led to his death.

Q   How did Douglas differ with President Buchanan over the question of secession?
A   Buchanan felt powerless to stop it. Douglas said it was better to lose a million men on the battlefield than to lose a single state – an unusual stand for a Democrat.

Q   What did Douglas propose the government do with free Negroes?
A   He suggested that they be sent to colonies in South America or Africa at government expense.

Q   How did Douglas make one last effort at compromise?
A   He and Crittenden led a Congressional Committee of Thirteen that tried to find a plan that would satisfy both sides, but neither Lincoln nor the southern firebrands would budge on their positions.

Q   What proposed constitutional amendment was supported by Douglas?
A   Congress would be prohibited from ever abolishing or interfering with slavery in states where it existed.

Q   How was the presidential inauguration date different back then?
A   Elections were held in early November, but instead of taking office in January, the oath was not administered until March. It took the 20th Lame Duck Amendment to change this.

Q   Where did Douglas and his wife stay when they went back to Chicago?
A   At the Tremont House hotel. His cottage near the lake was rented out and he never built his dream mansion.

Q   Douglas fell ill in Chicago in May of 1861, his acute rheumatism worsened by stress and years of smoking and drinking. When did he pass away?
A   June 4th – he was also in debt due to his recent election campaigns; Douglas was buried on his property near Lake Michigan.

HEINOUS CRIME

Q   Why is the Holy Family Church in **Cahokia** missing a candlestick?
A   Back in frontier times a member of the parish stole six candlesticks and hid them in Grand Marais Lake. His daughter told members of the church what had happened and they went to the shallow lake and were able to recover five of the candlesticks.

Q   What disappointed office seeker from Chicago assassinated President Garfield in 1881?
A   Charles Guiteau

Q   Was anyone in Illinois killed in a duel after it was outlawed by the legislature?
A   Yes - in **Belleville** two men got into a quarrel. It seems that **Timothy Bennett's** horse repeatedly got into Alfonso Stuart's cornfield and ate his crops. Each made serious threats against the other. Two of their friends, Nathan Fikes and Jacob Short, thought the affair to be silly and proposed that the matter be settled with a sham duel, using rifles with powder but no bullets. The duel was fought on a vacant lot according to code duello with Fikes and Short acting as seconds. Bennett loaded his rifle with ammunition, fired first, and killed his opponent. Bennett was the **first man in St. Clair County to be hanged**. It was done on September 3, 1821, in front of a large crowd.

Q   What **Ina** (near **Mount Vernon**) resident fell in love with her pastor and poisoned her husband and the pastor's wife - 1924?
A   Elsie Sweeten – she and Reverend Lawrence Hight were convicted, but she was acquitted in a second trial.

Q   Who was the last man hanged in Madison County?
A   Emil Fricker of **Highland** in 1926 - Fricker, a dairy farmer, was convicted of murdering the husband of a milkmaid on his farm with whom he had fallen hopelessly in love. He was also suspected of killing her first husband.

Q   What were the Banditti of the Prairie?
A   There was a criminal group in the **Oregon**, Illinois, area. Known as "**Banditti of the Prairie**," they terrorized the region for nearly a decade in DeKalb and Ogle counties. They were led by John Driscoll, a man named Taylor, and Driscoll's four sons. John Campbell, captain of the Regulators (vigilante group), was assassinated by these prairie bandits. A band of Regulators caught up with them around 1841 and killed Driscoll and a son named William. Each was shot by about 55 men. A third Driscoll son (Pierce) was spared because he was only thirteen. Over 100 Regulators were tried by a jury for committing this act but were acquitted.

Clay County Jail at Louisville

Q   The daughter of what Illinois U.S. Senator was stabbed to death in her **Kenilworth** suburban home near Chicago?
A   Charles Percy – Valerie's murder happened in 1966 while her father was campaigning for the U.S. Senate. The killer was never caught.

Q   Paula Sims was convicted in 1990 of murdering her baby daughter in a sensational trial that made national headlines. In what town did Sims live at the time of her conviction in *Peoria*? (A) Collinsville (B) Edwardsville (C) Alton (D) Granite City

A **Alton**

Paul Muni as "Scarface" 1932

Q Who once tried to poison Al Capone by putting prussic acid in his soup?
A Joe Aiello and his brothers offered to bribe the chef at the Little Italy Café to do the deed, but instead he informed on them. Capone's killers claimed six Aiellos within a month.

Q What was the only hotel to throw Al Capone out on his ear?
A The Biltmore in Los Angeles; Mayor Thompson told Capone to leave Chicago for a while so he could make a bid in the 1928 presidential race. It seems that Capone's presence was a big embarrassment to the city of Chicago. Capone decided to take a vacation on the west coast and checked in at the Biltmore in L.A. When the manager found out about it, he told Capone to leave.

Q How did insect phobia lead to Jake Guzik going to prison? (This is not a trick question.)
A. Mob cashier Fred Ries was sent to a grungy jail in **Danville** that was infested with cockroaches. He so abhorred the critters he sang like a canary in exchange for better conditions. The information he supplied sent Guzik away for five years.

Robert Stack as Eliot Ness

Q Why did Capone gunman Tony Napoli commit suicide in jail?
A Napoli was told by Capone to track down Eliot Ness and kill him. Ness became aware that someone was stalking him and turned the tables, capturing Napoli and sending him to jail. Napoli committed

suicide rather than testifying against Capone.

Q What were the actual names of The Untouchables?
A In addition to Eliot Ness there was Marty Lahart, Sam Seager, Barney Cloonan, Lyle Chapman, Tom Friel, Joe Leeson, Mike King, Paul Robsky, Bill Gardner and Frank Basile. Basile, Ness' driver, was the only one killed by the mob.

Q How did the term "bootlegging" originate?
A It went back to the Civil War when peddlers sold liquor illegally to Union troops by hiding it in their cowhide bootlegs.

Q Have any guards ever been killed in Menard Prison at **Chester**?
A Yes – three were killed during a 1966 riot.

Q Why did Al Capone drop out of school after the sixth grade?
A Al's grades in school were fine until his increasing truancy caused him to flunk. When the principal administered a paddling after Capone hit a female teacher, he quit.

Al and Ralph Capone in Florida

Q Who defended Leopold and Loeb, the killers of young Bobby Franks?
A Chicagoan Clarence Darrow – he also defended the Scottsboro boys in a famous Alabama rape case.

Q What Capone relative was called the "Father of Modern Gangsterdom?"
A Johnny Torrio

Q What famous evangelist visited Charlie Birger in his **Benton** jail cell shortly before the scheduled execution in 1928?
A Billy Sunday

Q What is Birger's chief claim to fame?
A He is the only Illinois gangster with a museum to preserve his memory. There is a Dillinger museum, but it's in Hammond, Indiana. Birger was also the last man publicly hanged in the state of Illinois.

Q What race riot during World War I resulted in more

African-American deaths than any riot in the nation's history?

A   39 lost their lives in the **East St. Louis** race riot

Q   Why is the SMC Cartage Company on Clark Avenue in Chicago famous?
A   It was the site of the 1929 St. Valentine's Day Massacre.

Q   What Chicago Black Panther leader was killed by Chicago police in a controversial 1969 raid?
A   Fred Hampton

Johnny "the Fox" Torrio recovering from his wounds in 1925 "beer war"

Q   What "World's Richest Reporter" was killed in a pedestrian subway under Michigan Avenue in Chicago?
A   Jake Lingle, a bought reporter, was killed in 1929

Q   What happened in 1929 to Chicago mobsters Joe Guinta, John Scalise, and Albert Anselmi?
A   They were beaten to a bloody pulp with a baseball bat by Capone who discovered they were traitors.

Q   What 1920's and 1930's gangster had a degree from the University of Illinois?
A   Fred Goetz, better known as "Shotgun" George Ziegler. He was thought to have participated in the St. Valentine's Day Massacre. In 1933 he joined the Barker-Karpis gang. The group killed him in 1934 at **Cicero** because his mind began to slip and they thought he might talk.

Q   What Lithuanian kid grew up in slums near Chicago's Stock Yards and became a famous 1930's bank robber?
A   Alvin "Creepy" Karpis; Fred Barker gave him the name "creepy" because of his cold piercing stare.

Q   What else was unusual about Karpis' looks?
A   He had no earlobes. Doc Moran gave him a plastic surgery job to correct the defect and botched the job.

Q   In September of 1934 Karpis decided things were too hot for him in Chicago. Where did he take a vacation?
A   Havana, Cuba

Q   What typically happened to molls – gangster girlfriends - when they were caught?
A   They were charged with harboring a fugitive and given five-year jail sentences.

Q   When the Barker-Karpis gang kidnapped the wealthy beer baron, William Hamm, what Chicago man was mistakenly arrested for it?
A   Roger Touhy and several members of his gang

Q   What Chicagoan became Karpis' childhood best friend?

A   Lester Gillis, better known as "Babyface" Nelson

Q   Who were the participants in the St. Valentine's Day Massacre?
A   John Scalise and Albert Anselmi, Verne Miller, Machine Gun McGurn, Shotgun Zeigler – all of the Capone gang - and Ed Fletcher and George Lewis of Detroit's Purple Gang.

Q   What was Machine Gun McGurn's trademark after he killed someone?
A   He placed a nickel in the dead man's hand.

Q   What was the famous 1924 quote by corrupt politician Fred Lundin who was Big Bill Thompson's campaign manager?
A   "To hell with the public. We're at the trough now and

Clyde Barrow of Bonnie and Clyde fame

we're going to feed."

Q   Was Clyde Barrow ever in Illinois?
A   After he broke out of a Waco, Texas, jail in March of 1930, he fled to **Nokomis**, Illinois, and robbed a B&O train

office and a dry cleaning establishment. Alert police captured him and sent him back to Texas.

Q How did Clyde Barrow and his girlfriend Bonnie Parker die?
A They were ambushed in their car by a posse at Arcadia, Louisiana, in May of 1934. Bonnie's head was nearly severed from her body and Clyde's body was hit 45 times.

Q How was the term G-Man invented?
A When Machine Gun Kelly was captured in Memphis he cowered and yelled, "Don't shoot, G-men, don't shoot!"

Bonnie Parker in a tough gun moll pose

Q Who captured Creepy Karpis without firing a shot?
A J. Edgar Hoover and 20 other G-Men in 1936

Q Most of the aforementioned criminals had an aversion to an honest day's work. To what extreme did Clyde Barrow carry out this lack of work ethic?
A He hated prison work so much he chopped off two of his toes to avoid it. Ironically, a week later he was pardoned, and he left prison on crutches.

Political cartoon in support of the G-Men

Q In what southern Illinois town was James Earl Ray born?
A **Alton** – Ray was the assassin of M.L. King Jr.

A typical Chicago handbook joint – Library of Congress

Q What town had five of its nuns murdered in 1992 while serving in war-torn Liberia?
A **Ruma**

Q What Springfield "godfather" was listed as one of Illinois' worst hoodlums by syndicated columnist Drew Pearson in 1962?
A Frank Zito

Q What Illinois company manufactured the bullet that killed John F. Kennedy in 1963?
A Winchester-Western Cartridge in **East Alton**

Q According to the Chicago Crime Commission, who were the top mob figures in 1967?
A The Chicago Crime Commission published a booklet that described the major geographical areas of Mob control in Chicago: The Loop – Gus Alex; Near North Side - Joseph DiVarco, Joseph Arnold; Northwest Suburbs – Leonard Patrick, Ross Prio; Far West and West Suburbs – Sam Battaglia, William Dadano, Sam Giancana; South Side – Ralph Pierce; South and Southwest Suburbs – Frank LaPorte, Fiore Buccieri.

MOO, MOO – OINK, OINK: ILLINOIS FARMS

It has been said that all of mankind's inventions, all of our accomplishments and dreams, would be for nothing were it not for six inches of topsoil and the fact that the sun shines and it rains.

Seventy thousand farms still cover 80 percent of Illinois' land area.

Note: About ten of these questions came from Jan McDonald Tribbett and the University of Illinois Extension. Her book, *Fascinating Agricultural Trivia*, came out in the summer of 2004. Call 618-236-4172 to order a copy.

Other questions were provided by Don Rogier of **Highland**, Jerry Mizell of South County St. Louis, and Gary Barber of Houston, a former **Edwardsville** resident.

Q   Where does Illinois rank among the 50 states in the value of exported agricultural products?
A   Second

Q   Where is the Illinois Farmers Hall of Fame?
A   In Morrow Hall at the University of Illinois

John Chapman – Johnny Appleseed

Q   In frontier Illinois, what was "broad-casting?"
A   Seed was placed in a cloth bag with straps that slung over the shoulders. As the far-mer walked along the field, he sowed the seed by scattering handfuls to his left and right.

Q   What legendary character by the name of John Chapman planted a grove of apple trees along the old Goshen Road?
A   Johnny Appleseed

Q   Where is the nation's oldest agricultural test plot?
A   University of Illinois – the Morrow Plot was planted in 1876.

Q   What town had the state's first county farm bureau?
A   **DeKalb**

Q   In pioneer times what animal was probably used for plowing more than the horse?
A   An ox – often yoked in pairs

Q   What is the name for a female donkey?
A   Jenny – the male is a Jack

Q   What term is used to describe the growing of fruits and vegetables for retail sale?
A   Truck farming - most think it's because these products can be hauled to town in a truck and sold for profit. But the word "truck" for these items was used by pioneer farmers, long before the advent of the car or truck.

Q   What was the minimum amount of land early settlers could buy from the government at a dollar or $1.25 an acre?
A   Forty acres or a quarter-quarter section; increased amounts had to be bought in multiples of 40.

Q   When the Illinois Central Railroad was completed around 1856 and the company sold land to prospective farmers, what were the terms?
A   Prices were low and terms were liberal. A down pay-ment of only fifty cents an acre was required with seven years to pay the remainder.

Q   Why was cholera so prevalent in pioneer days?
A   The concept of germs was unknown. Cholera occurred under conditions of filth, often caused when several families lived under one roof with no running water or indoor plumbing.

Q   What fruit (that could be made into wine) was thought by early pioneers to help them live to a ripe old age if they grew and consumed it?
A   Elderberry

Q   What do you call kernels of corn that have been soaked in a caustic solution and have had their husk removed?
A   Hominy

Q   What do you get when hominy is ground up into a coarse matter?
A   Grits

Q   When navigation on the Great Lakes at Chicago was opened in 1910, how many bushels of wheat were loaded onto ships from grain elevators?
A   4,500,000

Ceres – Goddess of Grain atop Chicago Board of Trade

Q   What are some interesting soil types found in Johnson County?
A   Yazoo clay, found near the Cache River basin; reddish-yellow Memphis silt loam; light brown Waverly silt loam

Q   How big is a township?
A   Six miles square consisting of 36 sections

Q   Section 16 was reserved for what purpose?
A   The money obtained from the sale of section 16 went to support public education, mostly to build one-room schoolhouses where students of several grades were combined.

Q   How were wagons designated in pioneer times?
A   By the number of bushels they could hold. A typical wagon was designated as an 80-bushel wagon.

Q   Much of Illinois is prairie. Why were settlers reluctant to try to farm the prairie in the early years of the state?
A   They mistakenly assumed that the lack of trees meant the soil was infertile.

Q What caused the lack of trees?
A Frequent prairie fires and thick grass that prevented tree seeds from taking root.

Cyrus McCormick's reaper cutting wheat

Q What were squatters?
A Some people moved on a piece of land and started herding or farming before it was put up for sale by the government.

Q What were squatter's rights and pre-emption laws?
A When the land was offered for sale, squatters were given the first chance to buy the property if they had a certificate of entry.

Q What is the cheapest price that land was ever sold for in Illinois?
A Twenty-five cents an acre; Uncle Sam was so hard up for currency after the Civil War that land near **Shawneetown** was sold at bargain prices.

Q How was the success of a farmer measured in 1855, other than his acreage?
A By the number of horses he owned

Q Why has red long been the predominant color for Illinois barns?
A When paints were first produced for barn use, it was discovered that the cheapest and most durable were from a red pigment that came from an iron oxide base.

Q Tripe and chitlins were common food items eaten by the poor during the Depression. What are they?
A Tripe is cow stomach and chitlins are hog intestines.

Q When farmers had large numbers of horses, what was their favorite feed crops for them?
A Timothy (hay) and oats

Q What was a "poor farm?"
A The Illinois General Assembly passed legislation in 1839 that established the almshouse system. This allowed county governments to build a place to house the indigent. Two story structures were often built in rural areas. The overseer and his family lived on the first floor and the poor lived in small rooms upstairs. The poor worked (farmed) small plots of land near the house and grew fruits and vegetables to assist in their keep.

Q What utilities mogul was responsible for making electricity available in rural areas of Northern Illinois?
A Samuel Insull

Q Is a tomato a fruit or a vegetable?
A Fruit

Q What unique method of rat control was invented by farmers?
A Rats can't burp so they set out quantities of Coca-Cola for them to drink. The carbonated beverage caused them to explode. (Yes, I know – unbelievable.)

Q What is tofu?
A It is a Japanese word that refers to soybean curd. Soybeans are rich in protein and are a favorite among health food faddists.

Q How many soybeans are in a pod, and what determines the number?
A Anywhere from 2-4, the number depending on how good the growing season has been.

Wild turkey

Q Is a soybean round like a pea or kidney shaped like a lima bean?
A They are round and yellow, marked with a black dot

Q What city bills itself as the "Soybean Capital of the World?"
A **Decatur**

Q Has Illinois ever been a significant tobacco producer?
A Yes – The soil and climate of Little Egypt was suitable for tobacco production in the state's early years. At one point Illinois ranked third in tobacco production, behind Virginia and Kentucky.

Q What price were farmers getting for a bushel of soybeans in 1943?
A Four dollars a bushel

Q What is the origin of the term "quarter horse?"
A In the old days race tracks were straight and a quarter of a mile long. Race horses were called quarter horses.

Q What weed (that cows won't eat) is found in fields and meadows, and if it isn't destroyed before it goes to seed practically takes over?
A Saurdock

Q   What type of cow generally is the best milk producer - Jersey, Guernsey, Holstein or Hereford?
A   Holstein

Q   Which of the following is raised mostly for beef, Jersey, Guernsey, Holstein or Hereford?
A   Hereford

Q   What weed commonly found on farms is used to make deadly ricin?
A   Jimson weed

Q   What **Galesburg** man served as Ronald Reagan's secretary of agriculture?
A   John Block

Q   What weed can be used to make rubber?
A   Milkweed

Illinois State Fair – A showcase for farm produce and livestock

Q   Has Illinois ever led the nation in the production of roses?
A   Yes – In 1969 it was the top producer of roses and gladioli

Q   What weed's seeds did the French immigrants bring with them because they were afraid it didn't exist here?
A   Dandelion – for greens and dandelion wine

Q   What is lambsquarter?
A   According to Mildred Rongey of **O'Fallon**, it was an edible weed that her mother sometimes mixed with dock and dandelion greens during the Depression.

Q   What is another name for a white-faced cow?
A   Hereford

Q   What type of cow generally is the best butterfat producer?
A   Jersey

Q   What price were farmers getting for a bushel of soybeans in 2002?

A   About $5.50 a bushel – not a whole lot more than what farmers were getting 25 years ago

Q   What was a general price for farmland in 1942?
A   About a hundred dollars an acre. This meant that one could buy a farm, raise a large crop of soybeans, and pay off the farm in about a year. This is impossible today due to low grain prices and the high cost of land.

Q   How many rows of kernels are there on a typical ear of corn?
A   Sixteen to eighteen – it's never an odd number.

Q   What caused the farm crisis of the 1980s?
A   In the mid 1970's, in the early years of the Carter administration, the price of farmland started to rise. Farmers decided to buy up as much cheap land as they could at a six percent variable loan from banks. Interest rates were deregulated in 1977. Farmers figured that in a few years their farm would be worth twice the amount they had paid for it. Then along came the energy crisis and interest rates shot up to nearly eighteen percent. With high interest rates farmers stopped buying acreage and prices fell from less demand. Instead of a three hundred dollar a month payment, the bank was now demanding almost $900 due to increased mortgage rates. When farmers couldn't make the payments the banks foreclosed and farms that had been in the family for over a hundred years were lost.

Q   Most people remember that pre cut homes could be bought from a Sears catalog. Was it also possible to order a pre-cut barn from Sears?
A   Yes

Q   Farmers are caught between a rock and a hard place. What is the negative side of having plenty of rain, no disease and an abundant harvest?
A   Increased yields generally lead to lower prices.

Q   Can you hear corn grow?
A   Farmers claim they can sit on their porch on a hot summer night, after a drenching rain, and hear the nearby corn in the field growing.

Route 66 advertising on Illinois barn at Cayuga by Dan Oberle

Q   Is it possible to hypnotize a chicken?

A Of course! First, it must be a pet chicken that is used to humans. You pick them up and start petting them. Then you cup your hand over their head and hold it there until they fall asleep, as if in a state of hypnosis. Marion Strohman of **Edwardsville** grew up on an Iowa farm. He and his sister had pet chickens and they made dresses for them to wear. Marion claims that he and his sister could put as many as eight chickens to sleep at one time.

Hawes Grain Elevator at Atlanta on old Route 66 by Dan Oberle

Q Is grain dust in storage silos explosive?
A Very – that's why they all have spark arrestors in their electrical systems.

Q In the old days were hogs driven to market the same as cattle?
A Yes – drovers brought hogs long distances to the Chicago market.

Q Why do you have white meat and dark meat on a chicken?
A Parts of the chicken where muscles get used a lot (such as the neck and legs) are dark. The muscles that get used the least, such as the breast and wings, are white meat.

Q Can chickens be trained to beat humans at tic tack toe?
A Yes – by rewarding them with grain. Chickens who can do this are popular attractions at state fairs and carnival sideshows.

Q Butter is made on a farm by churning cream long enough until all the fat particles clump together. What do you call the liquid substance that is left over?
A Buttermilk

Q How did Illinois farmers make cottage cheese in the old days?
A An animal enzyme called rennin was added to milk to make it curdle. Then the mixture was strained through a muslin cloth and the left over liquid was fed to hogs.

Q In the course of time, what name came to be applied to this cloth that was used to strain cottage cheese?
A Cheesecloth

Q When little Miss Muffet sat on her tuffet, eating curds and whey, what was she consuming?

A Cottage cheese – the lumps are curds and the whey is the milky substance. I have no idea was a tuffet was.

Q What principle of physics is used in a farmer's cream separator?
A Centrifugal force

Q What term does a chicken farmer use to describe a nest of several eggs?
A Clutch

Q In the fall, farmers went out into the woods and cut up dead trees, stacking the wood near the house in cords. This wood was used to heat the house in wintertime. What was done with the left over sawdust?
A When the pond or river froze, blocks of ice would be cut and stored in an icehouse. The sawdust was placed between the blocks to keep them from sticking together and freezing back into one big lump.

Q From what part of a cow is brisket obtained?
A The lower chest – it is very low in fat and it is cured in a solution of brine.

Q What generic newspaper was popular with farmers back in the 1950's?
A *Grit; Prairie Farmer* was another popular publication

Q Is there such a thing as "wheat rust?"
A Yes. It's a disease or fungus to which the plant is susceptible.

Q Where did the expression "rough as a cob" originate?
A Corncobs and the pages from Sears or Montgomery Ward catalogs were used instead of toilet paper in outhouses.

Q Why were three corncobs used per visit to the outhouse – two red and one white?
A You'll have to talk to a farmer or call this author if you can't figure this one out.

Q Where are most pumpkins grown in Illinois?
A Ogle and DeKalb counties grow the most pumpkins.

Q What use does limestone have on Illinois farms?
A It is pulverized and converted into lime or lime pellets and used as fertilizer.

Q What other use did Illinois farmers have for corncobs back in Lincoln's time?
A Corncob pipes for smoking

Q How did open grazing laws affect farmers?
A This meant that cattle were allowed to graze as they pleased, and that it was the farmer's responsibility to fence his crops for protection.

Q Farm fertilizer (often bought in 100-pound sacks) is associated with three numbers. What do these numbers represent?

A   The first number is the nitrogen content; the second is the percentage of phosphate; the third is the percentage of potash or potassium – NPK designation; currently it is often bought in bulk by farmers. (K is the symbol for potassium)

Q   Why are hogs able to kill poisonous snakes?
A   Their skin and fat layers are so tough and thick, the venom doesn't get into their bloodstream.

Q   What is NH 3?
A   Anhydrous ammonia (liquefied) that has a content of 82

"Start the Day With Pork" – Divernon, Illinois, by Dan Oberle

percent nitrogen

Q   Why do "druggies" steal anhydrous ammonia from farmers?
A   They use it to make "meth," known by the common name of "speed." The mixture is highly volatile and inexperienced people sometimes blow themselves to smithereens because they store it in propane tanks that are not made for high pressure.

Q   What high school club is popular with teenagers in rural areas?
A   FFA – Future Farmers of America

Q   In 1960, if you saw a Fordson tractor, what color was it?
A   Blue

Q   What color was a 1950 Allis Chalmers tractor?
A   Orange

Q   Did the Caterpillar Company make farm tractors?
A   Yes – but they had tracks – not wheels, and they could pull anything.

Q   What color were Caterpillar tractors?
A   Yellow, of course

Q   Rhode Island Red, Leghorn, Bardrock, and Plymouth Rock are all types of what farm animal?
A   Chickens

Q   What slang term do farm kids use to describe Cockleburs?
A   Porcupine eggs

Q   When land was purchased by a husband and wife in pioneer times, whose name was placed on the deed?
A   Only the husband's. However, whenever the land was sold, both names were required. The concept of joint tenancy, so prevalent today, was unheard of back then.

Q   What were primogeniture laws?
A   Before the Revolution, it was common practice that when the head of the household died and he had several sons, only the oldest inherited the land.

Q   What was the reasoning behind this?
A   It was done to prevent the large estate from being divided.

Q   This practice dates back to medieval times. What were the other landless sons expected to do when this happened?
A   Become monks or soldiers

Q   What New Deal agency was responsible for paving the first roads in rural parts of Illinois?
A   WPA – Works Progress Administration; opponents who thought the WPA was a big waste of taxpayer's money claimed WPA stood for "We Piddle Around."

Q   Why are authorities suspicious of non-farm people buying large amounts of farm fertilizer?
A   It can be used by terrorists for making bombs.

Q   Did Timothy McVeigh use farm fertilizer to make the Oklahoma City bomb?
A   Yes. It was mainly ammonia nitrate and fuel oil (anfo), stored in a rented van and ignited with a stick of dynamite.

Q   How did farmers in 1950 remove tree stumps?
A   They bought sticks of dynamite at a quarry and blasted them out.

Q   How did the original homesteaders remove tree stumps?
A   With a double-bladed axe. Remember the Alan Ladd/ Van Hefflin scene in *Shane*?

Q   What name was given to the 7-foot long saw that had handles on both ends?
A   Whipsaw or crosscut

Q   By what year had farms replaced most of the Illinois prairie?
A   1900

Q   What are the main products of Archer Daniels Midland Company, located in central Illinois?
A   Animal feed, fuel, and food products

Q   What Illinois county **leads the nation in corn production**?
A   McLean County (Bloomington/Normal) – it also usually leads the state in soybean production

Q   When did Illinois last lead the nation in the production of corn, soybeans, pumpkins, cheese, onions, and horseradish?

45

A 1996

Q What did farm kids often use for excitement on the Fourth of July instead of firecrackers?
A One-quarter sticks of dynamite

Q Farm kids also used calcium carbide for entertainment. How did this work?
A A can was placed over a small amount of calcium carbide with a small amount of water added. Then a fuse was added and lit. The water and calcium carbide produced acetylene gas that exploded, sending the can high into the air.

Q How is it possible to make a homemade fuse?
A Soak a piece of string in saltpeter and let it dry out.

Q What is saltpeter?
A Potassium nitrate

Q How did yeoman farmers make their own gunpowder?
A It was a mixture of saltpeter, charcoal, and sulfur.

Q Why were early Illinois settlers referred to as yeoman farmers?
A The term referred to small, independent freeholders who owned their own land.

Q What was the old farm prank related to saltpeter?
A If a small amount was mixed in with food, it led to temporary impotence.

Q Some pioneer plows required two men. How did this work?
A One man rode on a seat to ensure that the plowshares dug into the soil while the second man guided it. In most cases they took turns with the easier riding part.

Q Why did tractor makers switch from gasoline engines to diesel?
A Gasoline engines run hotter, wearing out the valves and other engine parts quicker.

Q Were baby chicks ever delivered to farmers through the regular mail by the postman?
A Yes – in reinforced cardboard crates that were perforated

Q What was the purpose of making hybrid plants?
A To produce healthier plants with higher yields. It's the same with humans – inbreeding produces hemophiliacs.

Q What town was home to Lester Pfister, the pioneer of new and better seed, who was subjected to much ridicule for placing paper bags over ears of corn?
A El Paso

Q How were hybrid corn plants first produced?
A Six rows of one type of corn were planted next to two rows of a different kind. Then the tassels were cut off the ears of corn on the six rows so that these plants were pollinated from the plants in the two rows. It was kind of like artificial insemination for plants.

Grain silos on old alignment of Route 66 at Ocoya by Dan Oberle

Q Why were paper bags placed over the ears of corn in the six rows of corn?
A To prevent premature accidental pollination caused by pollen settling on the silks

Q For each strand of silk, how many kernels do you get on an ear of corn?
A One

Q What determines the length of time it takes for corn to mature?
A The amount of sunlight it is exposed to. There is also a genetic factor. If a farmer gets his crop in late due to excessive spring rain, he buys seed that matures faster.

Q What determines the amount of time it takes for soybeans to mature?
A Soybeans mature based on the length of the nights. Soybeans planted near a streetlight or nightlight take forever to mature.

Q Rank the following animals according to the richness of nutrients in their manure – cows, chickens, pigs
A Chickens, pigs, cows

Q Do pigs eat just about anything, including snakes and dead cats?
A Yes

Q Why are potatoes planted in mounds instead of on flat ground?
A Too much water causes the potato plant to rot.

Q Are potatoes grown from seeds?
A No – they are grown from "shoots" or the "eyes" of the potato.

Q Is horseradish grown from seeds?
A No – it is grown from the tip of the root on the plant that is cut off.

Q What causes popcorn to pop?

A The heat causes moisture inside the kernel to expand and literally explode.

Q Can milo be popped similar to popcorn?
A Yes. It is often used for animal feed and popped milo is easier for animals to digest.

Q What is another name for milo?
A Grain sorghum – which is a drought re-sistant plant with heads of large yellow or brown seeds

Sketch of the horseradish plant

Q What is Indian corn?
A It has darker kernels and is often used with gourds and pumpkins as part of fall displays on front porches.

Q Will a single kernel of Indian corn grow if harvested in the fall and planted the next spring?
A Yes

Q What does the farm expression "laying by" mean?
A After corn was planted and it got about 2-3 feet high, a horse drawn tiller with disc blades would throw dirt in a ridge up against the stalk and give it better support.

Q What kind of unusual barn is located near **Peru**, Illinois?
A The St. Bede large, round barn constructed of brick. Scientific farming promoters after the turn of the century claimed that round barns were superior to traditional structures and had a better chance of surviving tornadoes. Some round barns were also made with better ventilation to dry ears of corn.

Q What was a "barn raising" in pioneer times?
A Neighbors often got together and helped a farmer erect a barn in a single day. Remember the barn raising in the Harrison Ford movie, *Witness*?

Q What was a "husking bee" in pioneer times?
A Again, neighbors got together and "shucked" corn, often followed by a large meal cooked by the women with music and dancing afterward.

Q What did early pioneer farmers do with the feet of a pig that had been butchered?
A Feet were cleaned and pickled – for eating.

Q Why did pioneer farmers eagerly buy the Farmer's Almanac?"
A It contained all kinds of advice and information about farming. It also predicted the weather a year in advance and told farmers when the best time was to plant, based on the position of the stars and the phases of the moon.

Q Did farmers really believe in these planting schedules?
A Many still do

Q Are phases of the moon related to Farmers Almanac recommendations?
A Yes – Charlie Oliver of **Belleville** was once getting ready to plant some fence posts. He was told by a neighboring farmer that the moon was in the *wrong phase*. "If you want the posts to be true and straight and firm, they should be inserted when the moon is dark (crescent moon)."
He explained that a bright (full) moon would pull the posts an inch or two out of the soil and they would lean and be weak.

Q What was a "witching stick?"
A When it came to digging a well on a farm, there was no way to tell where the best spot would be. Some people had the uncanny ability to take a forked branch and hold each of the Y sections in one hand. Then they would walk over the ground, like someone with a metal detector. When they reached a spot where there was water, an invisible force would cause the stick to bend and twist, pointing downward to where there was water.
It's hard to believe, but farmers actually hired professional "witchers" to find a spot for the well. Nowadays, I'm told, witching is done with two wires rather than sticks.

Q What other term beside "witching stick" was used?
A They were called "divining rods" and some referred to them as "dowsing rods."

Q What is a cistern?
A In parched areas where there is a risk of the well drying up for a spell in late summer, people direct rain water from their roof into a concrete cistern. This water is used for watering the garden, taking baths, and washing clothes.

Q What was a rain barrel?
A This was a smaller and cheaper version of a cistern. The downspout from a roof emptied into a rain barrel.

Q What old children's song made references to a rain barrel?
A *Playmate* – "Holler down my rain barrel/ Slide down my cellar door/ And we'll be jolly friends, for evermore."

Q What animal did farmers use in their front yards to trim grass instead of a lawn mower?
A Sheep; goats can be used but they also eat the bark off trees.

Q Do cows fall asleep while in the standing position?
A Most do after they are about a year old, giving rise to the teen sport of "cow tipping" since cows can't move laterally.

Q   What was the favorite mischief of farm teenagers at Halloween?
A   Tipping over outhouses

Q   Why was water from a rain barrel preferred to well water for washing clothes?
A   It was "soft water" because it had fallen from the sky. Groundwater in wells is often "hard water" because it contains dissolved minerals.

Q   What happened to odd parts of the pigs such as the ears at butchering time?
A   They became part of "head cheese." Some think the ears are used for making silk purses but there is an old saying about that.

Q   Were bees indigenous to Illinois?
A   No - they were brought in by settlers from the East. Indians called bees "white man's flies."

Q   What did early pioneer farmers use instead of glass on windows?
A   Greased paper or animal skins

Q   Metal door hinges were scarce for pioneer farmers. What was used instead?
A   Leather hinges

Q   What did John Deere modify to make his first steel plow?
A   An old Sheffield steel saw blade from a lumber mill

Q   Back in 1840 it was considered poor taste to buy land within how many acres of an existing neighbor?
A   Eighty (a half quarter section of land) – giving him the option to buy more land at $1.25 an acre when he could afford it.

Q   A human intestine is about twenty feet long. How long is the intestine of a horse?
A   One hundred feet

Q   Does Illinois raise ostriches in significant numbers?
A   Yes – at places such as **Mercola** and **Durand**

Q   Is it true or is it an urban legend that the eye of an ostrich is larger than its brain?
A   True

Q   Everyone knows ostriches cannot fly. How fast can they run?
A   Up to forty miles per hour

Q   What Rock Island County town is home to International Harvester?
A   **East Moline**

Q   What town in northern Illinois has a crashed plane with its nose stuck in the ground as a tribute to those who survived the agricultural crisis of the 1980's?
A   **Norway**, on the Fox River

Q   Since 2001, what is the official state soil?
A   Drummer silty clay loam

Grain storage along old Route 66 at Elkhart, Illinois, by Dan Oberle

Q   What is a female sheep called?
A   Ewe (pronounced *you*)

Q   What was the threefold purpose of a typical Illinois barn?
A   Storage place for crops, shelter for animals, workplace for the farmer

Q   How often do farmers milk their cows?
A   Usually twice a day but improved feed and breeding has bumped it up to three. Cows are given feed mix with hormones to improve productivity; some environmental groups consider this controversial.

Q   What Illinois crop has 60 percent more vitamin C than a lemon?
A   Horseradish

Q   What new word has replaced the old fashioned "farming?"
A   Agribusiness

Q   Is it true or an urban myth that rabbits and horses can't vomit?
A   True – it has something to do with the structure of their esophagus.

Q   Name two common Illinois farm animals that have four parts to their stomachs.
A   Cows and sheep are ruminants. When they eat grass it goes to the first of four stomachs. Later, when they are resting, they regurgitate and chew their cud.

Q   How many times does a cow chew on its cud before swallowing it again?
A   Approximately 47-50 times

Q   From what farm product is white vinegar made?
A   Corn

Q   From what farm product is malted milk made?
A   It consists of toasted barley, ground and mixed with powdered milk.

Q   Why was the U.S. Supreme Court case of *Munn v Illinois* an important victory for early Illinois farmers?
A   The Illinois legislature passed a law regulating railroad rates and setting limits on amounts charged by grain elevator operators. The law was challenged but the court held that it was constitutional because it was in the "public interest."

Q   Illinois produces large quantities of dairy products, including cheese. From what product source do most Illinoisans get their cheese?
A   Pizza

Q   What are the only livestock native to Illinois?
A   Turkeys – old timers called them "Carolina parrots."

Q   Is the following true or an urban myth? Some turkeys are so dumb they look up to see what is hitting them on the head when it starts raining and they drown.
A   Urban myth – although they *are* dumb; all birds are fairly dumb - hence the epithet, "birdbrain."

Q   What are the only two animals on an Illinois farm that must worry about sunburn?
A   Pigs and humans are only animals that can sunburn, unless it's an albino animal.

Q   Do pigs have teeth?
A   Yes

Q   Does a duck's quack echo?
A   No, although scientists don't know why

Q   What Illinois critter and its worldwide cousins out-number humans?
A   Chickens

Q   What meat is the most popular on earth?

White Fence Farm on old Route 66 at Romeoville by Dan Oberle

A   Pork – largely because over a billion Chinese eat tons of it

Q   How did soybeans originally come to this country?

A   They were originally brought over from Asia as *ballast in a ship*.

Q   Why are soybeans an excellent thing for crop rotation?
A   They are a legume – their underground nodules add nitrogen to the soil.

Q   In general terms, what is the current price of farm land in Madison County?
A $2,500 an acre to $3,500 per acre, depending on what soil type – of course there are a few other variables such as location.

Q   What traditionally was the signal for Illinois farmers that hog killing time had arrived?
A   This was usually done after the first killing frost of the season to prevent spoilage.

Q   What town was home to Gene Funk, a seed research scientist who developed hybrids?
A   **Bloomington**

Q   What Illinois town was named to honor David Bradley, the man who built a farm implement factory there?
A   **Bradley**

Q   When farmers took their hogs to the large slaughter-houses in Chicago or **East St. Louis**, what was the only part of the hog wasted?
A   The slaughterhouses bragged that they used every part of the hog except the squeal, and they were trying to sell that to Henry Ford for horns in his Model T Fords.

Q   What county was considered the castor bean and castor oil producing capital of the state in 1842?
A   **Randolph County**

Q   What county is the state's leading hog producer?
A   **Henry County**

Q   What is the number two dairy county in Illinois?
A   **Clinton County**

Q   What do you call a castrated male pig?
A   Barrow – a castrated bull is called a steer.

Q   What is the purpose of castration?
A   It makes the animal less aggressive, and in the case of a pig they put on more weight. It also makes the meat more tender.

Q   A blight on what crop in Ireland in 1846 caused thousands of Irishmen to migrate to Illinois?
A   The potato

Q   What causes the hair on a horse to grow longer in the winter?
A   Mike Gillespie of **Swansea** says it is caused by the days growing shorter and there is less sunlight. This triggers a hormonal reaction.

Q   Diesel fuel sold to farmers for agricultural purposes is taxed at a lower rate than urban fuel for highways. How are the two fuels differentiated?
A   A red dye is placed in farm fuel.

Q   What is one of the things the Highway Patrol checks when they pull over an eighteen-wheeler at a scale house?
A   They check the fuel in the tank to make sure it is legal.

Q   What crop did Illinoisans raise as a source of lubricant before oil wells came into existence?
A   Castor beans were once a big crop in the state. (Castor oil – ugh! I took it as a kid.) Castor beans on your property perimeter are also rumored to keep moles out of your yard.

Illinois hog farm

Q   In 1950, if you saw a gray tractor with red trim, what make was it?
A   Ford

Q   In 1950, if you saw a red tractor with white lettering, what brand was it?
A   International Harvester

Q   In 1950, if you saw a red tractor, what brand was it?
A   Farmall; it was very similar to International Harvester.

Q   In 1950, if you saw a green and white tractor, what brand was it?
A   Oliver

Q   In 1950, if you saw a beige and brown tractor, what brand was it?
A   Case

Q   In 1950, if you saw a green and yellow tractor, what brand was it?
A   John Deere

Q   What is succotash?
A   Corn and lima beans cooked together

Q   Why did farm residents sometimes have health problems with early lids used on canning jars?
A   The old one-piece lids had a zinc coating, and this sometimes leeched into the preserved food.

Q   When making a jar of jelly preserves, what kind of wax was poured over the top of the jar to preserve freshness?
A   Paraffin

Q   What is broomcorn?
A   Actually, it's a type of sorghum plant whose stiff-branched panicles are used for making brooms.

Q   What is a gelding?
A   A castrated male horse

Q   What county bills itself as the "Heart of Illinois Pheasant Country?"
A   **Champaign County**

Q   What term is used to describe the birthing process for a cow?
A   Calving. This term is also used to describe large chunks of glaciers falling off into the ocean.

Q   What do you call a female cow that has never borne a calf?
A   Heifer – If, like my wife, your answer was "unmarried virgin," that is a very poor alternate answer.

Q   What do you call a female pig that has never given birth?
A   Gilt – which becomes a sow after they have given birth to piglets

Q   What do you call a male pig?
A   Boar

Q   What new term has been devised to describe the process of raising fish as a source of Illinois food?
A   Aquaculture – although most simply say fish farming.

Q   About how many bushels of corn does Illinois produce annually?
A   10 billion

Q   How are Illinois farmers helping our nation to cope with gasoline shortages?
A   Illinois corn is used to produce ethanol to the tune of 690 million gallons a year.   www.siue.edu/ETHANOL

Q   Is ethanol about the same type of alcohol that was produced illegally during Prohibition?
A   Yes – the formula is $CH_3 CH_2 OH$

Q   How much are the construction costs to produce a gallon of ethanol?
A   Since 1982 it has dropped from $2.25 to $1.00

Q   What is done with the grain substance left over in the ethanol producing process?
A   It's used for animal feed.

Q   Are yeast and fermentation part of the ethanol making process?
A   Yes

Q   Can companies such as Pioneer and Monsanto develop hybrid corn that is more suitable for producing ethanol?
A   Yes – also more suitable byproducts/coproducts

50

Q   What are the two methods currently being used to make ethanol?
A   Dry Mill (corporations) and Wet Mill (farmer-owned cooperatives)

Ethanol research plant at SIU Edwardsville by Harold Zeigler

Q   How many ethanol plants are there in the U.S.?
A   About 76

Q   Does Illinois lead the nation in number of ethanol plants?
A   No – Illinois has about eight plants, Iowa eleven, Minnesota nine, and South Dakota ten

Q   About how many million gallons of ethanol does a typical Illinois ethanol plant produce in a year?
A   40

Q   What are the four components to a kernel of corn?
A   Germ, protein, fiber, and starch

Q   Which of the four is fermented into ethanol?
A   Starch

Q   Currently, Illinois gasoline is limited to what percent of ethanol content?
A   Ten percent

Q   Is process water used in the production of ethanol fully recyclable?
A   Yes

Q   What new plant product are scientists conducting research on as a possible more abundant source than corn?
A   Cellulose – plant fiber

Q   Is America the leading ethanol producer in the world?
A   No – It's Brazil. They decided to become free of dependence on OPEC oil back around 1970.

Q   How long does it take before a female chick begins laying eggs?
A   It takes a hen about seven months to mature, depending on the breed.

Q   What unit of measurement is used to describe the height of a horse?

A   Horses are measured by "hands" with one hand being the equivalent of four inches. A "hand" is also used to describe a bunch of bananas or a group of tobacco leaves tied together.

Q   What did a typical chicken house look like in 1947?
A   This author grew up in urban **East St. Louis** but the house we lived in had a chicken house in the back yard. It sat on five concrete blocks and was about 8x10 feet with a lean-to roof that sloped from front to back. The front had a human entry door, a large window and a small chicken-size door with a ramp leading to it. Inside were nesting boxes for the hens to lay eggs and horizontal poles for the chickens to roost on at night.

Q   Why did some farmers prefer mules to horses?
A   Mules are thought to better withstand heat and humidity and they eat less because they are smaller.

Q   Are mules sterile?
A   Usually

Q   Some Illinois farmers with artistic talent are getting creative with their crops. What does this mean?
A   Aerial shots of their crops reveal designs such as a picture of John Wayne or a replica of the U.S. flag.

Annual Great Godfrey Maze featuring the American Bald Eagle: courtesy Godfrey Parks and Recreation; 618-466-1483

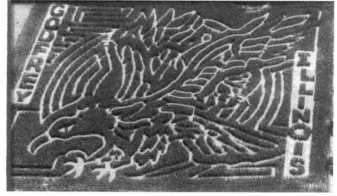

Q   How many pecks make a bushel?
A   Four

Q   What color was a 1950 Ferguson tractor?
A   Gray – it looked like a Ford, had a similar wide stance, but did not have any red paint.

Q   What was the price of a 1950 Farmall "M" tractor?
A $900

Q   Old time windmills had wooden gears. What was used to lubricate the gears?
A   Hog grease

Q   If you saw a Minneapolis-Moline tractor in 1950, what color was it?
A   Yellow and black

Q   What is the origin of the expression, "sucking the hind

teat?"

A   The weakest piglet always got shoved down to the last teat by the others. The first pair of teats produced more than the last, so that piggy became the runt of the litter.

Q   How many teats does a sow generally have?
A   Anywhere from ten to fourteen

Q   How many milk spigots are on a cow?
A   Four

Q   Where were eggs and butter stored on a farm before refrigerators?
A   In the well

Q   What is no till farming?
A   The seed, fertilizer and insect control are all planted together in a narrow strip of ground. The field is not plowed first.

Q   What is the main purpose of plowing?
A   To loosen the soil and get rid of the weeds

Q   For what purpose was GPS (global positioning system) originally sold to farmers?
A   For yield monitoring so they could determine what parts of their fields needed more fertilizer

Q   Why did GPS systems not catch on with most farmers?
A   After cost-benefit analysis, the farmers decided they weren't worth the price.

Q   What determines the straightness of row after row of corn or soybeans?
A   The skill level of the farmer driving the tractor

Q   How did farmers who weren't very good at plowing a straight row rationalize?
A   They claimed the yields from crooked rows were higher. (Think about it!)

Maple sirup harvested from trees at Funk's Grove in Shirley (Oberle)

Q   What is the secret to making a straight furrow?
A   Most farmers say you have to fix your gaze on an object at the end of the field and keep your eye on that object.

Q   What farm club sponsored by the University of Illinois Extension Services do many young people belong to?
A   The Four H Club resulting in projects for the State Fair at **Springfield**

Q   What do the four H's represent?
A   Head, Heart, Hands, Health

Q   What is a typical farmer's response to a dumb question where the obvious answer is "NO?"
A   It's something like – "Do pigs fly?" or "Do chickens have lips?"

Q   Is it true or is it an urban myth that a mule won't sink in quicksand but a donkey will?
A   Urban myth

Q   What logo is the symbol of 4- H Clubs?
A   Four leaf clover

Q   People who raise sheep often include a llama in the flock. Why?
A   The llama protects the sheep from predators. The llama has the uncanny ability to direct its caustic spit into the eyes of an attacker, causing severe pain, driving them off. (I know, I don't believe this one either.)

Pig Hip cartoon by Robert Waldmeier

Q   What happens to laying hens that fall off in production?
A   They are sold to somebody such as Campbell's and become chicken soup.

Q   What did farm wives in the 1930's and 1940's do with empty feed sacks?
A   They used the cotton material, imprinted with colorful designs, to make housedresses, pillowcases, aprons, and underwear.

Q   When chickens were killed for eating, what process had to be used before the feathers could be plucked?
A   They had to be dipped in boiling water – the smell was terrible.

Q   When it was time for chicken and dumplings on a farm, how did most housewives kill the chicken?
A   They cut the head off with a machete or axe. Many women were adept at "wringing" a chicken's neck. They would grab the chicken by its neck and swing it around in a circular fashion, causing the head to separate from the body.

Q   Who was thought to make better cow milkers, men or women?
A   Women are thought to be gentler and more patient

Q   What did farmers in 1945 do with empty burlap feed sacks?
A   They were placed over the seat of a tractor. The open weave of burlap was good for this purpose.

Q   What is a long ton of wheat?
A   2200 pounds – A regular ton is 2,000 pounds

Q   Is there such a thing as a spotted mule?
A   They are rare, but they exist (see a picture of one on page 106 of my *Illinois Crime*)

Q   If a farmer in a wagon yells the command "haw" to a horse, what does it mean?
A   Go left

Q   What is the command for a horse or mule to go right?
A   "Gee"

Q   In central Illinois, when is winter wheat normally harvested?
A   At the end of June

Q   During what month is winter wheat normally planted?
A   Late October, early November

Q   What part of corn is male and what is female?
A   The tassels are male and the kernels are female

Q   In Illinois, what was supposed to be "knee high by the Fourth of July?"
A   Field corn – with modern techniques it's "head high by the Fourth of July"

Q   What crop does Illinois lead the nation in production?
A   Soybeans

Q   What crop does Illinois run second in the nation, closely behind Iowa?
A   Corn – in past years there has been a few years where Illinoisans outproduced Iowans.

Q   What is the state's definition of a farm?
A   Mostly for tax purposes, it's a piece of land that produces crops or raises animals at a minimum value of $1,000

Q   What popular Illinois crop came from Manchuria and was not grown here until the 1920's?
A   Soybeans

Q   What determines the prices farmers receive for their crops and animals?
A   Market demand and the Board of Trade in Chicago

Q   What are the two main farmers' unions?
A   The NFO and the Farmer's Union

Q   What is the most profitable crop grown in Illinois?
A   Horseradish (legal crop)

Q   What part of the horseradish is used in making the condiment?

A   The upper part of the root.

Q   What unique geographic area in three counties bills itself as the Horseradish Capital of the World?
A   Madison, Monroe, and St. Clair counties on the American Bottom

Q   What percent of the U.S. total do these three counties produce?
A   Fifty percent

Dead Man's Curve - Route 66 Towanda farm country by Dan Oberle

Q   What rural Illinois school gives its prep sports teams the nickname "Cornjerkers?"
A   **Hoopeston** – the town once had a cannery

Q   Back in the 1920s, how did egg producers determine which eggs had chick embryos in them?
A   They held them up to a candle or a strong light

Q   About how often does a good laying hen produce an egg?
A   It used to be about one every five days but improved feed and breeding has improved on that.

Q   What is a big complaint among animal rights activists

Union Stockyards at Chicago (Chicago Chamber of Commerce)

about the way chickens are being raised?
A   They no longer run around the barnyard. They remain caged from birth until slaughter.

Q   Where did the phrase "pecking order" originate?
A   The barnyard. The dominant chickens exercise control and the subservient ones demure or wait their turn at the

feed or watering mechanism. To assert dominance, the aggressive ones peck at the weak ones.

Q   What bumper sticker do farmers use to counter criticisms?
A   "Don't complain about the cost of food with your mouth full."

Q   What is a pullet?
A   A young female chicken less than seven months old

Q   Where do forestry, fishing and agriculture rank in the Illinois economy?
A   Seventh – behind services, finance, manufacturing, government, transportation, retail trade, wholesale trade and construction; mining is ranked eighth.

MISSISSIPPI AND OHIO RIVER LORE

Introduction: Except for those bounded by an ocean, there is no state in the union blessed with better riparian access than Illinois. It kisses Lake Michigan and is bounded by the Wabash, Ohio and Mississippi rivers.

When settlers first came to the state, they usually settled along the banks of the rivers due to the commerce. In dozens of ways the lives of these people were affected by the actions of Mother Nature and the rivers. Rivers ate away embankments and by changing their course sometimes placed a town along the banks in another state. Occasionally whole towns were washed downstream. At least two southern Illinois towns have picked up and relocated farther inland to escape frequent floodwaters.

Water intake "castles" on the Mississippi near Chain of Rocks Bridge on old Route 66 (photo by Dan Oberle of Geneseo/Edwardsville

Farmers near rivers set their clocks by the punctual passing of boats, and sleepy little villages were awakened from their lethargy with cries of "S-t-e-a-m-boat-a-comin'! " Upscale homes built along the Ohio or Mississippi often had a widow's walk or a cupola from which people could watch the comings and goings on the river. Many a steamboat bell found itself sitting inside a church bell tower after the ship was retired.

Most people along the river took trips on the excursion boats at some point in their life. This author has seen several old time melodramas performed on the refurbished *Goldenrod*. And he has fond teen memories of the arcade section on the bottom deck of the Streckfus steamer *Admiral*. Somehow I just knew in my heart that living in a town along the river was more interesting than residing out in the middle of the prairie.

Q   How did the Mississippi River originate?

A   According to folklore artist S.S. Prentiss, when God made the world, He had a large amount of surplus water which He turned loose and told it to go where it pleased; it has been going where it pleases ever since, and that is the Mississippi River.

Q   What is the argument Missourians have with the Mississippi River?
A   They claim the Missouri River is the longest in the world and insist that the Mississippi empties into the Missouri. They also suggest a more appropriate name would be "Missourissippi."

Boatmen's Memorial at Cairo (Cairo Chamber of Commerce)

Q   In what year did railroads replace steamboats as a major source of travel?

A   1872

Q   Where is the Boatmen's Memorial - the Illinois tribute to those who lost their lives on the Ohio and Mississippi Rivers?
A   Cairo – at the confluence of the two rivers

Q   What was the last boat to make stops at Illinois river towns such as **Peoria, Quincy**, and **Savanna**?
A   *Delta Queen.*

Q   Where were the regular showboat stops along the Mississippi in Illinois?
A   **Galena, Rock Island, Moline, Quincy, Alton** and **Cairo**

Q   Where were the regular showboat stops along the Ohio River?
A   **Shawneetown** and **Metropolis**

Q   What nickname was given to the section of Mississippi River between St. Louis and Cairo in the 1850's?
A   The "Graveyard" because more than 300 steamboats sank on that dangerous stretch by 1867

Q   When Hungarian revolutionary leader Louis Kossuth steamboated on the Mississippi in 1851, what famous question did he have?

54

A He wanted to know why the people who lived along its banks didn't filter the water before drinking it. An equally famous reply: "Because we are such go-ahead people we don't have time to filter our water."

Q What similar reply was made to a female traveler who asked a question about drinking unfiltered Ohio River water?
A "Because it (sand and mud) scours out your bowels."

Q What did **Mike Fink** have to say about aquatic life and the food chain in the Mississippi?
A "I've seen trout swallow a perch, and a cat would come along and swallow the trout, and . . . the alligators use up the cat . . ."

Q What did Mike Fink have to say about the dirt and dust in the Mississippi River?
A He said there was so much of it you could occasionally see a catfish come up to the surface to sneeze.

Q What newer bridge across the Mississippi is considered by many to be the most beautiful in the state?
A The six-lane Clark bridge at **Alton**; the cable stays are wrapped in gold foil giving it a brilliant gleam.

Q How did writer George Fitch describe a steamboat?
A "A steamboat is an engine on a raft, with $11,000 worth of jig-saw work around it."

Q How was it possible to gain extra river bottom land without paying a cent for it?
A A group of men once owned some river bottom land near **Chester**. It probably wasn't much good for farming, but it made a handsome site for a factory or a warehouse. They were offered a princely sum for it but refused to sell. One day they noticed the strip was getting emaciated. A surveyor's tape found that half of it had been washed away. Now the men wanted to sell, but the market was sluggish. The next year the river ate so vigorously that only a narrow ribbon of ground was left, leaving the men much depressed. Suddenly the land began to increase. The Mississippi chose this site to deposit a 40-acre farm upon which it had foreclosed farther up the river. The men now sold the land and made a handsome profit.

Casino Queen gambling boat at East St. Louis

Q How much draft of water was necessary for steamboats to travel up the Illinois or Rock rivers?
A Some packet steamboats drew only three feet of water. A hackneyed expression said that steamboats on Western waters were built so they could run over a field after a heavy dew.

Q What did a roustabout do on a steamboat?
A It was the roustabout who unloaded bales of cotton or barrels of molasses. African-Americans were often used for this hard labor.

Q How did roustabouts pave the way for jazz music on Mississippi River steamboats?
A Roustabouts often played guitars for diversion, but their quarters were always on the lower decks. When upper deck passengers went down to lower decks to listen to them, this

New Clark Bridge at Alton: courtesy Robert Graul & *Alton Telegraph*

gave packet owners the idea of hiring jazz musicians.

Q When "St. Louis Blues" was recorded by W.C. Handy, what was on the flip side of that most famous record?
A "East St. Louis Blues"

Q What is this author's favorite tall tale about the Illinois River?
A A cook on board the steamboat **Peoria** decided to go fishing. He used as bait the carcass of a hog that had died on board. He attached the carcass to the stern by means of a meat hook. This type of line was usually left in the water overnight. When passengers awoke the next morning they were startled to find the boat going in the wrong direction. An enormous catfish had swallowed the bait and was now hurrying home, towing the steamship behind him. The captain, being used to such emergencies, got out his big bore buffalo rifle and shot the fish.

Q What happened to one steamboat that got stuck on a sandbar while taking on fuel at **Rockwood** in southern Illinois?
A The captain tried to get the ship unstuck but to no avail. He remembered that below the deck was a boatload of turkeys for delivery. He had the men take the turkeys out of their cages and brought up to the deck. The ship's carpenter fastened the turkeys down with staples over their feet. The captain blew the whistle and had everyone on board wave rags at the turkeys and yell, Shoo! Shoo! The startled birds flew up and lifted the boat back into deep water.

Q Why were early Illinoisans referred to as "suckers?"
A It goes back to the early lead mines at **Galena**. Many Illinoisans in 1830 went up the river to work the mines in

the spring, stayed all summer, and came back to their homes in late fall. This was similar to the migratory habits of the sucker fish, so Illinoisans became known as suckers.

An alternate theory is that the lower part of the state was settled by emigrants from the South where tobacco was grown. These poor people were sometimes seen as a drain on the state, much like offshoots called suckers on a tobacco plant that have to be removed or they detract from the main growth.

Q   Why did Illinoisans retaliate and call Missourians "pukes?"
A   It had been Missourians at the Galena lead mines that gave Illinoisans the derogatory name "suckers." These Missourians were themselves uncouth ruffians so Illinoisans retaliated from spite and called them "pukes." These terms remained common for about a hundred years but aren't used much in the current vernacular.

Q   What immigrant group was responsible for introducing this country to the drink known as the **mint julep**?
A   It was first concocted by the French **Cahokians** and **Kaskaskians**.   It consists of bourbon and molasses, garnished with a green mint leaf.

Q   What **East St. Louis** boat was the largest operating on the Mississippi in 1913?
A   It was the *Sprague*, used to haul bauxite to the **largest processing plant in the world**, Aluminum Ore on Missouri Avenue.

Eagle Packet Line at Alton

EAGLE
Packet Company,
STEAMER

Spread Eagle
W. LEVHE, Master.
EDWARD BLOCK, - First Clerk.
LEAVES ALTON
For St. Louis (except Sundays) 7 a.m.
For Grafton except Suts & Sundays 6 p.m.
LEAVES ST. LOUIS
For Alton. at   3 p.m.
Fare to St Louis 35c; round trip. 50c;
twenty   Ticket $1.00.
G. W. HILL, Agent.

Q   What is this author's favorite story about snakes along the Mississippi River?
A   Murray Schumach tells the story of a man fishing along the banks of a slough in the backwaters of the Mississippi near **Cairo**. He heard that frogs made irresistible bait for catfish but he couldn't find any. Suddenly he spotted a water moccasin with a frog in his mouth. He tried to pull the frog away but the snake doggedly hung on to its meal. In desperation, the man reached down and pulled a bottle of whiskey from his boot and poured it down the snake's mouth. The snake let go and slithered away.   A few minutes later, as the man was preparing to cast his line, he felt a tap on his boot. He looked down and there was the snake again with another frog in its mouth, looking for a drink.

Q   What famous naturalist visited southern Illinois in 1810 and came up with a tongue-in-cheek description of an unusual Mississippi fish?
A   **James Audubon** – "It's called the Devil Jack Diamond fish and it's about ten feet long and weighs 400 pounds. It lies sometimes asleep or motionless on the surface of the water and may be mistaken for a log or snag. The whole body is covered with scales impervious to musket ball."

Q   What myth did old timers believe about taking a fish out of the Ohio River and placing it into the Mississippi?
A   They reasoned that it would die as quickly as if you had pierced it with a bullet.

Q   There are many places in Illinois along the Mississippi that are lined with fifty-foot high levees. What was the purpose of "walking the levee" in times of high water?
A   It originated from a fear that Missourians on the other side of the river would come over and dynamite the levee to relieve the pressure on their side. Levee walkers had orders to "shoot to kill."

Q   What was a torch basket on a steamboat?
A   In lieu of searchlights the old steamboats had torch baskets. These were 18-inch iron kettles that were hung out over the river from the forward deck so as to allow burning embers to fall into the river and not the deck.

Q   What was a levee "boil?"
A   These were weak spots in the levee at the base on the dry side. Those who walked the levee were on constant lookout for boils – small geysers where the river had found a soft spot in the levee. Levee breaks usually came from boils enlarging themselves and not from the river running over the top. Once a boil was spotted it was quickly sandbagged.

Q   What was a calliope on a steamship?
A   They were keyboard instruments (much like steam operated organs) that did not become popular until after the turn of the century.

Q   What was the most innovative method devised for plugging a steamboat leak?
A   One captain felt a bump and went down to the hold of the ship to make sure everything was all right. He heard a terrible gurgling sound and saw a hole as big as a man in the prow where it had hit a piling. He yelled to his men and then jumped square into the breach to stop the leak. His men gave him cigars to smoke and whiskey to keep him warm. It took about an hour to ground the ship and when they pulled the captain out, he popped - just like a cork in a champagne bottle.

Q   According to Illinois fishing lore, why is it useless to fish after a night with a full moon?
A   Because the fish will gorge themselves feeding in the light of the moon and will not bite the next day.

Q   Why is 1811 in southern Illinois referred to as the year of the "great shakes?"
A   A massive earthquake, due to slippage at the New Madrid Fault, destroyed Fort Massac, near present-day **Metropolis**. It had been rebuilt after the Revolutionary War, so ordered by George Washington. It was quickly rebuilt after the earthquake as a fortification for the War of 1812.

Q   How strong was the 1811 earthquake?

A   The earthquake would have probably been about a 7.1 on the present Richter scale. It collapsed some bluffs along the river, caused the Mississippi to temporarily flow backwards, formed Reelfoot Lake on the Kentucky-Tennessee border, changed the course of the river, and formed new islands in it.

Because the region was so sparsely settled, there were few deaths. It rang church bells in Philadelphia, and people as far away as Quebec felt the tremors. The entire state only had a population of about 5,000 at this time. This "prime event," the "great shakes" as oldtimers called it, was said to have shaken the ground in long waves that would rock and roll. Due to the basket-like construction of pioneer homes, where no iron or nails were used, there was minimal structural damage.

One eyewitness said that the stock was very much disturbed and frightened; horses nickering, cattle lowing, hogs squealing, chickens squawking. The domestic animals all came running to the house for protection.

There were numerous aftershocks that lasted from November until March of 1812.

Q   What is the Indian version of how Reelfoot Lake was formed during this earthquake?
A   There was a Chickasaw Indian boy who was born with a deformity on one foot, and others in the tribe began calling him Reelfoot. The boy overcame this deformity and became a great warrior. However, because of his clubfoot, no maiden wished to marry him. He decided that he would steal a wife from the Choctaw tribe. When he informed the Sachem (medicine man) of his intent, the wise one warned that the Manitou (great spirit) would be angry because it was against his law to steal another man's wife.

Reelfoot ignored the warning and with a war party snatched a princess of the neighboring tribe. A great feast was prepared to celebrate the wedding, but as the people began to sing the wind started making its own music. Thunder began to roll and the earth rolled with it. Big cypress trees snapped like twigs. The Great Spirit was mad. He stamped his foot and the ground sank for miles around. He called to the Mississippi and it heard him and ran upstream till sundown. When the Great Spirit's anger was over, beautiful blue water covered the land once inhabited by Reelfoot and his people.

Q   What did the leadsman do on a steamboat?
A   It was his job to take soundings of the river to make sure the water was deep enough. He was called a "leadsman" because the chain that was used had a weighted lead pipe at the end of it. There were leather strips tied to the chain at certain intervals so measurements could be made at night.

Q   River towns in Illinois are notorious for flood stories. What is the author's favorite from the 1937 flood near **Shawneetown**?
A   For a number of days rescuers were trying to reach a stranded family, sure that food provisions were about to give out. When they found the family, up in the attic, they were hungry and exhausted. Rescuers noticed that the flood had brought in a half dozen fish that were swimming about in the shallow water that covered the attic. The rescuers asked why they hadn't captured the fish and eaten them. A gaunt survivor replied, "We couldn't eat them fish. They were fighting for their lives, same as us."

Q   When did the state of Illinois begin licensing and inspecting steamboats?
A   1852

Q   Samuel Clemens spent many a day navigating the Mississippi in Illinois waters. What is the meaning of his name Mark Twain?
A   It means two fathoms of water or 12 feet – safe waters for steamboats.

Q   What is the original meaning of the word *bushwhacking*?
A   It was used by men traveling *upstream* in small boats to make progress. They would grab hold of overhanging bushes to pull themselves forward.

Confluence of the Mississippi and Ohio rivers (Cairo C. of Comm.)

Q   How much did it cost to take a packet steamboat from **Alton** to St. Louis in 1904?
A   Ten cents

Q   What were the two main steamboat companies in Alton around 1900?
A   The Eagle Packet Company and the Diamond Jo Line. They were tied up at the wharves with rope that was 7/8 of an inch in diameter.

Q   What was the most popular showboat on the Illinois River in the heyday of steamboating?
A   The *Cotton Blossom;* Edna Ferber used the *Cotton Blossom* in her novel, *Showboat.*

Q   What daredevil (or fool) floated down the Ohio River from Pittsburgh to **Cairo** in an inflated rubber suit in 1881?
A   Paul Boynton

Q What **Collinsville** man in the 1930's and 1940's swam the Mississippi River at **East St. Louis** every Fourth of July?
A George Hopper

Q What is the difference between a flatboat and a keelboat?
A A flatboat is smooth on the bottom while a keelboat has a long narrow keel underneath, running most of the length of the boat for easier steering.

Q When was the "Golden Age of Flatboating" down the Ohio River to **Shawneetown**?
A 1790-1815

Players Casino Boat at Metropolis (Illinois Chamber of Commerce)

Q What was the first "snag boat" operating in Western Waters?
A The *Heliopolis* – designed in 1829 with a twin hull and a winch for pulling half-sunken trees and other snags out of the Ohio River that were hazardous to navigation. It operated at **Trinity**, Illinois, at the Grand Chain of Rocks in the Ohio River.

Q James B. Eads made a good living by salvaging engines and cargoes from sunken steamboats. What materials did he use to make his first diving bell?
A He took a whiskey hogshead and knocked one end out, fastened a seat inside, attached air hoses, and operated it from a barge that was anchored over the site of the wreck.

Q What was a hogshead?
A It was a large wooden stave barrel nearly four feet in diameter and about five feet tall.

Q What man painted the Mississippi River in 1847 with what was the **longest painting in the world** at the time?
A John Banvard first concocted the idea at age 15 when he floated down the river with his father. His panoramic canvas, three miles in length, was on rollers and depicted the Mississippi from **East St. Louis** to New Orleans. The opening night of his exhibition was rainy and not one person came to see it. Undaunted, he gave free tickets to riverboat men who then spread the word about its beauty and authenticity.

Q Although Mike Fink was a real person, the stories about him are tall tales. Why did he once eat a buffalo robe?
A He drank so much whiskey that it destroyed the lining of his stomach. The doctor told him before he could get well he would need a new coat for it. Fink made up his mind that a buffalo robe, hair and all, was just the thing to line his stomach. He swallowed it whole, and after that could drink as much as he pleased.

Q What legendary feat was accomplished by Mike Fink?
A He has title to the **longest jump on record**. He once boasted that he could jump across the Mississippi. When put to the test, he saw that he was going to fall short by about ten feet, so he changed course in midair and landed safely back at his starting point.

Q How did Mike Fink meet an untimely death?
A His drinking and womanizing were ended by a bullet from an angry husband.

Q **Jim Bowie**, who died with Davy Crockett defending the Alamo and invented the **bowie knife**, was an expert riverboat gambler and was the most celebrated duelist of his day. What is the famous story about Bowie saving a bridegroom from committing suicide?
A The young man and his wife were traveling on a steamboat going from Louisville to Natchez. He became involved in a card game and lost a sum of $30,000 in a crooked poker game. Jim Bowie came on board at **Cairo** and talked the man out of killing himself. Bowie sat in on the next game, caught the men cheating and took back the money. He gave three-fourths of the money back to the man and kept the rest as spoils of war. Bowie made the man promise that he would never gamble again.

Q Did Abe Lincoln ever see a slave auction?
A Yes – Lincoln and two other men were paid to build a boat, float down the Mississippi and take a load of hogs to New Orleans. While there, Lincoln witnessed the sale of a comely mulatto girl who underwent a thorough examination at the hands of bidders.
"Let's get away from this," Lincoln told his friends. "If I ever get a chance to hit that thing (slavery), I'll hit it hard."

Q What year was the famous race between the *Natchez* and the *Robert E. Lee*?
A 1870

Q What were the starting and ending points of the race?
A New Orleans to St. Louis

Q What ship was the oldest?
A The *Robert E. Lee* - the *Natchez* was built in 1869 and was specifically made to be a faster boat.

Q How great was the interest in this race?
A It was the Super Bowl of its era with hundreds of thousands of dollars wagered. Huge crowds lined the river for miles at the starting point. As the boats slowed down and took on more wood and coal at places like Vicksburg and Memphis, crowds along the banks cheered themselves

hoarse, rooting for their favorite. Telegraphers were on hand in each town to relay the progress to newspapers all over the country.

Q   Which boat took the early lead?
A   A gun was fired to start the race but the confident captain of the *Natchez* said he would not take off until after the *Robert E. Lee.*

Q   What incident happened at **Cairo**?
A   The *Robert E. Lee* stopped to prematurely celebrate and became stuck on a sandbar. The *Natchez* nearly caught up before the boat's crew dislodged it.

Q   What memorable event took place at Jefferson Barracks, several miles south of St. Louis?
A   The military there fired a cannon salute as each ship raced by. Jefferson Barracks is currently the third largest military cemetery in the U.S.

Q   What ship won the race?
A   The *Robert E. Lee* made the trip in record time – three days, eighteen hours and fourteen minutes. This was about an hour less than the old record.

Q   Where was the finish line?
A   At the St. Louis wharf, directly across from Bloody Island at East St. Louis

Q   What was meant by the expression, "She takes the horns?"
A   The fastest boat on the river sported a gilded pair of deer antlers (either on the hurricane roof or in front of the pilot house) until some other ship came along and bested the champion.

Q   What was the first steamboat in western waters?
A   Robert Fulton, the steamboat inventor, built a ship

Mississippi Great River Road logo

called the *New Orleans*. In 1810 it made a trip down the Ohio River and then from **Cairo** to St. Louis.

Q   What unusual event occurred when the ship arrived at St. Louis?

A   When the boat docked, it blew its shrill whistle. At that very moment a brilliant comet streaked across the sky. Hundreds of people on both sides of the shore came down to the river **to see if the comet had fallen into the Mississippi River**.

Q   What Illinois towns were brought into prominence by the Golden Age of Steamboats?
A   **East St. Louis, Chester, Grand Tower, Cairo, Elizabethtown, Cairo, Mound City, Metropolis, Golconda, Alton, Moline, Savanna, Quincy** and **Rock Island** were brought into prominence. Most river towns, especially East St. Louis and Cairo, became notorious for being lawless, wicked and immoral (reputations richly deserved).

Q   What code of rules were there for steamboats meeting each other going different directions on the Mississippi?
A   The right of way always went to the descending boat moving downstream. The ascending craft was expected to blow its whistle first to announce its intent. One whistle

Chain of Rocks Bridge across the Mississippi at Mitchell by D. Oberle

blast meant the right direction was going to be taken; two blasts indicated the left. Orders to the crew were given by a simple set of bells that were rung.

Q   Has there ever been a race between a train and a steamboat?
A   Yes – in 1874 from **Cairo** to Memphis. A passenger train pulled into Cairo from the East and the passengers prepared to depart the train and board the steamboat *American Empire*. The train's conductor told the passengers that if they stayed on board they would reach Memphis sooner. The ship's captain heard the remark and said that if he couldn't beat the train to Memphis, the ride was free. The train tracks paralleled the river, so the race was spirited. After nearly a four-hour trip, the steamboat arrived as the winner with about a quarter mile lead. Had the boat been going upstream, it would have been no contest.

Q   Was there ever a race riot on Illinois waters?
A   Yes – in 1869 the packet *Dubuque* took on a group of workers at St. Louis. They were headed north to help harvest wheat fields. A group of raftsmen tried to gain access to the upper deck but were prevented in doing so by a colored steward. The ship's captain suggested that the leader of the ruffians settle his quarrel by fisticuffs with the

steward on the forecastle. The man said it was beneath him to fight a colored man. Angry and frustrated, his men set fire to some bales of hay and began shooting and killing colored deckhands. Near the town of **Hampden**, Illinois, one deckhand jumped in the water and tried to escape. He was pelted with missiles until he sank from sight. A group of soldiers from the **Rock Island Arsenal** managed to quell the riot and make arrests. Eleven rioters were convicted and sent to the penitentiary.

Q   What Illinois river pirates were **America's first serial killers**?
A   The vicious Harpe brothers of Cave-in-Rock on the Ohio River

Steamer Grey Eagle passing under the Eads Bridge

Q   What was the Harpe brothers' modus operandi?
A   They would have a confederate flag people flatboating down the Ohio River. Their man said that the passage ahead was tricky, and for fifty cents he would safely steer them past the danger. Instead, he would run the boat aground near the mouth of the cave, and then the Harpes would kill everyone and steal their belongings. They slit the stomachs of the bodies, weighed them down with stones, and tossed them in the river.

Q   What other story illustrates the viciousness of "Big" Harpe and "Little" Harpe?
A   Once they stripped a male captive naked and tied him to a horse on the cliff above the opening of the cave. Then they blindfolded the horse and frightened the animal with yells and a gunshot. The horse raced over the cliff and fell to the rocky shore below. There was another instance where Big Harpe, in a fit of rage because his baby was crying, snatched the infant from his wife and bashed its brains out against a tree.

Q   What ultimately happened to Big Harpe?
A   A vigilante committee finally caught up with him and shot him to death. One of the men **cut off his head and placed it in the fork of a tree**. This was done to discourage future lawbreakers. The path became known as Harpe Head Road.

Q   What happened to Little Harpe?
A   Authorities caught up with him in 1804 near Natchez, Mississippi, and hanged him. His head was placed on a pole along the Natchez Trace as a warning to other evil doers.

Q   Why is the Kaskaskia River sometimes called the Okaw?
A   The area was first settled by the French, and they had a way of saying they were going au Kau - to Kaskaskia.

Q   How were keelboats pulled upstream?
A   Keelboats had a long line nearly a thousand feet long called a *cordelle*. It was fastened to a thirty-foot tall mast in the center of the boat. The boat was pulled upstream with this line by men on shore. The line was connected to the bow by means of a "bridle," a short line fastened to a loop on the bow and to a ring through which the cordelle passed. The bridle prevented the boat from swinging under the force of the wind or current when the speed was not great enough to accomplish this purpose by means of a rudder. The object of having the tow line fastened to the top of the mast was to keep it from dragging, and to enable it to clear the brush along the bank.
Keelboats were typically about 60-feet long and most were made in Pittsburgh at a cost of about $3,000 each.

Q   How was the "**Liberty Bell of the West**" brought up from New Orleans to Kaskaskia?
A   It took about four months for men to tow the bell up the Mississippi with the bell sitting on a raft.

Q   What was the origin of the "Liberty Bell of the West?"
A   King Louis XV presented the parish at **Kaskaskia** with a 600-pound cast metal bell in 1741. The bell, which is still preserved and on display, bears the inscription (in French): "For the church of the Illinois, with the compliments of the King from beyond the sea." The bell was made by Normand in the seaport town of LaRochelle in France.

Q   Did keelboats have sails?
A   Most of them did, but they were only useful in the case of an aft (rear) wind.

Q   What other terms are used to describe the front and rear of a ship?
A   Fore and aft, stem to stern

Q   How did the terms *starboard* and *port* come to be used for right and left sides of a ship?
A   Ships pull into ports or wharves on their left or port side. On the open seas, captains used a sextant on the right side of the ship to "shoot the stars" and determine their position.

Q   What is a packet steamboat?
A   The term packet means that it was a passenger boat rather one that hauled freight.

Q   What was the advantage of a sidewheel steamboat over a sternwheeler?
A   They could turn and maneuver better in the river.

SPORTS, LEISURE, AND THE CUBS

Q   When did the only all-Chicago World Series take place?
A   Nearly 100 years ago – 1906. Don't hold your breath for the next one.

Q   What **Granite City** native owns a World Series ring and became general manager of the St. Louis Cardinals.
A   Shortstop Dal Maxvill

Q   What famous golfer helped the Americans wrest the Walker Cup from the British in a series of matches in 1928 Chicago?
A   Bobby Jones

Q   What SIU **Carbondale** grad played pro baseball with Houston and the Arizona Diamondbacks?
A   Steve Finley – traded to the Dodgers in July 2004

Q   What town was the birthplace of Robin Yount, MVP of the American League in 1982?
A   **Danville**

Q   What town is home to Scott Spiezio who plays third base for the Seattle Mariners and won a World Series ring with the Angels?
A   **Morris** – his high school prep team was the "Redskins."

Q   What current U.S. Speaker of the House of Representatives was recently elected into the Wrestling Hall of Fame?
A   Dennis Hastert of **Aurora**, who coached at **Yorkville**

Q   What **Springfield** baseball executive was responsible for converting Babe Ruth from a pitcher to a slugging outfielder?
A   Ed Barrow

Q   What University of Illinois graduate was named "All Around Amateur Champion of America" in 1918, and in 1929 became president of the U.S. Olympic Committee, holding that position until 1952 when he was named Chairman of the International Olympic Committee?
A   Avery Brundage

Q   Why was Avery Brundage heavily criticized in 1936?
A   He declared that politics had no place in Olympic competition and urged that the Berlin Olympics, subsequently won by Nazi Germany, not be boycotted.

Q   What town's prep baseball team won the 1998 state championship and then went out to Las Vegas and won the American Legion **national championship**?
A   **Edwardsville**

Q   What tall, famous tennis star helped the American team defeat the Japanese in the 1928 American zone finals for the Davis Cup, held in Chicago?
A   Bill Tilden

Q   What superstar did the Chicago Bulls lose due to a flip of the coin?
A   Magic Johnson – they had to settle for David Greenwood

Q   In 1974 what Chicagoan set the NBA record by achieving the league's first quadruple double?
A   Nate "the Great" Thurmond of the Bulls who had 22 points, 14 rebounds, 13 assists and 12 blocked shots against Atlanta – awesome!

Old picture of Soldier Field in Chicago

Q   What Bulls player made the NBA 2004 All-Rookie Team?
A   Kirk Hinrich

Q   How many times have the Chicago Blackhawks won the Stanley Cup?
A   Three - 1934, 1938, 1961

Q   What Bears running back was the youngest player chosen as league MVP in 1977?
A   Walter Payton

Q   What St. Louisan won the U.S. Open at the Chicagoland Medinah golf course in 1990?
A   Hale Irwin

Pitcher and Cub announcer Steve Stone

Q   What Bears running back was considered one of their biggest busts for a high draft pick?
A   Curtis Enis – he had only about four touchdowns in three years.

Q   Who was the Bears' first se-lection in the 2004 draft?
A   Tommie Har-ris, a defensive tackle from Oklahoma

Q   What high school star from **Benton** became a crackerjack player for the Philadelphia 76ers?

A   Doug Collins, who also went into coaching and currently is color analyst for the NBA playoffs.

Q   What NBA team was Illini star **Frankie Williams** with in 2004?
A   The New York Knicks

Q   How does geography tend to determine baseball fan loyalty in Chicago?
A   Northsiders are Cub fans and southsiders are Sox fans.

Q   During the 1920's, where did the Chicago Cardinals play their football games?
A   Comiskey Park

Q   Who founded the nation's first professional women's softball league?
A   Cub owner P.K. Wrigley; this is depicted in the Tom Hanks/Geena Davis film, *A League of Their Own*.

Q   Just exactly how exciting was the 1927 Dempsey-Tunney title fight at the huge Amphitheater near the Chicago Stock Yards?
A   Of the 40 million who listened to the fight on radio, **five died from heart attacks**. This was the famous "long count" fight where Dempsey forgot to go to a neutral corner after knocking Tunney to the canvas. This gave Tunney about five extra seconds to beat the ten count, and he went on to win the fight.

Q   What happened after the Cubs traded pitcher Grover Cleveland Alexander to the Cardinals in 1926?
A   He pitched the Cards to a pennant and a World Series victory over Babe Ruth and company.

Q   Who portrayed Grover Cleveland Alexander in the 1952 Hollywood movie?
A   Ronald Reagan – *The Winning Team*

Q   How well did Rogers Hornsby play for the Cubs in 1929 after he was traded by the Cardinals?
A   He won the National League MVP with 40 homers, 149 runs batted in, and a .380 average.

Q   The basketball quintet from what Illinois school played in the first NIT in 1938?
A   The Bradley Braves of **Peoria**; Jack Brickhouse, a Peoria native, was broadcaster for their games

Q   Why is it somewhat easier for Chicago Bears kickers to make a field goal than their counterparts in the indoor Arena League?
A   Indoors there is no wind to contend with, but the uprights are only nine feet wide as opposed to nearly double that width for Bears kickers. The crossbar on the uprights is also slightly higher in arena football.

Q   Who was the leading receiver for the Chicago Bears in the 2003 season?
A   Marty Booker with 52 catches

Q   Roger Maris long held the American League record for home runs with 61. Who owned the National League record until it was broken by McGuire and Sousa?
A   Cubbie Hack Wilson with 56 in 1930

Q   What Cub manager was fired in August of 1932 while he had the Cubs in first place?
A   Rogers Hornsby. It was a personality conflict with management.

Cub slugger Dave Kingman

Q   What was the Cubs' unusual three-year pennant pattern of the 1930's?
A   They won in 1929, again in 1932, another in 1935, and a fourth title in 1938. No World Series wins for the lovable losers.

Q   In Cub folklore, what is the "homer in the gloamin'?"
A   In 1938, with the Cubs in a close race against Pittsburgh, a game was tied with two out in the bottom of the ninth. It looked as if the game would have to be finished the next day because of impending darkness. Gabby Hartnett, the player-manager, hit a two-strike Pirate fastball for a home run, leading the Cubs to a three game sweep and a pennant. It is considered the **most famous hit in Cub history**.

Bears field goal kicker Jeff Jaeger

Q   How was owner Chuck Comiskey partially responsible for the 1919 Black Sox Scandal?
A   The tightwad paid the lowest salaries in the league.

Q   What was unusual about the length of the World Series in that era?
A   It was best of nine instead of today's best of seven.

Q   What manager of the Washington Senators talked President Taft into throwing out the first baseball to start the season, thereby establishing an annual ritual?

A Clark Griffith of **Normal**, Illinois

Q What **Jacksonville** man was the PGA golf champion in 1961?
A Jerry Barber

Q Did **Jacksonville** High's Andy Kaufmann reach the 3,000 point scoring mark in his prep career?
A Yes – in 1988 for coach Mel Roustio of **East St. Louis,** this author's 1957 classmate

Q What Bears running back broke the career rushing mark set by Jim Brown?
A Walter Payton – 12,312 yards in 1984

Q Did Walter Payton ever get a Super Bowl ring?
A Yes – with the 1985 champs; he retired in 1988

Q What Bears offensive player started the trend of teams using linemen that weighed nearly 300 pounds?
A William "the refrigerator" Perry

Q What Chicagoan invented the idea of an annual baseball All-Star Game?
A *Tribune* sports editor Arch Ward came up with the idea as a way to promote the 1933 World Fair. The American League won 4-2 when Babe Ruth hit a two-run homer.

Q What other annual sports event was Arch Ward's idea?
A The annual College All-Star Football Game

Q How good at hitting was the 1929 Cub outfield?
A Kiki Cuyler hit .360, Hack Wilson hit .345, and Riggs Stephenson batted .362.

Q Did the Chicago Fire of the outdoor MLS ever win a championship?
A Yes – 1998

Q How many titles did Michael Jordan and the Beastly Bulls win?
A Six – there were two "threepeats"

Q What McKendree College (**Lebanon**) basketball coach has over 800 victories –
more than Bobby Knight or Lou Henson or Norm Stewart?
A Harry Statham

Q When is the last time SIU **Carbondale** made it to the NCAA Sweet Sixteen?
A In 2002 they made it by defeating Georgia and Bobby Knight's Texas Tech team at the United Center in Chicago

Q In what two cities

Grizzlie's semi-pro baseball Stadium in Sauget off Interstate 255

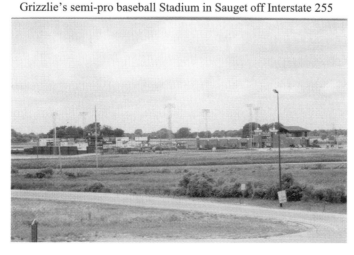

does the Big Ten basketball tournament alternate?
A The games are played at the United Center in Chicago and in Indianapolis

Q What **Galesburg** area native won the 2004 British Open golf championship?
A Todd Hamilton – he won by one stroke in a playoff against Ernie Els; the payoff was a cool $1.3 million

Q What Bears running back led the league in rushing from 1976-1980 and finished his career with the most rushing yards in history?
A Walter Payton

Brian Erlacher of the Bears

Q What Bears player has been to the most Pro Bowls?
A Mike Singletary – 10 times

Q What Bears player in 2003 was the highest paid player in the league at $15 million?
A Brian Erlacher

Q What Bears player has been in the most consecutive games?
A Steve Mc-Michael – 191 games from 1981-1993

Q Who is the Bears all-time leading scorer?
A Kicker Kevin Butler with 1,116 points

Q What Bears player scored the most points in a single game?
A Gayle Sayers – 36 points against San Francisco in 1965

Q What Bears player has the team record of scoring a touchdown in eight straight games?
A Running back Rick Casares in 1959

Q What Bears player kicked the most consecutive extra points without a miss?
A George Blanda –156

Q What is the longest field goal kicked by a Bears player?
A 55 yards by Bob Thomas in

Q   What Bears player has the most safeties in a career?
A   Steve McMichael with three

Q   What Bears player has the best lifetime rushing average?
A   Quarterback Bobby Douglas with a 6.6 yards average; Gayle Sayers had a 5.0 average.

Q   What Bears quarterback has the highest lifetime QB rating?
A   Erik Kramer with 80.7

Q   What Bears player had the best QB rating for one season?
A   Sid Luckman in 1943 with 107.8

Q   What Bears quarterback has the most career passing attempts?
A   Jim Harbaugh – 1,759

Q   What Bears quarterback holds the team record for most completions in a game?
A   Jim Miller – 34 against Minnesota in 1999

Q   What Bears quarterback has the record for most yards in a game?
A   Johnny Lujack with 468 in a 1949 game

Q   What Bears quarterback has the NFL record for most touchdown passes in a game?
A   Sid Luckman with seven against the Giants in 1943

Q   What Bears player has the most lifetime yards as a receiver?
A   Johnny Morris with 5,059

Q   What Bears receiver has the record for most career touchdowns?
A   Ken Kavanaugh – 50

Bobby Engram of the Bears

Q   What Bears player has the record for most lifetime interceptions - 38?
A   Gary Fencik

Q   What Bears player has the record for most interceptions in one season?
A   Mark Carrier with 10

Q   What Bear defender has the longest interception returned for a touchdown?
A   Rich Pettibon – 101 yards vs. Rams in 1962

Q   What Bear has the most lifetime kick-off return yardage?
A   Glyn Milburn – 4,444 yards

Q   What Bears player recovered the most opponent fumbles in his career?
A   Dick Butkus – 25

Running back Rashaan Salaam (C. Bears photo)

Q   What Bears lineman has the most lifetime sacks?
A   Richard Dent – 124.5

Q   What Bears player had the NFL's hottest selling jersey in 2002?
A   Brian Urlacher

Q   Did coach Dave Wannstedt have a winning record with the Bears?
A   No – he was 41-57 after six seasons from 1993-1998

Q   Who led the Bears in rushing every year from 1987-1993?
A   Neal Anderson

Q   What Bears quarterback was also a field goal kicker?
A   George Blanda

Q   What Bears player is credited with changing the tight end from a "third tackle" to an NFL receiving position?
A   Mike Ditka

Q   What Bears Hall of Famer is credited with becoming the **league's first middle linebacker** when he dropped off the line in 1954?
A   Bill George

Q   What Bears Hall of Famer was the last NFL player to play without a helmet?
A   Bill Hewitt

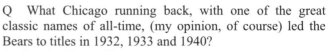
Bronko Nagurski

Q   What Chicago running back, with one of the great classic names of all-time, (my opinion, of course) led the Bears to titles in 1932, 1933 and 1940?
A   Bronko Nagurski

Q   Was Nagurski ever honored on a postage stamp?

A Yes – a 2004 old-timers postal issue

Q   What Bears Hall of Famer retired after eight seasons and became a professional wrestler to make more money?
A Bronko Nagurski

Q   What Bears Hall of Famer was the first to be named All-Pro at two different positions?
A George Musso at defensive tackle and guard

Q   When the Bears won the 1985-86 Super Bowl against New England, where was the game played?
A Louisiana Superdome

Q What Illinoisan **invented the game of indoor softball in 1887**?
A   George Hancock - a reporter for the Chicago Board of Trade, who *hated giving up baseball during the winter.*

Q   What Blackhawks star helped design the helmet that eventually became the standard for all NHL players?
A Stan Mikita

Q   Did Ernie Banks ever reach the 500 plateau of home runs in his career?
A Yes. He hit number 500 in 1970.

Q   What Chicago coach has the NCAA Division III championship football game named in his honor?
A   Amos Alonzo Stagg - he coached various teams for 70 years; it's called the Stagg Bowl.

Q   In what year did the Chicago Cubs win their last twenty-one games of the season to make it to the World Series?
A   1935 – They lost to Detroit, four games to two

Q What linebacker led the University of Illinois to a 17-7 Rose Bowl victory over the University of Washington in 1965?
A Dick Butkus

Q   What outrageous racial comment was made by Cubs manager Dusty Baker during the 2003 season?
A   Baker said he thought that black ball players could take the summer heat and humidity better than whites.

Q   What basketball team defeated Illinois in the second round of the NCAA Tournament in 2003?
A Notre Dame

Q   Where was Illinois ranked at the end of the 2004 basketball season, finishing 22-5.
A Eighteenth in the nation

Q   What **Belleville** native won the 1968 Masters golf tournament in Georgia when his opponent forgot to sign his scorecard?
A   Bob Goalby

Q   What billboard ad is being run by Hardee's to advertise their new thickburgers in the St. Louis/Metro East area?
A "Thinburgers are for Cub fans."

Q   What Chicago restaurant owner was highly critical of Governor George Ryan for issuing blanket pardons to 167 convicts on Death Row?
A Mike Ditka

Red Grange (courtesy USPS)

Q   What are the only original NFL franchises still in existence?
A   The Chicago Bears and the Chicago/St. Louis/Phoenix Cardinals

Q   What do sports analysts consider the two best rivalries in all of baseball?
A   The Giants vs. the Dodgers and the Cardinals vs. the Cubs; the Yankees vs. the Rex Sox is too one sided to be a contender.

Q   What Cub pitched the first ever night game at Wrigley Field in 1988?
A Rick Sutcliffe

Q   What Bear became the first player ever inducted into the Hall of Fame as a tight end?
A Mike Ditka – 1988

Q   What Illinois prep team, led by Dana Howard, became the state and **national** football champions?
A Mighty **East St. Louis** Flyers

Q   Where is the Illinois Basketball Hall of Fame located?
A   On the beautiful campus of Illinois State University at **Normal** – dedicated 1973

Ricky Proehl of the Bears

Q   What Bears receiver from Wake Forest led the team in receiving in 1997 and later in his career won a Super Bowl ring playing for the St. Louis Rams.
A Ricky Proehl

Q   What are some **Collinsville** High stars in the Illinois Hall of Fame?
A   Tom Parker, Ray Sonnenberg, Walt "Hoot" Evers, Ernie Wilhoit, Fred Riddle, Sam Miranda, Terry Bethel,

65

Tom Jackson, Bobby Bone, Jack Darlington, Marc Fletcher, Rich Knarr

Q   Who does Bogie Redmon think was the unsung hero on the 1961 **Collinsville Kahok** championship basketball team?
A   Guard Bob Meadows – the chaser on Collinsville's vaunted ball press

Q   What Chicago relief pitcher racked up an amazing 57 saves in 1990?
A   Bobby Thigpen

Q   What Cub second baseman hit an amazing 40 home runs in 1990?
A   Rhyne Sandberg; the only national leaguer to hit more at that position was Rogers Hornsby of the Cardinals.

Q   Did the football Illini win the Big Ten in Kurt Kittner's senior year?
A   Yes; in 2001 he led the Illini to a 10-2 record.

Q   What was admirable about five of the ten wins that year?
A   They were come-from-behind victories.

Q   Against what hapless team did Michael Jordan score 67 points in 1990?
A   The Cleveland Cavaliers

Q   Who did the White Sox manage to defeat in a 1990 game despite having a no-hitter thrown at them?
A   The hated New York Yankees

Q   What Blackhawk was Rookie–of–the–Year in 1991?
A   Ed Belfour

Q   What accounts for professional ice hockey being ignored except in cities like Chicago that have a franchise?
A   Its players are mostly Canadians and Europeans. Also, note that ESPN almost never broadcasts a college hockey game.

Q   Who owns the Chicago Cubs?
A   The *Chicago Tribune* bought the team in 1981. When Rhyne Sandberg signed a contract for $31 million in 1992, it cost more than the *Tribune* paid for the whole team.

Q   What **East St. Louisan**, with more tournament wins than anyone in the world, was proclaimed "Mr. Tennis" in 1990?
A   Jimmy Connors

Q   What White Sox knuckleballer was inducted into the Hall of Fame in 1985?
A   Hoyt Wilhelm

Q   What 1999 Bears quarterback from the Florida Gators was an accomplished golfer, winning the Chicago Celebrity Golf Classic?
A   Shane Matthews

Q   What wide receiver from NFL Europe became the first Bear receiver to notch four 135 yards-plus games in a season?
A   Marcus Robinson – 1999

Q   What Bears receiver from Southern Cal had 1037 yards and twelve touchdowns in 1995?
A   Curtis Conway

Q   What Illinois college did Bears linebacker Bryan Cox attend?
A   Western Illinois at **Macomb**

Q   What Bears running back from Colorado gained 1074 yards rushing in 1995?
A   Rashaan Salaam

Quarterback Erik Kramer

Q   What was Salaam's highest award in college?
A   Heisman Trophy

Q   What Bears rookie wide receiver in 1983 was a college track star?
A   Willie Gault

Q   What Bear run-ning back from Flor-ida State, obtained in a trade with the Green Bay Packers, led the 1998 Bears in rushing with 611 yards?
A   Edgar Bennett

Q   What Bears 1997 field goal kicker rewrote the NCAA record book as a Washington Huskie with 80 field goals?
A   Jeff Jaeger

Q   What Bear defensive back from Southern Cal had a total of 578 tackles from 1990 through the 1995 season?
A   Mark Carrier

Defense - Mark Carrier (courtesy Bears)

Q   What Bears linebacker from Oklahoma had 189 tackles in 1993?
A   Dante Jones

Q   How many years did the Bears play football games at Wrigley Field before moving to Soldier Field in 1971?
A   49

Q What 1999 Bears rookie receiver and third round draft pick played his college ball at Northwest Louisiana?
A Marty Booker

Q What Bears 1995 rookie punter from West Virginia led the nation as a collegian with a 48.4 yard average?
A Todd Sauerbrun

Q What Bears defensive back from Alabama started six games in 1997?
A John Magnum - he had an interception in a playoff game against New Orleans as a rookie in 1990.

Q What Bears defensive tackle from Notre Dame had 121 tackles in 1993?
A Chris Zorich

Q What 1996 Bears quarterback, who came over from the Seattle Seahawks, played his college ball at Milton College?
A Dave Krieg

Q What Bears quarterback, obtained in a trade with the Detroit Lions, threw a team record 174 passes without an interception in 1995?
A Erik Kramer

Q What was the nickname of the Bears running back Raymont Harris who rushed for 748 yards and caught 32 passes in 1996?
A "Quiet Storm"

Q What Chicago Bears lefty was from UCLA and shared quarterback duties with Shane Matthews?
A Cade McNown

Q What Bears 1996 rookie receiver and punt returner was a second team All-American at Penn State?
A Bobby Engram

Q Tom Seaver, a New York Mets pitcher, finished his career with the White Sox and had 311 wins. What was his nickname?
A Tom Terrific

Q What University of Chicago running back won the first Heisman Trophy?
A Jay Berwanger in 1935

Q For what pro team did Jay Berwanger play?
A He never had any desire to play pro ball.

Q Charles Radbourne of **Peoria** is in the Hall of Fame at Cooperstown. What impossible pitch did this old timer claim to have developed?
A He said he could throw a baseball *around a corner*. Witnesses claim to have seen him do it on one occasion, and the feat has never been repeated.

Q What feat did Radbourne accomplish in 1884?

A He won 60 games and lost 12 for the Providence Grays. In the first World Series ever, he won three consecutive games. His appropriate nickname? – "Old Hoss"

Q What was the original name of the Chicago Bears?
A **Decatur** Staleys

Q The Chicago Bears hold the record for the most lopsided score in history. What is it?
A The Bears scalped Sammy Baugh and the favored Redskins in 1940 by the score of 73-0 and won the title. Everything went right for the Bears that day.

Q What was the famous NFL championship "sneaker game" of 1934?

Quarterback Steve Stenstrom

A The Bears played the NY Giants on a field that was covered with ice. At halftime, the New York coach borrowed some sneakers from a local college and this proved decisive, winning 31-13. The Bears had easily beaten the Giants in two regular season games.

Q What 1998 Bears quarterback threw 72 touchdown passes in his collegiate career at Stanford?
A Steve Stenstrom

Q What 1997 Bears rookie had 1,452 yards for Northwestern his senior year?
A Darnell Autry

Q What Bears defensive back from Clemson had 101 tackles and made it to the Pro Bowl after the 1993 season?

Michael Jordan

A Donnell Woolford

Q What was the **largest enclosed sports stadium in the world in 1929**?
A It was the new Chicago Stadium, home of the Blackhawks.

Q Did the Chicago fire of 1871 destroy any sports facilities?
A Yes – it burned the fledgling Chicago Cubs' home field.

Q   How is Michael Jordan depicted in the statue that sits in front of the Bulls' United Center?
A   He is dunking the ball over a hapless opponent. The Blackhawks also play their home games at the United Center.

Q   What **Collinsville/Edwardsville** Bears lineman in the 1930s became sheriff of Madison County in the 1960's?
A   George Musso

Q   What Millikin University grad played football against two future presidents, Ronald Reagan and Gerald Ford?
A   George Musso – Milliken v Reagan's Eureka College and against Ford in a college all-star game

Q   How did the Chicago Blackhawks hockey team get their name?
A   Their owner (Fred McLaughlin) in 1926 named them in honor of his World War I Army division.

Q   What is the name of Chicago's entry in the spring/summer American Football League?
A   The Chicago Rush (2004)

Q   For years the Blackhawks labored under the "Muldoon curse" – what was it?
A   When management fired their first coach, Pete Muldoon, he said the team would be sorry and that it would never finish first. For years the Blackhawks were a hard luck franchise.

Q   When did the Blackhawks finally win Lord Stanley's Cup?
A   Not until the 1933-34 season against Detroit, led by goalkeeper Charlie Gardiner. They won again in 1937-38, defeating Toronto.

Q   What hockey innovation was developed by Fred Mc-Laughlin that is still in use today?
A   From his war experiences, he learned to rush fresh troops to the front when the first group became exhausted. He applied this to hockey and ordered rapid line changes whenever the unit on the ice seemed to tire.

Q   What **Mount Carmel** native pitched for the New York Giants in the 1954 World Series?
A   Don Liddell

Q   What White Sox player was the only man ever selected for the All-Star team in baseball and the Pro Bowl in football?
A   Everybody knows Bo – Bo Jackson.

Q   What Cubbie holds the record for RBIs in a single season?
A   Hack Wilson - the "ribbi" mark was set by him in 1930 with an incredible **190 RBIs in only 154 games**. Currently MLB plays a 162 game schedule.

Q   What **East St. Louisan** was an All-Star outfielder for the Cincinnati Reds and was Pete (the Gambler) Rose's idol when he was growing up?
A   Johnny Wyrostek, the Polish kid who was elected mayor of **Fairmont City** after he retired.

Q   Did SIUC win 20 games on the basketball court after losing their coach to the U. of Illinois in 2003?
A   On February 9, 2004, their record was 18-2 and they were ranked 23rd in the nation. Illinois' record was 15-5 and they fell out of the national rankings after losing a road game to Northwestern. Illinois later improved to 21 and 5 and SIUC won over 20 games.

Johnny Wyrostek

Q   **Coulterville** was home to George Khoury, the man who founded youth leagues for what sport?
A   Baseball

Q   Who became president of the National Football League in 1920?
A   Jim Thorpe, an Olympic champion and **great grandson of Chief Blackhawk**. Thorpe was voted the greatest athlete of the first half of the Twentieth Century.

Chicago Bat Column sculpture by Claes Oldenburg 1976 (Illinois Tourism)

Q   What Chicago sports figure narrowly avoided being part of the *Eastland* boat disaster in 1915?
A   George Halas, future coach of the Chicago Bears. He attended a football game that day and arrived too late at the dock to be allowed on board. The boat overturned in the Chicago River and 812 people drowned.

Q   What future evangelist set a record for stolen bases with a Chicago team in 1893?
A   It was Billy Sunday with 83 thefts. Ty Cobb broke the record in 1915.

Q   How did the University of Chicago get the nickname Maroons?
A   They started wearing maroon socks in 1894.

Q When Emmitt Smith of the Dallas Cowboys broke the career yards rushing mark in 2002, whose record did he break?
A Walter Payton's

Q Preston Pearson was a star receiver for the Dallas Cowboys. What was his college and what was his high school?
A U of I and **Freeport**; incredibly, Pearson never played football in college.

Q What White Sox pitcher invented the "spitter?"
A Hall of Famer Ed Walsh invented the pitch that was later outlawed – for the most part.

Q Why were the 1906 White Sox called the "Hitless Wonders?"
A They went to the World Series despite not having a single .300 hitter on the team. The Sox beat the Cubs in six games. It was the **first World Series between two teams from the same city**.

Q Who did the Cubs play in the 1945 World Series?
A The Detroit Tigers. The Tigers won in seven games. The Cubs won 20 out of 30 doubleheaders that year. Phil Cavaretta won the MVP award with a batting average of .355.

Q What was the Illinois connection concerning the coaches in the 2004 Elite 8 game between Duke and Xavier?
A The Xavier coach (Thad Matta) played his high school ball at **Hoopeston** and Chris Collins, the son of **Benton's** Doug Collins, is an assistant coach at Duke.

Q What Cub pitcher threw a no-hitter for nine innings but was defeated in extra innings when Jim Thorpe of Olympic fame drove home a run with a single?
A Jim Vaughn was the luckless pitcher. Cincinnati pitcher Fred Toney matched his no-hitter.

Q What Chicago Bears running back was the subject of the movie, *Brian's Song*?
A Brian Piccolo, who led the nation in rushing as a senior at Wake Forest. He died at an early age from cancer. Bears players rated it a "three hankie" movie.

Q Who was Rookie-of-the-Year for the White Sox in 1966?
A Tommy Agee

Q What Bears running back was Rookie–of–the–Year in 1965?
A Gayle Sayers, whose career was cut short by a knee injury.

Q How many touchdowns did Sayers score as a rookie in a game against the 49ers?
A Six

Q What Chicago Cardinals running back was elected to the Hall of Fame in 1967?

A Charlie Trippi

Q When did the Chicago Bulls become the new franchise in the NBA?
A 1966

Q What two Blackhawk players combined to win the NHL Hart MVP trophy four years in a row?
A Bobby Hull won it in 1965 and 1966 and Stan Mikita won it in 1967 and 1968.

Q Which Chicago team holds the record for the longest baseball game ever played in terms of elapsed time?
A In 1984 the White Sox defeated the Brewers in an affair that lasted two days because of a curfew. The total elapsed time was eight hours and six minutes.

Quarterback Rick Mirer (courtesy C. Bears)

Q What Chicagoan won the lightweight and welterweight boxing crowns in the early 1930's?
A Barney Ross

Q Who won the heavyweight boxing title fight held in Chicago in 1937?
A Joe Louis defeated Jim Braddock and took the title from him in an eight round match.

Q Who took the middleweight boxing title from Carmen Basilio in a 1958 fight at Chicago Stadium?
A Sugar Ray Robinson regained the title in the March 15th bout.

Bryan Cox (courtesy All-Star sports)

Q What major league baseball team plays the fewest night games?
A Chicago Cubs. Much of this is due to tradition, but part of it is due to fear of increased traffic problems and more public drunkenness - yikes!!!

Q. What **East St. Louisan** has eight World Series rings?
A Former Yankee outfielder Hank Bauer owns them. Only Yogi Berra has more with ten. Yes, the Yogi Bear cartoon character was named for him.

Q What celebrity did the Chicago Blackhawks pick as co-captain in 1991 to celebrate the NHL's 75th year?
A Jim Belushi, brother of John Belushi. Jim got his star on the Hollywood Walk of Fame in 2004.

Q What **East St. Louisan** and Hall of Famer played high school tennis at Assumption High?"
A Jimmy Connors, whose mother currently lives in **Belleville**. Remember when Jimmy married a Playboy model? Ooh la la!

Q Where was the nation's first automobile race (1895)?
A Contestants drove madly from Chicago to **Evanston** on Thanksgiving Day.

Q Why were basketball players once called cagers?
A Because crowds were so unruly in the early years the court was fenced off from the spectators.

Q What 12-year-old billiard player defeated the nation's champ in 1899 and caused him to go into retirement?
A Willie Hoppe. The match was held at the American Billiard Academy in Chicago.

Q What former Chicago Bulls coach was selected to be the color analyst for the 2004 Olympic basketball games?
A Doug Collins

Q What Cub player hit his 500th home run and was suspended for corking his bat, all in the same year?
A Sammy Sosa - 2003

Q What happened in a wild and exciting game on April 16, 2004, that caused Cub manager Dusty Baker to get thrown out of a game against first place Cincinnati?
A The Cubs were trailing 9-4 and Martinez, the leadoff hitter in the 7th, smacked a double. The umpire called him out, saying he batted out of order. Dusty Baker protested (went nuts) saying that he had pulled a double switch and according to his lineup card, the order was correct. He lost the argument. The Cubs went on to score a couple of runs, but it should have been three and maybe more.

Going into the bottom of the ninth, the Cubs trailed 10-9 and were up against Cincy's closer who already had four saves and no losses. Sammy Sosa and Moises Alou hit back-to-back home runs to win the game. Cub fans stayed around and cheered for twenty minutes before they left the park. For Sosa, it was Cub homer 512, tying him with legendary Ernie Banks. Unbelievable! - oi, oi, oi!

Q Who are the broadcasters for 2004 Chicago Cub televised games on WGN?
A Chip Caray (Harry's grandson) and Steve Stone

Q What mark of futility did Simeon Rice of the U of I/Tampa Bay Buccaneers manage to set in the 2004 Pro Bowl?
A He was kicked off the team for arriving late, missing meetings, creating a ruckus in the hotel lobby, and **coming to a meeting with his shoelaces untied.** Now there's a real sports felony!

Q Has Southern Illinois U. ever won the National Invitation Basketball Tournament at Madison Square Garden?
A Yes. They won in the 1966-67 season, destroying opponents with All-American Walt Frazier leading the way.

Q Two-thirds of the way into the 1998 season, what Cub hitter was predicted by a computer to break Roger Maris' home run record (61) before Mark McGuire?
A Sammy Sosa. The computer wrongly figured Sosa would win because McGuire took more walks and had a smaller "sweet zone" than Sosa. Busch Stadium is also a tougher park for a home run hitter than Wrigley Field.

Nelson Fox and his chaw of tobacco

Q What educator said that prep sports were a "disease" back in 1908?
A Dr. Otto Schneider, President of the Chicago Board of Education, made the remark. It was his belief that sports "didn't educate."

Q Where did the Chicago Bears play their home games while Soldier Field was recently being remodeled?
A At Champaign, home to the Fighting Illini. It took nearly two years but only one football season to remodel. (Please don't ask me to explain this.)

Q What town, noted for its watch factory, was nationally famous for hosting auto races in 1914?
A **Elgin**

Q What museum in **Mount Vernon** has a valuable 1930's Harley Davidson with less than 500 miles on its odometer?
A Dale's Classic Car and Motorcycle Museum

Q What **Wood River** High graduate was an outstanding quarterback at Mizzou and also played in the NFL?
A Gary Lane - who also became a prominent NFL official

Q What do Cub Bleacher Bums customarily do when one of them catches a home run hit by the opposition?
A They throw it back on the field.

Q Back in 1905, what were fans expected to do at Chicago Stadium when they caught a foul ball?
A Give it back.

Q What is the longest winning streak of the Chicago Bears?
A It is 18 games, an NFL record held by two other teams.

70

As of 2004 the New England Patriots were closing in on the record.

Q What **East St. Louisan** in the Soccer Coaches Hall of Fame is the only man to be the head coach in *two different* Olympic sports?
A Julie Menendez who coached Cassius Clay (M. Ali) to a gold medal at Rome in 1960; he was also the head soccer coach that year.

Q What **Edwardsville** Superintendent of Schools doubles as a referee for NCAA basketball games?
A Ed Hightower - he often does marquee matchups.

Q Why do many Illini basketball fans hate to see Hightower referee U of I games?
A The perception is that because he is an Illinoisan, he bends over backwards to be scrupulously fair, but ends up calling too many tacky fouls on the Illini.

Q What **Wood River** native and **Edwardsville** resident is in the NBA Hall of Fame?
A Harry "the Horse" Gallatin, who played for the New York Knicks.

Q How many games did the Chicago Cubs win in the 1906 baseball season?
A They set the Major League record for wins in a single season with 116.

Q What **Edwardsville** native is the current owner of the Harlem Globetrotters?
A Manny Jackson, who led his Joe Lucco-coached team to a second place finish at the IHSA state tournament back in 1956.

Q What 1954 **Edwardsville** High graduate made it to the NBA and was a prolific scorer?
A Don Ohl - who played the guard position

Q What are the Illinois origins of the Atlanta Hawks?
A The Ben Kerner-owned Hawks started out in **Moline** and **Rock Island** before he moved them, first to Milwaukee, then to St. Louis, where they defeated the Bill Russell-led Boston Celtics for the world title in 1958.

Q What NFL coach holds the record for most wins?
A George Halas of the Bears has 325 wins and seven NFL championships.

Q What Chicagoan was booed lustily when he attended a Northwestern football game in the 1920's?
A Al Capone

Q What future Chicago mayor was big into yachting?
A Big Bill Thompson's boat, the *Valmore,* finished first in a field of 12 in the 1908 Chicago-Mackinaw race. He won again in 1909.

Q The Chicago Bears set an NFL record for futility in 1938. What was it?
A They fumbled the ball an agonizing 56 times.

Q What White Sox pitcher won a doubleheader against the St. Louis Browns on July 1, 1905?
A 21 game winner Frank Owen

Q What was the worst performance by the Fighting Illini in the Rose Bowl?
A They played UCLA in 1984 and lost 45-9.

Q What **Waukegan** football star played for the Cleveland Browns at quarterback during the Jim Brown era?
A Otto Graham – arguably one of the best ever

Q What female bodybuilder took 4th in the Miss Universe competition in 1991?
A Terri LoCicero of **St. Charles,** Illinois

Q What legendary coach of the University of Chicago invented the huddle, end around, man in motion, and popularized the forward pass?
A Amos Alonzo Stagg

Q What three Illinois college teams have won national college NCAA basketball titles?
A University of Chicago, Wheaton College and Loyola of Chicago

Q Who won the heavyweight title fight held in Chicago in 1953?
A Rocky Marciano defeated Jersey Joe Walcott by scoring a knockout.

Q What Chicago Cub won the MVP award in 1984?
A Rhyne Sandberg

Q How many points per game did Michael Jordan average from 1987-1991?
A An incredible 37.6 points per game during that span

Q What was different about the NBA draft in the early 1960's?
A Teams like the St. Louis Hawks had regional and territorial draft choices so that fans in the area who had watched local stars play in college could also see them in the pros. Also, there were no lottery picks.

Q What Chicago Cardinal holds the record for most points scored in a single NFL game?
A Running back Ernie Nevers scored an amazing 40 points against the Bears in a 1929 contest.

Q Was Ernie Nevers ever honored on a postage stamp?
A Yes – a 37 cent 2004 issue

Q What baseball team first came up with the idea of using a pitching rotation to extend the life of their pitching staff?
A The Chicago White Stockings in 1880 under coach "Pop" Anson

Q Why was it so hard for Big Ten teams to get into the NCAA basketball tournament back in the 1960s?
A In a field of only 24, a team had to win the conference to make the tourney. If two teams tied for the conference championship, the team that had gone the longest without appearing in the tourney got the nod.

Q The University of Chicago won the collegiate basketball title in 1908 by beating Penn of the Ivy League. What was the score?
A 16-15 - they did a lot of clever passing back then.

Q Who did the Bears defeat in the 1985-86 Super Bowl?
A They smeared the New England (Boston) Patriots, 46-10

Q What controversial former Bears' linebacker is now a sports analyst for ESPN?
A Bryan Cox of **East St. Louis** – he's still controversial

Q When was the last time the Cubs won the World Series?
A Nearly 100 years ago – back-to-back in 1907 and 1908. We've had sixteen presidents since then.

Q What Cub infielder and Gold Glover was killed in a plane crash?
A Ken Hubbs, former Rookie-of-the-Year, died in 1964.

Q Why are Cub woes called the "Jinx of the Billygoat?"
A A Chicago tavern owner tried to gain admission to the local World Series in 1945 but was turned away because he brought along his goat. Angry, the man placed a curse on the team.

Q How did the Cubs partially break *the jinx* in 2003?
A They defeated the Atlanta Braves in a playoff series, but then lost to the Florida Marlins.

Q **Joliet**-born George Mikan played center for what NBA team?
A The Hall of Famer played for the Minneapolis Lakers.

Q What Cub pitcher was the first Canadian-born player elected to baseball's Hall of Fame?
A Ferguson Jenkins

Q What Chicago native became the first American to hold the world chess title?
A It was temperamental (spoiled rotten) Bobby Fischer who defeated Boris Spassky.

Q What Illinois city calls itself "Title Town" because it has so many prep state championships?
A It's **East St. Louis**, a powerhouse in football, basketball and track.

Q What **Troy/East St. Louisan** won the Cy Young Award in 1958?

A Bob Turley, pitcher for the New York Yankees

Q How did Joe Jackson acquire the nickname "Shoeless?"
A Jackson played in an exhibition game sans shoes, due to blisters, and hit a home run.

Q What Illinoisan from **Decatur** led the Brooklyn Dodgers to two National League pennants between the years 1951-1953?

U of I coach Harry Combes – courtesy University of Illinois)

A Chuck Dressen – he also managed them in 1958 when they were in Los Angeles.

Q Has anyone ever hit over .400 and lost the batting title?
A Shoeless Joe Jackson hit .408 for the White Sox in 1919 but lost the crown to Ty Cobb who hit .420.

Illinois coach and athletic director George Huff (courtesy State Farm Ins. & U of I)

Q Why was there so much sympathy for Shoeless Joe after he was banned from baseball for life after the Black Sox scandal?
A He proclaimed that he was innocent and backed it up with a .375 average in the World Series. However, a close inspection shows that he failed to deliver when men were on base.

Q How many games did Ed Cicotte win for the White Sox in 1919?
A He won 29 and probably would have won 30 but his tightwad owner Chuck Comiskey wouldn't let him pitch at

the end of the season to prevent him from collecting on a bonus.

Q   At what sport did gangsters Charlie Birger and John Dillinger excel?
A   Both belonged to organized baseball teams in their youth.

Q   At what sport did Al Capone excel?
A   None – unless you call killing people bloodsport. He was terrible at golf and softball.

Q   In what year did Illinoisan George Mikan lead the Chicago Gears to an NBA championship?
A   1947

Q   With what professional team did Red Grange play?
A   He signed with the Bears, but a knee injury later ruined his career.

Q   Why is boxing referee Dave Barry nicknamed "Long Count?"
A   In the 1927 title fight between Dempsey and Tunney, Dempsey knocked Tunney down and might have won by a TKO, but he had to be pushed to a neutral corner by Barry, giving Tunney five revitalizing seconds. Tunney made it to his feet and went on to win the match.

Q   Why was referee Dave Miller replaced at the last second by Dave Barry in the above match?
A   Boxing authorities learned just before the bout that Al Capone had intimidated Miller by telling him he had $50,000 on Dempsey to win.

Q   What is controversial about the third game of the 1932 World Series?
A   The Cubs were playing the Yankees, and this is the game where it has long been debated whether Babe Ruth pointed to centerfield before he hit the next pitch for a home run.

Q   What incredible feat was accomplished by Blackhawk hockey player Bill Mosienko?
A   In a 1952 game, **he scored three goals in 21 seconds**.

Q   What Bears quarterback led the league in 1953 in both completions and interceptions?
A   George Blanda – Mr. Adept and Mr. Inept

Q   What Northwestern University student was the top ranked amateur golfer in the country in 2000?
A   Luke Donald

Q   What **East St. Louisan**, while teaching at San Diego State, inspired John Carlos and Tommy Smith to make a statement at the 1968 Olympics with a raised clenched fist during the medal ceremony?
A   It's Harry Edwards who is also considered one of the preeminent sports sociologists in the country.

Q   When Loyola of Chicago won the NCAA basketball tournament title in 1963, who did they defeat?
A   Cincinnati – 60-58

Q   How were the White Sox responsible for causing a panic in Chicago?
A   When the Sox won the American League crown in 1959, the Fire Commissioner set off the air raid sirens for five minutes to celebrate. Nikita Khrushchev had just delivered his "We will bury you" speech, and frightened citizens thought nuclear war was imminent.

U of I player & Chicago Bear's coach George Halas (courtesy State Farm & U of I)

Q   What **East St. Louisan holds the consecutive game hitting streak record in World Series play**?
A   Hank Bauer - he hit in 17 straight games

Q   What Cubbie was Rookie-of-the-Year in 1961?
A   Billy Williams.

Q   Whatever became of the infamous Chicago Cub 2003 "Bartman ball?"
A   This sounds like an urban legend, but it was destroyed live on television on the MSNBC cable news show, ostensibly to appease the baseball gods and break the jinx.

Q   Who was the MVP when the Bears defeated the Giants 14-10 in 1963 to win the NFL title?
A   Linebacker Larry Morris

Q   What Blackhawk was probably the best goalie of the NHL in the early 1960s?
A   Glenn Hall

U of I star Andy Kaufmann

Q   What Cub pitcher led the National League in strikeouts in 1968?
A   Ferguson Jenkins had 160.

Q   How did Cub outfielder Rick Monday get the nickname "Mr. Red, White, and Blue?"
A   He prevented a war protestor from burning a flag in the outfield in a 1969 game at Dodger Stadium.

Q What White Sox Hall of Famer hit a home run at age 75 in an old timers game at RFK stadium?
A Luke Appling

Q What was the first Chicago school to win the IHSA prep high school basketball title?
A Chicago Marshall – 1958; for some strange reason, no Chicago team had won the tournament till then.

Q What prep **Springfield** basketball coach was elected as State Superintendent of Public Instruction, largely due to his sports recognition?
A Ray Page – 1962

Q What famed Dodger pitching duo led Los Angeles to a World Series victory over the Chicago White Sox in 1959?
A Don Drysdale and Larry Sherry. Khoufax had an 8.68 ERA and one loss in the Series. Sherry had two wins and two saves in the six games.

Q How many division titles have the Sox won since 1959?
A Three – but no pennants

Q When the new U of I Assembly Hall replaced the old Huff gymnasium, what did most observers think it resembled?
A A flying saucer

Q What 1954 Southern Illinois prep team won its 4th basketball tournament title by defeating Chicago DuSable 74-70?
A **Mount Vernon** – quite a feat for such a small town

Q What star of TV's *The Rifleman* once played in 66 baseball games but hit a paltry .239 for the 1951 Cubs?
A Chuck Connors

Q How did Chicagoan Eddie Gaedel make baseball history?
A In 1951 St. Louis Browns manager Bill Veeck inserted the *midget* into the lineup as a pinch hitter. To no one's surprise, he drew a walk.

Q What Chicago Cardinal receiver caught five touchdown passes in a 1950 game against the Baltimore Colts?
A Bob Shaw

Q How did George Halas help make pro football more attractive to fans in 1933?
A He convinced the rules committee to legalize the forward pass that had long been used in college.

Q Where did St. Louis wrestler Lou Thesz, considered by many to be the greatest wrestler who ever lived, have his first bout.
A The Social Center in **East St. Louis** (where he also practiced) in 1935. Thesz earned the grand sum of $3. He gave this author the information over the phone in 1996.

Q When and where was the first Roller Derby event held?

A 1935 at Chicago.

Q What DePaul University basketball star led the NCAA in scoring in 1945 and 1946?
A George Mikan

Q What did a Blackhawk player do in a 1947 hockey game that now is standard practice?
A When he scored a goal, Billy Reay raised his stick to make it easier on the official scorer to credit the proper player.

Q What Central Illinois town was home to baseball star

Remodeled Soldier Field – home of the Chicago Bears

Gary Gaetti?
A **Centralia**

Q What White Sox player became the oldest rookie in the majors at age 41?
A Satchel Paige, signed by Bill Veeck to a contract in 1948.

1947 University of Illinois Rose Bowl program

Q What **East St. Louisan** was the starting pitcher for the National League in the 1935 All-Star Game?
A Bill Walker

Q Did the Chicago Sting ever win a soccer championship?

A They defeated the New York Cosmos in 1981.

Q Where do the St. Louis Rams hold their summer training camp?
A Western Illinois University at **Macomb**

Q What three categories is Chicago-born Ricky Henderson the all time leader in major league baseball?
A Stolen bases, runs scored and walks

Q Who won the 500-meter speed skating event at the 1988 Winter Olympics?
A Bonnie Blair of **Champaign**, Illinois, winner of five gold medals

Q What Cub pitcher threw a no-hitter in his first start?
A Don Cardwell performed the feat in 1960 against the Cardinals.

Q Name at least four of the starting five on the Flying Illini team that defeated Michigan twice during the regular season but lost to them in the Final Four tilt.
A Kenny Battle of **Aurora**, Kendall Gill of Rich Township, Steve Bardo from **Carbondale**, Nick Anderson from Chicago, and Lowell Hamilton from Chicago. Alternates were Larry Smith of **Alton** and Marcus Liberty of Chicago

Q What town in southern Illinois was home to Whitey Herzog, coach of the 1985 World Champion Cardinals?
A **New Athens**

Q What southern Illinois town was home to Hall-of-Famer Red Schoendinst of the St. Louis Cardinals?
A **Germantown**

Q What guard from **Granite City** was inducted into the NBA Hall of Fame in 1960?
A Andy Phillip.

Q What incredible trio of quarterbacks did the Bears have in 1948?
A Their talented leaders were Sid Luckman, Johnny Lujack and Bobby Layne.

Q What southern Illinois town nurtured Olympic gold medal swimmer Tom Jaeger?
A **Collinsville**

Q What LSU coach turned down an offer to lead the Bears in 2004?
A Nick Sabin - whose team had just shared the national championship by beating Oklahoma. His salary at LSU is $3 million a year. The Bears settled for Lovie Smith, defensive coordinator for St. Louis whose Rams gave up nearly 500 yards of offense to the Carolina Panthers in their playoff game of 2004.

Q What prep southern Illinois school has won the most state soccer championships?

A **Granite City** has the state record for the most championships – the **Collinsville** Kahoks have four

Q Who was the first African-American to play for the Chicago Bears?
A Eddie Macon

Q What town won the 1953 Elks Club National Bowling Tournament in Chicago?
A **Litchfield**

Q Who was the National League Rookie-of-the-Year for the Chicago White Sox in 1956?
A Luis Aparicio

Q How many people attended the 1926 Army-Navy game

Memorial Stadium – home of the Fighting Illini

at Soldier's Field in Chicago?

U of I basketball star Steve Bardo

A One hundred thousand. Back in the old days the Army-Navy game was a really big event.

Q What Cub players formed the most famous double play combination in baseball history?
A It was Tinker to Evers to Chance - Joe, Johnny, and Frank, respectively.

Q How many touchdowns did Red Grange score against a vaunted Michigan team in 1924?
A He scored four times in the first twelve minutes and scored again in the fourth quarter. He also passed the ball for another touchdown. Because of the quality of the competition, it was **one of college football's greatest performances of all time.**

Q Who was the first Chicago Bulls player to have his jersey retired?
A Jerry Sloan of **McLeansboro**

Q Who is considered by many to be the second best current coach in the NBA?
A Jerry Sloan of the Utah Jazz is second to Phil Jackson of the Bulls/Lakers. Sloan got his 300th coaching win in February of 2004.

Q What University of Illinois player was the MVP at the 1919 Rose Bowl football game in California?
A George Halas

Q What **East St. Louisan** won the triple jump at the 1984 Olympics?
A Al Joyner, brother to Jackie Joyner-Kersee

Q What amazing feat did Lou Boudreau of **Harvey** accomplish in 1948?
A Not only was he baseball's MVP, he also managed Cleveland to a World Series victory.

Q What central Illinois town was the birthplace of Philadelphia Phillies 1950's pitching star Robin Roberts?
A **Springfield**

Q What Chicagoan offered to "fix" the Tunney-Dempsey title fight (in favor of Dempsey) in 1927 at Soldier Field?
A Who else but Al Capone! Dempsey turned him down and lost the fight.

Q Who was declared the Female Athlete of the Century by Sports Illustrated?
A **East St. Louisan** Jackie Joyner-Kersee.

Q The Chicago Bears signed Red Grange in 1925 for $100,000. He drew huge numbers of spectators but did he lead the Bears to a title?
A No. The Bears finished seventh out of about 18 teams and the Chicago Cardinals won the title.

Q Who managed the Cubs when they played the Philadelphia Athletics in the 1929 World Series?
A Joe McCarthy. Connie Mac managed the Athletics.

Q What Chicagoan hit the winning shot for Georgia Tech against Oklahoma State in the 2004 Final Four?
A Willie Bynum

Q In what town did **Edwardsville** win the 1991 AA state baseball championship?
A The AA and A championships back then were played in the **Springfield** stadium that was home to the Springfield Redbirds, a St. Louis Cardinals farm team.

Q What driver won the eight mile car race at **Libertyville** in August of 1913?
A Eddie Rickenbacker, the future World War I flying ace

Q Boxing was long considered barbaric because contestants had their eyes gouged and suffered brain damage. When was it first legalized in Chicago?
A 1897

Q Beside the University of Chicago and Chicago Loyola, what is the only other school in Illinois to win the NCAA basketball crown?
A **Wheaton** College in 1957

Q How many games did the Super Bowl winning Bears lose in the 1985 season?
A One

U of I basketball star Derek Harper

Q The USA women's soccer team won the World Cup in 1999. How did they fare against Nigeria in a game played at Soldier Field?
A They won 7-1 before a record crowd of 65,080 people.

Q What Illinois towns host minor league baseball teams?
A **Peoria, Rockford, Schaumburg**, and **Geneva**. A few years ago **Springfield** was home to the Redbirds, an affiliate of the St. Louis Cardinals.

Q What is the name of the trophy given to the pro football team that wins the NFC championship game?
A George Halas Trophy

Q Did Illini defensive back **Eugene Wilson** get to play in the 2004 Super Bowl as a rookie?
A Yes. He played for the Patriots and even recovered a fumble by a Carolina Panther receiver. Unfortunately, the refs ruled that the receiver never had possession so it was merely an incomplete pass. Replay footage showed that it was a fumble, but this was a ruling that coaches could not challenge.

U of I gridiron star Bobby Mitchell (courtesy U of I and State Farm Insurance)

Q Who defeated coach Bruce Weber's Southern Illinois University team by a single point in the 2002-03 NCAA Sweet Sixteen?

A Missouri – SIU was hurt by a bad call at game's end.

Q Kevin Stallings was an outstanding basketball player for the **Collinsville** Kahoks in the 1970's. What college team that made it to the 2004 Sweet Sixteen does he coach?
A Vanderbilt

Q What Illinois college did Doug Collins of **Benton** High attend and set scoring records?
A Illinois State

Q What town was home to Dan Issel, former NBA star of the Denver Nuggets?
A **Batavia**

Illini football coach John Mackovic (courtesy U of Illinois and State Farm Insurance

Q What basketball player from Dalton became the first ever to win a high school state championship, an NBA championship, and an Olympic gold medal?
A Quinn Buckner

Q What Chicago prep league football star drew a crowd of 125,000 in a 1937 championship game?
A Bill DeCorrevont – **no college or pro football player has ever drawn a crowd this large**. Décor-revont did not disappoint – scoring three touchdowns and passing for another to lead his Austin team to victory; in an earlier game, he ran the ball ten times and scored an amazing total of nine touchdowns.

Q What Southwest Conference high school team defeated a team of St. Louis All-Stars in a football game in the late 1930's?
A **East St. Louis Flyers** – they won 7-6 despite losing their starting quarterback to injuries in the first half.

Q What Cubs made the Top 100 Players of the Century list?
A Ernie Banks, Mordecai Brown, Ferguson Jenkins, Rhyne Sandberg, Greg Maddux and Grover Cleveland Alexander

Q How did "Merkle's Boner" enable the Cubs to win the pennant in 1908?
A It was the ninth inning and the Giants had runners at first and third with two out. The Giant batter Bridwell got a base hit to drive in the winning run. Cub players noticed that Merkle (a rookie), instead of going to second, turned and went to the dugout when he saw the winning run cross the plate. In the midst of a wild victory celebration by the Giants, the Cubs threw the ball to second base, and the umpire called the runner out. The game ended in a 1-1 tie. The two teams finished the season with identical records and the Cubs won the playoff game.

Q What poem immortalized the Cub double play combination of Tinker to Evers to Chance?
A It was composed in 1910 by New York sportswriter, Franklin P. Adams.

These are the saddest of all possible words
Tinker to Evers to Chance
Trio of bear cubs and fleeter than birds
Tinker to Evers to Chance
Thoughtlessly pricking our gonfalon bubble
Making a Giant hit into a double
Words that are weighty with nothing but trouble -
Tinker to Evers to Chance.

Q The trio of Tinker, Evers and Chance were just better than average ballplayers. How did they get into the Hall of Fame?
A When the balloting was ended in 1946, no candidate had received the majority of votes needed to make it into Cooperstown. Faced with this alarming prospect, a special committee was appointed and nine players were chosen, including the Cub double play trio. In one four season span, the trio completed only 54 double plays. **Never once did they lead the league in double plays**.

Q What two Cubbies were felled by "romantic bullets?"
A Billy Jurges and Eddie Waitkus. Jurges was shot three times in his hotel room by Violet Popovich after he told her *no more dates* back in 1932. Jurges declined to prosecute the woman.
Ruth Steinhagen was an obsessed Waitkus fan who shot him with a .22 rifle. The judge decided Steinhagen was a mental case and sent her to a ward.

Cub catcher Randy Hundley

Q What movie had a gun shooting scene based on the Waitkus episode?
A *The Natural*, starring Robert Redford

Q What was the last year the Cubs won the National League Pennant?
A 1945

Q What Cub player and manager nicknamed "Jolly Charlie" won four National League pennants?
A Charlie Grimm

Q Did the Cubs blow a 25 to 6 lead in a 1922 game against the Phillies?
A No – but they almost did with a final score of 26-23

Q Are the 49 runs in this game a National League record?
A Yes

Q Did the Cubs get rid of Grover Cleveland Alexander in time for him to become a World Series hero for the 1926 Cardinals?
A Yes

Q Why did the Cubs decide to get rid of Alexander?
A He was an alcoholic

Q Rogers Hornsby was the Cub manager in 1931. What National League hitting mark did he set in 1924?
A He batted .424 for the St. Louis Cardinals

Q How many World Series games did the Cubs win against the Ruth/Gehrig-led 1932 Yankees?
A None

Q What miracle finish allowed the Cubs to beat out the Cardinals for the 1935 pennant?
A They won their last 21 games, the second longest winning streak in major league history.

Q What achievement by the hated rival St. Louis Cardinals galls Cub fans?
A They are the only National League team (three or more head-to-head contests) to have an edge over the mighty New York Yankees (3-2). They defeated the Ruth-led Bronx Bombers in 1926, the DiMaggio-led Yanks in 1942, and the Mantle-led pinstripers in 1964.

Q What Cub pitcher went 2-0 in the 1935 Series against the Charlie Gehringer/ Hank Greenberg/ Mickey Cochrane-led Detroit Tigers?
A Lon Warneke, who later became a National League umpire

Q How did the Cubs fare in the Series against the '35 Tigers?
A They lost 4 games to 2.

Q In what year did the Cubs end up in last place for the first time in their history?
A 1925

Q What Cub pitcher was nearly killed by poison gas during World War I?
A Grover Cleveland Alexander

Sox catcher Carlton Fisk

Q How did Cub outfielder Lawrence Miller get the nickname "Hack?"
A It was said he resembled a noted wrestler of the 1920's by the name of Hackenschmidt.

Q How did the Cubs fare against the Yankees in 1938, bolstered by the addition of future Hall of Famer, Dizzy Dean?
A They lost four games in a row to the DiMaggio-led Yankees

Q Cub catcher Gabby Hartnett was reprimanded by Commissioner Landis for signing a baseball before a game. Why was this a problem?
A He gave it to Al Capone for the Big Guy's son.

Q What was Hartnett's famous reply after the reprimand?
A "If you don't want Capone talking to anybody Judge, you tell him!"

Q Who planted the famous ivy against the outfield walls at Wrigley Field?

Judge "Kennesaw Mountain" Landis – the man who banned eight White Sox players from baseball for life

A P.K. Wrigley took down all advertising signs and planted ivy instead in 1937.

Q What Cub pitcher won 20 games in 1940?
A Claude Passeau

Q What Cub outfielder led the National League in home runs in 1943 and 1944?
A Bill "Swish" Nicholson with 29 and 33 respectively

Q What Cub won the MVP title in 1945?
A Phil Cavaretta with a

.355 batting average and 97 RBIs

Cub hitting star Phil Cavaretta

Q What Cub centerfielder drove in more runs than Cavaretta that year?
A Andy Pafko with 110, but he only hit .302

Q The domination of what team in 1945 gave the Cubs the National League pennant?
A They took 21 out of 22 from Cincinnati.

Q   What National League team are the traditional rivals of the Cubs?
A   The St. Louis Cardinals

Q   How have the Cubs fared in the head-to-head rivalry?
A   The Cubs actually have a slight edge in total wins. But St. Louis has the last laugh with nine World Series championships, more than any other national league team, including the Giants and Dodgers

Q   What Cub threw a rare one-hit shutout in the 1945 Series?
A   Claude Passeau – the last time it happened was in 1906.

Q   How many games did the Cubs win in the 1945 Series?
A   They lost it, 4 games to 3.

Q   What was the Cubs record in World Series play at this point?
A   This was their 7th consecutive loss and their overall record was a miserable 2-8

Q   Who did the Cubs play in the 1932 World Series?
A   The New York Yankees

Q   Do most baseball observers think Babe Ruth pointed to the bleachers and predicted his home run in game three of the 1932 Series?
A   Most think it's a fairy tale.

Q   What is the basis of this fabled myth?
A   Joe Williams of the *New York World* was the only sportswriter out of dozens who said that Ruth had called the shot. He later recanted his version of events, but the myth still persists. What Ruth actually did was hold up two fingers to indicate that with two strikes, he still had one swing left.

Q   What did Ruth think of Wrigley Field?
A   He called it a "dump" and said he'd hit 100 homers if it were his home ballpark.

Q   What were the two worse decades of Cub baseball history?
A   The two decades following their appearance in the 1945 World Series

Q   When a sportswriter quipped, "The Cubs must have been chloroformed," what infamous deal was he talking about?
A   The one that sent Andy Pafko to the Dodgers. Pafko would go on to star on three pennant-winning teams.

Q   What is this writer's most memorable memory of Cub hitting star, Frank Baumholtz?

Sox emblem (courtesy White Sox)

A   I think it happened in the last game at the end of the 1952 season. Baumholtz and Cardinal Musial were neck and neck for the batting title. If Musial went hitless and Baumholtz had a good day, the Cubbie would win the crown. But Musial had a couple of hits early in the game and clinched it. On Baumholtz's next at bat, Musial, who started his career as a pitcher, was brought in from right field to pitch to Baumholtz. Baumholtz reciprocated by batting from the other side of the plate. Baumholtz hit a screaming liner to second base that Red Schoendienst muffed for an error. Musial signaled to the scorekeeper to change it to a hit, but the call stood. Musial went on to win seven batting titles in his career. He is the only player to hit 475 home runs or more in a career and never lead the league in homers.

Q   Who was the first African-American to play for the Cubs?
A   Second baseman Gene Baker who, at first, was considered a better prospect than Ernie Banks

Q   What team did Ernie Banks play for before his contract was purchased for $25,000
A   Kansas City Monarchs

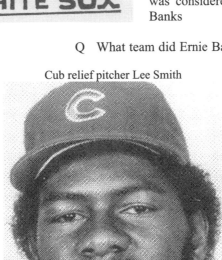

Cub relief pitcher Lee Smith

Q   What year did Banks break in with the Cubs?
A   September of 1953. He said he met more white people in that one month than in his entire life previously.

Q   What home run record did Banks break in 1955?
A   He hit 44 home runs, the most ever by a shortstop. Five of them were grand slams.

Q   What team slugging mark did the Cubs break in 1958?
A   As a team they hit 182 home runs, thanks to the addition of Pittsburgh slugger Dale Long. The Cubs acquired him in a trade for Gene Baker. Former Giant Bobby Thompson had 21 homers for the Cubs that year.

Cub strikeout artist Kerry Wood

Q   What year did Ron Santo break in with the Cubs?
A   1960 – he held sway at third base for the next 13 years.

Q What kind of a rookie year did Lou Brock have with the Cubs in 1962?
A Mediocre – he hit an un-spectacular .263 with nine home runs.

Q What infamous trade did the Cubs make early in the 1964 season?
A In a six-player deal, the Cubs sent future Hall of Famer Lou Brock to the Cardinals for pitcher Ernie Broglio. Broglio finished the season 4-7 and Brock led the Cards to a World Series victory over Mickey Mantle and the Yankees.

Q What clue did the Cubs have to Lou Brock's ability in the 1963 season?
A He stole 24 bases, the most of any Cub since Kiki Cuyler stole 37 in 1930.

Q What was ironic about the Brock for Broglio deal?
A Nearly everyone in Chicago was ecstatic when the trade was announced. Brock was hitting .258 at the time of the trade and Broglio was a former 21 game winner. Brock was elected to the Hall of Fame in 1985.

Q What Cub had more RBIs than sore-kneed Ernie Banks in 1961?
A George Altman, who had 96 to Banks' 80. Altman also hit 27 home runs that year.

Q What southwest city is home to spring training for the Cubs?
A Mesa, Arizona

Q What was spectacular about the Cub's hitting in 1965?
A They had three players with over 100 RBIs – Santo, Banks and Billie Williams.

Q How did Cub pitcher Bob Hendley lose a one-hitter in a 1965 game at Los Angeles?
A Sandy Khoufax threw a no hitter.

Q What was the name given to the zany Cub rotating managerial scheme of 1961 and '62?
A The College of Coaches – it was a dismal flop.

Q What manager led the Cubs to divisional titles in 1984 and 1989?
A Jim Frey

Q How many times did Ernie Banks win the MVP award in 19 seasons?
A Twice

Q What Cub player caught 160 out of 162 games in 1968?
A Randy Hundley

Q What Cub pitcher threw no hitters in 1969 and '71?

A Ken Holtzman

Q What Cub pitcher had six consecutive 20 win seasons in the 1960's and 1970's?
A Hall of Famer Ferguson Jenkins

Q What Cub hit 48 homers in 1979?
A Dave Kingman – but he was lackadaisical in the outfield.

Q What Cub was obtained from Philadelphia as a "throw in" in a 1982 trade?
A Rhyne Sandberg

Q What was Sandberg's greatest game as a Cub?
A Back in 1984 he twice homered off Cardinal closer Bruce Sutter late in the game to bring the Cubs even in the contest. Then he won the game with a third homer in extra innings.

Q Did the Cardinals ever get revenge?
A Yes – twenty years later in July of 2004. The second place Cubs were at home, playing the Cards in a critical two game series. The Cubs were already nine games off the pace, and it would be the last time the two teams faced each other in the season. The Cubs roared to an 8-2 early lead but three homers by Albert Pujols hammered the Cubs into submission 11-8.

Q Who led the Cub pitching staff in saves in 1983 and '84?
A Lee Smith

Q What innovative catching technique did Randy Hundley of the Cubs bring to baseball?
A Catching one-handed to keep his other hand from getting all banged up. The style was taught to him by his father.

Cub logo – courtesy Chicago Cubs

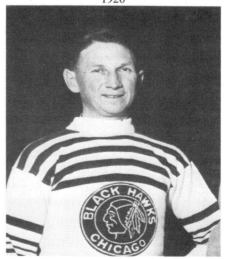

Pete Muldoon - manager of the Blackhawks, 1926

Q What outfielder led the Cubs in hitting in 1973?
A Jose Cardenal - .303

Q Who replaced Ron Santo at third base when he retired?
A Bill Madlock

Q Who is the only Cub player in the 20th century to win back-to-back batting titles?
A Bill Madlock

Q Who was the first "free agent" ballplayer signed by the Cubs?
A Dave Kingman

Q What magnificent comeback did the Cubs make in a 1979 game against the Phillies?
A They roared back from a 17-6 deficit to tie the game at 22-22. They lost 22-23 on a homer by Mike Schmidt.

Q What Cub player led the league in hitting in 1980?
A Bill Buckner with a .324 average

Q Who has the Cub record for best winning percentage in one year?
A Rick Sutcliffe, obtained in June from Cleveland, went 16-1 in 1984.

Q Who led the Cubs in RBIs in 1984?
A Ron Cey with 97

Q What crushing defeat did the Cubs suffer in the 1984 playoffs?
A They won the first two games against the San Diego Padres, but lost the next three.

Q What Cubbie won the 1987 MVP award?
A Outfielder Andre Dawson who hit 49 home runs and batted in 137 RBIs. He was the **first to win an MVP award playing for a last place club**.

Q Did Andre Dawson ever get his mug on a U.S. postage stamp?
A No – but he was honored with a 1988 Grenada issue available on E-bay.

Q What slick fielding Cub first baseman hit .296 his rookie year in 1988?
A Mark Grace

Q What Cub relief pitcher had the nickname "Wild Thing?"
A Mitch Williams who had 36 saves in 1989

Q How many games did Greg Maddux win in 1989?
A 19

Q Who defeated Don Zimmer's 1989 Cubs in the N.L. Championship series?
A The Giants 3 games to 2

Q What Cub led the National League with 40 homers in 1990?
A Rhyne Sandberg – the first second baseman to do it since Hornsby in 1925.

Q What Cub won the Cy Young Award in 1992?
A Greg Maddox

Q What Cub future Hall of Famer announced his early

Tommy John, Gary Peters, Joel Horlen (picture courtesy Chicago White Sox)

retirement in the middle of the 1994 season after 13 years?
A Rhyne Sandberg. He returned in 1996 and had 25 homers and 85 RBIs.

Q Who did the Cubs have to play in 1998 because of a tie in the "wild card" race?
A They defeated the Giants 5-3 and earned the right to face the Braves.

Q How did the Cubs fare against the Braves in the 1998 playoffs?
A They lost three straight.

Q What 1998 Cub Rookie of the Year was plagued with arm problems for the next two years?
A Kerry Wood

Sammy Sosa

Q Who won the 1999 homer derby between Mark McGuire and Sammy Sosa?
A McGuire hit 65 and Sosa hit 63.

Q Did Sosa beat out McGuire in 2000?
A Yes, but only because McGuire's knees and back gave out, prematurely ending his career.

Q What team did Mark Grace finish his career with after playing 13 seasons for the Cubs?
A Arizona Diamondbacks

Q How many home runs did Sammy Sosa hit in 1998, the year Mark McGuire hit 70 and broke Roger Maris' record?
A 66

Q How many homers did Sosa hit in 2000 when he led the major leagues in homers?

Harry Caray as a young announcer

A 50

Q What Cub pitcher struck out 20 Houston Astro batters in only his fifth start?

A   Kerry Wood

Q   Did Sammy Sosa ever play for the White Sox?
A   Yes – they obtained him from the Rangers in a trade for Harold Baines in 1989.

Q   What narrator of NFL films and announcer for the Philadelphia Phillies grew up in **Naperville**, Illinois?
A   Harry Callas

Q   What Chicagoan from **Mount Carmel** High was the last pitcher to win 31 games in one season?
A   Denny McLain in 1968 for Detroit

Q   What White Sox players made the Top 100 Players of the Century list?
A   Joe Jackson, Ed Walsh, Luke Appling, Eddie Collins, Luis Aparicio, Carlton Fisk

Chicago Stadium – home of the Blackhawks – 1929

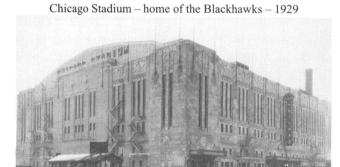

Q   What famed golfer in 1954 teed up a ball at home plate and hit the scoreboard at Wrigley Field with a golf shot?
A   Sam Sneed

Q   What was Harry Caray's trademark song that he sang with fans during the 7th inning stretch?
A   "Take Me Out To The Ball Game"

Q   What U.S. President accidentally started the 7th inning stretch tradition?
A   William Howard Taft - when he stood to stretch his muscles, fans followed suit out of respect.

Q   How long was Harry Caray an announcer with the White Sox?
A   Ten years – then he signed with the Cubs

Q   In what year did Harry Caray die after announcing 15 years for the Cubs?
A   1998

Q   What is the seating capacity of Wrigley Field?
A   39, 056

Q   What U.S. President, reluctant to admit a mistake, said in an April 2004 press conference that the worst mistake he ever made (as owner of the Texas Rangers) was trading Sammy Sosa to the White Sox?
A   George W. Bush

ILLINOIS CRITTERS

Q   What was the name of the World War II bond-selling pig from **Anna**?
A   Neptune – he sold more bonds than many movie stars

Q   What was the name of Abe Lincoln's dog?
A   Fido - it became a popular name for dogs for a hundred years. In Latin fido means *faithful*

Q   In what year was the last known bear shot and killed in Illinois?
A   1930

Q   What is the largest cottonmouth moccasin ever killed in Illinois?
A   A deadly snake measuring 49.5 inches met its demise at Mermet Lake in **Massac County**.

Q   The monarch butterfly was designated the state insect by the General Assembly in 1975 at the suggestion of a **Decatur** third grader. Where do monarch butterflies go to spend their winters?
A   They fly 2,000 miles from Illinois to Mexico.

Q   How fast is the state animal, the white tailed deer?
A   It can run up to 35 miles per hour.

Q   What town is famous for a cow named Harmilda?
A   **Harvard -** Harmilda is a Fiberglas replica of a milk cow in the middle of Main Street in Harvard, Illinois.

Amos Alonzo Stagg –2nd from left

Q   How did Harmilda get her name?
A   The name comes from **HAR**vard **MIL**k **DA**ys. Harvard is in the middle of the state's top milk producing region.

Q   What northeastern Illinois town is home to Tempel Farms, a 6,000-acre site with shows that feature Lipizzan stallions?
A   **Wadsworth**

Q   What northern town is home to the Effigy Tumuli, **the largest outdoor sculptures in the world**?
A   **Ottawa** – with earthen sculptures shaped like a catfish, snake, turtle, frog, and a water strider

Q Where in Illinois could one find a pig named Judas?
A Judas was a pig at the **East St. Louis** stockyards that was trained to lead other pigs to their doom at the slaughterhouse. They also had a Judas goat.

Q What kind of natural growth fence was used in Illinois before barbed wire was invented?
A Osage Orange – because it was "horse high, pig-tight, and bull-strong."

Q What was fairy compound?
A It was pioneer rat poison consisting of lard pellets laced with phosphorous and whiskey.

Q What southern Illinois prep sports team is called the Terriers?
A **Carbondale**

Q What Southwest Conference prep sports team is called the Redbirds?
A **Alton**

Q What southeastern Illinois town in Wayne County has prep sports teams called Mules?
A **Fairfield**

Q What central Illinois town east of Springfield has prep sports teams called the Panthers?
A **Decatur (Eisenhower)**

Q What is a cattalo?
A A cross between a cow and a buffalo - Charles Goodnight of **Macoupin** College went to Texas in 1846 and as a rancher established the Goodnight Trail to Wyoming. By crossing Angus cattle with buffalo, **he produced the nation's first cattalo**.

Q How big was Goodman's Texas ranch?
A One million acres

Q What was the name of Chicago's famous fighting pig, circa 1841?
A Pape. The pig took on all comers, even dogs, usually defeating them by ripping out their intestines.

Q Have bones of a T-Rex or brontosaurus been discovered in Illinois?
A No. About the fiercest thing we had eons ago was a mastodon or woolly mammoth. Early Chicagoans caught huge five-foot muskellunge pike fish but that species is long gone.

Q What name was affixed to hogs by pioneer Illinois farmers?
A They were called "land sharks" due to their voracious appetites and willingness to eat almost anything.

Q What is the name of the dog on a box of Cracker Jack?
A Bingo

New Salem team of oxen and conestoga wagon built by George Armstrong Custer's father in 1821

Q What name did the Waldmire family of **Springfield** give to hot dogs wrapped in fried cornmeal?
A Cozy dog

Q What critter is the sports and band mascot for **Lebanon** High School?
A Greyhound

Q What town's Lambs Farm has a Fiberglas 17-foot cow and a 10-foot tall milk bottle?
A **Libertyville**

Q What critter is the sports and band mascot for **Nashville** High School?
A Hornet

Q What southern Illinois town is known as the "Deer Capital" of the state?
A **Golconda** because of the fall hunting season

Q What was the name of the female circus elephant that was accidentally killed by lightning while chained to a tree at **Oquawka**?
A Norma Jean – She was buried on the spot; the town has a monument in her honor.

Q What is the name of the heroic three-legged dog whose barking saved lives on an Illinois Central passenger train that caught fire?
A Boomer - Boomer Hall at SIUC is named in his honor.

Q Tom Mix was a western cowboy star who worked for Essanay Studios in Chicago. What was the name of his famous horse?
A Tony. When listening to the radio program as a young lad, I can still remember what Mix said as he jumped on the horse to chase after fleeing badmen – "Dig dirt, Tony!"

Piasa Monster

Q What mythical (I think) creature terrorized Native Americans in the **Alton** area before the arrival of white men?
A Piasa monster

Q What was the name of U.S. Grant's horse, given to him by the grateful people of southern Illinois?
A Egypt

Q What famous animals are most associated with the town of **Olney**?
A White squirrels protected by local ordinance and the State Legislature; these albino "rats with bushy tails" are almost sacred in town so don't run over one with your car

when visiting or they'll lock you up and throw away the key.

Q   What was the name of the legendary gorilla at the Chicago Zoo?
A   Bushman - he died, was stuffed, and is currently on display.

Q   What is the name of the prehistoric animal that was named the state's official fossil?
A   It's the Tully monster, a 280 million year old invertebrate found only in Illinois and named for its discoverer.

Q   Near what town was the first Tully Monster found by Francis Tully in the 1950's?
A   **Braidwood** – they lived millions of years ago and probably fed on shrimp and jellyfish.

Q   What is the official state bird of Illinois?
A   The cardinal – a red crested finch that stays around all winter long

Tully Monsters

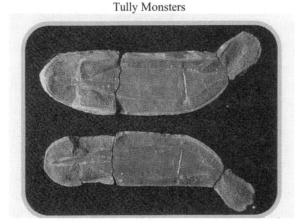

Q   What kind of a critter was Old Abe?
A   It was a bald eagle that served as mascot to a Wisconsin regiment. He compiled a combat record of twenty battles and sixty skirmishes in the Civil War.

Q   What is the official state insect of Illinois?
A   The beautiful orange and black monarch butterfly

Q   What is the official state animal of Illinois, chosen by our schoolchildren?
A   The white-tailed deer

Q   What is the name of the Tyrannosaurus Rex that is the featured attraction at the Field Museum of Natural History in Chicago?
A   Sue

Lions of Tsavo River – Field Museum of N. History

Q   What animal statues are famous for guarding the front entrance of the Chicago Art Institute?
A   Twin lions

Q   Where in Illinois can one find the Lions of Tsavo?
A   The Field Museum of Natural History where they are stuffed and on display. These are two critters that in real life killed dozens of workers trying to build a railroad bridge in British East Africa. They were featured in the first ever 3-

D film *Bwana Devil* and again in *The Ghost and the Darkness*.

Q   Early Chicago had a fish that could navigate over mud and sand on beaches. What was its name?
A   Mudskipper. It was an amphibious creature and it is currently on display at the Museum of Natural History.

Q   What Illinois town is famous for its purple martins?
A   **Griggsville** – they were brought to that town for the expressed purpose of ridding it of pesky skeeters.

Q   What was designated as our "state fish" in 1987?
A   Bluegill

Q   Does Illinois have its own Punxsutawney Phil?
A   Yes! Actually his stand in; it was the groundhog used in Bill Murray's film *Groundhog Day*, shot in **Woodstock**, Illinois, near the Woodstock Opera House. The town has a big hoop-de-do festival every February 2.

Q   What was the name of the Alsatian German shepherd that was the only survivor of the St. Valentine's Day Massacre in 1929?
A   Highball

Q   What famous reindeer was invented by an employee of Montgomery Ward in Chicago as a Christmas promotion?
A   Rudolph the red-nosed reindeer

Q   What ancient Egyptian royal hunting dog is the sports mascot of SIUE?
A   The saluki, a dog similar in looks to the greyhound

Q   What animal is the mascot of Southern Illinois University at Edwardsville?
A   Cougar – they had an old one (Chimega) and a young one (Keyna), both declawed. SIUE no longer keeps live mascots.

Q   What fierce animal is the prep sports and band mascot of **Edwardsville** High?
A   Tiger

Q   What tough animal is the prep sports and band mascot of **Staunton** High?
A   Bulldog

Q   What mythical creature is the mascot for **Pekin** prep sports teams?
A   Dragon

Q   What pyromaniac bovine has long been blamed for the 1871 Chicago fire that caused millions in damages?
A   Mrs. Patrick O'Leary's cow on DeKoven St.

Q What idea did a Chicago civic official bring back from a 2001 trip to Switzerland?

Those famous white squirrels of Olney, Illinois

A Cows On Parade – an artistic bonanza that caught on with the national media and was successful beyond anyone's wildest dreams.

ILLINOIS POLITICS –– CROOKED AND OTHERWISE

Q Who was the only territorial governor Illinois ever had?
A Kentucky aristocrat Ninian Edwards

Q What was his reward for giving up his seat as Chief Justice on Kentucky's Supreme Court and accepting the post?
A In addition to salary, he was given an estate of 1,000 acres in Kaskaskia.

Q Was Edwards a slave owner?
A Yes – he brought his slaves with him.

Q In what way was Edwards the state's most dominant political figure during its first 10 years?
A He was its only territorial governor (1809-1818), the state's first U.S. Senator (1818-1824), and the third governor (1826-30).

Q Who were his prominent relatives?
A His son-in-law was Daniel Pope Cook (U.S. Representative), his cousin was Judge Nathaniel Pope, and his

brother-in-law, Duff Green, was a St. Louis newspaper editor; his son married Mary Todd Lincoln's sister.

Q What were the circumstances of Ninian Edwards' death?
A He fell ill while heroically ministering to his St. Clair County neighbors during a cholera epidemic.

Q In the early days of the state, how were divorces obtained?
A It required passage of a bill by the state legislature. When Stephen Douglas first became a member of the General Assembly only 42 such petitions had been granted.

Q Who was the first governor of Illinois?
A Shadrach Bond

Q What man from **Murphysboro** was one of the managers of the radical Republican effort to impeach Andrew Johnson in the House of Representatives?
A John Logan

Q What future Illinois governor was famous for being prosecuted for bringing his slaves into the state and then illegally freeing them?
A Edward Coles of Virginia

Q Who was the first governor of Illinois Territory?
A Arthur St. Clair – our first county was named for him.

Q Who was our first representative to be elected to the territorial legislature?
A John McLean – his brother founded the town of **McLeansboro.**

Q What Illinois territorial delegate to Congress made the proposal that changed the course of our history – that of stealing land from Wisconsin and pushing our boundary north to include 14 more counties and the future city of Chicago?
A Nathaniel Pope

Birthplace of John Logan by Mike Coles of Anna, Illinois

Q What Illinois governor from **Belleville** was an investor in the state's first railroad – the Illinois & St. Louis?
A John Reynolds. The eight-mile long railroad was built to haul coal from the bluffs near **East St. Louis** to the thriving city of St. Louis. The railroad did poorly at first, but by 1867 the Short Line was the **richest dollar-per-mile railroad in the nation.**

Q What famous Illinois presidential candidate started out as a schoolteacher at **Whitworth** and **Winchester**?
A Stephen A. Douglas

Q   What was Douglas' nickname?
A   The Little Giant – short of stature, mighty of mouth

Q   What man was appointed postmaster of **New Salem** by President Andrew Jackson?
A   Abe Lincoln

Q   Was Abe Lincoln ever rejected in a marriage proposal?
A   Yes. Mary Owens turned him down for his lack of financial substance. Fortunately, he was only mildly in love with her.

Q   What Illinois U.S. Senator was the author of the Thirteenth Amendment, freeing the slaves?
A   Lyman Trumbull

Q   In the days of Lincoln and Douglas, how often and how long did the legislature meet?
A   Once every two years, the session lasting for about three months and paying the sum of about $400.

East St. Louis Mayor M. Stephens (far right)– courtesy Andrew Theising

Q   Why does the state of Illinois have a leg that once belonged to General Santa Anna?
A   The wooden leg was captured by the Third and Fourth Illinois Infantry during the Mexican War at the battle of Cerro Gordo. The brigade was led by Brigadier General James Shields, the same man who challenged Lincoln to a duel.

Q   What Illinoisan, who lived in St. Clair County, was a hero in the battle of Buena Vista in the Mexican War?
A   William Bissell – when the battle started, Colonel Bissell realized the Illinois men had never been under fire. "Steady boys, don't duck your heads," he encouraged. When a cannonball whizzed by his head, he flinched. "You may duck the big ones, boys," he shouted. Bissell restored order and led a brave counterattack.

Q   How did Bissell come close to killing Jefferson Davis, future President of the Confederacy?
A   In a heated 1848 debate in the House of Representatives about the extension of slavery into territories acquired from the Mexican War, a Southern congressman praised the actions of a Mississippi regiment at Buena Vista. Bissell, who was there, said the credit belonged to Illinois and Kentucky regiments. Jefferson Davis, a congressman from Mississippi, challenged Bissell to a duel. Bissell accepted and chose military muskets as weapons. The night before the duel was to be fought, friends on both sides talked Bissell and Davis out of it.

Bissell went on to be the first Republican governor of Illinois, and Davis became President of the Confederacy.

Q   What Illinois politician is known as the "Father of the Illinois Central Railroad?"
A   Stephen Douglas. He proposed the land grant bill in congress that authorized the building of a railroad to connect Chicago with Iowa and Alabama.

Q   What prominent Illinois politician advocated the annexation of Cuba?
A   Stephen Douglas, a firm believer in Manifest Destiny

Q   What first mayor of Chicago was disappointed when he first saw Chicago - a worthless marshland smelling of wild onion?
A   William Ogden – he was so astonished when he sold some worthless land at a profit, he went into the real estate business.

Q   What future presidential candidate earned about $3,000 a year as chief engineer for the Illinois Central Railroad in the 1850's?
A   George McClellan, who ran against Lincoln in the 1864 race

Lincoln, Stevenson and Dirksen

GALLANT MEN OF ILLINOIS

Q   What Chicago mayor got rid of an undesirable shanty town called "the Sands" by luring its residents to a dogfight and then setting fire to the shacks while they were gone?
A   Long John Wentworth – 1861

Q   What **Springfield** resident became a general in the Civil War and was U.S. Grant's rival for fame and recognition?
A   John McClernand of **Shawneetown**

Q   What two things worked against McClernand?

A   He was occasionally inept, and he was a Democrat.

Q   What Illinoisan met with African-American leaders in 1862 and suggested that Negroes leave the United States and establish a colony in Panama?
A   President Abe Lincoln

Q   What man handed Lincoln his only defeat at the hands of voters, besting him in 1832 for a seat in the General Assembly?
A   Peter Cartwright

Q   Who is regarded as the "Great Pioneer For Lutheranism" in Illinois?
A   Christian Bernard Thummel

Q   Why is **Bloomington** called the "Oberammergau of America?"
A   The first Passion Play, about the teachings and crucifixion of Christ, was performed in Ober-ammergau, Bavaria. The first such play in America was held at Bloomington in 1924.

Q   What school has one of the few Bible monuments in America?
A   It's in Bible Garden on the campus of Illinois Wesleyan at **Bloomington.** The inscribed marble, replicating an open book, is about four feet wide and four feet tall.

Q   What Civil War governor dismissed the Illinois General Assembly because it was controlled by Democrats who sought to hinder the prosecution of the war?
A   Richard Yates

Q   What Illinois senator was responsible for the act that created the Freedman's Bureau at the end of the Civil War?
A   Lyman Trumbull of **Alton**

Q   What Illinois general and politician helped establish the Grand Army of the Republic, a Union veterans group?
A   John Logan of **Murphysboro**

Q   What Illinois politician helped organize the first observance of Memorial Day in **Carbondale** (1866)?
A   John Logan

Q   Illinois counterfeiter Ben Boyd concocted an 1876 plot while in prison to kidnap a president and hold him for ransom. Who was the intended victim?

Pinkerton, Lincoln, McClernand

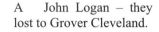
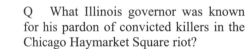

Lincoln the debater – Taylor Park, Freeport, IL

A   Abe Lincoln, our deceased President. His cohorts were caught and given a year in prison for **grave robbing**.

Q   What southern Illinois politician known as "Black Eagle" ran for Vice-president on the 1884 Republican ticket with James G. Blaine?
A   John Logan – they lost to Grover Cleveland.

Q   What ex-mayor of **East St. Louis** was assassinated near his home on College Avenue in 1885?
A   John Bowman – four-time mayor (His assassin was never caught.)

Q   What Chicagoan founded the American Socialist Party of America in 1894?
A   Eugene Debs – he later went to prison for his outspoken opposition to World War I.

Q   What type of labor organization did Debs lead?
A   American Railway Union – he led the Pullman strike of 1894 when Pullman cut wages due to the depression but failed to lower rents in his company town.

Q   What Illinois governor was known for his pardon of convicted killers in the Chicago Haymarket Square riot?
A   John Peter Altgeld

Q   How many senators do we elect to the state legislature?
A   59 – we send 118 to the house of representatives, and there are seven justices who serve on the supreme court.

Q   What group did the Illinois government formally apologize to in April of 2004 for running them out of the state in 1846?
A   The Mormons, during the governorship of Thomas Ford

Q   What Illinois governor was known for pardoning dozens of convicted killers on Death Row?
A   George Ryan

Q   What other move by Ryan angered Illinois motorists?
A   He roughly doubled the tax on automobile license plates.

Q   What current U.S. Speaker of the House wants to

eliminate the IRS?
A   Dennis Hastert – he wants to replace the current system with a national sales tax; it's estimated that tax accountants and lawyers cost the economy about $60 billion a year

Q   What Chicagoan, now a resident of **Bensenville**, has served as majority leader in the U.S. House of Representatives?
A   Henry Hyde

Q   What one word describes the dirty campaign carried out by Otto Kerner and William G. Stratton in the 1960 governor's race?
A   Mudslinging – on both sides

Q   Did Kerner go to jail for his actions as governor?
A   No, it was for bribery, mail fraud, perjury, conspiracy, and tax evasion while he was a Chicago judge.

Q   Approximately how much money does the General Assembly receive every year from legalized casino gambling?
A $300 million

Q   Why hasn't this solved the state's fiscal problems?
A   No matter how much you increase state income from sources such as gambling, politicians will find a way to spend it on pork barrel and social programs to get re-elected.

Q   What former U.S. Senator from **Troy,** and resident of **Makanda,** refused to give up his typewriter in favor of a computer?
A   Paul Simon

Q   What Chicago mayor sent two of his crooked cops to shoot and kill Frank Nitti?
A   Anton Cermak – Nitti survived the bullet.

Q   What was corrupt Mayor Anton Cermak's nickname?
A   "Ten Percent Tony" – this requires no explanation

Q   What Illinois governor was in John F. Kennedy's book, *Profiles In Courage*?
A   John Peter Altgeld

Q   What **Salem**-born Illinoisan was a three-time losing presidential nominee?
A   William Jennings Bryan – 1896, 1900, 1908. In case you're wondering, that's a record for futility shared with Henry Clay.

Governor's Mansion – Springfield, Illinois

Robert Ingersoll Monument – Glen Oak Park, Peoria

Q   What Illinoisan is famous for his "Cross of Gold" speech?
A   William J. Bryan – he favored a bi-metal monetary standard of gold and silver.

Q   When was the last time Abe Lincoln's casket was opened?
A   In 1900 – officials moved his body to its final resting place, and they wanted to make sure he was in the casket.

Q   What future Chicago mayor may – or may not - have participated in the 1919 race riot?
A   Richard J. Daley – he always refused to comment when asked about it.

Q   Who was the first African-American mayor of Chicago?
A   Harold Washington

Q   What town near the geographic center of Illinois was promoted as a successor to the state capital at **Vandalia**, but lost out to **Springfield**?
A   **Illiopolis** – the town currently has only 916 residents.

Q   Besides **East St. Louis**, Chicago, and **Springfield**, has the state had any other lynchings or race riots?
A   Yes – In 1893 Samuel Bush, accused of rape, was lynched from a telephone pole in **Decatur**. From 1880-1940 there were 30 recorded lynchings in the state.

Q   Has **Danville** ever had a race riot?
A   Yes – In 1895 two Negroes were kidnapped from the Vermilion County Jail and hanged from a downtown bridge. Two weeks later a race war erupted.

Q   Why did Illinois voters reject a new state constitution in 1922?
A   Mainly because it provided for a state income tax.

Q   What **Granite City** mayor was killed while trying to save his town from a 1903 flood?
A   John Edwards – an engine at a pumping station exploded when he lit a match in an effort to restart it.

Q   Who was the first President depicted on a coin?
A   Abe Lincoln appeared on the 1909 penny.

Q   What U.S. senator was responsible for getting the McKinley Bridge at **Madison** built?
A   William McKinley – no relation to President McKinley

Q   What **Danville** native was the powerful Speaker of the U.S. House of Representatives during the /Roosevelt/ Taft/Wilson administrations?
A   "Uncle Joe" Cannon – who served in the U.S. House of Representatives for 46 years

Q   What Illinois man was the **first person depicted on the cover of Time Magazine**?
A   Joe Cannon

Q   What Illinois town holds the record for hosting the most national political conventions?
A   Chicago – Convention City

Q   What Illinois governor was a serious candidate for U.S. President at the 1920 Republican nominating convention?
A   Frank Lowden - he lost out to Warren Harding.

Q   What **Carlinville** man, who was a U.S. Representative, was the pilot of the single-engine "Friendship Flame" on a round-the-world solo flight in 1951?
A   Peter Mack – he is buried at Arlington Cemetery.

Q   To whom was Frank Lowden married?
A   George Pullman's daughter, Florence

Q   In what Illinois city did a left-wing faction of the Socialist Party found/establish the American Communist Party in 1919?
A   Chicago

Q   What reform mayor of Chicago was responsible for forcing Al Capone to move his headquarters from Chicago to Cicero?
A   William Dever

Q   What blustery Chicago mayor launched a phony campaign to have pro-British bias removed from school textbooks?
A   Big Bill Thompson

Q   What woman, who was a onetime reporter for the *Chicago Tribune* and political activist, switched her allegiance

U.S. Grant's home given by citizens of Galena

Carlinville "Taj Mahal" Courthouse

Court House   Carlinville Il

from the Republican to the Democratic Party after hearing a speech by Clare Booth Luce?
A   India Edwards

Q   To what conservative Republican was Clare Booth(e) Luce married?
A   Henry Luce – onetime cub reporter for the *Chicago Daily News* and cofounder of *Time Magazine* and founder of *Life, Fortune*, and *Sports Illustrated.* The Time-Life Building in Chicago was constructed around 1966.

Q   What Chicago-born man might have come close to committing treason by giving classified documents about the Vietnam War to the *New York Times*?
A   Daniel Ellsberg – they became known as the Pentagon Papers.

Q   To many, of course, Ellsberg is a hero. What act of stupidity by government prosecutors led the trial judge to dismiss charges against him?
A   They broke into the office of his psychiatrist.

Q   What Illinois politician was known as "the man from **Libertyville**?"
A   Adlai Stevenson

Q   What Illinois U.S. President tried to annex the island of Santo Domingo?
A   U.S. Grant

Q   What U.S. President was responsible for making Thanksgiving an official holiday?
A   U.S. Grant

Q   How many cigars a day did U.S. Grant smoke?
A   Twenty – he died of throat cancer. Seward, Lincoln's secretary of state, smoked 40 a day.

Q   What Illinois governor was indicted for stealing state funds when he was treasurer?
A   Len Small – acquitted, but probably guilty

Q   On what grounds was Frank Smith, the 1926 U.S. senate winner, refused a seat in Washington, D.C.?
A   A senate committee said he *bought* the seat by spending too much on the campaign.

Q   What mayor of **West City**, near **Benton**, was murdered

by one of Charlie Birger's associates?
A   Joe Adams – Birger was hanged for the offense.

Q   What office was Chicagoan Ruth McCormick nee Hanna elected to in 1928?
A   U.S. House of Representatives as a Republican

Q   What honest reform governor was responsible for helping to run the Shelton Gang out of St. Clair County and **East St. Louis** in the 1930's?
A   Henry Horner

Q   What man broke precedent and flew to the Chicago Democratic National Convention in 1932 to accept the nomination?
A   Franklin Delano Roosevelt

Q   What was the main campaign slogan when Adlai Stevenson ran for President in 1952 and 1956?
A   "All The Way With Adlai"

Q   Who was the first foreign-born Governor of Illinois?
A   John Peter Altgeld

Q   What Chicago mayor was shot by Joe Zangara?
A   Anton Cermak – 1933

Q   What governor was responsible for initiating the state's first sales tax?
A   Henry Horner – three percent

Q   What **Jacksonville** native and daughter of William Jennings Bryan became the nation's first female ambassador?
A   Ruth Owens nee Bryan in 1933

Q   What Chicago banker won the Nobel Peace Prize?
A   Charles Gates Dawes

Q   What Illinoisan was Vice-president under Calvin Coolidge?
A   Charles Gates Dawes

Q   What former presidential candidate prosecuted John Scopes for teaching evolution in his Tennessee biology class?
A   William J. Bryan – Clarence Darrow of Chicago defended Scopes.

Q   What odd fact connects W.J. Bryan and John Scopes?
A   Both were born in **Salem**, Illinois.

Q   What Chicago politician wrote the song, "It's All In The Game?"
A   Charles G. Dawes – the song was a big hit for Tommy Edwards in 1959.

Q   What **Alton** woman ran for congress against **East St. Louisan** Mel Price and lost in 1952?
A   Phyllis Schlafly

Q   What political Republican activist was called "hysterical" by the press when she predicted in the 1970's that gays would eventually push for the right to be married?
A   Phyllis Schlafly

Phyllis Schlafly of Alton

Q   What author published her first book, *A Choice, Not An Echo* (Barry Goldwater) 1964?
A   Phyllis Schlafly – it sold three million copies.

Q   What Illinois governor died in office, probably due to the day-to-day strain of dealing with Depression problems?
A   Henry Horner

Q   What Chicagoan developed the first budget for the U.S. government?
A   Charles Dawes

Q   Who is our nation's greatest Vice-president?
A   Surprise – it's Charles G. Dawes – not Gore, the man who "invented" the Internet. Chicago banker Dawes, in addition to being our nation's first budget director, headed the RFC under President Hoover, won the Nobel Peace prize for his plan dealing with German reparations, and wrote a popular song.

Mayor Anton Cermak of Chicago

Q   What President tried to institute the nation's first income tax?
A   Abe Lincoln said the tax was needed to finance the Civil War. The courts declared it to be unconstitutional. We did not get an income tax until President Wilson and the 16th Amendment.

Q   What Illinois governor reduced the sales tax from three percent to two, but enacted the state's first cigarette tax?
A   Dwight Green in 1940

Q   What museum piece did the state legislature consider sending back to Mexico in 1942 as a goodwill gesture to secure cooperation in World War II?
A   General Santa Anna's wooden leg – we didn't.

Q   In what former Chicago mayor's home, after his death in 1944, was over a million dollars found stuffed in boxes?
A   Big Bill Thompson

Q   What Chicago mayor was an enthusiast of sailboat racing?
A   Big Bill Thompson

Q What **Rockford** man served with Admiral Richard Byrd and made six expeditions to the South Pole and two to the North Pole?
A George Dufek

Q What future Illinois U.S. senator was a "star witness" for the Kefauver Crime Commission in 1951?
A Young Paul Simon, crusading editor of the *Troy Tribune,* testified about gambling and corruption in St. Clair and Madison counties.

Q Did Gerald Ford or Jimmy Carter carry Illinois in the 1976 election?
A Ford

Q How much do some authors suggest legislator Paul Powell made annually in bribes?
A About 100,000

Q What **Abingdon** native was given the Medal of Honor by President Gerald Ford for meritorious service in Vietnam?
A Admiral James Stockdale

Q Who was the most famous man killed by a group of outlaws called the Banditti of the Prairie?
A George Davenport, a wealthy trader who lived on Arsenal Island between Davenport, Iowa, and Rock Island. Davenport was robbed and then shot and killed in July of 1845. The three men responsible were caught and hanged, marking the beginning of the end of this notorious group.

Q What two cities did Davenport establish?
A Davenport, Iowa, and **Rock Island**

Q Who built a castle-like home in 1928 on 300 acres in Ogle County near the town of **Oregon**?
A Walter Strong, publisher of the Chicago *Daily News*. He called the ostentatious estate *Stronghold.*

Q What **Elgin High** grad won the Nobel Prize for chemistry in 1974?
A Paul John Flory - the prize was a medal and $124,000

Q What man born Benjamin Kubelsky was known as the "**Waukegan Wit**?"
A Jack Benny – he originally carried his violin on stage just to give him a feeling of security.

Q Who are some famous actors who got their start performing at Chicago's Second City at 1616 North Wells?
A Alan Alda, Alan Arkin, Joan Rivers, John Belushi, Valerie Harper

Secretary of State/Governor George Ryan

Q When was **Lebanon's** Looking Glass Playhouse started?
A 1972 - Shirley Schafer and Dick Boyd staged the musical *Carousel* for the benefit of McKendree College. It was so successful that theatrical productions were continued.

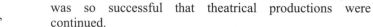
Joe Zangara – Cermak's assassin

Q Why the name Looking Glass?
A It comes from the nearby Lookingglass Prairie, east of town. It was so smooth it was like a looking glass.

Q What boxer from **Jacksonville** was one of the few to defeat Muhammad Ali?
A Ken Norton in 1973 – he broke Ali's jaw.

Q What entire municipal city council was indicted in 1946 for malfeasance in office - failing to take action against illegal gambling?
A **East St. Louis**. Tennis star Jimmy Connors' grandfather was mayor at the time. The charges were ultimately dismissed.

Q What governor vetoed a Republican bill that would have required teachers to sign a statement that they were not members of the subversive Communist Party?
A Democrat Adlai Stevenson

Q What small town was home to Josephine Williams, the mother of Senator Barry Goldwater who ran for President in 1964?
A **Bowen**

Q What member of the General Assembly from **Anna** won the Congressional Medal of Honor in World War II?
A Clyde Choate

Q What Illinoisan was Grover Cleveland's Vice-president?
A Adlai Stevenson (the first one)

Q What was the relationship between Adlai Stevenson the Vice-president and Stevenson the governor?
A Grandfather and grandson

Q U.S. Senator Paul Douglas was a former professor at what university?
A The University of Chicago – a university so infested with left-leaning teachers that the General Assembly wanted to investigate it in the 1950's.

Q Who was our state's first divorced governor?
A Adlai Stevenson

Q Why did Stevenson's wife divorce him?

A   She hated political life and thought he was obsessed with politics.

Q   Who was our nation's first divorced President?
A   Ronald Reagan

Q   Why did Jane Wyman divorce Ronnie?
A   She hated political life and thought her husband was obsessed with politics.

Q   What Illinois governor (with a straight face) told the Kefauver Crime Commission that Chicago was clean and had no illegal gambling?
A   Otto Kerner

Q   What **East St. Louis** Police Commissioner told the Kefauver Commission that there was no significant gambling in East St. Louis?
A   John English

Q   How many terms did Richard J. Daley serve as Mayor of Chicago?
A   Six

Q   What slogan did Daley use to get re-elected?
A   Chicago: "The City That Works"

Q   What title did Mayor Daley hate?
A   "Boss"

Q   What **Granite City** native and state auditor was sentenced to 12 years at Menard in **Chester** for embezzling state money?
A   Orville Hodge

Q   In what city was the first televised debate between Democrat and Republicans presidential nominees held?
A   Chicago – 1960, Kennedy v. Nixon. Kennedy won the televised debate, but radio listeners thought Nixon triumphed.

Q   What die-hard Democrat and New Deal supporter switched allegiances and supported Nixon with 200 speeches in this election?
A   Ronald Reagan.

Q   To whom was Governor Otto Kerner married?
A   Assassinated Chicago Mayor Anton Cermak's daughter

Q   In the 2004 U.S. senate race, which candidate sponsored tour buses to Canada to enable seniors to obtain cheaper drug prescriptions?
A   Blair Hull

Q   What Chicagoan and state comptroller ran for the U.S. senate seat in 2004 but lost?
A   Dan Hynes

Q   Before Rod Blagojevich became governor in 2003, who was the last Democrat to hold that office?
A   Dan Walker - 1973

Governor Rod Blagojevich

Q   What do Illinois lawmakers fight over every ten years, usually without coming to a compromise?
A   A new redistricting plan due to population changes. The stalemate is broken when either a Republican name or a Democratic name is drawn by the Secretary of State from an old Abe Lincoln stovepipe hat.

Q   Approximately what percent of the state's annual revenue comes from the lottery?
A   Only two percent

Q   What Illinois Senator secured enough Republican votes to pass Lyndon Johnson's Civil Rights Act of 1964?
A   Everett Dirksen of **Pekin**

Representative Jesse Jackson Jr.

Q   When Chuck Percy, president of Bell & Howell, won the U.S. senate seat in 1966, who did he unseat?
A   Democrat Paul Douglas

Q   What Illinois governor quit in the middle of his term to become a federal judge on a U.S. court of appeals?
A   Otto Kerner

Q   Who was the first Jewish governor of Illinois?
A   Sam Shapiro – he was the lieutenant governor when Kerner stepped down.

Q   Kerner headed a commission that investigated civil disorders following the assassination of M.L. King Jr. What was its conclusion?
A   We were rapidly becoming two nations, one black, one white – separate and unequal.

Q   How did Paul Simon become Lieutenant Governor of the state under a Republican governor?
A   Shapiro and Simon ran against Richard Ogilvie and his running mate. Ogilvie received the most votes for governor and Simon received the most for the second spot.

Q   Could such an oddity happen again?
A   No. The 1970 Illinois Constitution requires that both leaders be from the same party.

Q   What huge mistake did Ogilvie make as Republican governor?

92

A He spent tons of money on various new programs and then paid for the pork barrel by initiating the state income tax. Voters threw him out of office in the next election.

Q What conclusion did the Dan Walker Report come to concerning the actions of Chicago police during the 1968 Democratic National Convention in Chicago?
A The report called it a POLICE RIOT.

Q How did Ralph Smith of **Alton** become a U.S. senator?
A He was named by Governor Ogilvie to replace Everett Dirksen who died of lung cancer in 1969.

Q Who defeated Smith in the next election?
A Democratic state treasurer Adlai Stevenson III

Q How many times did Adlai Stevenson run for President?
A Twice - he was defeated in 1952 and 1956 by Dwight Eisenhower.

Q What label did Republicans manage to pin on Stevenson?
A "Egghead" (stuffy intellectual)

Q When Secretary of State Paul Powell of **Vienna** died in 1970, what was found in his hotel room?
A Hundreds of thousands of dollars in shoeboxes

Q Did his estate get to keep most of the money?
A No. Most of it went back to the state or was used to pay taxes.

Q Who became the state treasurer when Adlai Stevenson III became U.S. senator?
A Alan Dixon of **Belleville**

Q What former Illinois governor went to jail in 1971 on charges stemming from ownership of racing stock?
A Otto Kerner

Q How did this author first become acquainted with Paul Simon?
A When Simon was Lieutenant Governor, he came and spoke to my American Problems class at **Collinsville** High.

Q How did Dan Walker manage to defeat Paul Simon in the 1972 Democratic primary and become the state's next governor?
A He ran as an independent and managed to tie Simon in with the Powell and Daley political machine, although Simon was clean as a hound's tooth.

Q What **Nashville**, Illinois, man cast the deciding vote in the 1973 (5-4) Roe v. Wade Supreme Court decision?

Current Secretary of State Jesse White

Chicago State Senator Barack Obama

A Harry Blackmun. It is interesting that the lady known as "Roe" is now a "pro-lifer."

Q What Republican was elected to the first of his five terms as governor in 1976?
A James Thompson

Q What Illinoisan almost took the 1976 nomination away from Gerald Ford, despite Ford being the incumbent President?
A Ronald Reagan

Q What exciting rumor was spread around at the convention?
A Gerald Ford would step aside and become Reagan's running mate

Q Who became the first child born to a sitting Illinois governor in 72 years?
A Samantha Thompson - Governor Thompson married one of his former students at Northwestern, and they had a baby daughter.

Q What woman ran for Chicago mayor against the man who fired her when she worked for Mayor Daley?
A Jane Byrne defeated Michael Bilandic in 1979.

Q Alan Dixon served two terms as U.S. Senator and then fell victim to what sensational national event?
A The Clarence Thomas/Anita Hill brouhaha. Carol Mosley Braun, angered by Dixon's vote to confirm Thomas, defeated Dixon with a lot of sympathy votes despite national surveys that said most people believed Thomas rather than Hill.

Q What African-American was the state senator for the 13th legislative district in 2003?
A Barack Obama – a rising star in the Democratic Party

Q Who became the nation's **first female African-American Senator**?
A Carol Mosley-Braun - but she squandered her political capital with outrageous behavior and thriftless spending habits, becoming a one-termer.

Q Who did Mosley-Braun lose to in the 1998 election?
A Republican Peter Fitzgerald.

Q What political plum did President Clinton give Mosley-Braun after her loss?
A She became ambassador to New Zealand.

Q When Paul Simon retired from the senate in 1996, who replaced him?
A Richard Durbin - Assumption High of **East St. Louis** grad

Q What new position did Simon accept?
A He became the head of the Public Policy Institute at Southern Illinois University in **Carbondale.**

Q Who did Jim Thompson narrowly defeat in the 1982 race for governor?
A Adlai Stevenson III

Q When does Illinois begin its new fiscal year?
A July 1

Q After "Big Jim" Thompson decided to retire, what Republican secretary of state replaced him in 1991?
A Jim Edgar

Q What **Alton** woman's national campaign prevented the Illinois legislature from ratifying the ERA Amendment?
A Phyllis Schlafly. Illinois was the only northern state not to ratify ERA. You wouldn't think that one woman could make that much difference, but she did.

Q When did Paul Simon of **Makanda** first get elected to the U.S. Senate?
A 1984

Q What **Abingdon** native ran for Vice-president of the U.S. in 1992 on a ticket with Ross Perot?
A James Stockdale, a Medal of Honor winner. Their effort probably cost Bush the election the way Ralph Nader cost Gore the election in 2000.

Q What happened when Mayor Harold Washington tried to muster support for a 500-year celebration of Columbus – a repeat of the city's previous Columbian Exposition?
A There was little support for the idea. Due to this nutty thing called political correctness, Columbus is now seen as a "despoiler of paradise."

Q What Chicagoan, and head of the powerful Ways and Means Committee (finance), went to jail for mail fraud and mishandling his stamp fund?
A Dan Rostenkowski

Q What **Cicero** government official was convicted in 2002 of helping to loot the city's treasury of about $12 million?
A Betty Loren-Maltese – town president

ILLINI BASKETBALL 1904-2004

Q In its 95 year history, how many losing seasons have the Illini had?
A Only 12

Q What kind of buzzer sounded at the end of a basketball game in the old era before electronic scoreboards?
A None - an official fired a track starter's pistol to signal the end of a game.

Q In the very early days of basketball, what happened after every score?
A There was a jump ball at center court.

Q Why is the game called basketball instead of netball?
A When Dr, Naismith invented the game, the original goal was a peach basket. An official on a ladder had to retrieve the ball each time a "basket" was made.

Q What were the original 1906 teams of the Western Conference that evolved into the Big Ten.
A Wisconsin, Purdue, Northwestern, Minnesota, Chicago, Illinois and Michigan

Q What additional two teams in 1909 made it the Big Nine Conference?
A Iowa and Indiana

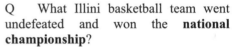

Q What Illini basketball team went undefeated and won the **national championship**?
A The 1914-15 team. They were 16-0 and held opponents to 13 points a game.

Q The old Illini gymnasium was named for George Huff. Who was he?
A Huff was the Illini football and baseball coach and athletic director in the 1920's and 1930's.

Q What football/basketball conference did George Huff help organize?
A He helped organize the Western Conference that later became known as the Big Ten.

Q Did George Halas ever play Illini basketball?
A Yes, he was a guard on the 1917 team. He was named captain for the 1918 season but went into the military.

Q Did basketball coach Harry Combs ever play for the Illini?
A Yes. He led them to two Big Ten titles in 1935 and 1937.

Q What *baseball* Hall of Famer led Illinois to a Big Ten basketball championship in the 1936-37 season?
A Lou Boudreau

Q Who starred for Illinois at center in 1939 and was later

elected to the Illinois Hall of Fame as the coach of the **East St. Louis Flyers**?
A Louis "Pick" Dehner

Q Who was this author's high school P.E. teacher?
A Louis "Pick" Dehner

Q In the decade of the 1940's, what Big Ten team had the best winning percentage?
A Illinois with a .725 percentage

Q Why was the Big Ten referred to as the Big Nine in those days?
A The University of Chicago dropped sports from its agenda in the late 1930's.

Q When did the Big Nine become the Big Ten?
A 1951 - when Michigan State joined

Q What Illini is considered the greatest all around athlete ever to attend the school?
A Dike Eddleman - he earned 11 varsity letters in basketball, track, football – the school record.

Q What high school did Eddleman attend?
A He was a **Centralia** Orphan and captain of their team that won the IHSA basketball title in 1942.

Q What other Illini record does Eddleman hold?
A He is the only Illini to make it to the Final Four, the Rose Bowl, and the Olympics (track).

Q What incredible feat did Eddleman's high school team accomplish in the playoffs?
A They were down by 13 points to the powerful 39-0 **Paris** team with five minutes to go. Eddleman won the game with a buzzer beater.

Q How well did Eddelman perform at the 1948 Olympics?
A He won the silver medal in the high jump.

Q What are the Eddleman Awards?
A Since 1992, the Illini male and female-of-the-year sports awards have been named for him.

Q Who holds the Illini record for punting average for a season in football?
A Dike Eddleman with a 43 yards per kick average

Q The Illinois cagers handed 14-0 Minnesota its first loss of the season in 1949. Who was the star of that team?
A Bill Erickson

Q Almost no one made jump shots back in 1949. What were the most common shots?
A Lay-ups, two handed set shots, hook shots, and one-handed push shots

Illini coach Lou Henson

Q How were free throws attempted back then?
A They were tossed underhanded

Q What was the first Big Ten team to score 92 points in a basketball game?
A In March of 1943 the Illini Whiz Kids defeated the University of Chicago 92-25 – a lopsided rout.

Q How many Big Ten records did Andy Phillip of **Granite City** break that night?
A He broke five records, including a scoring mark of 40 points in the game.

Q Did Illinois win the conference championship that year?
A Yes. It was their second in a row, the first team to win back-to-back since Wisconsin in 1914.

Q What was the overall record of the Whiz Kids for those two seasons?
A They were 35-6

Q How big was the NCAA tournament in 1942?
A There were only eight teams – the ones that won their conferences

Q What national defending champions did the Whiz Kids from Illinois defeat those two years?
A They beat Wisconsin and Stanford

Q In the 1942-43 season, how dominant were the Illini?
A Very dominating - they were 12-0 in conference play and won their games by an average score of 24.2 points.

Q How did the War ruin Illinois' chances for a national title?
A Three of the starting five got called up for service just before the NCAA tourney, so coach Mills didn't take the team. Wyoming won the title that year but most observers say Illinois was easily the best in the nation.

Q Name three of the Illinois basketball Whiz Kids from the 1941-42 team.
A Andy Phillip, Gene Vance, Ken Menke, Jack Smiley, Art Mathison

Q Illinois won a stunning upset in December of 1945. Name the number one nationally ranked team they defeated.
A They crushed DePaul at George Huff Gym, 56-37.

Q Who was the star of the 1945 Illini team?
A Jack Burmaster

Q Who was the great coach of DePaul in 1945?
A Legendary Ray Meyer

Q How big of a headache were Illini teams to Ray Meyer in the Whiz Kid era?

A   In three seasons his teams lost just eight games. Three of those losses were to Illinois.

Q   Who owns the Illinois rebounding record for a single game?
A   Skip Thoren hauled down 24 in a 1963 game against UCLA.

Q   What is the best game that Illinois has ever played against UCLA?
A   It was the opening game at home against the Bruins in 1964. They ended the defending champion's 30-game streak with a 110-83 triumph. Skip Thoren had 20 points, Bogie Redmon of **Collinsville** and Don Freeman of **Madison** had 17 apiece.

Q   Name the high school team that Harry Combes coached to a state championship before becoming the Illini coach.
A   His **Champaign Maroons** won the title in 1946.

Q   What do many Illini fans consider Combes' biggest recruiting failure?
A   Losing Cazzie Russell of **Carver High** to Michigan

Q   What two Illinois players were named All-Big Ten in 1960?
A   Manny Jackson and Govoner Vaughn, both from **Edwardsville**. They made the second team.

Q   Who is the Illini coach with the most wins?
A   Lou Henson with 423. Harry Combes had 316

Q   Did Harry Combes' teams ever defeat Adolph Rupp and mighty Kentucky?
A   Only once – 1964; Pat Riley and Lou Dampier were the Kentucky stars; Skip Thoren led the way for the Illini.

Q   What was unusual about where that 1964 Elite Eight game was played?
A   It was held at Kentucky's home court – Rupp Arena, before 20,000 screaming partisan fans. Current NCAA rules don't allow teams to play tournament games on their home floor.

Q   Did Illinois ever defeat a Cazzie Russell-led team at Michigan?
A   Yes. Don Freeman of **Madison** matched Russell's 33 points with a wild 99-93 upset victory in 1964. Rich Jones had 31 points. Preston Pearson played in the game but got into early foul trouble.

Q   Who holds the all time single season total points scoring mark for the Illini?
A   Don Freeman, the "Madison Marvel," had 668 and

Dave Downey and Jimmy Rahl

Don Sunderlage

Andy Kaufmann is a close second with 660.

Q   Who holds the four-year Illini scoring mark?
A   Deon Thomas - set from 1990-1994

Q   Why did Freeman play only three years?
A   Freshmen weren't allowed to play varsity ball back then.

Q   How many points per game did the Illini average during Freeman's junior year?
A   92.2 points per game, still the school record

Q   Who are the only two Illini to average over 20 points and ten rebounds per game?
A   Don Freeman and Nick Weatherspoon

Q   How did Freeman fare as a pro?
A   He scored over 12,000 points, playing mostly for the ABA teams. He won a championship with Indiana.

Q   Who was the Illini star when Illinois went to the Final Four in 1951?
A   Don Sunderlage. His team lost a last second heart-breaker to Adolph Rupp's Wildcats, but he led all scorers in the tournament with a 20.8 average.

Q   What Illini star made the All-Tournament Final Four team at Seattle in 1952?
A   John Kerr. Clutch shooting heroics in earlier games by Jim Bredar from **Salem High** helped the team make it to the Big Dance. Bredar also made the all-tourney team.

Q   What was Johnnie Kerr's nickname?
A   "Big Red" (his hair)

Q   What was remarkable about Kerr making the all-tourney team?
A   He wasn't the Illini starting center/forward – it was Bob Peterson

Q   What place did all three Harry Combes' teams ('49,'51, '52) finish at the final Four NCAA Tournament?
A   Third - back then the two teams that lost in the first game of the Final Four played for third place.

Q   Where does Kerr rank among all-time leading scores in Illini basketball history?
A   Second with a 25.3 points per game in 1953-54. Oddly, he only made second team All-America.

Q   How tall was Kerr?
A   He was 6-9, having played high school ball at Chicago's Tilden Tech

Q What NBA honor did Kerr win in 1969?
A He won Coach-of-the-Year with the Chicago Bulls.

Q What record did he set as an NBA player for Syracuse, Philadelphia, and Baltimore.
A The iron man record of playing in 844 straight games

Q What important statistics did Kerr accumulate in his NBA career?
A Kerr scored over 10,000 points and had over 10,000 rebounds – a rarity.

Q What position did Kerr hold after coaching the Bulls?
A He became their announcer.

Q How many times did coach Harry Combes' 1955 and '56 teams score 100 or more points?
A 25

Q What Michigan player blocked the Illini path to championships in the mid 1960's?
A Cazzie Russell

Q What feat did the Illini accomplish against the San Francisco Dons in December of 1956?
A They ended the Dons' 60 game win streak 62-33 – the longest in the nation. San Francisco had won two national titles with Bill Russell.

Q Who were the big names on this '56 Illinois team?
A Don Ohl of **Edwardsville**, Bill Altenberger of **East St. Louis**, Harv Schmidt, and George BonSalle.

Q What team's 60 game home winning streak did Illinois break in 1968?
A Houston – beating them 97-84. This was coach Harv Schmitt's second season. Greg Jackson and Dave Scholz each scored 21 points.

Q Did the Illini have any 20-win seasons in the 1970's?
A No - they didn't have a single 20-win season, a Big Ten championship, or a trip to the NCAA Tournament. Illinois would go 18 consecutive years without a trip to the NCAA tournament.

Q What amazing feat was performed by Illinois' Dave Downey in a 1963 game against Indiana?
A He set the school record and Big Ten record by scoring 53 points.

Q What was the big downside to that day?
A The Illini lost 103-100 at Bloomington to a team led by Jimmy Rayl. Rayl was such a prolific shooter that teams started guarding him as soon as he crossed half court. The slim Rayl set the new conference mark with 56 points a week later.

Q What incident crushed Illini football and basketball hopes in the mid-1960s?

John Kerr

A The NCAA hit Illinois hard for illegally dispersing over $21,000 to football and basketball players in the "slush fund scandal." Seven football players and five basketball players were suspended. Seventeen other players involved had already completed their eligibility.

Q What scoring and rebounding Illini star was selected in the first round of the 1973 NBA draft by the Washington Bullets?
A Nick Weatherspoon

Q What Illinois coach holds the record for most wins his first year with the team?
A Lon Kruger's team went 22-10 in 1997 before Bruce Weber, the former coach of SIU **Carbondale,** went 26-7 in 2004.

Q What marks did Kiwane Garris set at the end of his career in 1997?
A He finished second as the all-time scorer with 1,948 points and took the record for most free throws attempted and made in a career.

Q What amazing feat was accomplished by Lon Kruger's 1998 team?
A They were picked to finish seventh but ended up with a share of the title. In the process, they went undefeated against Indiana, Iowa, and Michigan for the first time in the school's history.

Q What was amazing about the 1999 Big Ten tournament?
A Illinois entered the tournament seeded 11th (last) and went on to defeat three top 25 teams before losing to Michigan State, ranked second in the nation. Sergio McLain, Fess Hawkins and Damir Krupalija were on that team that finished the regular season 14-17.

Q Did this team have the most league losses in Illini history?
A Yes

Q Who led the Illini in scoring during the 2000-2001 season?
A Cory Bradford

Q Who were the Illini players that led Illinois to a big upset of Indiana in a February 2000 game at Assembly Hall, televised by ESPN?
A Frankie Williams, Cory Bradford, Lucas Johnson, Sergio McLain and Damir Krupalija led the way to a 87-63 win over the 16th ranked Hoosiers.

Q What was Lon Kruger's record against Indiana during his tenure?
A An impressive 6-2

Q What hurt Andy Kaufmann's career scoring marks at Illinois?
A He missed a year due to a blood clot in his shoulder.

Q Who were the starters on the 2001 Illinois team that went 27-8 and won a share of the Big Ten title?
A Marcus Griffin, Brian Cook, Sergio McLain, Cory Bradford and Frank Williams.

Q Who was the sixth man on that team?
A Robert Archibald

Q What was Robert Archibald's best game as an Illini?
A In the 2001 NCAA tourney against Arizona where he scored about 25 points.

Q Who were the starters on the 2002 Illini team that went 26-9 and won a share of the Big Ten Crown?
A Robert Archibald, Brian Cook, Lucas Johnson, Cory Bradford, Frank Williams.

Q Who was the sixth man on that team?
A Sean Harrington

Q Who were the starters on Illinois' 2003 team that went 25-7 and won the Big Ten tournament?
A Brian Cook, James Augustine, Roger Powell, Deron Williams and Dee Brown

Q Who were the key alternates on that team?
A Nick Smith and Luther Head

Q What is Nick Smith's biggest physical problem?
A He has asthma and sometimes misses practice.

Q Who were the starters on the 2004 Illini team?
A James Augustine, Roger Powell, Luther Head, Deron Williams, Dee Brown. Nick Smith was the 6th man.

Q In the last seven years, how many times has Illinois either won the Big Ten outright, shared the title, or won the Big Ten tournament?
A Five

Q Since 1979, how many losing seasons have the Illini had?
A Two – 1992 and 1999

Q After Lou Henson retired as coach of the Illini, he came back and coached another team. What was it?
A New Mexico State

Q Who lured Lon Kruger away from the Illini after the 1999-2000 season?
A The Atlanta Hawks of the NBA. They paid him a cool two million dollars.

Q Who then was named the 15th coach of the Illini?
A Bill Self who had an impressive record at Tulsa

Q What **Collinsville** High star played four years for the Illini, 1993-1996?
A Rich Keene

Q In the seven-year history of an end of the year Big Ten tournament, how many times has the number one seeded team won the tournament?
A Only Michigan State in 1999, and they went on to win their second national title.

Q What national rankings oddity existed in the Big Ten at the end of the regular 2003-2004 season?
A Wisconsin was ranked tenth in the nation despite the fact that Illinois – ranked number 12 – won the Big Ten title and had a better overall record.

Q Who holds the all-time career rebound mark for the Illini?
A Efrem Winters set the mark in 1986.

Q Did Illinois ever defeat number one ranked Michigan State, led by Magic Johnson?
A Yes. The Illini beat the Spartans 57-55 before the largest crowd up to then to ever watch an Illini home game (16,209). Sophomore Eddie Johnson hit the winning jumper.

Q What former Illini has more total career NBA points than Magic Johnson, Kevin McHale or Pete Maravich?
A Incredibly, it's Eddie Johnson of Chicago Westinghouse.

Q Who won the NBA's Sixth Man award in 1989?
A Eddie Johnson

Q What two Illini career records did Derek Harper own when he finished his three-year career at Illinois in 1983?
A He had the all-time career record for steals and assists.

Q What prep achievement did Floridian Harper have?
A He was a McDonald's All-American and the best guard in the nation.

Q What hurt Derek Harper's Illini career statistics the most?
A He left after his junior year for the NBA. He had 10 brothers and sisters at West Palm Beach and the family needed the money.

Q With what Texas NBA team did Harper play 11 ½ seasons?
A The Dallas Mavericks

Q How many overtimes did it take for Illinois to defeat Michigan at Champaign in January of 1984?

Jim Dawson, Harry Combes, Don Freeman

A   Four. The Illini beat the bigger, deeper Wolverines 75-66. Efrem Winters had 23 points.

Q   Who was the sophomore point guard for Illinois that day?
A   Bruce Douglas - **Quincy** High's All-American. He played all 60 minutes for an Illinois record that may never be equaled.

Q   How many wins in a row did Douglas lead his Quincy team?
A   Sixty-four

Q   What son of a former Illini star played on the 1984 team with Bruce Douglas?
A   Doug Altenberger of **Peoria**. His father, Bill Altenberger, played for Illinois back in the late 1950's.

Q   Who did Illinois lose to in the March, 1984 Elite Eight game?
A   Kentucky – 54-51. An ankle injury held Efrem Winters to just seven points; Quinn Richardson had 16 points and Doug Altenberger had 13.

Q   How many points did Doug Altenberger score in his final home game as a senior against Indiana?
A   Twenty in a nationally televised game in 1987. Ken Norman had 24 that day and Altenberger outplayed and outscored Indiana's Steve Alford. Illinois defeated 3rd ranked Indiana 69-67.

Q   What Illini won the Big Ten scoring title in 1990?
A   Kendall Gill with a 20.0 scoring average. He was the first Illini to do this since Andy Phillip in 1943.

Q   What Illini guard made All-Big Ten in 1998?
A   Kevin Turner of **Rockford**

Q   What sanctions did the NCAA impose on Illinois in November of 1990?
A   Three years probation and no post season play for a year.

Q   What started the NCAA investigation?
A   Charges that cash payments had been made to Deon Thomas and LaPhonso Ellis of **East St. Louis**

Q   Why was the February 23, 1991, Illini win over Iowa particularly satisfying?
A   It was an Iowa assistant coach that ratted Illinois to the NCAA. Andy Kaufmann scored 31 points. Rennie Clemons, Deon Thomas and Larry Smith were his teammates.

Nick Weatherspoon – courtesy U of I

Deon Thomas – courtesy U of I

Q   What was particularly offensive about the Iowa tactics?
A   Their assistant coach Bruce Pearl phoned Thomas and secretly taped the conversation. He asked Thomas what it was like to be offered $80,000 and a new car to play for Illinois.

Q   Why are Illini fans so loyal to Thomas?
A   The NCAA said that if he left Illinois they would drop the investigation. Thomas stuck it out for four years and became the team's all-time scorer.

Q   What other marks did the 6-9 Thomas set?
A   He had 177 blocked shots and 803 field goals.

Q   What NBA team drafted Thomas in the second round?
A   The Dallas Mavericks, but he played most of his pro ball with Spain in the European league.

Q   The 1995 Illini team ended what opponent's incredible home win streak?
A   Duke - Bryant Notree, Jerry Gee, Kiwane Garris and Rich Keene ended the Blue Devil's record of 96 wins in a row over non conference teams at Durham, 75-65. Mike Krzyzewski's team was ranked 12th and at one point late in the game led 60-59. Four steals by Keene and Garris turned the tide.

Q   How many seasons did Lou Henson coach the Illini?
A   Twenty-one years, retiring in 1996. He was 214-164 in conference games.

Q   Only 12 other coaches have done something Lou Henson did in the tournament playoffs. What was it?
A   He took two teams to the Final Four, including New Mexico State.

Q   How many first round NBA draft picks played for Lou Henson?
A   Five – Kendall Gill, Nick Anderson, Kenny Battle, Derek Harper, and Ken Norman

Q   When Lou Henson retired, what assistant coach assumed he would become the new head coach?
A   Popular Jimmy Collins. When Lon Kruger got the job Collins took the head coaching position at Illinois – Chicago.

Q   How did Collins' U of I at Chicago fare during the 2003-2004 basketball season?
A   They won 22 games, had a winning streak of 12 in a row, and made the NCAA tournament. Collins led the singing of "Take Me Out to the Ball Game" at several Cub games in April of 2004. (He can't sing, but who cares!)

Q   What was the long term connection between Lou Henson and assistant coach Jimmy Collins?
A   Collins played for Henson at New Mexico State

Q   When Kruger and Collins went head to head in a November 1996 battle at Chicago, which team won?
A   Illinois won 68-63

Q   How did Iowa almost pull off an incredible win at Champaign on February 4, 1993?
A   With about three seconds left and the score tied, an errant Iowa shot bounced off Deon Thomas' shoulder and went in, giving them a two-point lead.

Q   Who snatched victory from the jaws of defeat with 1.5 seconds left?
A   Senior Andy Kaufmann took a deep inbounds pass and sunk a three pointer at the buzzer. He finished with 25 points.

Q   What was Illinois' most embarrassing loss in the NCAA?
A   It was a one-point loss to Austin Peay in the first round in March of 1987. Illinois had a third seed but second team All-American Ken Norman missed a jumper at the buzzer. Illinois had another embarrassing tourney loss one year to Chattanooga.

Q   How well did Indiana coach Bobby Knight handle an 82-72 Illini win at Bloomington on February 24, 1988?
A   In a nationally televised game, Knight went berserk with three technicals and was ejected from the game.

Q   What was Illinois' second most embarrassing NCAA tourney loss?
A   It was a 1990 loss to 12th seeded Dayton. Had Nick Anderson not jumped ship and left for the pros, Kendall Gill, Marcus Liberty and Anderson probably would have gone to another Final Four.

Q   Who upset Illinois in the 1986 NCAA tourney?
A   Villanova

Q   What was Nick Anderson's best game as an Illini?
A   He had 35 points against Ohio State in 1989.

Q   How many points did Nick score in the regionals against Louisville and Syracuse?
A   He had 48 points and 21 rebounds.

Q   Why was coach Jim Boeheim criticized by locals after his Orangemen lost 89-86 to the Illini?
A   They blew a 12-point lead and were out-rebounded by a

smaller, banged up Illini team. Boeheim said the close win against Missouri took a lot out of his team.

Nick Anderson

Q   What NBA team did Nick Anderson play with for ten years?
A   Orlando Magic

Q   Why did Nick Anderson always wear number 25 at Illinois and in the NBA?
A   He wore it to honor his Chicago Simeon teammate Ben Wilson who was killed in a drive-by shooting.

Q   Name three things Nick Anderson and Marcus Liberty have in common during their Illini careers?
A   Both were Illinois prep products, both were Prop 48s (they couldn't play as freshmen) and both skipped their senior years to go to the NBA.

Q   What was probably the biggest factor in the heart-breaking 1989 loss to Michigan in the Final Four, a team Illinois had easily defeated twice?
A   Both Kenny Battle and Lowell Hamilton, the two seniors, played with severe ankle sprains.

Q   How strong was the Big Ten in 1988-89?
A   Very. Two-thirds of the way into the season Illinois at 15-0 was ranked 2nd, Michigan at 14-2 was ranked 4th, Iowa at 13-2 was ranked 8th, Ohio State 12-3 was ranked 15th. Indiana wasn't even in the top twenty at this point, yet they won the Big Ten title.

Q   What was Lou Henson's nickname imposed by the media that Final Four season?
A   "Lou Do," because his hairdo looked artificial.

Q   How did Illini fans turn the hair thing into a positive?
A   They brought signs and banners to games that read "Lou Can Do."

Q   What fashion trend did the Illini sport that 1988-89 season?
A   Their shorts were the length of baggy Bermudas. Incredibly, nearly every college and NBA team now sport the ragamuffin look.

Q   How many players on the 1989 fabulous Final Four Illini team were home grown products?
A   Everyone on the team played their prep ball in Illinois. Michigan had two Illinois players on their team.

Q   Who dubbed that Illinois team the Flying Illini?
A   ESPN announcer, Dick Vitale

Q   Did the 1989 team ever reach the number one ranking in the polls?

TOP 20

THIS WEEK		LAST WEEK
1	DUKE (13-0)	
2	ILLINOIS (15-0)	
3	GEORGETOWN (12-1)	
4	MICHIGAN (14-2)	
5	OKLAHOMA (13-2)	
6	UNLV (11-2)	
7	LOUISVILLE (12-2)	
8	IOWA (13-2)	
9	NORTH CAROLINA (14-3)	
10	SYRACUSE (14-3)	
11	SETON HALL (15-1)	
12	ARIZONA (11-2)	
13	FLORIDA STATE (12-1)	
14	MISSOURI (14-3)	
15	OHIO STATE (12-3)	
16	N.C. STATE (11-1)	
17	STANFORD (12-3)	
18	GEORGIA TECH (10-4)	
19	KANSAS (14-2)	
20	TENNESSEE (11-2)	

A Yes, after their record was 17-0. They were the only undefeated Division I school in the country at the time. They finished at 31-5.

Q What was the last Illinois team before that to reach number one?
A The 1953 team

Q How long did the 1988-89 team hold the number one ranking?
A One week. Kendall Gill broke his foot in the overtime win against Georgia Tech and Illinois lost the next game.

Q What was the team's most incredible shot that season?
A Nick Anderson's 30-foot buzzer beater at Indiana. The Hoosiers tied the score with no time on the clock. Time had run out, but **Alton** official Ed Hightower put two seconds back on the scoreboard. Steve Bardo threw a long baseball pass to Anderson and the rest was history.

Q How poorly did Bardo, Hamilton, and Smith play in this game?
A After the first 28 minutes they were a combined 0-22.

Q In the 1988-89 season Kendal Gill, Nick Anderson, Kenny Battle and company were 17-0 at one point, yet they did not win the conference title. How did that happen?
A When Kendal Gill got hurt Illinois lost four conference games. Indiana, with three losses, won the Big Ten. Michigan, which won the NCAA Tourney, finished third.

Q What four Big Ten teams beat Illinois in the regular season that year?
A Iowa, Minnesota, Purdue and Wisconsin

Q How many Big Ten games did Kendall Gill play in 1988-89?
A Only six, but he was there to help "cream" Michigan twice.

Q Where was Illinois ranked nationally at the end of the regular season?
A Third – with a 27-4 record

Q What was the Flying Illini's biggest weakness?
A Lack of size. Their tallest player was Lowell Hamilton, slightly taller than 6-6. Nearly every one of Michigan's starters was taller. Fortunately, the Illini starters could all jump like Michael Jordan.

Q What was Illinois' biggest problem against Louisville in the regionals in 1989?
A Taller Louisville blocked 13 shots

Kenny Battle

Q How many times has Illinois been to the Final Four?
A Four times –1949, 1951, 1952, 1989

Q Who is the "forgotten man" on the 1988-89 team?
A Andy Kaufmann was sidelined midseason with a blood clot.

Q How close did Illinois come to winning the game in Seattle against Michigan?
A Kenny Battle of **Aurora**, who had 29 points, tied the game 81-81 with 30 seconds left. Michigan put in a rebound shot with 2 seconds left to win.

Q How many lead changes were in the game?
A Thirty-three

Q What connection did Steve Fisher, Michigan's interim coach, have with the state of Illinois?
A He was a native of **Herrin** and played for Illinois State; he also started his career as a high school coach in Illinois.

Steve Bardo

Q What was Illinois' record against the teams that made it to the Sweet Sixteen in 1989?
A 8-1 - Michigan's record was 4-5 but Michigan played superbly once they got into the tournament.

Q Was bench strength an Illinois weaknesses in 1989?
A They had an average bench; they weren't great shooters; they were average at the foul line

Q What were the Illini's main strengths in 1989?
A Excellent defense, great leaping ability, great in transition, great team speed and quickness; gritty and determined

Q Who did most sportswriters and computers pick to win the tournament?
A Illinois. Once Michigan got by Illinois they were favored to win because they were tall and had led the nation in field goal percentage two year in a row.

Q Why do many Illini fans fault Henson's strategy at the end of the Michigan game?
A They say the team should have used up about 15 seconds trying to make a steal and failing that, commit a foul. That way you have two chances to win. If Michigan only sinks one free throw, a two pointer wins it. If they sink both, a two pointer sends it into overtime and a three

pointer wins it. With the strategy Henson employed, there was no chance to win the game in regulation.

Q Was Michigan's superior height a problem for the Illini in the game?
A Yes. They scored five baskets in the last five minutes – all inside shots.

Q How good was the Illini team defensively that season?
A They had 341 steals, beating the old school record by 31

Q How many dunks did the Flying Illini have that season?
A 171 – disdaining easy layups

Q What was their biggest come-from-behind deficit that year?
A They were down by 18 to Mizzou in the annual "bragging rights" game back in December.

Q What other name do Illini fans have for the "bragging rights" game?
A "Border War"

Q Did this Flying Illini team set the school record for total points in a single game?
A Yes – 127 against LSU. They broke 100 eight times that year.

Q What was their shooting percentage against LSU that night?
A 68 percent – incredible for an away game. They were shooting 73 percent until Henson put in the substitutes.

Q What annual award is named for Kenny Battle?
A It's called the "Hustle and Grit Award."

Q What Illini defensive record did Kenny Battle set in 1988-89?
A Most steals in a season – 89; truly amazing for a forward

Q What former Illini currently does the color commentary on radio broadcasts?
A Steve Bardo of **Carbondale**

Q What Illinois basketball player won "Defensive Player of the Year" in 1985 and '86?
A Bruce Douglas, a long-armed guard

Q What Illini has the second highest total of points scored in a single game?
A **Jacksonville's** Andy Kaufmann had 46 against Wisconsin in 1990.

Q Assembly Hall opened in 1963. Where does it rank in age compared to other Big Ten arenas?
A Only two are older – Minnesota's Williams Arena (1928) and Northwestern's Welsh-Ryan Arena (1951)

Q What NBA team was Illini basketball star **Brian Cook** with in 2004?
A The L. A. Lakers. The rookie saw some playing time when Karl Malone was injured, but then he broke a finger and went back to the bench.

Q Kiwane Garris had a spectacular game against Mizzou in an annual Bragging Rights game a few years ago. Although he scored over 30 points, what do Illinois fans remember most about his performance in that game?
A With the score tied and no time remaining on the clock, Garris missed two free throws and Illinois lost in triple overtime, 108-107. He went from hero to goat.

Q What did Garris receive in the mail two weeks later?

Preston Pearson

A Two bricks from Columbia, Missouri. Ironically, the incident motivated Garris to never let his team down again at the end of a game. He went on to make 615 free throws, the most in team history.

Q Who sank the most three-pointers in Illini history?
A Cory Bradford (327) took the title away from Rich Keene (237).

Q What Illini announcer thinks Kiwane Garris was the best point guard in Illini history?
A Doug Altenberger

Q Did Kiwane Garris ever play in an NCAA tournament game?
A Yes. Illinois defeated Southern Cal 90-77 at Charlotte in 1997.

Q What was Lon Kruger's best win in 1997-1998?
A A February 12 Assembly Hall whipping of Tom Izzo's 12th ranked Michigan State Spartans, 84-63. Kevin Turner, Brian Johnson, point guard Matt Heldman of **Libertyville**, and Jerry Hester were on that team.

Kendall Gill

Q What member of that championship team lost his life in a car wreck?
A Matt Heldman

Q What near miracle enabled Illinois to get a share of the Big Ten title in the 1997-98 season?
A Purdue upset Michigan State 99-96 in overtime in the last game of the season.

Q What was coach Lon Kruger's record at Illinois in four seasons?
A 81-41 – not bad

Q Who did the Fighting Illini basketball team defeat to win the Big Ten tournament in 2003?
A Ohio State. Illinois finished second to Wisconsin in the conference race.

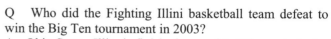

Q   What member of the Fighting Illinois roundball team was the Big Ten scoring champion in 2003?
A   Brian Cook

Q   Who is the tallest person ever to play for the Illini?
A   Nick Smith, who was on the 2004 Big Ten championship team. He stands about 7 feet 2 inches.

Q   When there was a technical foul and the 2004 Illinois team could send their best free throw shooter to the line, who did coach Bruce Weber choose?
A   Amazingly the tall timbered Nick Smith got the nod because he was the best free throw shooter on the team.

Q   When Illinois lost their final game to Wisconsin in the Big Ten tournament title game, how bad did this hurt them in the NCAA tourney selection?
A   The selection committee admitted that the late afternoon game was not considered in the process. Illinois drew a number five seed and played Murray State as a first round opponent.

Q   How bad did losing coach Bill Self to Kansas at the end of the 2003 season hurt Illini recruiting?
A   A lot, or so Illini fans thought. After Self left, Illinois lost Villenueva, one of the top players in the country, verbally committed to Illinois, to Connecticut, which won the title. However, that scholarship instead went to Calvin Brock, "Mr. Chicago Basketball."

Q   How many 20-win seasons has the Illini basketball team had the last four years?
A   They have won 20 games or more each year and three of the years they ended up winning the title. The only year they didn't win (losing out to Wisconsin) they won the end of the year Big Ten Tournament.

Q   What NBA team had both Kendall Gill and Glen Rice of Michigan on its roster?
A   Charlotte Hornets

Q   What NCAA shooting record does Cory Bradford have?
A   Hitting a three point shot in 88 consecutive games

Q   What Illini holds the team record for making 39 free throws in a row?
A   Kiwane Garris

Q   What Illini has the record for career three point field goal percentage?
A   Doug Altenberger at .475 percent

Q   What Illini has the team record for free throw per-

centage in a single season?
A   Brian Cook with 87.3

Jerry Hester

Q   What is generally the biggest complaint of Illinois football and basketball fans?
A   The Illini seem to lose many of the best prep players to teams in other states. A good example was Chicagoan Isiah Thomas going to Indiana and Cazzie Russell going to Michigan. Another problem is the inability to obtain good seating locations at home games.

Q   How many years in a row has Illinois led the Big Ten in scoring?
A   Four – 2001-2004

Q   What four Illinois teams made it to the NCAA tourney in 2004 – the most ever?
A   Illinois, DePaul, Southern Illinois, and Illinois Chicago

Coach Lon Kruger

Q   What team defeated DePaul?
A   Vanderbilt of Tennessee

Q   What team did Illinois defeat in the first round?
A   Murray State of Kentucky

Q   What four concerns did Illinois coach Bruce Weber have going into the game against Cincinnati?
A   They were ranked ahead of Illinois, were taller, more physical, and they were one of the best defensive clubs nationally.

Q   What rankled Illini players about the tournament selection committee in 2004?
A   They gave the Big Ten champions a lowly 5th seed.

Q   Did Illinois struggle in the first half vs. Cincinnati?
A   No – the Illini demoralized the Bearcats as they raced to an early lead, widened it to as much as 24 points with two minutes left, and led 49-33 at the buzzer.

Q   How good was Illini shooting in the first half?
A   With two minutes to go they were shooting at a 72 percent clip. Cincinnati cut into the lead with an 8-0 run by hitting a basket and two three pointers. Illinois finished at 19 out of 29.

Q   How many shots did Deron Williams miss the first half?
A   None

Q   What was the final score?
A   92-68

Q   Was this the most points Illinois had ever scored in an NCAA tourney game?

A Yes

Q What was Illinois' shooting percentage at the end of the game?
A 63.6 %

Q What other Illinois player had a sensational game?
A Junior forward Roger Powell was 9-11 shooting and finished with 22 points.

Q Who led the Illini in assists with nine?
A Luther Head; Dee Brown had eight

Q What freshman Illini made a couple of back-to-back three pointers?
A Richard McBride

Q What was the most spectacular play of the game?
A Dee Brown's behind-the-back fast break lay-up

Q What did Dee Brown have to say about Cincinnati's attempts to intimidate the Illini with "trash talk?"
A "Trash talk? Is that supposed to intimidate me? Come on, now. I'm from Chicago."

Q How did Illinois do in the assist and turnover department?
A They finished the game with 26 assists and only four turnovers, two each half.

Q How big a win was this for the Illinois program?
A It was their 22nd NCAA tournament win and the **first time they had defeated an opponent ranked ahead of them**.

Q Who led the way for Illinois in the first half?
A Deron William had 17 points, many from 3-point range.

Q Who was the tallest *starter* on this 2003-04 Illini squad?
A James Augustine at 6-10.

Q How many points did Deron Williams score?
A He finished with 31.

Q What was the score of the Illinois Sweet Sixteen game against Duke in March of 2004?
A Illinois played poorly and lost, 72-62.

Illinois 92, Cincinnati 68

ILLINOIS

	min	FG	FT	reb o-t	a	pf	pts
Augustine	28	5-6	1-2	2-3	0	3	11
Powell	37	9-11	3-3	0-0	0	2	22
Head	36	2-5	2-2	0-5	9	2	6
D. Williams	31	10-13	5-7	0-3	7	2	31
Brown	35	6-12	0-0	0-3	8	0	14
Spears	1	0-1	0-0	0-0	0	0	0
Howard	2	0-1	0-0	0-0	0	0	0
McBride	10	2-3	0-0	0-0	0	1	6
Nkemdi	2	0-0	0-0	0-0	0	0	0
Carter	2	0-0	0-0	0-1	0	0	0
Randle	4	0-0	0-0	0-1	0	2	0
Smith	10	1-3	0-0	0-4	1	1	2
Ingram	2	0-0	0-0	0-0	1	1	0
Totals	200	35-55	11-14	2-20	26	14	92

▶Shooting Percentages: FG .636, FT .786.
▶3-Point FG: 11-19, .579 (D.Williams 6-8, McBride 2-3, Brown 2-5, Powell 1-1, Head 0-2).
▶Team Rebounds: 1. Turnovers: 4.
▶Blocked Shots: 1. Steals: 9.

CINCINNATI

	min	FG	FT	reb o-t	a	pf	pts
Kirkland	25	3-7	0-1	2-2	5	1	6
Maxiell	36	6-10	3-5	4-8	1	2	15
Johnson	20	2-3	2-3	2-5	0	2	6
F. Williams	33	6-13	0-0	0-3	1	3	16
White	17	0-4	0-0	2-4	4	0	0
Moore	3	0-1	0-0	0-0	1	0	0
Meeker	1	0-0	0-0	0-1	0	0	0
N. Williams	13	0-0	0-0	0-0	0	1	0
Hicks	19	3-6	2-2	2-6	0	0	8
Bobbitt	29	6-12	0-0	1-4	2	3	15
Whaley	4	1-2	0-0	0-0	0	2	2
Totals	200	27-58	7-11	13-33	14	14	68

▶ Shooting Percentages: FG .466, FT .636.
▶3-Point FG: 7-16, .438 (F.Williams 4-8, Bobbitt 3-7, Moore 0-1).

Q Who played well in the game?
A Augustine and Powell each had 15; Dee Brown had 14 but was playing with a fractured foot.

Q Who had terrible games?
A Nick Smith and Deron Williams were pathetic. And the bench was a negative rather than a positive.

Q What was the only category in which the Illini did well?
A Offensive rebounding

Q How many trips to the NCAA Sweet Sixteen has Illinois had in the last four years?
A Three

Q What are the prospects for the 2004-2005 Illini?
A All the starters from this year will be back.

ILLINOIS RAILROADS

Q What Illinois town is noted for its railroad collection where fans can ride streetcars, diesels, and steam engines?
A **Union**

Q What was the first railroad in the state?
A The Illinois & St. Louis was built in 1837 by a syndicate headed by Vital Jarrot and former governor John Reynolds. It hauled coal seven-eight miles from the east bluffs at **Illinoistown** down to the Wiggins Ferry on the Mississippi River. The line originally ran on wooden rails across Grand Marais Lake and had coal cars that were pulled by mules.

Q What was the first people railroad in the state?
A The Northern Cross that ran between **Meredosia** and **Springfield**. It eventually connected both east-west borders at **Quincy** in the west and **Danville** in the east and going through **Decatur, Clayton, Mount Sterling,** and **Jacksonville**.

Q What railroad closely paralleled the Illinois and Michigan Canal?
A The Rock Island & Chicago

Q In 1837 the state legislature passed the historic Internal Improvements Act calling for the creation of a Central Railroad running north-south and four cross lines running east-west. What was the outcome?
A By 1840 the state was $14 million in debt, nearly bankrupting the state. Only 24 miles of railroad had been completed. Illinois got out of the railroad business and left development up to private enterprise.

Q Did Abe Lincoln and Stephen Douglas support this fiasco?
A Yes

Q Before Standard Time for railroads was adopted in 1883, how did people with pocket watches know if their timepiece was slow or fast?
A Each town dropped a large "time ball" at noon from a tower or the roof of a prominent building.

Chicago & Alton Railroad Depot – Illinois State Hist. Library

Q How did Abe Lincoln and a number of other Illinois legislators survive getting stuck in a blizzard while riding a train in 1855?
A They built a fire and used one of the cars on the train for kindling.

Q What was the longest railroad in the world in 1860?
A The Illinois Central

Q Besides water towers, what other structure was seen at frequent intervals along Illinois railroad tracks?
A Grain elevators

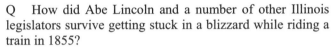

Chicago, Burlington & Quincy Depot at Oregon, Illinois

Q What was the famous slogan of the Illinois Central?
A "The Main Line of America"

Q When Sears started its catalog business, how did customers receive their mail order purchases?
A They picked them up at the local railroad depot.

Q What were "milk stops" for trains?
A Trains picked up milk cans from small towns every morning for fast delivery to larger cities.

Q What is unusual about the brick depots built by the Illinois Central in **Ashley** and **Arcola**?
A They were identical.

Q What state led the nation with miles of railroad track in the 1870's and 1880's?
A Illinois with over 10,000 miles of track

Q What town in Livingston County is noted for one of the worst train wrecks in state history, killing 85 people?
A **Chatsworth** - 1887

Q What town marked the highest point in Illinois on the Norfolk & Western Railroad and was called Fat Hill?
A **Cerro Gordo** in Piatt County

Q What **Tamaroa** resident used the Illinois Central to help slaves escape to freedom?
A B.G. Roots, an abolitionist who helped survey the line from **Centralia** to **Cairo**. The tracks were conveniently laid within 200 yards of his house.

Q What railroad marks the northern limits of southern Illinois?
A The Baltimore & Ohio

Q Where were the first steel rails in the country made?
A In Chicago – 1865

Q What was the first railroad bridge across the Mississippi?
A The Chicago, Burlington & Quincy built the bridge in 1856, much to the dismay of steamboat interests.

Q **Bellevillians** were crushed in the 1850's when what railroad from the East bypassed them and went through **Lebanon** and **O'Fallon** instead?
A The Ohio & Mississippi

Q What 14 mile long railroad connected **Belleville** and St. Louis in 1854?
A The Belleville & Illinoistown

Q The town of **Mendota** had the advantage of being at the crossroads of what two early rail lines?
A The Northern Cross and Illinois Central

Q Who was president of the Cairo & Vincennes Railroad?
A A.E. Burnside of Civil War fame, the man whose mutton chop whiskers gave us the term "sideburns"

Q The town of **Sandoval** had the advantage of being at the crossroads of what two early rail lines?
A The Ohio & Mississippi and the Illinois Central

Q Did the state ever build a railroad after the passage of the 1837 Internal Improvements Bill?
A Yes – a 51-mile long railroad from **Meredosia** on the Illinois River to **Springfield**. It was sold at public auction by the state a few years later for $21,000, much less than what it had cost to build. Had the state held on to it for five more years, it would have been worth twenty times the amount it received.

Q In 1950, what Illinois city was the second largest rail center in the world?
A **East St. Louis** - with twenty-seven railroads converging on it; only Chicago had more with about thirty-three.

Q   What was Abraham Lincoln's connection to the Illinois Central Railroad?
A   He was retained as an attorney for legal advice and he also defended the railroad's interests in several court cases.

Q   What railroad went through **Mokena**, Illinois?
A   Rock Island – Mokena comes from an Indian word that means "turtle."

Q   What famous English writer lost money in his 1837 investment in the Cairo City & Canal Company that planned to build a railroad from **Cairo** to **Galena**?
A   Charles Dickens – who came to Illinois to visit his brother (in St. Louis) and check out his investment; he wrote about Illinois in stinging rebuke in *American Notes* and *Martin Chuzzlewit*

Q   What is the origin of the railroad track width that is called "standard gauge" (4 ft. 8 ½ inches)?
A   It is the same width as the spacing of wheels on the old Roman chariots.

Q   In 1850, how many miles of railroad track were there in Illinois?
A   111

Q   Why did the metal rails used to build the Illinois Central in the 1850's have to be reheated and reshaped?
A   Our nation's iron and steel industry was in its infancy, so many of the rails were shipped from England. To better fit in the hold of a ship, they came here in a U-shape.

Q   What is the purpose of round domes that are seen perched on top of the old steam engines?
A   These domes often contained sand that was placed on rails when additional traction was needed.

Q   What kind of speedometer was used on the old steam engines?
A   They had none. Engineers made a guesstimate of speed by counting the amount of time it took to go from one mile marker to the next, or from one telephone pole to the tenth one down the line.

Q   What **Rushville** native (Schyler Cnty.) became a railroad builder and had a university in Iowa named for him?
A   Francis Drake – Drake College, famous for the Drake Relays track event; his railroads were big competitors of the Chicago, Burlington & Quincy.

Q   What Chicagoan was the **founder of the railway mail service in the USA**?

Central & Eastern Illinois Railroad – Ill. State Hist. Lib.

Chicago & Northwestern depot at Belvidere

A   George Armstrong – he established the system of sorting mail in traveling railroad cars in 1864.

Q   What Chicagoan was the first president of the Chicago & Galena Railroad, the Chicago & Northwestern Railroad, and the Union Pacific?
A   William Ogden – Chicago's first mayor

Q   What railroad man had a town in Illinois and a town in Missouri named for him?
A   John **O'Fallon**

Q   What was the first railroad from the East to reach Chicago?
A   The Northern Indiana Railroad in 1852

Q   What were the twelve most important Illinois railroads in 1860?
A   Illinois Central; Galena & Chicago Union; Chicago, Alton & St. Louis; Terre Haute, Alton & St. Louis; Great Western; Chicago & Rock Island; Logansport, Peoria & Burlington; Ohio & Mississippi (B&O); Chicago, Burlington & Quincy; Quincy & Chicago; Peoria & Oquawka; Chicago & Northwestern

Q   Approximately how many telephone poles along a railroad track equal a mile?
A   Forty

Q   Why were torpedoes placed on the tracks before the arrival of an approaching train?
A   As the engine passed over the torpedo it would explode and let officials know that another train was in front of it. Torpedoes had lead straps on them so they could be wrapped around a rail so as not to fall off. Railroad officials often carried them in empty Bull Durham sacks or in their coat pockets.

Q   What order did President Blanchard of Knox College in **Galesburg** give in 1850 to the local rail officials?
A   Not to run the train on Sunday and violate the Puritan Sabbath – the order was ignored.

Q   The destruction of Southern railroads was important to the Union victory in the Civil War. What were **Sherman neckties**?
A   During Sherman's "march to the sea" from Atlanta to Savannah, tracks were torn up and dismantled. To prevent rails from being reused, huge bonfires were built with the ties. Rails were heated in the middle and wrapped around the tree in the shape of a string necktie.

Q   What was rule G?
A   In the early days of railroading, there were no rules about employees drinking alcohol on the job. Rule G,

forbidding alcohol use while working, was implemented around 1910.

Q What was the "crane with the broken neck?"
A It was a subtle device used by railroad owners to "black-list" workers that had been active in union organizing. When such workers quit or were fired, they were given a letter with their service record on it. What they didn't know was that if their record was clean, the letter had a watermark on it that depicted a crane. For undesirables, their letter had a watermark of a crane with a broken neck. Watermarks can be seen by holding the paper up to a light.

Q Why were railroad "bulls" or policemen so hard on hoboes and tramps that endeavored to ride the rails for free?
A Because regular police weren't interested, and the scavengers sometimes turned into thieves. Railroad bulls put fear into the hearts of the vagrants by beating them, shooting them, or by tossing them off the train while it was moving.

Q How did the old steam trains improve on their time by eliminating frequent stops for water?
A When passenger trains went long distances time was important. A unique system was devised to eliminate the need to stop for water. The tender had a special scoop mechanism that picked up water in metal troughs below the tracks at designated points. Trains were able to secure the water on the fly, eliminating the need for stopping.

NY, Chicago & St. Louis Nickel Plate

Picking up water that way made a big splash. On one occasion there was a hobo catching a free ride on a freight train that secured water in this manner. He was drenched to the bone by the spatter. It happened in the dead of winter, and by the time the train arrived at its destination, **he was frozen stiff as a board.**

Q How much water did it take for a typical steam engine to travel 15 miles in 1869?
A An astounding 1,000 gallons of water

Q Where did hoboes like to hide and hitch rides on passenger trains?
A In the oblong battery boxes that hung beneath passenger coaches midway of the car length. The batteries were needed to furnish power for the lighting system of the train. Hoboes could usually find one box that was empty.

Q Did vagrants and migrant workers try to hitch rides on the cow catcher?

A Not often, but here is Glen Mullen's account of an 1890 ride. "I hops on the cow catcher and nobody saw me, and when the engine snorted out, there was yours truly smilin' like a basket o' chips. But I didn't smile long. That was a passenger engine and it kicked up an awful wind. Open yer mouth and she'd blow you wrong side out, and so cold she felt like an icicle laid against your eyeballs. The headlight attracted all the bugs in Kansas. My mouth, eyes, and shirt got full of 'em. One bloaty hoptoad jumped up from between the rails ahead of me and hit me smack between the eyes."

Q Did railroad detectives have nicknames for tramps?
A Yes – a *Timber* disguised his begging by selling pencils; a *Wangy* disguised begging by selling shoestrings; an *Alkee Stiff* was a drunkard; a *Shine* was a colored vagabond; a *Hay Bag* was a female vagrant; a *Blinkey* was a train rider who lost one eye.

Q What famous female railroad hitchhiker wrote a book called *Sister Of The Road*?
A "Boxcar Bertha"

Q What name did the Indians give to trains?
A Iron Horse

Q What are some examples of railroad jargon?
A Pike = rail line; hog = engine; reefer = refrigerator car; hotshot = fast train; drag = slow freight; Yardmaster = man who assembles trains in the yards; Hoghead = engineer; roundhouse = garage for storing and repairing engine; turntable = motorized platform, often at the roundhouse, that turned the engines around; car toads = car repairers; glory wagon = caboose; ground hogs = brakemen; lizard scorchers = cooks; monkeys = bridge workers; monkey suit = trainman's uniform; mud hops = yard clerks

Q When did engineers ring the locomotive bell?
A As they pulled into stations and at crossings

Q What was one of the shortest rail lines in Illinois?
A The 12.7 mile **Hooppole, Yorktown & Tampico**

Q What was the railroad man's prayer?
A "Now that I have flagged Thee, lift up my feet from the road of life and plant them safely on the deck of the train of salvation. Let me use the safety lamp of prudence, make all couplings with the link of love, let my hand-lamp be the Bible, and keep all switches closed that lead off the main line into the sidings with blind ends. Have every semaphore white along the line of hope, that I may make the run of life without stopping. Give me the Ten

Commandments as a working card, and when I have finished the run on schedule time and pulled into the terminal, may Thou, superintendent of the universe, say, 'well done, good and faithful servant; come into the general office to sign the pay roll and receive your check for happiness.' "

Q   In railroad parlance, what is a frog?
A   A device permitting the wheels on one rail of track to cross an intersecting rail

Q   Were trains ever wrecked on purpose as an exhibition?
A   Yes – back in 1896 W.G. Crush of the MKT line in Texas decided to stage a head on collision between locomotives as a promotion.   A place with a natural amphitheater was chosen as the site and with heavy advertising, a city of 30,000 people existed for one day.   Newspapers labeled it Crush City.   Engineers backed the locomotives up until they were two miles apart.   The two trains charged down the tracks with whistles shrieking at one another.   The crowd gasped in horror, realizing the two men were going to be killed.   At the last second both men slammed on the brakes and the behemoths shuddered to a stop, their cow-catchers clanging together. A roar went up from the crowd as they now perceived how spectacular the real thing was going to be.   Both trains returned to the starting positions.   Once more the whistles let out a yell – this time a death scream.   The engineers got the trains rolling and then set the throttles on wide open before they jumped. The two trains came together in a mighty crash.   A spectacular boiler explosion followed.   Clouds of smoke and dust leapt skyward.
    Then tragedy struck.   A man who had climbed a tree for a better view was hit in the head and killed by a piece of flying iron.   And a piece of chain flew through the air and struck a girl, killing her instantly.

Q   Did such an event ever take place in Illinois?
A   Yes – in 1931 the Rutland, **Toluca** & Northern, a short line, found itself bankrupt.   A train wreck was staged near **Magnolia**, Illinois, as a fund raiser to pay off creditors.

Q   What were some odd laws passed concerning railroads?
A   A Kansas law said: "When two trains approach each other at a crossing, they shall both come to a full stop and neither shall start up until the other has gone."   In South Dakota it was illegal to set firecrackers on a rail, "especially if you touch a match unto it."   In Montana it was illegal to show the movie, *The Great Train Robbery*.   Alabama's citizens were not allowed to wave a red flag at a train if there was no danger present.

Illinois rail lines in 1900

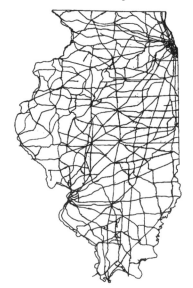

Q   What is the legend of John Henry?
A   John Henry was a steel driver, the man who hammers steel into a rock to bore a hole for explosives.   When the steam drill was invented, he was offended and challenged it to a race – man against machine.   For 35 minutes the great Negro, with a 20-pound hammer in each hand, slung them down on the steel, driving them into the rock.   When the contest was over, Henry, who worked for the Chesapeake & Ohio, had drilled two holes, each seven feet deep.   The steam drill had but one hole, nine feet deep.   According to the legend, the effort was supposed to have killed John Henry as he died from a stroke later that evening.

Q   Why did railroad men use flares?
A   They were dropped from a moving train to protect the rear.   When an engineer comes across one he is supposed to halt his train until the flare burns out.   Flares burn for about a ten-minute span.

Q   In railroad lingo, what are fishplates?
A   Metal plates that connect the rails

Springfield Railroad Depot 1947: Illinois State Historical Society

Q   What was the biggest railroad in the world?
A   Paul Bunyan had a brother named Cal who built the biggest railroad. Each rail tie was made from a giant redwood tree. Boulders were used for ballast.   The rivets for the engine boiler were 24 inches in diameter, and the boiler-makers drove them in place by firing canons at them.   The engine was so large that the fireman's scoop shovel held two tons. The gigantic train could haul 700 huge cars at a time.   On its first run, the **friction** burned up the rails and the train went so fast it defied the laws of gravity and flew off into outer space and was forever lost.

Q   Are there any "Illinois specific" verses to "The Wabash Cannonball?"
A   Yes – "Great cities of importance/ We reach upon our way/ Chicago and St. Louis/ **Rock Island**, so they say/ Then **Springfield** and **Decatur**/ **Peoria** above all/ We reach them by no other/ But the Wabash Cannonball"

Q   Who wrote the song, "Wabash Cannonball?"

A Illinoisan Billy Grammer, born in Franklin County in 1925; he also wrote "Gotta Travel On" and "Bonaparte's Retreat." He currently lives on a farm between **Valier** and **Sesser**.

Q What was the slogan of the Chicago & Alton Railroad?
A "The Only Way"

Q What is unusual about the logo of the Chicago & Northwestern Railroad?
A The word Northwestern slashes across a circle in a *northeastward* slant instead of northwestward.

Q What was unusual about the rail lines of the Chicago & Northwestern?
A It was the only major rail line in the country that operated left-handed; on double tracks its trains kept to the left instead of to the right.

Q How did the Nickel Plate Railroad get its name?
A The New York, Chicago & St. Louis was built in 1882 to be a competitor of the Lake Shore & Michigan Southern. Commodore Vanderbilt bought the line a year later and commented that for the price that was paid, it should have been nickel-plated, and that was the name that stuck.

Q How did people get killed walking on railroad bridges?
A Rail bridges were usually wide enough to only accommodate the width of the train. People walking on the bridges were sometimes taken by surprise and couldn't make it to the other end before the train caught up with them. Sections of planking were often removed from bridges to discourage pedestrian use.

Q When was the famous ballad "Casey Jones" popular in this country?
A Between 1906 and 1917, long after Illinois Central engineer Jones was killed in 1900

> Come, all you rounders, I want you to hear
> The story told of a brave engineer;
> Casey Jones was the rounder's name.
> On a high right-wheeler he rode to fame.

Q What connection did Casey Jones have to the Chicago Columbian Exposition of 1893?
A He operated a shuttle train from Van Buren Street to the Fair site.

Q Were engineers allowed to decorate their locomotives according to their own choosing?
A Yes – Jones trademark was a six-tone calliope whistle like a great whippoorwill: kaaaaseeeeeeeeejooooooooooones!

> The switchman knew by the whistle's moans
> That the man at the throttle was Casey Jones.

Chicago & Northwestern Depot 1959: Illinois State Historical Soc.

Q When Casey Jones was killed, how fast was he going before he realized that four cars from another train were sticking out from a siding onto the main line?
A Seventy miles an hour in an effort to be on time

Q Why wasn't Jones' fireman killed in the crash?
A He jumped

Q Why was Jones considered a hero in this crash?
A When they found Jones' body his hand was clutching the brake control.

Q Who wrote the lyrics to the "Ballad of Casey Jones?"
A Wallace Saunders, a Negro engine-wiper in the Illinois Central Railroad shops

Q What caused railroads to start installing sand boxes on their engines?
A There was a **plague of locusts** in 1836 and at first workers tried to clear the tracks with brooms but to no avail. The liquid from the crushed bodies made the rails slippery. Someone finally hit upon the idea of a mechanism that sprinkled sand on the tracks ahead of the wheels for traction.

Q Early railroads south of Illinois had a tendency to lay tracks using broad gauge. How wide are broad gauge tracks?
A Five feet

Q Why were narrow gauge tracks often used in mountainous regions out west?
A Narrow gauge allows for sharper curves.

Q What train company was known as the Military Tract Railroad?
A The Chicago, Burlington & Quincy, because of the section of land around **Quincy** called the Military Tract

Q What were gandy dancers?
A Irishmen employed to lay track - they often sang and did a little jig while performing their task.

Q Besides the *Green Diamond*, what other two Illinois Central passenger trains ran daily from St. Louis to Chicago (1936-58)?
A *Daylight* and *Night Diamond* (with sleeping cars)

Milwaukee Road passenger train in Chicago

Q What Chicago & Alton passenger trains ran daily from Chicago to St. Louis?
A *Alton Limited, Abraham Lincoln, Ann Rutledge, Midnight Special*

Q What two passenger trains did the Chicago & Eastern Illinois run daily from Chicago to St. Louis?
A *Zipper* and *Silent Knight*

Q Were *Blue Bird* and *Banner Blue*, the Wabash passenger trains from Chicago to St. Louis, painted blue?
A Yes

Q How many stops did the *Green Diamond* make between Chicago and St. Louis?
A Nine   (yes, it was painted green)

Q What was the fastest speed attained by the *Green Diamond* on its runs?
A Eighty-three mph

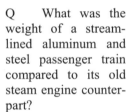

Tunnel Hill in southern Illinois (S. I. Tour.)

Q What was unusual about the *Green Diamond's* mail car?
A It contained a railway post office where letters were postmarked and delivered on arrival.

East St. Louis Junction Railroad courtesy Mark Godwin of Lebanon

Q What was the weight of a streamlined aluminum and steel passenger train compared to its old steam engine counterpart?
A It weighed 230 tons, half that of the steam engine type.

Q How many passengers could the *Green Diamond* carry?
A 100

Q What were the dining specialties of the *Bluebird* and *Green Diamond*?
A The *Bluebird* served world famous chicken pot pie and the *Green Diamond* served shrimp Creole.

Q How long did it take for the *Green Diamond* to make its 294-mile run from Chicago to St. Louis?
A About five hours

Q The five-car *Green Diamond* was "articulated." What did that mean?
A The cars were permanently joined.

Q What was the route of the *Twentieth Century Limited* and *Broadway Limited*?
A They ran from Chicago to New York

Q What irritants did passengers on early trains have to endure?
A The soot from the engine blackened their faces, and the sparks stuck to their clothing and ruined it.

Q What Northern Illinois town in Ogle County has a Railroad Park where the Burlington Northern, Santa Fe and Union Pacific crossed?
A **Rochelle**

Q What town in Marion County (on Route 50) was a freight transfer site where the IC crossed the B & O tracks?
A **Sandoval** – its economy was hurt by the overnight conversion of the B&O to standard gauge; thousands of workers were employed to complete this massive task.

Q What southern Illinois town is home to a railroad tunnel built in 1871 by the Pennsy Railroad?
A **Tunnel Hill** – 540 feet long

Q When George Pullman built his first sleeping-dining car, what ostentatious name did he give it?
A The Pullman Hotel Car

Q Is the Pullman name revered by railroad workers?
A No – he ran his company town of Pullman City in Chicago like a tyrant and treated his workers like serfs.

Q What Chicago land speculator conceived the idea of connecting Chicago and **Galena** with the Chicago Galena Union Railroad?
A William Ogden

Q In what northern Illinois town was America's first dining car, the *Delmonico*, built?
A **Aurora** – at the CB&Q roundhouse

Q What was the old Chicago CB&Q roundhouse converted to in 1996?
A The Walter Payton Roundhouse Complex with a microbrewery, a banquet facility, and his football museum

Q What three towns were connected by the Terre Haute & Western Traction Company?
A **Paris**, **Vermilion**, and Terre Haute

Q What unfortunate event caused the town of **New Philadelphia** to fail?
A When the railroad came along in 1869, it missed New Philadelphia by a half mile.

Q Warren truss bridges for railroads can be found all over the state of Illinois. What feature is true of a Warren truss bridge?
A The diagonals are composed of equilateral triangles.

Q What were railroad detectives called back in 1950?
A "Cinder dicks" – police at that time were called "bulls," "flatfoots," "coppers," "dicks," etc.

Illinois Central Railroad Bridge over Ohio River at Cairo

Q Vishnu Springs, a popular resort hotel in **McDonough County** with "curative" mineral water, enjoyed robust success from about 1889-1909. What was one of the main reasons for its demise?
A After twenty years of prosperity, Vishnu lay abandoned, in part, because it had no rail access.

Q What is the reason for the beginning of the town named **West Urbana**?
A The Illinois Central bypassed the town of Urbana by two miles, so a new town sprouted next to the rail line.

Q In railroad parlance, what was featherbedding?
A When railroads switched from coal and steam power to diesel, the job of the fireman was no longer necessary. Powerful unions pressured the railroads into keeping these men on the job, although they were no longer needed.

Q What eliminated the need for cabooses?
A Technology – a device called the ETD – it has an antenna on top and it tells the engineer if any part of the train comes uncoupled.

Q Whose job did the ETD eliminate?
A The rear brakeman was no longer needed.

Q What southern Illinois town is currently using an old Illinois Central water tower for steam engines as its municipal water supply?
A **Kinmundy** in Marion County

Q What kind of wood was used to build this 100,000 gallon structure?
A Cyprus staves held together with metal bands

Q There used to be five men on a train crew. Now there are only two. What positions are left?
A The engineer and conductor.

Q Who is in charge of the train, the engineer or conductor?
A The engineer follows the orders of the conductor.

Q What was the route of the Chicago & Northwestern rail line, and who was responsible for building it?
A The railroad went from Chicago to Milwaukee, Wisconsin, and it was built by William Ogden, the first mayor of Chicago.

Q What was the motto of the Chicago & Northwestern?
A The line with the "Best of Everything"

Q What line acquired the railroad in 1995?
A The Union Pacific

Q What were "end of the line" amusement parks?
A These were amusement parks built at the end of a streetcar line to encourage ridership. Admission to the park was often included in the cost of streetcar fare.

Q What did these "end of the line" parks often include?
A Croquet grounds, band concerts, peacocks, dance pavilions, small roller coasters, high wire acts, horseshoe throwing pits, vaudeville acts, swimming pools, walking trails, and floral gardens

Destroying Confederate railroad tracks

Riding the rails (track inspection vehicle)

Q How was the caboose invented?
A It was difficult for the official at the end of a long train to see what was going on up front. One enterprising railroader took a boxcar and refitted it with an observation cupola.

Q How much longer does the treatment of railroad ties extend the life of a tie?
A An untreated tie lasts about seven years, while a treated one lasts around 25 years.

Q   What became the standard method for treating railroad ties to extend their life?
A   Treating them with creosote inside a pressurized metal chamber.

Q   How did Illinois farmers in the 1890's earn extra money during the winter?
A   They could cut down trees and with a double bladed axe hack out a railroad tie. It took about an hour to do this, and they earned about ten cents per tie for their efforts.

Q   Why did companies that mass-produced railroad ties pound an S-shaped piece of metal into the ends of each tie?
A   These metal pieces were dated, and the procedure helped prevent the wood from checking or splitting. Today they use flat plates that seem to work better than the metal S.

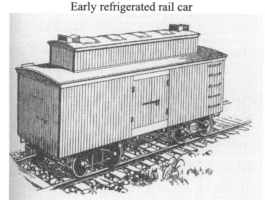
Early refrigerated rail car

Q   What kind of crushed rock was the most frequently used as Illinois railroad ballast?
A   Limestone

Q   Who was the third person inducted into the Railroad Hall of Fame?
A   Robert "Polecat" McMillan of **Centralia** (1889-1956) who contributed 67 years to the glamour of the rails, not retiring until the **age of 83 as the oldest railroad engineer ever**.

Q   What man holds the world record for traveling the most railroad miles?
A   Robert "Polecat" McMillan

Q   What is the name of the railroad company whose tracks closely parallel the B&O tracks in Illinois?
A   The Pennsylvania

Q   What college was noted for conducting classes in Pullman cars, bought from the railroad in 1927?
A   Blackburn College in **Carlinville** – even the library was housed in a old railroad car.

Q   What three towns were the three most distant tri-angulation points of the Illinois Central when it was first built?
A   **Galena, Cairo**, and Chicago

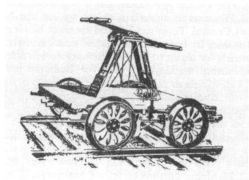
Two-man handcar

Hobo enjoying a free ride

Q   In what Illinois town did the Illinois Central line from **Cairo** to **Galena** split off and head for Chicago?
A   **Centralia**

Q   Where was the longest metallic structure in the world (spanning a river) in 1889?
A   It was the Illinois Central Bridge at **Cairo**, leading into Kentucky.

Q   How severe did the Great Depression hurt Illinois Central employment?
A   Because most people could no longer afford to ride trains, the Illinois Central was forced to lay off nearly half of its 60,000 work force during the 1930's.

Q   What railroad/passenger bridge in 1874 featured the longest steel trussed arches in the world?
A   The Eads Bridge between **East St. Louis** and St. Louis.

Q   What was the destination of the IC passenger train known as the *Panama Limited*?
A   It went from Chicago to New Orleans.

Q   What railroad did the students of Knox College at **Galesburg** write a song about?
A   The Chicago, Burlington & Quincy - "Oh the Lord made me and the Lord made you, and the Lord he made the CB&Q/ This must be true for the scripture sings/ the Lord he made all creeping things."

Q   What was the destination of the Chicago & Eastern Illinois passenger train known as the *Dixie Flyer*?
A   It ran every evening from Chicago to Atlanta.

Q   For many old railroads the tracks have been torn up and the roadbed paved over for bike trails. Yet the right of way along these roadbeds is being used for another high tech purpose. What is it?
A   Fiber optics cables are being laid for communication and broad-band internet purposes.

Q   What was America's first standard size diesel electric streamlined train?
A   Illinois Central's *Green Diamond* on the Chicago-Springfield-St. Louis run

Q   By 1956 how much money was the Illinois Central losing per day on its three trains that operated on a daily basis between Chicago and St. Louis?
A $2,000

Q The Illinois Central built the longest hinged (Bascule bridge) in the world to carry its Air Line across what river?
A The south branch of the Chicago River

Q What was one of the last major railroads in the country to dieselize?
A The Illinois Central

Q What was the first railroad in Madison County?
A The Alton & Sangamon, connecting **Alton** and **Springfield** (1852)

Q What was the main Illinois Central passenger train to Florida?
A *City of Miami*

Q When the IC engine 2500 was retired, what city's park was it sent to for display?
A **Centralia**

Q What was the first train in America to use refrigerated cars?
A The *Thunderbolt Express* of the Illinois Central – for shipping fruit from southern Illinois (1868)

Q What was the biggest disadvantage of strap iron rails?
A These were wood rails with iron fastened on top of them. They fell into disuse because of their tendency to curl up and stab the cars – and sometimes the passengers.

Q Were wooden rails ever used on railroads?
A Yes. The line in **East St. Louis** that carried coal from the bluffs down to the Mississippi riverfront had wood rails at first. The cars were originally pulled by horses and mules instead of a steam engine.

Q What was the first railroad to connect Chicago, **Alton**, and **East St. Louis**?
A The Chicago & Alton

Q Before the Eads Bridge was built in 1874, how were goods taken across the Mississippi River to St. Louis?
A Freight cars were loaded on special train barges owned by the Wiggins Ferry.

Q What are the cities referred to in the Big Four Railroad?
A Indianapolis, Cincinnati, Chicago, and St. Louis

Q What was the best-known passenger train from Chicago to St. Louis on the Wabash line?
A *Blue Bird*

Santa Fe "Superchief" Crossing Illinois River at Chillicothe
Skip Gatermann of St. Louis collection

Q Who was Billy Bryan?
A He was a railroad man in the tradition of Casey Jones. Like Jones, he also worked for the Illinois Central. He was a conductor on the Mudline Branch that ran diagonally from **Johnston City** to the Mississippi River Bridge at Cape Girardeau. Bryan supposedly started off each day with fifteen shots of Egyptian corn whiskey. A gregarious man, he became a legend with passengers and was known for regularly bending the rules to accommodate those he served. The company wanted to fire him but knew they couldn't because of his popularity. He retired in 1909 on the eve of his 70th birthday.

Q What two symbols have been used by the Illinois Central?
A The diamond and the big "I"

Q What did the Illinois Central start doing around 1970 to eliminate the old clickety-clack sound of metal wheels on the rail joints?
A The rails were welded together

Q The IC did not have its engine repair shops in the state of Illinois. Where were these shops located?
A Paducah, Kentucky

Q Where were the IC *car* repair shops?
A **Centralia**

Illinois Central Railroad 2-8-2 Mikado-type at Centralia by Misselhorn

Q What company built many of the old steam engines?
A The Baldwin Locomotive Works

Q How did diesel engines get the nickname "Geeps"
A The letters GP preceded number designations such as a GP 20

Q What did the letters GP signify?
A General Purpose

Q The IC switched from a black engine paint scheme to orange and white in 1967. Why did the orange and white colors not work?
A Engines with these colors always looked dirty.

Q In what year did Amtrack replace IC passenger service?
A 1971

Q What foreign company purchased the IC in 2002?
A Canadian National Railroad – the company that built the Canadian National Tower in Toronto

Q Does Illinois have any railroad tunnels?
A There aren't many but **East Dubuque** and **Tunnel Hill** in southern Illinois have them.

Q What old train track right-of-way is used by MetroLink as it goes from **East St. Louis** to **Belleville** and **Fairview** Heights?
A The Louisville & Nashville

Q The town of **Dwight** was named for a railroad surveyor, Henry Dwight. For what railroad was he the chief engineer?
A The Chicago & Alton

Q What is a unit train?
A A train that carries only one commodity such as coal

Q What rail line was nicknamed the "Tip Up?"
A Toledo, **Peoria** & Western

Q What rail line was nicknamed the "Pee Pooh?"
A The Peoria & Pekin Union

Q What was a cow-catcher?
A On early trains it was a V-shaped bumper fitted on engines to clear the track of animals and debris.

Q On early trains, what was a diamond stack?
A It was an oddly shaped stack or engine chimney designed to diminish the amount of hot embers emitted that might start disastrous prairie fires.

Q Who invented the pneumatic air brake for railroad cars?
A George Westinghouse – before that brakes were mechanical.

Q What two companies merged in the 1970's to form Conrail?
A The Pennsylvania and the New York Central

Q What was the shortest rail line in the state of Illinois?
A The **East St. Louis** Junction, owned and operated by the Stock Yards, operated within its confines of less than a square mile.

Q What is the only state to have more rail miles than Illinois?
A Texas

Q What Illinois writer said that railroads in our state "run as though it were the end of the world?"
A Theodore Dreiser

Q What was the first streamlined passenger train in Illinois?
A The Burlington *Zephyr* – first displayed at the 1933 Chicago Century of Progress Exposition

The "Abraham Lincoln" – first streamlined diesel between Chicago and St. Louis
Skip Gatermann collection

Q What was the top speed of the Zephyr?
A 112.5 miles an hour

Q In its heyday, how many miles of track did *East St. Louis* have in its 13 square miles of incorporated land?
A 550 miles

Q To what does the term "Illinois Traction System" refer?
A Streetcars

Q Who is considered the Father of the Illinois Traction System?
A Congressman William McKinley of **Danville**

Q Who is considered the Father of the Illinois Central?
A Stephen Douglas, although Sidney Breese made considerable efforts to secure a charter before Douglas

Chicago & Northwestern streamlined 4-6-2 Pacific-type locomotive 620 at Chicago

Q How much money did the Illinois Central pay back to the state of Illinois in return for its charter and nearly three million acres of land?
A Seven percent of its gross income, payable semi-annually; this sum amounted to over $100,000 in 1857.

Q What was odd about who controlled the Illinois Central Railroad in 1857?
A They were English shareholders, and the president of the company resided in England.

Q What did streetcar conductors do when they reached the end of the line and passengers disembarked?
A They went from front to rear flipping the backs of seats so that when the trolley went in the opposite direction, the passengers would be facing forward. The front and back of the trolley were mirror images.

Q What is the origin of the expression "trolley car?"
A The trolley is the mechanism on an electric streetcar that reaches up and connects with the overhead wires.

Q What Chicagoan coined an expression to describe trolley riders?
A Transportation mogul Charles Yerkes called them "strap-hangers."

Q What railroad did the Illinois Central merge with in 1972?
A The IC merged with Gulf, Mobile & Ohio to form the Illinois Central Gulf Railroad.

Q What engine type had two pilot wheels and eight driver wheels?
A Consolidated – known as a 2-8-0

Q What is a 2-8-2 engine type called?
A Mikado

Q What is the designated name for a 4-6-2 wheel alignment?
A Pacific

Peoria & St. Louis sleeping car on the "Line of Good Service"
Skip Gatermann collection

Burlington streamlined "Zephyr" at Chicago Fair in 1933

Q Approximately how many tons of freight are still carried each year by Illinois railroads?
A 450 million tons

CHICAGO – THAT TODDLIN' TOWN

Q What general defeated the Indians at Fallen Timbers, resulting in the 1795 cession of "One piece of land six miles square at the mouth of the 'Chicakgo' River?"
A Mad Anthony Wayne – "mad" as in "fought like a madman" – not mad as in "nuts."

Q Soldiers under the command of Captain John Whistler built Fort Dearborn. For what is one his descendents, James Whistler, noted?
A The famous painting – *Whistler's Mother*

Q When the Potawatomie Indians attacked Fort Dearborn (Chicago) in August of 1812, what happened to Captain William Wells?
A He was killed during the attack. The natives **cut out his heart and ate it** so that his courage would be transferred to them. His head was cut off and paraded around on a pole.

Q What was Chicago's first public building?
A A pen to hold wandering livestock

Q Who was the first editor of the Chicago *Daily Tribune*?
A John T. Scripps in 1847 – he later founded the great newspaper chain.

Q What was the Chap Book?
A It was a Chicago literary magazine founded around 1894 by Herb Stone and Hannibal Kimball.

Q Was *Main Street* by Sinclair Lewis set in north Chicago?
A No, it was set in Minnesota.

Q How did Burnham and Root's Rookery Building on LaSalle Street get its name?
A After the 1871 fire, the southeast corner of LaSalle and Adams streets was the site of an interim city hall. Pigeons took a liking to the structure and roosted there. The *area* became known as the rookery.

Q Was the 11 story Rookery Building Chicago's biggest office building when it was finished in 1888?
A Yes – possibly the largest in the world

Q   What is unique about the Rookery Building?
A   It has a large open court yard in the middle, giving light to interior offices.

Q   Where is the "Wall Street of the West?"
A   It's on LaSalle Street where the Chicago Board of Trade is located, between Randolph and Washington Streets. LaSalle ends at the building and because of the other tall buildings around, it's sometimes referred to as the "Little Grand Canyon."

Interior of the Chicago Theater

Q   What *Sun-Times* movie critic gave the controversial 2004 Mel Gibson film *The Passion Of The Christ* an enthusiastic "thumbs up?"
A   Richard Roeper. His partner Roger Ebert also gave it a *yes* vote. Many critics panned the film, claiming that it could cause a rebirth of anti-Semitism (Jewish hatred).

Q   Who said, "I have found a city – a real city – and they call it Chicago?"
A   Rudyard Kipling – he also had some unkind things to say about Chicago.

Q   What rival city's press referred to Chicago as that "Babylon on the mud?"
A   St. Louis

Q   In 1850 Chicago had a population of about 80,000. How many police constables did it have?
A   Only nine

Q   When the Chicago Club was organized around 1870, what sign did it post?
A   "No dogs, Democrats, women, or reporters."

Chicago Stage Office of Frank & Walker (courtesy Newberry Library)

Q   About 12,000 years ago, what body of water existed where the city of Chicago now sits?
A   Lake Chicago

Q   What do the call letters for WTTW, Chicago's public television, represent?
A   Window to the World

Q   Where is Jean Baptiste DuSable, the founder of Chicago, buried?
A   In a Catholic cemetery at St. Charles, Missouri

Q   Who committed Chicago's first homicide?
A   John Kinzie, considered by some to be the real father of Chicago, quarreled with rival Jean Lalime in 1812 and stabbed him to death.

Q   For what person was Fort Dearborn named?
A   Henry Dearborn, the U.S. Secretary of War

Q   A Chicago Historical Society sculpture depicts the heroic rescue of what white woman by an Indian?
A   During the Fort Dearborn Massacre (War of 1812), an Indian named Black Partridge saved the wife of lieutenant Helms by hiding her in Lake Michigan until the frenzy was over.

Q   Chicago's first tavern/hotel was named for what friendly Native-American?
A   The Sauganash - built in 1831 and named for Billy Caldwell, whose Indian name was Sauganash.

Q   What was Chicago's first newspaper?
A   The *Chicago Democrat* – 1831; The *Tribune* came along in 1847.

Q   Old time orators such as Stephen Douglas practiced what was called "spread eagle oratory." According to some, how powerful was Douglas' voice?
A   They claimed his booming decibels could shake the leaves on a tree 300 feet distant when he mounted the stump.

Q   How did Chicago earn the nickname, "Garden City?"
A   The depression of 1837, brought on by land speculation, caused residents to plant gardens to ensure a few greens and potatoes for the dinner table.

Q   How did George Mundelein end up as the archbishop of Chicago?
A   A Brooklynite, he was slated for promotion in 1915 to

bishop in Buffalo, New York, but Canadians, already at war with Germany, objected to a German of such prominence that close to their border. The pope sent him instead to Chicago as archbishop.

Q   How is it that the 28th Eucharistic Congress in 1926 met in Chicago – the first to be held in the USA?
A   Cardinal Mundelein used his influence with Rome.

Q   How can it be argued that Chicago is the cradle of the picture postcard industry in America?
A   The **first U.S. postcards** were printed for the 1893 Columbian Exposition in Chicago. Curt Teich later built a factory at 1733-1755 Irving Park Boulevard that became the **largest post card factory in the world.**

Q   How long was the Teich Company in business?
A   From 1898 to 1978

Q   Where are the Teich archives and museum located?
A   **Wauconda**

Q   Who won the famous fistfight between Alan Pinkerton (future detective) and Long John Wentworth (future mayor)?
A   Pinkerton - Wentworth was bigger but was out of shape. The fight took place at the corner of Lake and State.

Q   What Chicago Industrialist was said to be so mean and cantankerous that if you boiled him to broth, the devil wouldn't sup?
A   Cyrus McCormick of reaper fame

Q   The freighter *General Fry* made the first trip ever down what 1847 engineering marvel?
A   The Lake Michigan-Illinois River Canal

Q   What precipitated the famous Lager Beer Riot of 1855?
A   An anti-foreign faction called the Know-nothings gained control of city hall. They raised the price of an annual saloon license from fifty to three hundred dollars. The German element of the city found this discriminatory and rioted.

Q   What is the Waubansee boulder?

Ferris wheel at Chicago's Navy Pier

Lou Mitchell's Restaurant in Chicago – photo by Dan Oberle

A   It is a large stone on display at the Chicago Historical Society. It is thought that a crude face carved on it might be a Native-American artifact. Some think the work was done by a bored soldier at Fort Dearborn.

Q   What incident led to the formation of the Chicago Crime Commission?
A   The robbery and murder of two Brinks' Express agents in 1917

Q   What did city officials use in an unsuccessful effort to pave the mud streets of Wabash Avenue in Chicago?
A   Stove lids

Q   Who was Chicago's "Angel of the Stockyards?"
A   Mary McDowell – she worked tirelessly to improve the lives of those in south Chicago who worked at the stockyards. She even started the University of Chicago Settlement House. Some called her "The Garbage Lady" for she nagged the city council to see to it that refuse was collected regularly in the tenement house districts.

Q   What theory about the cause of the 1871 Chicago Fire was set forth by Mrs. O'Leary's son?
A   James O'Leary attributed the fire to *spontaneous combustion* from green hay in the barn.

Q   Chicago had 561 miles of sidewalks before the 1871 fire. Of what material were the sidewalks made?
A   Wood

Q   Who was placed in charge of Chicago's martial law after the 1871 fire?
A   General Philip Sheridan of Civil War fame

Q   How did Chicago try to deal with the downtown streets that seemed to be permanent marsh bogs?
A   In 1855 they raised the streets with fill, necessitating the jacking up of buildings and placing them on foundations. The five-story Tremont Hotel was raised six feet with jackscrews without making a single crack in the brick walls.

Q   Who was in charge of the Tremont Hotel raising?
A   New Yorker George Pullman, assisted by 1,200 workers. Pullman later became a Chicagoan and went into the railroad business.

Q   How did Pullman gain experience in raising and moving houses?

A He raised and moved many of them so that the Erie Canal in New York could be built.

Q What new word was coined to describe the lower basement levels after the streets were all raised six to ten feet high?
A Appropriately for Chicago, the **underworld.**

Q What Chicagoan grew tired of business and sold his interests to Marshal Field in 1867?
A Potter Palmer

Q What Chicagoan was responsible for making State Street the business center it is today?
A Potter Palmer – he got back into business after the Chicago Fire.

Q What were the only two Chicago buildings in the path of the 1871 fire to survive?
A The water tower and pumping station, both made of stone

John Kinzie's house 1833 – Chicago's first "American" home

Q What Chicagoan had the business slogan, "Give the little lady what she wants?"
A Potter Palmer

Q What president authorized the construction of the Great Lakes Naval Training complex in Chicago?
A Theodore Roosevelt – 1904

Q In what Chicago park is there a statue of Mayor Carter Harrison Sr.?
A Union Park – erected 1907

Pennsylvania Railroad locomotive on display at 1949 Chicago Railroad Fair (claimed world speed record in 1905)

Q What was the Great Lakes Experiment, a landmark event in Black history?
A During World War II, black naval musicians were integrated with white ones to form a band and entertain the troops to build morale. It was **the U.S. Navy's first effort at integration**, and it proved to be successful.
This story was told in one of the "JAG" television episodes in the 2003-2004 season.

Q In the 1920's, what part of Chicago was home to the city's self-styled Bohemians – Chicago's version of New York's Greenwich Village.
A Tower Town – so named because it was near the famed Water Tower at Michigan and Chicago avenues.

Q What is Bughouse Square?
A Washington Square Park in Chicago was nicknamed "Bughouse Square." It became a popular discussion site where people met to rehash issues of the day or give soapbox speeches on topics such as crime, woman's suffrage, the economy, or Marxism.

Q How many people were killed in the Chicago fire of 1871?
A About 300 – with 100,000 people left homeless and nearly $200 million in damages

Q What is the Gold Coast?
A After the Chicago fire turned his first hotel to ashes, Potter Palmer built a new hotel on a filled in frog pond on Lake Shore Drive, giving birth to Chicago's Gold Coast, named for the collective wealth of the people who live there. The Playboy Mansion is located in the Gold Coast.

Q What is Streeterville?
A In 1882 George "Cap" Streeter accidentally grounded his ship on a shoal at the edge of Chicago's shoreline, just west of the present day John Hancock Building. Stranded for good, Streeter convinced local builders to dump fill material at the site, creating the small burg that became known as Streeterville. Because the land had been reclaimed from the lake, Streeter said that the city of Chicago had no jurisdiction. He set himself up as the ruler. City officials and judges were vexed for decades by the legal technicalities this presented. Finally, old man Streeter was evicted for violating an old blue law prohibiting the sale of liquor on the Sabbath.

Q According to Norman Mailer, what is America's greatest city?
A Chicago

Q Did Douglas MacArthur and George Patton ever spend much time in Illinois?
A Yes – they were both stationed at Fort Sheridan.

Q In what part of Chicago was the Century of Progress World's Fair held in 1933-34?
A On Northerly Island by Lake Michigan

Q When did Chicago get its first permanent landing field for aeroplanes?

A In 1911 under the auspices of the Chicago Aero Club and its president, Octave Chanute

Q What Paris/Illinoisan published **Progress In Flying Machines** and was an inspiration and a mentor to the Wright brothers?
A Octave Chanute

Great Lakes Naval Instruction Building in Chicago (Skip Gatermann collection)

Q Where did Henry Ford build an airport hangar in Chicago?
A At the Lansing Municipal Airport of Cook County. Harold Gatty and Wiley Post flew to the airport after their record-setting airplane the *Winnie May* flew around the world in eight days.

Q What is the name of the cheap plaster-like material that was used on the exteriors of most buildings at the Columbian Exposition of 1893?
A Staff

Q Where is Chicago's "Black Metropolis?"
A It is a city within a city, centered at State and 35th streets on Chicago's South Side.

Q Chicago teachers had their salaries boosted to $3,200 a year in 1915. How much did this author make at his first teaching job at St. Louis in 1963?
A $4,200 – The extra $200 was for having a masters degree.

Q What all-black regiment of the Illinois National Guard had an armory built for them in 1915 on Forest Avenue in Chicago?
A The Fighting Eighth

Q Does Chicago have a subway?
A Yes – it opened in 1943

Q What year was the tragic Iroquois Theater Fire?
A 1903

Q What names are attached to famous Chicago expressways?
A Dan Ryan, Adlai Stevenson, J.F. Kennedy, Dwight D. Eisenhower

Q What African-American from Chicago was the first black from a northern state elected to Congress (1928)?
A Oscar DePriest

Q What African-American comedian ran unsuccessfully for mayor of Chicago in 1966?
A Dick Gregory

Q What Chicago pianist at the Panama Club wrote the million-dollar hit "Pretty Baby" in 1916?
A Tony Jackson

Q Who was Chicago's most generous philanthropist in the 1910-1935 era?
A Julius Rosenwald, who became president of Sears when Richard Sears left the company. When the stock market crashed in 1929 he guaranteed employees' margin accounts on all stocks, not just Sears. That move cost him seven million dollars. In 1929 he built Rosenwald Gardens, a modern low rent apartment complex in Chicago's Black Belt. His Rosenwald Fund is credited with establishing several thousand black public schools.

Chicago Municipal Airport (Teich Postcard collection)

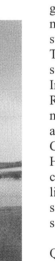

Q What Chicagoan is called the "Father of Modern Architecture?"
A Louis Sullivan

Q What Chicagoland high school was designed by Frank Lloyd Wright?
A Bloom High School

Q How many counties make up what is known as Chicagoland?
A Seven – Cook, DuPage, Kane, McHenry, Lake, Grundy, Will

Q What modernistic building was quickly nicknamed "Starship Chicago" as soon as it was completed in 1985?

A   The Thompson/Illinois Center, designed by Helmut Jahn

Q   What Chicago architect designed Crown Hall on the campus of the Illinois Institute of Technology?
A   Mies van der Rohe

Q   There are two statues guarding the entrance to Chicago's Mundelein College, built in 1930. Can you identify the two statues.
A   They are angels.

Q   What is unusual about the construction technique of the Mercantile Exchange Building?
A   It has no steel skeleton. Its stability depends on its thick walls.

Q   What is the famous slogan of Classic Rock 105.9 radio in Chicago?
A   "Of all the radio stations in Chicago . . . we're one of them."

Q   What controversial order did Chicago Mayor Richard Daley give to police during the riots after the Martin Luther King Jr. assassination?
A   "Shoot to kill"

Q   What singer, destined for stardom, did Chicago's Chess Record Company pass up a chance to sign?
A   Elvis Presley - because they had had just signed Bo Diddley and didn't think they needed a hillbilly singer.

Q   What Chicagoan won the "Best Supporting Actress" Oscar for her performance in *Written On The Wind* in 1955?
A   Dorothy Malone

Q   What was the year of the Great Chicago Flood, occurring after a dredge and dock company punched a hole in the bed of the Chicago River with pilings? (A) 1989 (B) 1990 (C) 1992 (D) 1993
A   April of 1992 – causing a billion dollars in damages from flooding

Q   What Chicago company went out of the catalog business in 1993? (A) Aldens (B) Sears (C) Montgomery Ward (D) J.C. Penney
A   Sears

Q   What symbols are on the municipal flag of Chicago?

Chicago's famous "Gold Coast" – Neal Strebel of Collinsville collection

A   Some years ago the city of Chicago decided that it needed an official flag. The original ensign was red, white, and blue with two stars. It was designed by Wallace Rice and was adopted in 1917. The flag currently has four stars, representing Fort Dearborn, the 1871 fire, the 1893 Columbian Exposition, and the 1933 Century of Progress Fair. The three white stripes represent Chicago neighborhoods: northside, southside and westside. One blue stripe pays tribute to Lake Michigan and the Chicago River. The other blue stripe stands for the south branch of the Chicago River and the Great Canal.

Q   When did Hugh Heffner open his first Playboy Club?
A   February of 1960 – in Chicago

Q   What theater in the Uptown Square district of Chicago is the largest free-standing theater building in America?
A   Uptown Theater – other theaters have more seating capacity, but they are housed in structures that offer other services.

Q   What Chicago neighborhood features the Green Mill, the Riviera Theater, and the Aragon Ballroom?
A   Uptown Square

Q   The Uptown Square part of Chicago was home to a Knights of Pythias Building. Why is it famous?
A   The seven-story building is thought to be the largest structure in the U.S. financed, designed, and built by African-Americans. It was demolished in 1981.

Holy Name Cathedral in Chicago

Q   How did Chicago get the name "Second City?"
A   Back in 1951 there was an article in *The New Yorker* that accused Chicagoans of trying to emulate New York City. Rather than complaining about the "put down," Chicagoans adopted Second City as an unofficial nickname.

Q   Did the famed **Peoria**/Chicago agnostic Robert Ingersoll fight in the Civil War?
A   Yes – reaching the rank of colonel and once being captured before he was exchanged. The "Fighting

Agnostic" was quite a mesmerist. While a prisoner, he was allowed to give a lecture and he nearly convinced the entire detachment to switch sides in the war.

Q   What Elvis Presley song mentions Chicago?
A   "In The Ghetto"

Q   What Chicagoan was the first war reporter to make a parachute jump in a combat zone?
A   Jack Thompson – 1942 in the North Africa campaign

Q   Who was Chicago's first notorious criminal outlaw?
A   Roger Plant. He was in charge of all sorts of criminal activity south of Madison Street during the Civil War Era. His emporium of underworld activity was called "Under the Willow."

Q   What Chicago newsman invented the term "Copperhead" to describe those who plotted Civil War treason?
A   Editor Joseph Medill of the *Tribune*

Q   What Chicago building, 25 stories high and two blocks long, has its own ZIP code, and contains a Merchant's Hall of Fame?
A   The Merchandise Mart

Chicagou – Illini chief who visited France in 1725

Q   What Chicagoan was secretary of state during the FDR and Truman administrations?
A   Edward R. Stettinius

Q   Ignatius Donnelly, the Wisconsin populist reformer, had a theory about the 1871 Chicago fire. What was it?
A   He claimed that the entire Midwest earth had been made combustible because of strange elements in the soil due to the close passage of a comet thousands of years before.

Standard Oil Building in Chicago (Neal Strebel collection)

Q   What was the most important thing saved from the 1871 Chicago Fire?
A   City records - John Van Osdel gathered the maps and ledgers and carried them to the Palmer House, dug a large hole, and buried them in the moist soil. These records of titles, marriages, mortgages, lawsuits and property ownership were vital in the rebuilding of the city.

Q   What were baked banknotes?
A   Paper money in safes did not burn but the intense heat turned them into detritus that was almost unrecognizable. These remains were sent to Treasury experts in

Washington, D.C. who were able to estimate the value and send new bills back to Chicago,

Q   The Chicago library lost all of its books in the fire. What person is credited with giving the library a new life?
A   Queen Victoria of England donated hundreds of books from her library to form a nucleus.

Q   How long did the Chicago fire last?
A   About 24 hours, destroying 17,450 buildings. The burning question is (pun intended), did the cow do it?

Q   When was the Chicago community called Dearborn Park built?
A   Construction was started in 1974.

Q   What Chicago radio station lasted from 1926-1978 and was sponsored by the Chicago Federation of Labor?
A   WCFL – with many programs devoted to the topic of labor

Q   What is unusual about Dearborn Park?
A   It was built on abandoned rail yards south of the Loop, and it is a walled suburban development plunked down in the middle of a city.

Q   Why did **Glenview** woman Susan Brenner, in March of 2004, threaten to sue Donald Trump if he tried to secure a trademark for the phrase, "You're fired?"
A   Because she owns a pottery store with the title, Your Fired (kiln). Trump, of course, thought about the trademark because of his popular reality television show.

Q   Did Queen Elizabeth II ever visit Chicago?
A   Yes – with husband Prince Philip in 1959 to celebrate the opening of the St. Lawrence Seaway, making the Great Lakes the nation's "fourth seacoast."

Q   What logo on top of a 20-story building, that can be seen from the Buckingham Fountain, is the largest of its kind in the world?
A   The torch and oval logo on the Standard Oil/Amoco Building on South Michigan Avenue can be seen for two miles.

Q   What Chicago Cardinal banned "rock and roll" from all Catholic school functions in 1957?
A   Cardinal Stritch

Q   What mobster became the 1,000 Chicagoan to be killed in gang-related wars since the advent of Prohibition?

A Roger "the Terrible" Touhy - 1959

Q What was the famous slogan of Chicago land and grain speculators?
A Buy low – sell high; Buy by the acre, sell by the foot.

Q What are some Chicago nicknames?
A Gem of the Prairie, Second City, Windy City, Garden City

Q What poet was responsible for the nickname, City of Big Shoulders?
A Carl Sandburg

Q Who said: "Chicago – first in violence, deepest in dirt, loud, lawless, unlovely, ill smelling . . . a spectacle for the nation."
A Writer Lincoln R. Steffans

Q What Chicago building was referred to as "The Old Lady On Harrison Street?"
A Cook County Hospital

Q Who said "Illinois (Chicago) has some of the most adroit and cunning political schemers on this continent?"
A 1896 national Republican campaign organizer, Joe Smith

Q What was Midway Gardens, designed by architect Frank Lloyd Wright?
A It was an entertainment complex that opened in 1914, located on a two-block area across the street from the southeast corner of Washington Park.

Q Chicago's Boyce Building, at Dearborn and Illinois streets, was the headquarters for what national organization?
A The Boy Scouts of America – W.D. Boyce was the founder.

Q What else was the 12-story building used for?
A Two newspapers were printed here – the *Chicago Ledger* and the *Saturday Blade.*

Q How were these newspapers different from other Chicago newspapers?
A They were aimed at rural audiences and had sensational news and human interest stories.

Q Beside the Boy Scouts, Boyce started another organization called the Lone Scout. How did they differ?

A Lone Scout was aimed at rural kids who were isolated and couldn't travel long distances to meetings or afford uniforms.

Q What is the official monthly magazine of the Boy Scouts?
A *Boy's Life*

Q What Chicago landmark was used for the establishing scene of the television program, "Married With Children?"
A Buckingham Fountain

Adler Planetarium in Chicago

Q Who said: "Chicago is a !@*@!! crazy place. Nobody is safe on the streets?"
A Lucky Luciano of New York

Q Who said: "Chicago has the best way of handling crooks. They get rival gangs to kill off each other, and all the police have to do is referee and count the bodies?"
A Humorist Will Rogers

Q Why were sewer grates stolen in Chicago during Prohibition?
A Alky cookers used them to set their stills on over an open fire.

Q What is the only city in America that is home to more major corporations than Chicago?
A New York City

Q What major airline makes its home in Chicago?
A United Airlines

Q What is unusual about the post office at 433 West Van Buren in Chicago?
A **It's the only one in the U.S. that you can drive through**.

Chicago Coliseum – Teich Collection

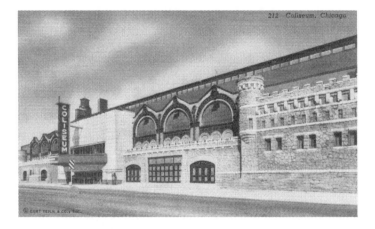

212 – Coliseum, Chicago

Q What is Chicago soul music?
A It's a brand of blues music that often features several lead singers, one of which uses an artificially high voice called falsetto.

Q Baxter industries has its headquarters in Chicago. What is its field of business?
A Baxter International is a producer of medicines and items for the sick and elderly.

Q What songwriter called Chicago "that toddlin' town?"
A Fred Fisher in a 1922 song

Q What is Chicago's motto?
A "I Will"

Q What Chicagoan, who was a faro banker and an expert at the confidence game known as three-card monte, coined the phrase, "Never give a sucker an even break?"
A Mike McDonald. Most Americans think it was W.C. Fields who uttered the line in a movie.

Q What female reformer claimed: "Drink and tobacco are the great separatists between men and women?"
A Frances Willard of **Evanston**, founder of the Women's Christian Temperance Union - WCTU

Q When the Chicago Commission decided to hold a fair honoring Christopher Columbus in 1893, what explorer got overlooked?
A Viking Leif Ericsson, whose North American explorations antedated Columbus by 500 years.

Q Was this Fair . . . fair? (Hmm)
A Probably. Ericsson's voyage did nothing to change the course of history in America. Anyone in the U.S. who drives a car or uses a computer should take his or her hat off to Columbus.

Q What famous military man was placed in charge of security at the 1893 Columbian Exposition?
A Nelson A. Miles – the man who captured Geronimo

Q What was probably the most mesmerizing speech ever given in Chicago?
A It was William Jennings Bryan's "Cross of Gold" speech in 1896.

Q About 835 people died when the *Eastland* capsized in the Chicago River in 1915. How many millions of dollars were paid out in lawsuit damages?
A Not a penny. A court of appeals said no one was negligent.

Q What name came to be applied to South Chicago after thousands of Negroes flocked there from Dixie during World War I, seeking employment?
A Bronzeville

Q Who was Ring Lardner?
A He was a 1920's Chicago sportswriter who wrote notable fiction about sports characters.

Q What Chicagoan created a character by the name of Pal

London Guarantee and Accident Company in Chicago

Hotel Wacker in Chicago

Joey?
A Writer John O'Hara. Frank Sinatra and Kim Novak had the main roles in the film.

Q What was the speed limit for automobiles in 1919 Chicago?
A Fifteen miles per hour

Q How many million did it cost to build the opulent Chicago Theater in 1921?
A Four million dollars

Q What other Chicago theater did Balaban and Katz build?
A The Tivoli on Chicago's south side

Q How many stories tall is the Chicago Theater?
A Eleven

Q Who supplied the original draperies and carpeting of the Chicago Theater?
A Marshall Field and Company

Q What building was erected on the original site of Fort Dearborn?
A London Guarantee and Accident Company; the entrance has a bronze bas-relief of the old fort and its surroundings.

Q What kind of an organ graced the Chicago Theater?
A A Mighty Wurlitzer

Q What Chicago building has been called the "world's most beautiful office building?"
A The Tribune Tower

Q A courtyard at the Tribune Tower has a statue of a Revolutionary War hero. Can you name him?
A Nathan Hale – "I regret that I have but one life to lose for my country."

Q What art and architecture critic's words are inscribed on the floor of the Tribune Tower's entrance hall?
A John Ruskin – "Therefore when we build, let us think that we build forever . . . and that men will say as they look upon the labor and wrought substance of them, 'See! This our fathers did for us.' " (I absolutely love that last line.)

Q What is State Street's challenge to Michigan Avenue's "Magnificent Mile?"
A The "Splendid Mile"

Q What type of architectural style describes the Tribune Tower, built in 1925?
A Gothic

Q What was the Chicago speed limit for taking curves in 1912?
A Six miles an hour

Q What was the favorite parlor game of Chicagoans in 1922?
A Mah Jongg – although some say it was "petting"

Q What was a "blind pig?"
A It was an innocuous building with a plain façade that fronted as a speakeasy in the 1920's.

Q Who announced Cub home games in the early years of radio?
A The legendary Tris Speaker on WENR/WLS

Q What did the Chicago radio call letters WLS stand for?
A World's Largest Store - the station was owned by Sears.

Q Who was the mainstay of the Saturday Night Barn Dance every week on WLS?
A Red Foley

Q What TV comedian started out as a singer in the 1930's on the WLS Barn Dance?
A George Gobel

Q What singing cowboy got his first big break on WLS Barn Dance?
A Gene Autry – in 1929 he recorded "That Silver-Haired Daddy of Mine," the first recording to sell five million copies.

Q What famous person heard Gene singing to pass the time while he worked as an Oklahoma railroad telegrapher and urged him to go into show business?
A Will Rogers

Q What Autry products were sold by Sears Roebuck?
A Records, guitars and songbooks

Q Who said: "Chicago did not invent municipal corruption, it merely perfected it?"
A Old saying – author unknown. Another old saying: "In Chicago, politics has always been a spectator sport."

Old Aragon Ballroom – Skip Gatermann collection

John Hancock Building and Old Water Tower

Q Who was the *Daily-News* referring to when it called him: "the most unbelievable man in Chicago history" when he died in 1944?
A Mayor Big Bill Thompson

Q Who was Chicago's best known and most durable social activist and professional radical?
A Saul Alinsky (1909-1972) – he championed the cause of troubled youth, the poor, and African Americans.

Q What was Alinsky's most famous quote?
A "To he- - with charity. The only thing you can get is what you're strong enough to take, so you had better organize."

Q Where is the Chicago neighborhood that was known as "Back of the Yards?"
A It was an Irish-American tenement neighborhood behind the Union Stockyards.

Q What is the Chicago neighborhood known as Woodlawn noted for?
A It was a black ghetto area.

Q How did First Ward alderman John Coughlin get the nickname "Bathhouse?"
A He once had been a masseuse in a bathhouse.

Q What editor of the *Chicago Defender* was said to be the first African-American millionaire in the U.S.?
A Robert Abbott

Q What **Bellwood** native became an astronaut and was part of the crew in Gemini 12 and Apollo 7 flights?
A Eugene Cernan – he was the one on Apollo 10 who dubbed the command module and lunar module "Charlie Brown" and "Snoopy."

Q What Chicagoan taught history at Bradley University in **Peoria**, was a political advisor to the Republican Party, and

was elected to the U.S. House of Representatives to fill a vacancy when Donald Rumsfeld resigned?
A Phil Crane

Q How many stories does the John Hancock Building have?
A 100

Q What Chicagoan is serving as Secretary of Defense under George W. Bush?
A Donald Rumsfeld, who also served as Richard Nixon's Chief of Staff and once was our representative to NATO.

Q For what field of endeavor is Chicago-born Frank Drake most noted?
A Physics and astronomy – he discovered Jupiter's radiation belt and with radio waves determined the true surface temperature of the planet Jupiter to be 3,000 degrees Fahrenheit, previously thought to be minus 189 degrees F. He is the author of the book *Intelligent Life in Space.* (He believes it's out there somewhere in Ozma.)

Q In 2004 Mayor Richard Daley tried to unite Chicago's diverse neighborhoods by urging them to read his favorite book on social justice. What is the name of the book?
A *To Kill A Mockingbird* by Harper Lee

Q How well did Daley's policy work?
A There was a big scandal when there were seven instances early in 2004 where racial slurs were broadcast over the Chicago Fire Department's radio system.

Q Name the Confederate Civil War prison that was salvaged and used to build the façade of the Coliseum in Chicago.
A Libby Prison

Q Chicago's Coliseum was long used as a convention center. What was its seating capacity?
A 15,000

Q What Chicago building on Lawrence near Broadway featured a "Ballroom of a Thousand Delights?"
A Aragon Ballroom

Q How many firefighters are employed by the city of Chicago?
A About 5,000

Q Going into the November 2004 election, what issue was probably hurting Republican candidate Jack Ryan the most?

Chicago's Dankmar Adler

A Speculation about sealed records concerning his 1999 divorce

Q To what prominent actress was Ryan married?
A Jeri Ryan – the sexy blonde counselor on the television show, "Boston Public"

Q What caused Ryan to drop out of the senatorial race in June of 2004?
A Revelations about him taking his wife to a kinky sex club

Q What seemed to be the determining factor for Blair Hull losing the Democratic primary?
A A nasty divorce and the fact that he was running as an Independent – Hull spent millions on the campaign and only got 15 percent of the vote, a landslide loss.

Q Who won the Democratic primary in March of 2004 for the U.S. Senate seat?
A Barack Obama, a Harvard grad who is currently a state senator

Q Who is going to be the first African-American President of the U.S?
A Many think it will be charismatic Barack Obama who gave the keynote address at the 2004 Democratic National Convention

Q What was Chicago's worst labor riot? – hint: 1937
A Three hundred striking workers at Republic Steel marched on the South Side plant and threw stones at the police who were guarding it. Shots were fired and ten demonstrators were killed. Several policemen were hospitalized.

Q During Prohibition Chicago speakeasies served Bronxes. Of what did this drink consist?
A Satan's drink was a concoction of ½ orange juice, ¼ gin, and a ¼ mixture of dry vermouth and sweet vermouth.

Q How is it during Prohibition that Chicago druggists could sell alcohol?
A Supposedly it was for medicinal purposes only, and a doctor's prescription was needed.

Streets of Shanghai at Century of Progress Exposition

Q What singing cowgirl came to the 1933 Fair and then joined a singing group called the Ramblers?

A   Patsy Montana – she starred on the Barn Dance for 15 years.

Q   What famous and rich man headed Chicago's *Herald-Examiner* in the 1920s?
A   William Randolph Hearst

Q   When famous viceman and restaurant owner Jim Colosimo was killed, on what grounds did Catholic authorities refuse to allow him to be buried in consecrated ground?
A   He was divorced

Q   By the mid Twenties Chicagoans had switched from the open car to the closed automobile with a roof. How did one Chicago judge describe the closed automobile?
A   "A house of prostitution on wheels."

Q   What was the Chicago Barbershop War of 1924?
A   Women started wearing their hair bobbed. Many began having their hair cut by male barbers since the popular pageboy was a male hairstyle. Enraged beauty shops pressured city hall to pass laws forbidding women from using barbers. Barbers retaliated by lobbying city hall to require a barber's license for women who cut hair in salons.

Q   What name was given to the 12 block long section of Michigan Avenue that features exclusive shops, specialty stores, and boutiques, ending at the Drake Hotel?
A   The Magnificent Mile

Q   When did Chicago movie houses start showing double features?
A   After the depression struck in October of 1929, people were looking for bargains.

Q   What does the 1928 sculpture (relief) on the Michigan avenue bridge show?
A   The massacre of women and children at Fort Dearborn by the Indians.

Q   What time did Sunday afternoon games start at Wrigley Field back in the Twenties?
A   One-thirty p.m. – to give everyone time to get home from church

Q   Where was the featured place for holding dance marathons and walkathons in 1920's Chicago?
A   The Coliseum

Q   Besides Riverview Park on the north side, what other amusement park did Chicago have in the 1920's and 1930's?
A   White City at 63rd and South Park Avenue

Q   What Chicago utilities mogul of the 1920's became a

Municipal flag of Chicago

pariah after the Depression hit and it was discovered that he paid himself $1.4 million a year and allegedly cooked the books?
A   Samuel Insull

Q   What Chicago writer in the 1920s referred to Chicago as "That Jazz Baby By The Lake?"
A   Ben Hecht

Q   What was Chicago Jazz?
A   Jazz started in New Orleans and flourished on riverboats and in a place known for its vice, Storyville. Toward the end of World War I the military declared Storyville off-limits. Musicians such as King Oliver and Louis Armstrong headed north and ended up in Chicago. Chicago soon became a Mecca for both musicians and singers. Chicago jazz is a combination of New Orleans jazz and Midwest influences.

Q   Is Gene Krupa a Chicagoan?
A   Yes. He played drums in the band for Fenger High. Chicago schools back then frequently had band contests at Riverview Park.

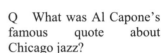
Elevated station; Union Stock Yards

Q   What was Al Capone's famous quote about Chicago jazz?
A   "Its got guts, and it doesn't make you slobber."

Q   Bandleader Paul Whiteman played many of the Chicago clubs in the 1920s. What three singers made up his Rhythm Boys?
A   Bing Crosby, Al Rinker and Harry Barris. Bix Beiderbecke played in Whiteman's band when he needed rent money, but he considered it prostitution.

Q   What Chicago singer was the first to make gospel singing profitable?
A   Mahalia Jackson

Q   What 1930's singer was a favorite with Chicagoans at the Drake Hotel?
A   The incomparable Hildegarde

Q   What opera star dominated Chicago theater in the Teens and Twenties?
A   Mary Garden

Q   What baseball player turned evangelist was good friends with Mary Garden?
A   Billy Sunday

Q   What was Carl Sandburg's favorite musical instrument?
A   The guitar

Q   What reactionary columnist started out as a sports writer

for the *Sun-Times*?
A Westbrook Pegler

Q What writer cut her literary teeth in the Windy City, authoring *So Big* in 1924?
A Edna Ferber

Q What author of *Winesburg, Ohio*, wrote of Chicago: "You know my city – factories and cars and roar of machine – Chicago triumphant; horrible, terrible, ugly and brutal . . ."?
A Sherwood Anderson

Q What University of Chicago artist made Chicago the sculptor capital of the world?
A Lorado Taft

Q What futuristic building at the 1933 Century of Progress had the world's largest unobstructed area enclosed under a roof?
A The Travel and Transportation Building with a roof suspended from metal cables. The dome was 200 feet across.

Q What admiral's ship (that went to the South Pole) was featured at the Century of Progress Fair?
A Richard Byrd's *City of New York*

Q Who became the chief benefactor of the Chicago Civic Opera when Harold McCormick ran out of money?
A Samuel Insull

Q What was Chicago's supreme Art Deco nightclub of the 1930s?
A The Chez Paree on Ontario Street.

Q When Sally Rand did her fan dance, what classical music piece accompanied her?
A *Clare de Lune* by Debussy

Q How did Missouri Ozarks-born Rand get her stage name?
A Born Helen Beck, she took her name from a Rand-McNally atlas.

Q How is it that Chicago became the early leader in the new medium of radio?
A New York was wedded to the stage, and Hollywood was committed to the screen.

Q What radio program made Illinoisan Arch Oboler, master of the macabre, famous?

A "Lights Out"

Q On what famous Chicago radio show did listeners hear the expression, "I'se regusted?"
A Amos 'n' Andy

Q What was the origin of the call letters of station WGN, owned by the *Tribune*?
A WGN stood for World's Greatest Newspaper

Aerial view of downtown Chicago

Q What acerbic *Baltimore-Sun* critic called Chicago "the only civilized city in the New World where they take fine arts seriously."
A H.L. Mencken

Q What Chicagoan shocked Americans with *The Man With The Golden Arm* and *A Walk On The Wild Side*?
A Nelson Algren

Q What Chicagoan sang the title song in the movie, *St. Louis Blues*?

A Two-hundred pound, contralto-voiced, Bessie Smith

Q At what Chicago school did clarinetist Benny Goodman play?
A He attended Lewis Prep School. The clarinet back then was referred to as a licorice stick. In the late 1930's Goodman became the "King of Swing."

Q What Illinoisan starred in *The Benny Goodman Story*?
A Steve Allen

Q What banjo playing music legend was nicknamed "Slick?"
A Eddie Condon, said to be a clothes horse, was born in Indiana and came to Chicago via **Momence** and **Chicago Heights**.

Phil Sheridan – in charge of martial law after 1871 fire

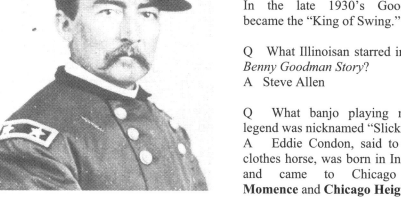

Q What Chicagoan associated with Hull House and the University of Chicago became F.D. Roosevelt's Secretary of Interior?
A Harold Ickes – who lived in **Winnetka**

Q What sticker did Chicago businesses place in their windows to indicate that they were doing their part to cooperate with economic recovery?
A The NRA Blue Eagle

Q   Why was Wacker Drive a favorite sleeping place for the homeless during the Depression?
A   Coverage. Actually it was only the lower part of double-decked Wacker Drive.

Q   What magazine was Colonel McCormick of the *Tribune* forced to sell because of the Depression?
A   Liberty Magazine

Q   Barnstormers were popular in the 1920s and '30s in small Illinois towns. What was the Chicago equiv-alent?
A   Air races. The tenth National Air Race was held in Chicago at the Curtiss-Reynolds Airport in 1930.

Q   What great hero of the 1920's alienated himself from many Americans by giving a speech at Chicago in 1940?
A   Charles Lindbergh spoke at Soldier Field on August 4th and told 40,000 America Firsters that what Hitler was doing in Europe wasn't our business and that he was too strong for America to defeat in a war.

Q   For what purpose was the *Chicago Sun* started?
A   The *Tribune* was anti-Roosevelt and isolationist. Marshall Field decided to start a new morning paper to give Chicagoans an alternative viewpoint.

Q   What Chicago Hotel on Michigan Avenue became a training center and barracks for World War II servicemen?
A   Stevens Hotel

Q   In March of 2004, dozens of gay and lesbians descended on Chicago's city hall, demanding that they be allowed to legally marry a person of the same sex. What was the result?
A   Police had to arrest several angry people for disturbing the peace because city hall replied that the Illinois legislature in 1996 had defined marriage as a union between a man and a woman. One of the people arrested was the daughter of a Chicago alderman.

Q   When John Kerry of Massachusetts was campaigning in Chicago in March of 2004, what embarrassing mistake did he make?
A   After addressing an AFL-CIO group, he went into the audience to talk with members of the audience. He didn't realize his microphone was still on, and he called the Bush administration a "bunch of liars and crooks."

Q   Why is baggage sent to O'Hare Airport in Chicago marked ORD?
A   Orchard Place was the original name of the airfield and that designation is still used.

Q   What Chicagoan won on Donald Trump's show, "The Apprentice" in April of 2004?
A   "Bill Rancic, you're hired at $250,000 a year," said Trump. When offered the chance of managing a beautiful golf course in California or a new skyscraper in Chicago, Rancic said he couldn't leave such a great city – YES!

Sally Rand

CHICAGO GANGSTERS

Q   What Chicago gangster was a mild-mannered florist by day and a murderous bootlegger by night?
A   Dion O'Banion - said to be directly responsible for the deaths of at least 25 men

Q   What head of Chicago's Unione Siciliano was honored with a life size wax figure of himself at his funeral procession?
A   Mike Merlo

Q   What social activist wrote his doctoral thesis on Capone's henchmen?
A   Saul Alinsky

Q   How was Al Capone's brother (Frank) killed?
A   Frank died in a blazing shootout with police during an election-day dispute at **Cicero** in 1924.

Q   Why did Capone pump six bullets into Joe Howard in 1924?
A   Because Jake Guzik went running to Capone and told the Big Guy that Howard had slapped him around.

Crosby's Opera House 1866 (Bettman Archives)

Q   What big time bootlegger turned everything over to Al Capone and left for Italy after an attempt on his life?
A   Johnny Torrio

Q   What harrowing event caused Torrio's hasty retirement?
A   Hymie Weiss, Bugs Moran, and Schemer Drucci put five bullets into Torrio in an assassination attempt.

Q   What northside jazz bar that was popular with gangsters and celebrities in the 1920's is still going strong?
A   The Green Mill

Q   How much life insurance did Capone have?
A   None. He applied to several companies, but they all wisely turned him down.

Q   When Capone went somewhere public, such as the theater, how many bodyguards did he normally take along?
A   Eighteen

Q   How did Chicago extortionists deal with cleaning establishments that refused to pay protection?
A   They hid explosive chemicals in the lining of suits that needed to be cleaned.

Q   Was Capone responsible for the killing of Jake Lingle?
A   Probably not. St. Louisan Leo Brothers did ten years for the crime, but it was more likely done by Jack Zuta who was hired by Bugs Moran. Moran later had Zuta killed so he couldn't talk. Moran probably blamed Lingle for the sudden closing of a roadhouse on Sheridan Road, costing Moran big bucks.

Q   What did Capone do after the Depression hit to make himself popular with Chicago citizens?
A   He set up soup kitchens to feed the hungry and the unemployed

Q   Was Al Capone ever in the comic strips?
A   Chester Gould invented the character Dick Tracy and modeled him after Eliot Ness. He took ideas for the strip from Chicago headlines. Capone was never used in the strip but a similar character named Big Boy was a featured bad guy.

Q   Why did Capone send some of his goons to Hollywood looking for Ben Hecht?
A   Hecht was screenwriter for the film *Scarface*. When they confronted Hecht about the title character, he said it wasn't really Capone, and that the title was used merely to attract more patrons.

Q   What Chicago gangster invented the "drive-by shooting?"
A   Hymie Weiss - who killed a competitor in a drive-by shooting. The man had stolen a shipment of Dion O'Banion's beer and Weiss was working for O'Banion.

Q   How was Frankie Yale killed?

Gangster Frank Nitti

Al Capone

A   Yale was an old friend of Capone's, but the Big Guy thought Yale was chiseling him, so he sent Jack McGurn to New York to gun him down.

Q   Why was Edward O'Hare, Butch O'Hare's father, gunned down on Chicago streets in 1939?
A   Edward O'Hare was one of the informers responsible for sending Al Capone to prison for tax evasion. He was killed shortly after Capone was released from prison as a "present." from the gang.

Q   What did Capone do for a diversion at Alcatraz?
A   He went out for the softball team but was so clumsy he was relegated to the bench.

Q   What kind of an estate did Capone leave his wife and son after he died in 1947 at age 48?
A   He apparently squandered millions and did nothing in the way of investments to take care of his family. He basically died penniless.

Q   What Chicago gangster was the first to take the Fifth Amendment on the witness stand?
A   Murray "the Camel" Humphreys

Q   What big time Chicago gangster started out as a choirboy and a singing waiter?
A   Dion O'Banion

Q   How did Louis Alterie, a good friend of Dion O'Banion, get the nickname "two gun?"
A   He was an enthusiast of western movies and the Wild West. He owned a ranch in Colorado and always carried two six shooters with him – even in Chicago.

Q   How did Vincent "the Schemer" Drucci come to an untimely death?
A   He was arrested after committing intimidating violence during a Chicago election. As he was being taken in for questioning, he got into an argument with detective Dan Healy. Healy slapped him and when he tried to grab Healy's gun, Healy drilled him.

Q   How did Capone get the scars that earned him the nickname "Scarface?"
A   In his Brooklyn youth Capone made some crude remarks to a young woman at a dance hall. Her brother Frank confronted him and when Al mouthed off, Galluccio took out a knife and carved him up.

Q   Who is the "lost Capone?"
A   An older brother, Vincenzo, who left home and went out

West. He became fascinated with the cowboy lifestyle and did not return to the city. He changed his name and became a lawman known as "Two-gun Hart."

Q Did Capone ever hold down a traditional job?
A During World War I he worked for three years in a munitions factory.

Q What kind of huge mansion did Capone live in?
A Interestingly, he lived in a rather unpretentious two-story brick dwelling on Prairie Avenue. It still exists.

Q Who were the two most famous residents of Chicago's Parkway Hotel?
A George "Bugs" Moran and Reinhardt Schwimmer, the dentist and gangster wannabe who happened to be in the wrong place at the time of the St. Valentine's Day Massacre.

Q Why was Bugs Moran's bodyguard Ted Newberry killed in January of 1933?
A Newberry was implicated in an attempted killing of Frank Nitti by two Chicago detectives. This action had the blessing of Mayor Anton Cermak. Newberry's killing was payback by Nitti's boys. Some think that the "accidental" 1933 shooting of Cermak in Miami by Joe Zangara was also payback.

Q What did Cermak say before he died – probably one of the great quotes of all time?
A "I'm glad it was me instead of him." Most historians believe the shots were intended for Roosevelt.

Q Who was the only gangster feared by Al Capone?
A Dion O'Banion's successor, Al Wajciechowski, a Polish thug who changed his name to Earl "Hymie" Weiss. Weiss and his men nearly killed Capone when they shot up his Cicero headquarters with over a thousand slugs.

Q What Chicago gangster is credited with inventing the phrase, "You're going for a ride?"
A Hymie Weiss

JOHN DILLINGER

Eliot Ness (Chicago Historical Society)

John Dillinger (courtesy Dillinger Museum)

Q Was Dillinger born in Chicago?
A No – he was born in 1903 at Indianapolis but was killed in Chicago.

Q How well did Dillinger do in school?
A Most of his teachers and classmates barely remembered him. His grades were average, but he was not a trouble-maker. He quit at age 16.

Q Dillinger read stories about the Old West. Who was his hero?
A Jesse James

Q What teenage gang did Dillinger lead?
A The Dirty Dozen

Q Was Dillinger good at any sports?
A Yes – he was adept at baseball.

Q What did Dillinger decide to do with his life at age 19 in 1923?
A On impulse, he joined the Navy.

Q Did Dillinger secure an honorable discharge when his military stint was over?
A No – he went AWOL when his ship, the *Utah,* docked in Boston. He went back to his father's farm near Mooresville, Indiana, and told everyone he'd been kicked out. He was never prosecuted by the military for desertion.

Q Did Dillinger ever marry?
A Yes – he married a 16-year-old girl from Indiana in April of 1924, Berl Hovious

Q Where did they live?
A Dillinger had no job, so they took turns living with each other's parents.

Q Did Dillinger have any children?
A No

Q What major crime did Dillinger commit in September of 1924?
A He pulled a street holdup and tried to rob a store owner of his weekly receipts.

Q How long of a prison sentence did the judge give Dillinger?
A Fourteen years - the judge didn't like Dillinger's surly attitude and gave him the max.

Q What were Dillinger's vital statistics?
A He was about five feet, seven, brown hair and brown eyes, medium build, 160 pounds.

Q Was Dillinger afraid of hard work?
A Yes. Most gangsters hated physical labor and while in

prison he maimed himself to get out of performing work assignments.

Q   What unsavory characters did Dillinger become buddies with at Pendleton Reformatory? (I know, "reformatory" is an oxymoron.)
A   Harry Pierpont and Homer Van Meter. The latter had already done time at Menard Prison in **Chester**, Illinois.

Q   What happened when Dillinger came up for parole in 1929?
A   He was turned down because of several escape attempts.

Q   When was Dillinger finally paroled?
A   Not until the end of May in 1933 after serving nearly nine years in prison.

Q   What made the parole board sympathetic this time around?
A   His stepmother was dying.

Q   What did Dillinger do not long after being released from prison?
A   He joined the "white caps" gang and began robbing banks.

Q   What nickname did the working press first ascribe to Dillinger?
A   He was called the "athletic bandit" after he vaulted over railings and counters in banks.

Q   What did Dillinger do with his ill-gotten loot?
A   He used it to bribe and pay the right people to break his old buddies out of prison.

Q   How did Dillinger end up in jail at Lima, Ohio, September 28, 1933?
A   After helping his buddies escape, he was captured by authorities.

Q   Did his prison buddies return the favor?
A   Yes – they busted him out of jail by posing as prison authorities, saying they wanted to question Dillinger. A local sheriff was shot and killed in the process.

Q   Since Dillinger's gang frequently holed up in Chicago after their robberies, what action did local authorities take?
A   They formed a special Dillinger Squad dedicated to his capture.

Q   Who was the head of Chicago's Dillinger Squad?
A   Captain John Stege

Q   What head of the Indiana State Police fabricated

Anna Sage – the woman in red

in Tucson, Arizona.

Dillinger stories in hopes of making Harry Pierpont jealous of Dillinger and breaking up the gang?
A   Matt Leach

Q   What book did Dillinger mail to Leach in jest?
A   *How To Be A Detective*

Q   What did law enforcement officials use for target practice instead of the traditional bullseye?
A   A picture of Dillinger; according to Jerry Mizell of south St. Louis, the FBI still trains with Dillinger targets.

Q   What other nickname did the press give Dillinger?
A   "Jackrabbit" – due to the way he leaped over railings at banks.

Q   When did Dillinger kill his first man?
A   During a bank robbery at East Chicago, Indiana, in January of 1934, after which the gang holed up

Q   Who became Dillinger's girl friend at this stage of his career?

G-Man Melvin Purvis

A   Evelyn "Billie" Frechette. His first wife divorced him after he had been in prison about four years.

Q   Where did Dillinger and Billie meet?
A   In a Chicago nightclub where she was working.

Q   What did Dillinger say to a newsman who asked him why he gravitated toward a life of crime?
A   "We can't all be saints."

Q   How was Dillinger captured by Tucson authorities?
A   There was a fire in the Congress Hotel where he was staying. After firemen put out the fire, he drew attention to himself by giving them a huge tip.

Q   Did Dillinger ever fly in an airplane?
A   Yes – he was dragged from his cell, kicking and screaming and flown back to Chicago from Tucson. From there he was transferred to the county jail at Crown Point, Indiana.

Q   What famous photo of Dillinger was taken at Crown Point?
A   When Dillinger arrived in Crown Point, he was surrounded by lawmen, newsmen and photographers.

131

Someone yelled and told prosecuting attorney Robert Estill to put his arm around Dillinger. Dillinger reacted first and put his arm on Estill's shoulder. The picture of Estill acting chummy with Dillinger ruined his career.

Q   What was Dillinger's nickname in prison?
A   The guards called him "whittling Johnny" because he was always whittling on a piece of wood.

Q   Did Dillinger ever carve anything useful?
A   Yes – he carved a crude wooden gun, darkened it with shoe polish, and used it to make an amazing escape.

Dillinger in the picture that ruined Robert Estill's career

Q   Who did Dillinger take with him when he escaped?
A   A Negro named Herbert Youngblood. The man was later shot and killed by authorities after he and Dillinger split.

Q   What federal law did Dillinger violate that enabled the feds to get involved in his case?
A   The Dyer Act that prohibited the transportation of a stolen vehicle across state lines. He did this when he escaped from the prison at Crown Point, Indiana, stole a car, and then fled to Illinois near the town of **Peotone**.

Q   Did Dillinger have a lawyer?
A   Yes – Louis Piquette of Chicago. Piquette was ultimately jailed and disbarred for his criminal associations.

Q   Where did Dillinger, now joined by Billie Frechette, decide to go instead of staying in Chicago?
A   St. Paul, Minnesota

Q   Who were the main members of the new gang he formed?
A   Homer Van Meter and Lester Gillis, better known as Baby Face Nelson

Q   After several bank robberies in Minnesota, where did Dillinger and Frechette hide out?
A   Back in Chicago – April of 1934

Q   Where did the gang get together to plan their next batch of robberies?
A   The Little Bohemia Lodge in Wisconsin

Q   What happened at the Little Bohemia shootout between the Dillinger gang and the G-Men, led by Melvin Purvis of the Chicago FBI?

A   After a fierce shootout, most of the gang escaped into the woods. The feds captured Billie Frechette and the wife of Baby Face Nelson, but several innocent bystanders were injured. Purvis offered his resignation to Hoover after the debacle, but it was declined.

Q   What kind of a sentence was given to Mrs. Helen Nelson and Billie Frechette?
A   A year and a day in jail for Frechette – a year's probation for Helen Nelson

Q   What operation did Dillinger undergo at the end of May in 1934?
A   Plastic surgery – arranged by his lawyer and performed by Dr. Wilhelm Loesser.

Q   How well did the operation succeed?
A   The surgeon botched the job. He also tried to alter Dillinger's fingerprint by scraping away flesh and using acid.

Dillinger girlfriend Polly Hamilton (Wide World)

Q   What happened to Dillinger during the operation?
A   He swallowed his tongue, but the doctor saved his life by retrieving it with forceps and administering artificial respiration.

Q   After Dillinger's face and fingers healed, what two women did he befriend?
A   Polly Hamilton (who became his girlfriend) and Anna Sage, a Romanian immigrant who ran the boarding house where Polly lived.

Q   What was Dillinger's boldest move when he was on the lam?
A   He attended the Chicago World's Fair with Anna Sage and girlfriend Polly Hamilton.

Q   Why did Anna Sage turn Dillinger in to the cops?
A   She also ran a bawdy house and had been caught. To avoid being deported, she cut a deal with the police who, in turn, notified Melvin Purvis and the feds.

Q   How much was the reward being offered for Dillinger at the time of his death?
A   Twenty thousand dollars – state and fed money combined

Q   What was the name of the Chicago Theater where John Dillinger was gunned down by G-Men?
A   Biograph Theater

Q   What alias was Dillinger using at the time he was killed?
A   Jimmy Lawrence

Q   How much money did Dillinger have on him that night?
A $7.80 and a gold pocket watch.

Q   How old was Dillinger when he died?
A   Only 31

Q   Besides photos, what other evidence do we have of Dillinger's physical dimensions?
A   A death mask was made from a moulage. This author bought a good replica off E-Bay a couple of years ago.

Q   What other famous people are buried with Dillinger at Crown Hill Cemetery in Indianapolis?
A   Gun inventor Richard Gatling, President Benjamin Harrison, novelist Booth Tarkington, and poet James Whitcomb Riley.

Q   How did the ticket taker at the Biograph almost blow the operation?
A   She became alarmed when she saw so many men in suits standing around. She thought the feds were possibly a gang that was getting ready to rob her of the night's receipts.

Q   What signal did Melvin Purvis give to the other federal agents at the Biograph Theater to let them know that the man coming out was Dillinger?
A   He lit up a cigar.

Q   What other Chicago theater did Dillinger and the two girls consider going to that Sunday night?
A   The Marbro on Chicago's west side, about nine miles away. Shirley Temple was featured there in *Little Miss Marker*.

Q   What coincidence was there between the St. Valentine's Day Massacre and the Dillinger shooting?
A   The SMC Cartage Company and Biograph Theater were only blocks from each other.

Q   How many shots hit Dillinger?
A   Four – the fatal one piercing his brain. Melvin Purvis was credited with the shot. Purvis tore the buttons off his coat in his haste to draw his weapon.

Q   After Dillinger went down, what did several ghoulish female souvenir hunters do?

A   They stooped down and dipped handkerchiefs or the hem of their dresses in Dillinger's blood.

Q   How many people came to look at Dillinger's body after it was placed on display at the morgue?
A   Five thousand

Q   What did Dillinger think of Bonnie Parker and Clyde Barrow?
A   He thought they were a couple of gun-crazy young punks.

Q   What automaker did Dillinger send a letter to, thanking him for making such a great car that was perfect for getaways after a bank robbery?
A   Henry Ford

Q   Why was Dillinger considered a hero by many Illinoisans?

Louis Piquette – Dillinger's lawyer

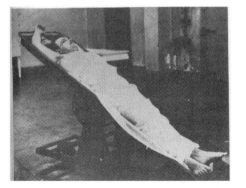

A   Because he robbed banks, and huge numbers of people lost money in banks that failed in the early years of the Depression. The common man felt as though he had been robbed.

Q   Why was Anna Sage called "the Lady in Red?"
A   She told authorities that when she went to the theater that night, she would wear a bright orange dress for easy identification. Under the marquee lights, it looked red to reporters.

Q   How long did John Dillinger's bank robbing crime spree last?
A   For as famous as he became, it was remarkably short – a little over a year – 14 months.

Q   Who gave the most memorable performance portraying Dillinger in the movies?

Dillinger's body

A   Warren Oates in the 1973 film, *Dillinger*. Lawrence Tierney gave a good performance in *Dillinger*, 1945.

Q   What was Dillinger's best quote?
A   "I don't smoke much, and I drink very little. I guess my only bad habit is robbing banks."

Q   What federal law did Dillinger violate that warranted his being gunned down in cold blood by the feds?
A   The only federal law he violated was driving a stolen car across state lines. Crooks seldom get gunned down for such a petty crime. Dillinger's mistake was in becoming so notorious and being such a braggart.

Q   Why were Dillinger bank holdups harrowing for by-standers?
A   He often took hostages and made them stand on the running board of the getaway car, releasing them after they lost their pursuers.

Q   What happened to Anna Sage, the woman in red who fingered Dillinger?
A   The government paid her $5,000 and deported her back to Romania. She died in 1947 from a liver ailment.

Q   What did Dillinger's father, John Sr., do after his son's death?
A   He toured the country and made money with a "Crime Doesn't Pay" show where he gave lectures and told stories about his son. He died in 1943.

Q   What happened to Billie Frechette after she got out of prison?
A   She joined the "Crime Doesn't Pay" traveling show and made money talking about her relationship with John Dillinger.

Q   What happened to Melvin Purvis after the death of Dillinger?
A   He wrote a book called *American Agent*, then he organized the Junior G-Men for Post Toasties breakfast cereal. He didn't get along with Hoover and resigned from the force. In 1960, in ill health, **he shot himself**.

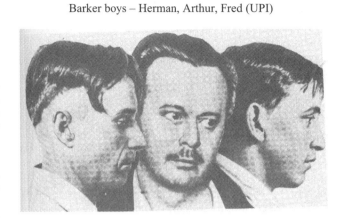
Barker boys – Herman, Arthur, Fred (UPI)

Alvin Karpis (Famous Photos)

BABY FACE NELSON

Q   What was Nelson's given name?
A   Lester Gillis

Q   What was Nelson's lineage?
A   He was born in Chicago, 1908, to Belgian immigrants.

Q   In what part of Chicago did Nelson live?
A   Near the stockyards in a neighborhood called the Patch

Q   How tall was Nelson?
A   Only five feet, five inches

Q   Who was his best friend while he was coming of age?
A   Alvin Karpoviecz (Lithuanian) or Alvin Karpis – both were misfits.

Q   What was Nelson's first major brush with the law?

A   He was arrested in 1922 for stealing a car and was sent to reform school at **St. Charles**.

Q   When was he released?
A   April of 1924, but he was in and out several times after that.

Q   When did George Nelson get married?
A   Late in 1928 he married 16-year-old Chicagoan Helen Wawrzyniak over the strong objection of her parents.

Q   Did they have any children?
A   They had two boys, but they unloaded both of them on his grandmother, Mary Gillis.

Q   Where was his first bank robbery?
A   He had a minor role as a lookout and a wheelman in a robbery at **Spring Grove**.

Q   Where was his next robbery?
A   First National Bank of **Itaska**

Q   Where was his third hit?
A   A bank in **Hillside**

Q   Who was Nelson's first murder victim?
A   For reasons that are unclear, he shot and killed Ted Kidder, a paint salesman.

Q   When did Nelson hook up with Dillinger?
A   Shortly after Dillinger escaped from the Crown Point Jail in 1934.

Q   What curious thing happened when Dillinger and Nelson robbed a bank at Mason City, Iowa?
A   Nelson was posted outside the bank as lookout. Soon a large curious crowd began to form. He took particular delight in firing bursts from his machine gun in the general direction of the crowd to hold them at bay.

Q   Did Nelson kill any FBI agents?
A   Yes – he machine gunned Carter Baum who was chasing him after the shootout at Little Bohemia Lodge in Wisconsin. He severely wounded two others. Nelson hid out in Chicago after the incident at Little Bohemia.

Q   How did Nelson almost get caught on April 30th, 1934?
A   Three policemen, while driving in their car, recognized Nelson and Homer Van Meter. The police chased the pair down and pulled them over, but Nelson got the drop on them. He wanted to shoot the policemen, but Van Meter talked him out of it. Instead, he shot up the police car.

A Nelson stood watch outside and a jewelry store owner figured out that a holdup was taking place. The proprietor came out shooting and hit Nelson with a shot, but a steel vest saved his life. A policeman heard the ruckus and came running, but Nelson shot him dead.

Incredibly, a 16-year-old high school youth jumped on Nelson's back and clung like a cocklebur. Nelson finally shook him off. When Nelson fired and wounded him in the hand, the kid fainted.

The gang made their escape and then split up. Nelson picked up Helen and they went to a hideout in **Barrington**.

Q What kind of a car did Nelson drive?
A A 1933 Ford V-8, license 639-578

Q Was Nelson jealous of Dillinger?
A Yes. It always bothered him that the press referred to the bunch as Dillinger's gang instead of Nelson's gang.

Q What happened at the June 30th, 1934 South Bend bank robbery?

Q How was Nelson finally apprehended?

A   He was spotted by the feds while driving on a road near **Barrington**.

Q   What happened in the ensuing gun battle?
A   Nelson exchanged blistering gunfire with agents Samuel Cowley and Herman Hollis. He killed both of them but was mortally wounded. Nelson's wife Helen and his partner, John Chase, helped him into agent Hollis' Hudson and they fled the scene. Nelson died the next morning at a house in **Skokie**.

Q   How did authorities find Nelson's body?
A   John Chase and Helen Nelson dumped his body in a drainage ditch and then called a local undertaker and told him there was a body at Lincoln and Harms Avenue.

Q   What happened to the police car?
A   It was found all shot up on the side of the road in **Winnetka**.

Q   What happened to Helen Nelson Gillis?
A   She read in the newspapers that she was the new Public Enemy Number One, and that the police and FBI had orders to shoot on sight. Two days later she surrendered to the FBI.

Q   Where was Lester Gillis/George Nelson buried?
A   St. Joseph's Cemetery in **River Grove**

Q   How did Helen Nelson get her sentence reduced?
A   By informing on her husband's chief lieutenant, John Paul Chase. Chase was apprehended and sentenced to life in prison at Alcatraz.

ILLINOIS TOWN FESTIVALS

Note: Some of these old festivals may have been discontinued.

Q   What northern Illinois town on the Fox River has an annual Scarecrow Festival every October?
A   **St. Charles**

Q   What town on the St. Clair/Madison County line has an annual Horseradish Festival and Italianfest?
A   **Collinsville**

Q   What town has a Dog-a-Thon Festival every June?
A   **Pekin**

Q   What southeastern town has a Shrimp Festival every third Saturday in September?

Dillinger Map

A   **Golconda**

Q   What town has an annual Scarecrow Festival?
A   **Galesburg** – the first weekend in October

Q   What town has a Chautauqua festival every June?
A   **Jacksonville**

Q   What town hosts a Labor Day craft show that attracts over 100,000 people?
A   **Frankfort,** off Interstate 80

Q   What town has a Guitar Festival the weekend after Labor Day?
A   **Mundelein** – home of Washburn International Guitars

Q   What town near Mundelein has an annual Oktoberfest the third week in September?
A   **Libertyville**

Q   What town on I – 176 has a Johnny Appleseed Festival in late September?

George "Baby Face" Nelson

A   **Crystal Lake**

Q   What town has a Strawberry Fest the third weekend in

May?
A **Plainfield**

Q   What town in Tazewell County has an annual Marigold Festival?
A **Pekin**

Q   What town features a festival the second week in June that includes food, carnival rides, games and entertainment?
A **Elmhurst** – the Elmfest

Q   What town hosts a 4th of July parade and a Four Bridges bike race?
A **Elgin**

Q   What town recently had a Jack Benny Festival this past June?
A   **Waukegan**

Q   What northern town off I–57 has over 165 art and antique dealers?
A   **Blue Island**

Q   What northern town has a Classic Car Cruise Night every Thursday evening during the summer months?
A   **Crystal Lake** – showcasing about 500 cars every week

Q   What northern Illinois town has a Rhubarb Festival every June?
A   **Aledo**

Q   What Illinois town of Ernest Hemingway's youth did he allegedly describe as having "broad lawns and narrow minds?"
A   **Oak Park**

Q   What town on Route 40 is noted for its annual Schuet-zenfest (shootfest)?
A   **Altamont**

Q   What Illinois town is noted for its annual Broomcorn Festival in September?
A   **Arcola**

Q   What St. Clair County town has an annual Art Festival every May?
A   **Belleville**

Q   What Swedish community has an annual Harvest Fest every September?
A   **Bishop Hill**

State Fair at DuQuoin courtesy Terry Farmer/Ill Tourism

Old toboggan and ski slide at Swallow Cliffs, Palos Hills

Frank Lloyd Wright's Robie House

Q   What town in Eastern Illinois on Route 1 is noted for its annual Rooster Day?
A   **Carmi**

Q   What McHenry County town of 15,000 is noted for its annual Norge (Norway) ski meets?
A   **Cary**

Q   What town on Route 40 is noted for its annual Bocce Ball Tournament?
A   **Casey**

Q   What southern Illinois town on the Mississippi has an annual Popeye Festival?
A   **Chester**

Q   What town on the Mississippi has an annual Miles Davis Festival?
A   **East St. Louis**

Q   What cabbage growing community has an annual Sauer-kraut Festival?
A   **Forreston**

Q   What Whiteside County town has an annual Dutch Days Festival?
A   **Fulton**

Q   What town has an annual Stearman Fly-In for 1930's type double wing airplanes?
A   **Galesburg**

Q   What seat of Kane County has an annual Swedish Festival?
A   **Geneva**

Q   What southern Illinois town on the Mississippi River has an annual Lewis and Clark Festival at an Interpretive Center on route 3?
A   **Hartford**

Q   What northeastern town near the Wisconsin border has an annual Milk Days Festival?
A   **Harvard**

Q   What Williamson County town has an annual Italianfest in May?
A   **Herrin**

Q   What southern Illinois town has an annual Superman celebration?
A   **Metropolis**

Q   What Kankakee County town is noted for an annual Gladiolus Festival?
A   **Momence**

Q   What Illinois town has an annual Wyatt Earp Festival?

A **Monmouth**

Q What did Wyatt's father (Nicholas) do for a living?
A He was a constable at Monmouth and a Union supporter until Lincoln issued the Emancipation Proclamation.

Q What eastern Illinois town has an annual Lone Ranger Festival?
A **Mount Carmel** – home to Brace Beemer, the radio voice of the Lone Ranger

Q What central Illinois town and seat of Washington County has an annual Fall Festival the third week in September?
A **Nashville**

Q What southern Illinois town has an annual Pumpkin Land Festival every October?
A **Ozark**

Q What town is noted for an annual Rodeo Festival every Labor Day in September?
A **Palestine**

Q What seat of Pike County has an annual Pig Days Festival?
A **Pittsfield**

Q What southern Illinois town has annual October Encampment Days, recreating the life of frontier Illinois?
A **Prairie du Rocher**

Q What town on the Rock River was famous for its Booster Rooster Day Festival?
A **Prophetstown**

Q What Illinois towns were named All-America City by Look Magazine at various times in the 1950's and 1960's?
A **Quincy, Peoria, Granite City, Alton, East St. Louis**

Q What Illinois town is famous for its annual Hot Air Balloon races and World Freefall Skydiving?
A **Rantoul**

Q What town's Grandview Drive was declared by Teddy Roosevelt, when he visited, to be the most beautiful in the world?
A **Peoria**

Q What Western Illinois town has an annual Dogwood Festival every May?
A **Quincy**

Q What town has an annual Popcorn Day Festival?

A **Ridgway**

Q What town has an annual Saint Anne's Day?
A **Saint Anne** – because it was founded on Saint Anne's Day. Anne was Jesus' grandmother.

German U-boat at Museum of Science & Industry

Q What town is home to the annual Melon Days Festival on Labor Day?
A **Thomson**

TOWNS WITH NATIVE-AMERICAN NAMES

Q What town in Henry County is named for an Indian tribe?
A **Algonquin**

Q What town name translates from the Indian name for Half Day?
A **Aptakisik**

Q What oldest town in southern Illinois in St. Clair County was named for a local Indian tribe?
A **Cahokia**

Q What town in Bureau County translates to "he walks in his sleep?"
A **Neponset**

Q What northern Illinois town was named for an Indian peace pipe?
A **Calumet City**

Q What town is an Indian word that means "meeting of the waters?"
A **Channahon** in Will County

Q What town on the Iroquois-Kankakee County line translated into "little duck?"
A **Chebanese**

Q What town name translates into "white dove?"
A **Chenoa**

Q What town name translates from an Indian word that means "stinking onion?"
A Chicago – Checagu

Q What Perry County town in southern Illinois is a corruption of the name of a Kaskaskia chieftan?
A **DuQuoin**

Q What town name translates from the Indian word that means "beautiful land?"
A **Kankakee**

Judge David Davis Mansion in Bloomington

Q   What Illinois town was named for a tribe of Sioux Indians?
A **Kansas**

Q What town in Henry County translates from the Winnebago word for "prairie chicken?"
A **Kewanee**

Q What Tazewell County town name translates from the Ojibwa word that means "turtle?"
A **Mackinaw**

Q What Champaign County town is named for a local Indian tribe?
A **Mahomet**

Q What southern Illinois town is named for the Kaskaskia Chief Kanda?
A **Makanda**

Q What Mason County town is a variation of an Indian word that means "great spirit?"
A **Manito** – from Manitou

Q What town is named for the Kankakee half-Indian daughter of a French scout?
A **Manteno**

Q What St. Clair County town was named for the Mascouten Indians?
A **Mascoutah**

Q What Northeastern Illinois town comes from Algonquin words that mean "good land?"
A **Minooka**

Q What Illinois town was named for the half-breed daughter of a Potawatomie chief?
A **Momence**

Q What Shelby County town near **Decatur** gets its name from an Indian word that means "muddy water?"
A **Moweaqua**

Q What town in Cumberland County translates from Indian words that mean "place of the gods?"
A **Neoga**

Q What Montgomery County town is named for the grandmother storyteller in Longfellow's "Hiawatha?"
A **Nokomis**

Q What Henderson County town on the Mississippi River comes from an Indian word that means "yellow banks?"

A **Oquawka**

Q What Winnebago County town name comes from Indian words that mean "river of many bends?"
A **Pecatonica**

Q What large town on the Illinois river is named for one of the five tribes of the Illini?
A **Peoria**

Q What Bond County town is named for the daughter of Powahatan, the chief who nearly killed Captain John Smith of the Jamestown Colony in Virginia?
A **Pocahontas**

Q What town on the Rock River is named for White Cloud, the Sauk Indian who railed against the encroachment of the whites?
A **Prophetstown**

Q When Beatles star George Harrison visited his sister in **Benton** in 1963, at what town did he join a local group called the Four Vests and play a gig?
A **Eldorado** – at the VFW Hall

Q What LaSalle County town is named for a tribe of Indians that lived in New York state?
A **Seneca**

Salt pans used by Native-Americans

1816 Indian treaty map negotiated by W. Clark, Ninian Edwards and Auguste Choteau

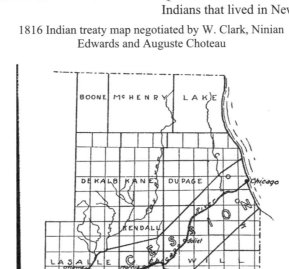

Q What seat of Gallatin County was named for a local tribe of Indians?
A **Shawneetown**

Q What DeKalb County town in Northern Illinois was named for an Indian who was loyal to the whites?
A **Shabbona**

Q What DeKalb County town derives its name from an Indian word that means "paw paw?"
A **Somonauk**

Q What town in Perry County is the French name for the Kiawkashaw Indians?
A **Tamaroa**

Q What town in McLean County derives its name from Indian words that mean "where we bury the dead?"
A **Towanda**

Q What seat of Douglas County gets its name from Indian words that translate to "level plain?"
A **Tuscola**

Q What Iroquois County seat takes its name from the wife

of a Potawatomie Indian who married fur trader Gurdon Hubbard?
A **Watseka**

Q What Pulaski County town is named for a tribe of Cherokee Indians?
A **Wetaug**

Q What Cook County town gets its name from an Indian word that means "beautiful land?"
A **Winnetka**

NOTABLE ILLINOIS TOWNS

Q What town is noted for its collectable pottery and an 83-foot tall totem pole?
A **Abingdon**

Q What Knox County town's station WMBI was the voice of the Moody Bible Institute?
A **Addison** – D.L. Moody founded a Chicago church, a Bible institute, and a radio network.

Q What seat of Edwards County was known as the English Settlement and was founded by Morris Birbeck and George Flower?
A **Albion**

Q What is unusual about the Haskell House in **Alton**?
A It isn't a real house, it's a one-room child's playhouse, built in 1885 in the Queen Anne architectural style. The only other such playhouse in the state is the Ellwood playhouse in **DeKalb**. It looks like a regular house except it is only thirteen by fifteen feet in outside dimensions.

Q What northern Illinois town has five buildings designed by Chicago architect George G. Elmslie?
A **Aurora** – the Healy Chapel, the Graham Building, Second National Bank, Keystone Building, American National Bank

Q The student newspaper at SIUE is named the *Alestle*. Can you name the three towns that give the newspaper its title?
A **Alton, East St. Louis**, and **Edwardsville** – where SIU has had campuses

Shabbona – Chief of the Potawatomie

Q What Illinois town had the state's first municipal library in 1819?
A **Albion**

Q What Mercer County town has a restaurant called "The Slammer" where meals are served in old jail cells?
A **Aledo**

Q How was Aledo's town name chosen?
A The founding fathers drew five letters out of a hat.

Q What Henry County town is home to Raging Buffalo Snowboard Park?
A **Algonquin**

Q What town in Marion County was named for a Crimean War battle?
A **Alma**

Q What town in Effingham County, on Route 40, was named for a rise of high ground?
A **Altamont**

Q What southern Illinois town has the Smallpox Needle, a monument to 1,300 Confederates who died there while in prison?
A **Alton**

Q Why was Upper Alton sometimes called "**Pie Town**?"
A It started back in 1846 when the women of the area began baking pies for soldiers going off to fight in the Mexican War.

Q What was amazing about the creation of Illinois Glass Company of **Alton** in 1873, which became the largest in the world?
A William Smith and Edward Levis bought a small glass factory, a business venture that had already failed on three occasions in Alton. Most of their knowledge came from a chemistry book (borrowed from a druggist) that had a chapter on glass making.

Q By the 1890's, how large was the expanded glass plant?
A It covered 45 acres and employed 3200 men and women. The plant consumed well over 80 tons of coal

Map showing Illinois Indian tribes in 1765

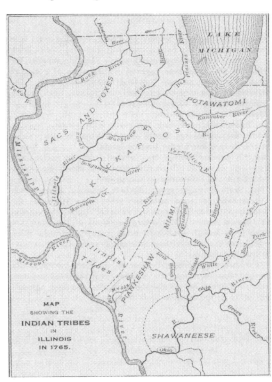

daily.

Q   What is the name of the beautiful suspension bridge across the Mississippi at **Alton**?
A   The Clark Bridge, honoring William Clark of the Lewis and Clark expedition

Q   Name the town where Charles Dickens' brother started a newspaper in 1854?
A   **Amboy**

Q   What Henry County coal mining town was settled mostly by Belgians?
A   **Atkinson**

Q   What Logan County town on old Route 66 was originally called Xenia?
A   **Atlanta**

Alton Little Theater

Q   What is the name of the town close to the point where the Rock River flows into the Mississippi?
A   **Andalusia**

Q   What town has a chapel that was endowed by the Swedish Nightingale, Jenny Lind?
A   **Andover**

Q   What Union County town was home to Bunny Bread and the man who created the comic strip, "Moon Mullins?"
A   **Anna**

Q   What Pike County town, named for a mythical strong man, was once the residence of Brigham Young?
A   **Atlas**

Q   What Illinois town came from the oldtimers expression, "See you at the wood?"
A   **Atwood**

Q   What Kane County town is named for the goddess of dawn?
A   **Aurora**

Q   What was the first Illinois town to have electric street lights?
A   **Aurora**

Q   What Lake County place with a biblical name is the principal town in the Chain O' Lakes?
A   **Antioch**

Q   What Illinois town in Fulton County was named for a Swedish ruler during the Napoleonic Era?
A   **Bernadotte**

Alton Glass Factory – 1873

Q   What Douglas County town was home to the creator of Raggedy Ann and Andy?
A   **Arcola**

Q   What town, known for its starchy name, was home to Cincinnati Red's slugger, Ted Kluszewski?
A   **Argo** – home to Argo Corn Starch

Q   What Illinois town is also a style of men's dress socks?
A   **Argyle**

Q   What Kankakee County town is at the confluence of the Kankakee and Iroquois rivers?
A   **Aroma Park**

Q   What Amish town uses the slogan, "Where You're a Stranger Only Once?"
A   **Arthur**

Q   What Christian County town was named for a parish in Louisiana?
A   **Assumption**

Q   What Fulton County town was named for fur mogul John Jacob Astor?
A   **Astoria**

Q   What town near **Decatur** was originally called Marrowbone, by two fur traders who survived a blizzard by sucking on bone marrow?
A   **Bethany**

Q   What town in southern Illinois has a bed and breakfast called "Hard Day's Night" because Beetle George Harrison once stayed there?
A   **Benton**

Q   What Lake County town is named for a place in Scotland?
A   **Bannockburn**

Q   What northwest Chicago suburb is home to Jewel Tea?
A   **Barrington**

Q   What Pike County town is a misspelling of Barre, Vermont?
A   **Barry**

Q   What Kane County town called itself the "Windmill Capital of America?"
A   **Batavia**

Q   In 1930 about 75 percent of **Cicero's** population came from what European country?

A Czechoslovakia

Q What African-American town in southern Illinois was known as "Pistol City" in the 1930's?
A **Colp**

Q What Illinois town was named for the father of the woman who wrote *Uncle Tom's Cabin*?
A **Beecher** – for preacher Henry Ward Beecher, noted abolitionist and father of Harriet Beecher Stowe

Q What Southern Illinois town is the seat of the oldest county in the state?
A **Belleville** – St. Clair County

Q What southern Illinois town has the **second oldest symphony orchestra in the nation**?
A **Belleville**

Q What suburb of Peoria has a name that is French for "beautiful view?"
A **Bellevue**

Q What Chicago suburb is home to Borg-Warner and Chicago Screw?
A **Bellwood**

Q What southern Illinois town was named for a famous Missouri senator during the Jacksonian era?
A **Benton** – for Thomas Hart Benton

Q What town was hit by a two million dollar fire in May of 1900?
A **Bloomington**

Q What town has a Franklin Avenue that is the **only street in America with a university at both ends**?
A **Bloomington** – Illinois State and Illinois Wesleyan

Q What Illinois town has a newspaper called the *Pantograph*?
A **Bloomington**

Q Where is the Prairie Aviation Museum?
A At the Bloomington-Normal Airport on Route 9 east of **Bloomington**. It has displays of jet aircraft and helicopters. The facility also has a nice Ozark Airlines DC-3.

Q What town north of Kankakee is home to Olivet University?
A **Bourbonnais**

Q At what town did King

Edward VII of England go hunting near the Santa Fe Bottoms in 1860?
A **Breese**

Q What town in Lawrence County was once known as Hardscrabble?
A **Bridgeport**

Q What town in Madison County was founded by ex-slaves and was the largest all-black community in Illinois?
A **Brooklyn**

Q What southern Illinois town is home to the Irvin S. Cobb Bridge across the Ohio River?
A **Brookport**

Q What large Kentucky town does this Illinois bridge lead to?
A Paducah

Jenny Lind Chapel – Andover

Q What southern Illinois town near **Vienna** is home to the Vertical Rock Climbing School?
A **Buncombe**

Q What Macoupin County town is named for an early battle in the Revolutionary War?
A **Bunker Hill**

Q What Illinois town, south of **Waterloo** and near Route 3, is home to Illinois Caverns State Natural Area offering tourists a chance to explore caves?
A **Burksville**

Q What is the technical name for a cave explorer?
A Spelunker

Monument at Bible Garden – Illinois Wesleyan at Bloomington

Q What town, south of **Rockford**, was named for an English poet?
A **Byron** – for Lord Byron

Q What town was named by its founder because he believed it was antipodal (directly opposite) a town in China?
A **Canton**

Q What southern Illinois town, founded by Daniel Brush, has a name that means "coal valley?"
A **Carbondale**

Q What town is home to Blackburn College?
A **Carlinville**

Q What town in Woodford County buried Democrats in one cemetery and Republicans in another?

A   **Carlock**

Q   What town has the only foot and wagon suspension bridge in Illinois?
A   The General William Dean Suspension Bridge at **Carlyle**, named for a town hero captured at the beginning of the Korean War.

Q   What eastern Illinois town is named for the biblical character that was the son of Reuben and grandson of Jacob?
A   **Carmi**

Q   What seat of Greene County was home to Marcus Reno, who fought alongside George A. Custer against Indians?
A   **Carrollton**

Q   What town had a miner who initiated the practice in Illinois of taking a canary into the coal mines to detect deadly fumes?
A   **Carterville**

Q   What five governors called **Edwardsville** their home?
A   Edward Coles, Ninian Edwards, John Reynolds, Thomas Ford and Charles Deneen

Q   What seat of Hancock County has a famous jail where Mormon leader Joseph Smith was murdered?
A   **Carthage**

Q   What Illinois politician has two towns named for him?
A   Zadoc Casey – **Caseyville** and **Casey**

Q   What town in Hardin County has a cave that was once home to river pirates and counterfeiters?
A   **Cave-in-Rock**

Q   What Stephenson County town is the burial site of Jane Addams, the woman who started Chicago's Hull House?
A   **Cedarville**

Q   What central Illinois town, that bills itself as the Gateway to Egypt, hosted a state fair in 1858?
A   **Centralia**

Q   What town near Decatur translates to "Fat Hill" and was named for a battle in the Mexican War?
A   **Cerro Gordo**

Q   What southern Illinois town has the oldest courthouse in the state?
A   **Cahokia** – its courthouse dates back to 1737.

Q   What southern Illinois town has the oldest brick building in the state?

A   **Cahokia** – the Jarrot Mansion, 1810

Q   How old is the Holy Family Church in **Cahokia**?
A   It is the oldest in the state, dating back to early 1700.

Q   What southern Illinois town once had the highest per-capita commercial valuation in the U.S.?
A   **Cairo**

Q   What Illinois "Sin Town" was originally called West Hammond?

A   **Calumet City**

Dean Suspension Bridge at Carlyle

Q   What town in Henry County was home to Benjamin Walsh, an entomologist (bugs) who co-founded "The American Entomologist" magazine?
A   **Cambridge**

Q   What Illinois town has the Orendorff House, built by Chicago architect Robert C. Spencer, an early proponent of the Prairie Style?
A   **Canton**

Q   What town's courthouse, dismantled and stored in the backyard of East St. Louis businessman Alexander Cella, was rebuilt and displayed at the St. Louis World's Fair in 1904?
A   **Cahokia** – it is the oldest west of the Appalachians

Q   What town was the site of **our nation's first observance of Memorial Day**?
A   **Carbondale**

Q   What famous newspaper columnist and avid baseball fan was born at **Champaign** in 1941?
A   George Will

Q   What happened when the town of **Urbana** tried to annex West Urbana?
A   Citizens revolted and renamed their town **Champaign** after a county in Ohio.

Q   What town is home to the **tallest Abe Lincoln statue in the world**?
A   **Charleston** – six stories tall, it shows him clutching a copy of the Emancipation Proclamation.

Jarrot Mansion in Cahokia – oldest brick building in the state – photo by Bill Jacobus

Q What town in north central Illinois (Bureau County) was home to one of the state's worst mine disasters?
A **Cherry** – 1909; 259 miners were killed.

Q What northern Illinois town is home to Kegel Harley Davidson, the **world's oldest Harley Davidson dealer**?
A **Cherry Valley**

Q What southern Illinois town on the Mississippi is home to Menard Prison?
A **Chester**

Q What town was home to Vitreous Enamel Products that produced a 12-ton assembly line steel Lustron Home, popular with returning WW II vets?
A **Cicero**

Lustron all-metal house in Highland

Q How many house units could the plant turn out in a single day?
A 26

Q Of what material were the interior walls of Lustron homes made?
A Enameled porcelain over metal

Q Where was the first Lustron house erected in 1946?
A Suburban **Hinsdale**

Q What were the dimensions of the early Lustron home models?
A 31 feet x 35 feet – two bedrooms

Q What is the easiest way to spot a Lustron home?
A The exterior is done in metal panels that are about two feet square.

Q Where are the two Lustron homes in **Highland**?
A There is one at 717 Poplar, near the hospital, and another at 1423 Laurel on the east end of town.

Q What is the biggest enemy of a Lustron home?
A Rust (Note: For more info on this topic, buy a copy of Tom Fetters' book, *The Lustron Home*.)

Q What Illinois towns are known to have had one or more Lustron homes?
A Addison, Albion, Algonquin, Arlington Heights, Ashland, Aurora, Bedford Park, Belleville, Bensenville, Bloomington, Brookfield, Bushnell, Cambridge, Canton, Carlinville, Carthage, Centralia, Champaign, Chicago, Cicero, Clinton, Colchester, Colfax, Columbia, Danville, Decatur, Deland, Des Plaines, Dixon, Downers Grove, Dwight, East St. Louis, Edwardsville, Elgin, Elmhurst, Evanston, Fairbury, Fairview Heights, Farina, Farmer City, Freeport, Geneva, Gibson City, Glen Ellyn, Grand Ridge, Griggsville, Hamilton, Harvard, Havana, Hazel Crest, Highland, Hinsdale, Homewood, Jacksonville, Joliet, LaSalle, Le Roy, Leland, Lincolnshire, Litchfield, Little York, Lombard, Macomb, Mansfield, Marengo, Mascoutah, Mattoon, McHenry, Mendota, Meredosia, Moline, Monmouth, Monticello, Morton Grove, Mount Carmel, Mount Morris, Mount Prospect, Mount Vernon, Moweaqua, Naperville, Normal, Oak Lawn, Olney, Onarga, Orion, Palatine, Peoria, Peoria Heights, Peotone, Peru, Pisgah, Pittsfield, Pleasant Plains, Poag, Polo, Pontiac, Princeton, Prospect Heights, Quincy, Rochester, Rock Island, Rockford, Roselle, Sandwich, Saunemin, Savanna, Sheridan, Skokie, Somonauk, South Beloit, Springfield, Strawn, Sycamore, Urbana, Vandalia, Vermilion, Villa Park, Waterloo, Watseka, West Chicago, Westmont, Wheaton, Wilmette, Windsor, Woodstock, York Center, Yorkville

Q What town in DeWitt County is a nuclear power site and has a Days Inn featuring a series of **luxury fantasy suites** with various esoteric décor such as jungle, desert, Roman, Cupid (heart-shaped bed), etc.?
A **Clinton**

Q What company town near **Carbon Hill** has a newspaper called *The Courant* and was home to William Somerville who had an airplane factory circa 1910?
A **Coal City** – the 1875 Diamond Coal Mine disaster was near here.

Q What Rock Island County town is home to the Niabi Zoo, featuring lions and tigers?
A **Coal Valley**

Q What southern Illinois town was home to Agnes Ayers, who starred in silent movies with Rudolph Valentino?
A **Cobden**

Jail where Joseph Smith killed at Carthage

Q What southwestern Illinois town features a 1904 full-size Bull Durham mural?
A **Collinsville**

Q Where is an annual observance of the spring equinox, held at 5:45 A.M. at a reconstructed ancient sun calendar?
A Cahokia Mounds State Historic Site near **Collinsville**

Q How high is Cahokia Mound?
A 100 feet

Q When was the mound occupied by the Cahokia Indians?
A A.D. 700-1400

Q What was the Native-American population of the mound area at its zenith?
A Ten to fifteen thousand

Q How many distinct terraces are on the mound?
A Four

Q How many acres does the great mound cover?
A Fourteen

Q How was the mound built?
A The dirt was carried there in baskets or in pottery.

Q Which is larger in total volume, the Great Pyramid of Egypt, or the Great Cahokia Mound?
A Cahokia Mound

Q Was the great mound a burial site?
A No – there was a large building on top and it is believed the chief ruled from this site.

Q Why is Cahokia Mound also called Monks Mound?
A A group of Trappist monks from France lived there from around 1808-14.

Q Who owned the mound at that time?
A Nicholas Jarrot, a prominent resident of **Cahokia**

Q In recent years, large sections of the mound have slid downslope as a unit. This is called slumping. What is being done to prevent further deterioration?
A The mound sits on a high water table and water build up is the problem. Horizontal pipe drains that are perforated carry excess water away from the mound to a drainage pit.

Q Has new dirt ever been added to the mound in recent years?
A Yes – to repair the slump areas

Q Are there other smaller mounds in the area?
A Originally there were about 100. Some of the mounds in **East St. Louis** were simply bulldozed as the town grew and developed.

Interpretive Center near Cahokia/Monks Mound

Old time circus comes to Carlinville by James Denby

Q What is Woodhenge?
A It's the name given to a circle of wooden posts east of the Great Mound that were used as a solar calendar by local natives, much like Stonehenge in England.

Q What town in Jersey County took its name from a lake in New York where summer camps were held to train Sunday School teachers?
A **Chautauqua** – established by the Methodist Episcopal Church that built cottages for education, religion and recreation; automobiles are still discouraged on the narrow tree-lined streets.

Q What southern Illinois town in Monroe County was named by George Rogers Clark for Lady Liberty?
A **Columbia** – its old name was Grand Ruisseau (Great Run)

Q What town, whose prep teams are the Hornets, is home to the Thompson Mill covered bridge, built in 1843?
A **Cowden**

Q What town in Will County, near **Joliet**, holds an annual memorial service for Czech citizens of Lidice, who were murdered by the Nazis in retaliation for the killing of Hangman Heydrich by the Resistance?
A **Crest Hill**

Q What Will County town has a name that was picked from the Bible at random?
A **Crete**

Q What town in Tazewell County has a name that translates to "broken heart?"
A **Creve Coeur**

Q What Fulton County town was so named because the many lakes and ponds reminded founders of an island in the Caribbean?
A **Cuba**

Q What southern Illinois town is home to a sandstone formation called Rainbow Arch?
A **Cypress**

Q What town near **Nauvoo** was named for a Vice-president of the U.S.?
A **Dallas** – after George Dallas

Q What Illinois city has two parks with the name Scovill?
A **Decatur**

Q What town is home to Milliken University?

A Decatur

Q What company recently closed its doors in **Decatur** with the loss of several thousand jobs?
A Firestone

Q What town was home to A.E. Staley who first proposed that soybean be used for animal feed and industrial raw materials?
A **Decatur**

Q What seat of Macon County was named for a hero in the Tripolitan War?
A **Decatur** – for Stephen Decatur

Q What town is home to Northern Illinois University?
A **DeKalb**

Q What town is named for a German baron who volunteered his services in the Revolution and was killed at the Battle of Camden, S.C.?
A **Dekalb**

Q What was the only Illinois town to build a movie theater with an Egyptian motif?
A **DeKalb** – the 1928 Egyptian theater; Egyptian design became very popular in Illinois after the discovery of King Tut's tomb in 1922.

Q What southern Illinois town is named for the Spanish explorer who discovered the Mississippi River?
A **DeSoto**

Ellwood Child's Playhouse in Dekalb

Q What Northern Illinois town on the Rock River was home to Charles Walgreen, founder of the drug store chain?
A **Dixon**

Q What town has a Lowell Park with a swimming pool where Ronald Reagan once was a lifeguard?
A **Dixon**

Q What **Dixon** man was the creator of the comic strip "Buck Rogers" - 1929?
A John F. Dille, a graduate of the University of Chicago; Ray Bradbury said it was the "Buck Rogers" strip that inspired him to write about science fiction.

Q What Illinois town was the longtime residence of pool/billiards champion Minnesota Fats?
A **Dowell**

Q What town was home to Alan Pinkerton, founder of the Pinkerton Detective Agency?

A Dundee

Q What southern Illinois town with a French name is home to Falling Springs Park?
A **Dupo**

Q What southern Illinois town was the site of the Hambletonian, a world-famous harness race?
A **DuQuoin**

Q In what town did this author attend a state fair during his 1960 Labor Day weekend honeymoon?
A **DuQuoin** – My wife and I were both sophomores in college at the time. I wasn't cheap, just poor. Well, maybe some cheap.

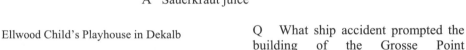

Fischer Theater in Danville

Q What town on Route 66 was home to the Keeley Institute, a home for the treatment of alcoholism?
A **Dwight**

Q During the 1880's what was thought to be the remedy for a morning hangover?
A Sauerkraut juice

Q What ship accident prompted the building of the Grosse Point Lighthouse at **Evanston**?
A The *Lady Elgin* in 1860

Q What is the translation of the French phrase, Grosse Point?
A Great Promontory

Q What honor was achieved by Alex Holsinger of **Normal**, Illinois?
A He earned the rank of Eagle Scout by cleaning up and documenting names in the cemetery at **Shirley** in McClean County. Alex was declared to be the one millionth young man to earn the distinction.

Q What southern Illinois town is home to Winchester Western Cartridge small arms?
A **East Alton** – it's next to the Olin Brass mill; they use Olin brass for their cartridges.

Q What Madison County town bills itself as the third oldest in the state?
A **Edwardsville**

Q What southern Illinois town has a LeClaire historic district where N.O. Nelson had a company town?
A **Edwardsville**

Q   What was manufactured at the 1895 N.O. Nelson plant?
A   Plumbing fixtures

Q   Why was the 200-acre area called LeClaire?
A   Nelson named it for a Frenchman named Mason LeClaire, a man who advocated cooperative efforts.

Q   What was unusual about Nelson's company town?
A   He built houses for his workers and allowed them to purchase the property at a reasonable price. He also built them a park, a lake, a ball diamond, and a school.

Q   What southern Illinois town has the Propellex Corporation that makes explosives for pilot ejection seats and explosives to help cap oil well fires?
A   **Edwardsville**

Q   What town in central Illinois on Route 40 is home to the John Boos Company, the **nation's oldest maker of butcher blocks**?
A   **Effingham**

Q   What town in Saline County was named for Judge Samuel Elder?
A   **Eldorado** – Elder-ado

Q   What central Illinois town bills itself as "The Heart of the USA?"
A   **Effingham**

Q   What northeastern Illinois town's Board of Trade once largely set the nation's dairy prices?
A   **Elgin**

Q   What was the first rural community in Illinois to get electricity?
A   **Elmwood** – 1889

Q   What is the only town in the U.S. platted and surveyed by the U.S. government in addition to Washington, D.C.?
A   **Equality** in Gallatin County near the salt licks

Q   Near what southern Illinois town is a fifty-foot restored stone

University Center at SIU Edwardsville (courtesy SIUE)

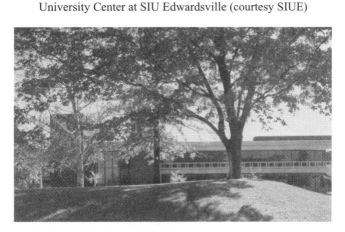

A   **Elgin**

Greyhound Depot and Post House at Effingham

Q   How far back does the Rose Hotel go?
A   1812

Restored Iron Furnace at Elizabethtown

furnace that was used to smelt limonite ore to make pig iron?
A   **Elizabethtown** – it operated from 1839-1883, except for the years during the Civil War.

Q   What did the call letters at station WTMV in **East St. Louis** at the Broadview Hotel represent?
A   Watch The Mississippi Valley

Q   What municipal park, with well over 1,000 acres, was the **third largest in the nation** when it was created in **East St. Louis** around 1930?
A   Grand Marais (great swamp) – later renamed Frank Holten State Park to honor a long-serving state legislator

Q   What town was home to **Frederick Maytag**, the man who made washers and dryers so reliable that the repairmen have little to do?

Q   What town in Jo Daivess County is named for Mrs. Armstrong, who inspired and rallied frontier fort defenders at Apple River?
A   **Elizabeth** – known by some as E-town

Q   What southern Illinois town is home to the Rose Hotel, until 1978 the oldest continuously operated hotel in the state?
A   **Elizabethtown**

Q   What Chicago suburb is home to McDonald's Hamburger College?
A   **Elk Grove**

Q   What diminutive structure, near the entrance to Principia College at **Elsah,** seems to be a collection of errors?
A   The Mistake House – actually built from a variety of materials to field test them since they would be used for campus buildings. Some call it the Sample House.

Q   What Jersey County town is home to Principia (Christian

Scientist) College?
A **Elsah** – The college moved here from St. Louis in 1935

Q What city in Illinois was the ultimate destination for many escaped slaves?
A Chicago - because Chicago was a large city and many residents were sympathetic to the plight of the slaves.

Q What southern Illinois town has the old Crenshaw House, where slaves were kept for the purpose of producing salt?
A **Equality**

Q How was salt processed at Gallatin County's Half Moon Lick near **Equality**?
A There were actually two salt licks on the Saline River, and archaeological evidence shows that Woodland and Mississippian people produced salt there from 100 B.C. to 1600 A.D. The French government first started processing salt there around 1735. The American government took over around 1802 and leased them with the requirement that ten percent of the proceeds would go to the U.S. Treasury. The lessees had to produce at least 120,000 bushels annually.

The brine was boiled in large iron kettles on furnaces fueled by wood. After the nearby wood supply was depleted, new furnaces were built two miles away closer to wood sites, and the brine was carried to the furnaces by wood (log) pipes with six inch holes drilled through them. A complex bucket system was used to hoist the brine to a thirty-foot high cistern with the brine flowing to the furnaces by gravity.

So important was the backbreaking task of making salt that this was the **only place in Illinois where slavery was legal**.

Q What were the names of the two salt licks at **Equality**?
A Half Moon Lick and Great Salt Spring

Q By 1810 what was the annual production of Half Moon lick?
A 126,000 bushels of salt

Q What town has the school where Ronald Reagan played college football?
A **Eureka**

Scenic Elsah by Robert Graul

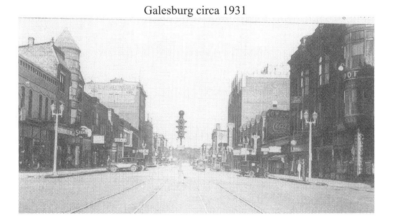

Galesburg circa 1931

Q What town was the birthplace of noted columnist Drew Pearson?
A **Evanston**

Q What town is home to the only private school in the Big Ten?
A **Evanston** - Northwestern

Q What percent of Northwestern University's students rank in the top ten percent of their high school graduating classes?
A 83 percent

Q What town was home to captain Adam Bogardus, the national shooting champion who traveled with Bill Cody's Wild West Show?
A **Elkhart**

Q What southern Illinois town is home to the Pierre Menard house, the man who was the first lieutenant governor of the state?
A **Ellis Grove**

Q What town in Peoria County is home to Lorado Taft's "Pioneers of the Prairie" statue whose inscription reads: "To the pioneers who bridged the streams, subdued the soil, and founded a state?"
A **Elmwood**

Q What town was home to Bishop Fulton J. Sheen, a noted 1950's radio and television commentator on life and theology?
A **El Paso**

Q What northern Illinois town is the national headquarters for Rotary International?
A **Evanston**

Q What northeastern Illinois city (not Chicago) is home to five institutions of higher learning?
A **Evanston**

Q Civil War general Lew Wallace spent some time in **Fairfield,** attending to legal business. While there, he worked on the manuscript of what famous novel?
A *Ben Hur*

Q What town on the American Bottom was home to American Zinc, the nation's second leading processor of that commodity?
A **Fairmont City**

Q Who owns the **Rock Island** home of lumber baron

Frederick Weyerhaeuser?
A Augustana College

Q What town is home to St. Clair Square, one of the most profitable malls in the entire state?
A **Fairview Heights**

Q What town near Lake Shelbyville has an annual Christmas Festival of Lights drawing over 200,000 visitors annually?
A **Findlay**

Q What Chicago suburb has a Scottish name that means "gently rolling meadow?"
A **Flossmoor**

Q What Chicago suburb is said to be more dead than alive because of its many cemeteries?
A **Forest Park** – Elizabeth Taylor's husband Michael Todd is buried here.

Q What Lake County town is named for the cavalry officer who once said that the only good Indian was a dead Indian?
A **Fort Sheridan** – for Phillip Sheridan

Q What Stephenson County town was the site of the second Lincoln-Douglas debate in 1858?
A **Freeport**

Q What town in Stephenson County has one of the tallest Civil War monuments in the state?
A **Freeport** – built in 1871 and it's 96 feet tall

Q What Whiteside County town on the Mississippi has a large nine-story windmill celebrating the town's Dutch heritage?
A **Fulton**

Q How did **French Village,** on the outskirts of **East St. Louis,** get started?
A According to research by Don Rogier of **Highland**, if newly arriving French immigrants to **Cahokia** were suspected of having cholera, they were placed in a stockade at French Village, about nine miles away.

Q What Northeastern Illinois town was home to America's first mining boom?

A **Galena**

Q What metal was mined at **Galena**?
A Lead

Q What percent of the nation's lead supply came from **Galena** in 1834?
A 85 percent

Q What town is home to Knox College?
A **Galesburg**

Q What town had the Purington Brick Works that produced bricks used in the construction of the Panama Canal?
A **Galesburg**

Q What town has the Riverbank Laboratories, a place where prominent scientists lived and worked?

Freeport Fire Station Number One

A **Geneva**

Q What is the Sabine formula?
A It is an equation that is still used to determine sound absorption coefficients. Paul Sabine developed this formula while working in the acoustics lab at Riverbank in **Geneva**.

Q What World War II related science was taught at the Riverbank Lab in **Geneva**?
A Cryptology – code breaking

Q What southern Illinois town in Madison County has a translated name that means "coal valley?"
A **Glen Carbon**

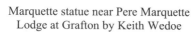
Marquette statue near Pere Marquette Lodge at Grafton by Keith Wedoe

Q What Illinois town was home to the poet Archibald MacLeish?
A **Glencoe**

Q What town's Curtiss Airport hosted the International Air Races during the 1933 Chicago World's Fair?
A **Glenview**

Q Where in Illinois did 19 year-old George H. Bush learn how to land a Navy plane on the deck of an aircraft carrier?
A **Glenview** – Naval Air Station Glenview trained thousands of World War II Navy pilots. A Lake Michigan steamship (U.S.S. Sable) was refitted to simulate the deck of a carrier.

Q What other future President finished out his tour of duty with the U.S. Navy at the Glenview base that had formerly been the Curtiss Airport?

A   Gerald Ford

Q   Where was the *U.S.S. Sable* and its sister ship, the *U.S.S. Wolverine*, berthed at night?
A   **Navy Pier** – each morning they steamed northward on Lake Michigan to receive Navy planes and their pilots.

Q   What landmark in **Wilmette** was a rendezvous point for **Glenview** World War II Navy pilots before they were given final instructions for carrier landings on Lake Michigan?
A   Baha'i Temple – code name Point Obo

Q   What Hollywood actor was a flight instructor at **Glenview** Naval Air Station and lived with his wife Barbara Stanwyck in nearby **Park Ridge**?
A   Robert Taylor

Q   What future astronaut was in the naval reserves at **Glenview** Naval Air Station?
A   Neil Armstrong

Naval Air Station at Glenview

Q   Where was the first major nursery in northern Illinois?
A   Kennicott Grove in **Glenview**, established by horticulturalist Dr. John Kennicott in 1836

Q   What Illinois town is the birthplace of Red Schoendienst, the baseball Cardinal Hall of Famer?
A   **Germantown**

Marston Hall at Greenville College

Q   What Illinois town was named for a circuit judge who was a friend of Lincoln's?
A   **Gillespie** – for Judge Joseph Gillespie

Q   What river town is home to beautiful Pere Marquette Park?
A   **Grafton**

Q   What town's Demoulin Brothers factory is noted for making circus outfits and uniforms for high school and college marching bands?
A   **Greenville**

Q   How many generals did **Galena** furnish in the Civil War?
A   Nine – Grant, Rawlins, Chetlain, Duer, Parker, Rowley, John E. Smith, John S. Smith, Maltby

Q   What town was the birthplace of singer/actor Howard Keel?

A   **Gillespie** – he starred in *Carousel, Showboat* and *Kiss Me Kate*

Q   What town near **Alton** was home to Monticello College for women?
A   **Godfrey**

Q   What southern Illinois town was known as the "Pittsburgh of the West" because of its numerous steel mills?
A   **Granite City**

Q   What southern Illinois town was originally called "Six Mile Prairie" because it was located six miles from St. Louis?
A   **Granite City**

Q   What native of **Granville** was in a mine accident that cost him four toes? This led to his becoming a pitcher instead of an outfielder.
A   Red Ruffing - he was a star for the NY Yankees.

Q   What town on Route 40 has a covered bridge over the Embarras River, the longest of its type in the state?
A   **Greenup**

Q   What town in Bond County was the boyhood home of Robert Ingersoll, noted agnostic?
A   **Greenville** – also home to a college founded by free Methodists

Q   What were some beliefs of early free Methodists?
A   Free Methodists were formed in the state of New York around 1860. According to Jim Reinhard of **Greenville**, the split in the Methodist church occurred for several reasons: (1) Free Methodists were anti-secret societies - such as the Masons (2) Free Methodists were abolitionists (3) they were egalitarian; mainstream Methodists had fundraisers where affluent members bought and sat in their own pews while the poor were relegated to the balcony.

Q   What town was the site of the Abolition Riot of 1838 between pro-slave forces and abolitionists?
A   **Griggsville**

Q   What northern Illinois town, named for a Chicago mayor, is home to a Six Flags amusement park and a huge shopping mall?
A   **Gurnee**

Q   What Hancock County town on the Great River Road is

the site of Keokuk Dam?
A **Hamilton**

Q What Kane County town is noted for its Eberly's Honey Hill apiaries?
A **Hampshire**

Q What town in JoDaviess County calls itself the "Mallard Capital of the World?"
A **Hanover**

Q What seat of Calhoun County is famous for its lift bridge on the Illinois River?
A **Hardin**

Q What did the call letters of radio station WEBQ in **Harrisburg** represent?
A We Entertain Beyond Question

Q What seat of Saline County is close to the Garden of the Gods?
A **Harrisburg**

Q What southern Illinois town on the American Bottom was founded by International Shoe in 1890?
A **Hartford**

Q What Mason County town on the Illinois River was called the "Catfish Riviera of Illinois?"
A **Havana**

Q What town near the Wisconsin border was named for a Scottish hymn?
A **Hebron**

Q What town in Mon-roe County was founded by a leader of a failed German revolutionary movement in 1848?
A **Hecker** – by Frederick Hecker

Q What town in Putnam County was the site of Ben Lundy's abolitionist newspaper, *The Genius of Universal Emancipation*?
A **Hennepin**

Q What town in Marshall County (on the Illinois River) had the slogan, "Best Town in Illinois by a Dam Site?"

Riviera Roadhouse on Old Route 66 courtesy Dan Oberle

A **Henry**

Q What town in Williamson County was the site of an infamous massacre of scab coal miners in 1922?
A **Herrin**

Q What town in McLean County is home to the Simkins War Museum?
A **Heyworth**

Q What town on Route 40 was called "Little Helvetia" because of its large Swiss population?
A **Highland**

Q What Chicago suburb became home to the famed Chicago Symphony?
A **Highland Park**

Q What Montgomery County courthouse was forced by a judge to remove its "The World Needs God" sign from a front third floor window a few years ago?
A **Hillsboro**

Q What town is home to Portuguese Hill – with a large contingency of people with Portuguese ancestry?
A **Jacksonville** – they were a persecuted group from the island of Madeira and had been converted to Protestantism, incurring the wrath of dominant Catholics. In Jacksonville, they slavishly voted Republican.

Q What town is home to Illinois College and MacMurray College?
A **Jacksonville**

Q What two towns were bitter rivals after the Civil War in a bid to become the home of a new land grant university in Illinois?
A **Jacksonville** and **Champaign** – the University of Illinois site was won by Champaign boosters and lobby forces.

Dunlap Hotel – Jacksonville

THE DUNLAP HOTEL
JACKSONVILLE, ILLINOIS

Q What community was home to the large estate (20,000 acres) of Jacob Strawn, sometimes referred to as the **"Cattle King of America?"**
A **Jacksonville** – he erected the Strawn Opera House in 1861; Jacksonville was the meat processing center of Illinois until the role was usurped by Chicago.

Q What community

billed itself as the "Athens of the West?"

A **Jacksonville** – due to its emphasis on culture and education; it was also called the "City of Institutions" for its schools, churches, and state hospitals for the "insane," the blind, and the "deaf and dumb."

Q   What new town in Morgan County, named for the African Reverend A.W. Jackson, was planted in its center for the expressed purpose of becoming the county seat?
A **Jacksonville**

Q   What was unusual about the naming of **Jacksonville**?
A   It is one of the few towns in the USA named for an African-American, and he was a slave at the time.

Q   What frontier town did William Cullen Bryant visit and denigrate by calling it a "horridly ugly village composed of little shops and dwellings stuck close together around a dingy square?"
A **Jacksonville**

Hotel Moraine on the Lake at Highland Park

Q   What town was home to Hertzberg Bindery, inventors of Perma Bound, a method of rebinding library books?
A **Jacksonville** – circa 1960

Q   What is unusual about the intersection of Church and State streets in **Jacksonville**?
A   There are churches on all four corners – a rarity in the USA.

Q   What town is home to Eli Bridge, the state's only producer of Ferris wheels?
A **Jacksonville** – Capitol Records also located here in 1965.

Q   What does the Kordite-Mobil Corporation of **Jacksonville** produce?
A   Hefty brand trash bags (20 billion a year); it is the city's largest employer.

Q   What town in Vermilion County was named for an island in the West Indies?
A **Jamaica**

Q   What town was originally named Juliet to match a nearby town named Romeo?
A   **Joliet** – it was mistakenly renamed at the time of incorporation to honor Joliet (original spelling Jolliet) the explorer.

Q   What northern Illinois town underwent a city-sponsored mural campaign in the period from 1991-1999?
A **Joliet**

Q   What town's high school was the **first in the state to install an observatory**?

A **Joliet**

Q   What recently deceased **Joliet actress** was a star on the television series "The District?"
A   Lynn Thigpen – officials recently named a school in her honor

Q   What lead singer on the Commodores hails from **Joliet**?
A Lionel Ritchie – "Say You, Say Me," "Dancing On The Ceiling," "Hello, Is It Me You're Looking For?"

Q   What town had a prison known as the "Rock Pile?"
A **Joliet**

Q   What U.S. President visited **Joliet** and stayed at the National Hotel?
A   Martin Van Buren – the hotel was famous for a loud gong that was rung by a black man to summon its patrons to meals; Abe Lincoln also stayed at the hotel

Q   In what southern Illinois town did Lincoln sit on a porch one night and watch Donati's comet?
A   **Jonesboro** – Lincoln was there for one of the debates with Douglas.

Q   Which of the seven Lincoln debates with Douglas was the most poorly attended?
A The one at **Jonesboro**

Q   How many people attended the last debate at **Alton**?
A   6,000; The debate was held very close to the spot where Elijah Lovejoy was killed.

Q   What Cook County town is home to one of the most famous ghosts in Illinois, Resurrection Mary?

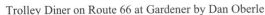
Trolley Diner on Route 66 at Gardener by Dan Oberle

A **Justice**

Q What town is at the part of the Illinois River called the "Nile of North America?"
A **Kampsville**

Q What important archaeological site is at **Kampsville**?
A The Koster farm, sometimes called the Koster dig

Q What southern Illinois town was the last to be named for a place in Egypt?
A **Karnak**

Author in front of Mermaid House at Lebanon, Illinois

Q What town is home to the "Liberty Bell of the West," rung to commemorate victories by George Rogers Clark?
A **Kaskaskia**

Q What town in Cook County is named for one of Sir Walter Scott's novels?
A **Kenilworth**

Q What town in Henry County was home to Boss Glove Factory and Walworth Valve?
A **Kewanee**

Q What town in Christian County was planned by officials of the Peabody Mine?
A **Kincaid**

Q What town near **Salem** is home to Ingram's Log Cabin Village?
A **Kinmundy**

Q What Knox County town is home to the Wolf covered bridge over the Spoon River?
A **Knoxville**

Q What Illinois River port is the seat of Marshall County?
A **Lacon**

Q What Illinois town was named for LaFayette's homestead in France?
A **LaGrange**

Q What town has been described as a "rich man's dormitory for Chicago?"
A **Lake Forest**

Q What Hancock County town was named for a French explorer?
A **La Harpe** (Benard)

Q What Chicago suburb has a museum with replicas of all the inaugural ball gowns of the U.S. first ladies?
A **Lansing**

Q What LaSalle County town was the western terminus for the Illinois-Michigan Canal?
A **LaSalle**

Q What town features the Wild Bill Hickok state memorial?
A **LaSalle**

Q What town has the Lincoln Trail Monument?
A **Lawrenceville**

Q From what town in Fulton County did Edgar Lee Masters use characters for his Spoon River Anthology?
A **Lewistown**

Q What is the name of the Lewistown cemetery visitors flock to, guidebook in hand, to see the tombstones of the characters in Masters' book?
A Oak Hill Cemetery

Q What Cook County town is noted for its elm trees that were planted back in the 1830's?
A **Lincolnwood**

Q What Chicago suburb is home to the Morton Arboretum?
A **Lisle**

Joliet's Rialto Theater Route 66 by D. Oberle

Q What historic three-story building in **Litchfield** was converted to apartments while retaining its basement bowling alley and top-floor ballroom?
A Elks Lodge 654

Q What town has a building that was the Mermaid Inn, named by a sea captain who claimed to have seen mermaids?
A **Lebanon** (see picture above)

Q What Chicago suburb town has the only Cookie Jar Museum in the world?
A **Lemont**

Q How many entries does Illinois have on the National Register of Historic Places?
A Over 1,200

Q What Fulton County town, near the Spoon River was on the Burlington Northern route, has prep teams named *Indians*, and was near Camp Ellis?
A **Lewiston**

Q What seat of Fulton County is near Dixon Mound State Museum?
A **Lewistown**

Q   What was the first town laid out in the Military Tract?
A   **Lewistown**

Q   What town has the log cabin home that once belonged to Lincoln's parents, Thomas and Sarah?
A   **Lerna**

Q   Name the town where Marlon Brando once lived and worked as an usher in a local theater.
A   **Libertyville**

Q   What town on the Sanitary Ship Canal has the lock that determines the amount of water that is stolen, er, withdrawn, from Lake Michigan?
A   **Lockport**

Q   What town is at the point where the Sanitary Ship Canal joins the DesPlaines River?
A   **Lockport**

Q   What Chicago suburb is called "Lilac Town" because of the William Plum estate?
A   **Lombard**

Q   What town is home to Benedictine College?
A   **Lyle**

Q   What Cook County town, located on the portage between the Chicago and DesPlaines rivers, calls itself the "Gateway to the West?"
A   **Lyons**

Q   What town is home to the eight-story Hoffman Tower on the DesPlaines River?
A   **Lyons** – it was an advertising symbol for Hoffman Brothers Brewing Company.

Q   What town is home to Western Illinois University?
A   **Macomb**

Q   Who gave his "Prince of peace" speech while staying at the Lem Young House in **McLeansboro** in 1909?
A   William Jennings Bryan

Rasmussen Blacksmith shop at Lewistown by William Ulmer

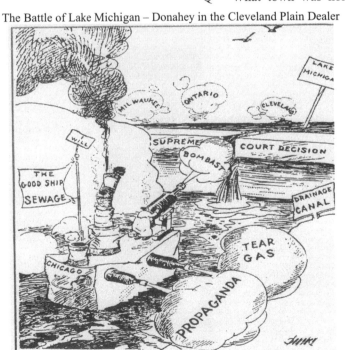

The Battle of Lake Michigan – Donahey in the Cleveland Plain Dealer

Q   What town, with an Eagle Park, was platted by St. Louis industrialists in 1889 for the purpose of building the McKinley Bridge?
A   **Madison**

Q   What town boasts Giant City State Park and was home to Paul Simon at the time of his death?
A   **Makanda**

Q   What town in Williamson County was home to actress Judith Ivey?
A   **Marion**

Q   What building in **Marion** has an Egyptian identity with a pyramidal roof and lotus leaf details?
A   The Veterans Administration Hospital

Q   What St. Clair County town is named for the biblical Hebrew town of Mareshah?
A   **Marissa**

Q   What town was named for a supreme court justice and was home to James Jones who wrote, *From Here to Eternity*?
A   **Marshall**

Q   What town was home to Grover Cleveland's Vice-president, Adlai E. Stevenson?
A   **Metamora**

Q   What southern Illinois town is home to Fort Massac Park?
A   **Metropolis**

Q   What famous male union organizer, nicknamed "the General," is buried at **Mt. Olive's** Coal Miners Cemetery?
A   David Bradley

Q   What new name was chosen for the industrial park known as **Monsanto**, Illinois?
A   **Sauget** - the name honors the prominent Sauget family. It was changed because every time one of the other factories located there had a chemical spill, the Monsanto Company received a black eye from the media coverage.

Q   What town has the Archer House, the state's oldest operating hotel?
A   **Marshall**

Q   How did the town of **McLean** get its name?

A   It was named for John McLean, the first representative in the U.S. Congress for Illinois.

Q   What Cook County town is named for a shire in Scotland where golf was invented?
A   **Midlothian**

Q   What town in Iroquois County comes from "mill by the ford?"
A   **Milford**

Q   What Carroll County town takes its name from "mill at the edge of town?"
A   **Milledgeville**

Q   What northwestern town translates from the French for the word "mill?"
A   **Moline** – from "moulin"

Q   What southern Illinois town name comes from the German words for mill town?
A   **Millstadt**

Q   What northern town's name is a Potawatomie word that allegedly means "good earth?"
A   **Minooka** – home to actor Nick Offerman who is slated to play the bad guy in Sandra Bullock's *Miss Congeniality II*

Q   What Quad City town is home to John Deere Company?
A   **Moline**

Q   Did John Deere ever "plow" into politics?
A   Yes – he became mayor of **Moline**

Q   What Illinois town was home to Wyatt Earp?
A   **Monmouth**

Q   In what town can the statue of Apollo called "The Sun Singer" be found?
A   **Monticello** - at Robert Allerton Park

Q   What town in central Illinois is home to "Millionaires Row?"
A   **Monticello**

Q   What town on the Fox River was known as "Child City" because of its large orphanage complex?
A   **Mooseheart**

Q   What seat of Grundy County is near the Dresden nuclear plant?
A   **Morris**

Q   What Cook County town was home to the Revelle

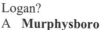

Dixie Truckers Route 66 Hall of Fame at McLean by Dan Oberle

Sun Singer statue at Allerton Park, Monticello

Company, maker of plastic model kits?
A   **Morton Grove**

Q   What southern Illinois Town was home to the Western River Fleet during the Civil War?
A   **Mound City**, home to a large military cemetery

Q   What seat of Wabash County was home to ornithologist Robert Ridgway who wrote *The Birds of North America*?
A   **Mount Carmel**

Q   What town is called "King City" because it "crowns" southern Illinois?
A   **Mount Vernon**

Q   What Chicago suburb was named to honor a popular Catholic bishop in Chicago?
A   **Mundelein**

Q   What town is known as "Golf Country?"
A   **Mundelein** – due to a dozen golf courses

Q   What southern Illinois town was the birthplace of Civil War General John Logan?
A   **Murphysboro**

Q   What town has remnants of old brick kilns off Highway 149 that were once used to make charcoal?
A   **Murphysboro**

Q   What town is home to North Central College?
A   **Naperville**, named for early settler, John Naper -1830

Q   What Chicago suburb has a downtown riverwalk that follows the DuPage River?
A   **Naperville**

Q   In what town did pioneer settlers take refuge during the Blackhawk War?
A   **Naperville**

Q   What **Naperville** native is credited with firing the first shots at the Civil War battle of Gettysburg?
A   Marcellus Jones

Q   What seat of Washington County was named for a town in Tennessee?
A   **Nashville**

Q   What northwestern town, north of **Quincy,** was the

155

largest city in the state in 1840?

A **Nauvoo**

Q How much did it cost to build the Mormon Temple at **Nauvoo**?

A A million dollars – it was 128 feet long, 88 feet broad, 60 feet high, and to the top of the tower 165 feet; 30 hewn pilasters cost $3,000 each; built in 1841, burned in 1848

Q What small town in Pike County has a marker to commemorate a landing made by Cal Rogers who made the nation's first transcontinental flight?

A **Nebo**

Q How did the town of **Newark** in Kendall County get its name?

A Originally called Georgetown, this Anglo-Saxon settlement takes its name from Newark, England.

Q What is **Newark's** chief claim to fame?

A It was the second town in America that saw Abe Saperstein's Harlem Globetrotters play basketball. **The town of Hinckley in DeKalb County was the first**.

Q What southern Illinois town was famous for its walking canes, made from a catalpa tree that grew from a riding whip, angrily thrust into the ground by the niece of Daniel Boone?

A **New Haven**

Q What town was named for the son-in-law of famed circuit rider, Peter Cartwright?

A **Newman**

Q What architectural style describes the University of Illinois classroom buildings and library at **Urbana** on the southern part of the campus?

A Georgian Revival – these buildings, still in use, are about 100 years old.

Q What man and his colleagues isolated a pure compound of plutonium in August of 1942 in room 405 of the Chemical Lab at the University of Chicago?

A Glen T. Seaborg, who would later become the head of the AEC – Atomic Energy Commission

Q Where can one see a restored octagonal toll house that once was on the plank road between **Canton** and **Liverpool**?

First Baptist Church at Nashville

.Cracker Jack

Old restored toll booth near Dixon Mounds by William Ulmer

A It is at the Dickson Mounds Museum at **Lewistown**

Q What town, northwest of **Springfield**, lived in by Abe Lincoln, has a reconstructed pioneer village?

A **New Salem**

Q What Cook County town is home to the Bradford Museum of **collector plates, the largest collection of its kind in the world**?

A **Niles**

Q What town has a replica of the Leaning Tower of Pisa?

A **Niles**

Q What town had a horse named Louis Napoleon that helped make it the "Norman Horse Capital of the U.S.?"

A **Normal**

Q What town is home to Illinois State University?

A **Normal**

Q What famed tree planter was responsible for the founding of **El Paso, Pontiac, Towanda, Lexington, Clinton and Le Roy**?

A Jesse Fell

Q What Chicago suburb has a factory that produces the snack, Cracker Jack?

A **Northbrook**

Q What Chicago suburb was originally called South Waukegan?

A **North Chicago**

Q What Chicago suburb is home to Kraft Foods?

A **Northfield**

Q What is the only remaining nineteenth century hotel building left in **Rockford**?

A The Chick House at Main and Elm streets, built in 1857

Q What town on the Fox River was home to the first permanent settlement of Norwegians in America?

A **Norway**

Q What Chicago suburb has 14 polo fields and is the "Polo Capital of Illinois?"

A **Oakbrook**

156

Q   What Chicago suburb had a training center during World War II that was only one of two places in the U.S. where African-American aviators could earn their wings?
A   **Oak Lawn** – the other place was Tusgegee Institute in Alabama.

Q   What Chicago suburb was home to Frank Lloyd Wright and has several of his homes as tourist attractions?
A   **Oak Park**

Q   What is memorable about Frank Lloyd Wright's Unity Temple in **Oak Park**?
A   It was the first time that concrete was used as an integral part of surface design in a major building.

Q   How many Frank Lloyd Wright structures does the city of **Oak Park** boast?
A   25

Q   What town between **Newton** and **Robinson** derives its name from the shape of its incorporated area?
A   **Oblong**

Q   What town was called "Hellhole of the Illinois Central," due to scalawags who stole passenger's luggage?
A   **Odin**

Q   What site near **Nashville**, off Interstate 64, was famous for its hotel complex and mineral springs?
A   **Okawville**

Q   What town in St. Clair County on Route 50 was named for a railroad developer?
A   **O'Fallon** – for John O'Fallon

Q   What town has a nationally famous prep Panther Marching Band, a restored 1961 IC caboose, and is the fastest growing community in southwestern Illinois?
A   **O'Fallon**

Q   What important early cement-making center was named for an Illinois Governor?
A   **Oglesby**

Q   What seat of Richland County (and once an oil center) was named for a Civil War lieutenant?
A   **Olney** – for John Olney

Q   What Cook County town was home to coach Amos Alonzo Stagg?
A   **Olympia Fields**

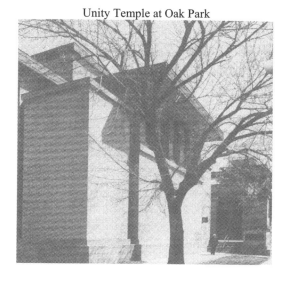

Mormon Temple at Nauvoo

Unity Temple at Oak Park

Q   What town is called the "Nursery Capital of the Midwest?"
A   **Onarga** – for its trees and shrubs – not children

Q   What town in Henderson County, on the Great River Road, is home to the Henderson covered bridge?
A   **Oquawka**

Q   What seat of Ogle County was visited by Transcendentalist Margaret Fuller who called it the "Capital of Nature's Art?"
A   **Oregon**

Q   Who designed the Soldiers Monument on the grounds of the Ogle County Courthouse in **Oregon**?
A   Lorado Taft

Q   What town is near Lorado Taft's statue of Chief Blackhawk, overlooking the Rock River in Lowden State Park?
A   **Oregon**

Q   What Illinois town is named for a famed mythological hunter?
A   **Orion**

Q   What Illinois town was home to W.D. Boyce, **founder of the American Boy Scouts**?
A   **Ottawa**

Q   The Plainfield Halfway House was a tavern stop for a stage line that was halfway between what two cities?
A   Chicago and **Ottawa**

Q   What is unusual about Ahlgrim's Funeral Home in **Palatine**?
A   It also has a miniature golf course.

Q   What Crawford County town was home to Illinois' first businesswoman – Auntie Gogin?
A   **Palestine** – she was a milliner (hat maker).

Q   What Christian County town in its early history was named "City of Roses," for its prolific rose production and sales?
A   **Pana**

Q   In what Bond County town did Iowa-born John L. Lewis, of United Mine Workers fame, start his career in coal mining?
A   **Panama** – he also lived a while in **Springfield**.

Q In what town was Lincoln's kinsman, Dennis Hanks, killed by a team of runaway horses?
A **Paris**

Q What seat of Edgar County is the town where the "sport" of goosepulling originated?
A **Paris**

Q What Chicago suburb came into existence in 1948 as a planned community, second in size only to Levittown in New York?
A **Park Forest**

Q What town calls itself the "Honeybee Capital of the Nation?"
A **Paris**

Q What eastern Illinois town has one of the most beautiful court-houses in the entire state?
A **Paris** – Edgar County

Pecan Grove Creamery at Okawville –courtesy Skip Gatermann

Q What Chicago suburb was founded by George Penny who operated a brickyard?
A **Park Ridge**

Q What town in Ford County was settled by Swedes in the 1850's?
A **Paxton**

Q What east-central town has a Carnegie library with a prominent copper dome?
A **Paxton** – it is now a prominent green due to patina.

Q Name the seat of Tazewell County where the Union League of America, a patriotic organization, was founded in 1862?
A **Pekin**

Q What central Illinois town is home to astronaut Scott Altman?
A **Pekin**

Q What unusual type of bridge is at **Pekin** on the Illinois River?
A Hydraulic lift bridge (see photo above)

Q What was unusual about the town of **Pembroke**?
A In Kankakee County, it was an African-American town that now goes by the name of **Hopkins Park**. They have an African-American Rodeo every Memorial Day weekend.

Pekin Bridge over the Illinois River

Q What small town, in the northeast corner of Champaign County, is due east of **Rantoul** on Route 22 near the intersection of Route 136, not far from the middle fork of the Vermilion River?
A **Penfield** - The Church of St. Lawrence, built around the turn of the century by Irish Catholics, is prominent.

Q What town on the Illinois River goes by the nickname "Whiskey City," "Progressive Town," and the "Capital of Central Illinois?"
A **Peoria**

Q Identify the alliterative phrase for the town of **Peoria** that became **famous as the national measuring stick** for what policy would or would not work in Middle America.
A "Will it play in Peoria?"

Q The Spring Valley "Halfway House," situated between the towns of **Utica** and **Ottawa**, obtained its name from the fact that it was half way between Chicago and what other town?
A **Peoria**

Q What Illinois town is home to the Caterpillar Company and calls itself the "earth moving capital of the world?"
A **Peoria**

Q What town's GAR Hall has a bust of General John Logan by Frederick Triebel?
A **Peoria** – Logan and Ben Stephenson of **Springfield** helped found the Grand Army of the Republic after the Civil War.

Q What Will County town was home to Bennett Industries, the company that first developed five-gallon plastic industrial pails for shipping purposes?
A **Peotone**

Q What town in Randolph County was originally named "Short's Prairie?"
A **Percy**

Q What city adjoining **LaSalle** had a company that made Wesclox Big Ben clocks?
A **Peru**

Q What town is the burial site of Edgar Lee Masters, Vachel Lindsay, and Ann Rutledge?
A **Petersburg**

Q What town name was determined by the outcome of a card game?
A **Petersburg** – two original settlers could not agree on a name, so the winner (Peter Lukins) got to choose.

Q   What Chicago suburb is home to Washington Park racetrack with a replica of Mount Vernon for a clubhouse?
A   **Phoenix**

Q   What seat of Perry County was named for a congressman who said about the Barbary pirates: "Millions for defense but not a cent for tribute?"
A   **Pinckneyville** – for C.C. Pinckney of S. Carolina

Q   What seat of Pike County calls itself the "Pork Capital of the World?"
A   **Pittsfield**

Q   What town sports an annual Fall Color Tour?
A   **Pittsfield**

Q   What town in Will County, founded by the Frenchman DuPazhe back in 1790, was an early rival of **Joliet**?
A   **Plainfield**

Presbyterian Church at Pana

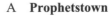

Q   What town in Kendall County called itself the "biggest little industrial city in the world," because it manufactured grain reapers by Hollister and Marsh?
A   **Plano**

Q   What town is home to the Farnsworth House, designed by Mies van der Rohe?
A   **Plano** – it's considered one of the landmarks of modern architecture.

Q   What town in Bond County on old Route 40 is named for an Indian princess who lived near the Jamestown colony in Virginia?
A   **Pocahontas**

Q   What Ogle County town is named for an Italian adventurer who traveled to China?
A   **Polo** – for Marco Polo

Q   What town in Jackson County is home to Saltpeter Cave and a famous natural stone bridge?
A   **Pomona**

Buffalo Township Library at Polo

Q   What seat of Livingston County was named for a famous Indian who led a war against the settlers in Illinois?
A   **Pontiac**

Q   What town near Chicago is called "the most Polish town in America?"
A   **Posen**

Q   What town was named one of the "Best Ten Small Towns" in the U.S. in 1997?
A   **Pontiac**

Q   What town, near the Modoc Rock Shelter, has a name that translates to "prairie by the bluff?"
A   **Prairie du Rocher**

Q   What town near **Chester** was home to James Thompson, the man who platted much of Chicago and named its Randolph Street after his own Randolph County?
A   **Preston**

Q   What seat of Bureau County is home to an 1863 covered bridge that is the only one in Illinois open to traffic?
A   **Princeton**

Q   What **Princeton** resident's home was perhaps the state's leading site on the Underground Railroad?
A   Owen Lovejoy, a minister and abolitionist who helped found the Republican party in Illinois

Q   What town on the Rock River is on the site of an Indian encampment where White Cloud warned his people about the encroaching whites?
A   **Prophetstown**

Q   What town in western Illinois has the Apparition Tree that has an outer bark that seems to bear the image of Jesus carrying a lamb?
A   **Quincy**

Q   What city, once the 2nd largest in the state, was a Look Magazine All-America-City in 1968?
A   **Quincy**

Q   What western Illinois town is often referred to as "Gem City?"
A   **Quincy**

Q   What town on Interstate 57 is home to Chanute Field?
A   **Rantoul**

Q   What town near **Champaign** was the original home of the Tuskegee Airmen (African American pilots)?
A   **Rantoul**

Q   Beside the museum at **Rantoul**, what city in central Illinois has an airport hangar devoted to vintage aircraft?
A   **Springfield** has the Air Combat Museum at the Capital Airport.

Q   What Randolph County town, named for a type of tree, was near Horse Prairie, an area roamed by wild horses that escaped from the French settlers?
A   **Red Bud**

Q   What town in McHenry County was named for the Frenchman who first brought slaves to Illinois?
A   **Renault**

Q   Orsolini's, known locally as Whiskey Corners, was a Cabin Court for motor tourists located at **Richmond**, Illinois, on the southeast corner of Routes 12 and 31. Where can one find one of its restored circa 1946 cabins?
A   Inside the McHenry County Historical Society Museum. One of the old cabins was sawed in two, placed inside the museum, and restored.

Q   What town is named for a famed Illinois naturalist?
A   **Ridgway** – for Robert Ridgway

Old Peoria skyline

Q   What Illinois town and Chicago suburb is home to Triton College?
A   River Grove

Q   What Chicago-land town was laid out and planned by Frederick Law Olmstead, the man who planned Central Park in New York?
A   **Riverside**

Q   What nearly all-black town was settled by African American workers who helped build the 1893 Columbian Exposition in Chicago?
A   **Robbins** – named for worker Eugene Robbins

Villa Katherine at Quincy

Q   What southern Illinois town is home to Milestone Bluff, an ancient Indian dwelling and burial site?
A   **Robbs**

Q   What seat of Crawford County is home to Marathon Oil?
A   **Robinson**

Q   What Northern Illinois town in Ogle County calls itself the "Asparagus Capital of Illinois?"
A   **Rochelle**

Q   What northern town is separated from the town of Sterling by Lawrence Park, an island in the middle of the Rock River?
A   **Rock Falls**

Q   What is the state's second largest city?
A   **Rockford** – 150,000 plus; Aurora is a close third.

Q   Germanicus Kent is considered the founder of what northwestern Illinois city?
A   **Rockford** – he arrived there from **Galena** in 1834 and built a sawmill and established a ferry service.

Q   How did **Rockford** get the nickname "Forest City?"
A   From a New York *Tribune* article due to its many trees

Q   What town near the Wisconsin border was located on a shallow river crossing site on the Chicago to **Galena** stage route?
A   **Rockford** – a *ford* on the *Rock* River

Q   What town's Time Museum has a valuable collection of watches and timepieces?
A   **Rockford** – the city also has a large Swedish population.

Q   Where was "Little Rockford?"
A   Antarctica – Admiral George Dufek raised the **Rockford** and United States flags on a parcel of land there during a 1958 expedition.

Q   What town was home for a while to Dred Scott when he lived with his master at Fort Armstrong?
A   **Rock Island** – this was the basis of Scott's claim that he should be a free man because he lived on free soil.

Q   What town in the 1880s was home to Watch Tower Amusement Park?
A   **Rock Island**

Q   What Mississippi River town is home to Augustana College?
A   **Rock Island**

Q   What southern Illinois town is home to James Anderson, the man who discovered Illinois fluorspar while digging a well?
A   **Rosiclare**

Q   What Madison County oil town was named for the wife of the owner of Royal Dutch Shell?
A   **Roxana** – for Roxanne

Q   What town is the site of a famous wrestling match between Abe Lincoln and Dow Thompson while Abe was serving in the military during the Blackhawk War?
A   **Rushville**, seat of Schuyler County

Q   What town features a scenic Spoon River Drive?
A   **Rushville**

Q What town was named for a doctor and patriot of the American Revolution?
A **Rushville** – for Dr. Benjamin Rush

Q What town was the birthplace of Edward Scripps of the famous Scripps newspaper chain?
A **Rushville**

Q What first settlement in Champaign County was along the "Potawatomie Trail of Death" when the state of Indiana sent its remaining Indians in 1838 to Kansas?
A **Sadorus**

Q What town is named for Jesus' grandmother and claims to have a bone fragment from her body?
A **St. Anne** in Kankakee County

Q What hotel on the Fox River at **St. Charles** was called the "Crown Jewel of the Fox?"
A The Hotel Baker, built by Colonel Edward J. Baker

Q What Fayette County town on Route 40 is named for the patron saint of mariners?
A **St. Elmo**

Q What three Madison County towns make up the Triad school district?
A **Troy, St. Jacob** and **Marine**

Q What town is the birthplace of William Jennings Bryan?
A **Salem**

Q What town's American Legion Hall was the birthplace of the GI Bill of Rights?
A **Salem**

Q What graduate of Illinois College at **Jacksonville** went on to become the twice-elected governor of Nebraska?
A **Salem**-born Charles Bryan, brother of William Jennings Bryan

Q What Carroll County town has a name that means grassy plain?
A **Savanna**

Q What Cook County town was home to bandleader Wayne King and silent film actress Dorothy Dalton?
A **Schaumburg**

Q What LaSalle County town was called the "shipyard of the prairie" for the LST boats it made during World War II?

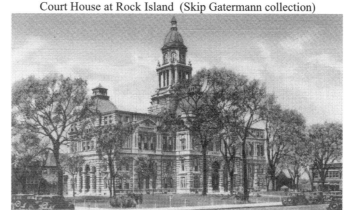
West Side Senior High, Rockford (Teich collection)

Court House at Rock Island (Skip Gatermann collection)

A **Seneca**

Q What German suburb of Chicago had Illinois' first female governor, Julia Kolze, elected in 1934?
A **Schiller Park**

Q What town in DeKalb County was named for an Indian who was loyal to whites?
A **Shabbona**

Q What seat of Gallatin County is famous for its bank that turned down Chicago officials for a development loan?
A **Shawneetown** – they said Chicago was too far north and would never amount to anything. (see picture on next page)

Q At what town was the U.S. stamp commemorating the Illinois Sesquicentennial issued?
A **Shawneetown** – 1968

Q What Bureau County town was the first site of a Danish Evangelical Lutheran congregation in the USA?
A **Sheffield**

Q What town did Queen Margrethe of Denmark visit in 1976 to see the St. Peter's Danish Lutheran Church?
A **Sheffield** – it is the church of the first Danish Lutheran congregation in America.

Q What town on Route 66 is home to Funk's Maple "Sirup?"
A **Shirley**

Q Six hundred and forty acres were taken from **Shiloh** Valley in southern Illinois to create what air base after World War I?
A Scott Field – one of the nation's oldest air bases

Q What northwestern Illinois town has a two-block long Hero Street, named for young Mexican men who fought in World War II?
A **Silvis** – Defense Department statistics say that **no area of comparable size sent as many men to fight in the war**.

Q What southern Illinois town is home to Buffalo Rock, a petroglyph with the outline of a buffalo, thought to be drawn by early Indians?
A **Simpson**

Q What Chicago suburb was settled by large numbers of immigrants from Luxembourg, and bills itself as the "world's largest village?"
A **Skokie**

Q What Northeastern Illinois town in Kane County was home to "Ma" Sunday and husband evangelist Billy Sunday?
A **Sleepy Hollow**

Q What Dutch Community on the Calumet River called itself the "onion set capital of America?"
A **South Holland**

Q What southern Illinois town printed most of our nation's comic books back in the 1950's?
A **Sparta**

Q What town has an airport named for Charles Lindbergh because he helped plan it and delivered mail there?
A **Springfield**

Q Where is the Illinois Vietnam War Veterans' Memorial?
A Oak Ridge Cemetery at **Springfield**

Q In what central Illinois town did the Independent Klan of America try unsuccessfully to establish an African-American auxiliary group?
A **Springfield** in 1925

Q What northern Illinois town bills itself as the "Heart of American Hardware" for its manufacturing concerns?
A **Sterling**

Q In what year did **Springfield** become the permanent home of the Illinois State Fair?
A 1894

Q What Chicago suburb is home to Hawthorne Downs racetrack?
A **Stickney**

Q What northern Illinois town was the site of the first battle of the Blackhawk War?
A **Stillman Valley** – Major Stillman and his militia were defeated by Blackhawk.

Q What town near the Wisconsin border bills itself as "Illinois' Highest Town?"
A **Stockton** – this writer assumes they are referring to elevation.

The Shawneetown Bank that refused Chicago a loan

Q What Chicago suburb bills itself as "The City With a Smile?"
A **Streamwood**

Q What town was home to Clarence Mulford, the man who created the character **Hopalong Cassidy**?
A **Streator**

Q What town in Moultrie County was home to the Little Theater on the Square, famous for its summer stock plays?
A **Sullivan**

Q What do Betty Grable, Pat O'Brien, Ann Miller, and Margaret Hamilton all have in common?
A At one time or another, they all performed at the Little Theater in **Sullivan.**

Q What Chicago suburb is known for its Argo corn starch plant that was the **largest in the world**?
A **Summit**

Cozy Dog Drive-in on Route 66, Springfield by Dan Oberle

Q What southeastern Illinois town is home to Red Hill Raceway?
A **Sumner**

Q What is the connection of **boxer Joe Louis** with the Kankakee County town of **Sun River Terrace**?
A After a match with Jersey Joe Walcott in 1948, Louis established a training camp at the town's Sunset Hills Club. Sun River Terrace did not incorporate until 1980.

Q What southern Illinois town is named for a seacoast town in Wales, England?
A **Swansea**

Q What seat of DeKalb County, once named Orange, is named for a type of light bark tree?
A **Sycamore**

Q What Perry County town is the French name for a local tribe of Indians?
A **Tamaroa**

Q What Alexander County town is home to a noted correctional facility?
A **Tamms**

Q What town in Effingham County translates to "city of Teutons" and was settled by Catholic Germans?
A **Teutopolis**

Q What Illinois town was named for a battle in the Mexi-

can War?
A **Tampico**

Q   What seat of Christian County was a noted coal mining area and had a very active KKK in the 1920's?
A   **Taylorville**

Q   What town on the Mississippi was originally called Sparhawk's Landing and has a courthouse where the slave Dred Scott is said to have been detained?
A   **Thebes**

Q   What southern Illinois town has the only cantilever bridge in the state?
A   **Thebes** – built in 1905

Q   What Vermilion County town was named for the president of the Northern Cross Railroad?
A   **Tilton**

Q   What Chicago suburb was called "Fungus Town" due to a large mushroom canning plant?
A   **Tinley Park**

Q   What town in Marion County was named for LaSalle's faithful lieutenant who did much to help establish a French foothold in Illinois?
A   **Tonti** – for Henri Tonti

Q   What coal mining town in Marshall County was named by Mexican coal miners for a town in Mexico?
A   **Toluca**

Q   What Tazewell County town translates to "three hills?"
A   **Tremont**

Q   What town was home to the famous lawman Wild Bill Hickok?
A   **Troy Grove**

Sheffield – St. Peters Church

St. Francisville Bank (courtesy Mike Brasel)

Q   What poker hand was Hickok holding when he was shot in the back and killed by Jack McCall?
A   Two pair – aces and eights – now the famous "dead man's hand"

Q   What town was the first stage stop out of St. Louis on the old National Road?
A   **Troy** – home to Senator Paul Simon and St. Louis Cardinal's third baseman Ken Oberkfell

Q   What seat of Douglas County was the place where Uncle Joe Cannon, the famous Speaker of the House, once practiced law?
A   **Tuscola**

Q   What McHenry County town is home to a 56-acre Illinois Railway Museum that features working steam engines?
A   **Union**

Q   What town, named for another in Ohio, has the Frasca Air Museum that features planes used in the movies *1941* and *Midway*?
A   **Urbana**

Q   What town calls itself the Burgoo Capital of Illinois?
A   **Utica** – burgoo is a thick stew with vegetables and meat from assorted critters.

Q   What Monroe County town on the floodplain was once home to a vast feudal empire owned by Steven Miles?
A   **Valmeyer**

Q   What town at the juncture of routes 40 and 51 is the seat of Fayette County?
A   **Vandalia**

Q   Billionaire oilman **H.L. Hunt** was born on a farm in 1889 near what Illinois town?
A   **Vandalia**

Q   How did Hunt become one of the **richest men in America**?
A   He would ask a farmer how much he wanted for his land, go back in town and then offer that same land to an oil speculator at a higher price. He bought and sold the land simultaneously, making a profit without investing a penny. Eventually, he began buying oil properties for himself in Oklahoma and East Texas.

Q   How many wives and children did Hunt have?
A   Three wives and twelve children; he died in 1974.

Q   What Madison County town, known for frequent flooding, was named for a place in Italy?
A   **Venice**

Q   What southern Illinois town is home to the Trail of Tears Park, commemorating the removal of 8,000 Cherokee Indians from their homeland?
A   **Vienna**

Q   What Douglas County town once called itself the "Pancake Capital of the World" due to an annual festival?
A   **Villa Grove**

Q   What town near **Springfield** was the site of a famous

1898 mine riot where ten miners and six guards were killed?

A **Virden**

Q   What hamlet in northeastern Illinois has a St. Peter's Church modeled after the one in England near Stonehenge?

A   **Volo**

Q   What town near **Freeport** calls itself "Little Russia?"

A   **Vladimirovo**

Q   What Chicago suburb has a six-story replica of a pyramid that is the home of a local contractor?

A   **Wadsworth** – the exterior features a statue of Ramses II.

Q   What town is situated in three counties and derives its name from the first letters of each county?

A   **Wamac** – for Washington, Marion and Clinton counties

Q   What DuPage County town was named for early settler Julius Warren?

A   **Warrenville**

Q   What place in Hancock County is named for the town in Mrs. Porter's novel, *Thaddeus of Warsaw*?

A   **Warsaw**

Q   What town in Monroe County is named for the castle where Martin Luther translated the Bible?

A   **Wartburg**

Q   What suburb of East St. Louis, and home to an Emerson Electric war plant, is where this author spent the happy days of his youth?

A   **Washington Park**

Q   What seat of Monroe County was the Gretna Green of the area, noted for its "quickie" marriage laws?

A   **Waterloo**

Q   What southern Illinois town's St. Paul's Protestant church has a rooster on top instead of a cross?

A   **Waterloo** – in the old days, crosses on churches and statues of Christ were seen by many as trappings of Catholicism.

Q   What town is named for the site of Napoleon's final

Valmeyer flood of 1993

Kurt Teich postcard plant (courtesy Lake County Museum)

defeat by Lord Wellington in 1814?

A   **Waterloo** – there was an argument between two factions over the town's name, and they were deadlocked; when someone quipped, "It looks as if you've met your Waterloo," that name became the compromise

Q   What Iroquois County town is named for the Indian wife of Gurdon Hubbard, the man who made famous Hubbard's Trace from Chicago to Vincennes?

A   **Watseka**

Q   What town's Henry Bacon designed the Lincoln Memorial in Washington, D.C.?

A   **Watseka**

Q   What town in Lake County has a fabulous collection of postcards by Curt Teich, the "father of Illinois postcards?"

A   **Wauconda**

Q   What Illinois town was home to Jerry Orbach ("Law and Order"), Ray Bradbury (*Fahrenheit 451*) and Otto Graham (Cleveland Brown's quarterback)?

A   **Waukegan**

Q   What town's Orion Howe, a 14-year-old drummer boy, won the Congressional Medal of Honor in the Civil War?

A   **Waukegan**

Q   Who is known as the "Drummer Boy of Shiloh?"

A   Edward Hager, a 14 year-old from **Greene County**, who was mortally wounded after taking up a fallen comrade's weapon to join the battle

Q   What was unusual about Robert Sabonjian serving six terms as mayor of **Waukegan?**

A   Three terms were as a Democrat and the other three were as a Republican – a street in town is named for him

Q   What town's pioneer newspaper probably had the state record for length of title?

A   **Waukegan's** *The Little Fort Porcupine and Democratic Banner*

Q   What Morgan County town was named for a series of novels by Sir Walter Scott?

A   **Waverly**

Q   What town in Marshall County features a gob pile on it's official "Welcome to - - - - - -" sign?

A   **Wenona** – gob piles are waste material left over from coal mining.

Q What Chicago suburb was organized by utilities mogul Samuel Insull?
A **Westchester**

Q What small northern Illinois town was named for a place in Scotland and was home to Alan Pinkerton, "America's First Detective?"
A **West Dundee**

Q What Cook County town was once home to John Dillinger for a brief spell?
A **Western Springs** – Dillinger drove a taxi here until police ran him out of town after customers complained that he was surly.

Q What southern Illinois town has a pyramid-shaped memorial that pays tribute to all coal miners?
A **West Frankfort**

Q Is **West Frankfort** named for Frankfurt, Germany?
A No – the name comes from Frank's Fort (Frank Jordan)

Q What town near Route 34 is home to the Illinois Pet Cemetery platted in 1926?
A **Westmount**

Q What is the name of the light rail service from Chicago to **Westmount**?
A Metra

Q What southern Illinois town was named for a tribe of Cherokee Indians that passed through along the Trail of Tears?
A **Wetaug**

Q What Illinois town was home to Elbert Gary, chairman of U.S. Steel - the man who planned the town of Gary, Indiana, made famous by the song in Meredith Wilson's *The Music Man?*
A **Wheaton**

Q What seat of DuPage County is called "The Button of the Bible Belt" and its college was the alma mater of Reverend Billy Graham?
A **Wheaton**

Q What Macoupin County city took its name from 52 structures brought there from the St. Louis World's Fair to house coal miners?
A **White City** – the white houses had been used as temporary residences for Fair workers and were purchased when it was over to start a company town.

Route 66 Café at Braidwood by Dan Oberle of Edwardsville/Geneseo

Q What Greene County town is the gravesite of the "Little Drummer Boy of Shiloh?"
A **Whitehall**

Q What Cook County town is home to the beautiful Baháí Temple, the North American headquarters of that religion?
A **Wilmette**

Q How did the small town of **Wartrace** in southern Illinois get its name?
A Originally called Grantsburg, the town received its moniker from the hanging of a horse thief by a mob shortly after the Civil War. Townsfolk said they hoped it would be the last *trace* of *war* in the area.

Q What Will County town, on the Kankakee River, is called "Island City" because the river splits the downtown area?
A **Wilmington**

Q What seat of Scott County received its name when parched surveyors told a Kentucky man he could have the honor in exchange for a jug of whiskey?
A **Winchester**

Kornthal Church – Union County

Q What Chicago suburb is home to New Trier High, the school where Ann Margret was a cheerleader?
A **Winnetka**

Q What Northeastern town near the Wisconsin border was named for the dock and harbor company that planned it?
A **Winthrop Harbor** – Winthrop Harbor and Dock Company

Q What town gets its name from a lake that was formed by damming Nippersink Creek?
A **Wonder Lake**

Q What town in DuPage County gets its name from a wooded valley?
A **Wood Dale** – Edward Lester of Vermont was the first settler.

Q What Madison County town on the American Bottom was home to a huge Standard Oil refinery complex?
A **Wood River**

Q What was the Wood River Massacre, July 1814?

A   The Moore family from North Carolina first moved into the area and gave it the name, Wood River.   Seven members of the family were murdered by renegade Indians. The territorial legislature was so incensed that it enacted a system of fifty-dollar bounties for the killing of hostile Indians.

Q   What seat of McHenry County is home to an opera house where Orson Welles and Paul Newman once performed?
A   **Woodstock** – the Woodstock Opera House

Q   What town, north of **Edwardsville** in Madison County, is named for a land developer who donated land for the Wabash Railroad to come through?
A   **Worden**, named for John Worden

Q   There is a town in Stark County named **Wyoming**.   Is it named for the state of Wyoming?
A   No – it's named for settlers who came here from the Wyoming Valley in Pennsylvania.

Q   What town in Franklin County is named for a coal company and was laid out with a hub and radiating spokes, like the city of Paris, France?
A   **Zeigler** – Napoleon favored this design because a cannon at the hub could fire on several streets.

Q   What town in Lake County was founded by religious zealot John Dowie who imposed blue laws, blew whistles when it was prayer time, and believed that the earth was flat?
A   **Zion** – Dowie also predicted shortly before his death that he would return to earth in 1,000 years.

ILLINOIS OLD TIME RADIO

Q   What central Illinois town was home to radio personality Fizz Singer?
A   **Springfield**

Q   What Illinois radio personality played the violin?
A   Jack Benny

Q   What was tightwad Jack Benny's famous reply to a holdup man who stuck a gun in his ribs and said, "Your money or your life?"
A   When the impatient thief asked a silent Benny, "Well . . . ?" Benny replied, "I'm thinking."

Q   What Chicago radio personality wrote an entry for Encyclopedia Britannica under the topic of ventriloquism?
A   Edgar Bergen

Q   What Chicago personality started singing on station WLS at age eleven for no pay due to child labor laws?
A   Mike Douglas – whose "Mike Douglas Show" became daytime television's most popular program

Q   What brand of coffee sponsored the Edgar Bergen and Charlie McCarthy show?
A   Chase and Sanborn

Q   What Chicago radio show was so popular, theaters would shut down the movie when it came on and broadcast the program over the speakers to audiences?
A   "Amos 'n' Andy"

Q   What couple from **Peoria** became famous as Fibber McGee and Molly?
A   Jim and Marian Driscoll Jordan

Q   What Illinoisan from **Mount Carmel** was the voice of the Lone Ranger on radio?
A   Brace Beemer

Q   What popular Chicago variety show was hosted by Don McNeil?
A   "The Breakfast Club"

Q   What was McNeil's nickname?
A   "The King of Corn"

Q   What Illinois radio and television personality was most similar to Don McNeil?
A   Steve Allen, who was an early host of "The Tonight Show" on NBC

Q   *The Breakfast Club* holds the national record for broadcast longevity.   How many years did it run?
A   35 years

The incomparable Hildegarde

Fibber McGee and Molly on WMAQ radio

Q   What town has a radio station with the call letters WROK?
A   Appropriately, **Rockford**

Q   What radio program caused a national panic when it announced that the Mount Jennings Observatory in Chicago had discovered life on Mars and that the Martians had landed on Earth?
A   Orson Welles with his "War of the Worlds" thriller.   Americans should have known that Chicago is flat as a pancake and has no Mount Jennings.

Q   What conservative ABC radio commentator has a street

named for him in Chicago?
A   Paul Harvey

Q   What Tampico-born man started his path to fame as a baseball radio announcer?
A   Ronald Reagan

Q   What radio announcer has the words "Holy Cow" on his tombstone?
A   Harry Caray

Q   What Illinois town was considered the radio capital of the world in the 1920s and '30s?
A   Chicago

Q   What two presidential candidates set a precedent by debating on Chicago radio in 1960?
A   Kennedy and Nixon

Q   What town's radio station was the first to play a Beatles record in America?
A   **West Frankfort**.

Q   What Chicago radio was responsible for the second half of a White Sox doubleheader being cancelled?
A   Steve Dahl – he announced a disco record destruction ceremony between games (1979) and rock loving – disco hating fans went berserk.

Q   What Chicago company was the first to make radios that would fit in automobiles?
A   Motorola

Q   What Chicago company gave the nation its first portable radio?
A   Zenith

THE NOTORIOUS SHELTON GANG

Q   Who has written the definitive book on the Sheltons?
A   My friend Taylor Pensoneau of **Belleville/ New Berlin** – *Brothers Notorious*

Q   How many kids did Ben and Agnes Shelton have?
A   Seven: Roy, Carl, Earl, Dalta, Bernie, Hazel and Lula

Q   What two were never really members of the gang?
A   Roy and Dalta

Q   What musical instrument did Carl Shelton play?
A   He played the organ at the Methodist Church in **Merriam**.

Gene Autry on "National Barn Dance"

"Gang Busters" – cast and sound men

Q   Which Shelton spent the most time in jail?
A   Roy Shelton – he managed to get in trouble on his own.

Q   Which Shelton was the only one to serve in World War I?
A   Big Earl, Carl was thought to be the smartest

Q   Which Shelton was considered the dumbest by Shelton enemies?
A   Big Earl

Q   Which Shelton was the youngest?
A   Bernie

Q   Which Shelton didn't drink, smoke or gamble?
A   Carl

Q   What three brothers learned to hate hard work by toiling in coal mines at **Carterville**?
A   Carl, Earl and Roy

Q   What was the favorite song of the Shelton brothers?
A   "That Old Gang of Mine"

Q   What were Carl Shelton's best social skills?
A   He was a good roller skater and an excellent dancer.

Q   Who was the nemesis of the Sheltons in **Marion**, Illinois?
A   Rival bootlegger Charlie Birger

Q   What were the Sheltons doing in the early years of Prohibition?
A   At first they drove cabs in **East St. Louis**, then they bought a tavern at Nineteenth and Market.

Q   What Prohibition agent harassed the Sheltons and caused them to move from **Herrin** back to **Fairfield**, some 70 miles away?
A   S. Glenn Young

Q   Why was Carl Shelton sentenced to jail by a **Danville** judge in the spring of 1931?
A   Carl was charged with violating the Prohibition laws and with being in possession of a stolen vehicle that had been transported across state lines.

Q   Did Carl ever serve his sentence?
A   Yes – six months in Vermilion County Jail and five years probation

Q   What sensational news did Carl make while he was in jail during jury deliberations?
A   He subdued two convicts trying to escape after beating the jailer. Then he called for a doctor.

Q   What Methodist minister in **Herrin** is thought to be the author of S. Glenn Young's 1925 biography?
A   Reverend P.R. Glotfelty

Q   How many men did Young claim to have killed before he himself was gunned down? (picture of his **Herrin** grave on p. 289 in *Incredible Illinois*)
A   Twenty-one, giving rise to the title **"world's greatest lawman"**

Q   What was Young's self-imposed title?
A   The Little Napoleon of Williamson County

Q   What Klansman administered a beating to Earl Shelton in a 1924 raid on a Shelton roadhouse?
A   Ceasar Kagle, one of Young's assistants; Earl refused to tell them what officials the Sheltons were paying off

Q   How did the Sheltons get revenge on Cagle?
A   There was a disturbance at the Rome Club (February 8, 1924) in **Herrin** and when Cagle went to see what was going on, someone from the mob fired a shot that killed him. The Sheltons and an ally named Ora Thomas were part of that crowd.

Q   What opposition group to the Klan was formed in Williamson County?
A   The Knights of the Flaming Circle

Q   How did the name **Bloody Williamson** come to be applied to that part of southern Illinois?
A   Due to the Herrin Massacre of scab coal mine workers, Klan violence, and strife between Birger and the Sheltons

Q   What two Sheltons were singled out for indictment by the grand jury for the death of Cagle?
A   Carl and Earl

Q   What KKK leader did the Sheltons ambush on a road along the Okaw Bottoms in May of 1924?

A   S. Glenn Young – he and his wife were on their way to East St. Louis on a Klan assignment; Young was wounded in the leg, and his wife was permanently blinded from the attack

Q   Were the Sheltons charged by authorities for attempted murder?
A   Yes, Carl and Earl surrendered to the Sheriff of Clinton County and posted bond of $20,000 each at **Carlyle**

Q   Which Shelton was considered the brawler?
A   Bernie

Q   Which Shelton was a womanizer?
A   Carl chased anything in skirts

Q   What **East St. Louis** madam financed the Shelton brothers foray into bootlegging?
A   Bess Newman and husband Art, owners of the Arlington Hotel

Q   In what East St. Louis vice district did Bess Newman's business flourish?

Southern Illinois during the Shelton/Birger rivalry – courtesy Southern Illinois University Press

A   The Valley

Q   How and when was the Valley vice district formed in East St. Louis?

A   After the flood of 1903 a number of homes on Third Street near City Hall were abandoned.   A group of prostitutes moved in and the place flourished from 1904-1943.

Q   Why was it called the Valley?
A   Cars driving through the area after heavy rains formed deep ruts with their wheels.   These ruts caused drivers cruising through the area to have to slow down, giving the girls more opportunity to display their wares

Q   Why did Bess and Art Newman finally throw the Sheltons out of the Arlington?
A   They had the nasty habit of sitting around and cleaning their guns in the lobby.

Q   When the Sheltons expanded to southern Illinois, in what town did they run a roadhouse?
A   **Herrin**

Art Newman – at various times allied with both the Shelton gang and Charlie Birger

Q   Why did the KKK become the enemy of the Sheltons?
A   They were opposed to the illegal consumption of alcohol and they were more effective upholding Prohibition laws than most police forces.

Q   In what southern Illinois town did the Klan stage a huge rally with 10,000 members?
A   After holding a big meeting at Monk's Mound in May of 1923, they paraded through downtown **East St. Louis**.

Q   Why didn't the Klan flourish in **East St. Louis**?
A   The town had too many Irish Catholics and beer-loving Germans.   They prospered in places like **Williamson County** where Baptists and Methodists dominated.

Q   Which Sheltons were wounded in a shootout with Klan members at a garage in **Herrin**?
A   Carl and Earl, Saturday, August 30, 1924; six men were killed in the fracas.

Q   What prevented further violence?
A   The state militia was called in from **Carbondale** and **Salem.**

Q   When did Young and Ora Thomas, bitter enemies, manage to kill each other?
A   In a shootout at the Canary Cigar Store in the **Herrin** European Hotel, January, 1925

Q   What happened in **Collinsville** on January 27th, the day of Thomas' funeral in **Marion**?
A   There was a $15,000 holdup of a mail messenger who was delivering a payroll for the Lumaghi Zinc Mine.

Q   When was the Shelton trial for the mail robbery?

A   Two years later - in **Quincy** because it was a federal case involving mail robbery?

Q   Who lied at the Shelton trial to get them convicted?
A   Art Newman, Charlie Birger and Harvey Dungey

Q   What sentence was imposed on the three Shelton brothers?
A   Twenty-five years at Leavenworth

Q   How did the Sheltons get off the hook?
A   Harvey Dungey admitted to a *Post-Dispatch* reporter that he had lied at the trial and was upset because Charlie Birger hadn't paid him the money he'd promised.

Q   The Sheltons had been blamed for the murder of Lory Price, a state policeman. How did it come out that Art Newman and Charlie Birger had killed him?
A   After Newman had been arrested in May of 1927, he confessed to a *Post-Dispatch* reporter and gave him all the gory details. Newman was given a life sentence.

Q   Whatever happened to Helen Holbrook, the Shawnee-town dame who had slept with both Birger and Carl Shelton?
A   She was found dead in St. Petersburg, Florida, poisoned in February of 1927.   Many suspected one of the Sheltons did it because she knew too much.

Q   What were the Sheltons arrested for in late August of 1927?
A   Along with four other men, they were charged with the September 27, 1924 robbery of a bank in **Kincaid**, located in Christian County.   The safe contained $60,000 to cover the Peabody mine payroll.

Q   How much money did the robbers get?
A   A bank official pushed an alarm button and there was a shootout between the robbers and angry town citizens.   The man holding the money satchel dropped it when he was wounded.

Q   Where was the trial held?
A   At the courthouse in **Taylorville**

Q   What alibi did the Sheltons claim?
A   Like the previous trial in **Quincy**, they said they were in **East St. Louis** at the time of the holdup.

Q   Who was the prosecution's star witness?
A   Art Newman said that Earl had told him several months before the robbery that he and his brothers were going to hit the bank and flee by a back road to **Mascoutah** and stash the money there in a brewery.

Q What was the Sheltons' ace in the hole?
A A desk sergeant with the East St. Louis police produced an arrest blotter that showed Earl and Bernie had been arrested and booked on the day in question.

Q What was suspicious about the blotter?
A The book appeared to have been altered and the Shelton names were written with fresh ink while names before and after them were faded.

Q Were the Sheltons convicted?
A Yes – they were sentenced from a year to life at Menard Prison in **Chester.**

Q What happened when the Shelton lawyers filed an appeal?
A The state Supreme Court overturned their convictions, ruling that eyewitness testimony was shaky, at best. The case was never retried.

Q What young newcomer joined the Shelton gang about this time, according to Taylor Pensoneau in *Brothers Notorious*?
A Frank "Buster" Wortman, son of an **East St. Louis** fireman

Q After Charlie Birger was hanged in the spring of 1928, what did the Sheltons do about the Cuckoo gang of St. Louis?
A They ordered Cuckoo leader Herman Tipton and the rest out of East St. Louis.

Q What happened when the Cuckoo gang didn't cooperate?
A The Sheltons started an inter-gang feud by having some of the leaders killed at a cabin near the Mississippi River at **Valmeyer**

Q What happened to three men whose bodies were found in a ditch near **Granite City** in February of 1931?
A It was thought that the Sheltons got into it with the owner of Red Top Taxi of East St. Louis. They were lured to a meeting at "Wide Open" Smith's tavern at 330 A East Broadway, not far from the Eads Bridge. Just before they entered, a friendly taxi driver warned them they were walking into a trap. They went into the speakeasy with Thompsons blazing. A nervous Wide Open Smith took the next train out of town and never returned to East St. Louis.

Q What newly elected sheriff of St. Clair County ran the Sheltons out of East St. Louis?
A Jerome Munie – with the backing of Governor Hoerner; Munie began putting pressure on the Sheltons in 1932 by arresting them one at a time. By 1934 the Sheltons had left East St. Louis. Additionally, all three of the Sheltons were charged for failure to pay property taxes on their residences. Munie also harassed them by arresting them on vagrancy charges – no real jobs. A discouraged Carl Shelton went back to the farm in **Fairfield**.

Q What company in East St. Louis hired the Sheltons in 1930 to protect their property during a strike?

A Phillips Petroleum on Route 3 near East St. Louis

Q When the Sheltons tried to move in on labor racketeering, what business agent for the boilermakers did they offer $30,000 to "get lost?"
A Ollie Moore

Sheriff Jim Pritchard of Franklin Cnty

Q When Moore refused the offer, what happened to him?
A Moore was gunned down on Collinsville Avenue by shots from a moving car. Police figured Monroe "Blackie" Armes did the job for the Sheltons, but couldn't prove it. This was in 1932.

Q What St. Louis gang did the Sheltons enlist in an effort to get control of **East St. Louis**?
A The Cuckoo gang

Q When did the Newmans have a falling out with the Sheltons and switch over to the Birger gang?
A 1926 - the Sheltons retaliated by blowing up Newman's house on North Park Drive in East St. Louis.

Q Did the Sheltons ever join forces with the St. Louis Cuckoo Gang?
A Yes. They teamed together in the fight against the Birger gang.

Q How did the St. Louis group get the name "Cuckoo?"
A The Capone mob on several occasions sent representatives down to St. Louis to "get them on board." The Capone boys were sent home in pine boxes. Capone threw up his hands and decided to leave them alone. They were nuts, fanatical – cuckoo.

Q Birger and the Sheltons had formed an alliance against S. G. Young and the KKK. What caused the breakup?
A (1) The demise of Young and the Klan – mutual enemies (2) Rivalry over Helen Holbrook – the **Shawneetown** Dame (3) Charlie Birger skimming mutual slot machine profits

Q What was the "armored tank" like that was devised by the Sheltons?
A They took an old tanker and mounted a machine gun on the rear. They also cut out gun ports on the sides.

Q Describe Charlie Birger's tank.
A He took an old REO truck and armor plated it, turning it into a war wagon.

Q When did the Sheltons and Charlie Birger temporarily join forces?
A Carl visited Charlie in the hospital and proposed the truce to join forces against the anti-wet KKK.

Q Who was the "Shawneetown dame?"

170

A   Helen Holbrook – she lived in a Shawneetown mansion and apparently had liaisons with both Birger and C. Shelton

Q   What was the name of Charlie Birger's gang hangout in **Marion**?
A   Shady Rest

Q   How was Shady Rest the site of the first aerial attack carried out on American soil (according to Ripley's Believe-It-Or-Not)?
A   The Sheltons found some barnstorming pilots and hired one of them to fly the plane over Shady Rest while one of them tossed homemade bombs.

Q   How successful was the attack?
A   The bombs missed their targets, killing only Birger's pet eagle and favorite hunting dog.

Q   When Earl Shelton was hospitalized in **East St. Louis** with a mild case of malaria, who hatched a plot to kill him?
A   Art Newman. Art and buddy Fred Wooten planned to dress up as women, sneak into the hospital room, and stab Earl to death.

Q   What foiled the plot?
A   An alert East St. Louis policeman spotted them, realized it was men dressed as women, and arrested them on a concealed weapons charge.

Q   What happened in 1927 when the Sheltons were put on trial in **Quincy** for a mail robbery in **Collinsville**?
A   At first they were convicted, but the charges were dismissed when it was discovered that Harvey Dungey and Charlie Birger perjured themselves with their testimony.

Q   After Charlie Birger was executed in 1928, who became a leading nemesis of the Sheltons?
A   Charlie "Blackie" Harris

Q   How did Harris get the nickname "Blackie?"
A   It was due to his swarthy complexion.

Q   What was Carl's favorite weapon?
A   A .44 frontier-type revolver

Q   Where did the Sheltons move their base of operations after Birger's death?
A   **East St. Louis**

Q   Did Bernie ever get married?

A   He married an **East St. Louis** girl named Carrie Stevenson, and they built a dude ranch near **Millstadt** and called it Happy Hollow. Bernie was a big horse lover and loved to play polo.

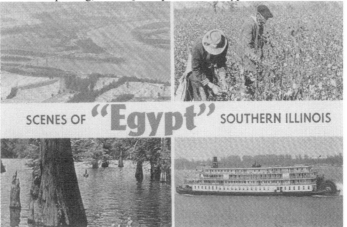
Scenes from Little Egypt –Confluence of Mississippi and Ohio rivers; Cotton picking; Delta Queen packet boat; Cypress tree "knees"

Q   How did Bernie meet Carrie Stevenson?
A   The pretty young blonde was the widow of bootlegger Ray Stevenson. She ran The Pines, a popular restaurant and motel in **Collinsville**. Bernie was a frequent patron of the place.

Q   What did Bernie and Carrie have in common?
A   They both loved fancy cars and horses. Both also had volatile tempers.

Q   How did Carl get himself arrested in **East St. Louis** in 1935?
A   He was booked for vagrancy and fined for carrying a concealed weapon. He told police that he had retired and was raising mules on his farm in Fairfield.

Q   How did the Sheltons become involved with **Peoria**?
A   In 1930 the Capone mob tried to muscle in on Clyde Garrison, the city's gambling czar. The owner of the Windsor Club on Fulton Street decided to form an alliance with the Sheltons for survival.

Carl Shelton

Q   What did Bernie do after his wife Carrie divorced him in 1937?
A   He moved his base of operations to **Peoria**

Q   Where was Bernie's new base of operations in Peoria?
A   The Palace Club, located near city hall

Q   Did Carl Shelton ever kill anyone accidentally?
A   Yes – in 1943 he hit a nine-year-old girl on State Route 121 near **Decatur** while driving from **Peoria** to **Fairfield**

Q   What caused Carl to quit **Peoria** and go back to his farm in 1945?
A   Peorians elected a new mayor, and Carl Triebel had a meeting with Carl Shelton and told him in no uncertain terms that he was closing down the gambling parlors.

Q What did Bernie do?
A He stayed but moved his headquarters to the modest **Parkway Tavern** on Farmington Road, just outside the city limits.

Q When Carl Shelton was killed in October of 1947, what were his last words?
A "Don't shoot me anymore, Charlie (Harris). It's me, Carl Shelton. You've killed me already."

Q How many bullets hit Carl Shelton's body?
A 17

Q How many shooters were there at the Shelton farm on Pond Creek road?
A Four

Q According to the newspapers, how many people showed up for Carl's funeral at the First Methodist Church?
A 1,200

Q What previous incident led authorities to believe that "Blackie" Harris was Carl's killer?
A Carl and Ray Walker had severely beaten a Pond Creek neighbor in a dispute over some stolen cattle. The bloodied man was a relative of Blackie Harris.

Q Was Blackie Harris arrested and held for the murder of Carl Shelton?
A Yes

Q Did Harris do prison time for the killing?
A No – a grand jury refused to indict.

Q What was odd about Carl Shelton's estate?
A He died without a will, but his real and personal property was worth about $100,000; he only had $9.20 on deposit in a Fairfield bank

Q How many deaths can be directly or indirectly traced to the Sheltons?
A 35

Q How long were they in power?
A 25 years

Q How long did **East St. Louis** businessman Frank Wortman stay in power?
A From 1941 to his death from cancer in 1968 – 26 years

Q What famous actor once called **East St. Louis** the "Hellhole Of The Nation?"
A W.C. Fields

Q Who was the heavy drinker among the Shelton brothers?

A Bernie

Q After sheriff Munie ran the Sheltons out of East St. Louis, what did Carl Shelton do?
A He retired to a farm in **Fairfield** but then later helped Bernie run things in **Peoria.**

Birger Gang (courtesy Illinois State Historical Society)

Q What happened to Earl Shelton?
A Earl was arrested on a liquor charge and was sent to prison in Atlanta

Q Who gained control of the gambling establishment in **East St. Louis** after the Sheltons left?
A According to Taylor Pensoneau, Frank "Buster" Wortman, after he was released from prison in 1941, stemming from a run in with federal agents while protecting a Shelton still in 1933

Q Why did Wortman and Blackie Armes switch allegiances from the Sheltons to the Chicago syndicate?
A Both said the Sheltons forgot to take care of them in prison and did nothing for them when they got out.

Q What was Bernie Shelton's response to new peace overtures by the Chicago syndicate after Carl's death?
A He rebuffed them, saying he intended to run things in **Peoria** and southern Illinois; this probably sealed his fate.

Q What trap was set for Bernie by gunmen in 1948?
A Bernie was driving to Muscatine, Iowa, to sell some of his palomino horses from his ranch. The gunmen were waiting for him along a highway near **Galesburg,** but Bernie took a different route.

Q How was Bernie killed in July of 1948?
A He had just left the Parkway Tavern and was shot before he reached his car. The killer, firing from a thicket, hit Bernie in the chest with a high-powered rifle.

Q Where was Bernie buried?
A Bernie died at St. Francis Hospital and was buried, according to his second wife's wishes, in **Peoria**. **Bernie** was only 49-years-old. His wife (Genevieve Paulsgrove) had him buried at Parkview Cemetery, close to the murder scene.

Q Was this murder ever solved?
A No

Q What gambling spot did Bernie own in neighboring **Tazewell County**?
A The Paradise Club

Q After Bernie's death, what gubernatorial candidate rode the coattails of unfettered gambling and corruption to the statehouse?
A Adlai Stevenson, defeating Dwight Green's bid for a third term

Q How close did an assassin come to killing Earl Shelton in May of 1949?
A Earl was wounded when someone, from the roof of a nearby building, fired several shots at him through a window at the Farmer's Club in **Fairfield**.

Q What **East St. Louis** policeman was the nemesis of the Sheltons?
A Robert "Tree" Sweeney

Q How tough was Sweeney?
A He killed as many men in the line of duty (12) as Frank and Jesse James combined.

Q What happened to Blackie Armes?
A He was killed in December of 1944 when he got into a shootout with **Herrin** tavern owner, Thomas Propes who was also killed.

Q What former Sheltonites threw in their lot with Wortman as he began to push his empire southward?
A Tony Armes from **Herrin** and Blackie Harris.

Q According to the FBI, how many killings were attributed to Blackie Harris?
A 21

Q What happened to Wortman associate Ray Daugherty in 1947?
A His body was found at Crab Orchard Lake near **Carbondale**. The murder was never solved, but many attributed it to the Sheltons.

Bernie Shelton

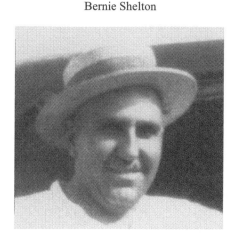

Q What happened at a secret meeting between gambling interests and state officials at a 1941 meeting at the Broadview Hotel in **East St. Louis**?
A Officials agreed not to put the brakes on a burgeoning gambling empire in return for regular payoffs. Carl Shelton was one of the gamblers who delivered the payoffs to the collectors. This went on for about eight years before the scheme was exposed.

Q What was Earl Shelton doing in 1944?
A He ran a gambling house in Fairfield.

Q Desperate to remove the Sheltons from power, what action was taken by the Chicago Syndicate?
A They let it be known that there was a $10,000 contract on the head of each Shelton brother.

Q Did the Sheltons ever partner up with the Chicago Outfit?
A No – they turned them down repeatedly; some think this is what led to their demise.

Birger gang at Shady Rest near Marion

Q Which Shelton was the first to be murdered?
A Carl was shot and killed while driving a Jeep on his farm in **Fairfield**.

Q Who was convicted of the crime?
A The murder was never solved. Charles "Blackie" Harris was the prime suspect.

Q What was the name of Bernie's ranch on the outskirts of **Peoria**?
A Golden Rule Ranch

Q Was Bernie buried in **Fairfield** or **Peoria**?
A Peoria

Q What man was elected governor by promising to clean things up in places like East St. Louis and **Peoria**?
A Adlai Stevenson

Q Whatever happened to Blackie Harris?
A He was convicted of murdering two people in the Pond Creek area of Fairfield and sent to prison.

Q What happened to "Little Earl" Shelton on September 9, 1949?
A When he pulled in his driveway on Elm Street, his car was riddled with bullets from an unknown assailant. Earl, who had been at the scene of Uncle Carl's shooting two years earlier, narrowly missed death as bullets flew around

him. At the time of this shooting, he was working on the farm for Big Earl and doubled as his bodyguard.

Q What happened to Big Earl in May of 1950?
A He was wounded in the arm while inspecting oil rigs in the Pond Creek area.

Q What happened to Roy Shelton on June 7, 1950?
A Roy got out of prison in 1943. He was shot in the spine while driving a tractor on a farm in the Pond Creek area, close to where Carl had been killed. He fell off the tractor and the plowshares ran over his body, leaving him a bloody mess. Roy was the oldest and quietest of the Sheltons.

Q What happened to Big Earl in December of 1950?
A Someone tossed a bomb through a window of his home. He and his wife Earline were lucky to escape the blast and ensuing flames.

Q What action was then taken by Dalta, Big Earl and Little Earl?
A The three Sheltons sold their holdings in **Fairfield** and moved to Florida.

Q What happened to Big Earl's barn in June of 1951?
A It was burned by an arsonist.

Q What happened to tenants who tried to farm the Shelton property?
A They were shot at and run off.

Q What happened to oil machinery on the Shelton farms?
A It was frequently hit with rifle fire and damaged.

Q What happened to Lula Shelton Pennington, the Shelton sister, in June of 1951?
A She and her husband were wounded by a shooter in a residential neighborhood in broad daylight. They, too, left for Jacksonville, Florida, along with Lula's mother (Agnes) who was over 90-years-old.

Q How did Big Earl prosper in Florida?
A He got into real estate and did quite well. He was in his 90's when he passed away.

Q How did Blackie Harris finally end up at Menard Prison in **Chester**?
A He bought up much of the Shelton land and farmed over 1,000 acres. In 1964 he was charged with the killing of two people that had testified against him in an earlier civil lawsuit. He was sentenced to 18 years and was let out on parole a few years before he died.

Q Who has written the definitive biography of the Sheltons?
A Taylor Pensoneau of **Belleville/New Berlin**; for an autographed copy of *Brothers Notorious* send $18.95 to Downstate Publications, Box 320, New Berlin, IL 62670

CHARLIE BIRGER - BOOTLEGGER

Q Where was Charlie Birger born?
A Western Russia (Lithuania) - 1883

Q In what town did Charlie live and sell newspapers as a youth?
A St. Louis - where he sold papers for the *Post-Dispatch*

Q What southern Illinois town has a street named for Birger's upstanding entrepreneur brother, Sam?
A **Glen Carbon**

Q In what branch of the military did Birger serve?
A The U.S. Cavalry – Fort Assinnibone, Montana, 1901; when he enlisted, Birger said he had been a bricklayer in **Glen Carbon.**

Q Did Birger ever return to Glen Carbon?
A Yes, in 1904, after his three-year stint in the Army.

Q What famous horse did Birger tame?
A Maneater – said to be as cantankerous as Pecos Bill's horse, Widowmaker

Q Why was Birger able to collect a monthly pension from the U.S. government?
A He spent a month in the hospital when a horse fell on him.

Q Why was Charlie Birger **missing a finger** on his left hand? (see picture on page 178)
A It was bitten in a barroom brawl, became infected, and had to be amputated. Birger displayed the finger, preserved in alcohol, in a jar in his living room.

Q What label was applied to Birger by some members of the press?
A The "Scourge of Egypt" (southern Illinois)

Q Why did some apply the Robin Hood label to him?
A He gave pennies and nickels to local children and bags of groceries to those in need.

Q Charlie bought his wife Beatrice a washing machine but put it to what innovative use?
A Mixing water with 190 proof alcohol

Q Did Birger ever do time in prison?
A He was caught in a Williamson County dry raid and did a year in **Danville** prison – 1924.

Q How many times did Birger marry?

Birger Avenue in Glen Carbon – named for Charlie Birger's brother – photo by Bill Jacobus

A   Three – **East St. Louisan** Edna Hastey (1909), Beatrice Bainbridge (1921), Bernice Davis (1926)

Q   What mine did Birger work at when he lived a spell in **Belleville**?
A   The Nigger Hollow Mine in **O'Fallon**

Q   What did Birger do for a living when he lived in the Edgemont section of **East St. Louis** from 1906-08?
A   He operated a small store

Q   When did Birger kill his first man – William Oughten?
A   Around 1908 when he got into an argument at Phil Traband's Saloon at 89th and State in **Edgemont**. Authorities ruled it was self-defense.

Q   Where did Charlie Birger live from 1908-1913?
A   Staunton

Q   What other Illinois towns did Birger call home?
A   The 1910 census had him living in **Virden,** and in 1913 he was in **Christopher**.

Q   When did he go to the **Marion, Harrisburg, Herrin** area?
A   Late 1913 - this is where he lived the rest of his days on earth.

Q   Who did Birger kill in 1917?
A   He shot a rival liquor competitor by the name of Crip Yates. Again, it was held to be self-defense.

Q   Why was Birger sent to Massac County jail in 1918?
A   The sheriff found three stolen cars in Birger's barn at **Ledford**.

Q   How many children did Birger have?
A   Two – one by Edna Hastey and another by Beatrice Bainbridge

Q   Where did Birger live when he married Beatrice Bainbridge?
A   Above the Busy Bee Candy Kitchen in **Harrisburg**

Q   How did Birger get along with his in-laws?
A   Bob Bainbridge said Charlie was destined to "die with his boots on," and Mrs. Bainbridge hated his living guts.

Charlie Birger hanging

Q   Who was Charlie Birger's favorite movie star?
A   Tom Mix

Q   What was Charlie Birger's favorite drink?

A   An Egyptian cocktail – corn liquor mixed with port wine

Q   When did Beatrice learn Charlie was having an affair with the "Shawneetown Dame?"
A   When she saw the woman come out of Birger's hospital room in **Herrin** after his 1923 shootout with Whitey Doering at the Half Way roadhouse.

Q   What did Birger do with his ailing, senile father from 1919 to 1921.
A   He cared for him at his home in **Harrisburg**. When his father died, Charlie buried him in a Jewish Cemetery in St. Louis.

Q   What did Birger purchase in 1923?
A   Forty acres of ground in **Williamson County**

Q   What did he build on it?
A   His gang's clubhouse, which his wife named Shady Rest; it was on Route 13 halfway between **Harrisburg** and **Marion** on the north side of the road.

Q   Where did Beatrice and the kids live?
A   They lived in town on Poplar Street in **Marion**

Q   Who did Birger kill in November of 1923?
A   A man named Cecil Knighton in an argument over a woman. Again, it was ruled self-defense

Q   What was the name of Birger's business establishment in **Marion**?
A   It was a roadhouse by the name of Half Way. It was on **Johnson City** Road in Marion.

Q   What bank did Birger and his gang rob in November of 1926?
A   The gang made off with about $5,000 by robbing the bank at **Pocahontas**; it was payroll money for the Pocahontas Mining Company.

Q   How was Charlie Birger wounded in late November of 1923?
A   Charlie got into a fight with St. Louis gangster, Whitey Doering, killing him.

Q   Who was a surprise visitor while Birger was recuperating at a hospital?
A   Carl Shelton. This was when the two rivals formed a temporary alliance.

Q   What Birger facility was located across the road from Birger's Shady Rest?

A A barbecue stand

Q What was the use for a shallow pit near Shady Rest?
A Dogfights and cock fights

Q When did Birger have his falling out with the Sheltons, ending their brief alliance?
A April, 1926, in a meeting at Shady Rest

Q Why did the Birger gang kill Lyle Worsham, one of their own, in September of 1926?
A They suspected him of giving information to the Shelton gang.

Q What member of the Birger gang was an artist of sorts and drew pictures depicting some of the shootouts?
A Harvey Dungey

Q What special vehicle was used to make an attack on Birger's Shady Rest by the Sheltons?
A Blackie Armes and Joe Adams helped them build a crude tank that had a revolving turret. It lumbered along at a top speed of ten miles an hour.

Q What happened at the confrontation?
A When the tank approached the barbecue stand near Shady Rest, occupants began firing at it. Reinforcements came out from Shady Rest and drove the tank away.

Q What was Birger's next step?
A He had a car shop in **Harrisburg** armor plate an old Lincoln. They used it several times to attack some of the Sheltons' roadhouses. It was so slow and heavy, it wasn't very useful, but Birger parked it near Shady Rest for deterrence.

Q What two other suspected traitors were killed by Birger's men in October of 1926?
A High Pockets McQuay and Ward Casey Jones

Q Who paid for their funeral expenses?
A A generous Charlie Birger

Q Who threw a stick of dynamite at Birger's barbecue stand in November of 1926?
A Blackie Armes, but he did it from a fast moving car and missed his target.

Q Who killed Joe Adams, mayor of **West City** near **Benton,** and an ally of the Sheltons?
A Charlie Birger sent two young men (Harry and Elmo

Thomasson) from his gang. They shot him after knocking on his door and handing him a fake note from the Sheltons.

Q What state highway patrol officer was murdered by Art Newman and Birger's men?
A Lory Price. Not only was Lory killed, his pregnant wife was also shot and thrown down an abandoned mine shaft.

Lory Price of the Illinois Highway Patrol - murdered by Birger gang

Q What happened to Shady Rest in January of 1927?
A It burned to the ground. Authorities found four bodies in the smoldering ruins.

Q What happened in March of 1927 to Birger's house on West Poplar?
A Someone tried to set fire to it while Birger and his family were asleep.

Q What was the result of the fire?
A Birger woke up, heard a noise, smelled smoke, ran outside and put out the fire.

Q What evidence did authorities have as a basis for arresting Charlie Birger for the murder of Joe Adams?
A After Harry Thomasson was arrested for the shooting, he confessed and told authorities he was acting on orders from Birger. Mrs. Adams had seen the two boys shoot her husband. Authorities also had the fake note written by Charlie Birger.

Actor John Malkovich of Benton in the same jail cell once occupied by Charlie Birger (Franklin County Hist. Soc.)

Q When Charlie Birger was arrested, how was he tricked?
A Sheriff Prichard told him he would likely wriggle out of this jam, and that while he was in jail he could keep his machine gun with him. When it was time to go before the judge, he convinced Birger to leave the weapon behind because guns weren't allowed in the courtroom.

Q When and where was Birger's trial?
A It started at **Benton** in July of 1927.

Q How long did it take the jurors to deliberate?
A They came back with a death penalty after 24 hours.

Q If the state had previously outlawed execution by hanging, why was Birger sentenced to die on the gallows?

A   Because hanging was the penalty when he had Joe West killed.

Q   What famous Chicago evangelist visited Birger while he was waiting execution?
A   Billy Sunday

Q   What NBA basketball star lived as a youth in a bedroom above the **Benton** jail rooms when his father was sheriff of Franklin County?
A   Doug Collins – who later coached the Bulls and Pistons

Q   Did Birger ever undergo an insanity hearing?
A   Yes – requested by his lawyer in a last ditch effort to avoid execution; Birger was found to be sane after only 12 minutes of questions.

Q   Was Birger allowed conjugal visits with his wife while he was in jail?
A   Yes

Q   After all appeals were exhausted, when was the date for execution?
A   April 19, 1928

Q   Approximately nine months passed from the date Birger was convicted and his execution date. How long does it take in current death penalty cases before all appeals are exhausted?
A   Fifteen years is not uncommon.

Q   Did Birger try to commit suicide in his cell?
A   Yes

Q   What were Birger's famous last words as he joked and bantered on the scaffold?
A   "It's a beautiful world!"

Q   Who was Charlie Birger's hangman?
A   Phil Hanna of **Epworth/Carmi**. He executed dozens of men and was called the "human hanging machine"

Q   Why did Hanna get into the hanging business?
A   He once attended a hanging that was botched, and the poor man strangled to death. Hanna prided himself on his skill.

Q   How many knots were in Birger's noose, and how many steps led to the platform of the gallows?
A   An unlucky Thirteen

Q   Why did Birger choose a black hood rather than a white one to be placed over his head?
A   He said white ones were for the KKK.

Q   How many doctors listed to Birger's heart before he was pronounced dead?
A   Three

Q   Where was Birger buried?
A   In the same St. Louis Jewish cemetery as his father

Q   What is on Birger's tombstone?
A   Shachna Itzik Birger

Q   Was Birger a practicing Jew?
A   No - but there was a St. Louis rabbi with him at his execution.

Q   Did any of Birger's wives attend the execution?
A   Only Edna Hastey, Birger's first wife. Birger told reporter Roy Alexander that she had been the best of the three.

Official pass to Birger execution

STATE OF ILLINOIS
Franklin County ss.
I, JAMES S. PRITCHARD, Sheriff of Franklin County, Illinois, do hereby appoint
J. J. Entsminger.
as Special Deputy Sheriff to assist at the execution of Charles Birger, for murder, at Benton, Illinois. Execution at County Jail, in Benton, Illinois, Friday, April 13, 1928, at 10 o'clock A. M.
(Not Transferable)   James S. Pritchard
Sheriff.

Charlie Birger with black hood, moments before his hanging

Q   How many times did Birger kill someone and have a coroner's jury rule it was self-defense?
A   Four

Q   What happened to Birger's daughter Charline in 1949?
A   She died in childbirth at St. Louis and was buried near her father; daughter Minnie died in 1992 at Wyoming

Q   What insurance executive is mostly responsible for the conversion of the **Franklin County** Jail into a museum?
A   Robert S. Rea of **Benton**

Q   Who is the only criminal in the state that has a museum devoted to him?
A   Charlie Birger – the old jail at **Benton** is now a museum.

Q   How long was Birger in the jail before he was

executed?
A   Nearly a year – April 29, 1827 – April 19, 1928

Q   What country singing star recorded the song, "The Hanging of Charlie Birger?"
A   Vernon Dalhart – the song was written by Carson Robinson

Q   Who has written the definitive biography of Charlie Birger?
A   My friend Gary DeNeal of **Herod**, Illinois– *A Knight of Another Sort;* For an autographed copy send $19.95 to Springhouse, Box 61, Herod, IL 62947

Birger in jail cell – notice missing finger

ILLINOIS WRITERS AND ARTISTS

Q   What Illinois novelist wrote the book, *Vessel of Wrath,* about temperance advocate Carrie Nation?
A   Robert Lewis Taylor

Q   What **Winnetka** author wrote the anti-capitalist book, *Wealth Against Commonwealth*?
A   Henry Demarest Lloyd

Q   Who do many think the facial image on Lorado Taft's Blackhawk statue looks like?
A   Taft's writer friend, Hamlin Garland

Q   What was the first monthly magazine west of the Appalachians?
A   *Illinois Monthly*, published in **Vandalia** from 1830-32

Q   What famous writer called Chicago the literary capital of the world in 1920?
A   H.L. Mencken of the *Baltimore Sun*

Q   What writer from **Bloomington** became famous for his work, *A Message to Garcia*, a story about the Spanish-American War?
A   Elbert Hubbard

Chautauqua Auditorium at Shelbyville

Q   What town was home to Jesse Williams, the first playwright to win a Pulitzer (for "Why Marry?") in 1917?
A   **Sterling**

Q   What Chicago author invented the detective known as Philip Marlowe (*The Big Sleep*) and later became a Hollywood screenwriter for financial security?
A   Raymond Chandler – his *Double Indemnity* was nominated for an Academy Award.

Q   What **Galesburg** historical writer became one of the leading authorities on the antebellum South?
A   Frederick Bancroft

Q   What Chicago writer of oral history won a Pulitzer for *The Good War*?
A   Studs Terkle

Q   What Chicago woman won the Pultizer Prize in 1931 for *Years of Grace*?
A   Margaret Barnes

Q   What **Oak Park** native wrote the best seller, *Jonathin Livingston Seagull*?
A   Richard Bach – a descendant of composer Johann Sebastian Bach

Q   What University of Chicago book has served as a guide for writers and editors since 1969?
A   *The Chicago Manual of Style*

Q   What Illinois writer authored *U.S.A., The Big Money* and *Manhattan Transfer*?
A   John Dos Pasos, who thought writers should be "architects of history"

Q   What Chicago journalist authored *Inside Europe* and a series of other books beginning with the title, "*Inside?*"
A   John Gunther

Q   What state song was written by Theodore Dreiser's brother, Paul?
A   "On The Banks Of The Wabash," the state song of Indiana. Theodore wrote most of the words while Paul composed the music.

Q   What town was home to George Barnard, a noted sculptor?
A   **Kankakee**

Q   What Illinoisan hit the top of the charts in 1963 with the song, "Sugar Shack?"
A   Johnny Gilmer

Q   What **Winnetka** author created the character Auntie Mame?
A   Patrick Dennis, a.k.a. Everett Tanner III

Q   What Chicago author of *Herzog* and *Humboldt's Gift*

won both a Nobel Prize and a Pulitzer Prize in 1976?
A   Saul Bellow

Q   What type of books were written by Wesley Brinke of **Edwardsville** back in the nineteenth century?
A   Books about Illinois counties

Q   What town was the setting for Booth Tarkington's *Penrod?*
A   **Marshall**

Q   What county seat of Hamilton County is home to the People's Bank, a classic example of American Baroque architecture?
A   **McLeansboro**

Q   What town was home to Helen Hockison, a cartoonist for the *New Yorker* magazine?
A   **Mendota**

Q   What town was home to Boyd Button Company and called itself the "Button Capital of America?"
A   **Meredosia**

Q   What southern Illinois town has an architectural marvel designed by Prairie School architect Walter B. Griffin?
A   **Anna** - Its Stinson Library is named for a Union Army officer who left $50,000 to the city.

Jean Kirkpatrick of Mount Vernon at the U.N.

State Song

"By thy rivers gently flowing,
Illinois, Illinois,
O'er the prairies, verdant, growing,
Illinois, Illinois,
Comes an echo on the breeze,
Rustling through the leafy trees,
And its mellow tones are these,
Illinois, Illinois,
And its mellow tones are these,
Illinois."

A   Stan Hitchcock of **Nashville**

Q   Who is the most prolific Illinois writer on matters of military affairs?
A   Walter Boyne of **East St. Louis** – his dozens and dozens of works that include both fiction and non-fiction

Q   What Illinois town was home to author Edgar Lee Masters?
A   **Lewistown**

Q   What town was home to Zez Confrey who wrote the popular song, "Kitten on the Keys?"
A   **LaSalle**

Q   Peter Newell was from **Bushnell**, Illinois. What famous book by Lewis Carroll did he illustrate?
A   Alice In Wonderland

Q   What **Herrin** resident wrote *The Origin of the Brunists*, a novel about a coal mining accident?
A   Robert Coover – who also wrote some pretty far out stuff that he had trouble getting published.

Q   What English writer visited **Cairo** and called it a "detestable morass . . . a place of ague and death?"
A   Charles Dickens

Q   What southern Illinois town has a nude statue named *the Hewer*, by George Barnard?
A   **Cairo**

Q   What Oak Park woman, whose uncle was Frank Lloyd Wright, wrote books about the fictional Melendy family?
A   Elizabeth Enright (1909-1968) – her second book, *Thimble Summer*, won a Newbery Award in 1939.

Q   What Chicago playwright wrote screenplays for *Nicholas and Alexandra, They Might Be Giants, Robin and Marian*, and *The Lion in Winter*?
A   James Goldman – he won the Oscar for *Lion in Winter*

Q   Where is Marc Chagall's "Four Seasons" mosaic in Chicago?
A   First National Plaza at Dearborn and Monroe streets

Q   What Chicago-born novelist wrote screenplays for *The Marathon Man, Harper, The Stepford Wives, All the President's Men* and *The Great Waldo Pepper*?
A   William Goldman

Q   Who wrote the song, "The Ballad of Dan Walker?"

Q   What **Park Ridge** composer was a direct descendent of John Alden of Plymouth Rock and *Mayflower* fame?
A   John Alden Carpenter – he studied under Edward Elgar and composed a number of works for children; he ventured into jazz with his 1922 ballet, *Krazy Kat,* based on the cartoon comic strip.

Q   What writer from **Bloomington** wrote *A Message to Garcia*?
A   Elbert Hubbart – it was about the Spanish-American War.

Q   Dorothy – the girl in the story *The Wizard of Oz* – was named for what person?
A   Dorothy Gale of **Bloomington**, niece of writer Frank Baum, who died about a year after her birth

Q   What was the book, written by **Oak Park** native Ernest Hemingway, that won the 1954 Nobel Prize for literature?

A *The Old Man And The Sea.* Curiously, much of it was written in Cubero, New Mexico, situated along **Route 66,** far from any body of water

Q What southern Illinois town has an old railroad depot museum dedicated to sketch artist Roscoe Misselhorn?
A **Sparta**

Q What **Galesburg** native won a Pulitzer Prize for poetry in 1951?
A Carl Sandburg

Q What Chicago novelist wrote *Manhattan Transfer*?
A John Dos Pasos

Q What Chicago novelist wrote *The Man With The Golden Arm*?
A Nelson Algren

Q What **Hope**, Illinois, native won the Pulitzer Prize in poetry in 1940?
A Mark Van Doren

Q What Chicago company is famous for making maps and atlases?
A Rand-McNally

Q What native of **Glencoe**, noted for his poetry, also served as Librarian of Congress?
A Archibald MacLeish

Q Who authored *The Wonderful Wizard of Oz* while living in Chicago?
A Frank Baum

Q What Upton Sinclair novel resulted in the passage of the Pure Food and Drug Act?
A *The Jungle*

Q What **Oak Park** resident created a character by the name of Lord Greystoke?
A Edgar Rice Burroughs created the Englishman known as Tarzan.

Q How many trips did Burroughs make to Africa before writing his first book in 1912, *Tarzan of the Apes*?
A None – everything came from his imagination and things he had read.

Q What Chicago-born attorney wrote the novel, *Presumed Innocent*?
A Scott Turow

Q What Illinois town was home to Alan Nevins, historian and Pulitzer Prize winner?

Hemingway as ambulance driver during World War I (Hemingway Foundation)

Willie and Joe by Bill Mauldin

A **Camp Point**

Q What friend of Carl Sandburg started out by writing advertising copy for a Chicago newspaper?
A Sherwood Anderson - who wrote *Winesburg, Ohio*

Q What Robert Lewis Taylor novel won the Pulitzer Prize in 1958?
A *The Travels of Jamie McPheeters*

Q What two men from the University of Chicago started the Great Books program in 1952?
A Mortimer Adler and Robert Hutchins

Q What years was *The Dial*, a journal of literary criticism, published in Chicago?
A From 1880 to 1917, then it moved to New York

Q What two brothers won Pulitzer Prizes for history and poetry?
A Carl and Mark Van Doren of **Hope**, Illinois

Q What future Pulitzer Prize winner covered the 1919 Chicago race riot as a reporter for the *Daily News*?
A Carl Sandburg

Q What Illinois poet is often called the "Western Walt Whitman?"
A Carl Sandburg

Q What Illinois-born war correspondent wrote *The Rise and Fall of the Third Reich*?
A William L. Shirer

Q What *Chicago Sun-Times* cartoonist created the characters "Willie and Joe" during World War II?
A Bill Mauldin

Q What famous general hated Willie and Joe?
A George Patton – our greatest general of WW II

Q What native of **Camp Point** and distinguished historian wrote over fifty works on U.S. and Illinois history?
A Alan Nevins

Q What Chicago publisher printed a nude photo of Marilyn Monroe in the first issue of his magazine?
A Playboy Hugh Hefner

Q Back in 1895, what was the price of most Chicago newspapers?

A   One penny, but it quickly went to two cents after the turn of the century. When this author was in high school in 1955, newspapers cost a nickel.

Q   What was the first University in the United States to go into the business of printing scholarly books?
A   The University of Chicago

Q   What **Robinson**-born man wrote the best seller, *From Here to Eternity*?
A   James Jones

Q   What publisher opened its first retail store at the Woodfield Mall in **Schaumberg** in 1991?
A   Encyclopedia Britannica

Q   What Chicagoan wrote a play based on his experiences selling worthless land in Florida and Arizona?
A   David Mamet – *Glengarry Glen Ross*

Q   How did Mamet learn to capture the essence of writing the natural way people really talk?
A   He spent weeks wandering through the streets of Chicago with a tape recorder.

Q   What screenplays has Mamet written?
A   *The Untouchables*, *The Postman Always Rings Twice*, *The Verdict*, *House of Games*

Q   Who wrote the classic book on southern Illinois, *Legends and Lore of Southern Illinois?*
A   John W. Allen in 1964

Q   What noted soprano, who studied voice in Chicago, was an important performer for the Chicago Grand Opera Company?
A   Mary Garden (1874-1967)

Q   What Chicago oral historian wrote *Working* and *Hard Times?*
A   Studs Terkle – this master of gritty realism is a Pulitzer Prize winner

Q   What **Albion** writer attracted settlers from England to frontier Illinois with *Notes on a Journey to the Territory of Illinois* and *Letters From Illinois?*
A   Morris Birbeck

Q   *Ebony* magazine is based in what Illinois city?
A   Chicago

Q   What Chicagoan wrote *The Pit* and *The Octopus*, novels that criticized the Robber Barons?

® Popeye by Elzie Seegar of Chester

Tarzan by Edgar Rice Burroughs

A   Frank Norris

Q   What **Springfield** native, who was born and died in the same house, was known as "The Vagabond Poet?"
A   Vachel Lindsay

Q   What *Chicago Tribune* reporter wrote *Andersonville*, the story of an infamous Confederate prison camp?
A   MacKinley Kantor

Q   What is Chicagoan Richard Kiley's most memorable role on Broadway?
A   Don Quixote in *Man of LaMancha*

Q   For what television mini-series did Kiley win a Golden Globe and an Emmy?
A   *Thorn Birds*

Q   Chicago movie executive Sherry Lansing helped make the movie about an accident at a nuclear power plant called *The China Syndrome*. What happened 12 days after her picture was released?
A   The nuclear power accident in Pennsylvania at Three Mile Island

Q   What four famous Illinoisans were all ambulance drivers in World War I?
A   Ray Kroc, Walt Disney, John Dos Pasos and Ernest Hemingway

Q   What was the name of the place near **Oregon** that was home to a colony of artists that included Lorado Taft and Hamlin Garlin?
A   Eagle's Nest

Q   What Richard Wright novel is about an African-American postal worker in Chicago?
A   *Lawd Today*

Q   What novel by Chicagoan Michael Crichton got a little preachy as it warned about the economic dangers posed by Japan to America?
A   *Rising Sun* – but it was still a good story.

Q   What first novel by Theodore Dreiser was about a poor girl in Chicago?

A   *Sister Carrie*

Q   What Chicago writer hated the fact that he became known as "The Children's Poet?"
A   Eugene Field – "Little Boy Blue," "Wynken, Blynken and Nod," etc.

Q   What Frank Harris novel is about the Haymarket Square incident in Chicago?
A   *The Bomb*

Q   What is the subject of the Chicago sculpture called "Bat-column?"
A   A baseball bat

Q   What **Newton**, Illinois, man, famous for singing folk songs and Christmas songs, won an Academy Award for his acting role in *The Big Country*?
A   Burl Ives

Q   What were Ives' two most famous movie roles?
A   He was Big Daddy in *Cat on a Hot Tin Roof*; in *East of Eden* he was the one who loaned James Dean money to invest in beans.

Q   What writer had his novel, *Reversible Errors*, turned into a four hour CBS mini-series starring Tom Selleck and William Macey?
A   Scott Turow

Q   What year did Chicagoan Walt Disney open Disneyland in Anaheim, California?
A   1955

Q   Who won the Pulitzer Prize for fiction in 1949?
A   Chicagoan James Cozzens for *Guard of Honor*

Q   What Chicago author saw several of his novels, such as *The Prize*, turned into films?
A   Irving Wallace

Q   What **Waukegan** native wrote a book about censorship and book burning?
A   Ray Bradbury wrote *Fahrenheit 451* (the temperature at which books burn)

Q   With what comic strip is **Anna**-born native Frank Willard associated?
A   "Moon Mullins"

Q   What Illinoisan was a Pulitzer Prize winning political cartoonist for the *Washington Post*?
A   Herbert Block – Herblock – the man responsible for coining the term "McCarthyism"

Q   What **Chester** native drew the popular Popeye comic strip.
A   Elzie Seegar

Q   With what Illinois town is Chester Gould, the creator of Dick Tracy, associated?

Don Hesse of Belleville (courtesy Post-Dispatch/Globe) "Risky way to cross the desert"

Little Orphan Annie by Harold Gray (author collection)

A   **Woodstock**

Q   What humorist and author created the cartoon character Mr. Dooley, an Irish saloon keeper who made wry commentary on contemporary life at the turn of the century?
A   Chicagoan Finley Peter Dunne

Q   With what comic strip is Chicago native Bud Fisher associated?
A   "Mutt and Jeff"

Q   Rollin Kirby was a nationally famous political cartoonist of the 1920's and 1930's. With what Illinois town in Henry County is he associated?
A   **Galva**

Q   In what southern Illinois town did conservative political cartoonist Don Hesse live when he drew for the *St. Louis Post-Dispatch*?
A   **Belleville**

Q   What **Kankakee** cartoonist originated the "Little Orphan Annie" comic strip?
A   Harold Gray

Q   What Chicago native was famous for drawing the comic strip, "Blondie?"
A   Chic Young

WHAT'S IN A NAME?

Q   Why was Cub pitching ace Mordecai Brown called "Three Finger?"
A   He only had three fingers on his right hand. He once won both ends of a doubleheader in 1908.

Q   What town in Illinois did "Long John" Wentworth name after his hometown in New Hampshire?
A   **Sandwich**

Q   What town bills itself as the "City of Murals?"
A   **Belvidere**

Q   For what is the town of **Marengo** named?

A It was the scene of Napoleon's victory in Austria.

Q How did the town of **Monee**, south of Chicago, get its name?
A It's a corruption of the name Marie.

Q What is the meaning of the town name of **Normal**, Illinois?
A It comes from the word "normal" – a term applied to colleges and universities that trained teachers.

Q What county's name comes from an Indian word meaning "white potato?"
A **Macoupin**

Q What Illinois town is named for a constellation?
A **Orion**

Q What is the translation of **Jacksonville's** Riviere Mauvaise Terre?
A Badlands – though no one seems to know why the French gave the creek that name since it is an oxymoron.

Q How did Northwestern University in Chicago get its name?
A Illinois was part of the old Northwest Territory.

Q How did Eliot Ness and his men in Chicago come to be called "the Untouchables?"
A Chicago was very corrupt and the fact that Ness and his men couldn't be bought led to the moniker coined by the newspapers.

Q How did Chicago's 1893 fair fan dancer Sally Rand come up with her stage name?
A She took it from a Chicago Rand-McNally atlas.

Q What was Bears running back Walter Payton's nickname?
A "Sweetness"

Q What Chicago White Sox Hall of Famer was referred to as "Old Aches and Pains?"
A Luke Appling

Q What was Blackhawk star Bobby Hull's nickname?
A "The Golden Jet" – his son is called "The Golden Brett."

Q What put-down nickname is given by Chicagoans to the newspapers of southern Illinois?
A They derisively call them the "pygmy press."

Billy Goat Tavern in Chicago by Pascale Lacor

Q What Chicago nickname was actually invented as a put-down by New Yorkers?
A The Windy (windbag) City

Q What nickname was given to the legendary U of I basketball teams from 1941-43?
A "The Whiz Kids" - Andy Phillip of **Granite City** played on that team.

Q What was Ernie Banks' nickname?
A "Mr. Cub"

Q What was Mike Ditka's nickname?
A "Iron Mike"

Q What was Yankee pitcher Bob Turley's nickname?
A "Bullet Bob" – he was from **East St. Louis.**

Q What was Red Grange's nickname?
A He was called the "Galloping Ghost" and the "Wheaton Iceman."

Q What was Gayle Sayers' nickname?
A "The Kansas Cyclone"

Q What southwestern city was originally called Illinoistown?
A **East St. Louis**

Q What is the French translation of **Belleville**?
A Beautiful town

East St. Louisan Candy Tockstein (Toxton) who married Mel Torme (courtesy Candy Toxton)

Q How did **Albion**, seat of Edwards County, receive its name?
A The town was settled by the English, and the name for England in 1066 was Albion.

Q What Chicago singer with a mellow voice was called "The Velvet Fog?"
A Mel Tormé

Q How did the town of **Aledo** get its name?
A City fathers drew five letters of the alphabet from a hat.

Q What town name comes from the Algonquin word for fort?
A **Waukegan** – originally called Little Fort

Q   How was the town of **Murphysboro** named?
A   The names of three county commissioners were placed in a hat and a man named Murphy from Perry County won.

Q   What was the nickname of Bears' coach George Halas?
A   "Papa Bear"

Q   What new name did Ned Buntline of **Carlyle** suggest for William F. Cody?
A   "Buffalo Bill"

Q   Why was this nickname appropriate?
A   When the transcontinental railroad was built, officials paid him $500 a month to keep workers supplied with buffalo meat.

Q   Why does Phoenix have a football team named the Cardinals?
A   Because they were originally the Chicago Cardinals, named for Illinois' state bird.

Q   What is the meaning of the Algonquin word, "Illinois?"
A   Loosely translated it means "warriors" or "superior men" – pretty cool, huh!

Q   What is the meaning of the Ojibwa word "checagou?"
A   Chicago is named for a word that roughly translates to "stinking onion"

Q   What nickname was explorer Henri de Tonti's given by the Indians?
A   "Iron Hand" - he lost the extremity in a naval battle and replaced it with one made of metal.

Q   What central Illinois town bills itself as the "Pride of the Prairie?"
A   **Decatur**

Q   What is the translation for the French town named Prairie du Rocher?
A   It means "prairie by the bluff" because of the nearby limestone outcrop near the Mississippi River.

Q   What nickname did the Native-Americans give to George Rogers Clark?
A   "Long Knife"

Q   What is the translation for the French town of Prairie du Pont?
A   Prairie du Pont – prairie across the bridge – became **Dupo**.

Calder's Flamingo by Pascale Lacor of Chicago

Hugh Heffner's Mansion, courtesy Kirsten and Charles Viola

Q   How did the town of **Benld** get its name?
A   The town was named for early settler Ben L. Dorsey. When city officials hired an artist to paint a sign for the railroad depot disaster struck. Already tipsy from "eleven o'clock bitters" the night before, the man took a few more drinks before beginning. He got as far as **BEN L D**orsey when he fell off the ladder in a drunken stupor and broke a leg. The sign was never finished and that was the name that stuck. (Honestly, I didn't make this up to sell more books.)

Q   What Illinois town was named for a place in Scotland by Illinois Central officials in the hope that it would attract immigrant settlers from that country?
A   **Kinmundy**

Q   What was the name of the Rock Island Railroad passenger train to Los Angeles?
A   *Golden State Limited*

Q   What Illinois town was named for a Spanish lieutenant under Cortez by Illinois Central Railroad officials in the hope that it would attract settlers from Spain?
A   **Sandoval**

Q   What town was given a French name by I.C. railroad officials with the expectation that it would draw settlers from France?
A   **Beaucoup**

Q   What town was named for a Norse god by I.C. railroad officials in the belief that it would bring Scandinavian immigrants to the state?
A   **Odin**

TRAILS, ROADS, HIGHWAYS & CARS

Q   What three nationally significant roads wind their way across Illinois?
A   Route 40 (National Road); Route 30 (Lincoln Highway); Route 66

Q What name was given to the wide-bodied wagons used by early settlers to come to Illinois?
A Prairie schooners

Q What other name was used to describe these wagons?
A Conestoga wagons – named for the stogies (cigars) smoked by the drivers

Q How did the Indians mark trails and directions?
A They bent saplings and forced them to grow in the desired direction.

Q What was the first trail used in Illinois by white men?
A The portage path between the Chicago and Illinois rivers, traveled by Marquette and Joliet

Q What was the path of the Vincennes Trail?
A It ran from Vincennes, Indiana, on the Wabash to **Illinoistown** (East St. Louis).

Q What was the path of the Goshen Road?
A It went from **Shawneetown** on the Ohio River to **Edwardsville**; another branch of it went over to **Kaskaskia.**

Q In what year did the National Road (Route 40) reach **Vandalia**?
A 1842

Q What was the route of an early Illinois road known as the Sucker Trail?
A It went north from **East St. Louis** to **Galena.**

Q What later names were applied to the Sucker Trail?
A The Great Northern Stage Route; it evolved into the Great River Road.

Q What was the route of the northern Illinois road known as Hubbard's Trace?
A It ran from Chicago directly south to Vincennes and was blazed by Gurdon Hubbard, a fur trader.

Q What Illinois highway did Hubbard's Trace become?
A Route 1

Q What towns did Hubbard's Trace go through?

A **Blue Island, Crete, Grant, Momence, Beaverville, Iroquois, Hoopeston, Myersville** and **Danville**

Q What was the route of the Kiswaukee Trail?
A It went from **Danville** to the **Rockford** vicinity.

Illinois in 1820

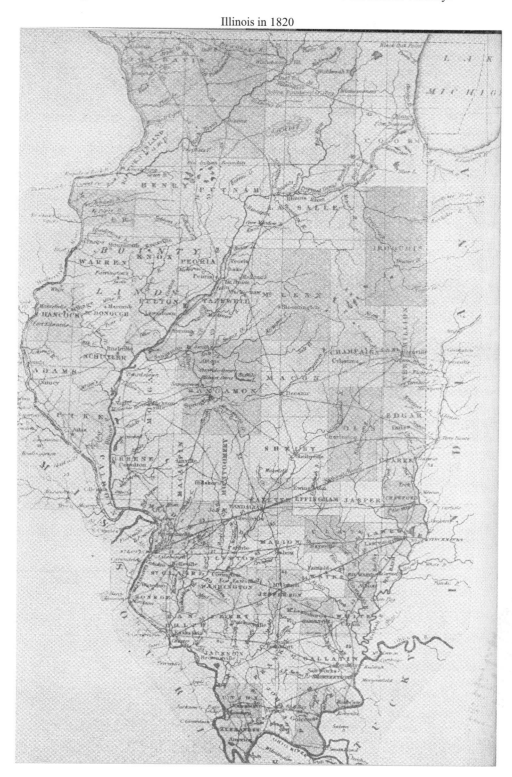

Q What was the route of the Army Trail, built by Winfield Scott in 1832?
A It went from Chicago to **Dixon's Ferry** on the Rock River and passed through **Aurora** and **Naperville**. From Dixon's Ferry it ran up to **Galena**.

185

Q   What road ran from Chicago to **Ottawa**, **Moline** and **Rock Island**?
A   The Grand Army of the Republic Highway – GAR

Q   What was the route of Oliver Kellogg's Trail, built in 1825?
A   It went from **Peoria** to Ogee's Ferry on the Rock River, and from there it went to **Galena.**

Q   What later road connected **Bloomington** with Chicago?
A   The Old Chicago Trail

Q   What were corduroy roads?
A   Roads that consisted of trees that were felled and stripped of their branches and placed side by side.

Q   Why were they called corduroy roads?
A   Because they looked ribbed like corduroy cloth.

Q   What were plank roads?
A   This was an improvement over the bone-jarring corduroy roads. These were merely thick boards laid across stringers that were parallel to the gravel roadbed.

Q   Were plank roads an Illinois invention?
A   No – they were a Russian invention that had been tried successfully in Canada.

Q   What was the cost per mile of plank roads in 1840?
A $3,000

Q   When did plank roads fall out of favor in Illinois?
A   Around 1856 because they were expensive to maintain and railroads were becoming increasingly popular

Q   What was invented to help pay for the cost and upkeep of plank roads?
A   The turnpike – a barrier or gate (*pike*) across the road that was raised or *turned* after a toll was paid - turnpike

Q   What was the split-log drag process for improving roads?
A   Invented in Missouri, the device used several teams of horses or mules that dragged logs over a dampened roadbed

Illinois Route 66

1929 Chicago police began phasing out motorcycles with Fords (Chicago Historical Society)

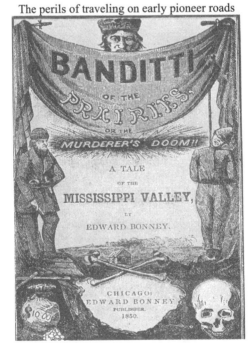

The perils of traveling on early pioneer roads

BANDITTI OF THE PRAIRIES OR THE MURDERER'S DOOM!! A TALE OF THE MISSISSIPPI VALLEY, BY EDWARD BONNEY. CHICAGO: EDWARD BONNEY PUBLISHER. 1850.

to smooth it. Mechanized road graders built by the Caterpillar Company of **Peoria** would later achieve the same results more quickly and economically.

Q   Macadamized roads became popular around the turn of the century. What were they?
A   Named for John MacAdam of Scotland, the road was a mixture of crushed rock on a convex roadbed for drainage.

Q   Where was the first macadamized road in Illinois?
A   The St. Clair County turnpike from **East St. Louis** to **Belleville** (State Street).

Q   What was Semple's Folly?
A   James Semple of **Alton** took an old steam engine from the Northern Cross Railroad and refitted it with broad, flat wheels. He called it a "land schooner," and it made its maiden run from Alton to **Edwardsville.** As he continued on toward **Springfield,** the smoke-belching behemoth fell into a hole, broke an axle, and was abandoned.

Q   What was the first Illinois group that began pressing authorities for better roads?
A   Velocipede enthusiasts – bicycle lovers

Q   How many automobiles were registered in the state of Illinois in 1900?
A   600

Q   When were Illinois motorists first required to register their autos and pay two dollars for identification plates?
A   During the second term of Governor Charles Deneen – 1909-1913

Q   What did owners of early motor vehicles do with their cars in winter time?
A   Because the roads were frozen and dangerous, they garaged them and stored their batteries with a local mechanic who attached them to low voltage lines to keep them charged.

Q   What was the Tice Law?
A   Homer Tice of **Greenview** sponsored state legislation in 1913 that established a uniform licensing system and fees that went to support road maintenance.

Q What unique source of labor did the Tice Law authorize for road maintenance?
A Convict labor

Q What were the first counties to respond to the Tice Law and approve bond issues for road improvement?
A **Cook, Vermilion, St. Clair** and **Jackson**

Q What were "dusters?"
A Overcoats used by those who drove early cars with open cockpits to keep road dust off suit clothes; a matching hat and a pair of goggles completed the ensemble.

Q What were "tourist camps?"
A In the old days of motoring there was no such thing as a motel, but around 1915 many towns began to build tourist parks that were free to campers. Early motorists had to bring along such items as tents, sheets, washcloths, soap, frying pans, and so forth.

Q What were "tin can tourists?"
A It's a mostly derogatory term that was applied to road "gypsies" who sometimes spent a whole season at a free camp site.

Q When tourist camps first became popular in the early 1920's, what criticism was leveled at them by J. Edgar Hoover?
A Hoover called them "dens of iniquity" that threatened the morals of the nation and had his men launch an investigation. This led to registration books, but visitors got around that by giving phony names. According to the History Channel, a follow up survey was done to check names with auto registrations, and it was found that only seven percent of the people were using actual names.

Q When did cement/concrete roads come into widespread use in Illinois?
A 1919 – directly after World War I; Governor Frank Lowden helped push through the legislation.

Old gas pumps at Wood River Museum

A Round

Turkey track imprints on old Route 66 at Nilwood – photo courtesy Dan Oberle of Edwardsville/Geneseo

paths?
A 93 percent

Q When was the word motel first copyrighted?
A 1925 – it was spelled mo-tel – with a dash.

Q The word "motel" was a contraction of what two words?
A Motor hotel

Q Does Illinois claim the famous motel units along Route 66 that received national attention in 1953?
A No – that distinction belongs to the Coral Courts, just outside the city limits of southwest St. Louis. Their art deco styling, terrazzo floors and glass blocks made the units a classic; Coral Courts received national attention in 1953 when the kidnapper of Bobby Greenlease hid out there for two days.

Q What name was applied to motel units that provided enclosed garages?
A No-tell motel

Q What shape were road signs in 1922 that indicated a state road?

Q What shape was given to a sign in 1922 that indicated the road crossed state boundaries?
A A shield

Q Before filling stations existed in urban areas to dispense gasoline, what idea was tried?
A *Curbside pumps* with underground storage tanks located near the owner's store; many of these were dry goods stores.

Q How much did a Model T Ford cost in 1916?
A $360 - through mass production techniques Henry Ford lowered the price from $950 in 1909 to $360 in 1916.

Q What was the first year more cars were made than wagons and carriages?
A 1914

Q In 1904 what percent of Illinois roads were mere dirt

Q In the 1920's, what was a "domestic style" gas station?
A It was a station built to resemble a small house, usually with a gabled roof. It was meant to blend in with its residential surroundings.

Q In order to disguise the utilitarian purpose of these "house stations," where were the pumps located?
A Behind the building

Q When was the AAA – American Automobile Association - organized in America?
A In 1906 by the influential Chicago Motor Club

Q When did Illinois adopt its first motor vehicle code?
A 1911

Q How many cars were in the state by 1918?
A 340,000

Q What famous architect said that the automobile was going to ruin the city of Chicago?
A Frank Lloyd Wright

Q What **Kankakee** banker ran for governor in 1920 with the promise to "pull Illinois out of the mud?"
A Len Small

Forrest Park - one of the early camping places for road gypsies at Bloomington by Dan Oberle

Along the Pontiac Trail at Pontiac by Dan Oberle

Q What was the speed limit imposed on the first Illinois hard roads?
A Reasonable and prudent

Q When the State Highway Patrol was organized in 1922, how many officers were there to cover the entire state?
A Eight

Q When did full service stations along highways in Illinois convert to self-service?
A Around 1974

Q What state had the finest system of roads in the nation by the end of the 1920's?
A Illinois – with 75 percent of the state's 10,098 miles of roads fully paved

Q Why were brick roads popular during the Depression?
A They were more labor intensive than concrete roads and made good WPA projects that put unemployed men to work.

Q What mistake did some early highway engineers make in road construction?
A The edge of the road was made with a slight rise or curb to warn motorists they were dangerously close to falling off. This slight rise caused some motorists to lose control of the car, resulting in an accident.

Q What type of number designations are usually given to roads that run from north to south in Illinois?
A Odd – such as 1, 3 and 157 and 159 in **Glen Carbon, Edwardsville** and **Collinsville**; roads that run east-west are mostly even numbered such as Routes 16 by **Mattoon**, 14 through **McLeansboro** and 146 through **Anna**

Q What name was given in the old days to the area of a filling station where cars were greased?
A Lubritorium

Q Before lifts operated by air compressors were installed, how were cars greased?
A One bay of the station had a grease pit.

Q What was "skunk oil?"
A In 1913 Standard Oil introduced a substitute for gasoline called "motor spirits," but the yellowish substance never caught on with a public that derided it as skunk oil.

Q Neon signs were popular along old highways. What was their approximate life span?
A 30 years

Q Why was lead introduced into fuel for motorcars in 1923?
A Higher octane rating for better engine performance; the higher the compression ratio of a car's engine, the greater the need for higher octane gas.

Q Why did Dupont's Ethyl Corporation start placing red dye in leaded gasoline in the 1930's?
A To discourage housewives from using it as a cleaning agent because tetraethyl lead is soluble and penetrates the skin, causing lead poisoning

Q What were gravity pumps at old filling stations?
A Old gas pumps were mechanical. A lever was pushed back and forth by the attendant to bring the gasoline up from the storage tank into a glass container that had markings to show the number of gallons. After the hose nozzle was placed in the car's gas tank, another lever allowed the gasoline to drain from the glass into the car by gravity.

Q Why were buckets of water with floating corncobs placed next to gas pumps?
A The corncobs were used to clean bugs off windshields.

Q What type of containers were used to store quarts of oil at filling stations?

A   They were glass with a tapered metal spigot that screwed on.   Such glass containers are hard to find nowadays because attendants usually removed the metal top and smashed the glass for trash storage in 55-gallon metal drums.

Q   Why did newsboys in the old days often locate their stand at a corner filling station?
A   Because on cold days they could build a fire in one of the 55-gallon metal drums and burn used crankcase oil for warmth.

Q   What did cash-poor teenagers in the early 1950's do when they needed to add oil to their hot rod engines?
A   They took their used crank-case oil and strained it through a cotton cloth to remove most of the dirt.

Q   How did Fifties teens get flames to shoot from their exhaust pipes?
A   They placed a spark plug inside the tailpipe, and when they turned on a dashboard switch it ignited the fumes.

Q   Why did some of these teens place mothballs in their gas tanks?
A   Mothballs are made of naphthalene, and it was believed this added a "kick" to the fuel mixture.   They also thought they could get a "high" by placing an aspirin in their bottle of Coke or Royal Crown Cola.

Q   Why is there no such thing as a 1943 Ford?
A   Due to World War II, auto plants were converted to wartime production, and no cars of any kind were made between 1942 and 1945.

Q   When was the Great River Road completed in western Illinois along the Mississippi River?
A   1965

Q   Where is the longest highway incline in the state?
A   It's the **Goreville** incline in southern Illinois.

Q   What limitation was placed on gasoline during the war?
A   Most drivers were limited to three gallons a week.
Q   What was a hot patch?
A   Tires prior to the 1970's had inner tubes.   When the inner tube was punctured, it was usually patched rather than

replaced.   Rubber cement for the patch was applied, then it was briefly set on fire and blown out, ensuring a more secure hold for the patch.   Bicycle inner tubes were repaired in the same manner.

Q   What speed limit was imposed on Illinois highways during World War II for safety and improved gas mileage reasons?
A   35 MPH

Q   What nickname was given to two-seat cars of the 1920s with open cockpits?
A   Roadsters

Red brick road on Route 66 at Auburn – Dan Oberle photo

Q   What were rumble seats?
A   Small coupes often had fold out seats in the trunk that were exposed to the elements.

Q   What did people begin calling vehicles that took passengers from train stations to hotels?
A   Station wagons

Q   What were suicide doors?
A   Rear doors on old cars were often hinged in back.   If a passenger stepped out of a car and the driver absentmindedly pulled forward before the door was shut, the passenger could be knocked down and run over.

Q   In the glory days of highway travel in the 1950's, why did so many people get lost as they went through **Joliet**?
A   About five or six major highways converged on that town.

Q   What name was given to cheap cars of the 1920's?
A   Flivvers or tin lizzies

Q   What practical option did the 1940 Nash Ambassador have?
A   A rear seat folded out into a bed that extended into the trunk

Q   What were running boards?
A   Step up devices that ran along the bottom of the car from the front fender to the rear fender. (see picture at left)

Several interesting old cars on an annual Route 66 road tour in Illinois – Dan Oberle photo

Q   What was the top speed imposed by a 1903 Illinois law on "horseless carriages?"
A   15 miles per hour?

Q   What ridiculous community laws were imposed by some Illinois towns on motor cars in 1900?
A   A man holding a red flag had to walk in front of the vehicle as it crawled down the road.

Q   What was the Illinois speed limit in 1936?
A   80 MPH

Q   How did improved Illinois highways give a boost to the postcard industry?
A   As more and more people began making long distance trips, they often sent a penny postcard back home to friends and relatives to keep in touch. The card frequently showed a roadside motel where they were staying or a tourist attraction they had visited.

Q   What does Route 66 author Michael Wallis call these postcards?
A   "A slice of Americana in visual shorthand"

Q   What was the first big year of car model change after World War II was over?
A   1949 – there wasn't much difference between a 1948 Ford and a 1942 Ford.

Q   What was the first year Chevrolet introduced "power-glide?"
A   1949 – it was an automatic shift

Q   Where does the dirt come from to build a modern cloverleaf for an Illinois interstate highway?
A   Typically it comes from a nearby farm by the process of eminent domain. The government digs a 20-acre hole in the ground and typically pays the farmer close to a million dollars. The result is a large depression called a "borrow pit." It soon fills with rainwater, and it is usually stocked with fish.   One of these can be seen on the Keller farm between Route 157 and Interstate 255 near **Collinsville**.

Q   Where did President Eisenhower get the idea for a U.S. system of interstate highways?
A   From the autobahn in Germany when he was the head of NATO; Ike perceived that interstates could double as emergency landing strips for airplanes in the Strategic Air Command

Q   This author lives near exit 12 of Interstate 270. What does the number 12 represent?
A   It is approximately 12 miles from the Mississippi River.

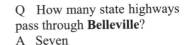
An early 1990's Route 66 road tour sponsored by State Farm

Q   Where does Illinois rank nationally in total miles of roads?
A   Fourth – with 34,000 miles of state highways and 2,000 miles of interstate highways.

Q   How many state highways pass through **Belleville**?
A   Seven

Q   What relatively new Illinois interstate parallels interstate 55, but is farther east?
A   Interstate 57 – from Chicago to Cairo

Q   What is the longest interstate highway in Illinois?
A   I-57 at 293 miles long

Q   How many district state police headquarters are in Illinois?
A   22 – at **Sterling, Elgin, Harrison, Lockport, Pontiac, East Moline, Metamora, Springfield, Pesotum, Collinsville, Effingham, DuQuoin, Macomb, Downers Grove, Pecatonica, LaSalle, Litchfield, Carmi, Pittsfield, Ashkum** and **Ullin**

CARS OF A BYGONE ERA

American Austin – A small car made in Butler, Penn. by Roy Evans
Auburn – Made in Auburn, Ind. by Frank and Morris Eckhart.
Blackhawk – A cheaper version of the Stutz Bearcat
Buick – Made in Detroit by David Buick, inventor of the cast iron enameled bathtub.

Cadillac – First built by Henry Ford and named for Antoine Cadillac, the founder of Motor City; both Capone and Eliot Ness drove Cadillacs
Chandler - Built in Cleveland until acquired by Hupmobile
Chevrolet – Established in 1911 by Will Durant and race car driver Louis Chevrolet
Cord – Named for Errett Cord, the head of Auburn Motors which built the car
DeSoto – First manufactured in 1928 and slightly lower in price and quality than a Chrysler
Detroit Electric – Attained a glorious maximum speed of

Typical old truck used by John Steinbeck's Oakies – Dan Oberle

190

25 mph; had a tiller for a handle since drivers sat in the back seat

Diana – Built by the Moon people in St. Louis

Doble – A steam powered car that required a 24-gallon tank of water

Dodge – First built by the Dodge brothers of Detroit in 1914.

Duesenberg – Built by Paul and August Duesenberg of Indianapolis. Greta Garbo and Mae West popularized the car. "Ain't that a doozie" was a popular expression in the Twenties and Thirties.

DuPont – A luxury car built by those hoity toity Duponts of Delaware

Essex – Built by the Hudson Motor Co. of Detroit

Ford – The 1903 Ford looks exactly like a 1903 Cadillac because Henry Ford quit that company, took his plans with him and launched his own firm. John Dillinger drove a V-8 Ford as his getaway car.

Franklin – An air cooled car made by H.H. Franklin of Syracuse, NY, and driven by famous people like Amelia Earhart and Charles Lindbergh.

Graham – Built by the three Graham brothers in Detroit; for a while sold quite well

Christening the Paul Bunyan giant at Atlanta with mustard, 2004, a Route 66 icon – courtesy Dan Oberle

Old Route 66 at Lincoln, Illinois, courtesy Dan Oberle

Hudson – Named for a Detroit department store mogul – not the explorer.

Hupmobile – Named after the company founder, Robert Hupp of Detroit

Jordan – Started at Cleveland in 1916 by an ex-newspaper man

LaSalle – A lower priced version of a General Motors car

Lincoln – Founded in 1920 by Henry Leland, but he ran into financial problems and was bought out by Ford.

Marmon – A large car built in Indianapolis; a favorite of big time gangsters

Nash – Founded in 1917 by Charles Nash of Kenosha, Wis.

Oakland – A GM car whose sales declined rapidly in 1924 after the Pontiac was introduced

Oldsmobile – Designed in 1901 by Ransom Olds as a one-cylinder car

Packard – This luxury auto dates all the way back to 1899

Peerless – A Cleveland bicycle firm that decided there was more money to be made in cars

Pierce-Arrow – A prestigious car that came out of Buffalo N.Y., and made by George Pierce

Plymouth – A cheap car offered by Chrysler and named for those hardy settlers in New England because the car was said to embody their qualities of ruggedness and durability; became the number three seller in America behind Chevy and Ford.

Reo – Headed by Ransom Olds and made in Lansing. Michigan

Roamer – This beauty came out of Kalamazoo, Michigan, and bore a slight resemblance to the Rolls-Royce.

Rickenbacker – Named for Captain Eddie, the race car driver turned ace aviator

Stanley Steamer – A very popular steam powered car in 1912

Studebaker – Studebaker started out selling wheelbarrows to miners during the California Gold Rush. Then the family progressed from making carriages to horseless carriages.

Stutz – Founded in 1911 by Harry Stutz. The Bearcat was the darling of Sheiks and Shebas during the Roaring Twenties.

Tucker - Illinoisan Preston Tucker acquired the old Dodge plant and began making cars in Chicago. He was charged with fraud and securities violations. He ultimately won vindication, but the controversy wiped out his capital and only **51 innovative Tucker cars** were produced.

His car had a number of features that were ahead of their time. The car had a center "swivel" headlight that moved left or right, depending on the direction of the car. There was a flat six engine that gave it a top speed of 120 mph. The aircraft-inspired doors made it easier to enter and depart. Rear fender vents cooled the helicopter-inspired engine located in the trunk.

Willys-Overland - Organized by John Willys who built cars in Indianapolis and Toledo; the company would produce the famous World War II vehicle, the Jeep, so named because it was a General Purpose Vehicle.

ROUTE 66 – CAN YOU DIG IT?

Q When were all the Burma Shave signs taken down along Route 66?
A 1963

Q How many states, including Illinois, does Route 66 cover?
A Eight

Q What has been the most visited site on all of Route 66 for many years?

A   The Route 66 Hall of Fame at Dixie Truckers Home in **Mclean**

Q   When and where was the Illinois Route 66 Association formed?
A   In May of 1989 at **Lexington**

Q   Who was the Grand Marshall of the first annual Route 66 road tour held in 1989?
A   Harry Abrams, a contestant in the 1928 Bunion Derby foot race that traveled the entire length of Route 66

Q   What company helped promote the first annual road tour?
A   State Farm Insurance

Q   By 1990, how many members were in the Illinois Route 66 Association?
A   350 – currently there are close to 1,000

Q   What was important about the year 1992 for Route 66?
A   It was the highway's 66th anniversary.

Q   Robert Close was the owner of the Standard/Sinclair gas station at **Odell** in Livingston County. When he took a lunch break in the 1950's, he used the honor system for customers. How did that work?
A   Customers wrote their names and the amount of the purchase on the side of the gas pump. When the customer returned and settled the bill, his name was erased.

Q   How wide was Illinois Route 4, the forerunner of Route 66?
A   Only 14 feet wide

Q   What singers and groups have recorded "Get Your Kicks on Route 66?"
A   Nat King Cole, Perry Como, the Rolling Stones, Asleep at the Wheel, Buckwheat Zydeco, Chuck Berry, Paul Anka, Anita Bryant, Perry Como, Buddy Greco, Roy Hamilton, Harry James, Johnny Mathis, Mel Tormé, Natalie Cole and about 125 other singers

Q   Route 66 was originally slated for the number designation Route 60. Why was it changed?
A   A Route 60 from Newport News, Virginia, to Springfield, Missouri, was already in the works. When several governors complained about the proposed new road, the number was changed to 66 in the spirit of compromise.

Ariston Café at Litchfield, Illinois, courtesy Dan Oberle

Q   What dirt path existed from Chicago to **East St. Louis** before Route 66 came along?
A   The Pontiac Trail

Q   What improved road, built in 1918, did Route 66 mostly follow?
A   State Route 4, sometimes designated as SBI 4 (state bond issue)

Q   In what famous book does Jack Kerouac talk about his travels on Route 66?
A   *On The Road*

Q   What was the first restoration project by the Illinois Route 66 Association?
A   A marker on a bridge on Route 4 (the forerunner of Route 66) in **Pontiac**

Q   How many subscribers are there to the Illinois Route 66 Association newsletter?
A   About 1,000 members from about 26 countries

Memory Lane on old Route 66 at Lexington

Q   Who is the author of *Route 66: Going Somewhere, The Road in McLean County*?
A   Terri Ryburn-LaMonte

Q   What Springfield man is the author of *Searching For Route 66*?
A   Tom Teague

Q   Where did Route 66 bisect Route 30, the nation's first bicoastal highway?
A   **Joliet** – Route 30 went from Chicago and bisected Route 66 at Joliet, then north to **Aurora**, and then due west from there to exit the northwestern part of the state near **Fulton**.

Q   Including Illinois, how many miles long was Route 66?
A   2,448 miles

Q   How wide was the original Route 66 pavement in Illinois?
A   Two strips, each nine feet wide, six inches thick

Q   There is a stretch of Route 66 highway north of **Auburn** that passes over Panther Creek. What is significant about the pavement on this stretch of road?
A   It's brick and drivable.

Q   What company took advantage of the Route 66 shield and incorporated it into its logo in 1929?
A   Phillips 66

Q   Who wrote the definitive journey guide to Illinois Route 66?
A   John Weiss – *New, Historic Route 66 of Illinois*

Q   Signs along Route 66 originally were made so they were large enough to be read at what speed?
A   40 miles per hour

Our Lady of the Highway at Raymond, Illinois, on old Route 66 by Dan Oberle

Q   How many miles long was Route 66 in Illinois – Chicago to **East St. Louis**?
A   295 miles

Q   How much per mile did it cost to build the original Route 66 in Illinois?
A $40,000 a mile to pave it in 1926

Q   By what early name was the Chicago road that led to **Springfield** known?
A   The Southwest Road – planked around 1845

Q   Who is considered the "Father of Route 66?"
A   Cyrus Avery of Oklahoma, the former head of the American Association of State Highway Officials

Q   What governor was responsible for widening Route 66 in the mid-1950's?
A   William G. Stratton

Q   Who penned the lyrics to "Get Your Kicks on Route 66?"
A   Bobby Troupe

Q   What Chicagoan made the song a popular hit?
A   Nat King Cole – his father was a clergyman

Q   What killed off billboard signs along Route 66?

Earnie's Roadhouse, Route 66 at Hamel, Illinois, courtesy Dan Oberle

A   The 1965 Highway Beautification Act, pushed by Lady Bird Johnson. Merramec Caverns and Mail Pouch barn signs survived because they probably were far enough away from the road to be exempt.

Q   What two actors were the stars of the hit *Route 66* television series?
A   Martin Milner and George Maharis

Q   What were their names in the program?
A   Tod Stiles and Buz Murdoch

Q   What kind of a car did they drive?
A   1960 Corvette

Q   How many years did the *Route 66* television series on CBS last?
A   Four years

Q   Who drove the Corvette most of the time on the program, Martin Milner or George Maharis?
A   Martin Milner usually drove.

Q   Why did the shiny wax and polish have to be removed from the car?
A   The reflected sun caused problems for the recording cameras.

Q   What actor replaced George Maharis after he fell ill with hepatitis?
A   Glen Corbett

Q   What orchestra leader wrote the stunning music score for the opening credits of *Route 66*?
A   Nelson Riddle

Q   Who starred in the 1993 remake of "Route 66?"
A   Dan Cortese as Arthur Clark and James Wilder as Nick Murdock; the series lasted for four episodes.

Q   What color was the Corvette used on the 1993 program?
A   Red

Q   What writer called Route 66 "The Mother Road?"
A   John Steinbeck in *The Grapes of Wrath*.

Q   What other nicknames are used for Route 66?
A   The Colossus of Roads, Great Diagonal Highway, The Main Street of America, Bloody 66

Q   What three Mississippi River bridges were used by Route 66 at various times to cross into Missouri?

A   McKinley Bridge; McArthur Bridge; Chain of Rocks Bridge

Q   What site in a Route 66 town was named one of the *USA Today's* "Best 50 Places in America?"
A   **Springfield's** Cozy Dog Restaurant

Q   What are "ghost signs" on Route 66?
A   These are painted signs that have faded over the years and are barely discernable.

Q   What town had an inn/restaurant that was jacked up and moved at a different angle so it would face a new Route 66 alignment?
A   **Pontiac** - the Log Cabin Inn

The Old Log Cabin at Pontiac courtesy Dan Oberle

Q   How many different main alignments did Route 66 have in Illinois?
A   Three – 1926-30; 1930-40; 1940-1977

Q   Who organized a famous footrace in 1926 that went along Route 66 from LA to Chicago and on to New York?
A   Promoter C.C. Pyle

Q   What sports star was used to promote the event?
A   Football star Red Grange

Q   Who won the event?
A   Oklahoma Native-American Andy Payne

Andy Payne, winner of Route 66 foot race, courtesy Dan Oberle

Q   Of all eight states, which was the first to complete Route 66 from dirt to Slab All The Way?
A   Illinois

Q   What railroad tracks did Route 66 parallel for much of the way in Illinois?
A   The Chicago & Alton

Q   What was the speed limit on Route 66 in 1937?
A   80 miles an hour

Q   What town was the eastern terminus of Route 66 before it was extended to Lake Michigan?
A   **Cicero**

Q   What Route 66 site in Chicago would you visit to get some Milk Duds??
A   Lou Mitchell's Restaurant is famous for its Milk Duds instead of after dinner mints.

Q   Henry's Hot Dogs is a Route 66 landmark in what town?
A   **Cicero**

Q   What Route 66 town features Del Rhea's Chicken Basket Restaurant?
A   **Willowbrook**

Q   What town along Route 66 is noted for its large Bohemian population?
A   **Berwyn**

Q   What Route 66 town is split in two by the Kankakee River?
A   **Wilmington**

Q   What town in McLean County claimed to be the highest point along Route 66 between Chicago and St. Louis?
A   **Towanda**

Q   What Route 66 town's Pioneer Gothic Church was host to England's Prince of Wales in 1860?
A   **Dwight** – the prince became King Edward VII

Q   What Route 66 town features the Launching Pad Restaurant (with its Gemini Giant) and the Eagle Hotel?
A   **Wilmington**

Q   What Route 66 coal mining town, named for a railroad official, was the site of one of the first commercial oil well productions in the state?
A   **Litchfield**

Q   In what Route 66 town can one find the Riviera Roadhouse?
A   **Gardner**

Q   What McLean County Route 66 town was named for a Revolutionary War battle near Boston?
A   **Lexington**

Q   There were numerous drive-in movie theaters built along Route 66. What was their nickname?
A   Passion Pits

Q   How was the Route 66 town of **Shirley** named?
A   The town was platted by John Foster in 1866, but locals say the name came from a novel that resident Mrs. Corydon Weed was reading.

Q   What Route 66 town was famous for its Correctional Center for Women?

A   **Dwight**

Q   What are the two most noteworthy towns with male correctional centers on Route 66?
A   **Joliet** and **Pontiac**

Q   What Route 66 town is noted for its vintage billboards along Memory Lane during its summer celebration?
A   **Lexington**

Q   What Route 66 town has the beautifully restored Rialto Theater?
A   **Joliet**

Q   What Route 66 town had a famous restaurant run by Gus Belt?
A   **Normal**, home of the original Steak 'n' Shake

Q   What is one of the newest Route 66 relocated landmark at **Atlanta**?
A   A "gentle giant" Bunyan Statue (with a hot dog in his hands); it came from the Bunyan Restaurant in **Cicero** and is now in a park at Atlanta.

Q   What Route 66 town was famous (still is) for its maple "sirip?"
A   **Funk's Grove** at **Shirley**

Q   **Braidwood** once was the center of a huge mining district. How many mine shafts were sunk near that town?
A   90

Q   What town was home for years to the Dixie Truckers Home Route 66 Hall of Fame?
A   **McLean**

Q   What town will be the new home for the Illinois Route 66 Hall of Fame?
A   **Pontiac**

Q   What Route 66 town is famous for its octagonal library and interesting bell tower?
A   **Atlanta**

Q   What town (on its outskirts) had a dangerous section of highway that was labeled "Dead Man's Stretch?"
A   **Lincoln**

Q   What Route 66 town once featured Ernie Edwards' Pig Hip Restaurant?
A   **Broadwell** – it now features the Pig Hip Museum

Q   What Route 66 town features the Cozy Dog Restaurant?
A   **Springfield**

Clock Tower at Atlanta on Route 66, courtesy Dan Oberle

Q   What Route 66 town features a stretch of road that was imprinted with wild turkey tracks before the cement hardened?
A   **Nilwood** (picture on page 187)

Q   What Route 66 town is famous for its courthouse that was called the Taj Mahal of the Midwest?
A   **Carlinville** – due to enormous cost overruns

Q   What Route 66 town had a famous dance hall called the Coliseum and a beautifully preserved Russian Orthodox Church?
A   **Benld**

Q   What town has Henry's Route 66 Emporium?
A   **Staunton**. The town also features an annual Tour d' Donut bike race where contestants can improve their official time by consuming donuts.

Q   A Catholic statue referred to as "Our Lady of the Highway" is located near what town?
A   **Raymond**

Q   What are five prominent Route 66 landmarks in **Litchfield**?
A   Niehaus Cycle Sales for road nomads, Litchfield Drive-In Theater, Ariston Café, The Gardens, and the Route 66 Café

Q   Russell Soulsby's restored Shell gas station can be found in what town?
A   **Mt. Olive**

Q   The former Tourist Haven Roadhouse can be found at what Route 66 town?
A   **Hamel**

Q   What color were the Burma Shave signs seen on Route 66 in Illinois?
A   Red and white

Q   What was the original color of the old Merramec Caverns signs painted on barns along Route 66 in Illinois?

Towanda history/geography project on Route 66, courtesy Dan Oberle

A   Black and white

Q   Is **Collinsville's** famed Brooks Catsup water tower located on an old stretch of Route 66?
A   No. It's on Route 159.

195

Q   What town has an original stretch of Route 66 that is now submerged beneath a lake?

A   **Springfield** – at the north end of Lake Springfield that was formed by damming the Sangamon River

Shea's Service Station at Springfield on Route 66, courtesy Dan Oberle

Q   Did this author marry a girl who lived on Route 66?

A   Yes! Lorna Sanders lived at 2404 Vandalia in north **Collinsville**. Old Route 66/Route 40 once passed directly in front of her home.

Q   Route 66 went past a Gothic revival Catholic Church named St. Boniface. This was in what town that features a Route 66 Festival every June?

A   **Edwardsville**

Q   Where was Dead Man's Curve on Route 66 in **Edwardsville**?

A   Near the current entrance to the ESIC subdivision. Cars headed east encountered a steep downhill slope that went under the Nickelplate Railroad underpass. Drivers sometimes failed to negotiate the sharp turn to the left and crashed into the concrete support pier.

Q   Route 66 entered **East St. Louis** at what point?

A   Route 66 came into East St. Louis along Route 40. It entered East St. Louis after it passed the town of **Fairmont City**. Then it dropped below the B&O and Pennsy double overpass and crossed St. Clair Avenue at 9th Street.

Q   The Mother Mary Jones Memorial is in a cemetery at what Route 66 town?

A   **Mt. Olive**

Q   What Madison County town is home to the McKinley Bridge?

A   **Venice**

Old Route 66 at Berwyn courtesy Dan Oberle

Q   Is this bridge currently open for traffic?

A   No, but the state has authorized money for repairs and hopefully it will be reopened in a year or two.

Q   The Luna Café is in what Route 66 town on the American Bottom?

A   **Mitchell**

Q   In what Route 66 town can one find Bill Shea's gas and oil products museum?

A   **Springfield**

Q   What town was the original site of the Ariston Café owned by the Adam family?

A   **Carlinville** – it was moved to **Litchfield** when Route 66 was reconfigured and bypassed Carlinville.

Q   Did Route 66 ever intersect with Route 50?

A   Yes. Route 66, heading south, crossed St. Clair Avenue at 9th Street in **East St. Louis** and St. Clair Avenue is also Route 50. Route 50 was originally called the Cahokia-Vincennes Trace.

Q   What is the most notable bridge on the entire stretch of Route 66 from Chicago to Santa Monica?

A   The Chain of Rocks Bridge near **Granite City**

Q   What is the most memorable feature of the bridge?

A   A dogleg in the middle

Q   What is the Chain of Rocks Bridge being used for today?

A   It is the **World's Longest Pedestrian Bridge,** and it is part of a bicycle trail; it is also used for watching eagles catch fish in the winter along the Mississippi River.

Q   What is the function of the interesting stone castles in the river, not far from the bridge?

A   They are pumping stations that send river water to a nearby Missouri water treatment plant.

Q   What famous amusement park in Missouri sat on the bluffs overlooking the Chain of Rocks Bridge?

A   Chain of Rocks Amusement Park

Q   What is the significance of the term "chain of rocks?"

A   Mother Nature placed a series of rocks or boulders at this point in the Mississippi River. These rocks can sometimes be seen when the river is low. The Army Corps of Engineers built a canal around this dangerous stretch.

ILLINOIS GOVERNORS

Q   What governor was born in Maryland, married a distant cousin, settled near Kaskaskia, and died on his farm in 1832?
A   Shadrach Bond

Q   What first governor of Illinois from **Monroe County** pushed for a canal to connect Lake Michigan with the Illinois River?
A   Shadrach Bond – who has a county named in his honor; his salary as governor was $1,000 a year

Q   What governor was born in Virginia, was a friend of Thomas Jefferson, freed his slaves when he arrived in Illinois (giving each 160 acres of land), and had a slave-owning son who died fighting for the Confederacy?
A   Edward Coles

Q   What second governor of Illinois was a Virginian and a good friend of Thomas Jefferson and James Madison?
A   Edward Coles

Q   What third governor of the state and resident of **Edwardsville** and **Belleville** pushed hard for the removal of all Indians within the border of the state?
A   Ninian Edwards

Q   What governor, born in Maryland, married his cousin, was governor of Illinois Territory, was pompous and vain, and was an Illinois Indian fighter during the War of 1812?
A   Ninian Edwards

Q   What fourth governor of the state oversaw the prosecution of the Blackhawk War and in his later years advised Southerners to take up arms against the Union?
A   John Reynolds of **Cahokia**

Q   What governor was born in Pennsylvania, fought Illinois Indians in the War of 1812, was a known agnostic, spent part of his boyhood at the **Edwardsville** Goshen settlement and died in **Belleville**?
A   John Reynolds

Q   What Governor wrote a *Pioneer History of Illinois*?
A   John Reynolds – with help from John Mason Peck

Q   What man was governor of Illinois for only 16 days?
A   William Ewing, who served out the unexpired term of John Reynolds who resigned so that he could serve as a congressman

Q   What former governor twice defeated Abe Lincoln in a contest for speakership of the Illinois House?
A   William Ewing

Q   What Kentuckian moved to Kaskaskia and when he became governor pushed hard for public education?
A   Joseph Duncan (1834-38) – although nobody listened to his proposals for public education

Q   Who was the only Whig governor of the state?
A   Joseph Duncan 1834-38 – he died at *Jacksonville* in 1844

Q   What governor had great physical prowess, hated Yankees, was pro-slavery, and is considered one of the state's worst chief executives?
A   Thomas Carlin – 1838-42

Q   What governor had 13 children and granted the Mormons a charter for their city at Nauvoo while he was in office?
A   Thomas Carlin of **Quincy** and **Carrollton** (1838-42)

Q   What did Mormon "saints" call their neighbors?
A   Gentiles

Q   What man, destitute after his term as governor ended, wrote a history of the state in a vain effort to solve his financial problems?
A   Thomas Ford – 1842-46; he lived in **New Design, Waterloo, Edwardsville, Versailles** and **Oregon**

Q   What governor closed the state banks and reduced the state's indebtedness by instituting tolls on the Illinois-Michigan Canal?
A   Thomas Ford of **Peoria** (1842-1846)

Q   What man became Illinois' first two-term governor and was known for his stinginess?
A   Augustus French – 1846-1853; he lived in **Albion, Paris, Palestine** and **Lebanon**

Q   What governor advocated war with Mexico?
A   Augustus French (1846-53) – a new state constitution was also adopted during his tenure.

Q   Who was the first "Yankee-born" governor of Illinois?
A   Augustus French, born in New Hampshire

Q   What governor, who lived in **Joliet** and **Chicago**, defrauded the state by redeeming fraudulent canal script (bonds) to the tune of $253.23?
A   Joel Matteson – 1853-57

Q   What 9th governor of the state held office during the great railroad building boom?

Governor Shadrach Bond

Governor William Henry Bissell

A   Joel Matteson (1853-57) – he was also president of the Chicago & Alton Railroad.

Q   What governor, who lived in **Belleville**, served with distinction in the Mexican War and established the state's first tax-supported institution of higher learning in **Normal**?
A   William Bissell – 1857-1860; also the first Illinois governor to die in office

Q   Who was the state's first Republican governor?
A   William Bissell (1857-60), who supported Salmon P. Chase of Ohio for the 1860 presidential nomination instead of Lincoln

Q   What founder of **Quincy** became governor of Illinois?
A   John Wood – 1860-61, after the death of Governor William Bissell

Q   What future Illinois governor went off to California in 1849 because he contracted "gold fever?"
A   John Wood – he found no gold and came back to Illinois.

Q   What graduate of Illinois College in **Jacksonville** was a Republican governor during the Civil War?
A   Handsome Richard Yates – 1861-1865; he lived in **Springfield** and **Jacksonville.**

Q   What governor supported national homestead legislation, favored using Negro troops in the Civil War, and supported suffrage for women?
A   Richard Yates – although a friend of Lincoln's, he was a thorn in the President's side and pressed for an unrealistic early military victory and the immediate emancipation of slaves

Q   What Republican "war governor" of Illinois strongly supported Abe Lincoln's prosecution of the Civil War and when he was obstructed by a Democratic legislature, sent them home?
A   Richard Yates (1861-65) - a **Jacksonville** lawyer

Q   What governor fought at Cerro Gordo and Vera Cruze in the Mexican War, went to the California gold fields and came back $5,000 richer, and was wounded at Corinth in the Civil War?
A   Richard Oglesby, who lived in **Decatur** and **Springfield**

Q   What man was the first to serve three terms as governor?
A   Richard Oglesby – 1865-1869; 10 days in January of 1873; and 1885-1889

Q   What governor was adept at "waving the bloody shirt?"
A   Richard Oglesby – accusing practically anyone who was a Democrat of being a traitor

Q   What future governor gave an electrifying speech at the Republican Convention in 1860 and named Lincoln the "Railsplitter Candidate?"
A   Richard Oglesby

Q   What **Decatur** man was the twelfth (1865-69), fourteenth (1873), and eighteenth (1885-89) governor of the state?
A   Richard Oglesby – serving two full terms and only part of another, re-signing after only ten days to serve in the U.S. Senate

Governor Richard James Oglesby

Q   What future governor presided over the **Bloomington** convention in 1856 that established the Illinois Republican Party?
A   John Palmer – 1869-1873

Q   What **Bloomington** Republican lawyer was the nineteenth governor of the state?
A   Joe Fifer (1889-93)

Q   What governor declined to run for another term because he did not want to support (campaign for) a second term for U.S. Grant as President?
A   John Palmer

Q   What man served as a Republican governor and a Democratic senator?
A   John Palmer

Q   Why the switch in party allegiance?
A   Palmer could not support Republican policies and became an independent "mugwump."

Pierre Menard

Q   Who was the last Civil War general to become governor of Illinois?
A   John Beveridge – 1873-77

Q   Who was the first governor of the state to come from Cook County?
A   John Beveridge, who became governor when Oglesby resigned in 1873 to become U.S. Senator

Q   What governor served for 30 years in the U.S. Senate after his term of office and was one of the best known nationally of all governors, except for Frank Lowden and Adlai Stevenson?
A   Shelby Cullom – 1877-1883

Q   What Republican governor bore a striking resemblance to Lincoln, crafted the Illinois Granger Law in 1873 when he was a member of the General Assembly, and is the "**Father of the Interstate Commerce Commission?**"

A   Shelby Cullom

Q   Except for Illinois, what state has been the birthplace of more Illinois governors than any other?
A   Kentucky

Q   What Republican lieutenant governor became the chief executive when Shelby Cullom resigned and left for the U.S. Senate?
A   John Hamilton – 1883-85

Q   What governor from **Bloomington** oversaw legislation that gave Illinois women the right to vote in school elections and provided for the secret or Australian ballot?
A   Joe Fifer – 1889-1893

Q   What twentieth governor was the first foreign-born man elected governor of Illinois?
A   Democrat John Peter Altgeld (1893-97) was born in Germany

Q   What man became the state's first governor from Chicago?
A   John Peter Altgeld

Q   What governor was responsible for opening normal schools at **DeKalb** and **Charleston**, for insane hospitals at **East Moline** and **Peoria**, and for the soldiers' widows' home at **Wilmington**?
A   John Peter Altgeld, nicknamed the "Little Dutchman"

Q   What man from **Carbondale** and **Clay County** was a friend of labor and sent troops to prevent the unloading of black strike-breakers from Alabama during coal mine strikes at **Virden** and **Pana**?
A   John Tanner – 1897-1901

Q   What twenty-first governor had to deal with the Spanish-American War?
A   Republican John Tanner

Q   Who was the first Illinois-born governor? (**Jacksonville**)
A   Richard Yates – 1901-1905, son of the Civil War governor

Q   Was Yates an activist governor who sought progressive reforms?
A   No – he had no program of his own and rejected the Progressive Movement that sought to disturb the status quo.

Q   What Republican governor, born at **Edwardsville**, was

the son of a Latin professor at McKendree College in **Lebanon**?
A   Charles Deneen (1905-1913) – under his tenure the state's first primary election law was enacted.

Governor John Peter Altgeld

Q   What Illinois governor was a straight-laced Methodist who abstained from alcohol and invited evangelist **Billy Sunday** to hold prayer sessions at the governor's mansion?
A   Charles Deneen (pictured below in top hat)

Q   Who was the only mayor of Chicago to become an Illinois governor?
A   Democrat Edward Dunne – 1913-1917

Q   What Irish Catholic governor had 13 children?
A   Edward Dunne - he also supported better roads in the state by holding meetings with the Illinois Highway Improvement Association

Q   What governor was married to Florence Pullman, daughter of railroad millionaire George Pullman?
A   Frank Lowden – 1917-1921

Q   What Republican governor's reforms exceeded those of any other state to that time?
A   Frank Lowden

Q   What future governor quit his Chicago law practice and moved to a large feudal-style estate (Sinnissippi) on the Rock River near **Oregon**?
A   Frank Lowden – Sinnissippi is the old name for the Rock River

Q   What governor announced early in his term that he would not run for a second?
A   Frank Lowden

Q   What single event probably prevented Frank Lowden from securing the Republican presidential nomination in a landslide year - 1920?
A   His feud with Big Bill Thompson, Mayor of Chicago; Thompson was an isolationist while Lowden had supported our entry into World War I.

Q   What World War I governor supported women's suffrage, enacted a $60 million road improvement program, reformed and modernized state government, sent troops to quell race riots in **East St. Louis** and Chicago, and constructed the Centennial Building to help celebrate the state's 100th anniversary?
A   Frank Lowden

Q   What twenty-fifth governor of Illinois could have been

Vice-president of the U.S. with Harding, but declined the nomination?
A   Frank Lowden

Q   What **Kankakee** governor was known as "the Great Road Builder?"
A   Len Small (1921-1929) – when he retired to his farm he also published the Kankakee *Daily Republican.*

Q   What governor ended 16 years of progressive state reform and threw in his lot with Big Bill Thompson's Chicago machine?
A   Len Small

Q   What governor legalized pari-mutuel betting at racetracks, created the state conservation department, and replaced hanging with electrocution as a method of capital punishment?
A   Len Small

Q   What governor had a background as a furniture salesman and an embalmer?
A   Louis Emmerson – hard to believe, but it was quite common back then for furniture salesmen to make extra money in the embalming business

Q   What Republican twenty-seventh governor was born in **Albion** and lived in **Mount Vernon**?
A   Louis Emmerson (1929-33) – after the Depression hit, he perceived that no Republican could win the next election, so he didn't bother to run.

Q   Who are the state's two oldest governors at the time they were elected?
A   Governors Emmerson and George Ryan were both about 65 years-old when they took office.

Q   Why was Governor Emmerson's state income tax proposal, needed to deal with the Depression, declared unconstitutional?
A   Because it was progressive (graduated) rather than uniform as required by the Illinois constitution

Q   What man, born in Cook County, was the state's first Jewish governor?
A   Henry Horner – 1933-1940

Q   What twenty-eighth governor instituted relief measures to help the state cope with the Depression, and abolished the state real estate tax, replacing it with a two percent sales tax to cover revenue losses?
A   Henry Horner (1933-40) – the Father of the Sales Tax; he won reelection in 1936, but the pressures of dealing with the Depression caused him to resign in ill health, leading to his death in 1940.

Governor Frank Orren Lowden

Q   How did the State Historical Library gain 5,000 volumes on Abraham Lincoln in 1940?
A   Henry Horner, a bachelor, amassed the collection and left it to them in his will.

Q   How often did the legislature meet in the old era of the Thirties?
A   From January to June – every other year

Q   What lieutenant governor of Illinois (from **McLeansboro)** became governor after the death of Governor Horner?
A   John Stelle (1940-41) - He was a graduate of Western Military Academy in **Alton.**

Q   What was John Stelle's main accomplishment after he was out of office?
A   A World War I veteran, as an American Legion national leader he **helped craft the GI Bill of Rights** and lobbied it through congress.

Q   How many Illinoisans served in World War II?
A   670,000

Q   Who was probably the most handsome of all Illinois governors?
A   Republican Dwight Green – 1941-1949

Q   What Republican governor during World War II previously earned his claim to fame by helping to successfully prosecute Al Capone for tax evasion?

Governor Dwight Green (Illinois State Hist. Society)

A   Dwight Green – after he was re-elected, he secured a new law that required Illinois schools to teach U.S. History.

Q   What important precedent did Green establish?
A   Republican governors should start cooperating with Democratic mayors of Chicago for the good of the city.

Q   What governor is the "Father of the Cigarette Sales Tax?"
A   Dwight Green – he implemented it to replace lost revenue after he convinced the legislature to reduce the sales tax from three to two percent.

Q   What hurt Green in his bid for a third term?

A Adlai Stevenson accused him of being lax on gambling. He also assailed the governor's handling of a mine disaster in **Centralia** that killed 111 men. Green had accepted contributions from coal mine operators and allowed them to be lax on safety regulations.

Q What Illinois governor placed the state police under the merit system?
A Adlai Stevenson (1949-53)

Q What Illinois reform governor broke up syndicated gambling and prostitution in **Peoria, East St. Louis, Rock Island, Joliet, Springfield**, and **Decatur**?
A Adlai Stevenson

Q To what prominent family did Adlai Stevenson's mother belong?
A Helen Davis' parents owned the *Bloomington Pantagraph*. Stevenson was once assistant managing editor of the **Bloomington** *Daily Pantagraph*.

Q What claim to fame did Stevenson's great grandfather have?
A Adlai E. Stevenson was Grover Cleveland's Vice-president.

Q What place of prominence did Stevenson's maternal grandfather hold in Illinois history?
A Jesse Fell was **Bloomington's** first lawyer. It was he who suggested that Lincoln challenge Douglas with a series of debates in 1858.

Q What work did Stevenson accomplish with the U.N. before he become governor?
A He was our alternate delegate to that body, and he assisted in its creation after World War II ended.

Q How was Stevenson hurt by the Alger Hiss communism case?
A Stevenson testified to his "good character" dating back to the time they worked together in the State Department. Hiss was convicted of perjury and sent to jail. From that point on, Republicans accused Stevenson of being soft on communism.

Q How many terms did Stevenson serve as governor?
A One – 1949-1953

Q How did Stevenson manage to secure the Democratic nomination for President in 1952?
A Delegates at the Chicago convention drafted him.

Q How did Stevenson fare against Ike in 1952 and 1956?
A He was trounced by the war hero.

Q Did Stevenson try for a third run at the presidency in 1960?

Governor William G. Stratton

A Yes – but he lost out to JFK. He wanted to be Kennedy's secretary of state, but JFK chose Dean Rusk instead and named Stevenson ambassador to the U.N.

Q Why did Stevenson fall under heavy criticism during the Bay of Pigs fiasco?
A It was Stevenson who convinced JFK to withhold air cover for the invading troops, saying it would make us look bad in the eyes of the world.

Q How did Stevenson redeem himself during the Cuban Missile Crisis in October of 1962?
A Everyone remembers his gutsy reply to the Soviet ambassador. He said that the U.S. was prepared to "wait until hell freezes over" for a reply to the charge that the Russians were installing offensive missiles in Cuba.

Q What line did Stevenson steal from Lincoln when a reporter asked him about losing to Ike?
A He said "I'm too big to cry, but it hurts too much to laugh?"

Q Who are considered the two wittiest politicians of the Twentieth Century?
A Adlai Stevenson and John F. Kennedy

Q What Republican governor was born at **Ingleside** in Lake County?
A William G. Stratton – 1953-1961

Q Who was Stratton's wife?
A Marion Hook of **Gurnee** – he divorced her after he was out of office and married Shirley Breckinridge of Chicago.

Q What future Republican governor was in the U.S. Congress, helping to override six Harry Truman vetoes?
A William G. Stratton (1953-60)

Q What reapportionment of the legislature was accomplished by Stratton, the first since 1901?
A The house districts would be apportioned according to population while the senate seats were distributed geographically. This gave Chicagoland and the north control of the house and downstate control of the senate.

Q What big scandal broke during Stratton's administration?
A State auditor Orville Hodge of **Granite City** went to prison for embezzling state money.

Q What was Stratton accused of after he left office?
A Income tax evasion – stemming from the way he spent campaign funds

Q What task force did Stratton later chair?
A Campaign finance – it recommended that personal use of campaign funds be prohibited.

Q What Republican governor in 1953 appointed the first

woman to serve in the governor's cabinet?
A William G. Stratton

Q What did Stratton do to help schools during his second term of office?
A He increased the state sales tax.

Q What Democrat defeated William G. Stratton in 1960?
A Otto Kerner – 1961-1968

Q How does historian Robert Howard describe Otto Kerner?
A Popular, but naïve and indecisive – our second most handsome governor

Q What was Kerner's domestic albatross?
A His wife developed a serious drinking problem.

Q What thirty-second governor raised taxes to pay for the state's first three billion dollar budget?
A Otto Kerner

Q How did Kerner increase state revenues?
A He increased the state sales tax and a new tax was levied on motel and hotel rooms.

Q What did Kerner convince the Atomic Energy Commission to do in 1967?
A Locate its new high energy accelerator at **Weston** in DuPage County

Q What was the "**bedsheet ballot**" of 1964?
A After the 1960 census, Republicans and Democrats couldn't agree on a new reapportionment map. In accordance with the law, an "at large" ballot was drawn up with 118 names from each party. The unusual ballot was nearly a yard long. Democrats won control of the house, but Republicans now had control of the senate.

Q What prominent Republican helped prosecute Kerner in the horse racing stock scandal?
A Future governor, Jim Thompson

Q Who was Illinois' second foreign born and second Jewish governor?
A Sam Shapiro of **Kankakee** – 1968-69, finishing out Otto Kerner's term after he resigned the governorship to become a federal judge

Q What man was governor of Illinois during the disturbances/riots by protestors during the 1968 Democratic National Convention in Chicago?
A Sam Shapiro

Q At the end of Shapiro's term, what last minute action by him was vetoed by the Supreme Court?
A In accordance with Mayor Richard Daley's wishes, he appointed ten Democrats and one Republican to judgeships.

Q What future governor and graduate of Chicago-Kent Law School started his career by winning election as Cook County sheriff?
A Republican Richard Ogilvie – 1969-1973

Civil War Governor Richard Yates

Q What charisma handicap did Ogilvie have?
A He always seemed to have a stern look due to a World War II wound to his face and jaw.

Q What new budget law was passed during Ogilvie's tenure?
A The budget making process was taken from a legislative committee and placed in the executive branch - the governor's budget director

Q Has this prevented pork barrel spending waste?
A No – because legislators get their pork barrel tossed in before they have a final vote on the budget.

Q What Republican brought in a group of young executives known as the "whiz kids" to help streamline government?
A Richard Ogilvie

Q What governor doubled the state's revenue with its first income tax, but then was thrown out of office by disgusted voters?
A Richard Ogilvie

Q What new cabinet department was created under Ogilvie?
A Department of Transportation

Q How did the new Illinois EPA hurt Ogilvie in the next election?
A The agency angered voters by ordering a ban on leaf burning

Q What two successful tactics did Dan Walker use to defeat Paul Simon (the favorite) in the 1972 Democratic primaries?
A First, he depicted Simon as a lifelong insider who was a tool of Richard Daley's Chicago machine. Next, he walked all over the state glad-handing voters and kissing babies to garner grass roots support.

Q What new law hurt the favorite, Paul Simon, in the 1972 Democratic gubernatorial primary?
A The open primary – Republican voters crossed over and voted for Dan Walker over Paul Simon, thinking Walker would be easier to beat.

Q What "sound bite" did reporters come up with to describe this race?
A "Bandana Dan" (he wore a red bandana) versus the Bow Tie" – Simon's trademark

Q Why did Walker, after winning, become a one-termer?
A He alienated the powerful Daley forces in Chicago and he had difficulty working with the legislature. He did manage to trim the state payroll by ten percent.

Q What governor signed a bill that created the Illinois lottery?
A Democrat Dan Walker – 1973-1977

Q What unusual style did Dan Walker bring to the governorship?
A Confrontational – us against them, similar to his courtroom tactics as a successful lawyer

Governors Stratton, Ogilvie, Walker, Shapiro and Kerner (courtesy Illinois State Historical Society

Courtesy of the Illinois State Historical Library

Q What effect did this have on his tenure?
A It helped doom him to one term.

Q What other misstep cost Walker support from Mayor Richard Daley?
A His "Walker Report" was critical of the way Chicago police handled demonstrators at the 1968 Chicago convention.

Q What happened to Dan Walker after his term as governor?
A He began living in the fast lane, divorced his wife, bought a yacht, and was sent to a Minnesota prison for perjury and fraud after bilking money from a savings and loan institution.

Q What did the judge say when he sentenced Walker to seven years in prison for savings and loan fraud?
A Walker had "placed himself above the law" and used the S&L as his "personal piggybank"

Q What later happened to Paul Simon's political career?
A He was elected U.S. Senator in 1974 and later ran for U.S. President on the Democratic ticket.

Q What was a big area of disagreement with Simon and fellow Democrats in D.C.?
A He was a fiscal conservative and supported a balanced budget amendment.

Q What Republican became the state's most popular governor, serving four terms in that capacity?
A Jim Thompson (1977-1991)

Q What was unusual about Jim Thompson's first term as governor?

A Due to a new state constitution, his term was limited to two years so that gubernatorial elections did not coincide with presidential elections.

Q Was this new law a good idea?
A Yes – it meant that candidates had to win on their own merits and not count on being swept into office on the coattails of a popular presidential candidate. It also helped create more interest in dull "off-year" elections.

Q What was Thompson's best move in his early years as governor?
A Signing a bill that increased the minimum drinking age from 18 to 21. When it was previously lowered to 18, teenagers began killing themselves in car accidents in record numbers.

Q What incident caused a citizen revolt that saw a voter initiative that reduced the size of the House of Representatives by 1/3?
A Legislators voted themselves a hefty raise during troubled fiscal times.

Q What man holds the Illinois record for having the longest tenure as governor?
A Republican Jim Thompson – 1977-1991

Q Who is the only woman to become the governor of Illinois?
A That has yet to happen.

Q What accounts for Thompson's longevity?
A No personal or political scandals, good charisma, good speaking skills, excellent campaigning skills, good ability to get along with Democrats, good decision making skills

Q What politician began reading political news when he was in grade school and at that young age decided he wanted to be a politician?
A Jim Thompson of DeKalb County and **Oak Park**

Q What new class of crimes deserving stiffer penalties were earmarked during the Thompson administration?
A Class X felonies that included arson, attempted murder, rape and armed robbery

Q What was the "three strikes" law passed during the Thompson administration?

A   After a third felony conviction, life without parole as a habitual offender

Q   What serious penalty was brought back by Thompson after an absence of 28 years?
A   The death penalty

Abe Lincoln? No, it's Governor Shelby Cullom

Q   What Democratic U.S. Senator challenged Thompson twice for the governorship?
A   Adlai Stevenson III – capable, but a lackluster speaker totally lacking his father's charisma.

Q   What nearly cost Jim Thompson the 1982 election?
A   Chicago African-Americans who were energized by Harold Washington's announced bid to become Chicago's next mayor; Thompson won by a meager 5,074 votes.

Q   What messed things up for Stevenson in the 1986 election?
A   Lyndon LaRouche (an extremist) disciples won the primary races for lieutenant governor and secretary of state. Stevenson refused to run with them and sought election as an independent, but lost.

Q   What happened to governor Thompson's efforts to bring a 1993 World's Fair to Chicago?
A   They were blocked by Chicago mayor Harold Washington who was generally uncooperative with the Republican governor. Also, Columbus had fallen out of favor due to an insane new mania called "political correctness."

Q   What was the U.S. Supreme Court ruling in the landmark case of *Rutan v. Illinois*?
A   Contrary to Thompson's wishes, the court ruled in 1990 that governmental hiring based on party affiliation was an abridgment of free speech.

Q   What hurt Thompson's political ambitions nationally?
A   It was the Reagan Era, and Thompson was too much of a moderate for many Republicans.

Q   What was Thompson's biggest failing as governor?
A   He was a liberal spender and left office with the state a billion dollars in debt.

Q   What **Charleston** man and secretary of state succeeded Jim Thompson as governor?
A   Republican Jim Edgar – 1991-1999

Q   Governor Jim Edgar signed a Kimberly Bergalis bill into law. What was the nature of this new law?
A   It required dentists infected with the AIDS virus to notify their patients.

Q   What political stepping stone led to Edgar's election?
A   Thompson appointed him secretary of state when Alan Dixon of **Belleville** left that office to become U.S. Senator.

Q   What caused Dixon to lose his office to Carol Mosley Braun?
A   Braun decided to challenge him after his vote to confirm Clarence Thomas to the U.S. Supreme Court.

Q   Why is the office of secretary of state a better stepping stone than that of lieutenant governor?
A   Name recognition – the secretary of state issues drivers' licenses and license plates; the office also has tons of patronage.

Q   What insurance reform did Edgar help get enacted when he was secretary of state?
A   All Illinois drivers were required to carry insurance.

Q   What governor won election by the highest margin in state history?
A   Jim Thompson in 1976

Q   What governor has the second highest margin?
A   Jim Edgar – 1996

Q   What nickname did Edgar acquire?
A   "Governor No" – due to his fiscal conservatism

Q   What amazing feat did Edgar accomplish?
A   When he took office that state was in debt; when he left it was in the black – all without raising taxes.

Q   How did Edgar reform the welfare system?
A   He supported "Earnfare" legislation that required able bodied welfare recipients to get jobs.

Q   What school reform effort by Edgar was opposed by most teacher unions in the state?
A   The creation of charter schools

Q   What was Edgar's Illinois Teacher Corps?
A   Since there were shortages of teachers in science and math, an alternative certification program allowed people with degrees (but no teacher training) into classrooms.

Q   Where did Edgar meet his future wife, Brenda Smith of **Anna**?
A   At Eastern Illinois University

Q   What was Edgar's worst idea as governor?
A   Allowing local school districts to levy an income tax on residents to support education – fortunately it never happened.

Q   What was the "Baby Richards" brouhaha during

Edgar's governorship that gained national attention?
A   Edgar disagreed with a state supreme court ruling that favored parental rights over that of the welfare of the child. Edgar specifically thought Judge James Heiple was wrong-headed.

Q   What ex-pharmacist from **Kankakee** succeeded Edgar as governor?
A   Republican George Ryan – 1999-2003

Q   What led to Ryan becoming a one-termer?
A   This is a no-brainer: he raised taxes, spent money like a drunken sailor, and was tainted by corruption in his office when he was secretary of state. Ryan also made an ill-advised visit to see Fidel Castro, and he alienated many voters by issuing blanket pardons to inmates on death row.

Q   What motivated Ryan to issue these blanket pardons?
A   It was either conscience, stupidity, or a desire to win the Nobel Peace Prize.

Q   What positions did Ryan hold before becoming governor?
A   He was lieutenant governor under Thompson and secretary of state under Edgar.

Q   How did Ryan get support from the Illinois Education Association in the 1998 election?
A   He promised that 51 percent of all new state income would go to schools.

Q   When Ryan was speaker of the house in the 1980's, did he support the ERA Amendment?
A   No – protestors wrote his name in blood on the Capital floor.

Governor Jim Edgar

Q   When Ryan was secretary of state, what reform did he make in the drunk driving laws?
A   The legal intoxication limit was lowered from .10 to .08, winning him top awards from MADD – Mothers Against Drunk Driving.

Q   What fiscal crisis did Ryan face after his first two years in office?
A   The economy started going south at the end of the Clinton administration and continued for two and ½ years under Bush, causing shortfalls in state income.

Q   Who is the current governor of Illinois?
A   Democrat Rod Blagojevich - only 30 percent of voters know this; he's also our first governor with four vowels and seven consonants in his name.

Q   What former governor was a member of the 9-11 Commission investigating our response to terrorism?
A   James Thompson

Q   What criticism did Thompson make on June 17, 2004, concerning *New York Times* and *Washington Post* headlines?
A   The newspapers said there was no *link* between Al Qaeda and Saddam Hussein. Thompson pointed out that the report says there were *links*, but no *collaboration* – a huge difference.

CHICAGO WHITE SOX

Q   What Sox player has the team's highest batting average for one season?
A   Luke Appling - .388 in 1936

Q   What Sox player has four of the team's top ten highest single season batting averages?
A   Eddie Collins – his highest was .369 in 1920.

Q   What 1972 Sox player has the team's highest slugging percentage for one season?
A   Dick Allen with .603

Q   Did Nellie Fox ever have 200 hits in a season for the Sox?
A   Yes, in 1954

Q   What 1962 player set the Sox record for doubles in one year with 45?
A   Floyd Robinson

Q   Did Minnie Minoso ever hit 20 triples in one season?

Ed Walsh, White Sox pitcher 1906

A   No - his best was 18 in 1954.

Q   Did Ron Kittle ever hit 40 home runs for the Sox?
A   No – his best was 35 in 1983

Q   What Sox player scored an astounding 135 runs in 1925?
A   Johnny Mostil

Q   Luke Appling had 128 runs batted in for 1936. What teammate that same year had more?
A   Zeke Bonura with 138

Q   What 1950's and 1960's Sox spark plug frequently had a big chaw of tobacco in his left cheek?
A   Nelson Fox

Q   What Sox slugger was with them only three years in the early 1970's but was called "Savior of the Franchise?"
A   Dick Allen

Sox 2nd baseman, Eddie Collins

Q   Have the White Sox ever played the St. Louis Cardinals in the World Series?
A   No

Q   Since 1900, do the St. Louis Cardinals have more World Series titles than the Cubs and White Sox combined?
A   Yes – the Cards have nine

Q   What 1983 Sox player set the single season team mark in stolen bases with 77?
A   Rudy Law

Q   Has any Sox player ever had 100 extra base hits in a season?
A   No – Shoeless Joe Jackson had 74 in 1920

Q   What 1931 Sox player had 127 bases on balls (walks) that year?
A   Lu Blue

Q   What Sox player struck out 175 times in 1963?
A   Dave Nicholson

Sox pitcher Ted Lyons

Q   What hitter led the Sox team in 1966 with 21 pinch hits?
A   Smokey Burgess

Q   What 1957 Sox player led the team in pinch hitting with a .355 average?
A   Walt Dropo

Q   What Sox relief pitcher appeared in a team record 88 games in 1968?
A   Wilbur Wood

Q   What Sox pitcher had 40 wins in 1908?
A   Ed Walsh – he had 42 complete games that year.

Q   What 1904 Sox pitcher had a miniscule .171 earned run average in 1904?
A   Doc White

Q   Who is the best strikeout pitcher the Sox ever had?
A   Juan Pizarro – his average was 8.69, almost one per inning.

Q   What Sox pitcher had an improbable 15 wins pitching in relief in 1965?
A   Eddie Fisher

Q   What 1954 Sox pitcher never lost a game in relief?
A   Sandy Consuegra

Q   What two Sox outfielders played entire seasons without making an error?
A   Ken Berry in 1969 and Sam Mele in 1952

Q   What Sox player is the lifetime team leader in triples?
A   Shano Collins – 104

Q   What Sox player is the team leader in career strikeouts?
A   Jim Landis – 608

Q   What Sox player pitched in the most number of games in his career?
A   Red Faber - 669

Q   What Sox player holds the team record for *wins* in relief?
A   Hoyt Wilhelm – 41

Q   Who founded the American League in 1899?
A   Chuck Comiskey and Byron Johnson

Q   How did the expression "farm team" originate?
A   The parent club *harvested* the better players from its minor league affiliate.

Q   What was Ed Walsh's most effective pitch?
A   Spitball

Q What was the team batting average of the 1906 Sox team that beat the Cubs in the World Series?
A The Hitless Wonders finished last in the league with .230

Q In 1907 the Sox became the first team in baseball to hold spring training outside the U.S. borders. What was the location?
A Mexico City

Q In what year was the first game played at the old Comiskey Park?
A 1910

Q What was Ed Walsh's nickname?
A "The Big Reel"

Q What did Ed Cicotte, Wilbur Wood, Hoyt Wilhelm and Ted Lyons have in common?
A They were all knuckleball pitchers.

Q How did the Sox fare against Red Sox pitcher Babe Ruth in his 1915 Comiskey Park debut?
A They routed him, 11-3

Q What year did the Sox win their last World Series?
A 1917 – defeating the New York Giants

Q What Sox pitcher won three games in the Series?
A Red Faber

Q What Sox player was suspended in 1918 by manager Comiskey who said he was "chicken?"
A Joe Jackson – because he chose to work in a shipyard rather than fight in France under the government's World War I "work or fight" edict.

Q How much did it cost to buy a ticket for a seat in the grandstands at Comiskey Park in 1917?
A Fifty cents

Q What was the greatest Sox team of all-time?
A Probably the 1919 team – they had speed, pitching, hitting and defense.

Q How many White Sox players in 1919 had 200 or more hits?

Sox slugger Al Simmons (author's collection)

Luke Appling "old aches and pains" for 21 seasons

A Three – Eddie Collins, Joe Jackson, and Buck Weaver, a rarity that has happened only one other time in American League history.

Q How many years did Eddie Collins play?
A Twenty-five – he might be the best second baseman of all time in the American League.

Q What White Sox player was described by Casey Stengel as "the strangest player of all time?"
A Moe Berg. He was an intellectual and an expert on French Renaissance literature. He also served as a spy for the U.S. government before World War II.

Q What famous quip best describes Berg, a good field, no hit, utility infielder who played for the Sox from 1925-30?
A "He could speak 12 languages but couldn't hit any of them."

Q During World War II, what physicist did the OSS want Berg to assassinate?
A Werner Heisenberg – but only if he was close to developing an atomic bomb; he wasn't.

Q What four Sox players each won twenty games in 1920?
A Lefty Williams, Ed Cicotte, Dickie Kerr, Red Faber

Q What player was banned from baseball by Judge Landis because he left the Sox in 1922 to play for the Famous Chicagos?
A Dickie Kerr

Q What Sox player caught a baseball dropped from the top of the Tribune Tower in 1925?
A Ray Schalk – Carl Laemmle of Universal Pictures dropped three balls. Schalk missed the first two and caught the last. A crowd of 10,000 witnessed the stunt.

Q What two things usually happened when a Sox player was honored with a special day?
A The player performed well that game and inexplicably was not on the roster the next season.

Q What Sox player was elected to the Hall of Fame in 1984?
A Luis Aparicio

Q What White Sox manager was the only manager besides Casey Stengel that won an American League pennant in the 1950's?
A Al Lopez

Q What were the all-time ugliest Sox uniforms?
A The ones worn in 1983 with the wide stripe across the chest and a large horizontal stripe on each sleeve – they looked like softball uniforms.

Q Who was the American League Rookie of the Year in 1983 (despite being saddled with an ugly uniform)?
A Ron Kittle

Q What dubious milestone was reached by the 1932 Sox?
A They lost 100 games

Q What Sox player received more votes than Babe Ruth for the 1933 All-Star Game?
A Al Simmons

Q What Sox pitcher lost a leg and a career in a 1938 hunting accident?
A Monte Stratton

Q What famous pitch did Stratton throw?
A A looper called the "gander" pitch

Q Who portrayed Stratton in the film version of *The Monte Stratton Story*?
A Jimmy Stewart

Q One of the worst Sox trades in history was in 1938 when they sent what outfielder to the Brooklyn Dodgers?
A Dixie Walker

Q What late 1930's and early 1940's Sox manager was hated by umpires because he disputed so many of their calls?
A Jimmy Dykes

Q What 1942 Sox player, near the end of his career, pitched only on Sundays?
A Ted Lyons

Q Because of wartime travel restrictions, where did the Sox in 1943 conduct spring training?
A French Lick, Indiana – the future home of Larry Bird.

Q What are the most common nicknames for the White Sox?
A Pale Hose and ChiSox

Q Karl Scheel was a batting practice pitcher and "bench jockey" for the 1945 Sox. What is the main job of a bench jockey?
A Make wisecracks at opposing teams and try to get their goats by taunting

Q What was a typical taunt in those days?
A "Hey, meathead!"

Sox pitcher Red Faber (author's collection)

Q What Sox manager fell ill in 1946 due, in part, to his daily consumption of 15 cigars?
A Jimmy Dykes

Q How many games did the sad Sox lose in 1948?
A 101

Q How well did the Ed Lopat for Bill Wight trade work out for the Sox in 1948?
A Lopat won 17 games for the Yanks and Wight went 9-20

Q What do most current managers do to prevent one of their pitchers from losing 20 games in a season?
A Fearing psychological damage, they don't let them pitch anymore after 19 losses.

Q What were the two worst decades for the Sox?
A The Twenties and Forties – they played sub-.500 ball both decades.

Sox slugger Hack Wilson

Q What magic did front office man Frank Lane pull off for the Sox in 1950?
A He "stole" shortstop Chico Carrasquel from the Dodgers for $25,000

Q What outstanding trade did the Sox pull off in 1951?
A They acquired Minnie Minoso from the Indians for Gus Zernial and Dave Philley

Q At what did Minoso and centerfielder Jim Busby excel?
A Stolen bases

Q Who resigned from the 1952 Sox in disgust when his mother refused to give him a raise?
A Chuck Comiskey Jr.

Q In 1953 the Yankees tried, in vain, to swap Gil McDougald for what Sox pitcher?
A Billy Pierce

Q Who won the last American League game played at Sportsman's Park in 1953?

A   The Sox defeated the St. Louis Browns who then moved to Baltimore.

Q   How successful was Marty Marion's first year as Sox manager in 1955?
A   The Sox went 91-63. They were in first place on September 3, a lofty spot they hadn't held that late in the season since 1920.

Q   What was lanky Marion's nickname?
A   Slats (presumably this moniker came from bed slats that are long and narrow).

Q   The Cubs have long labored under the "billy goat curse." What name is given to the Sox curse?
A   Comiskey Curse – after their tightwad owners

Q   When Frank Lane was finally fired in 1955, what were his Sox totals for trades over a seven-year period?
A   241 deals involving 353 players – unbelievable!

Q   What huge mistake was made by the St. Louis Cardinals after Lane quit?
A   They hired him and he traded away all their talent.

Q   What did Sox management do after Marty Marion finished 85 and 69 in 1956?
A   They fired him and hired Al Lopez.

Q   Who had controlling interest of the Sox in 1958?
A   Dorothy Comiskey, Chuck Comiskey's sister

Q   Who bought Dorothy's 54 percent controlling interest?
A   Bill Veeck

Q   How many big names were on the 1959 Sox team?
A   Earl Torgeson, Nellie Fox, Luis Aparicio, Bubba Phillips, Jim Landis, Sherm Lollar, Early Wynn, Bob Shaw, Billie Pierce, Gerry Staley, and Dick Donovan. The bench consisted of Billy Goodman, Norm Cash, Ted Kluszewski and Sammy Esposito

Q   What major awards were won that year?
A   Fox won the MVP and Wynn won the Cy Young

Q   What prediction did Mayor Daley make for the 1959 World Series?

Charlie Grimm

A   He said the Sox would win in four straight.

Q   Who was the Sox hitting hero in the 1959 World Series?
A   Ted Kluszewski hit .391 and had three homers

Q   How spectacular was Ted Kluszewski in the Series?
A   He drove in 10 runs, a record for a six game Series

Q   What was unusual about "Killer" Kluszewski's uniform?
A   His sleeves were cut off at the shoulders to show his huge biceps, something he started doing when he played for Cincinnati.

Q   Who defeated the Sox in the 1959 World Series?
A   Sandy Khoufax and the Dodgers

Q   Did the Sox have a winning edge against the Yankees in 1959?
A   Yes – something they hadn't done since 1925.

Q   What record did the Sox set in the 5th game of the 1959 series?
A   They won 1-0, using three pitchers in the process.

Q   What year of the "great flop" was the most disappointing in team history?
A   1969 - they collapsed late in the year with a team that was loaded with talent and lost out to Baltimore who lost the Series to the "Miracle Mets."

Q   What zany nickname was given to pinch hitter Jim Rivera on the 1960 team?
A   "Jungle Jim"

Q   What two *very good* players were traded away for peanuts by Veeck after the 1959 season?
A   Norm Cash (Tigers) and Johnny Callison (Phillies)

Q   What did Veeck do in 1960 that angered the baseball establishment?
A   He placed player's names on the back of their road jerseys.

Sox manager Eddy Stanky (author collection)

Q   What other spectacular stunt was pulled by Veeck?
A   An exploding scoreboard

Q   Who did Veeck sell the Sox to in the middle of the 1961 season?
A   Chicago businessman Arthur Allyn. Chuck Comiskey then sold his 46 percent to a Chicago group.

Q   What famous person was turned down after making a bid to buy the Sox?
A   Danny Thomas

Q   Who was the pitching ace on the 1964 Sox team?
A   Juan Pizarro – a 19 game winner

Q   The 1964 Sox won 98 games and lost the pennant to the Yankees by one game. How did it happen?
A   The Sox won nine in a row at the end of the season, but the Yankees won ten in a row. However, Mickey Mantle and Company lost the Series to the Cardinals.

Q   Who was the only .300 hitter on that 1964 Sox team?
A   Floyd Robinson at .301

Q   The 1965 Sox won an impressive 95 games. Who beat them out for the pennant?
A   The Minnesota Twins

Q   Who had the highest batting average on that team?
A   Don Buford at .283

Q   Who was the star pitcher on the '65 Sox team?
A   Tommy John

Q   What two Sox players were injured that year in a car accident after a Chicago Black-hawks game?
A   Tommy John and Pete Ward. The neck injury ruined Ward's career.

Q   Who replaced Al Lopez, who was in failing health, as the Sox manager?
A   Eddie "the Brat" Stanky

Q   What did Stanky order his pitchers to do that caused them to be a hated team elsewhere in the league?
A   Throw beanballs

Q   Who won Rookie-of-the-Year honors for the Sox that season?
A   Outfielder Tommy Agee

Q   What was Black Wednesday for the 1967 Sox Team?
A   They blew the pennant to the Red Sox by losing a September 27th doubleheader to the last place Athletics.

Q   What did opponents accuse manager Eddie Stanky of doing to win games with his poor hitting '67 ball club?

Sox speed merchant Minnie Minoso

A   They accused him of freezing the baseballs to keep the scores low.

Q   Where did the 1968 Sox play ten home games in an effort to boost their sagging attendance?
A   Milwaukee – rumors abounded that the Sox were moving north

Q   Did the Sox draw well in Milwaukee?
A   The attendance for those ten games amounted to one third of the season's total attendance.

Q   What happened to manager Eddie Stanky in the middle of the 1968 season?
A   He was fired and replaced by Al Lopez. The team finished with 95 losses.

Q   What happened to Carlos May, a promising rookie in 1969?
A   He blew off a thumb in National Guard exercises – the Comiskey Curse

Q   What first did the Sox achieve in 1969?
A   They replaced their infield with artificial turf – the first American League team to do so.

Q   What outrageous offer was made by Charles Finley of the Athletics in 1969?
A   The flamboyant owner offered to swap complete teams with the White Sox. Sox owner Allyn turned him down.

Sox player Bill Nicholson

Q   The 1970 Sox set the team record by losing how many games?
A   106

Q   Who was the only .300 hitter on that team?
A   Luis Aparicio - .313

Q   Who became the first Sox player to hit 30 home runs?
A   Bill Melton hit 33 in 1970

Q   Who became the new Sox manager with just 16 games left to play in the 1970 season?
A   Chuck Tanner

Q   Did the "new look" Sox have a winning record in 1971?
A   No - they won 79 and lost 83.

Q   What controversial announcer joined the Sox in 1971?
A   Harry Caray

Q   Who were the leading hitters on the 1971 team?
A   Carlos May and Walt Williams each hit .294

Q Who was the best pitcher on the '71 staff?
A Wilbur Wood was 22-13

Q What newly acquired player broke the Sox record for homers in the 1972 season?
A Richie Allen hit 37

Q Why was Allen one of the most hated players in baseball?
A He was angry about Vietnam and racism and had trouble showing respect for the Star Spangled Banner. He hit 30 homers in one year for the Cardinals, who acquired him from Philadelphia, but they got rid of him after one season. He was then traded to the Dodgers who also only kept him for one season.

Q Did Allen win the league MVP in 1972?
A Yes - with 133 RBIs and a .308 average; for some strange reason batting averages were low in the decade of the Seventies. John Bauer of **Collinsville**, a nephew of Yankee great Hank Bauer, says it's because the pitching mound used to be higher.

Q What was unusual about two of the homers Allen hit in one game that year?
A They were both inside the park jobs – a rarity.

Q What key injury killed the Sox chances in 1973?
A Dick Allen was hitting over .300 and had 16 homers when he fractured a kneecap halfway through the season.

Q What hitting statistic did the White Sox lead the American league in for the first time ever in 1974?
A Home runs

Q Who was the pitching star of the 1974 team?
A Jim Kaat, a sore-armed castoff of the Twins with 21 wins

Q What four Sox players from the 1975 team made the All-Star team?
A Bucky Dent, Jim Kaat, Rich Gossage and Jorge Orta

Q What was Gossage's nickname?
A "Goose"

Q What two excellent players were picked up by the Sox in a June, 1975 trade?

Charlie Root (author's collection)

A Chet Lemon and Dave Hamilton; Lemon was later traded for Steve Kemp.

Q Having lost $8 million over the last five years, to what west coast city were the Sox rumored to be headed?
A Seattle

Q Who bought the Sox and kept them in Chicago?
A Bill Veeck

Q Why was Sox announcer Harry Caray controversial?
A Because he shamelessly rooted for the home team (that's why this author loved him as a Cardinal announcer) and he really got down on players that weren't performing up to par.

Q What two Sox pitchers combined for a no hitter during the 1976 season?
A Blue Moon Odom and Francisco Barrios

Q What 56 year-old player was activated by the Sox in an effort to boost attendance?
A Minnie Minoso

Q Who was the only .300 hitter on the '76 team?
A Ralph Garr - .300

Q What was the most games won by any Sox pitcher in '76, a season that saw them lose 97 games?
A Ken Brett won 10 games

Q Who became the Sox new manager in 1977?
A Bob Lemon replaced Paul Richards

Q What nickname was given to the 1977 team that slugged 192 home runs – the team record?
A The South Side Hitmen

Q What derisive song was played by organist Nancy Faust when opposing pitchers were batted out of the game?
A "Na-Na-Hey-Hey – Goodbye"

Q Who were the two home run leaders that season for the Sox?
A Richie Zisk (30) and Oscar Gamble (31)

Richie Zisk (courtesy of the White Sox)

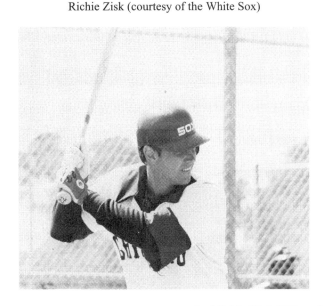

Q Who led the Sox pitching staff in '76 with 15 wins?
A Steve Stone

Q What player, traded from the Angels to the Sox, was a big flop in 1978?
A Bobby Bonds hit for a low average in 26 games before he was traded to Texas.

Q What Sox pitcher was 10-5 at the All Star break but never won another game?
A Wilbur Wood

Q Who became the new Sox manager halfway through the season?
A Larry Doby

Q What distinction did this move give to Larry Doby?
A He was baseball's second African-American player and second African-American manager.

Q What statement did Bill Veeck make in 1979 that brought down the wrath of the umpires?
A He said the striking umpires were bums who should be kept on the road.

Q What ex-Cub did a good job for the Sox in 1977, 1978 and '79?
A Don Kessinger

Q What nickname did the press give to the young Sox pitching staff in 1979?
A Kiddie Corps – led by Ken Kravec with 15 wins

Q What player-manager stepped down in the middle of the 1979 season?
A Don Kessinger gave way to Tony LaRussa

Q When the Sox invested heavily in the free agent market for 1980, what players did they sign?
A Carlton Fisk, Jim Essian, Greg Lizinski, and Ron LeFlore

Q Who was the star rookie pitcher for the Sox in 1980?
A Britt Burns

Q Who led the team in homers in 1980?
A Jim Morrison and Wayne Nordhagen each had 15

Q What was unusual about the 1981 season?
A Two months of play in the middle of the season were missing due to a players strike.

Q Did this create an oddity in either of the two leagues?
A Yes – the St. Louis Cardinals had the best overall record in their division, but in order to make the playoffs, a team had to win at least one of the two halves of the season. They missed the playoffs.

Q Who were the only Sox .300 hitters in 1981?

A Bill Almon at .301 and Chet Lemon at .302

Q Who won the most games for the Sox in 1981?
A Britt Burns with 10

Sox manager Al Lopez 1957-65; 68-69

Q How many games in a row did the Sox win in 1982?
A Eight – a club record

Q What was accomplished by the Sox 85-75 record in 1982?
A 1981 and 1982 were the first back-to-back winning seasons for the Sox in 20 years

Q Who led the Sox with 25 homers in 1982?
A Harold Baines

Q Who led the '82 Sox with 19 pitching wins?
A LaMarr Hoyt

Q What Seattle ace fastballer did the Sox sign for 1983?
A Floyd Bannister

Q Was the addition of Bannister enough for LaRussa and the Sox to win the division?
A Yes – but they lost the AL crown to Baltimore on a Tito Landrum home run.

Q Did this 1983 team finally bring out the crowds?
A Yes – they drew over two million – a Sox record at the time.

Q What honor did LaRussa win?
A Manager of the Year

Q What honor did LaMarr Hoyt win?
A Cy Young Award

Q How many games did the Sox finish ahead of second place Kansas City?
A 20 games

Q Who was the team's only .300 hitter?
A Tom Paciorek at .307

Q What four Sox players had twenty or more homers?
A Harold Baines, Ron Kittle, Carlton Fiske, Greg Luzinski

Q How many games did Bannister win?
A 16

Q What is the White Sox record in World Series play?
A They are 2-2. They won against the Cubs in 1906, defeated the Giants in 1917, lost to Cincinnati in 1919, and lost to the Dodgers in 1959.

212

Q What member of the Sox team in 1983 is credited with originating the phrase that became a rallying cry – "Win Ugly?"
A Doug Rader from **Northbrook**, Illinois

Q What 1990's Sox star drove in 100 runs or more for 8 consecutive seasons?
A Frank Thomas

Q What Sox third baseman tied a Major League record by hitting two grand slams in one game in 1995?
A Robin Ventura – against Texas

Q Who were the main sluggers on the 1996 Sox team?
A Frank Thomas (40 homers), Harold Baines (22 homers), Danny Tartabull (27 homers and Robin Ventura (34 homers)

Q The Sox went with a youth movement in 1998, using 18 rookies. In what year did they mature into a club that won the division title?
A 2000

Q How did the Sox do against the Mariners in the 2000 playoffs?
A They lost three straight

Q Which team has had the most managers, the White Sox or the Cubs?
A The Cubs have had over 50 while the Sox have had about 38

ILLINOIS ACTORS AND ACTRESSES

Q What Chicagoan starred in his own TV show in 2004, "According to Jim?"
A Jim Belushi

Q What actor, who attended the University of Illinois, played Clyde Barrow's brother in the film *Bonnie and Clyde*?
A Gene Hackman

Q What Chicago actress got her first big break in the movie, *Flashdance*?
A Jennifer Beals

Knuckleball pitcher Hoyt Wilhelm (courtesy Sox)

Q What Chicago actress played special agent Dana Scully on "The X Files?"
A Gillian Anderson

Q What Chicago actor was the villain in *Titanic* and the hero in *The Phantom*?
A Billy Zane

Q What Chicago actress starred in the 2004 Showtime series, "The L Word?"
A Jennifer Beals

Q What Chicago woman was extremely successful as a character actress in legitimate theater from about 1910 to 1925 and appeared in several 1929 films?
A Louise Glosser Hale

Q What Chicago actor was in the television program "T.J. Hooker," starring William Shatner?
A Adrian Zmed

Q What **Peoria** actor portrayed Charles Emerson Winchester III on the TV series "M*A*S*H*?"
A David Stiers

Q Did Chicagoan Bill Murray ever get to give his "Best Actor" speech for the Academy Award nominated film, *Lost in Translation*?
A Murray lost out to Sean Penn but gave a parody of his speech on the David Letterman Show in March of 2004.

Q What **Normal**, Illinois, man played Lt. Colonel Henry Blake on "M*A*S*H*?"
A McLean Stevenson

Q What Chicago actor of the 1940's and 1950's was married to Shirley Temple?
A John Agar – *Sands of Iwo Jima*

Q What **Rock Island** native was the star of the popular television series, "Green Acres?"
A Eddie Albert

Bill Murray

Q Where was director John Sturgis born?

A **Oak Park** – he directed *Bad Day At Black Rock*, *The Great Escape*, and dozens of other films.

Q What **Carrollton** native was featured with Jeff Bridges in *Starman* and with Harrison Ford in *Raiders Of The Lost Ark*?
A Karen Allen

Karen Allen

Q What Evanston-born actor portrayed Father Mulcahy on "M*A*S*H*?"
A William Christopher

Q What Chicagoan directed the popular horror movie, *The Exorcist*?
A William Friedkin

Q Who portrayed Bozo The Clown on station WGN in Chicago?
A Bob Bell - he played the character for more than two decades, retiring in 1984.

Q Where was film director Vincent Minnelli born?
A Chicago – he married Judy Garland and was the father of Liza Minnelli.

Q What Chicago comedian starred on the "Dick Van Dyke Show?"
A Morey Amsterdam.

Q What Chicago jazz great with a gravely voice had a big hit with the song, "We Have All The Time In The World," from the James Bond film, *On Her Majesty's Secret Service*?
A Louis Armstrong

Q What **Quincy** actress starred with Humphrey Bogart in *The Maltese Falcon* and ended her 50-year career with *Youngblood Hawke*?
A Oft-wed Mary Astor

Q What **Carbondale**-born, **Cobden** reared (you raise corn and rear children) actress starred with Rudolph Valentino in *The Sheik*?
A Agnes Ayres

Mandy Patinkin – Chicago Hope

Q What 1920's Chicago western actor married Clara Bow, the "It Girl?"
A Rex Bell

Q What Chicago actor starred in *Shoot To Kill*, with Sidney Poitier, and in *Someone To Watch Over Me*?
A Tom Berenger

Q What **Park Ridge** actress with unusual eyes played a floozie in *The Great Gatsby*?
A Karen Black

Q What Chicago actor starred in the TV's "Happy Days," "Charlie's Angels," and "Father Dowling Mysteries?"
A Tom Bosley

Q What Chicago actor starred in *Iron Eagle* and portrayed a young fighter jock who was adept only when listening to rock music; he also starred in *Bad Boys, Backdraft, Born on the Fourth of July*.
A Jason Gedrick

Q What was comedian Sam Kinison's home town?
A **Peoria**

Q What **Elgin**-born actor is married to Melissa Gilbert of "Little House on the Prairie" fame?
A Bruce Boxleitner

Susan Dey

Q What singer/pianist was born in **Danville** in 1936 and despite little formal training played Carnegie Hall?
A Bobby Short

Q What **Rochelle** native starred with Tom Hanks on "Bosom Buddies?"
A Peter Scolari

Q What **Kewanee** actor played Al Capone in the Robert Stack "Untouchables" television series?
A Neville Brand

Q What Chicagoan was a famous choreographer (*Sweet Charity, Cabaret*) and wrote the screenplay for the autobiographical movie, *All That Jazz*?
A Bob Fosse – who married dancer Gwen Verdon

Q What **Evanston**-born actor starred in *City Hall, Serendipity*, and *Runaway Jury*?
A John Cusack – sister Joan is also an accomplished actress

Q What **Winnetka** actor, who played in **Black Sunday**, is known for portraying freaks and psychotics?
A Bruce Dern – Laura Dern (*October Sky*) is his daughter.

Q What blonde **Pekin**-born actress starred in "The Partridge Family" and "LA Law?"
A Susan Dey

Q What recently deceased **Belleville** actor starred in "Davy Crockett," "Beverly Hillbillies," and "Barnaby Jones?"
A Buddy Ebsen

Q What **Park Ridge** actor starred in the *Star Wars* trilogy (Han Solo) and as Indiana Jones?
A Harrison Ford

Q What Chicago-born actor studied acting at SIU in **Car-bondale** and is the number one star on "NYPD Blue?"
A Dennis Franz

Tina Turner

Q What Chicagoan was the star of "Baa Baa Black Sheep" and "Wild Wild West?"
A Robert Conrad

Q What **Cairo** actor starred in the television series, "Peter Loves Mary?"
A Peter Lynd Hayes

Q What Chicago actress starred in *South Pacific* and *Les Girls*?
A Mitzi Gaynor

Q What Chicagoan started out as a disc jockey and later became the first host of the "Today Show?"
A Dave Garroway

Q What Chicago actor played Michael Fox's father on "Family Ties?"
A Michael Gross

Q Who is Michael Gross' fairly well known sister?
A Tall, lithe Mary Gross, the "Saturday Night Live" comedienne

Q What **O'Fallon** actor won an Academy Award for *Stalag 17?*
A William Holden

Q What **Evanston** actor starred in *Ben Hur, Planet of the Apes*, and *The Ten Commandments?*
A Charlton Heston

Q What actor alienated himself from liberal Hollywood by becoming president of the NRA?
A Charlton Heston – who was recently diagnosed as having Alzheimer's disease

Q What **Winnetka** actor was born with the name Roy Sherer?
A Rock Hudson

Q What **Alton** actress starred in *Young Man With a Horn* and *Dressed to Kill?*
A Mary Beth Hughes

Q What **Cairo** actor starred in *Hurry Sundown* and *Elmer Gantry?*
A Rex Ingram

Q What **Hunt/Newton** man was a noted folksinger and actor?
A Burl Ives

Q What **Marion** High School cheerleader starred on "Designing Women?"
A Judith Ivey

Q What Chicago actor was famous for wearing a German military helmet on "Laugh In?"
A Arte Johnson

Q What **Gillespie** actor was known for his rich baritone voice in movie musicals?
A Howard Keel

Q What Chicago actor was in *Kismet?*
A Richard Kiley

Q What Chicago actor was featured on the "Carol Burnette Show" and "Hollywood Squares?"
A Harvey Korman

Burl Ives

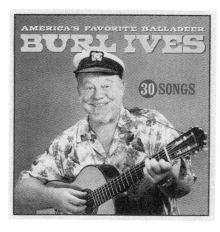

Q What Chicago actor starred in *The Hunchback of Notre Dame* and *The Shadow Strikes?*
A Rod LaRocque

Q What **Melrose Park** actress/dancer married Robert Goulet?
A Carol Lawrence

Q What Chicago actor was in "The Big Valley" and "77 Sunset Strip?"

A Richard Long

Q What **Kankakee** actor starred in *The Shaggy Dog, The Absentminded Professor*," and in television's "My Three Sons?"
A Fred MacMurray

Q What Chicago actor played the fearless treeswinger in *Tarzan The Magnificent* and *Tarzan Goes To India?*
A Jock Mahoney

Q What Gary-born, Chicago reared actor starred with Michael Douglas in "The Streets of San Francisco" and in the TV movie, "Miracle on Ice?"

A   Karl Malden

Q   What Chicago actress starred in *Splash, Steel Magnolias* and dated John Kennedy Jr.?
A   Darryl Han-
nah

Marlee Matlin (Famous Photos)

Q   What **New Trier** cheerleader was called "The Female Elvis?"
A   Ann Margret

Q   What **Morton Grove** deaf actress won an academy award for acting in *Children of a Lesser God*?
A   Marlee Matlin (1987)

Q   What award-winning **Joliet** actress was "the voice" in *The Exorcist*?
A   Mercedes McCambridge

Q   What **Evanston** actress won an Oscar for her performance in *Ordinary People*?
A   Elizabeth McGovern

Q   What **Carbondale/Edwardsville** actress played the role of Jackie on the "Roseanne" television comedy show?
A   Laurie Metcalf

Q   What blonde Chicago actress was known for her role on "Knot's Landing?"
A   Donna Mills

Q   What Chicagoan played the Lone Ranger on about 220 televised episodes?
A   Clayton Moore

Q   What Chicago actor portrayed Franklin D. Roosevelt in *Sunrise At Campobello*?
A   Ralph Bellamy

Q   What Chicago actor defeated Rocky Balboa (Sylvester Stallone) in a movie title fight?
A   Clubber Lane (Larence Tero) – Mr. T

Q   What **Wilmette** actor was featured in *Stripes, Ghostbusters,* and *Caddyshack*?
A   Bill Murray – a big Cubs fan

Q   What Chicago native starred in "Mary Hartman, Mary Hartman?"
A   Martin Mull

Q   What **Oak Park** comedian/actor won a Grammy for "The Button Down Mind Of . . ."
A   Bob Newhart

Q   What **Danville** native starred in several Francis the talking mule movies?
A   Donald O'Connor

Q   What Chicago man directed *Animal House* and *The Blues Brothers*?
A   John Landis

Q   What Chicago-born actor starred on the television series, "Chicago Hope?"
A   Mandy Patinkin

Q   What Chicago actor starred in *Blink, Legends of the Fall,* and *Practical Magic*?
A   Aidan Quinn

Q   What **Highland Park** native was father to six children on "The Brady Bunch?"
A   Robert Reed

Q   What **Oak Park** resident and band leader was called the "King of Percussion?"
A   Bobby Christian

Q   What Chicago actor married Lauren Bacall after Humphrey Bogart died?
A   Jason Robards

Mercedes McCambridge

married to Jessica Lange?
A   Sam Shepard

Q   What Chicago-born actor starred in *The Wild Bunch, Executive Action,* and *The Dirty Dozen?*
A   Robert Ryan

Q   What young **Highland Park** actor starred in "The Wonder Years?"
A   Fred Savage

Q   What Fort Sheridan (Chicago)-born actor portrayed Chuck Yeager in *The Right Stuff* and is

Q   What **Park Ridge** actress played the lead in *Diary of a Mad Housewife*?
A   Carrie Snodgress

Q   What blonde Chicago native played in the 1970's television series, "Starsky and Hutch?"
A   David Soul

Q   What Chicago actress married and divorced Wallace Beery, was Joe Kennedy's girlfriend, and starred in numerous pictures including *Sunset Boulevard*?

A Gloria Swanson

Q What **Christopher** native hosted television's popular "Match Game?"
A Gene Rayburn

Donna Mills (Famous Photos)

Q What **Paris**, Illinois, actor was Alfalfa in the Our Gang movie comedies?
A Carl Switzer

Q What Chicagoan, known more for his singing, starred in *Higher And Higher*, *Walk Like A Dragon*, and was a frequent guest on "Night Court?"
A Mel Tormé

Q What **East St. Louis** rock and roll singer was the main performer at the 2001 Super Bowl?
A Tina Turner

Q What **Danville** native was the chimney sweep in *Mary Poppins*?
A Dick Van Dyke

Q What rugged **Hartford/Alton** actor played the lead role on the television series, "Cheyenne?"
A Clint Walker

Marilu Henner (Famous Photos)

Q What **Danville** native starred in the television series, "My Mother The Car?"
A Jerry Van Dyke

Q What Chicago actor starred in *Death on the Nile*, *Deceptions*, and *Private Benjamin*?
A Sam Wanamaker

Q What Chicagoan was the swimming star of the 1924 and 1928 Olympics?
A Johnny Weissmuller, who had polio as a child

Q What Chicago television show of the 1950's starred Fran Allison and two puppets?
A "Kukla, Fran, and Ollie"

Q What sexy Chicago actress starred in *Fathom*, *Lady in Cement*, and *The Four Musketeers*?
A Raquel Welch

Q What Chicago actor portrayed Norm on the popular comedy, "Cheers?"
A George Wendt

Q What Emmy-winning **Oak Park** actress starred on "The Mary Tyler Moore Show" and "The Golden Girls?"
A Betty White

Q What **East St. Louis** blonde twins starred with Mickey Rooney in "Andy Hardy's Blonde Trouble?"
A Lee and Lyn Wilde

Q What Chicago actor got his big break portraying an alien on "Mork And Mindy?"
A Robin Williams

Q What **Granite City** native became a cowboy movie star famous for using a bullwhip?
A Whip Wilson

Q What Chicago actor was the star of "Father Knows Best" and "Marcus Welby M.D.?"
A Robert Young

THE BLUES BROTHERS

Q What was the basis for the idea of *The Blues Brothers*?
A A five-minute "Saturday Night Live" sketch

Q What name does John Belushi go by in this film?
A Joliet Jake Blues

John Belushi

Q What is Dan Aykroyd's name in the film?
A Elwood Blues

Q What Illinoisan directed *The Blues Brothers*?

A   John Landis

Q   Who wrote the script for *The Blues Brothers*?
A   John Landis and Dan Aykroyd

Q   What year was *The Blues Brothers* released?
A   1980

Q   Why are the Blues brothers trying to raise money?
A   To help keep an orphanage open by paying its taxes

Q   Where is the orphanage located?
A   **Calumet City**

Q   What Academy Award-winning musician did the score for *The Blues Brothers*?
A   Elmer Bernstein

Dan and John

Q   Who plays Belushi's crazy girl friend in the film?
A   Carrie Fisher

Q   What kind of car do the Blues brothers drive in the film?
A   1974 Dodge sedan

Q   What singer, married to Edie Gorme, gives the Blues Brothers advice while they are all in a sauna?
A   Steve Lawrence

Q   What musical instrument does Dan Aykroyd play when the Blues Brothers are on stage?
A   Harmonica

Dan, John and Aretha Franklin

Q   Who does the singing when the Blues brothers are on stage?
A   John Belushi

Q   What Chicago street is showcased in the chase scene?
A   Lower Wacker Drive

Q   Who played the part of Mrs. Murphy in the film?
A   Aretha Franklin

Q   What Guiness World Record is established by the film?
A   The total number of police cars wrecked in one film

Q   How fast are the Blues brothers going on Wacker Drive in the film?
A   Over 100 miles per hour

Q   What famous piece of Chicago artwork is showcased as the Blues Brothers screech to a halt at Daley Plaza?
A   The Chicago Picasso

Q   The film ends with the Blues Brothers being sent to prison. What song concludes the film?
A   "Jailhouse Rock"

Q   What famous African-American performers are featured in the film?
A   Cab Calloway, Aretha Franklin, Ray Charles, James Brown

Q   What other famous faces are in the film?
A   John Candy, Paul Reubens, and Twiggy

Q   What Chicago and metro area sites are featured?
A   Stateville Correctional Center at Joliet
East 95th Street Bridge
Pilgrim Baptist Church on 91st Street
Dixie Square Mall in Harvey
Stag Hotel on West Van Buren
Chez Paul at 660 North Rush
Jackson Park Lagoon on Lake Shore Drive
Wrigley Field
Nate's Delicatessen on West Maxwell
Palace Loan Company on East 47th Street
McCormick Place on Lake Shore Drive
Lyric Opera
Richard Daley Civic Center
City Hall at North LaSalle

Q   Who replaced John Belushi in the 2000 remake that was a flop?
A   John Goodman

MUSIC, THEATER AND DANCE

Q   What warbler from **East St. Louis** became the featured singer on the Arthur Godfrey television show?
A   **Bill Lawrence**; before that he was the featured vocalist with the Jimmy Dorsey band. When drafted by the Army due to the Korean War, he was replaced on the program by Julius LaRosa.

Q   In the film *Runaway Bride*, Julia Roberts gives Richard Gere a record album featuring what **East St. Louisan**?

A   Miles Davis

Q   What Chicago-born composer did the music for "Happy Days Are Here Again?"
A   Milton Ager

Q   What President used the song for his campaign theme in 1932?
A   Franklin D. Roosevelt

Q   Name two other notable Milton Ager songs.
A   "Hard-Hearted Hannah" and "Ain't She Sweet?"

Q   What **Metamora** man formed a big band group known as the Casa Lomas?
A   Glen "Spike" Gray – his group in the 1930's became one of the leading dance bands in the nation.

Q   What **Princeton**, Illinois, man was one of America's greatest organists?
A   Virgil Fox – 1912-1980

Benny Goodman

Q   What **Meredosia** native did the music score for *Shenandoah* and *Bedtime For Bonzo*?
A   Frank Skinner

Q   What **Chicagoan** became the first black choreographer for the Metropolitan Opera in New York?
A   Katherine Dunham, who was also in the 1943 film, *Stormy Weather*.

Q   What University named a performing arts theater in Katherine Dunham's honor?
A   SIU at **Edwardsville** where she was a professor in the 1960's and 1970's

Q   What early jazz song paid tribute to the Elgin Watch Company in **Elgin**, Illinois?
A   "I've Got Elgin Movements In My Hips With Twenty Years Guarantee"

Q   What **East St. Louis** singer became a huge star after she divorced her abusive husband and switched from singing rhythm and blues to angry rock and roll?
A   Tina Turner, who was born in Tennessee, grew up in St. Louis and lived with Ike Turner in East St. Louis.

Q   What **East St. Louisan** was one of the first American males to earn a decent living performing ballet?
A   **William Dollar,** who was born in 1907 and became the leading dancer for the American Ballet in New York. He created the ballet used by Ford Motor Co. at the 1939 New York World's Fair, and George Balanchine choreographed several ballets especially for him.

Q   What **Evanston**-born man invented the electric organ, an instrument that he did not know how to play?
A   Laurens Hammond

Q   What **Newton** man was a noted folksinger and had a hit with "A Little Bitty Tear Let Me Down?"
A   Burl Ives

Q   What Chicagoan did the music score for *The Color Purple*?
A   Quincy Jones

Q   What Chicagoan, who almost became a priest, was frequently voted the nation's outstanding drummer?
A   Gene Krupa

Q   How old was Krupa when he became a professional drummer?
A   Seventeen

Q   What **Peoria**-born singer entertained the troops in Vietnam and sells religious CDs via television advertising?
A   Christy Lane

Q   What Chicagoan, born Frank Vecchio, sang the title song to television's "Rawhide?"
A   Frankie Laine

Q   What Chicago zoo did Marlin Perkins ("Wild Kingdon") direct?
A   Lincoln Park Zoo

Teen heartthrob Tommy Sands

Q   What Chicago choral director has sold millions of records?
A   Norman Luboff

Q   What **Danville** native became famous as a 1920's torch singer? (the word "torch" relating to a one sided love affair)

219

A Helen Morgan

Q What Chicagoan was head of the American Federation of Musicians in the 1940's?
A James C. Petrillo

Q What victory did Petrillo win in 1942?
A The recording industry agreed to pay royalties to musicians for every record sold. Some say the downside of higher salaries for musicians was the death of the Big Band Era.

Q What West Side Chicagoan and showman's "Follies" launched many a career?
A Flo Ziegfield

HOLLYWOOD IN THE HEARTLAND

Q What bouncy musical, set in Roaring Twenties Chicago, won six Oscars in 2003?
A *Chicago* – starring Catherine Zeta Jones, Renee Z., and Richard Gere

Q What 2002 movie has Tom Hanks fleeing the **Quad Cities** area and coming to Chicago, asking Frank Nitti for protection from the Looney (Rooney) gang?
A *Road To Perdition;* Note: In the 1920's **East Moline** didn't have enough population so the area was referred to as the Tri Cities.

Joan Cusack

Q What 1960's movie, with gum chewing Rod Steiger and Sidney Poitier, is set in Sparta, Mississippi, but was filmed in **Sparta**, Illinois?
A *In The Heat of the Night*

Q What movie, based on Richard Wright's novel about Chicago racism, uses the Wrigley Building as an establishing shot?
A *Native Son*

Q In the silent movie *Safety Last*, was the famous scene where Harold Lloyd dangles from the hands of a huge clock filmed in Chicago at the top of the Wrigley Building?

A No - it was filmed in Los Angeles

Q What 1965 movie has Elvis Presley as part of a musical combo employed by a Chicago nightclub owned by a

Mother's Bar in Chicago, courtesy Kirsten and Charles Viola

mobster?
A *Girl Happy*

Q What 1969 film is based on Ben Hecht's autobiography?
A *Gaily, Gaily* - the film starts out in **Galena** and then moves on to Chicago.

Q What Keifer Sutherland movie is about a bunch of University of Chicago medical students pushing the envelope when it comes to life and death?
A *Flatliners*

Q What movie is about the Chicago Black Sox baseball scandal?
A *Eight Men Out*

Q What movie has lawman Tommy Lee Jones chasing after an innocent Harrison Ford?
A *The Fugitive* – the film features an exciting chase scene on Chicago's El.

Q What 1991 Ron Howard movie (with Kurt Russsell) is about Chicago firefighters combating an arsonist?
A *Backdraft*

Q What movie is about a bunch of suburban Chicago teenagers serving Saturday morning detention?
A *The Breakfast Club* introduced us to the Brat Pack – Molly Ringwald, Ally Sheedy, Emilio Estevez, Anthony Michael Hall, and Judd Nelson.

Q What futuristic movie, starring a patch-eyed Kurt Russell as "Snake," was set in New York but had its final scene filmed at the old Chain of Rocks Bridge, the western terminus of Illinois Route 66 near **Mitchell/Granite City**?
A *Escape From New York*

Q   What movie has sexy Chicago babysitter Elizabeth Shue using the F word?
A   *Adventures in Babysitting.*   The Richard Daley Civic Center is featured in one of the scenes.

Q   What charming 1984 movie, partially filmed at the town square in **Pontiac**, is about small-town life in America?
A   *Grandview U.S.A.* - starring Jamie Lee Curtis, C. Thomas Howell, Patrick Swayze, Troy Donahue, John and Joan Cusack

Q   What spooky 1996 movie features supernatural monsters chasing hero (Tom Sizemore) through the Field Museum of Un-natural History?
A   *The Relic* – the coal tunnels in the museum's lower bowels provide a good hiding place for the devouring demon.

Q   What 1986 film about young love in suburban Chicago stars Corey Haim, Kerri Green and Charlie Sheen in his first major role?
A   *Lucas*

Q   What 1975 film features John Wayne as a Chicago cop who tails the bad guys all the way to England. The

Chicago's Marina Towers, courtesy Charles & Kirsten (Barber) Viola

long gone S curve of Lakeshore Drive is featured in the film's opening credits.
A   *Brannigan*

Q   What 1992 film used the red granite arched entrance of the Rookery Building on LaSalle Street as the entrance to a huge toy store labeled Duncan's Toy Chest?
A   *Home Alone II.* The Rookery Building, 11 stories tall, was designed by Burnham and Root in 1907.

Q   What 1986 film has Matthew Broderick deciding to skip school for some fun and relaxation in a production aimed at teenyboppers?
A   *Ferris Bueller's Day Off* - The skydeck on the Sears Tower gets a featured role in the film. Bueller also tours the Chicago Art Institute with girlfriend Mia Sarah.

Q   What film has Tom Berenger as a hating white supremacist in a 1988 thriller?
A   *Betrayed* - Debra Winger is an FBI agent with office in the Dirksen Building.   The filmmakers used the R.R.

Pilgrim Baptist church, courtesy Kirsten and Charles Viola

Donnelley Building while it was still under construction as Berenger's assassination site. Will Winger get there in time to prevent the killing? Hmm.

Q   What movie about Indy 500-type racecars, starring Burt Reynolds, has Sylvester Stallone driving 195 mph in downtown Chicago? (The fine was $25,000.)
A   *Driven*

Q   In what Chuck Norris film does he fall into the Chicago River from the Wells Street Bridge during a fight scene in a 1985 Chicago cop movie?
A   *Code of Silence*

Q   Name the film with the following plot: Michael Keaton (Batman) is a Chicago Blackhawks star hockey player who forms a relationship with a struggling single mother (Maria Alonso) with a precocious son who is sometimes endearing, sometimes exasperating; heart-warming tale with a happy ending.
A   *Touch And Go*

Q   Identify Willard Motley's story about Chicagoan Nick Romano, an impulsive young man whose wayward ways will lead to the electric chair. Humphrey Bogart starred (as Derek's attorney) in this film that introduced moviegoers to John Derek.
A   *Knock on Any Door.* **East St. Louisan** Candy Toxton, (Tockstein) who later wed Chicagoan Mel Tormé, has a minor role in this film.

Q   Name the film that is a continuation of Motley's Nick Romano's saga. This time it's his wayward, illegitimate son (James Darren) who suffers through a plethora of trials and tribulations from youthful rebellion and irresponsibility.

A *Let No Man Write My Epitaph.* Burl Ives (from **Newton**, Illinois) and Shelly Winters join forces with a motley

Rock and Roll McDonalds, courtesy Kirsten and Charles Viola

bunch of North Clark Street do-gooders who help get Darren's engine back on the right track of life.

Q Name the first American movie to graphically deal with the problem of drug addiction. Frank Sinatra portrayed Nelson Algren's Frankie Machine in this 1955 shocker with the hip music score.
A *The Man With the Golden Arm*

Q Name the 1966 film in which Tony Franciosa and Jill St. John starred that was a remake of *Chicago Deadline*, the 1949 Alan Ladd and Donna Reed story about a Chicago reporter.
A *Fame is the Name of the Game*

Q Identify the 1961 film based on Lorraine Hansbury's novel about a black Chicago South Side family that encounters discrimination when they move to a white suburb.
A *Raisin in the Sun.* Sidney Poitier, Claudia McNeil, and Ruby Dee starred in the film. The title came from a line in a Langston Hughes poem: What happens to a dream deferred/Does it dry up/Like a raisin in the sun?

Q What 1974 movie was originally written as a play in 1928 by Ben Hecht and Charles MacArthur?
A *The Front Page.* Billy Wilder directed the 1974 version starring Jack Lemon and Walter Matthau. It dealt with a hard-bitten editor and wise-cracking, street-cynical newspaper men writing about political corruption and police stupidity.

Q Identify the 1932 chick flick based on Chicagoan Edna Ferber's novel of the same title; this film has been made three different times.
A *So Big.* Critics like the 1932 Barbara Stanwick version best, but most readers remember the 1953 edition starring Jane Wyman. The novel won the 1924 Nobel Prize for literature, the first Chicago novel to do so.

Q Name the movie where Jennifer Lopez is a Chicago cop who falls in love with a man who has difficulty living day-

to-day because of the memory of his wife and son who were killed in an accident while he was driving.
A *Angel Eyes.* J-Lo has family problems of her own due to a father who is a wife-beater.

Q Name the movie about a Chicago suburban family (Treat Williams and Michelle Pfiffer) whose son was kidnapped at a very young age by a mentally unstable woman. Chicago detective Whoppi Goldberg helps them find their son about ten years later.
A *The Deep End of the Ocean.* The happy family reunion is marred by the older son's angst due to guilt. He was supposed to be watching his three-year-old brother in the store at the time of the abduction. But there is a bigger problem. The victim has no memory of his first family and wants to go back and live with the father who raised him.

Q Name the 1995 movie where Sandra Bullock, a Chicago Transit Authority clerk, rescues Peter Gallagher (bushy eyebrows and all) from the path of an oncoming train.
A *While You Were Sleeping.* Gallagher falls off the platform at the Sedgwick Avenue station and goes into a coma. Then along comes handsome Bill Pullman and . . . .

Q Identify the 1994 slapstick comedy where Joe Mantegna and his bumbling kidnapper buddies have difficulty keeping

Navy Pier from Lake Michigan, courtesy Kirsten and Charles Viola

track of a baby they've snatched.
A *Baby's Day Out.* Marshal Field's has a cameo role in a scene where the baby crawls out of the store and into a taxi. Chicagoans who split up to do shopping traditionally meet again under Field's streetside clock.

Q Name the 1959 film with Bradford Dillman and Orson Welles (Clarence Darrow) that retells the Leopold and Loeb thrill killing of young Chicagoan Bobby Franks; based on the novel by Meyer Levin.
A *Compulsion.* Levin was a University of Chicago classmate of the two disturbed young men.

Q Identify the film where *Chicago Sun-Times* writer Julia Roberts falls for Nick Nolte, a rival at the *Tribune*.
A *I Love Trouble*

Q Name the film where bounty hunter Steve McQueen drives a tow truck helter skelter through the serpentine parking lots of the Chicago Marina Towers in pursuit of his prey.
A *The Hunter.* The villain ends up crashing through a guard gate and ends up in the Chicago River.

Music Box Theater, courtesy Kirsten and Charles Viola

Q What 1951 film is about that hootchie coochie dancer from the "Streets of Cairo" who performed before wide-eyed yokels at the 1893 Columbian Exposition in Chicago?
A *Little Egypt*

Q What 1938 Darryl Zanuck film perpetuates the myth that Mrs. O'Leary's bovine, who lived in a shed at 137 DeKoven Street, was a pyromaniac and an accessory before the fact.
A *In Old Chicago*

Q What is the hokey 1964 film about two scientists who are transported in time back to 1871 Chicago, one day before the big fire?
A *The Time Travelers*

Q Name the film: Clark Gable is the featured gangster in this 1931 vehicle, and Joan Crawford is a "cub" reporter. The 1929 St. Valentine's Day Massacre and the slaying of reporter Jake Lingle are woven into the story.
A *Dance Fools Dance*

Q What 1998 film showcases the R.R. Donnelley Building on Wacker Drive? Samuel Jackson is falsely accused of a money laundering scheme. Desperate, he takes hostages in the building and matches wits with police negotiator Kevin Spacey.
A *The Negotiator*

Q What film starring Tommy Lee Jones/Robert Downey Jr./Wesley Snipes; was partially filmed in/at the wooded Mermet swampland near **Metropolis**, the Irvin S. Cobb Bridge at **Brookport**, the Massac Memorial Hospital, Veach's Truck Stop, and Roy Willy's Barbecue at **Bay City** in Pope County?
A *U.S. Marshals.* The plane crash scene was filmed near **Golconda**.

Q In what movie does Aidan Quinn star as a Catholic **Chicago** firefighter who saves the life of a young Jewish boy.
A *Stolen Summer* - Quinn's son becomes pals with the Jewish boy and learns that he is dying from leukemia. Some interesting viewpoints about religion are entwined with a remarkable story of hope and friendship. Brian Dennehy has a cameo as a Catholic priest. Kevin Pollack, a Jewish rabbi, is the terminally ill boy's father. Bonnie Hunt (*The Green Mile*) stars as Quinn's long-suffering wife trying to raise eight children.

Q Name the 1964 movie where Frank Sinatra, Dean Martin, Bing Crosby, and Sammy Davis Jr. star in a "Rat Pack" parody of Chicago gangster films; contains Sinatra's melodic ode to the Windy City – "My Kind of Town."
A *Robin and the Seven Hoods*

Q In what 1967 bloody tale do Jason Robards (Capone) and George Segal star in an awful, bloody, and ultra violent story of the single most famous event of the 1920's?
A *The St. Valentine's Day Massacre*

Q Name the movie: Mary Tyler Moore and Donald Sutherland are husband and wife in Judith Guest's 1976 story (directed by Robert Redford) about a Lake Forest couple and their son (Timothy Hutton) who have difficulty coping with the accidental drowning of another son in Lake Michigan.
A *Ordinary People*

Q In what movie do Paul Newman and Robert Redford

Chicago's Blackstone Hotel courtesy Kirsten and Charles Viola

shine in an Oscar-winning film set in 1937 Chicago.
A *The Sting*

Q Name the movie where John Belushi and Blair Brown provide the war between the sexes fireworks in a 1981 romantic comedy.
A *Continental Divide.* Belushi portrays a *Sun-Times* Mike Rokyo-type Chicago reporter (Ernie Souchak) who finds that roughing it in the Rocky Mountains with a birdwatcher is tough on a city boy.

Q Name the 1975 film about four black high school buddies attending a fictional Chicago vocational school. Naturally one of them gets killed at the end.
A *Cooley High*

Biograph Theater where Dillinger was killed, courtesy Kirsten and Charles Viola

Q Name the lightweight 1959 biographical story of a legendary Chicago jazz drummer, played by Sal Mineo.
A *Gene Krupa Story*

Q Name the 1948 film where Jimmy Stewart is the intrepid reporter who answers a newspaper ad placed by a Chicago scrubwoman who is convinced that her son was wrongly convicted of killing a policeman.
A *Northside 777*

Q What 1991 film stars John Goodman as the frolicking, woman chasing, cigar-smoking, fun-loving Bambino in a biography of the man who helped make baseball America's Sport?
A *The Babe* - some of the baseball scenes were filmed at **Danville** Stadium in Illinois, built in 1946 for the Brooklyn Dodgers' farm team. *A League of Their Own* was also filmed at Danville Stadium.

Q The Chicago Theater has a featured segment in what 1988 Robert DiNero/Charles Grodin vehicle?
A *Midnight Run* - Sally Rand and her ostrich feathers once performed at this ornate theater.

Q Name this oldie but goodie! James Cagney stars in the best of the 1930's gangster films. It's better than *Scarface* (Paul Muni) and *Little Caesar* (Edward G. Robinson).
A *The Public Enemy*

Q What 1989 film is about a Nazi war criminal who flees to America in disguise at the end of World War II?
A *Music Box* - the federal prosecutors who help nail him have offices in the Thompson Center, that architectural oddity of steel and glass that no one seems to be able to properly air condition.

Q In what 1996 film does Keanu Reeves have a crackerjack chase scene where he scrambles up a raised Michigan Avenue Bridge on the Chicago River?
A *Chain Reaction*

Q In what movie do Julia Roberts and Dermot Mulroney take a tour on the Chicago River, courtesy of Wendella Tour Co.? (312-337-1446)
A *My Best Friend's Wedding*

Q What 1996 movie has Kevin Dillon and Shannen Doherty ("Beverly Hills 90210") completely miscast as a Chicago couple that find themselves accused of murdering their own daughter.
A *Gone In The Night* - Ed Asner also stars in this Lifetime TV drama based on a true story. David and Cindi Dowaliby are the real life couple that find themselves victimized by the system and an overzealous prosecutor seeking a career boost from the case.

Q What movie features Tom Cruise as a high school senior who lives in suburban Chicago? He wants to be accepted at Princeton but might have to settle for the University of Illinois.
A *Risky Business* - Cruise accidentally dunks the expensive family Porche in Lake Michigan and devises an ingenious way to earn some quick cash to get it fixed. Rebecca DeMornay is his girl friend who likes making out while riding the "El." Tom Cruise's parents wait endlessly at O'Hare Airport.

Chicago's Natural History Field Museum, courtesy Charles and Kirsten Viola

Q What 2001 film has the following plot? A small town white girl (Julia Stiles) must go live with her father in South Chicago after her mother is killed in a car accident. Her new boyfriend from school (Sean Patrick Thomas) is a black teen with a keen interest in hip-hop music and a checkered past. Theirs is a rocky romance, but he helps lead her to a revitalized interest in her lifelong ambition, demonstrating the cathartic power of dance.
A *Save The Last Dance*

Q What Chicago airport is used in all three of the Home

Alone series, representing airports in Paris, New York and San Francisco?
A O'Hare Airport

Flatiron Building, courtesy Charles and Kirsten Viola

Q   What movie has the following plot? Kevin Bacon and his wife (Kathryn Erbe of *Law And Order*) rent a middle class home in North Chicago. Life is good in this 1999 film until one night at a party he undergoes hypnosis by his sister-in-law. From that moment on he sees haunting images of a young girl and a mystery begins to unfold around her. One day the ghost tells him to dig. And dig he does – all over his house, searching for an answer that will unknowingly put him and his family in grave danger.
A *Stir of Echoes*

Q In what movie does Diane Keaton star as a young woman looking for love in all the wrong places – barhopping along Chicago's Rush Street?
A *Looking For Mr. Goodbar* - this teacher with a double life meets a violent end after a pickup on New Year's Eve.

Q What film has the following plot? Andy Garcia, a homeless man turned hero, decides to end his life by jumping off a ledge at Chicago's Drake Hotel (312-787-2200).
A *Hero* - Geena Davis plays the love interest.

Q   In what movie does Andrew McCarthy get seduced by Jacqueline Bisset in the trademark glass elevator of Chicago's Water Tower Place on Michigan Avenue?
A *Class*

Q   In what movie do Demi Moore and Rob Lowe star in a yuppie romance with lots of angst and indecision?
A *About Last Night* - Mother's, a Chicago singles bar on Division Street, was one of the places featured in the film.

Q Name the film where good ol' boy Patrick Swayze takes on the Chicago Mob when they kill his brother.
A *Next Of Kin* - The final showdown takes place in a Chicago cemetery and machine guns prove no match for a good hunting dog, a knife, and a bow and arrow.

Other films shot in Chicago or its suburbs:

Above The Law - 1988, Adam's Rib – 1923, Appoint-ment With Danger – 1951, The Babe Ruth Story - 1948, Bad Boys – 1982, The Big Score - 1983, The Big Town – 1987, Blink – 1994, Bullet on a Wire – 1996, Candyman - 1992, Chain Reaction –1996, The Chamber – 1996, Chicago Deadline – 1949, Chicago Syndicate – 1955, Child's Play - 1988, National Lampoon's Christmas Vacation – 1989, The Color of Money – 1986, Curley Sue 1991, Damien: Omen II – 1978, Dennis the Menace – 1993, Doctor Detroit – 1983, Eight Men Out - 1988, Endless Love - 1981, Eyes of an Angel – 1991, A Family Thing – 1996, Four Friends – 1981, Girls Just Want to Have Fun – 1985, Hambone and Hilly - 1984, Harry and Tonto – 1984, Hoffa – 1992, Home Alone - 1990, Hoop Dreams – 1994, Hudsucker Proxy (Paul Newman) – 1994 The Jackal – 1997, Kalifornia – 1993, Let's Get Harry – 1986, Little Big League - 1994, Mad Dog and Glory – 1994, Major League – 1989, Medium Cool – 1969, Meet the Parents - 1992, Men Don't Leave - 1990, Mercury Rising – 1998, My Bodyguard (Chris Makepeace) - 1980, The Naked Face - 1984, Natural Born Killers - 1994, North By Northwest – 1959, Opportunity Knocks – 1990, The Package – 1989, Payback – 1998, Personal Foul – 1987, Planes, Trains and Automobiles – 1987, Prelude to a Kiss – 1992, Pretty in Pink – 1986, The Public Eye – 1992, Rent-a-Cop – 1988, Richie Rich – 1994, Rookie of the Year – 1991, Rudy – 1993, She's Having a Baby – 1988, Sixteen Candles – 1984, Solstice – 1993 (lonely people on Christmas Eve), Something Weird – 1966 (ESP and witchcraft), They Call

Chicago's Due Pizzeria, courtesy Kirsten and Charles Viola

Me Bruce – 1982 (Bruce Lee), Thief – 1981 (James Caan, Tuesday Weld), Three Days – 1997 (losing a loved one), Union Station - 1950, Vice Versa – 1988 (Judge Reinhold and Fred Savage – father and son – trade places), Wayne's World – 1992 (Mike Meyers and Dana Carvey), Weird Science – 1985 (two nerds create the perfect woman – Kelly LeBrock, Wildcats – 1986 (Goldie Hawn coaches a football team), Windy City - 1984.

ILLINOIS SONGS AND MUSIC

Q   What is the state song?

A   It's called *Illinois*. "By thy rivers gently flowing, Illinois, Illinois . . . ! " "Not without thy wondrous story . . . Can be writ the nation's glory, Illinois!   Illinois!"

Chicago's Second City, courtesy Charles and Kirsten Viola

Illinois adopted it as the official state song in 1925. *Illinois* was written by Charles H. Chamberlain and sung to the tune, "Baby Mine." You can color me dumb, but the hair on the nape of this author's neck still stands on end when I hear the state song.

Q   What Illinoisan is mentioned in the Jimmy Dean hit song, "PT – 109?"

A   Patrick Henry McMahon of **Wyanet** was on the PT 109 when it was cut in two by a Japanese destroyer in the Solomon Islands. McMahon's life was saved when **skipper John F. Kennedy**, swimming with him on his back and the strap of McMahon's life jacket clinched between his teeth, made it to safety.

Q   What Chicago record company's first hit song was "Maybeline" by St. Louisan Chuck Berry?

A   It was Chess Records in 1955. The company was the creation of Leonard and Phil Chess, two Polish-born Jews who had previously run nightclubs in Chicago that featured Billy Eckstine and Ella Fitzgerald. Chess Records was also the home of Muddy Waters, a Mississippi transplant who was a deliveryman by day and played the nightclub circuit at night. A financially strapped Sam Phillips of Sun Records once offered to sell his label to the Chess brothers. They had just signed **Bo Diddley** and couldn't see buying up a contract of some hillbilly singer from Tupelo, Mississippi, named **Elvis Presley**.

Q   What happened when George Harrison came to visit his sister at **Benton**, Illinois, in 1963?

A   George Harrison came to **Benton** to visit his sister, Louise Harrison Caldwell, for a month. The Beatles were already popular in England but were just getting ready to begin a tour known as the British Invasion. The radio station in **West Frankfort** became the **first in the nation to play a Beatles song**.

Q   What Illinoisan is considered by many to be the greatest ballad singer of all time?

A   Burl Ives of **Newton**

Q   What is the most famous song ever written about an Illinois highway?

A   "Get Your Kicks on Route 66" by Bobby Troupe. It was written during the 1950's and recorded by Nat King Cole.

Q   What **Peoria**-born country/western/religious singer entertained our troops in Vietnam?

A   Christy Lane (real name Eleanor Johnston), the singer whose songs include: "One Day at a Time," "Footsteps," and "I Believe in Angels."

Q   What African-American, Mississippi/Chicago singer was depicted on a U.S. stamp?

A   Muddy Waters – he earned his nickname from playing in mud as a kid; Waters left Mississippi and came to Chicago as part of the black migration; he brought a new blues sound with him that became known as the Chicago blues; Rolling Stone Magazine, Mick Jagger's band, and Bob Dylan's "Like a Rolling Stone," was named after Waters' original "Rollin' Stone" composition; he recorded for Chess Records; played Carnegie Hall in 1959; played his hit song, "Got My Mojo Working," at the 1960 Newport Jazz Festival; died in 1983

Actor David Soule released a song or two

Q   What Illinoisans wrote popular songs about the Civil War?

A   Chicagoan Henry Clay Work wrote the popular Civil War song, "Marching Through Georgia." Chicagoan George Root wrote the wildly popular, "The Battle Cry of Freedom."

Q   What Chicago singer had a large gun collection and was a fast-draw expert that enabled him to appear in several television and movie westerns?

A   Mel Torme, "The Velvet Fog." He wrote "The Christmas Song" ("chestnuts roasting on an open fire") during a July 4 cookout; he married actress Candy Tockstein of **East St. Louis** in 1949.

Q   What Illinoisan wrote one of the most popular wedding songs of all time in 1901?

A Carrie Bond of Chicago published a book of songs, one of which was "**I Love You Truly**," still popular at weddings.

Q What Chicagoan wrote "Solidarity Forever," a popular union organizing and strike song?
A Ralph Chaplin, a member of the radical IWW (Wobblies) labor group, wrote it in 1914.

Q What Chicago rock and roll singer married Nancy Sinatra?
A Tommy Sands, who also appeared in a few movies. Some of his hits were "Sing Boy Sing" and "Teenage Crush." (picture on page 226)

Q What **Rochelle** native wrote the song, "When You and I Were Young, Maggie?"
A Charles Butterfield

Q What **Marengo** native wrote, "In The Shade of the Old Apple Tree?"
A Egbert Van Alstyne

Carl Sandburg

Q What Illinoisan, who wrote a multi-volume biography of Abe Lincoln, was a noted folksinger in his early years?
A Carl Sandburg (see picture above)

Q What Chicago-born singer sang the title song in the movie, *Gunfight at the OK Corral*?
A Frankie Laine – he was born Frank Vecchio in 1913. Some of his other hits include: "That's My Desire," "Mule Train," "A Woman in Love," "Jezebel," "Rawhide," and "Love is a Golden Ring."

Q W.C. Handy is considered the "Father of the Blues." What was on the flip side of his recording of "The St. Louis Blues?"
A "The East St. Louis Blues."

Q Who wrote "In the Good Old Summertime?"
A George Evans. **Streator** was home to George "Honey Boy" Evans, a member of Chicago's Mastodon Minstrels (black face) in the 1890's.

Q What **Alton/East St. Louis** jazz great released the 1956 album, "Birth of the Cool?"
A Miles Davis

Q Who wrote the 1922 jazz ballet, *Krazy Kat*, based on the famed comic strip?
A John Alden Carpenter, a direct descendant of John Alden of *Mayflower* fame

Q What Mississippi River classic song comes from the

film, *Showboat*, based on the novel by Edna Ferber of Chicago?
A "Old Man River." The town of **Thebes** is mentioned in the novel.

Q What was the most widely known song in *Cahokia, Kaskaskia and Prairie du Rocher* that was sung by the French at New Year?
A "La Guillannée" – sung as part of a celebration of wine, song and dance combined with a collection of money for the poor

Q What famed engineer on the Illinois Central was killed in a train wreck and has had numerous songs written about him?
A Casey Jones, the **first person inducted into the Railroad Hall of Fame.**

Q What is the more recognizable name of the music group known as the Chicago Transit Authority?
A Chicago

Q What New Orleans/Chicago female singer became famous for her signature song, "Precious Lord?"
A Mahalia Jackson – Queen of Gospel Music

Q What hit song, recorded in 1958 by Tommy Edwards, was written by a Vice-president of the United States from Illinois?
A "All in the Game" was written by Charles G. Dawes of **Evanston**, Vice-president under Calvin Coolidge.

Q What Chicago Montgomery Ward employee wrote a famous Christmas song in 1939?

Banker; Vice-president; songwriter; C. G. Dawes

A Robert May wrote "Rudolph the Red-nosed Reindeer" as part of a seasonal sales promotion. Cowboy singer Gene Autry's recording of the song was a smash hit.

Q What popular hit song of the early 1950's was about a northern Illinois railroad?
A "Rock Island Line" - the Rock Island & St. Louis Railroad was completed in 1867. It was **made famous in a song by Lonnie Donnigan** - "Oh, the Rock Island Line, she's a mighty good road . . . ."

Q What song about a passenger train on the Wabash line became a big hit?

227

A "**Wabash Cannon Ball.**" Certainly the most famous Wabash passenger train was this one immortalized in song.

Chicago drummer Gene Krupa with Buddy Wise on saxophone

Interestingly, the song predated the train by many years, and the lyrics refer to stations never served by the real Cannon Ball.

Q What Illinois circuit-riding preacher became famous, in part, because of his rivalry with the legendary Mike Fink?
A Peter Cartwright, a man of broad chest and powerful arms, became the subject of stories and legends due to his rivalries with that scalawag, **Mike Fink**, "King of the Keelboats." Fink's exploits were showcased in the 1950's Disney TV movie, *Davy Crockett and the River Pirates*. Following is a typical Mike Fink swagger song:

I'm a ring-tailed roarer and a ring-tailed screamer too!
I was raised on grizzly bear milk and cradled with a wildcat.
I'm half horse and half alligator and people call me the Mississippi Snag.
I can eat a dozen rattlesnakes for breakfast and drink a barrel a' whiskey besides.
I can out-run, out-hop, out-jump and out-fight any man in this whole country!
Ya-hoooooooo! Yip-eeeeeeee!
Stand back and gimme room!

Q In the only fight between Fink and Cartwright, who won?
A Cartwright bested Fink and made him recite "The Lord's Prayer"

ILLINOIS ENTERTAINERS

Q On his radio program, what kind of car did Jack Benny say he drove?
A Maxwell - Benny was born in **Waukegan** on Valentine's Day in 1894.

Q Folk singer Dan Fogelberg was born in what Illinois river town?

A **Peoria**

Q What **Moline** native was Captain Parmenter of "F-Troop" (Where Indian fights are colorful sights, and nobody takes a likkin') and starred in *The Cat From Outer Space*?
A Ken Berry

Q What Illinois native played the role of Big Daddy in *Cat on a Hot Tin Roof*?
A Burl Ives of **Newton**

Q Peter Scolari of **Rochelle** starred on "Bosom Buddies." Who was his co-star?
A Tom Hanks

Q What Chicago-born star of "Thirtysomething" married costar Patricia Wettig?
A Ken Olin, who has since moved on to directing. He is not related to actress Lena Olin who is Swedish.

Q What Chicago actor with a bulbous nose recommended that you not leave home without your American Express card?
A Karl Malden

Q Mike Nichols and Elaine May, who later married, started their careers at what theater that featured acerbic satire?

Harpo Studios in Chicago, courtesy Charles and Kirsten Viola

A Chicago's Second City - Nichols divorced May and is currently married to Diane Sawyer.

Q What **Oak Park** actress was married to Alan Ludden and starred on "The Golden Girls?"
A Betty White

Q What is the name of Oprah Winfrey's production Company?
A Harpo Productions - derived from Oprah spelled backwards.

Q   What Chicago native starred in *Alien Nation* and *Princes Bride* and played Dr. Geiger on "Chicago Hope?"
A   Mandy Patinkin

Q   What Chicago African-American actress played Vanessa Huxtable on the "Bill Cosby Show?"
A   Tempestt Bledsoe

Q   What Chicagoan was the lead singer for the group, Jefferson Airplane?
A   Grace Slick

Q   What **New Trier** cheerleader is currently teamed with Andy Williams at a show in Branson, Missouri?"
A   Ann Margret

Ann Margret (Famous Photos)

Q   What **Christopher/Benton** actor starred as the bad guy with Clint Eastwood in *Line of Fire*?
A   John Malkovich

Q   What Chicago writer and former real estate salesman wrote the screenplay for Kevin Kostner's *Untouchables*?
A   David Mamet

Q   What Chicago actress, inadvertently omitted from my *Incredible Illinois* book, starred on "Taxi" and with Burt Reynolds on "Evening Shade?"
A   Marilu Henner – that red-haired beauty

Q   What Chicago comedian has recently tried his hand at playing the villain in such movies as *One Hour Photo*?
A   Robin Williams

Q   What diminutive **Zion**-born actor tried to defeat Arnold Schwarzenegger in the 2003 governor's race in California?
A   Gary Coleman

Q   Chicago native Martin Mull is probably best known for his role in what TV program?
A   "Mary Hartman, Mary Hartman"

Q   Chicago western star John Agar married what princess from the 1930's?
A   Shirley Temple

Q   What **Rock Island** movie star was an undercover spy for the U.S. in World War II?
A   Eddie Albert

Q   What **Carrollton** native starred with Harrison Ford in *Raiders of the Lost Ark*?
A   Karen Allen

Q   What **Hyde Park** comedian, pianist, and actor was associated with the "Tonight Show" in its early years?
A   Steve Allen – who was married to Jane Meadows

Q   What **East St. Louisan** became a dance sensation in Paris at the age of 19 and was noted for her skimpy outfits.
A.   Josephine Baker

Q   What **Danville** native played Luther on the TV sitcom "Coach" and was a hit in "My Mother The Car?"
A   Jerry Van Dyke

Q   What movie did John Dillinger watch at the Biograph Theater in Chicago shortly before he was gunned down by Melvin Purvis and the G-men?
A   *Manhattan Melodrama*, starring Clark Gable as the bad guy

Q   What **Galena** native was fired for incompetence from his radio job and later hosted one of the longest running shows ever – the "Breakfast Club?"
A   Don McNeill

Q   What blonde Chicago actress was best known for her role in the prime time soap opera, "Knots Landing?"
A   Donna Mills

Johnny Weissmuller and Maureen O'Sullivan (author's collection)

Q   What veteran Chicago movie actor got his big break in *The Big Chill*?
A   Tom Berenger

Q   What was Chicago-born John Chancellor best known for on TV?
A   He replaced Dave Garroway on the "Today Show" and later was the anchor for "NBC Nightly News."

MOVIES MADE IN ILLINOIS OR ABOUT ILLINOIS

229

Q   What silent film, made by Essanay Studios in Chicago (1909), has become a favorite for comic melodrama players at dinner theaters?
A   *Ten Nights in a Barroom*, written by Tim Arthur

Q   When was Frank Baum's *Wizard of Oz* first made into a film?
A   1910. It was done as a silent by Selig Polyscope Co. in Chicago. The color/sound remake with Judy Garland was in 1939, the year this author was born.

Q   What was the name of the film about bootlegger Roger Touhy?
A   *Roger Touhy, Gangster* starring Preston Foster - it was made in 1944.

Q   What 1983 film is about Chicago crime kid Sean Penn accidentally killing another boy and being sent to reform school?
A   *Bad Boys*, which also featured Ally Sheedy

Wizard of Oz poster (author's collection)

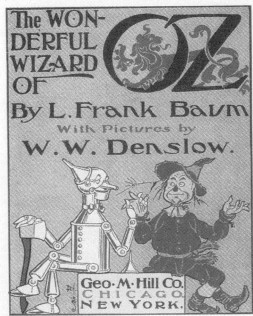

Q   What 1984 film centers on Molly Ringwald's sixteenth birthday. It is anything but sweet as she suffers through every embarrassment imaginable.
A   *Sixteen Candles,* which also has **Evanston's** John Cusack in it.

Q   What 1985 Chuck Norris action film is about a Chicago cop caught up in the middle of a gang war?
A   *Code of Silence*, featuring Henry Silva as the villain.

Q   What film, based on a novel by Chicagoan Richard Wright, has the famous line, "I didn't mean to kill her!"
A   *Native Son*, the 1951 film about Bigger Thomas. Richard Wright played the main character. In a 1986 remake, Matt Dillon and Illinoisan Elizabeth McGovern were the featured stars.

Q   What 1955 movie about infiltrating the Chicago Outfit starred Dennis O'Keefe and Abbe Lane?
A   *Chicago Syndicate*

Q   Did the Route 66 TV series ever do a program based in Chicago? (picture on next page)

A   Of course – this is Illinois trivia. Tod Stiles and Buz Murdoch tooled around in their Corvette in two 1962 episodes filmed by Screen Gems.

Q   How was Illinois featured in the 1963 Cinerama film, *How The West Was Won*?
A   The river pirates who operated at Cave-in-Rock in southeastern Illinois on the Ohio River were depicted early in the film.

Q   What is the plot of the 1971 film, *T.R. Baskin*, starring Candace Bergen?
A   "Dear Mom and Dad: I have gone to Chicago to seek fame and fortune, T.R. Baskin."

Q   What Chicago era is depicted in the 1973 movie, *The Sting*?
A   In 1930's Chicago, Paul Newman and Robert Redford team up to pull off the ultimate con. Interestingly, actor Paul Newman honed his craft early in his career at the **Woodstock**, Illinois Opera House.

Q   What is the plot of the 2002 Lifetime TV movie, "Obsessed?"
A   In a Chicago jail cell, Ellena Roberts tells her attorney that she is totally innocent of the harassment she is charged with and claims she has had a torrid affair with the man (Sam Robards) who has filed the charges. In court, the doctor's version differs entirely.
    Blonde, clever and fetching, Jenna Elfman plays the **Skokie** High School grad now working as a medical writer. Who do you believe in this "he said, she said?" As the plot unfolds, Ellena's lawyer begins to learn some startling facts in this better than average television movie. (mostly because Jenna Elfman is so fetching)

Q   What is the lesson of *Mahogany*, filmed in Chicago and starring Diana Ross and Billy Dee Williams?
A   In this 1975 flick, the Ross character yearns to climb to the top in the world of fashion design, but she learns that success is hollow unless you have someone to share it with.

Elizabeth McGovern (Famous Photos)

Q   Who was Betty Grable's co-star in *Wabash Avenue*, a 1950 musical about life and love in old Chicago, set during the 1893 World's Fair?
A   Victor Mature plays the role of Andy Clark who

finagles his way into a partnership with Phil Harris as co-owners of a dance hall. Betty Grable is the wisecracking burlesque queen involved in a love-hate relationship with the Mature character.

Route 66: George Maharis and Martin Milner

Q In what 1976 film does Gene Wilder keep getting thrown off the train?
A *Silver Streak* - with Jill Clayburgh and Richard Pryor of **Peoria**. The train ride from L.A. to Chicago is a highlight of the film. The big crash scene at Chicago's Union Station is a real gem.

Q What movie has Timothy Bottoms trying to blow up people while they are riding on a suburban Chicago roller coaster?
A *Rollercoaster* – a 1977 Richard Widmark and George Segal thriller.

Q What is the featured attraction in the 1977 Kirk Douglas film, *The Fury*?
A Once again a suburban Chicago roller coaster steals the show as death rides the rails courtesy of Andrew Stevens and his telekinetic powers.

Q What 1986 John Hughes film is about a Chicago suburban high schooler determined to take a day off from school.
A *Ferris Bueller's Day Off* - naturally Matthew Broderick convinces his buddies to do it with him, and they tool around in a hot Ferrari.

Q What 1986 film stars Richard Gere as a maverick Chicago cop who poses as a hit man to meet with someone in New Orleans looking to have a job done?
A *No Mercy*. Kim Basinger provides the plot's romantic interest.

Q What is the plot of the 1988 film, *Red Heat*?
A Moscow's toughest detective (Arnold Schwarzenegger) teams with Chicago's craziest cop (Jim Belushi) to track down a Russian drug dealer who has fled to the Windy City.

Q What is the plot of the 1989 film, *Uncle Buck*?

A John Candy, a bachelor and all around slob, is reluctantly asked to baby sit his Chicago sister's rebellious teenage daughter and two other siblings while she visits her sick father in Indianapolis. **Edwardsville's** Laurie Metcalf has a featured role in the film.

Q What is the plot of the 1993 film, *Groundhog Day*?
A Harold Ramis (**Highland Park**) directed Bill Murray in this amusing story of a sarcastic Chicago weatherman who experiences the worst day of his life . . . over and over.

Q Who is Chicago's most famous female private eye?
A It's *V. I. Warshawski*, based on the novels of Sara Paretsky. In the 1991 film, Kathleen Turner is stuck babysitting her new boyfriend's daughter. When he gets murdered, Turner and the victim's daughter set out to solve the crime.

Q What 1992 film set in Chicago was based on a "Saturday Night Live" sketch?
A *Wayne's World,* starring Mike Meyers and Dana Carvey as two slacker buddies trying to promote their public access cable show.

Q What 1986 movie started the craze about serial killer Hannibal Lecter?
A *Manhunter,* starring William Peterson as the FBI agent. The river scene in the movie was shot near **Chester**.

Q What 2000 movie, starring Sean Young and Tony Denman, was shot in **Benton**, Illinois?
A *Poor White Trash*, a story about a southern Illinois family who resorts to crime so they can afford to send their teenage son to college.

Richard Pryor of Peoria

Q What Paul Newman movie had its main pool scenes shot at a hall in Chicago at Fullerton and Southport?
A *The Color of Money,* co-starring Tom Cruise. Paul Newman finally won his Academy Award for this one.

Q In what Bill Murray movie does he inherit an elephant?
A In *Larger Than Life,* Murray is a motivational speaker whose life is going nowhere until he inherits an elephant. One of the scenes in the film was shot in **East St. Louis**.

Q In what Kevin Kostner movie is there a shot of the St.

Louis Arch and the Veteran's/Martin Luther King Bridge in **East St. Louis**?
A *American Flyers – a 1985 film*

Red Heat - Schwarzenegger and Belushi

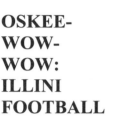

OSKEE-WOW-WOW: ILLINI FOOTBALL

Q Who is considered the "Father of Illinois football?"
A Student Scott Williams who secured permission from authorities for a team from Illinois to play Illinois Wesleyan in 1890

Q What color was the team uniform for the first three years of Illinois football?
A Green – they changed to orange and blue in 1894

Q Who was center on the 1890-93 teams and later became the Illini coach?
A George Huff

Q Did Illinois have a winning record after its first decade of football?
A Yes – they were 61-27-6

Q Who was Illinois' first passing quarterback?
A Pomeroy Sinnock – 1908

Q What is the most lopsided win in the school's history?
A 87-3 over Illinois Wesleyan in 1912; they defeated Illinois College 79-0 in 1895.

Q How many times has Illinois won or shared the national football title?
A Four

Q What was amazing about the 1910 Illini team that went 7-0?
A They were unscored upon.

Q What was the best seven-year span in Illini history?
A From 1923-1929, under coach Bob Zupke, they were 45-8-3 with two national titles in 1923 and 1927.

Q What was the amazing thing about Red Grange's four touchdowns in 12 minutes against Michigan in 1924?
A Michigan was a powerhouse – shutting out its previous three opponents as well as its next three.

Q How bad was the 39-14 "whupping" Illinois gave to Michigan that day?
A It would be the most points scored by a Michigan opponent over a 43 year period.

Q How many members were there on a typical Illinois team of the 1920's?
A Thirteen or fourteen – everyone played both ways, offense and defense

Q What famous sportswriter gave Grange the nickname "Galloping Ghost?"
A Grantland Rice

Q What was the seating capacity of Illinois Field, the team's stadium of the early 1920's?
A A mere 17,000

Q Why was the new 1924 building called Memorial Stadium?
A To pay tribute to the 183 Illini men and one woman who lost their lives in World War I.

Q Why were many critical of athletic director George Huff's plans for a new stadium?
A The new stadium had 75,000 seats, but there were only 11,000 students.

Buddy Young

Q What new feature was installed at Memorial Stadium in 1974?
A Artificial turf

Q What is the current seating capacity of Memorial Stadium?
A 70,904

Q Who has coached all of the following: Robert Holcomb, Erik Kramer, Jim Harbaugh, Rodney Peete, and David Krieg?
A Ron Turner – at various places

Q Who is Ron Turner's more famous brother?
A Norv Turner, former offensive coordinator for the Super Bowl Champion Dallas Cowboys and former head coach of the Washington Redskins

Q What are the only five Big Ten teams that the U of I has lifetime winning records against?
A Iowa, Indiana, Wisconsin, Northwestern and Purdue; they are nearly .500 against Michigan State and Minnesota and are pathetic against Ohio State and Michigan.

Q   What is the record for the longest U of I losing streak?
A   Eighteen games starting at the end of the 1996 season, all of the 1997 season, and one game into the 1998 season

Q   Who was the MVP on the 1998 (3-8) team?
A   Linebacker Danny Clark; passer Kurt Kittner was ranked last in the conference and Rocky Harvey was ranked third in kickoff returns.

Ray Nitschke (courtesy U of I and State Farm)

Q   Who has the Illini single game rushing record?
A   Robert Holcomb – 315 yards vs. Minnesota in 1996

Q   What Illini has the most career rushing touchdowns?
A   Howard Griffith had 31 from 1987-1990

Q   What Illini passer finished his two-year career with an average of 300.4 yards per game average?
A   Tony Eason

Q   Has any Illini quarterback thrown for 10,000 yards in a career?
A   No – Jack Trudeau finished with 8,725 and Jason Verduzco (1989-92) finished with 7,532

Q   Has any Illini quarterback thrown for 600 yards in a single game?
A   Yes – Dave Wilson threw for 621 yards against Ohio State in 1980 (I don't know how that was possible.)

Q   How good of a receiver was David Williams?
A   In 1984 he caught 101 passes for 1,278 yards, the 2nd highest total in NCAA history at the time

Q   What unusual use did the Memorial Stadium see on September 22, 1985?
A   The Farm Aid concert to raise money and advertise the plight of Illinois farmers

Q   What kind of scholarships did Illinois football players receive in the 1930's?
A   There was no such thing as athletic scholarships

Q   What **Tuscola** native won All-America honors as a tackle in 1939?
A   Jim Reeder

Q   What 1934 play, drawn up by coach Zupke, is in the College Football Hall of Fame?
A   The Flying Trapeze, a complicated flea-flicker-type play that enabled Illinois to knock off a powerful Ohio State team, 14-13.

Q   Who became the new coach in 1942 after coach Zupke was forced to step down after back-to-back losing seasons?
A   Lineman coach Ray Eliot

Q   How did a Ray Elliot team pull off an incredible upset against Michigan, led by All-Everything quarterback Tom Harmon? (father of actor Mark Harmon)
A   Winless in four games, the Illini had only one star on the team, Mel Brewer of **Carbondale**. He was expected to miss the game because his mother's funeral was the day before the game. When he unexpectedly showed up, he asked coach Ray Eliot if he could speak to the team. With tears in his eyes, he said a few words about the funeral and then told the team that he didn't come back to lose. He asked his teammates to repeat those words over and over – "I didn't come back to lose." Illinois won the game 16-7.

Q   What diminutive 5-5 Illinois running back was 5th in the Heisman balloting in 1944?
A   Buddy Young – who went pro with the Baltimore Colts

Q   Who did Illinois defeat in the 1947 Rose Bowl in Pasadena?
A   UCLA by the score of 45-14; UCLA entered the game with an unbeaten record

Q   Who was the first black player to score a touchdown in the Rose Bowl?
A   Buddy Young

Q   How did All-American defensive guard Alex Agasee of **Evanston** score two touchdowns against Minnesota in a 1940's game?
A   He stole the ball from a runner and recovered a fumble in the end zone.

Q   Who did the Fighting Illini defeat in the 1952 Rose Bowl?
A   Stanford – 40-7

J.C. Caroline (courtesy U of I and State Farm)

Q   Did Illinois play in the **first nationally televised bowl game**?
A   Yes – it was the 1952 Stanford game.

Q   Who did the University of Illinois defeat in the 1964 Rose Bowl?
A   Washington's Huskies -17-7

Q   How well did Buddy Young do in a summer college all-star game against the Chicago Bears?
A   He was named MVP and his team won.

Q   What Illini became the **first African-American executive in any sports league**?

A   Buddy Young - in 1963 when Pete Rozell named him as liaison between players and the league office

Q   How many conference championships did the Illini win in the 1950's?
A   Two – 1951, 1953

Q   Who was the quarterback of the 1951 team?
A   Tommy O'Connell

Q   Who were the 1953 Illini "touchdown twins?"
A   J.C. Caroline and Mickey Bates

Q   What team did they annihilate in the 1954 opener with Caroline rushing for 192 yards and Bates for 152?
A   Ohio State and Woody Hayes

Jim Grabowski (courtesy U of I and State Farm Insurance)

Q   How many times did Michigan beat Illinois in the 1950's?
A   Only three times

Q   What Illini **led the nation in rushing in 1953**?
A   J.C. Caroline

Q   Does Caroline hold the Illini mark for yards rushing in a single season?
A   No – Jim Grabowski gained 1,258 yards, two more than Caroline's best effort

Q   How did Caroline fare as a senior with the Illini?
A   He quit school and signed a contract to play Canadian football.

Q   Did Caroline ever play for the Bears?
A   Yes – from 1956-65

Q   What Illini player was a four-time Pro Bowl selection with the San Francisco 49ers?
A   Abe Woodson

Q   What Illini lineman went on to star with the St. Louis Cardinals?
A   Ernie McMillan

Q   What Illinois fullback went on to star as a player for the Green Bay Packers?
A   Ray Nitschke

Q   Who did Illinois defeat in the 1963 Rose Bowl 17-7?

A   Washington State

Q   Who were the stars of that team?
A   Jim Grabowski (MVP), Dick Butkus, and safety George Donnelly

Q   Who intercepted two passes in the 1963 Rose Bowl victory?
A   George Donnelly

Q   How were field goals scored back in the 1920's?
A   Drop kick – with no one holding the ball; Frosty Peters was Illinois' standard setter

Q   What Illini player was the number three pick in the 1961 draft, selected by the Washington Redskins?
A   Joe Rutgens of **Cedar Point,** a great pass rushing lineman who played both offense and defense

Q   What Illinois teams of the Sixties went winless?
A   The 1961 team went 0-9 and the 1969 team was 0-10

Q   What caused coach Pete Elliot to resign in 1967?
A   A slush fund scandal

Q   How did Illinois fare against Ohio State and Michigan in the 1970's?
A   They were 0-20

Q   What Illini kicker was the first to boot five field goals in one game?
A   Dan Beaver in 1973 against Purdue; he finished his career with more field goals than any player in Big Ten history.

Q   What defensive standout from the Seventies played with the Minnesota Vikings for fourteen years?
A   Scott Studwell

Scott Studwell (courtesy U of I and State Farm)

Q   What defensive standout broke Dick Butkus single game and career mark for tackles at U of I?
A   Scott Studwell

Q   Who was the first Illinois player to be picked on Walter Camp's All-America Team?
A   Ralph "Slouie" Chapman - 1914

Q   How many bowl games did Illinois play in during the 1980's?
A   Five

Q   What was the only bowl game they won that decade?
A   Citrus Bowl

Q   What incredible feat did California quarterback Dave

234

Wilson accomplish against Ohio State in the 1980 Illini season?
A   He set an NCAA record by passing for 621 yards in a 49-42 loss.

Q   Why was Mike White the National Coach of the Year in 1983?
A   Illinois was undefeated against Big Ten opponents, 9-0

Q   What Illini won the Big Ten MVP in 1983?
A   Don Thorp of **Arlington Heights**, the 6th Illini to do so; he tackled 18 runners for losses in the 1983 season.

Q   What lineman from **Wheaton** is possibly the greatest offensive lineman in Illini history?
A   Jim Juriga – All Big Ten 1983,1984,1985

Q   How many times did receiver David Williams make All-American as an Illini?
A   Twice

David Williams (courtesy U of I and State Farm)

Q   What forced Mike White to quit as the head coach of the Illini?
A   He was nailed for recruiting violations

Q   Who had more total yardage as an Illini, Tony Eason or Jeff George?
A   Tony Eason

Q   Why did Jeff George only play two years for the Illini?
A   He started his college career at Purdue.

Q   What Illini was second in the nation as a kickoff return specialist in 1989?
A   Mike Bellamy with a 28.7 average

Q   What team did Illinois (led by Jeff George) defeat 31-21 in the 1991 Citrus Bowl, their first such victory in 26 years?
(A) Alabama (B) Penn State (East Carolina (D) Virginia
A   Virginia

Q   What Illini player in 1990 signed for more money to play for the Indianapolis Colts **than any rookie in NFL history**?
A   Jeff George

Q   What do Illini fans remember most about Jeff George?
A   His come-from-behind victories and his quick strike capability

Q   What team is Illinois' traditional rival in football and basketball?
A   Purdue – although Purdue sometimes seems more preoccupied with Indiana and Notre Dame

Q   Who is the all-time leading scorer for the Illini?
A   Kicker Chris White with 262 points (1983-85); Chris Richardson is a close second with 259.

Q   Who is the all-time Illini scorer as a running back?
A   Red Grange of **Wheaton** with 186 points (1923-25)

Q   What Illini has the most touchdown in a single season?
A   Red Grange (1924), Buddy Young (1944), and John Karras of **Argo**, Illinois, (1951) had 13 scores

Q   Who holds the single game rushing mark for the Illini?
A   Jim Grabowski gobbled up 239 yards against Wisconsin in 1964 beating a Red Grange performance against Penn in 1925 by two yards

Q   Who kicked the longest punt in Illini history?
A   Dike Eddleman – 88 yards against Iowa in 1948

Q   What was the Illini record for the 2003 season?
A   A dismal 1-11

Q   What Illini *punt return* record will probably never be broken?
A   Dike Eddleman returned 8 punts in 1948 for 262 yards – an impossible 32.8 yards per try; the next best on the list is a paltry 14.8 average.

Q   Who holds the Illini career *kickoff return* average?
A   Red Grange had 15 returns from 1923-35 for an astounding 30.2 average. Mike Bellamy is second with a 26.4 average.

Q   What Illini quarterback threw for 413 yards against Purdue in 1985?
A   Jack Trudeau

Q   What two former Illini players were on the 1967 and 1968 Green Bay Packers championship teams?
A   Jim Grabowski and Ray Nitschke

Al Brodsky (U of I and State Farm)

Q   What Illini receiver totaled 177 yards against Ohio State in a 1982 game?
A   Mike Martin

Q   What number did Dick Butkus wear?
A   50

Q   What number was on the jersey of Red Grange?
A   77

235

Q Who holds the NCAA mark of 15 games in a row with an interception?
A Al Brodsky (a record that will probably never be broken)

Q Who set the NCAA record with back-to-back passing games that totaled 1,024 yards?
A Dave Wilson against Ohio State and Indiana (1980)

Tony Eason (courtesy U of I and State Farm)

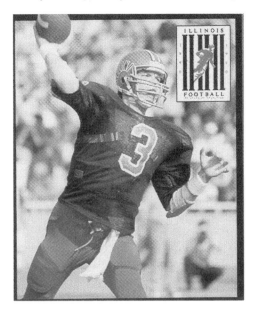

Q Who set an NCAA mark for career interceptions with 29 in 27 games?
A Al Brodsky (1950-52) My question: Why did opponents keep throwing the ball in his direction?

Jack Trudeau (courtesy U of I and State Farm)

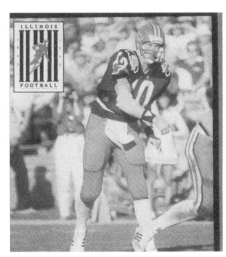

Q What Illini quarterback set an NCAA record for pass attempts **in a quarter** with 32 in a 1985 game against Purdue?
A Jack Trudeau

Q What Illini set an NCAA record with 215 consecutive pass attempts without an interception?
A Jack Trudeau – 1985

Q What Illini quarterback set an NCAA record with 66 pass attempts in a game with no interceptions?
A Jack Trudeau against Purdue in 1985

Q What are some of the more recent 1st place finishes for the Illini as Big Ten football champions?
A 1946, 1951, 1963, 1983, 1990 (tie)

Q In what year did Illinois rack up its most impressive wins over ranked opponents?
A In 1983 they defeated Michigan State (19), Michigan (8), Iowa (4) and Ohio State (6)

Q What greatest of band musicians called the Marching Illini the "**world's greatest college band**?"
A John Phillip Sousa

Q What is the only other Big Ten marching band "respected" by the Illini?
A Michigan

Jeff George (courtesy U of I and State Farm)

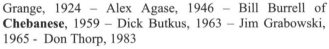

Q Who are the only two Illini players to have their jerseys retired?
A Dick Butkus and Harold "Red" Grange

Q What Illini players have won the Chicago Tribune's MVP of the Big Ten award, dating back to 1924?
A Red Grange, 1924 – Alex Agase, 1946 – Bill Burrell of **Chebanese**, 1959 – Dick Butkus, 1963 – Jim Grabowski, 1965 - Don Thorp, 1983

Bill Burrell (U of I/State Farm)

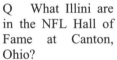

Q What Illini are in the NFL Hall of Fame at Canton, Ohio?
A Dick Butkus, Red Grange, George Halas, Bobby Mitchell, Ray Nitschke

Q Who was the sixth U of I player to win the Silver Football Award as the Big Ten's Most Valuable Player?
A Defensive standout Don Throp of **Arlington Heights** - 1983

Q Why is the term Big Ten a misnomer?
A Penn State was added to the fold in the 1990's, making the total membership 11. Conference officials and fans persist in calling it the Big Ten. (Irrational fans think there is something *magical* in the old name.) Come on, folks! When the Big Eight added four teams they called it (gulp) The Big Twelve.

THE SPECTACULAR EADS BRIDGE

Q   The Eads Bridge connects what two cities?
A   East St. Louis and St. Louis

Q   When was it completed?
A   1874 – work started in 1867

Eads Bridge abutment and west approach

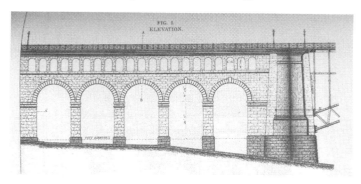

Q   Which bridge is older, Roebling's Brooklyn Bridge or the Eads Bridge?
A   The Eads Bridge

Q   From what school did Captain James B. Eads learn engineering?
A   The terms "captain" and "engineer" were self-applied. Eads was not a military man and he was a self-taught engineer, reading periodicals and books about the subject.

Q   When was the idea of such a bridge first conceived?
A   A schoolmaster named Russell, who lived in **Bluffdale**, Illinois, had a dream about such a bridge at St. Louis in the 1820's.

Q   Where was the first railroad bridge across the Mississippi in 1856?
A   Between **Rock Island** and Davenport, Iowa

Q   When the steamboat *Effie Afton* hit the Rock Island pier, caught fire, and burned the wooden trusses, what claim was made by railroaders?
A   That rival steamboat interests conspired to stage the "accident" on purpose

Q   What Chicago engineer built the Rock Island Bridge?
A   Lucius Boomer

Q   Before the Eads Bridge was built, what powerful East St. Louis company had a monopoly on traffic between St. Louis and East St. Louis?
A   The Samuel Wiggins Ferry Company

Q   What kind of monopoly was granted to the Wiggins company by the Illinois legislature in 1819?
A   It was allowed to purchase one mile of waterfront on the Illinois side of the river and no rival company could locate within two miles.

Q   How did railroad traffic cross the river before the Eads Bridge was built?
A   On special Wiggins barges called "transfer boats."

Q   Did the Eads Bridge put the Wiggins Ferry Company out of business?
A   No – the ferry company also owned the land that became rail facilities and warehouse storage sites. It also became a partner in the Terminal Railroad Association. Ferries did not stop crossing the river until just before the start of World War I.

Q   The west end of the bridge was at the foot of Washington Avenue in St. Louis. What famous spot was at the east end?
A   West Broadway on the old Bloody Island at E. St. Louis

Q   Why did Eads choose Washington Avenue as the site for his bridge?
A   It was in the middle of the wharf on the riverfront.

Q   What did Eads do to make a living before the Civil

Eads Bridge caisson for east pier (Missouri Historical Society)

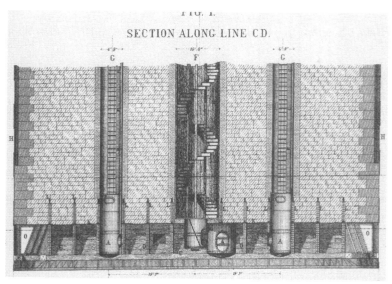

War?
A   He was in the ship salvage business – diving to the bottom of the Mississippi to reclaim cargo from wrecked ships.

Q   What was the prevailing rule of law concerning sunken ships?
A   If the ship had been at the bottom of the river five years or longer, anyone could salvage it.

Q   Was Eads ever an advisor to Abe Lincoln?
A   Yes – when the Civil War broke out, Eads was called to

Washington, D.C. to advise Lincoln on the best way to utilize western rivers for winning the war.

Q What job did Eads have during the Civil War?
A He built "alligator ironclads" at the **Mound City** facility in southern Illinois.

Q What rival group competed with Eads and his people to get the consent to build the bridge?
A The Lucius Boomer Bridge Company of Chicago

Q Where did the Boomer Company propose to build their bridge in relationship to the Eads Bridge?
A About a mile north of it close to the present site of the M.L. King Bridge

Q What hurt Eads and his Illinois and St. Louis Bridge Company's chances in this bridge rivalry?
A Eads had never before built a bridge.

Q What hurt Boomer's chances the most in the bridge rivalry?
A St. Louisans didn't trust a Chicagoan, their bitter city rival, to be looking out for their best interests.

Q What was the biggest difference between the two bridge designs?
A Boomer planned to have more piers and more spans than Eads.

Q Is the Eads Bridge mostly made of steel or wrought iron?
A Wrought iron. Steel did not come along until the 1880's.

Q How many piers in the water did Eads propose?
A Only two piers and three arched truss spans

Q What was the main criticism of Eads' design?
A Critics said the 520 foot center span was too long and, like other poorly designed bridges, it would fall in the water.

Q In 1851 Eads descended to the bottom of the Mississippi River at Cairo during the flood. How deep was the water at Cairo?
A Sixty-five feet

Eads Bridge

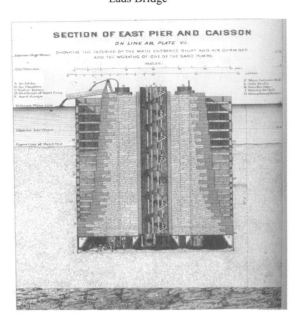

Q What famous eastern industrialist was involved with Eads in planning and financing the bridge?
A Iron and steel magnate, Andrew Carnegie

Q Eads planned to use compressed air caissons for building the piers in the water. Was this the first time they had ever been used?
A In America, yes – in France, no; caisson is a French word that translates to "diving box."

Q How was the construction work protected from floating logs, ice and other debris coming downstream?
A Wood poles/pilings were driven into the river north of the work on each side of the piers.

Q What provided a platform for the men to work on?
A Floating barges that were secured with anchor

Q Was it painful going up and down the caisson from the top of the river to the bottom?
A Yes. When visiting dignitaries were allowed to use the caissons, it was discovered that women, for some strange reason, suffered less than men from the compressed air.

Q What did workmen discover they couldn't do in compressed air at the bottom of the river?
A Whistle

Q What caused "the bends?"
A Descending below the water in a caisson that was pressurized allowed nitrogen bubbles to form in the bloodstream. Ascending too quickly didn't give the nitrogen enough time to dissipate, and this was very

Eads Bridge – elevation of one-half the center span (M. Hist. Society)

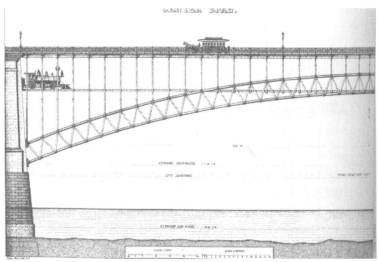

painful, sometimes causing death.

Q Not knowing the cause of the problem, what did the men resort to in an effort to ward off the disease?

A Copper bracelets that were useless but gave some peace of mind. There are people today who wear these copper bracelets to ward off arthritis or back pain and swear by

Eads Bridge: erection of west arch cables (Missouri Historical Society)

them.

Q What engineer came to observe Eads work and ended up stealing his caisson design?
A Washington Roebling for his Brooklyn Bridge

Q How many deaths occurred from decompression sickness – the bends?
A 13

Q What kind of stone was used as a facing for the limestone piers?
A Granite

Q How did Carnegie raise needed capital for the bridge project?
A He went to London and secured capital by selling bonds.

Q What weather disaster struck the construction site March 8, 1871?
A A tornado struck East St. Louis and the construction work on the east abutment. It sunk a $15,000 bridge tugboat, destroyed machinery and scaffolding, and killed several workmen.

Q What was the strength of this tornado?
A One man was killed when the storm dropped an entire house on him. A twenty-five ton locomotive was picked up and thrown to the bottom of a fifteen-foot embankment.

Q Why is there a section of ground west of Denverside near the riverfront in East St. Louis called the Ames Addition?
A Edgar Ames was on the board of directors for the Union Pacific Railroad. He guessed correctly that the bridge would be a boon to East St. Louis and invested in land there. (see map on p. 179 in this author's *Southern Illinois: An Illustrated History*)

Q Who built the approaches to the Eads Bridge?
A This work was sub-contracted to the Baltimore Bridge Company for $378,000.

Q What objection did steamboat officials make to the government after they saw the erection of the arched tube trusses?
A They complained to the corps of engineers that the clearance for river traffic was going to be too low and sought an injunction.

Q How was this problem resolved?
A President Grant intervened and ordered that all opposition should cease and work should continue on the bridge.

Q Once trains crossed the bridge going from east to west, how were they supposed to reach Union Station?
A By a tunnel that went under the streets of St. Louis. However, construction on the station had not even started at the time the bridge was completed.

Q What main problem did the tunnel present?
A The tunnel was often filled with choking smoke and cinders, nearly asphyxiating passengers.

Q What test was administered in July of 1874 to challenge the structural integrity of the bridge?
A Fourteen locomotives with loaded tenders were parked in the middle of the bridge.

Q What was used to test the structural integrity of the upper deck for wagons and pedestrians?
A A man led an elephant across. It was widely believed that **elephants had some sixth sense and would not cross a structure that was unsafe**.

Q When was the dedication and opening ceremony?

Eads Bridge – work on deck begun (Missouri Historical Society)

A July 4, 1874, with celebratory cannon bursts, a long parade, a fireworks display, a huge picture of Eads, and long winded speeches by the governors of Illinois and Missouri.

Q Was the 520-foot center arch span the longest in the world?
A Yes

Q Was the bridge completed on time and under budget?

A   No and no. It took three years longer and $6 million more than anticipated.

Q   When the bridge opened, what was the only railroad with tracks that actually connected to the bridge?
A   The St. Louis, Vandalia & Terre Haute

Eads Bridge completed (courtesy Missouri Historical Society)

Q   What was one method used by the Wiggins Ferry Company to compete successfully with the new bridge?
A   It offered customers free whiskey

Q   Why did the rail yards of about twenty-seven railroads locate in East St. Louis rather than St. Louis?
A   St. Louis was larger and had built close to the river's edge, leaving no room for rail yards. East St. Louis started on the east side of Cahokia Creek. The large level expanse of ground added by the attachment of Bloody Island was the perfect site for roundhouses, repair facilities, and storage terminals.

Q   Who was responsible for forming the St. Louis Terminal Railroad Association in 1889?
A   Railroad mogul Jay Gould. It was a combination of the terminal railroads of St. Louis and East St. Louis. This group was responsible for building Union Station in St. Louis in 1894, creating the **largest terminal system in the United States**.

Q   What did St. Louis businessmen decide to build in an effort to get around the new bridge monopoly?
A   The Merchant's Bridge for railroads only, completed in 1890 and located north of the present McKinley Bridge.

Q   What new bridge did the city of St. Louis build in 1912 in another effort to circumvent the bridge monopoly?
A   The Municipal Bridge, located slightly south of the Eads Bridge and later renamed the MacArthur Bridge

Q   What town was founded by the Niedringhouse brothers of St. Louis as a site for their metal stamping plant and as a way to circumvent the excessive bridge tolls?
A   **Granite City**

Q   What other bridges have been built at St Louis?

A   McKinley Bridge (1910), Chain of Rocks Bridge (1929), Jefferson Barracks Bridge (1944) Veterans Bridge (1951), the Poplar Street Bridge (1967), and the 270 Bridge (1965)

Q   The Eads Bridge was closed to vehicular traffic in the mid 1990's due to structural weaknesses in the eastern approach ramps. When did it reopen?
A   July of 2003

Q   Who currently owns the McArthur Bridge and the Eads Bridge?
A   The city of St. Louis gave the MacArthur Bridge to the Terminal Railroad Association and the Terminal group turned over the Eads Bridge deed to St. Louis for MetroLink electric passenger rail facility use.

FAMOUS FIRSTS OF ILLINOIS

Q   Who was the first governor of the state?
A   Shadrach Bond

Q   In what Illinois town was the first improvement made to the type of penicillin discovered by Alexander Fleming?
A   **Peoria** – Dr. Rod Bothast worked with a group that used milk sugar, corn steep liquor, and moldy cantaloupe

Q   Who was the first child born in Illinois?
A   Eulalia Pointe du Sable – daughter of Jean Baptiste du Sable and his Potawatomie Indian wife

Q   What town had the **first game preserve in the nation**?
A   **Ottawa** – established in 1868 by Judge J.D. Canton

Q   Where was the **first free and integrated school in the nation?**
A   The stone school at **Otterville**

Hamilton School at Otterville by Keith Wedoe

Q   What town had the state's first medical college?
A   **Jacksonville** – it was a part of Illinois College, but the department folded in 1848, in part, due to the **controversy of using cadavers to study anatomy**.

Q   What entomologist and naturalist from **Silver Creek**

was the first in America to advocate the study of ecology?
A Stephen Forbes 1844-1930

Q What company of Chicago introduced the nation's *first electric Mixmaster*?
A Sunbeam – 1930

Q What town had the state's first zinc smelting facility?
A **LaSalle** – 1860

Chicago Sun-Times – courtesy Charles and Kirsten Viola

Q What air base is named for the first enlisted man to be killed in an aviation accident?
A   Scott Air Base near **Belleville/O'Fallon,** named for Corporal Frank S. Scott

Q   Where was the **nation's first "planned" industrial town**?
A   Chicago – at George Pullman's model town for employees at his sleeping car factory

Q   Where was the **first planetarium in America**?
A   Chicago's Adler Planetarium, built for the Century of Progress Fair in 1933

Q   What town council passed Illinois' first zoning ordinance?
A   **Evanston** - 1921

Q   What is the Illinois connection of John Law, the man who talked the King of France into printing **the world's first paper money**?
A   Law convinced the French to print the money to finance a huge development plan in Upper Louisiana (Illinois). It was a grand scheme about trade, settlers, and mining, based on the assumption that gold and silver were in Illinois country since lead had been found at **Galena**. This speculative scheme was known as the "**Mississippi Bubble.**"

Q   When were the **first slaves** brought to Illinois?
A   They arrived at **Prairie du Rocher** around 1720 to work the gold and silver mines – part of John Law's scheme to develop Illinois. When little gold or silver was found, the slaves were sold to French inhabitants.

Q Who founded the **nation's first professional women's softball league**?
A Cub owner P.K. Wrigley. This is depicted in the Tom Hanks/Geena Davis film, *A League of Their Own.*

Q What town was home to Richard Rhoades, the man who patented the first hearing aid in 1879?
A **River Park**

Q Where was the first regular mail service in Illinois?
A   Fort Dearborn at Chicago in 1803. Mail was brought on foot once a month from Fort Wayne, Indiana. Mail service from Vincennes to **Cahokia** was established in 1805. Mail service from Vincennes to **Shawneetown** came along in 1806.

Q   What book is generally considered to be America's **first best-seller poetry volume**?
A   *Spoon River Anthology* by Edgar Lee Masters

Q What Illinois town had the **first 18-hole golf course in America**?
A **Wheaton** - 1893

Q Where was America's first automobile race?
A It was held in 1895, and it went from Jackson Park in Chicago to **Evanston**. The winning car averaged about 6.7 miles per hour.

Q Where did Henry Ford get the idea for making automobiles by using the world's first assembly line?
A By observing the overhead trolley system used by meat packers at Chicago's Union Stock Yards

Q Where was America's first "automobile row" – a string

Drake Hotel, courtesy Kirsten and Charles Viola

of buildings that were custom made to showcase and market cars?
A   Chicago's "Motor Row" was located on South Michigan Avenue between 14th and 24th streets. Many of the buildings are still there.

Q   When did Illinois become the **first state east of the Mississippi River to give women the right to vote in state and presidential elections**?
A   1913 – it became known as the "Illinois Law" and quickly became the model for other states.

Q   What was the first prison newspaper in America to be published on a regular basis?
A   The *Menard Time* at **Chester**, a prison that was built in 1877 by 200 other prisoners from **Joliet**

Q   What was the **first streamlined passenger train in America**?
A   The Illinois Central's "art moderne" *Green Diamond* – 1936

Admiral Richard Byrd's polar ship on display at Chicago Fair

Q   Who was the first person to fly under the Eads Bridge at **East St. Louis**?
A   Thomas Baldwin, a daredevil aviator from **Quincy** in 1910.

Q   What Chicago physicist conducted the "countdown" for the **world's first nuclear explosion** at Alamogordo, New Mexico in April of 1945?
A   Sam Allison – who later received a Medal of Merit from President Truman

Q   Near what Illinois town was the **first coal in America** discovered by Joliet and Marquette?
A   **Utica** -1673

Q   What town had the first bank in Illinois?
A   **Shawneetown** – the financial capital of the state

Q   What town had the first steam-operated mill in Illinois?
A   **Belleville** – on South High Street, owned by Thomas Harrison - 1831

Q   What Illinois town had the **nation's first junior college**?
A   **Joliet** – in 1901

Q   When and where was the nation's first aeronautical air show?

A   It was held at Chicago in 1910, organized by Harold McCormick.

Q   What and where was the nation's **first commercial aviation disaster**?
A   It happened in 1919 at Chicago when the Goodyear blimp *Wingfoot Express* caught fire and crashed through the roof of a bank in the Loop, killing thirteen.

Q   Where was the **world's first juvenile court**?
A   Cook County - 1889

Q   What **Springfield** incident was responsible for the first national organization to look after the interests of African-Americans?
A   The NAACP was formed directly as a result of the 1908 **Springfield** race riot.

Q   Who were the first baseball players banned for life from the game?
A   Eight members of the Chicago White Sox who conspired to "throw" the 1919 World Series

Q   What facility was responsible for producing the world's first nuclear powered generator?
A   The Argonne National Laboratory at **Lamont** in 1951

Q   What was the nation's first skyscraper?
A   William L. Jenney designed Chicago's Home Insurance Co., **the first skyscraper in the world in 1884**. It was torn down in 1931. A cast iron frame was used and walls were simply "hung" on the frame. This is still the basis of modern skyscrapers, although steel has replaced iron. Some earlier tall structures, like the Monadnock Building, had to be raised on stones that were six feet thick.

Q   When was the **nation's first forensic crime lab** established at Northwestern University?
A   Not long after the St. Valentine's Day Massacre in 1929

Q   When did the first wagon shipment of lead ore from

Chicago's famous Green Mill (courtesy Charles and Kirsten Viola)

Galena arrive in Chicago?
A   1829 – a trip that took 11 days

Q   When did Illinois become the **first state to establish an environmental protection agency**?
A   1970 under Governor Richard Ogilvie

Station WGN in Chicago (courtesy Charles and Kirsten Viola)

Q   Where and when was the **nation's first Rotary Club founded**?
A   Rotary International was founded in Chicago in 1905. In 1955 the U.S. government issued an 8-cent stamp commemorating the organization.

Q   What graduate of Northwestern University was the first to call television a "vast wasteland?"
A   Newton Minnow

Q   What was the first church building erected in America by Swedish Lutheran immigrants?
A   The Jenny Lind Chapel at **Andover** – 1854

Illinois Central's "Green Diamond" –world's first streamlined train

Q   What was the **first university in the nation to hold homecoming** for its alumni?
A   University of Illinois

Q   What was the **first university in the nation to publish a student newspaper**?

A   University of Illinois

Q   What was the **first university in the nation where fans began the practice of "tailgating"** at football games?
A   University of Illinois

Q   What was the **first U.S. bridge depicted on a postage stamp**?
A   The Eads Bridge at **East St. Louis** in an 1898 Trans-Mississippi issue

Q   Who was the first gangster to be depicted on the "Man Of The Year" Time Magazine cover?
A   Al Capone in 1930

Q   What Illinois town had the state's first Jaycees?
A   **East St. Louis** holds that distinction; their group was the second oldest in the nation, started in 1920.

Q   Where was the state's first radio station?
A   Station WDZ of **Tuscola/Decatur** in 1921

Q   Who was the first native-born Illinoisan to win the Nobel prize?
A   Robert Millikan in 1923

Q   Who was pro football's first $100,000 a year football player?
A   Harold Red Grange of the Chicago Bears, 1925

Q   What Illinois governor became the **first foreign-born governor elected in any state in the union**?
A   German-born Peter Altgeld 1892

Q   When and where was the **first aerial bombing attack ever carried out on American soil**?
A   It happened at **Marion** in 1926. The Shelton brothers rented a Curtiss "Jenny" to fly over rival gangster Charlie Birger's hangout at Shady Rest. Several nitro/dynamite bombs were tossed, but they all missed their targets, killing only Birger's pet eagle and dog.

Q   Who was the first black woman to have a play produced on Broadway?
A   Lorraine Hansbury of Chicago - *A Raisin in the Sun*

Q   What Illinoisan was the first to be inducted into the Railroad Hall of Fame?
A   It was Illinois Central engineer Casey Jones of **Centralia**

ILLINOIS MOST CALAMITOUS

Q   How many major race riots have there been in Illinois?
A   Three – **Springfield** in 1808, **East St. Louis** during World War I, and Chicago in 1919.

Q   Which of the three riots was the most disastrous?
A   The **East St. Louis** riot set the **national record** for African-American lives lost in a riot – thirty-nine.

Q   What outlaw and counterfeiter, whose farm was about six miles from the town of **Morrison**, plotted with his gang to steal the body of Abe Lincoln?
A   Ben Boyd

Q   What northeastern Illinois town made the national media due to severe flooding from heavy rains May 25, 2004?
A   **Gurnee**

Q   What was the most famous murder in **Mt. Pulaski** history?
The brutal slaying of farmer Charles McMahon and his two farmhands in 1882

Q   What criminal, who became known as the **Birdman of Alcatraz**, is buried at **Metropolis**?
A   Robert Stroud

Q   What **Mendota** schoolteacher was responsible for the murder of 180 civilians in his "sack of Lawrence" during the Civil War?
A   William Quantrill

Q   What town was home to Elizabeth Reed, the **only woman hanged** in the state of Illinois?
A   **Lawrenceville** – she poisoned her husband

Q   What did Illinois judges of old frequently do to remind convicted felons of their crime?
A   They ordered that on each anniversary of their foul deed they were to be placed in solitary confinement to ponder their actions.

Q   Where and when did Illinois' worst earthquake occur?
A   It happened in southern Illinois near the New Madrid Fault in 1811. It was stronger than the famed San Francisco quake, but there was little loss of life because the area was largely unsettled.

Q   When and where was the most deadly tornado in Illinois

Long John Wentworth raids "The Sands" in Chicago

history?

A   Southern Illinois in 1925. It went across the entire southern part of the state and claimed over 1,000 lives.

Q   What was significant about the May 26, 1917 tornado

Chicago's Pinkerton Detective Agency "We Never Sleep"

that hit Illinois?
A   It was one of the state's ten deadliest, killing 101 people.

Q   What was the most deadly tornado to hit **East St. Louis**?
A   The 1896 tornado came across the Mississippi River and claimed about 113 lives.

Cartoon: "Frontier Illinois is the graveyard of the West"

Q   What state has the most tornadoes?
A   Texas, largely due to its size, but Illinois cyclones rank second and ours are the **deadliest in the nation**. In the Midwest the weather does the 136 things Mark Twain gave it credit for.

Q   Was Ted Kazynski from Illinois or Wisconsin?
A   Theodore Kazynski, better known as the *Unibomber*, attended **Evergreen Park High School** in South Chicago.

Q   How many lives were lost when a great ice sheet covered most of Illinois about 15,000 years ago?
A   Sorry, we don't know the answer to that because it was in the Pleistocene Era, and no one kept records.

Q Besides making travel faster, what was another main reason for decertifying Route 66 and building Interstate 55?
A Many people got planted because Route 66 was narrow, winding, and dotted with dozens and dozens of deadly concrete bridge abutments.

Q In early Illinois pioneer days (1790-1825), what percent of the settlers were killed due to Indian warfare?
A Estimates usually fall around the ten percent category.

Killers of Bobby Franks, Richard Loeb and Nathan Leopold

Q What was the worst Mississippi flood in recorded Illinois history?
A It was the most recent one in 1993. Damages were in the millions. The entire town of **Valmeyer** was washed downstream and it relocated on top of the bluffs overlooking the floodplain.

Q What was the most destructive fire in Illinois history?
A The one allegedly started by Mrs. O'Leary's cow in 1871.

Q What calamitous Chicago event determined the outcome of a mayoral race?
A Democrat Jane Byrne was elected mayor after there was a big snowfall; she blamed traffic snarls on inept incumbent leadership.

Q What happened to the **Chester** Bridge over the Mississippi River in 1944?
A A 640 foot span fell into the river during high winds that some thought to be a tornado.

General Santa Anna's captured wooden leg

Q How many incumbent Chicago mayors have been assassinated?
A Two. Carter Harrison was assassinated during the Columbian Exposition, and Anton Cermak was killed in Miami by a bullet thought to be meant for President-elect Franklin Delano Roosevelt.

Q In the 1909 **Cherry Mine disaster** only about half of the 480 men in the mine were saved before officials sealed it to contain the fire. Did anyone survive when the shaft was unsealed a week later?
A Yes – miraculously 20 men emerged alive from the once raging inferno. Read all about it in the 2002 book *Trapped* by Karen Tinton

Q How did President Ronald Reagan (of **Tampico** and **Dixon**) beat the curse placed on the presidency by Tecumseh and his brother, Tenskwatawa - The Prophet?
A Before The Prophet was killed at the battle of Tippecanoe, he placed a curse on the Great White Father before he died. Starting with Harrison in 1840, every President elected in a year ending in zero died in office. The curse struck down Harrison (the victor at Tippecanoe), Lincoln, Garfield, McKinley, Harding, Roosevelt, and Kennedy. Reagan was elected in 1980 and narrowly survived John Hinckley's bullet.

Q According to legend, what monster was terrorizing the Native-Americans that lived in the **Alton** area before the arrival of the white man?   (see picture below)
A The dreaded **Piasa monster**, which translated means "creature that devours man." The beast was said to have lived in a cave and feasted on locals, swooping down and carrying them away to be devoured in its lair. Finally, the brave young chief of the Illini, Ouatoga, took twenty armed warriors with him and stood brazenly on a rock to defy the monster. The evil one swooped down to kill its intended victim and, at the last second, the hidden warriors emerged and killed the creature with their poisoned arrows.
The original petroglyph of this beast was considered the most significant Indian painting of its kind in America.

Q Where exactly was the original (30-foot long by 12-foot high) painting of the Piasa monster?
A On a limestone bluff at **Alton**, near the site of the state prison. It was quarried for railroad ballast by convicts in 1856. The Native-Americans who painted the petroglyph used three colors – black (representing death), red (emblematic of war and vengeance) and green (expressive of hope and triumph over death). It was replicated in recent years as a Boy Scout project.

Chief Ouatoga awaits the evil Piasa monster

Q What northern Illinois town was hit by a tornado in late April of 2004, killing eight people?
A **Utica**

Q How many men were killed in March of 1947 in an explosion at

Mine No. 5 near **Centralia**?
A 111

Q What two men are considered the **nation's first serial killers**?
A The Harpe brothers at **Cave-in-Rock**

Q What mass murderer is thought to have killed dozens of women during the 1893 Columbian Exposition in Chicago?
A Herman Mudgett

Female Prison at Joliet 1896

Q What Chicago mass murderer was known to have the tattoo that read "born to raise hell?"
A Richard Speck - 1966

Q What **DesPlaines** mass murderer was put to death in 1994 by lethal injection?
A John Wayne Gacy – who killed more than 30 young men back in 1980

Chicago race riot of 1919 (Chicago Historical Society)

Q How many people were killed at O'Hare Airport in 1979 when an engine fell off a DC-10 airplane?
A 275

Q What prominent **Eldorado** doctor committed suicide after being convicted of killing his son?
A Dale Cavaness – 1986

Q What caused the Great Chicago Flood in April of 1992?
A The Great Lakes Dredge and Dock Company punched a hole in the bed of the Chicago River driving pilings. The estimated damage was a billion dollars.

Q What 1991 graduate of Wheaton College had the student union building named in his honor for his actions during 9-11-01?
A Todd Beemer led the passenger revolt on flight 93 over Pennsylvania that probably saved the White House from a terrorist attack.

ILLINOIS TASTE BUDS

Q What did the Illinois Indians do with the acorn from the white oak?
A They ground it up, bleached it, and ate it.

Q Where did Illinois Indian corn originally come from?
A Mexico or Central America – called maize

Q When was the snack food known as Cracker Jack invented?
A This confection first made its appearance at the Chicago Columbian Exposition of 1893.

Q In what year did Cracker Jack start placing toy prizes inside its boxes?
A 1912

Q If you order a Chicago sundae, what kind of fruit will it have on it?
A Pineapple

Q What Chicago company is the **largest cracker and cookie maker in the world**?
A Nabisco – they make over six billion Oreo cookies a year.

Q What **Peru**, Illinois, man moved to Chicago, became a candy maker, and **invented the confection known as caramel**?
A Charles Gunther – who was also a collector of rare books and manuscripts which his family sold to the Chicago Historical Society

Q Did Louis Rich start his meat product company in Iowa or Illinois?
A Chicago, Illinois

Q In what town did the nation's **first Dairy Queen** open back in 1938?
A **Kankakee** – but it was called Sherb's, operated by Sherb Noble. The first *store* with the name Dairy Queen opened in **Joliet**.

246

Q   What was the first candy bar in Illinois?
A   The Tango Bar, it was made in Chicago around 1904.

Pizzeria Uno in Chicago, courtesy Charles and Kirsten Viola

Q   What town is home to the Keebler Company that uses those cute little elves to make cookies?
A   **Elmhurst**

Q   What was the first brand of chewing gum made by P.K. Wrigley of Chicago in 1893?
A   Juicy Fruit – back in the 1950's there were machines that sold gum a stick at a time for a penny.

Q   What Illinois town has a Choo Choo Restaurant where meals are delivered by toy trains?
A   **DesPlaines**

Q   What northern Illinois town is home to Sarah Lee Bakery?
A   **Deerfield**

Q   In what Illinois town was Miracle Whip salad dressing invented?
A   **Salem's** Max Crosset concocted the recipe for his restaurant. Kraft Food of Chicago bought the recipe in 1931.

Q   What family invented the corn dog?
A   Originally called the "Crusty Cur," the Waldmire family of **Springfield** came up with this one. It is also known as the "cozy dog."

Quaker Oats

Q   What Illinois food has the slogan, "Nothing is better for thee than me?"
A   Quaker Oats

Q   Where was the foot-long hot dog invented?
A   At Chicago's Riverview

Amusement Park

Q   Where was the first MacDonald's franchise in Illinois?

A   **Des Plaines** - Ray Croc bought the company from the McDonald brothers in California.

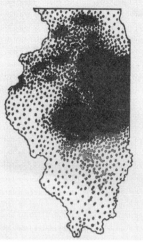
Where Illinois corn grows

Q   Why did the early MacDonald restaurants fail to become teen hangouts?
A   Kroc refused to install jukeboxes or pay phones.

Q   In what year did MacDonald's first reach the goal of selling a million hamburgers a day?
A   1963 – the Big Mac was invented in 1967 by a franchise owner.

Q   In what Illinois town was the idea for Krispi Kreme donuts first mulled over?
A   In 1937 **Peoria**, Vernon Randolph and his friends had just purchased some doughnut making equipment and were standing around trying to decide where to set up the business. He lit up a Camel, noticed it was made in Winston-Salem, North Carolina, and moved his business there.

Q   How did deep pan pizza come to be invented in Chicago?
A   Deep-pan pizza was first made by Ric Riccardo and Ike Sewell and served up at Pizzeria Uno on East Ohio in Chicago. Up until then (1945), pizza served in Chicago's Little Italy was thin crusted and thought of as an appetizer.

Dairy Queen

Thus was born **Chicago-style pizza**.

Q   Who invented the snack food known as Twinkies?
A   Twinkies were concocted by James Dewar of the Continental Baking Company in **Schiller Park.**

Q   Where and when was Kool-Aid invented?
A   In 1930 Edwin Persins, a Nebraskan, built a plant in Chicago to produce Flavor Smack, which later became

known as Kool-Aid. The company was acquired by General Foods in 1953.

Q Are tomatoes one of the ingredients on a Chicago-style hot dog?
A Yes – plus mustard, relish, onions, and a pickle wedge on a poppy seed bun

Dying the Chicago River green, courtesy Charles and Kirsten Viola

Q In what Illinois city was the ice cream sundae invented?
A **Evanston**

Q What town has a Carnation plant that produces "Coffee-mate" a non-dairy cream for coffee?
A **Jacksonville**

Q What big Chicago cheese company bought out Philadelphia Cream Cheese in 1927?
A Kraft Food

Q What happened in 1977 to Mrs. Helen Brach, whose late husband was president of Chicago's **Brach Candy Company**?
A She disappeared while on her way home from a trip to Minnesota.

Q What Illinois town calls itself the Popcorn Capital of America?
A **Ridgway**

Q What Illinois town claims the first Steak 'n' Shake restaurant?
A **Normal** is home to the original **Steak n' Shake** restaurant that first opened in 1934. "In sight, it must be right," was one of their early slogans; the black and white colors were chosen because it was believed this combination would show off the restaurant's cleanliness.

Q What Illinoisan invented the popcorn machine in 1893?
A Charles Cretors

Steak and Shake in Normal by Dan Oberle

Q In what Illinois town did **Paul Beich** establish a candy business?
A **Bloomington** - on East Front Street. His business grew to become one of the best-known candy companies in America.

Q In what town was Morton Salt Company founded?
A Morton Salt Company was founded at Chicago in 1848 and quickly became the *largest domestic producer of that commodity*.

Q Are Milk Duds, Tootsie Rolls and Jelly Belly candies all made in Illinois?
A Yes

Collinsville's Brooks tangy catsup

Q For whom did the Curtiss Candy Company of Chicago name its Baby Ruth candy bar in 1920?
A President Cleveland's daughter. Most people think it was named for the Yankee baseball slugger.

Q Did the Chicago Curtiss Candy Company sell penny size Baby Ruth and Butterfinger candy bars during the Depression?
A Yes – it was all people could afford.

Q What popular candy bar did the Mars Company of Chicago come out with in 1929?

Luna Café in Mitchell, Illinois, by Dan Oberle

A Snickers – the most popular candy bar in America (also this author's favorite)

Q What was the most popular candy bar produced by Chicagoland's Shutter-Jonhson in 1929?
A Bit-O-Honey

248

Q What was the most popular candy bar produced by Chicagoland's Williamson Candy Company in 1929?
A Oh Henry!

Q What was the most interesting candy put out by the Ferrara Pan Candy Company of Chicago?
A Boxes of little sugar-coated pellets called Boston Baked Beans

Q What city in America has long led the nation in the production of candy bars?
A Duh! – Chicago

Q What northeastern Illinois city is home to Pepperidge Farm bakery company?
A **Downers Grove**

Q In the 1960's what town had the Hollywood Candy Company that made Zero and Smooth Sailing candy bars?
A **Centralia**

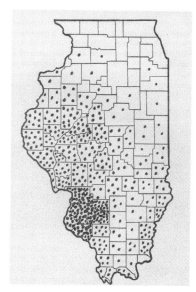

Where Illinois wheat is grown

Q What Illinois town is the home to the company that makes Chuckles candy?
A **Danville**

Q What Illinois town is home to Peter Pan peanut butter?
A **Downers Grove**

Q What Illinois towns are home to Quaker Oats?
A **Danville and Chicago**

ILLINOIS INVENTORS

Q Who had the most popular ride at Chicago's Columbian Exposition?
A George Ferris, inventor of the Ferris Wheel

Q What **DeKalb** resident invented barbed wire?
A Joseph Glidden - barbed wire was called "the devil's rope."

Q What **DeKalb** man invented the S–type barbed wire

Jacob Haish - barbed wire rival of Joseph Glidden

and was a huge competitor of Joe Glidden?
A Jacob Haish – see picture above

Q What Illinoisan invented a device to make passengers more comfortable on long distance train trips?
A George Pullman invented the Pullman sleeper car.

Q What University of Chicago scientist/pathologist has a disease named for him?
A Howard Taylor Ricketts – ricketts is a bone disease caused by lack of vitamin D

Q What man from **Winchester** invented numerous surgical tools and is called the **Father of Modern Dentistry**?
A Greene V. Black

Q What man from **Wheaton** invented the radio wave telescope?
A Grote Reber

Q What Illinoisan invented celluloid?
A John Hyatt, a native of **Kankakee**

Q What man, who once lived in **Carlyle,** invented a long-barreled Colt revolver that became a favorite for lawman **Wyatt Earp?**
A Ned Buntline, who once edited a newspaper in **Carlyle.** The gun was called the Buntline Special.

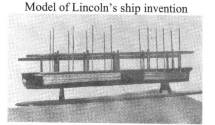

Model of Lincoln's ship invention

Q Who was the inventor of the steel plow?
A John Deere of **Grand Detour**

Q What aid to navigation was invented by a young Abe Lincoln?
A A device that enabled boats to navigate shallow waters such as the Sangamon River – see picture above

Q Who is considered the "Father of the Dime Novel?"
A **Carlyle's** Ned Buntline first popularized the Wild West with his pulp fiction stories.

Q The European Jethro Tull invented the seed drill. Who made an improved version in 1858?
A Phillip Gundlach of **Belleville**

Q Who "invented" the nation's first mail order catalog?
A Aaron Montgomery Ward in 1872

Q What Illinoisan invented the grain silo?
A **Spring Grove** farmer Fred Hatch in 1873

Q Who invented the world's first glass ashtray?
A William Smith of the **Alton** Glass Works in 1873

Q What American was the first to use caissons for working on bridge piers below the surface of a river?
A Captain James B. Eads, the man who completed the

Eads Bridge at East St. Louis in 1874

Q   Who invented the Wienermobile?
A   The Oscar Meyer company of Chicago

Q   Who invented the Mickey Finn?
A   There actually was a Chicago saloonkeeper by that name who concocted a drink with knockout drops.

Q   Who invented an envelope with an address window?
A   A.F. Callahan of Chicago in 1902

Q   Who invented shoe inserts for people with fallen arches and bunions?
A   William Scholl of Chicago in 1904

Q   What company invented the pinball machine?
A   It was invented at Chicago in 1930 by the In And Outdoor Games Company.

Q   What inventor of shorthand, long taught in public schools, founded a secretarial school in Chicago to teach his method?
A   John Robert Gregg

Q   Who invented the children's toy known as Lincoln Logs?
A   J.L. Wright, the son of Chicago architect Frank Lloyd Wright - 1916

Q   Who invented Tinker Toys?
A   Charles Pajeau of **Evanston**, a stone mason by trade,

Drug store innovator Charles Walgreen

got an idea from watching children play with empty spools of thread. In 1914 he marketed a toy with wooden pieces that children could tinker with and invented an American classic.

Q   What **Waukegan** man invented the "magniscope," the world's first practical motion picture projector?
A   Edward Amet (1894) – Edison's Kinetoscope was a peep show-type projector for only one person; Amet made films in his back yard with local actors and showed them on a screen at George Spoor's Phoenix Opera House; Amet sold his interest in the machine for $10,000 thinking that public interest in motion pictures had run its course.

Q   What **Mount Prospect** resident invented the Weber Grill?
A   George Stevens, who originally called it George's Bar-B-Q Kettle

Q   What man's research at Riverbank Labs in **Geneva** led to the development of the **electronic hearing aid**?
A   Paul Sabine
Q   At what university did the world's first nuclear chain reaction take place in 1942?
A   Chicago University under the Stagg Field football stands at a squash court

Q   What two Chicago scientists conceived the idea of using an atomic pile with graphite rods to control a nuclear reaction?

Inventor James Semple

A   Italian Enrico Fermi and Hungarian Leo Szilard

Q   Why did Fermi come to America?
A   To escape Mussolini's Fascist government

Q   Who invented a steam engine that would travel without rails across the prairie?
A   James Semple of **Alton/Elsah**. He fitted an old steam engine of the Northern Cross Railroad with wide wheels. People laughed and called it "Semple's Folly." The land schooner broke down near **Carlinville** on its way to **Springfield** in 1847. Semple left it there and gave up on the idea.

Q   What inventor and **Alton** native advocated the construction of the Panama Canal in 1845?
A   Senator James Semple

Q   What **Peoria** inventor built the world's first "real" automobile?
A   Charles Duryea, who was born in **Canton**, Illinois, in 1895. His car had pneumatic tires, a steering tiller, a

Earl Prince's Multimixer

gasoline engine, and a gear shift mechanism with three speeds forward and a reverse.

Q   What **De-Kalb** resident invented the six spindle Multimixer used at soda fountains for making malted milks?
A   Earl Prince (in 1930), who was born at **Downers Grove**

Q   What inventor, born in **Mendota**, who worked at the **Peru** Plow Company and later the **Moline** Plow Company, invented metal wheels and gears for farm implements that were named for him?
A   William Bettendorf

Illinois Glassworks at Alton where the glass ashtray was invented

Q   Why did Bettendorf establish the town of **Gilbert**?
A   It was his company town for workers at a farm implement factory he built there. The name was later changed to Bettendorf, Iowa.

Q   What was Abe Lincoln talking about when he said "the system has added the fuel of interest to the fire of genius?"
A   The U.S. Patent Office that protects those who come up with inventions

Q   What **Bloomington** man invented the black and white safety gate that comes down and blocks traffic at railroad crossings?
A   Harry Sampson of the **Alton Railroad** who was born in **Gardner.** He secured a patent in 1936.

Q   What **Rock Island** man invented the toboggan ride?
A   J.P. Newberg – the one at Rock Island in 1890 was called "Shoot the Chutes." It was a 300-foot long greased wooden slide and flat-bottomed boats slid down the track and skimmed out over the water at the bottom.

Q   What **Moline** man invented the self-starter for automobiles?
A   Vincent Bendix – his company also sponsored transcontinental air races and awarded the Bendix Trophy

Q   What resident of **Morrison,** in Whiteside County, invented the time lock for banks?
A   James Sargent

Q   What invention was designed by Lee Hobart and manufactured by Earl Roof of **Pontiac**?
A   A weed mowing machine composed of bicycle wheels, a gas engine, a belt, one blade, and a housing unit. This eliminated cutting weeds by hand with a scythe.

Q   What graduate of **Crane Technical High** in Chicago made improvements on the wire recorder and secured a

number of patents for the nation's first tape recorder around 1946?
A   Marvin Camras, a graduate of the Illinois Technical Institute and an employee of Armour Research Foundation

Q   What Illinoisan invented the mechanical grain reaper?
A   Cyrus McCormick

FAMOUS ILLINOIS WOMEN

Q   Who was once called "the most dangerous woman in America" by industrialists?
A   Mother Mary Jones, a union organizer – Gene Autry paid her tribute with a 1952 song, "The Death of Mother Jones."
She is buried at **Mount Olive.**

Q   What **Joliet** native became "Miss America" in 1927?
A   Lois Delaner

Blondie by Chic Young

Q   Who made the first statue of Abe Lincoln?
A   Miss Vinnie Ream – it now stands in the Rotunda of the National Capitol.

Q   What **Waukegan** reared actress starred in a 2003 movie with Harrison Ford and Josh Hartnett?
A   Lolita Davidovich – *Hollywood Homicide*

Q   Who was the first woman novelist in Illinois?
A   Sarah Marshall of **Shawneetown** who wrote *Early Engagements* in 1841

Lolita Davidovich

The Feminine Mystique in 1963?
A   Betty Goldstein Friedan

Q   Who was the first woman to be appointed by a governor to his cabinet?
A   Vera M. Binks of **Kewanee**, appointed by William G. Stratton in 1953; she oversaw the Department of Registration and Education.

Q   What **Peoria** woman launched the feminist movement in America by writing

Q What was meant by the title of her book?

A She called it the *innate siren call* that led women to give up their identity by marrying, becoming a housewife and raising children – "Women of the world unite; you have nothing to lose but your vacuum cleaners."

Q What **Carlinville** woman wrote novels and essays about Native-American culture in the Southwest?

A Mary Hunter Austin

Q What **Mendota**-born woman became a famous cartoonist for the *New Yorker*?

A Helen Hockinson

Q What product has Illinoisan Joan Cusack been pushing recently on television commercials?

A Direct TV – satellite television; Joan also starred in *Runaway Bride, Nine Months, Class, Arlington Road and Grosse Pointe Blank*

Q What woman donated money for the founding of Bradley University?

A The widow Lydia Moss Bradley of **Peoria**

Mary Astor, star of *The Maltese Falcon*

Q Who helped Jane Addams found Chicago's Hull House in 1889 to help immigrants?

A Ellen G. Starr

Q What Chicago woman sang at JFK's inauguration and Martin Luther King Jr.'s funeral?

A Mahalia Jackson

Q What Chicago woman was a high school cub reporter with the *Tribune* and due to a twist of fate was one of the first people on the scene after the St. Valentine's Day Massacre?

A **Virginia Graham** – she would later be one of the founders of the Cerebral Palsy Foundation.

Heroine Annie Keller Memorial

Q Did Chicagoan Virginia Graham ever have her own radio show?

A Yes – the "Virginia Graham Show" in the early 1950's

Q When the Mormons left Nauvoo in

1846 and headed for Utah, why did Joseph Smith's first wife and widow stay behind?

A She disliked polygamy and later married a non-Mormon.

Q Who became the first woman elected to the Illinois Senate (1924)?

A Florence Fifer Boher, daughter of governor Joseph Fifer

Jane Addams – 1902

Q What woman's testimony before the General Assembly in **Springfield** led to the construction of a state mental hospital at **Jacksonville**?

A Famed reformer Dorothea Dix – 1847

Q What was Dorothea Dix's main criticism of the prison at Alton?

A It had dirt floors that could not be washed.

Q Why is there a statue of Annie Keller at **White Hall** in Greene County? (picture below)

A Her brave actions saved the lives of many school children during a 1927 tornado. While protecting the children, she was killed by a door that was ripped from its hinges. Lorado Taft did the monument honoring her using pink marble. (see picture below)

Q What **St. Charles** woman is the author of *Misty*, a story about a horse?

A Marguerite Henry

Q What Alton woman was responsible for the founding of the **Alton** Little Theater Showplace

A Alton High English teacher Dorothy Colonius

Q What young woman from **Belvidere** disguised herself as a man and fought in the Civil War?

A Jenny Hodgers – her hoax was not discovered until 1911 – **the national record.**

Q What **Mendota** native was a popular cartoonist for the New Yorker Magazine?

A Helen Hokinson

Q What **Alton** woman is given credit for **singlehandedly defeating the ERA amendment** to the U.S. Constitution?

A Conservative spokesperson Phyllis Schlafly

Q What woman was responsible for lobbying the Illinois legislature into adopting a state flag?

A Mrs. Ella Park Lawrence of the DAR – the flag was adopted in 1915.

Q What famous dancer from **Oak Park** was closely associated with choreographer Martha Graham?

A Doris Humphrey

Q Who was the first woman elected to the Illinois General Assembly?
A Lottie Holman O'Neill. She was first elected in 1922 and she held that position for 38 years.

Q In 1892 what Chicago woman became the first female admitted to the Illinois Bar?
A Myra Bradwell, who passed the test in 1871 but was refused admission because she was female. Instead she became the publisher of *Legal News*

Frances Willard of the WCTU

Q Who was the first woman in the nation to become president of a major university?
A Hannah Gray – University of Chicago, 1978

Q What Chicagoan is an Olympic medalist and world famous figure skater?
A Dorothy Hamill – she now does Vioxx TV commercials

Q What **Urbana**-born actress played Kelly Taylor on the television series "Beverly Hills 90210?"
A Jenny Garth

Q What woman became the first to be appointed to the Illinois supreme court in 1992?
A Mary Ann McMorrow

Q What **Peoria** native founded NOW, the National Organization For Women?
A Betty Friedan

Q What **Morrison** woman was an associate of suffragette Carrie Catt and helped establish the League of Women Voters after helping secure ratification of the 19th Amendment?
A Gertrude Foster Brown

Q What **Evanston** actress had featured roles in *Freaky Friday, Family Plot, Nashville,* and *Plaza Suite*?
A Barbara Harris

Q What **Rockford** native has appeared in a number of television shows including "Roseanne," "Dallas," and "Knots Landing?"
A Andrea Walters

Q What young Illinois girl co-starred with Macaulay Culkin in the movie *My Girl*?
A Anna Chlumsky

Q What **DeKalb** actress is best known for her role as Perry Mason's "Girl Friday?"
A Barbara Hale was Della Street

Q What founder of the American Red Cross converted a building on West Main into a hospital after a tornado struck **Mt. Vernon** in 1888?
A Clara Barton

Q What **Jacksonville**-born woman was a founder of the DAR – Daughters of the American Revolution?
A Ellen Hardin Walworth – 1912

Q What **Jacksonville** native became America's first woman ambassador to a foreign country?
A Ruth Bryan Owens, daughter of William Jennings Bryan, became ambassador to Denmark in 1933.

Q What distinction was achieved by Chicagoan Ella Flagg Young in 1909?
A She became the first woman in the nation to become superintendent of schools in a large city.

Q What woman, who attended Catholic University, authored *Mary, Mary* and *Please Don't Eat The Daisies*?
A Jean Kerr

Q What woman's social activism led to an 1892 Illinois law limiting women's working hours and prohibiting child labor?
A Florence Kelley

Q What fashion debate was sparked in 1889 by Mrs. Marshall Field?
A A huge debate occurred when the question of appropriate female attire for attending the Chicago Opera arose. A new fashion coming into vogue was the low-necked dress known as the décolleté gown. Mrs. Marshall Field expressed a preference for the high neck dress, similar to those worn by European actress Sarah Bernhardt. Mrs. Reginald De Koven, wife of the composer who wrote, "O Promise Me," pooh-poohed rumors that wearing such revealing dresses was unhealthy and would lead to pneumonia.

Q What famous female sharpshooter entertained people at the 1893 World's Fair in Chicago?
A Annie Oakley – Little Sure Shot – who performed with Buffalo Bill Cody's Wild West Show

Q What wife of Paul Douglas was elected to the seventy-ninth congress and wrote a biography of Margret Sanger (founder of Planned Parenthood)?
A Emily Taft Douglas, who was defeated for a second term by Republican William G. Stratton in 1946.

Q What former Queen of Hawaii visited Chicago in 1897?
A Liliuokalani

Q What famous posh Chicago brothel was run by a couple of sisters whose father was a judge in Kentucky?

253

A   The Everleigh Club – run by the Everleigh sisters

Q   What woman became a big star with the New York Metropolitan Opera and in 1957 portrayed the ill-fated Carmen in the Bizet opera?
A   Jean Browning Madeira, who was born in **Centralia** but grew up in **East St. Louis**.

Q   What famous 1920's dancer founded a dog and cat facility near **Deerfield** called Orphans of the Storm?
A   Irene Castle McLaughlin

Q   What **Rockford** native and friend of Jane Addams was appointed by President Taft to be the first head of the U.S. Children's Bureau?
A   Julia Lathrop

Writer Edna Ferber (1885-1968)

Q   What Chicago woman made her literary debut with "Columbian Ode," a tribute to Columbus?
A   Harriet Monroe who helped launch the Chicago Renaissance

Q   What woman founded **Mount Carroll** Seminary as a co-educational facility in 1856?
A   Frances A. Wood

Q   What woman from **Freeport** wrote a Hollywood gossip column and was noted for her stylish hats?
A   Hedda Hopper

Q   What Chicago-born platinum blonde actress starred in *Picnic* and *Pal Joey*?
A   Kim Novak

Q   What **Quincy** actress started out in silent films and starred with Humphrey Bogart in *The Maltese Falcon*?
A   Mary Astor

Q   What Chicago actress starred in the film, *South Pacific*, back in the 1950's?
A   Mitzi Gaynor, who also starred in a Broadway production of "Hello Dolly."

Q   What big scandal was Marjorie Lindheimer Everett involved in during the late 1960's?
A   Everett was a dominant figure back then in the horse racing world. In return for favors and influence, she sold racing stock to Otto Kerner at bargain basement prices and later bought it back with a big return to Kerner. Kerner paid about $15,000 for the stock and sold it for around $150,000. Kerner claimed no criminal wrongdoing and that Republicans were out to "get him" as revenge for the Democrats "stealing the election for Kennedy in 1960." Kerner was sent to a federal prison.

Q   What Northwestern University student was the bride in the 1991 film, *Father of the Bride*?
A   Kimberly Williams who starred with Steve Martin and Diane Keaton

Q   What woman challenged Republican governor Jim Edgar in the 1994 race?
A   Dawn Clark Netsch, the state comptroller – she carried only one county, largely because she wanted tax increases and opposed the death penalty.

Q   What sexy **Park Ridge** actress had a role with Robert Redford in *The Great Gatsby*?
A   Karen Black

Q   Mary Gross, Chicago star of the movie *Feds*, was featured on what TV comedy program?
A   "Saturday Night Live." Mary is the sister of actor Michael Gross, featured on "Family Ties."

Q   What woman, who lived in **East St. Louis** for three years, is considered the quintessential actress of the silent screen?
A   Lillian Gish, who was the star in D.W. Griffith's *Birth of a Nation* in 1915

Q   What state representative became Illinois' first woman elected lieutenant governor?

Lowney Turner Handy at her writer's colony

A   Corinne Wood – 1999; an attorney from **Lake Forest**, she was George Ryan's running mate.

Q   What **Evanston** woman was the first in America to become the dean of a college?
A   Frances Willard in 1873 at Northwestern

254

Q Who is considered the first female doctor in Illinois?
A Frances Ballew Piggott - During the Revolutionary War in 1782 there was a certain Captain James Piggott who brought settlers into the Illinois country from Pennsylvania. Piggott had participated in earlier battles of the war at Germantown and Brandywine Creek. The state of Virginia, which claimed to own Illinois by right of her original sea-to-sea charter, was granting 400 acres to each family that moved in to help settle southern Illinois.

Piggott and his settlers built the fort of Grand Ruisseau, located near present-day **Columbia** in Monroe County. One of the settlers at Grand Ruisseau was a woman named Frances Ballew. She and her children had been abandoned by Bennet, her husband. She began living in a blockhouse home with Piggott, who had lost his wife to disease a few years earlier. Frances had four children. The other women at the fort resented Francis and the casual liaison with Captain Piggott. Most of them had been close friends with Piggott's wife, Eleanor. The first child of the Piggott-Ballew alliance was conceived while the settlers were living at **Kaskaskia**.

In the spring of 1789 Frances found a wounded man in a growth of underbrush. **He had been scalped** and was bleeding from an ugly head wound. He was taken to the blockhouse where she cleansed his wounds. After the man had sufficiently regained his strength, several men held him down while she used an awl to **drill holes in his skull** about an inch apart. She had to be careful not to go too deep and pierce the brain. In a short time proud flesh appeared around the holes and true skin eventually covered the bone.

Frances slowly won the community's respect by earning the title of frontier surgeon-doctor. Her fame as both a surgeon and doctor began to spread around the American Bottom. She had probably picked up knowledge of rudimentary medical and surgical procedures in her affluent home while growing up in Maryland. While tending to the medical needs of her four children, other medical knowledge had been picked up along the way. Frances knew how to deal with scalping wounds from medical tracts passed around frontier forts. She also learned how to stitch wounds and apply herbal medications.

Frances and James Piggott eventually married, moved to **Cahokia**, and had several more children. James Piggott, at the suggestion of his Pennsylvania friend Arthur St. Clair, established a ferry service on the Illinois side of the Mississippi, directly across from St. Louis. This business formed the basis of a small community at the site that eventually grew into the city of **East St. Louis**.

After James died in 1799 Frances and her children sold the ferry business and moved to St. Louis. Sixteen members of the Piggott family are buried in Bellefontaine Cemetery in north St. Louis. One of the Piggott heirs was **Virginia Mayo** who became a distinguished actress in the early 1950's and has a star on the St. Louis Walk of Fame in University City.

Q What woman from **Evanston** is considered the main leader of the WCTU (Women's Christian Temperance Union)?
A Frances Willard (picture on p. 253)

Q What wife of one of Chicago's founders wrote a novel about frontier life called *Wau Bun*?
A Mrs. John Kinzie – her husband, a prosperous trader, later acquired the du Sable property at the land office in **Palestine** and enlarged and improved it. Kinzie Street in Chicago is named for him since it was he who strove to make Chicago a thriving and prosperous city.

Q What southern Illinois woman discovered the cure for "milksick?"
A Dr. Anna Bixby - a legendary and romantic figure from **Hardin County**. She studied medicine in Philadelphia but came to practice in southern Illinois. Her fame spread quickly when she solved the riddle of milksick that caused mysterious deaths every fall. **Abe Lincoln's** mother, Nancy Hanks, died in 1818 from the disease when he was only ten years old. **Superstition attributed the sickness to witches**, but Bigsby proved it was caused by the white snake root plant, also known as nightshade. Farmers eliminated the problem by destroying the plant wherever it was found.

Harriet Monroe in 1892 (Brown Brothers)

Q What town is home to Erika Harold, the 2002-03 Miss America?
A **Urbana**

Q What **Evanston** woman is the only one in America whose likeness appears as a statue in the rotunda of the U.S. Capitol?
A Frances Willard

Q Who were the Wilde Twins?
A Lyn(n) and Lee Wilde, from the Lansdowne area of **East St. Louis**, went to Hollywood and landed roles in the movies. Their biggest film was with Mickey Rooney, *Andy Hardy's Blonde Trouble*.

Q What is the most popular name given to female newborns in Illinois?
A Emily – for boys it's Jacob, having recently replaced the long popular Michael

Q What Chicago reporter covered stories about "blood, guts and sex" and once dated actor George Raft?
A Virginia Marmaduke from **Herrin/Carbondale**

Q What is the title of Phyllis Schlafly's newest book?
A *Feminist Fantasies* – a collection of columns she has written about radical feminism in America

Q What southern Illinois college has a statue of Sacajawea, the Native-American woman who was invaluable to the Lewis and Clark expedition?
A Lewis and Clark Community College in **Godfrey**

Q What **Mount Vernon/Galesburg** woman was known as the "Angel of the Battlefield?"
A Mary Ann Bickerdyke. She traveled with U.S. Grant in nearly all of his western campaigns nursing the sick and wounded. She was also known as the "Cyclone in Calico" for her strong will and determination.

Q What woman from **Cairo** gained a similar reputation during the Civil War?
A Mary Jane Safford

Mrs. Potter Palmer (Bettman Archives)

Q What Chicago feminist/artist changed her last name as a statement of her independence from male dominance?
A Judy Cohen Gerowitz became Judy Chicago in 1970.

Q What woman became the first major league baseball owner in American League history?
A Grace Comisky – after the death of her husband in 1939

HILLARY RODHAM CLINTON

Q What Chicago suburb did Hillary Rodhan-Clinton live in as a youngster?
A **Park Ridge** on Wisner Avenue

Q What frozen river did Hillary ice skate on as a teenager?
A DesPlaines

Q Where did her father, Hugh Rodham, have a drapery fabric store in Chicago?
A Merchandise Mart

Q Was Hillary ever a Girl Scout?
A Yes – and she earned most all of the merit badges

Q According to Hillary's Republican father, why did Nixon lose the 1960 race to Kennedy?
A Richard Daley's "machine" bought and stole enough votes to swing the election.

Q Was Hillary a Cub fan or White Sox fan?
A Cubs – Ernie Banks was her favorite player.

Q When did Hillary start wearing thick glasses?
A In late grade school

Q What high school did Hillary attend?
A Main Township East

Q What top award did Hillary win?
A The Good Citizen Award from the DAR – she also graduated in the top five percent of her class.

Q What University did Hillary attend?
A Wellesley (Massachusetts) and Yale Law School

Q Was Hillary a Republican or a Democrat in her youth?
A Republican – a fan of Barry Goldwater in high school

Q Was Hillary active politically in college?
A Yes – she was President of the Young Republicans club

Q What was Hillary's major at Wellesley?
A Political Science with a minor in Psychology

Q What transformed Hillary into a Democrat?
A Most university professors are Democrats and most university students were against the war in Vietnam – Wellesley was PC before PC was invented.

Q Was Hillary at the 1968 Democratic Convention protests in Chicago?
A She went to Grant Park with a friend, but when things started turning ugly, they left.

Q What was Hillary's religion as a youth?
A Methodist

Hillary in 1992

Q What was the subject of Hillary's senior thesis at Wellesley?
A The work of Chicago activist, Saul Alinsky and solutions to poverty

Q Did young Hillary give the commencement speech at her graduation?
A Yes – it was liberal but not radical.

Q Where did Hillary first meet Bill Clinton?
A In the library at Yale

Q Why did Hillary choose Yale over Harvard?
A A Harvard professor told her, "We don't need any more women."

Q Did Hillary say yes to Bill's first marriage proposal?
A No – They were living together, but she turned him down several times.

Q Did Hillary marry Bill or follow him to Arkansas and teach at a nearby law school?
A She followed him to Arkansas and agreed to marry him about a year later in 1975.

Q How did Hillary's close friends feel about her marriage to "hillbilly Bill?"
A They were disappointed because they thought *she* had a shot at becoming our nation's first woman President.

Q When was daughter Chelsea born?
A 1980

Q How was Chelsea named?
A For the Joni Mitchell song, "Chelsea Morning"

Q Did Hillary stay home and raise her daughter?
A No - Chelsea was reared by live-in babysitters and grandparents.

Q Is Chelsea a daddy's girl or mommy's girl?
A Daddy's girl

Q Did Clinton, Jerry Brown, or Paul Tsongas win the 1992 Democratic primary in Illinois?
A Clinton

Q What article of Hillary's clothing became an issue in the campaign?
A Her headbands

Q What was the most harmful Republican remark against Hillary during the campaign against George Bush?
A "Hillary Clinton in an apron is like Michael Dukakis in a tank."

Q What slashing remark about Hillary did Pat Buchanan make?
A "Hillary believes that 20-year-olds should have the right to sue their parents, and Hillary has compared the institutions of marriage and the family to slavery and life on an Indian reservation."

Q Did Chelsea Clinton attend a public or private school after her father became President?
A Chelsea attended Sidwell Friends private school run by Quakers. Ironically, the NEA, strong supporters of the

Hillary Rodham Clinton (author's collection)

Clintons, had no comment at this slap in the face at public education.

Q What was the tuition at that school?
A Ten thousand dollars a year

Q What did Hillary regret most about the *60 Minutes* interview following the Gennifer Flowers accusations?
A Her reference to the Tammy Wynette song, "Stand By Your Man."

Q While campaigning in the 1992 Illinois primary at the Busy Bee Coffee Shop in Chicago, what new gaffe did Hillary make?
A When asked whether her law work might have been a conflict of interest when Bill was governor, Hillary replied: "I could have stayed home and baked cookies and had teas, but what I decided to do was fulfill my profession. . . ." This was seen as a slam at housewives.

Q What Illinois town did the Clinton-Gore Campaign Bus pay a visit?
A **Vandalia**

Q What was Hillary's Secret Service code name?
A Evergreen

Q What was Hillary's biggest defeat in the White House?
A She was put in charge of the task force on health care reform, and it went down to defeat.

Q Did Hillary ever convince her Republican father to become a Democrat?
A No

Q What new fashion trend did Hillary introduce?
A She thought her legs were too thick and gave up dresses for pants suits – a first for First Ladies.

Q What book did Hillary write while in the White House?
A *It Takes A Village*

Q What two issues did Hillary fight for as first lady?
A Children's rights and women's rights

Q What "first" did Hillary achieve as First Lady?
A She was the first to keep her maiden name – Hillary Rodham-Clinton. Back when they were in Arkansas, she insisted on being called Hillary Rodham, not Hillary Clinton.

Q Who was Hillary's role model?
A Eleanor Roosevelt

Q What is ironic about this?
A Eleanor's husband (FDR) was also unfaithful, and she stuck by him.

Q What precedent did Hillary establish as First Lady?
A By helping to shape domestic legislation, she redefined the role of First Lady, although current First Lady Laura Bush has chosen not to follow that controversial path.

Q To those who imagine Hillary is a cold fish, what is her nickname?
A "Sister Frigidare" – Norman King says in his biography that her high school newspaper in its senior prediction issue said Hillary was destined to become a nun.

Q What was Hillary's experience with presidential impeachment?

Hillary Clinton

A As a lawyer she worked with Democrats to help draw up articles of impeachment against Nixon – which she thought was fair. When her husband was impeached, she thought it was unfair and called it a "Republican conspiracy"

Q Is Hillary's blondish hair color natural?
A No – her real color is medium-dark brown.

Q When Bill Clinton was President, what woman from Waukegan was his personal secretary?
A Betty Currie – an African-American

Q What was the chief criticism of Hillary's activist role as First Lady?
A Hillary was not elected to anything, yet she was usurping the role of the Vice-president.

Q What embarrassment did husband Bill suffer when he visited **Champaign** in 1998?
A Air Force One got stuck in the mud at Willard Airport and experienced a two hour delay.

Q Why are many Illinoisans somewhat saddened at the recent turn of events in Hillary's life?
A Instead of running for the U.S. Senate from Illinois, she and Bill moved to Chappaqua, New York, leaving her Illinois roots behind.

THE BIGGEST, HIGHEST, GREATEST, SMALLEST, MOST SPECTACULAR

Q What Chicago library was the largest in the world when it was built?
A The Harold Washington Library, which opened in 1991

Q What Illinois company is the **largest land owner in the United States**?
A McDonald's has the title that was once owned by Sears of Chicago, but Wal-Mart is closing fast.

Q What unusual statistic about personalized license plates does Illinois claim?
A It has more drivers with "vanity" plates than any other state.

Q What unusual statistic concerning units of government does Illinois claim?
A It has more city, county, and township units of government than any other state – over 6,000

Q What southern Illinois town is home to the largest Christian cross in the nation?
A **Alto Pass**

Q Where is the state's biggest Ferris wheel?
A Navy Pier in Chicago – 150 feet tall

Q What town has the **largest pick-your-own orchard in the United States**?
A **Belleville** – Eckert's Orchards

Q Where was the **largest concrete swimming pool in America** in 1925?
A **Wood River** had the largest concrete swimming pool in America, built by Standard Oil refinery located there.

Q What town is home to the B.R. Pierce family whose herd of cattle is said to be the **oldest in the nation**, reproducing itself generation after generation?
A **Creston**

Q Where is the world's largest indoor marine mammal pavilion in the world?
A Shedd Aquarium in Chicago – it features whales, dolphins, sea otters, seals and penguins.

Q Where is the world's largest commodities exchange in the world?
A Chicago's Board of Trade (wheat, soybeans, corn, pork bellies, etc)

Q Where was the first planetarium in the Western Hemisphere?
A Chicago – the Adler planetarium that opened for the Century of Progress fair in 1933

Q What Chicago publication is the **world's largest selling encyclopedia**?
A The World Book Encyclopedia

Q According to Ripley's "Believe It Or Not," what are the only two abutting towns in the world with a common street that has a university at each end?

A **Bloomington** (Illinois Wesleyan) and **Normal** (Illinois State)

Q What was the **only electric railroad in the world to operate sleeper cars**?
A The McKinley Lines of the Illinois Traction System for service between **Peoria, Springfield,** and St. Louis

Q What geographical feature in the Mississippi River is the **smallest national park in the world**?
A Tower Rock (near **Grand Tower**), first sighted by Marquette and Joliet, is only 62 feet tall. There were thoughts in 1867 about removing it as an impediment to steamboat traffic, but President Grant thought it might serve as a bridge pier some day and prevented its destruction.

Q What man in frontier Illinois was known as "**America's Greatest Agnostic?**"
A Robert Ingersoll – the noted lecturer and politician had a statue erected in his honor at Glen Oak Park in **Peoria.**

The Plantation Club at Moline

Q What city has the most movable bridges in the world?
A Chicago has 45 movable bridges for the purpose of letting large ships pass.

Q Where in Illinois is the nation's oldest, free public zoo?
A Chicago – Lincoln Park Zoo, 1868

Q Where was the largest simple truss span in the world in 1917?
A **Metropolis** – built by the Burlington Railroad across the Ohio with a span of 720 feet.

Q What was the **richest dollar-per-mile railroad in America** in 1860?
A The seven mile long Illinois & St. Louis, built in 1837. It nearly went bankrupt in its early years because the owners overestimated the demand for coal in St. Louis.

Q In what year did Chicago's O'Hare Airport become the world's busiest facility?
A 1961

Q What southern Illinois town has the **largest outdoor Catholic shrine in the world**?
A **Belleville** – Our Lady of the Snows

Q What southern Illinois town has the McPike Mansion, built by the man who established the largest box and container factory in America?
A **Alton** – the Alton City Mills

Q What **Granite City** manufacturing firm was the largest in the world when it came to making pots and pans for kitchen use?
A Graniteware by the Niedringhaus brothers.

Q Why does Illinois hold the record for being the **smallest state to ever be admitted to the union**?
A Census fraud! There was such a rush to admit Illinois to the union that census takers were bribed to include visitors to the state, count some families twice, and round *up* estimates of distant villages to higher numbers. The final tally was 40,258, barely reaching the minimum of 40,000. It was later discovered that the actual number was about 35,000.

Q What Illinois university has the largest campus in terms of acreage?
A SIU at **Edwardsville**, with 2,660 acres, is ranked in the top three in the nation.

Q Where is the world's largest lock and dam facility in the world?
A The one near **Golconda** on the Ohio River with gates that weigh 250 tons

Q Where is the largest comic book mural in the nation?
A At **Metropolis** on Ferry Street; it's a replica of the first issue of a Superman comic book in 1938

Q Where was the second largest hanger in the world for dirigibles in 1921?
A Scott Field near **O'Fallon**; it was 178 feet high and 810 feet long.

The Lincoln Boulder at East Douglas and North State in Freeport

Q What unusual service did these dirigibles see since there was no war in the 1920's or 1930's?
A They were used for flying over local terrain to help spot **illegal stills** during Prohibition.

Q What library claimed to have the largest circulation in

259

the world in 1896?
A   Chicago Public Library

Q   What is the tallest building in Illinois?
A   Sears Tower with 110 stories, 1,454 feet tall; also the tallest in the USA

Q   What town bills itself as Illinois' highest town?
A   **Stockton** – near the Wisconsin border

Q   What St. Clair County town claims to have the largest Catholic church building in Illinois?
A   **Belleville** - massive St. Peter's

Q   What was the largest artificial lake in southern Illinois (1991)?
A   Crab Orchard Lake near **Carbondale** covering 7,000 acres

Split Rock between Ottawa and LaSalle

Q   Statistically, what space on a Monopoly board is landed on more frequently than any other?
A   That pretty red property known as Illinois Avenue

Q   What southern Illinois town once billed itself as the Comic Book Capital of the World because it printed most of the nation's comic books?
A   **Sparta**

Q   Where is the oldest cast metal bell in the nation?
A   There is a Spanish bell, presumably cast in the 8th century, in the chapel at **McKendree College in Lebanon**. It came from an old mission in Santa Fe, New Mexico, and was brought to the Illinois State Fair in 1858. **President Cobleigh** was taken with the heirloom and purchased it for the college after the fair was ended. Mounted in a relatively new tower, the bell has been deemed the **oldest in the nation**.

Q   What are some incredible facts about Robert Wadlow, the world's tallest man?
A   1. Robert Wadlow of **Alton** was about eight feet and eleven inches tall.
2.   Wadlow's nickname was the "Gentle Giant."
3.   All of Wadlow's brothers and sister were "normal" size.

4. Wadlow was born in 1918 and weighed eight and a half pounds.
5. By the time Wadlow was 12 months, he weighed 45 pounds.
6. When Wadlow entered the first grade at school he was the size of a typical 17-year old.
7. Wadlow's IQ was 124, way above normal.
8. Robert's shoe size at age 20 was size 37AA.
9. Robert's extraordinary growth was blamed on that overactive bean-shaped pituitary gland.
10. Wadlow's hobbies were stamp collecting, photography, and scouting, and he was a member of the DeMolay.
11. Robert weighed in on a livestock scale at 480 pounds.
12. In 1937 Wadlow signed a contract with the Ringling Brothers to make two circus appearances a day.
13. When Robert stayed in hotels, two double beds were placed side-by-side for him to sleep on.
14. Wadlow never drove a car because there simply wasn't enough room for him in the driver's seat. When he rode in a car, he sat in the back seat and stretched his legs out to touch the windshield.
15. Robert became a popular attraction at conventions, state fairs, and other like gatherings. He traveled all over the country as a guest of honor, visiting 41 states, Canada and Mexico.
16. Robert died in 1940 from an infected blister on his ankle, rubbed raw by a metal brace on his leg. His casket was 10 feet long and 32 inches wide.

AMAZING FACT: After Wadlow's death the family did not allow medical science to examine his body or his brain. They were upset with the fact that the American Medical Association had backed one of its members who wrote an untruthful medical article about Robert.

Q   What Chicago suburb bills itself as the "Biggest Village in the World?"
A   **Skokie**

Billy Rose (5-3) with Robert Wadlow (8-11)

Q   What distinction does Sand Cave in southern Illinois hold?
A   It is the **largest sandstone cave in North America**.

260

Q   What boast could Illinois make about its roads in 1928?
A   It had more miles of paved roads than any other state in the union or any comparable area in the world.

Partial view of the famous Caterpillar Tractor Company in Peoria

Q   What are thought to be the oldest living things east of the Mississippi River?
A   The bald cypress trees of the Cache River wetlands in southern Illinois

Q   Where is the Shawnee Trail (River-to-River Trail)?
A   It's in southern Illinois and is 115 miles long, extending from **Grand Tower** on the Mississippi River to Battery Rock on the Ohio River.

Q   Where in Illinois is the **tallest church in the world**?
A   Chicago's First United Methodist Church makes that claim. It is housed in a skyscraper topped by a steeple 568 feet tall.

Q.   What newspaper billed itself as the "World's Greatest Newspaper?"
A   The *Chicago Tribune*, which dropped the brag line from its masthead in 1977.

Q   In 1893 what was the **largest amusement ride in the world**?
A   The wheel built by George Ferris of **Galesburg** for the Columbian Exposition; each car held about 30 people.

Q   Where is the **nation's smallest National Monument**?
A   It's Tower Rock in the Mississippi River near **Grand Tower**

Q   Where is the **nation's smallest grave marker** – according to Ripley's "Believe It Or Not?"
A   **West Salem** - actually located east of Salem, settled by Moravians; Ripley's "Believe It Or Not" says the tombstone of Emma Pfeil is world's smallest tombstone at 5 and 7/8 x 10 and ½ x 2 inches

Q   What town was home to Robert Hughes, the **World's Heaviest Man**, weighing over 1,000 pounds?
A   **Fish Hook** – he died in 1958

Q   Where is the **nation's smallest** active post office with a lobby?
A   **Muddy**, Illinois - postal authorities wanted to tear it down and build a new one, but residents objected.

Q   Where was the **biggest amusement park in the world in 1935**?
A   It was Riverview Amusement Park on the north side of Chicago.

Q   What is considered the **biggest newspaper headline mistake of all time**?
A   The 1948 *Chicago Tribune's* "Dewey Beats Truman" issue the next morning after the November election

Q   Where was the largest maker of glass products in the world in 1940?
A   Owens Glass Company at **Alton**

Q   For decades, what company has been the largest supplier of numismatic metal for the U.S. Mint?
A   The Olin Corporation of **East Alton.**

Q   What is the chief interest of numismatists in this company?
A   Olin perfected the "sandwich" metal that is used on dimes and quarters by the U.S. Mint.

Q   What town in Pope County, with less than 1,000 pop-

Fort Armstrong Hotel in Rock Island

ulation, is the smallest county seat in Illinois?
A   **Golconda**

Q   What Washington County town was home to Bat Masterson – famed lawman and friend of Teddy Roosevelt?
A   **Golden Gate**

Q   A "low bridge" is built just above the surface of a river while a "high bridge" is built high enough to allow boats to pass underneath. Does Illinois hold the national record for the size of each of these two types of bridges?
A   Yes – a low bridge usually has a swing or vertical lift section to allow boats and barges to pass.

Q   What southern Illinois town is home to Ferne Clyffe State Park?
A   **Goreville**

Q What town's Hangar One at the U.S. Naval Air Station was the largest in the world when built in 1929?
A **Glenview**

Q Where was the **largest inland beach in America** in 1913?
A Jones' Park in **East St. Louis**. The large sand bottomed swimming pool was fed by an artesian well.

Cross of Peace at Bald Knob (southern Illinois) – largest in the USA by volume

Q Where is the tallest catsup bottle in the world?
A **Collinsville**
- the Brooks catsup water tower there is the tallest, though I've heard that the flabbergasted Heinz people plan to build a larger one.

Q Where in Illinois is an Indian mound that is greater in volume than the Great Pyramid of Egypt?
A **Collinsville** - the great Cahokia Mound in the State Park area

Q In 1922 what company was the **largest maker of burlap-type sacks in the world**?
A American Fiber of **East St. Louis** held that title. The bags were made from a fiber-like material that came from a yucca plant grown on their plantations in Arizona.

Q What Illinoisan owned so many acres of land and so many head of cattle that he was called the "Cattle King of the World?"
A John Gillette of **Elkhart**

Q What Illinois town has the **tallest fountain in the world**?
A **East St. Louis** has a fountain on the riverfront that shoots 627 feet, nearly as high as the St. Louis Arch. It was built by St. Louisans who wanted something nice to look at when they went to the top of the Gateway Arch.

Q An SIU at **Edwardsville** student was seen wearing a T-shirt that read: "SIUE football – undefeated since 1960." How is that possible?
A SIUE has never fielded a football team.

Q What piece of history in southern Illinois is called the "Liberty Bell of the West?"
A **Kaskaskia** is the location, and it's the bell that was rung to celebrate George Rogers Clark wresting that part of Illinois from British rule. The bell is older than the famed Liberty Bell in Philadelphia.

Q What city in 1910 was the world's largest producer of processed bauxite (aluminum ore)?
A **East St. Louis**

ILLINOIS AFRICAN-AMERICANS

Q What musician from **Alton** and **East St. Louis** dropped out of Julliard Music School in New York because he felt they weren't teaching him anything?
A Miles Davis

Q What Illinois jazz musician pioneered "cool jazz" in the late 1940s and was one of the first jazz musicians to use electronic instruments?
A Miles Davis

Q What athlete attended SIU **Carbondale** on a track scholarship and became a noted comedian?
A Dick Gregory, who this author saw perform an early routine in 1962 at the East St. Louis campus of SIU before it was moved to **Edwardsville**. Gregory later became a noted Chicago Civil Rights activist and wrote his autobiography, *Nigger*.

Q What Chicago singer hit the top of the charts with "You'll Never Find Another Love Like Mine?"
A Lou Rawls

Q How many slaves are estimated to have escaped via the Underground Railroad in Illinois?
A 75,000

Q What famed dancer was living in Boxcar City on the riverfront at the time of the **East St. Louis** race riot?
A Josephine Baker

Oprah Winfrey (Illinois Tourism)

Q What Chicago poet from **Bronzeville** won the first Pulitzer Prize ever given to an African-American?
A Gwendolyn Brooks

Q What graduate of the University of Illinois and reporter for the *Daily Illini* wrote, *Feminist Fatale*, a study of the women's movement?
A Paula Kamen, a 1989 grad – the same year as this author's son, Steven Nunes

Q What Chicagoan is known as the "Queen of Gospel?"
A Mahalia Jackson

Q What singer, who started her career in Chicago, married

Chicago Cardinal defensive back Dick "Night Train" Lane
A   Dinah Washington – "What a Difference A Day Makes"

Q   What Chicago dancer later adopted **East St. Louis** as her home and has a performance theater at SIU **Edwardsville** named for her?
A   Katherine Dunham

Q   What Chicagoan was the first African-American priest in America?
A   Father Augustine Tolton, who died in 1897 while serving as pastor of Saint Monica's Church

Q   What Chicagoan was the founder of PUSH and the Rainbow Coalition?
A   Jesse Jackson

Q   What Chicagoan was the first African-American female to earn a pilot's license?
A   Bessie Coleman – a manicurist

Q   How many times has Jesse Jackson been elected to public office?
A   None

Q   What Chicago surgeon performed the first successful repair of the sac around the heart, the pericardium?
A   Daniel H. Williams

Q   What **East St. Louisan** was the featured halftime performer at the 2000 Super Bowl, won by the St. Louis Rams?
A   Tina Turner

Q   What **East St. Louisan** and SIU Edwardsville teacher was named Illinois Author of the Year in 1990?
A   Eugene Redmond, who currently sponsors a literary group called Drumbeat.

Q   What event was Jackie Joyner-Kersee's specialty in the Olympics?
A   The heptathlon (seven events) where she became the only woman to win back-to-back in 1988 at Seoul and 1992 at Barcelona. She also took the bronze in the long jump at Barcelona.

Q   What **East St. Louisan** founded the National Theater of Harlem, cited by President Reagan as one of 63 important cultural institutions in America
A   Barbara Teer

Q   What new name did rhythm and blues artist Yvette Stevens adopt?
A   Chaka Kahn

Q   What Chicagoan started a phenomenon called Gospel

Heavyweight champ from Jacksonville, Ken Norton

Writer Richard Wright (R) & Count Basie

Music by writing a song in 1932 called "Take My Hand, Precious Lord?"
A   Thomas Dorsey, whose wife and baby daughter died in childbirth.

Q   What blues singer with a powerful voice lived in Chicago from 1960 until his death in 1991?
A   B.B. Odom

Q   What famous actress wed jazz musician Miles Davis?
A   Cicely Tyson. He and the actress were wed in Bill Cosby's home and Andrew Young performed the ceremony.

Q   What Chicagoan had a number one hit with the song, "Duke of Earl" in 1962?
A   Gene Chandler

Q   Who founded the town of New Philadelphia?
A   Frank McWorter, a free African American, moved to **Pike County** from Kentucky and founded the town of **New Philadelphia**. Through hard work and diligence he was able to purchase the freedom of 13 family members.

Q   What **East St. Louisan** was National League Rookie of the Year in 1951 and led the league in stolen bases?
A   Sam "Jet" Jethro

Q   What **East St. Louisan** was elected to the football Hall of Fame in 1995?
A   Kellen Winslow who played nine years as tight end for the San Diego Chargers when Dan Fouts was quarterback. He did not play football until his senior year at East Side because his mother feared injury. He played for the chess team instead.

Q   What Chicagoan became the first black from a Northern state to be elected to Congress?
A   Oscar DePriest - but he was a one-termer because he voted against most of Roosevelt's New Deal.

Q   What **East St. Louisan** made national news when he went straight from high school to the NBA?
A   Darius Miles, who was selected third in the draft by the L.A. Clippers, a record then for a high schooler. He was traded to Cleveland who, in turn, traded him to Portland.

Q   What notable event was accomplished by southern Illinoisan Oscar Micheaux in 1919?
A   The noted filmmaker of the 1920s and 1930s created his first movie, *The Homesteader*.

Q   What **East St. Louisan** played for the University of

Illinois and won the Butkus Award?
A   Dana Howard - along with Simeon Rice, John Holecek and Kevin Hardy, they were the nation's best linebacking corps two years in a row. Dana won the Butkus Award his senior year for being the **best linebacker in the nation**.

Q   What Illini holds the career mark for sacks?
A   Simeon Rice with 44.5

Q   What Illini holds the career record for tackles?
A   Dana Howard with 595 although John Sullivan set the single game mark with 34 against Minnesota in 1977

Q   What do Sergio McLain, Marcus Griffin and Jerry Hester have in common?
A   These University of Illinois basketball stars all came from **Peoria Manual High School**.

Q   What **East St. Louisan** played the acerbic part of Aunt Esther on "Sanford and Son?"
A   Lawanda Page

Q   What **East St. Louisan** owns four Super Bowl rings?
A   Eric Wright – he played cornerback with Joe Montana and the 49ers in the 1980's.

Q   What woman who lived in the Alta Sita neighborhood of **East St. Louis** appeared with Mel Gibson in the film, *Mad Max, Beyond Thunderdome*?
A   Tina Turner

Q   What **Peoria** comedian performed in several movies with Gene Wilder?
A   Richard Pryor

Q   What **East St Louisan** replaced controversial Andrew Young as our U.N. representative after Young was forced to resign in 1979 due to unauthorized contact with the PLO?
A   Donald McHenry, who was **our nation's youngest to head our U.N. delegation**

LEWIS AND CLARK IN ILLINOIS

Q   What was the background of Lewis and Clark?

Chicago drummer "Baby" Dodds

Oscar DePriest – first African-American to serve in U.S. Congress since Reconstruction

A   William Clark was the younger brother of George Rogers Clark. Meriwether Lewis was Thomas Jefferson's personal secretary.

Q   What was their mission?
A   To explore the newly acquired Louisiana Territory.

Q   What was a secondary objective?
A   To search for the fabled (and non-existent) Northwest Passage

Q   Did Lewis and Clark know each other before the joint mission?
A   Yes – they had both served under Anthony Wayne at the battle of Fallen Timbers against the Indians.

Q   What was the starting point of the expedition?
A   Clarksville, on the Ohio River across from Louisville, Kentucky

Q   Was Sacajawea, the female Indian guide with them at this point?
A   No – they met her along the Missouri River in Dakota Territory

Q   How long were Lewis and Clark in Illinois as they made preparations for the trip?
A   181 days

Q   What was their first stopping point in Illinois?
A   Fort Massac on the Ohio River at **Metropolis**

Q   Were any African-Americans part of the expedition?
A   Yes – a man named York was William Clark's slave

Q   What was their second stopping point in Illinois?
A   **Cairo** – near present day Fort Defiance

Sacajawea (courtesy Illinois Tourism)

Q   What man did they visit with at Kaskaskia?
A   Pierre Menard – his home, built later, was called the "Mount Vernon of the West."

Q   How difficult was it for the men to go upstream against the current of the Mississippi River?

A   The men rowed and only progressed about ten or twelve miles a day

William Clark (Ill. State Hist. Lib.)

Q   Did the expedition visit Fort Chartres?
A   No – by now it was abandoned and in ruins

Q   Who did Lewis and Clark confer with at **Cahokia**?
A   Nicholas Jarrot who built a two-story house in 1799 that is the oldest brick building in Illinois

Q   What famous site was owned by Nicholas Jarrot?
A   The Great Cahokia Mound

Q   What place was used as a posting place where Lewis and Clark communicated by letter with Thomas Jefferson back in Washington D.C.?
A   **Cahokia**

Q   What were Jefferson's plans for the land directly west of the Mississippi River?
A   He was thinking about relocating all Indians in the East across the river. All whites west of the river would be expected to move back on the other side.

Q   What happened when Lewis asked the Spanish officials in St. Louis permission to explore the Louisiana Territory?
A   They said they could only give their permission after the actual transfer had taken place.

Q   Where did Lewis and Clark and their Corps of Discovery group spend the winter?
A   At Camp Dubois, a hastily constructed log fortification across from the mouth of the Missouri River

Q   How many stars were on the American flag they flew at Camp Dubois?
A   Fifteen – it did not reflect the fact that several new states had recently been added to the union.

Q   What member of the expedition later went on to make a name for himself?
A   **John Colter**, the famed mountain man

Q   Once the expedition started in May of 1804, how long were they gone?
A   Twenty-eight months

Q   What happened to William Clark after the expedition?
A   He settled down and married a St. Louis woman. Clark died in 1838 and was buried in Bellefontaine Cemetery in north St. Louis.

Q   What happened to Meriwether Lewis after the expedition?
A   He fell upon hard times and died in 1809 at Grinder's Inn along the Natchez Trace. It has long been debated whether his death was murder or a suicide.

www.lewisandclarkillinois.org

POTPOURRI

Q   What does the prep sports logo for Hoopeston High "Cornjerkers" look like?
A   See picture below

"Jerky" – Hoopeston's sports mascot

Q   What southwestern town claims a bridge that saw the first use of underwater caissons in its construction?
A   **East St. Louis** - John Roebling used caissons to build the Brooklyn Bridge, but their first use was by James Eads when he constructed a bridge over the Mississippi at East St. Louis in 1874.

Q   What 1998 TV Lifetime movie was about an **Evanston** mother whose 16-year-old daughter is kidnapped into the world of porn as a result of contact with a stranger via an Internet chat room?
A   *Every Mother's Worst Fear*, starring Cheryl Ladd and her real life daughter

Q   What did Oprah Winfrey do in August of 2004 that earned her less than twenty dollars a day?
A   She served on a Chicago jury that convicted a man of murder.

Q   What semi-controversial law was passed by the state legislature in 2004?
A   Mothers are now allowed to breast feed their babies in public.

Q   Is former football star Mike Ditka a Republican or Democrat?
A   Republican – After Jack Ryan declined to run for the U.S. Senate seat in November of 2004, Mike Ditka gave serious thought to making a bid for the seat. After intense media speculation for a couple of days, Ditka announced that he had too many prior commitments.

Q   What Rockford/Chicago man was the **first casualty of the Civil War**, May 24, 1861?

A Elmer Ellsworth, a law student and friend of Lincoln's, was the leader of some Zouaves he had recruited. They were stationed in Alexandria, Virginia, at the beginning of the war. A local hotel owner raised the Confederate flag on the roof and Ellsworth and a couple of men went upstairs to remove it. On his way back, the hotel owner shot and killed Ellsworth. Ellsworth's men, in turn, shot James Jackson, the owner.

Death of Colonel Elmer Ellsworth at Alexandria, Vir.

Q. What southwestern town has the **world's tallest fountain**?
A **East St. Louis** on the Mississippi riverfront and it shoots 627 feet high.

Q What southern Illinois town did Buffalo Bill visit once a year in the 1890's to buy Indian arrowheads for his Wild West show?
A East St. Louis – the arrowheads came from nearby Cahokia Mounds; he usually stayed at the Berry Hotel

Q Can Illinois private citizens buy an adult lion and keep the animal on his or her property?
A No – Illinois is one of 19 states that forbids such an act.

Q What county claims to be the **Chowder Capital of Illinois**?
A Edwards – Midwest chowder is a thick soup with meat, vegetables, and tomatoes.

Q What is unusual about the Union Tank Car repair facility in **Wood River**?
A It's a geodesic dome, a construction technique invented by Buckminster Fuller of SIU. It was constructed from the top down over an inflated balloon.

Q Has Spiderman ever climbed the Sears Tower?
A Yes – Daniel Goodwin did it in seven hours while wearing a Spiderman costume in 1981.

Q What honor was accorded Cahokia Mounds in 1982?
A It was the tenth site to de declared of "universal human value" by UNESCO

Q What town in southern Illinois was named for a place in

Homer's *Iliad*?
A **Troy**

Q What unusual event takes place twice a year at LaRue Swamp in southern Illinois?
A LaRue Swamp, on the western edge of Pine Hills, is designated a National Heritage Landmark. The ecological miracle was formed thousands of years ago when it was the alluvial plain of the Mississippi and Big Muddy rivers. The last glacial period, called the Liman Advance, pushed the rivers away to their present beds. For several weeks in the spring and fall the access road is closed to traffic to enable snakes and reptiles to migrate without loss of life. This unusual event has been reported in Ripley's "**Believe It Or Not.**"

Q What two Illinois towns in the 1920's and 1930's were known as Gretna Greenes?
A **Metropolis** and **Waterloo** - Gretna Greene is a place in Scotland noted for its lax laws concerning marriage. These two towns had road signs that offered "quickie" marriages by justices of the peace to young people who were only 16 years old.

Q What site in **Springfield** is the only non-Lincoln attraction that draws tourists?

Charles Duryea and the world's first real automobile

A The Dana House designed by Frank Lloyd Wright

Q What famous television comedian was a graduate of Northwestern University?
A Paul Lynde, who had a drinking problem

Q What Lifetime channel television movie starred Jean Smart as Candy Delong, the FBI's first female profiler?
A "Killer Instinct" – Delong, after helping to break the Theodore Kazynski "Unibomber" case, now tries to catch a Chicago serial rapist/killer; Kazynski was a graduate of Evergreen Park High in south Chicago

Chicago writer James T. Farrell

Q What is the largest Protestant group in Illinois?
A Methodists – followed by Lutherans, Baptists and Presbyterians; there are over 1,000 Catholic church buildings in Illinois

Q   How many Illinoisans were killed in the Mexican War?
A   About 1,000 including Colonel John J. Hardin

Q   How many Illinoisans were killed in the Civil War?
A   5,857 were killed in action and 23,000 died from wounds and disease.

Chicago's "Jelly Roll" Morton

Q   When did Chicago pass Pittsburgh as the nation's largest steel producer?
A   1953

Q   What is the largest industrial county in the nation?
A   Cook County

Q   When did oil production begin in Illinois?
A   1906 in Clark, Crawford and Lawrence counties

Q   What Mississippi River town has the most significant Native American painting in the United States?
A   **Alton** boasts the Piasa Monster, a creature painted on the bluffs. The original was bulldozed for railroad roadbed ballast.

Q   What southwestern town has a life-size statue of the world's tallest man?
A   **Alton**. The likeness is of Robert Wadlow who was known as the Alton Giant. He died in 1940. Wadlow was about a foot taller than Kareem Abdul Jabbar.

Q   What southeastern town has a reconstructed stone furnace that was used for making iron back in the 1838?
A   **Rosiclaire** in Hardin County has this fifty-three foot high treasure.

Q   Where can you go on St. Patrick's Day to see a green river?
A   Chicago. City officials place green dye in the Chicago River every March 17th. Inebriated tourists who stumble out of a pub can't believe their eyes.

Q   Why was Illinois author Ray Bradbury critical of Michael Moore's film, *Fahrenheit 911* on the Dennis Miller show on CNBC (July 2004)?
A   *Fahrenheit 451* is a copyrighted phrase, and Moore used a form of it without asking Bradbury for permission.

Q   What southwestern town has a Popeye statue?
A   **Chester** was hometown to Elzie Seegar, creator of Popeye.

Q   What towns have the state's largest collection of Sears pre-cut homes ordered from a catalog?
A   **Carlinville** has the most; about 155 homes were brought in to house local coal miners; **Elgin** ranks second;

the "Jeopardy" television show had a whole category devoted to Sears homes in July of 2004

Q   What town has a railroad car facility in the shape of a geodesic dome?
A   **Wood River**. The geodesic dome was invented by Buckminster Fuller of SIUC.

Q   What **Carmi** man was in charge of the military expedition that **captured and killed John Wilkes Booth**, Lincoln's assassin?
A   Everton Conger

Q   Where is the statue known as the Madonna of the Trail?
A   **Vandalia** - it's is a tribute to the pioneer women of Illinois commissioned by the DAR.

Q   In what Illinois place have the oldest human remains been found?
A   The Modoc Rock Shelter, three miles east of the Mississippi and south of **Prairie du Rocher**.

Harold Ickes – member of FDR's Cabinet

Q   What was unusual about the Civil War wound of Josiah Nicholson of **Eddyville**?
A   He was shot in the back of the head and the ball lodged in the roof of his mouth, barely missing his cervical cord. Surgeons advised against trying to remove the ball.
Twenty-one years later he sneezed violently and dislodged the ball, which he then proudly kept on display.

Famed evangelist Billy Sunday

Q   How did the town of **Golden**, in Adams County, get its name?
A   Settled by Germans, it was originally called South Prairie. So much grain was planted that it became known as Golden Prairie, later shortened to Golden.

Q   What governor of Illinois lived in the town of **Lebanon**?
A   Augustus French – he founded McKendree's law department.

Q   What southern Illinois town in Pope County has a town named for a successful washing machine salesman?
A   The town of **Robbs** is named for Robert Robbs.

Q   What town in Knox County has a college whose two

main buildings were called East Bricks and West Bricks?
A **Galesburg** – Knox College

Q What 20-acre estate in **Highland Park** was designed by famed landscape architect Jens Jensen?
A The A.G. Becker estate

Q What is misleading about the name of Lake **Peoria**?
A Lake Peoria is merely a bulge in the Illinois River - two miles at its widest point

Q Why did Illinois Native Americans tend to use the pirogue instead of the birch bark canoe?
A Very few birch trees were native to Illinois.

James Stockdale – Ross Perot's running mate

Q Did Vice-president Aaron Burr ever visit Illinois?
A Yes – he stopped at Fort Massac near **Metropolis** to confer with commander James Wilkinson in 1805. It is thought that he was plotting to organize an expedition to separate the western territories from the U.S. and set himself up as king under Spain's protectorate. **He was tried for treason but acquitted.**

Q What was the life span of most settlers in frontier Illinois?
A Anyone who made it past fifty was fortunate. Stephen Douglas died from "secession stress" and acute rheumatism at age 48.

Q What Illinois college did Jesse Jackson attend?
A The University of Illinois

Q What is the oddest thing about Jesse Jackson's resume?
A He has never held an elective office

Q What drug bill for seniors was the Illinois legislature considering in the July of 2004?
A One that would allow them to purchase prescriptions from Canada.

Q Why are drugs cheaper in Canada than Illinois?
A Prices are regulated in Canada because it is a socialist country.

Q What was George Rogers Clark's nickname?
A The "George Washington of the West"

Q What ethnic group introduced the Christmas tree to Illinois?
A German immigrants – the Christmastide custom of the

tannenbaum dates back to St. Boniface. Martin Luther reportedly was the first to add lighted candles to the tree.

Q What man from **Carlyle** became a notorious western outlaw?
A Jack Slade

Q What immigrant group introduced the log cabin to Illinois?
A It was the Swedes who first built log cabins

Q What one-armed man from **Carbondale** was an early explorer of the Grand Canyon?
A John Wesley Powell – the men with him were from **Bloomington;** he was honored on a 1969 postage stamp

Q What ethnic group introduced the idea of the Easter Bunny to Illinois?
A German immigrants, although it was called the Easter Hare

Sportswriter Ring Lardner

Q From what source does Scott Air Base, located near **O'Fallon**, secure its water supply?
A From the Mississippi River. Two large pipes run from the water treatment facility at **East St. Louis** all the way to the base; two are used to insure a continuous flow in case one might rupture or be broken.

Q What other town in Illinois (besides Chicago and East St. Louis) raised its street level about ten feet to prevent flooding?
A **Cairo**

Q What sometimes made the night landscape of Illinois coal mining towns unusual?
A The weird flickering light of gob piles (coal refuse) that occasionally caught fire

Postcard king Curt Teich – courtesy Lake County Museum

Q What product did Granite City's Corn Refining Products Company begin making in 1907?
A World famous Karo Syrup

Q What **Granite City** man designed the ***Dutch Boy logo*** for the brand of paint made by United Lead?
A Lawrence Earle

Q What **Golconda** man was called the "Patton of the Pacific?"
A General John Hodge – who commanded divisional forces at Guadalcanal, Bougainville, and the Philippines.

Q Why is the Metro East light rail system known as MetroLink (St. Louis, **Fairview Heights, Belleville, East St. Louis**) considered a white elephant?

A   A recent government study concluded it was so expensive to operate that it would be cheaper to buy its patrons a new car every five years.

Q   When drilling for Illinois oil back in 1920, what was a "go-devil?"
A   About 200 quarts of nitro send down 1,500 feet of casing to explode and release trapped oil. The resulting gushers of oil and rock were spectacular.

Q   Where was the only Indian reservation in Illinois?
A   Sand Ridge near **Murphysboro**

Q   What outspoken Chicago rabbi became one of the first to support Dr. Herzl's Zionism movement – a call for the creation of a new Jewish state in Palestine?
A   Bernhard Felsenthal – 1897

Q   What Chicago surgeon developed the operating technique of removing a lung in a one-step operation instead of two?
A   Ambrose Graham – who also discovered a way to make the gall bladder visible on an X-ray

Q   Who was Chicagoan William Chalmers?
A   He was the other half of the Allis-Chalmers heavy machinery and earth moving equipment company that was formed in 1901. He married the daughter of detective Alan Pinkerton.

Q   What Chicagoan defeated the Russian world champion Boris Spassky at Reykjavik, Iceland, in 1972?
A   Temperamental Bobby Fisher; he forced the International Chess Federation to change its rules that allowed collusion among the Russians

Q   Where is the *U.S.S. Cairo*, a Civil War Union gunboat on display?
A   Vicksburg, Mississippi

Q   What **Humboldt** iconoclast publisher was killed in an 1898 duel?
A   William Brann – whose combative style and acerbic remarks also got two of his brothers killed

Q   What Chicago actor received death threats after he killed John Wayne in *The Cowboys*?
A   Bruce Dern

Q   What Chicago man, who died in 1965, was one of

Feminist Betty Friedan (author's collection)

SIUC Quarterback Jim Hart

America's best-known magicians?
A   Harry Blackstone – he once performed for President Calvin Coolidge at the White House.

Q   What Chicago motion picture executive donated the original copy of the Bill of Rights to the Library of Congress?
A   Barney Balaban –whose Central Park Theater was the **first in the world with air conditioning**

Q   What **LaSalle** native produced the following TV shows: "Have Gun, Will Travel," "The Rifleman", "The Donna Reed Show," "The Munsters" and "77 Sunset Strip?"
A   James Aubrey

Q   What **Shawneetown** resident was in charge of the forces that captured Jefferson Davis at the end of the Civil War?
A   Cavalry commander James Wilson

Q   Did Illinois volunteers fight the Civil War with muskets or repeating rifles?
A   Most of them had single shot weapons furnished by the government, but some saved up their money and bought Henry repeating rifles. Tyler Henry designed the gun for the New Haven Arms Company that evolved into the Winchester firm.

Q   How much did the Henry lever action rifle cost?
A   Fifty dollars – the soldiers earned a salary of $13 dollars a month.

Q   Have father and son ever been elected to the Illinois governorship?
A   Yes – Richard Yates, during the Lincoln Era, and son Richard Jr., in 1900

Q   In what Illinois county was Idaho Senator William E. Borah born?
A   **Jasper** – Borah is best known for his opposition to the U.S. joining the League of Nations

Q   Where can the captured World War II German submarine U –505 be seen by Illinois tourists?
A   Museum of Science and Industry in Chicago; it was the first enemy warship captured in battle on the high seas by the U.S. Navy since the War of 1812.

Q   What **Bloomington** man, due (in part) to his exceptional

Collinsville High Kahoks Fred Riddle, coach Virgil Fletcher, Bogie Redmon - 1961

typing ability, became John J. Pershing's chief of staff in World War I?
A   James Harbord – who became President of RCA in 1923

Q   Did Nixon, Ford, Reagan, and George H.W. Bush all carry Illinois in the 1968, 1972, 1976, 1980, 1984 and 1988 presidential elections?
A   Yes

Q   What **Cairo** man quit his trade of sign painting and became a well-known artist and etcher?
A   George "Pop" Hart – 1868-1933

Q   What Illinoisan is considered the Father of the 13th Amendment abolishing slavery?
A   Owen Lovejoy

Q   What **Oak Park** priest has written numerous books and took a critical stand in 1969 against the Church's position on celibacy, divorce, and abortion?
A   Andrew Greeley – author of *The Jesus Myth* and *The Moses Myth* and several novels, including *Thy Brother's Wife*

Q   How many stars did the 1968 Illinois Sesquicentennial flag have on it?
A   Twenty-one – to indicate Illinois was the 21st state to join the Union in 1818; Jerry Warshaw designed the flag.

Q   What is this author's favorite story about gauging Illinois storms?
A   "Measuring a Storm, Illinois Style" by Marillyn Kinsella of **Fairview Heights**

The knock-knocks happened on stormy nights. I hated storms, especially at night. We had huge elm trees that died, but their skeletal arms reached menacingly over the roof of our house. I was convinced they acted as the perfect conductors for any and all electricity that a storm could muster.

When I was real small, I jumped into Grandpa's bed and hid under the covers. After all, his bedroom was right next to mine. In fact, the only thing that separated my bed from his was the wall. But, as I got older, even I had to agree that it seemed a tad childish; so I stuck it out in my own bed.

Often times, I could hear the thunder miles away before it ever reached our home. Grandpa Joe taught me how to figure out how close a storm was. You just counted how many times you could say "Mississippi" between the flash of light and the clap of thunder. So, if I saw a flash

SIUC/Chicago comedian/activist - Dick Gregory

of blue-white light, I started counting. "One Mississippi, two Mississippi, three Mississippi." Boom! The storm was three miles away. I restarted counting again and again until "One" and boom! The storm was overhead. I resisted running into Grandpa's room. I didn't want to be a baby.

Then I heard the knock-knock. It's the universal call and response. "Knock, knock-knock, knock, knock!" I answered, "Knock, knock." Grandpa was saying, "Are you okay over there?" And I was answering, "I'm fine." The strange thing was, I was fine, because after that, the storm always subsided."

Q   Where was the first significant *American* settlement in Illinois?
A   **New Design** in 1782

Q   What Chicago publisher at Prentice-Hall talked Art Linkletter into writing *Kids Say The Darndest Things*?
A   Bernard Geis

Brace Beemer (radio's Lone Ranger) and J. Edgar Hoover

Q   What year did the defense department close Chanute Air Base at **Rantoul**?
A   1993 – But it still has a great museum.

Q   By law, what must be presented to Illinois voters every 20 years?
A   The question of whether to hold a convention to modify the state constitution

Q   Why were flatboats called "the boats that do not return?"
A   Since they were unpowered their trip was always one way – downstream

Q   What was the famous dictum of architect Daniel Burnham, the man who designed much of the 1893 Columbian Exposition?
A   "Let your watchword be 'order' and your beacon 'beauty.'" "Make no little plans. They have no magic to stir men's blood..."

Q   What four Illinoisans have served on the U.S. Supreme Court?
A   David Davis, Harry Blackmun, John Paul Stevens and Arthur Goldberg

Q   What famous person landed on the deck of the carrier *U.S.S. Abraham Lincoln* in 2003?
A   President George Bush – despite having said repeatedly that the road ahead would be long and difficult, he was chided by the press for declaring that

Illinois coal fields

"major military operations in Iraq are over."

Q When Illinois became a state in 1818, what was the ratio of Indians to whites?
A Indians outnumbered whites 3-1

Q Why was the 33rd Regiment of the Illinois Volunteers (Civil War) called the "Brains Regiment?"
A Large numbers of them were from Illinois State University (Normal)

Opera singer Mary Garden's perfume

Q How did taverns and inns in early pioneer days deal with flies at mealtime??
A Sometimes a tree branch with leaves was swished around to keep flies away. Ostrich feathers were also employed for this same purpose. In one tavern a cord was hung about three feet above the table with attached strips of paper hanging down nearly touching the meal. At mealtime the cord was manipulated in such a manner as to keep the flies away.

Wild Bill Hickok

Q What was shoo fly pie?
A Old-time pie that was so sweet and delicious it could be set in a far corner of the kitchen and it would draw flies away from the dinner table.

Q What were typical Illinois tavern prices in 1830?
A Supper, six cents; breakfast, six cents; lodging six cents; cider three cents

Q What were table manners like at early taverns and inns?
A One traveler told the story: "At breakfast there was a very large party who occupied two tables, and exhibited the usual American celerity of eating and drinking. No change of knife, or fork, or plate, no spoon for the sugar basin; no ceremony whatsoever observed, every man for himself, and none for his neighbor; hurrying, snatching, gulping, like famished wildcats; victuals disappearing like magic."

Q Was the above example typical or an aberration?
A Frontier manners, especially when women were absent, were commonly bad. Another example: "The inn was filled with company who had more the appearance of penitentiary society than gentlemen. Hard scuffle for breakfast. Ran an old hen down and cut off the head with an axe. An old sow and a starved dog made a grab before

the feathers were stripped. One got the head, the other the body. All hands were mustered to join in the chase. The cook with her broom, the hostler with his spade and boys with sticks and stones. In about ten minutes, after hard fighting, the materials for breakfast were recovered, and in twenty minutes the old hen made her appearance on the breakfast table."

Q What was significant about the Prairie Division in World War I combat?
A Illinois was one of only four states to contribute an entire division (four or five brigades) to the war.

Q How did the early pioneers deal with rampant crime?
A Vigilantes: in one place, the **Ogle County Lynching Club** was formed in 1841 to deal with the problem.

LINCOLN STUFF

Q What happened to the original Illinois log cabin that belonged to Lincoln's parents?
A It was displayed at the 1893 fair in Chicago. When the fair was over and its future was being considered, it disappeared and was never found.

Q What was Lincoln's favorite sport as a youth?
A It was a game called "fives," although sports did not catch on in this country until after the Civil War

Q What kind of fence did Abe Lincoln like to build?
A Split rail fence – remember, his nickname was "the railsplitter."

Q What is considered the most famous Lincoln statue in Illinois?
A The bronze standing statue of Lincoln, designed by Augustus Saint-Gaudens in Chicago's Lincoln Park

Q What Lincoln statue in **Vandalia** has him seated and reading a book?
A "Sitting With Lincoln" by R. Program

Gutzon Borglum's bronze bust of Lincoln

Q With what three states are Abe Lincoln associated?
A Kentucky (born), Indiana (lived), and Illinois (elected President).

Q Due to his gaunt frame and stature, some think Lincoln may have suffered from what disease?
A Marfan's syndrome

271

Q   Who is the most revered living Lincoln scholar?
A   David Donald who writes with a profound clarity and grace; Paul Angle held that position when he was alive.

Q   What are some Lincoln nicknames?
A   "The Railsplitter," "Honest Abe," and the "Savior of the Union."

Q   What cousin of Abe Lincoln's claims to have taught him how to read?
A   Dennis Hanks – probably a dubious claim

Lincoln and Ann Rutledge in their courting days

Q   Who won the fabled wrestling match between Lincoln and local bully, Jack Armstrong?
A   It was probably a draw, but Lincoln won the respect of Armstrong's followers by his performance.

Q   How did Lincoln's mother die a tragic death in Indiana?
A   Nancy Hanks died from "milksick" – passed on to humans by cows that ate the poisonous nightshade plant.

"Abraham Lincoln From New Salem"

Q   What two Civil War leaders were born in Kentucky, less than 100 miles apart?
A   Lincoln and Jefferson Davis

Q   What was the name of Lincoln's stepmother?
A   Sarah Bush Lincoln – whom he visited just before he left Illinois for the White House

Q   How much formal schooling did Abe receive?
A   He attended school for only about a year.

Q   What did Abe Lincoln do during the Blackhawk War that was unusual?
A   He reenlisted twice, something only six percent of the men did.

Q   How long did Lincoln live in New Salem?
A   Six years

Q   Who did Lincoln purchase his home from in 1844?
A   Reverend Charles Dresser – the man who married Abe and Mary Todd

Q   Was this the only home Lincoln ever owned?
A   Yes

Q   Who was the young girl that was Lincoln's first love?
A   Ann Rutledge, although some historians doubt this story. She took ill with a fever and died at a young age.

Some historians attribute Lincoln's melancholy to losing his first love.

Q   What Illinois town where Lincoln lived has been restored and is now a popular tourist attraction?
A   **New Salem**

Q   What was Lincoln's ambition as a young man?
A   He wasn't sure, but he knew he didn't want to be a farmer.

Q   Did Abe attend his father's funeral?
A   No – Lincoln thought his father was too hard on him and was a slave driver when it came to working on the farm. He also never bought a headstone marker for his father's grave.

Q   Who was Abe Lincoln's most noteworthy teacher?
A   Mentor Graham – he is buried in a cemetery near **New Salem**

Q   How many relative deaths did Lincoln have to deal with as a youngster?
A   His younger brother died when he was three; his mother, aunt and uncle died when he was nine; his sister died when he was eighteen.

Q   Did Thomas Lincoln ever administer whippings to his son Abe?
A   Yes – usually for spending time reading instead of doing his chores

Q   Where are Lincoln's parents buried?
A   Shiloh Cemetery S.E. of **Mattoon** and south of **Charleston**

Q   The movie *Lincoln*, starring Sam Waterson and Mary Tyler Moore, was based on a book written by what author?
A   Gore Vidal

Q   In what Illinois town did Lincoln make his first political speech?
A   **Decatur** – at age 21

Q   Where can one find the bronze statue of Lincoln that shows him at a critical period of his life when he discarded the axe of the frontiersman and turned to the study of law?
A   **New Salem** State Park – sculptor Avard Fairbanks executed the piece, donated by the Sons of Utah Pioneers in 1954

Q   Where is the only surviving structure in which Lincoln maintained a law office?
A   **Springfield's** Lincoln-Herndon law office

Q   What poem by Vachel Lindsay is about Abe and the

city of **Springfield**?
A "Abraham Lincoln Walks at Midnight"

Q How many novels did Abe Lincoln read in his lifetime?
A None – he read bits and pieces of *Ivanhoe* and that was it

Q What were the most popular Shakespearian plays performed in **Springfield** during Lincoln's era?
A Richard III, Othello, Hamlet

Q Who were Lincoln's close friends?
A Although at ease and gregarious in large groups, he never had a "best friend," either as a youth or a mature man.

Q What law school did Lincoln attend?
A There were no law schools in Illinois back then. He merely read law books and then took an oral and written test to be admitted to the Illinois Bar.

Q What is most likely one's view of Mary Todd Lincoln if you are an Ann Rutledge advocate?
A Author Don Winkler asserts that Mary trapped Lincoln into matrimony by seducing him into impregnating and marrying her. Then Mary's nagging made his life intolerable. She was also responsible for Abe's death by hiring an incompetent guard the night he was murdered.

Q What kind of books did Lincoln like to read?
A For fun and relaxation he liked poetry. He did not care to read biographies because he felt they were all puff pieces, designed to make their subject look good.

Q For decades Abe Lincoln lagged behind George Washington as a national icon. When did he zoom to the top?
A During the Progressive Era, 1900-1915

Q What is the name of the motor route that goes through Kentucky, Indiana and Illinois past all the Lincoln landmarks?
A Lincoln Heritage Trail

Q What was Lincoln referring to when he said, "this honor gave me more pleasure than any I have had since?"
A Being elected captain of the New Salem militia unit by his friends and neighbors

Abe Lincoln shrine at Postville Courthouse – Lincoln, Illinois

Abe Lincoln

Warren G. Harding

Q Did Lincoln ever have his horse stolen?
A Yes – at the end of the Black Hawk War. He was forced to share a horse with a friend. They sold the horse and bought a canoe and paddled down the Illinois River from **Peoria** to **Havana**. From there they walked back to **New Salem.**

Q Did Lincoln participate in the battle of Stillman's Run?
A No – but he helped bury the dead after the battle.

Q Have we ever had any presidents taller than Lincoln?
A No. He was a bit taller than 6-4, but his lanky build and stovepipe hat made him seem even taller. James Madison (Madison County) was our shortest President.

Q Tad Lincoln had two pets of the same species. What were they?
A Goats

Q Name the town where Lincoln as lawyer won the "almanac case" in defending a young man accused of murder.
A **Beardstown** – The almanac proved there was no full moon on the night in question, casting doubt on the testimony of an accuser.

Q Was Lincoln a "snappy" dresser?
A No. He was careless in his appearance, giving him the look of a country bumpkin.

Q Was Lincoln an abolitionist?
A No, but his firm stance against the *extension* of slavery in the territories made it seem like he was.

Q Why did Lincoln give his youngest son Thomas the nickname Tad?
A Because he had a large head like a tadpole.

Q Did Lincoln invent the phrase, "Founding Fathers?"
A No. Although Lincoln often talked about "our fathers," the phrase Founding Fathers was first used by

Q Are there any towns in Illinois named for Lincoln?
A Yes. Lincoln was legal advisor in locating and platting the town. He christened the town of **Lincoln** with the juice from a watermelon. He thanked the town fathers for the honor but told them that a town with a name like Lincoln probably wouldn't amount to much.

Q What would be an appropriate summary of Lincoln's political views as a Whig?

A   He was an advocate of individual initiative, self-improvement, free-wage labor capitalism, and economic mobility

Q   What religion were his parents?
A   They were hard-shell Baptists

Q   What was Lincoln's religion?
A   Abe belonged to no church but he thought like a Calvinist/deist.

Q   How important was keeping Kentucky out of the Confederacy in Lincoln's mind?
A   Lincoln once said that he *hoped* to have God on his side but he *had* to have Kentucky.

Q   Who is Lincoln's best-known biographer?
A   Carl Sandburg - his "Prairie Years" and "War Years" contain more words than all the works of William Shakespeare.

Q   How was the Lincoln penny received when it was first issued in 1909?
A   Southerners hated it. Many in the North thought it smacked of Caesarism.

Q   What was the only war Lincoln served in as a volunteer?
A   The Blackhawk War of the 1830's. Lincoln joked that he never fought any "redskins" but that he killed a lot of bloodthirsty mosquitoes.

Q   Was Abe ever a "war protestor?"
A   Yes. He was against the Mexican War of the 1840's because he saw it as a Southern plot to acquire more territory in the southwest and make states from it where slavery would be allowed.

Q   What was the first political party Abe joined?
A   He became a member of the Whig Party whose symbol was the raccoon. The party traced its roots back to Alexander Hamilton and George Washington. The name came from the English Whig Party that opposed the Tories - a faction that usually sided with the king.

Q   How did Lincoln first meet Mary Todd?
A   Mary, a Kentuckian, was visiting her sister in **Springfield**. Her sibling was married to the prominent Ninian Edwards Jr., son of the former Illinois governor.

Q   Did Mary Todd's family own slaves?
A   Yes. Her Kentucky family, though not rich, was

Lincoln Monument – Lincoln Park

considered upper class. Her family did not approve of her marriage to backwoodsman Abe Lincoln.

Q   With whom did Abe Lincoln nearly fight a duel with broadswords?
A   James Shields, a Democratic political rival. The two (and their associates) traveled to **Alton**, then rowed to an island in the Mississippi on the Missouri side. The duel was called off at the last second when Lincoln apologized for having written a critical "letter to the editor."

Q   What was Lincoln's biggest accomplishment in Illinois politics?
A   Getting the state capital moved from **Vandalia** to **Springfield**. He teamed with a group of legislators called the "Long Nine" because they were all at least six feet tall.

Q   What scientific achievement did Lincoln do that no other President can claim?
A   He is the **only President to secure a patent**. He invented a flotation device to help boats navigate shallow rivers such as the Sangamon. Lincoln never followed up on the patent.

Q   What is the thesis of a 2000 book about Abe Lincoln, *Moonlight: Abe Lincoln and the Almanac Trial?*
A   Author John Walsh argues unconvincingly that Lincoln's future in politics was in question so he suppressed evidence, tampered with a witness, and possibly suborned perjury. I say poppycock!

Q   Was Mary Todd Lincoln supportive of Lincoln's political ambitions?

"Gulliver Abe" - tied down by office seekers
-courtesy American Antiquarian Society

A   Yes. She pushed and prodded, believing that some day he would be President. Abe had serious doubts that this would ever happen.

Q   What major structural change did the Lincolns make to their home in **Springfield**?
A   Their famous home was only a one-story frame. As the boys increased the size of the family, Abe and Mary had the roof raised and a second story added. Most of the existing furniture is not original but merely similar to furniture of that period.

Q   What three sons were born in Lincoln's Springfield home?
A   Edward, William, and Thomas; Edward also died here

Q   What 1854 incident revived Lincoln's sagging political career.

A The passage of the Kansas-Nebraska Act, sponsored by Stephen Douglas. The act nullified the Missouri Compromise of 1820 and said that the people of Kansas could decide for themselves whether their state would be slave or free.

Q In what town did Lincoln and Douglas meet to plan their seven debates?
A **Bement**

Q How many Lincoln-Douglas debates were there?
A Seven

Q Who won the Lincoln-Douglas debates?
A Douglas was elected to the contested U.S. senate seat, but the debates gained Lincoln the national recognition that led to his presidential nomination on the Republican ticket.

Q Where is the bronze statue of Lincoln known as "Lincoln The Debater?"
A Taylor Park in **Freeport**

Q Who was the favorite to get the Republican Party's presidential nomination in 1860?
A William Seward of New York was the early leader, but Lincoln supporters were organized at the Chicago convention. They secured the nomination for him after several ballots.

Q Did Lincoln attend the nominating convention?
A No – he stayed in **Springfield**

Q In what way could Lincoln be considered a minority President?
A The three other candidates (Stephen Douglas, John Bell, and John Breckinridge) had more popular votes combined than Lincoln, but Lincoln won the electoral majority that was needed. It was kind of like the Gore-Bush 2000 election.

Q What Illinois town, at the crossroads of the Illinois Central and Great Western railroads, is the place where Lincoln gave his "farewell address" to the people of Illinois before he left for Washington D.C.?
A **Tolono**

Q Toward the end of the Civil War, black troops comprised about 15 percent of the Union army. This incensed the South which threatened to massacre black troops that were captured in battle. How did Lincoln handle this problem?
A He largely averted the disaster by threatening to do the same to captured Confederate soldiers.

Abe Lincoln election as seen from the Southern point of view

Abe Lincoln's election as the North sees it

Q What were some other Lincoln's nicknames?
A Honest Abe, Lincoln the Rail-splitter, Baboon, Ape, Black Republican, Savior of the Union, Longshanks, Illinois Sucker, Little Giant Killer, Divider of the Union, American Caesar, Cincinnatus of the West, Illinois Tyrant, Destroyer of the Constitution, Northern Scalawag, Lincoln the Martyr. Midwest Sambo, The Great Emancipator, Southern Oppressor.

Q Was Lincoln responsible for the transcontinental railroad getting built?
A Yes – he realized that connecting the East with the West was vitally important and pushed congress to pass enabling legislation.

Q What great land giveaway was involved in the act that enabled the transcontinental railroad to be built?
A For every mile of track that was laid, the government gave the Central Pacific and Union Pacific 20 square miles of land.

Q How did this benefit the federal government in the long run?
A In return for the free land, the railroads had to haul federal cargo at reduced rates. This practice was not ended until 1946. By then the value of this deal turned out to be twenty times that of the original value of the land given away.

Q What town was home to both of Lincoln's White House secretaries?
A **Pittsfield**

Q Did Lincoln ever meet George A. Custer?
A Yes – they met when Lincoln visited George McClelland in October of 1862. At the time, Custer was merely McClellan's aide-de-camp. When Lincoln met Custer's wife Libby at a Washington, D.C. party, he remarked: "And so you are the wife of the man who goes into the cavalry charges with a whoop and a yell." Lincoln liked Custer because he showed daring virtues lacking in most of his generals. Custer was a real hero at the battle of Gettysburg.

Q In a humorous vein, what affliction did Lincoln ascribe to his commander of the Army of the Potomac, George McClellan?
A He said the overly cautious commander had a bad case of the "slows."

Q Why did Abe Lincoln stop the practice of exchanging captured prisoners with the Confederacy?
A He realized that it benefited the South which had a smaller population than the North.

Q What famous consoling letter did Lincoln write to a grieving mother who lost five of her sons in the war?
A The Bixby letter - actually, two of Mrs. Bixby's sons deserted, but this was unknown by Lincoln when he wrote the letter.

Q What diminutive P.T. Barnum attraction entertained Lincoln at the White House?
A Tom Thumb

Q When Lincoln was assassinated, what cabinet member was stabbed and seriously injured by other conspirators?
A William Seward, secretary of state

Q Which leader is considered by most historians to be the most capable, Abe Lincoln or Jefferson Davis?
A Abe Lincoln – no contest

Q What were the provisions of the Morrill Land Grant Act signed by Lincoln in 1862?
A Federal lands were sold for the benefit of aid to state universities. Illinoisan Jonathan Turner pushed for the idea and representative Morrill introduced the bill in congress.

Q What did Lincoln have to do that was never a problem for Jefferson Davis?
A Lincoln had to stand for re-election in 1864. The Confederate Constitution gave the Southern President a six- year term.

Q Why was Mary Lincoln severely criticized by the press while she was First Lady?
A She greatly overspent her $25,000 budget allocated for redecorating the White House.

Q What was unusual about Lincoln's estate considering that he was a lawyer?
A He died without a will.

Q Was Lincoln concerned about his wife's excessive grieving over the death of her sons?
A Yes. One day he took her to a White House window and pointed to a nearby sanitarium. He told her that if she didn't pull herself together, that was where she was headed.

Q Was Mary Lincoln ever committed to a sanitarium?
A Yes. Her only surviving son, Robert, had her committed to a place in **Batavia**.

Q Does Abe Lincoln have any living direct descendents?
A No. Robert Lincoln had a son, but he died while yet a teenager.

Abe Lincoln in 1860

Abe Lincoln watermelon christening site: Lincoln, Illinois

Q Were any women hanged as a result of the assassination conspiracy that killed Lincoln?
A Yes – Mary Surrat was hanged with several others. Some think she was an innocent victim.

Q When you visit the Lincoln tomb at Oak Ridge in **Springfield**, what are you supposed to do when you see his sculptured bust?
A Rub his nose for good luck – with your hand, not your nose.

Q What famous sculptor did the bust of Lincoln?
A Gutzon Borghum, who also sculpted Mount Rushmore in South Dakota

Q Where was Lincoln's body kept from 1869 to 1874?
A In a vault built into a hillside at Oak Ridge Cemetery. Called the First Burial Place, it was guarded day and night for several years by Union soldiers out of respect for the Great Emancipator.

Q Where did Lincoln give his famous "house divided" speech?
A In the Hall of Representatives at the Old Capitol Building in Springfield

Q Who portrayed Abe Lincoln in the movies?
A Henry Fonda and Raymond Massey

Q What were the film titles?
A Fonda was in *Young Mr. Lincoln* – 1939, and Massey starred in *Abe Lincoln in Illinois* - 1940

Q Did they ever make a film about Lincoln's Vice-president, Andrew Johnson?
A Yes – Van Hefflin starred in *Tennessee Johnson*

Q Was Lincoln a popular subject for silent films?
A Yes, because he was the first President to be widely photographed. In all, Lincoln appears in about 150 films and theatrical productions

Q What Chicago company did **Springfield** native Robert Lincoln serve in the capacity of president from 1897-1911?
A Pullman Company

Q What Lincoln book was recently written by former New York governor Mario Cuomo?
A *Why Lincoln Matters* – a criticism of President Bush

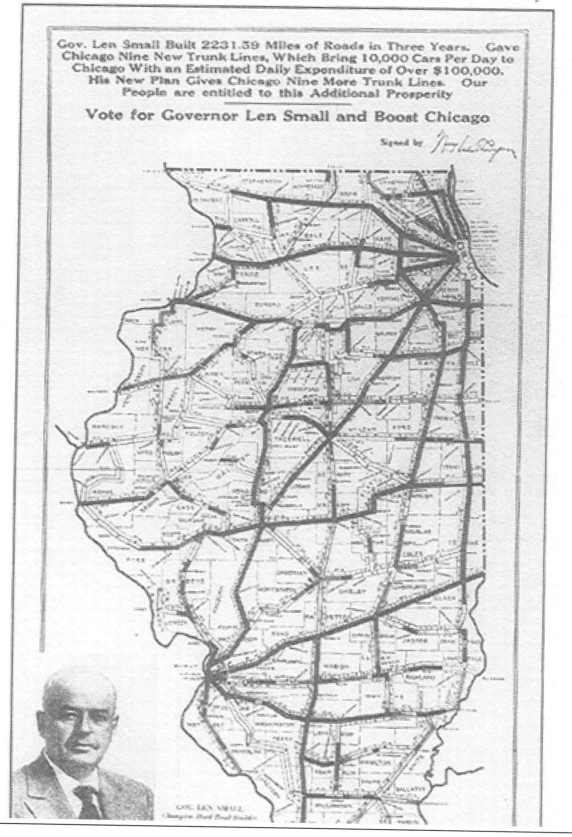

Henry's in Cicero, Illinois, on old Route 66 – courtesy Dan Oberle of Edwardsville/Geneseo

Del Rhea's Chicken Basket in Willowbrook, Illinois – old Route 66, courtesy of Dan Oberle of Edwardsville

Law Building at the University of Illinois at Champaign/Urbana (Teich collection)

"Tad" Lincoln

Mary Todd Lincoln

John & Cyrill Craig at Aluminum Ore in East St. Louis

Chicago Mayor Richard M. Daley 1996

Beer Nuts plant at Bloomington – photo courtesy Mike Brasel

Bob Then's new 1961 Shell station and tow trucks at the corner of Kingshighway and Caseyville Avenue, Washington Park/Rosemont

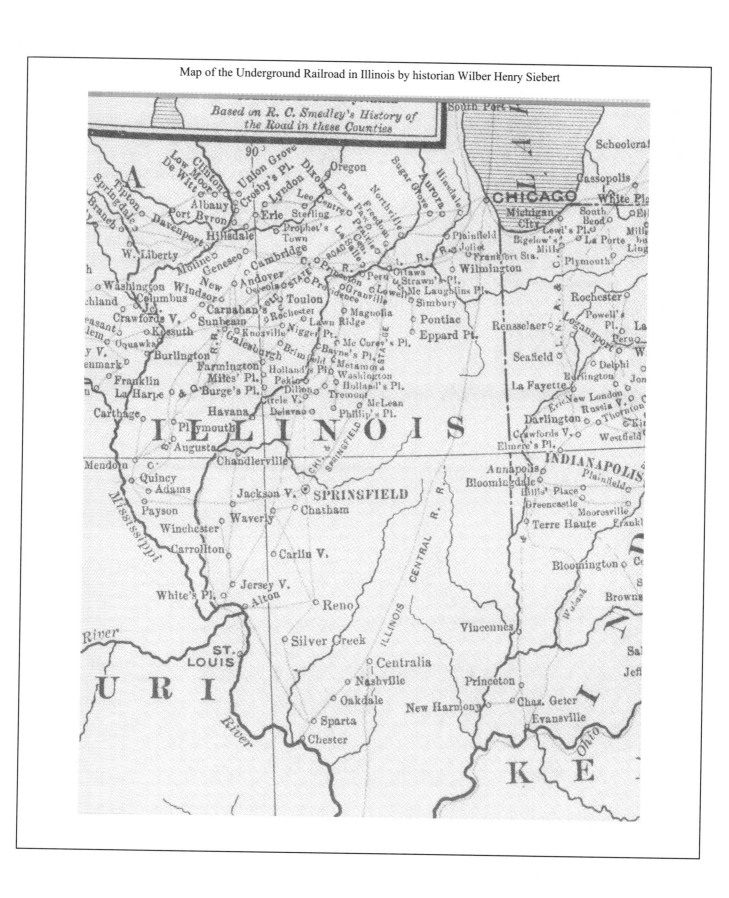

Map of the Underground Railroad in Illinois by historian Wilber Henry Siebert

Chicago author and Hollywood screen writer
Ben Hecht -1915

Writer Eugene Field at his desk

Chicago writer Nelson Algren 1950

Historic sites in Illinois

U. S. GRANT HOME STATE MEMORIAL
OLD MARKET HOUSE STATE MEMORIAL

HAYMARKET
HULL HOUSE
DOUGLAS TOMB

CHICAGO PORTAGE NATIONAL HISTORIC SITE

ILLINOIS MICHIGAN CANAL TERMINUS

BISHOP HILL STATE MEMORIAL

NAUVOO STATE PARK

FORT CREVE COEUR STATE PARK

FORT EDWARDS MONUMENT

POSTVILLE COURT HOUSE STATE MEMORIAL

MT. PULASKI COURT HOUSE STATE MEMORIAL

LINCOLN'S NEW SALEM STATE PARK

LINCOLN HOME STATE MEMORIAL

MARQUETTE CROSS
PERE MARQUETTE STATE PARK

VANDALIA STATE HOUSE STATE MEMORIAL

CAHOKIA COURT HOUSE STATE MEMORIAL
CAHOKIA MOUNDS STATE PARK

ALBION

FORT CHARTRES STATE PARK
KASKASKIA STATE PARK
PIERRE MENARD HOME STATE MEMORIAL

SHAWNEE NATIONAL FOREST

CAVE IN THE ROCK STATE PARK

Chicago boxer Barney Ross

Motorola founder Paul Galvin (right) and son - 1952

Illinois writer James Jones on the set of "From Here To Eternity" with actor Montgomery Clift

Marshall Field in 1906

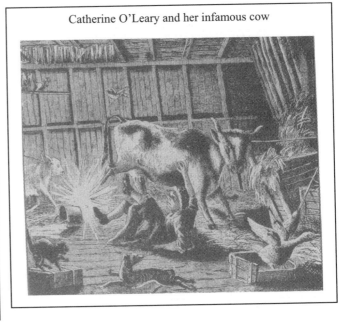

Catherine O'Leary and her infamous cow

Rush Medical College at Dearborn & Indiana streets after 1871 Chicago fire – Chicago Historical Society

Retired farmer George Mecherie, founder of State Farm Insurance 1922

Midland Shopping Plaza at Kewanee by Dan Oberle

"It Will Soon Be Here" by Olaf Krans 1838-1916

Lincoln's law partner, William Herndon

Scott Field in 1923 – world's 2nd largest dirigible hangar in background

Photos in this book are courtesy the Edwardsville *Intelligencer*, the East St. Louis *Journal*, the St. Louis *Post-Dispatch*, the Belleville *News-Democrat*, St. Clair County Historical Society, the author's personal collection, the *Miami Herald*, the Chicago *Tribune*, Wide World, UPI, Chicago Historical Society, Bettman Archives, AP, Newberry Library, Famous Photos, Illinois Department of Tourism, Illinois Chamber of Commerce, Illinois Department of Transportation, Illinois State Historical Library, University of Illinois, "Illinois History," "Journal of Illinois History," and the "Journal of the Illinois State Historical Society."

Edwardsville Certificate of freedom -1848

UNITED STATES OF AMERICA,

STATE OF ILLINOIS,
Madison County, }ss.{ To all to whom these Presents may come—GREETING:

𝕶𝖓𝖔𝖜 𝖄𝖊, That Mary Jane Long wife of John Long a person of Color, about ___twenty four___ years of age, five feet ___three & ½___ inches high, ___Mulatto___ complexion, has two small pitts on each side of her fore head Daughter of Elijah & Dicey Richardson has exhibited, presented and filed, in the Office of the Clerk of the Circuit Court of the County and State aforesaid, a 𝕮𝕰𝕽𝕿𝕴𝕱𝕴𝕮𝕬𝕿𝕰, duly authen= ticated, of **FREEDOM,** as such person of Color.

Author Bill Nunes and his Chevy Caprice

Harold Zeigler in front of Dr. Jazz, the author's favorite ice cream and sandwich shop on St. Louis Street in Lebanon, Illinois